2005

VOICES

in dialogue

VOICES
in dialogue

Reading Women
in the Middle Ages

LINDA OLSON

AND

KATHRYN KERBY-FULTON

EDITORS

University of Notre Dame Press
Notre Dame, Indiana

Manufactured in the United States of America

Library of Congress Cataloging-in-Publication Data
Voices in dialogue : reading women in the Middle Ages /
edited by Linda Olson and Kathryn Kerby-Fulton.
p.   cm.
Includes bibliographical references and index.
ISBN 0-268-03717-5 (cloth : alk. paper)
1. Women—History—Middle Ages, 500–1500.   2. Women and literature—History—
To 1500.   3. Literature, Medieval—History and criticism.   4. Civilization, Medieval.
I. Olson, Linda, 1962–   II. Kerby-Fulton, Kathryn.
HQ1143.V67   2005
305.42'094'0902—dc22

2005004936

To our mothers, who taught us to hear and respect all voices

Irma Koren Natalie Hammill
(August 13, 1932–July 11, 1990)

Doreen Margaret Kerby
(June 10, 1928)

▣ CONTENTS ▣

Voices in Dialogue begins with an engaging discussion of the women with whom Augustine of Hippo exchanged letters, and it does so even though none of the letters written by these elusive women have survived. This scenario may seem strange to many, perhaps even anathematic to some, coming at the beginning of a volume which deals so extensively with women's cultural history, and there might be several reasons for surprise and objection. For one, Augustine has been seen as one of the worst of villains by many adherents of modern feminism. Now, at the beginning of the twenty-first century, young people, particularly young women, walk into my seminar on women writers in the Middle Ages with the assumption that all medieval women experienced lives so oppressed and spoke in voices so unrecorded that they simply cannot imagine them as authors and teachers and visionaries. Many of these students—especially the well-read ones—feel no qualms whatsoever about laying blame for this catastrophe squarely on the shoulders of Augustine, whom they label the progenitor of medieval misogyny.

Despite his enormous influence in the Middle Ages (and I would be the last to slight it in any way),[1] Augustine cannot possibly accept so grand a title alone. He must share this crown with such notables as his contemporary Jerome, the apostle Paul, the philosopher Aristotle, the theologian Thomas Aquinas, the poet Jean de Meun, and hundreds of other medieval clergymen, many of whom interpreted and used Augustine in their own ways, and some of whom wrote absolutely horrible things about women— things I suspect Augustine would never even have thought. Still, then, we have a gross generalization, for these same men wrote very different things depending on time and circumstance, personal agenda and intended audience. At times they also wrote horrible things about kings and popes, knights and bishops—about men, that is—and certainly not everything they wrote about women, or actually did in relation to women in their lives, was negative.[2] Far from it, in fact, a point well demonstrated by the Augustine revealed in the exchange between Catherine Conybeare and Mark Vessey, for this

Augustine hardly deserves the almost universal criticism he has received in modern scholarship for his views of women. Quite the contrary, in fact, since he treats his female correspondents not only as intelligent, learned individuals with their own souls and thoughts, their own responsibilities and interpretive skills, but even as worthy and useful colleagues in the work of God he has taken upon himself. It is, then, a somewhat unusual image of Augustine, surrounded not by learned male associates but by accomplished female correspondents, which opens this volume, and one which seems to me as a student of Augustine and his medieval readers both valid and long overdue.[3]

Yet some readers might also raise questions about the methodology used in the dialogue between Conybeare and Vessey, for the letters of these women simply have not survived, which means that we must work from what Augustine's own letters imply—work, that is, from the "spaces between letters" so carefully read by Conybeare. Short of the sort of miraculous manuscript discovery that all students of lost texts dream of at some time in their research, the solid evidence generally sought and studied by the historian and literary scholar alike simply does not exist. This raises a couple of essential questions: What do we accept as valid literary and historical evidence? How do we then use the evidence we do accept? To be more specific to Conybeare's and Vessey's dialogue, can we with any hope of accuracy gauge the authorial activities, and thus the literacy and learning, of the women with whom Augustine corresponds solely through his half of the correspondence? Conybeare's study would suggest that much can be gleaned in this way, and both her logical approach and reasonable results hold up well, even providing a "methodological model" for exploring gaps in the historical record (Vessey), when confronted by the sophisticated contextualizations and qualifications of Vessey's response.

Yet the problem of evidence—what constitutes evidence and how it is used—rises again and again in *Voices in Dialogue.* Mary Jane Morrow and David Bell, for instance, see and use the Anselmian prayers in the Shaftesbury Psalter in very different ways, just as Elizabeth Schirmer and Steven Justice read *The Chastising of God's Children* with significantly different implications, and Nicholas Watson and Felicity Riddy view the evidence for the production of the *Book of Margery Kempe* in strikingly different ways: in each case, the conclusions reached differ accordingly. Perhaps the most notable of our dialogues for the way in which it raises the question of evidence, however, and certainly the one which addresses a topic hotly debated at present, is that by Stephen Jaeger and Giles Constable, who discuss the attribution of the *Epistolae duorum amantium* to Abelard and Heloise. Here the literary scholar meets the intellectual historian, and the textual analysis of the one, with its subsequent arguments and conclusions, does not satisfy the academic need for positive historical evidence on the part of the other. They simply disagree, explaining their academic rationale and citing both evidence and adherents on either side of the debate to support their views. Though the reader can hardly fault such carefully presented arguments and the quintessential right to hold them, she might still respond to stalemates like these with Bell's post-colonial question: "Where do we go from here?"

From another perspective, however, dialogues like these highlight the multivalent nature of academic interpretation: one reader will quite simply see the evidence differently from another, for our individual views and experiences—our academic desires and intentions—play a central role in the scholarship we do. In all of our researches and methodologies, no matter how scholarly and carefully designed to achieve objectivity or authenticity in relation to the past, as in the arguments and results that grow from our work, there is an element of desire: what we want to achieve as academics and what we want to discover in the past in order to achieve it inevitably influence what we in fact do and find in our research and writing. This can no sooner be avoided than it should be regarded as a negative aspect of historical studies, though we too often speak of the disastrous descent into the uncertain realm of "subjective scholarship." Our scholarship has always been subjective and always will be: there is little point in either denying it or making it the focal point of our writing. We need only think of fine old terms of western learning like *philosophia* ("love of knowledge") and *studium* ("zeal" or "enthusiasm") to remind ourselves of the emotional or affective element of our quest for knowledge, and the ambiguity of the term *historia* itself (both "history" and "story") should highlight how one person's fact is another person's fiction, whether we refer to poets or scholars, modern or medieval. As John Van Engen puts it, "It makes all the difference what we imagine possible." Were we never to desire a different picture of the past, never to conjecture or speculate beyond certainties, our knowledge would not advance at all: our individual subjectivities are as essential to our academic activities as concrete external evidence and wide-ranging scholarly consensus.

So it has not been our aim as editors in gathering the essays that make up *Voices in Dialogue* to suppress these individual scholarly impulses in our contributors, though we have been pleased with how many of them have emphasized in the course of their discussions the nature of their evidence—solid or fragmentary, certain or ambivalent, as the case may be. Following at least vaguely in the footsteps of Augustine, who encouraged multivalent interpretations of scripture[4] and advised his women correspondents to sort through theological problems via "the inward teacher of the inner self" (interioris hominis magister interior) (Conybeare), we have made every effort to foster the unique nature of each essay and dialogue. In fact, the dialogue format of the volume was designed to allow various academic desires and approaches free expression, while providing a built-in scholarly discussion—one might even call it a test of sorts— of the methodology used and results achieved when these desires manifest themselves in writing about certain thorny problems in women's history. Thus each contributor's essay is paired with a response from a different scholar, with the two together forming a dialogue focusing on a particular problem, or person, or text, or set of texts. The varying perspectives and approaches—the different ways of doing research into the past—and the many suggestions and conclusions presented by the eleven dialogues brought together in this collection become, therefore, as much a self-reflection of and on our scholarship (and one, I think, that has held surprises for us all) as they are a demonstration of academic exchange in action.

Yet in bringing so many different perspectives on some of the persistent problems of women's cultural history together in what we believe are valid and fruitful ways, this volume has become extremely diverse. Our twenty-two contributors approach various problems through literary, codicological, paleographical, linguistic, liturgical, historical, and theological channels. At one extreme, texts that no longer exist are the focus and theories are extrapolated from surrounding evidence, while at another a single extant manuscript is examined more closely, or a defined aspect of a single text or hypothesis or problem is studied in detail. In addition, this is not a volume simply about the Middle Ages, for we begin in Late Antiquity with Augustine (354–430) and end in the early Renaissance with Anne Askew (*Examinations* 1546, 1547). Its contributors were not given word limitations or paradigms for shaping their essays and responses, but encouraged to exchange ideas and write and respond pretty much as they wished; hence, some dialogues (and individual essays within dialogues) are very short, while others are very long; one includes a response by the contributor to the initial reply given by the respondent, and another presents "afterwords" co-authored by both members of the team.

This is also not a volume rigidly dedicated to women and women's history, which, if we listen to one of the primary messages echoing through many of the dialogues, is an impossibility in any case. The voices of women we find in textual history are so irretrievably intermingled with the voices of those around them—the voices of advisors and critics, co-authors and scribes, readers and imitators, both male and female—that careful and thorough study of the women necessitates study of their male associates, and vice versa. This broader view, which aims always to include women in (rather than exclude them from) the larger framework of historical studies, means also that the scholars gathered here are not exclusively experts in women's history. Some are, certainly, but many are students of different, sometimes wider, sometimes more specialized fields: music and liturgy, history and epistolography, paleography and codicology, literature and languages, prophecy and heresy, and so on. What this volume does focus upon, however, is textual records, whether they be in Latin or vernacular languages, whether they be historical or literary, theological or liturgical, epistolary or homiletic. *Voices in Dialogue* is, then, very much a book about texts, about how they were written and how they were read by both women and men from the fourth to the sixteenth century.

This is hardly a narrow focus, however, and it would be both impossible and reductive to attempt here a summary of a volume as broad and diverse and lengthy as *Voices in*

Dialogue has grown to be. It is our belief in any case that our readers would much rather reflect on the research and arguments of our contributors, the primary texts and new discoveries they present, than hear us summarizing work too subtle and complex to be effectively presented in such a way, and generalizing prematurely on the conclusions associated with the individual cases studied here. This is to say that we think the dialogues gathered here speak eloquently for themselves, and the introductory material that follows deals accordingly not with surveying the contents of the various essays, but with six topics which weave their way through the eleven dialogues, like threads stitching the essays together, uniting their discussions even as they highlight methodological differences and contradictory conclusions. The literacy, authorship, and relationships of the women studied in several of the essays are the focus of my discussion, while my co-editor looks at the history of homiletic, liturgical, and sacramental roles for medieval women. In discussing these topics, both of us have allowed our own scholarly work—the products of our personal academic desires and researches—to form a commentary on that of our contributors, and thereby extended the dialogic principle of the volume into its introductory material. There are no certain answers provided here any more than in the individual dialogues—no conclusive comments on the problems presented by the volume—but there are many questions raised, many revelations made and challenges thrown out, many suggestions offered for the future progress of our scholarship, as there should be in an informed and lively academic dialogue.

Linda Olson

Notes

1. Much of my own scholarship has focused on Augustine and the influence of his *Confessiones* in the Middle Ages. See "The Textual Construction of Monastic Interiority: Reading Augustine's *Confessiones* in England c. 1066–c. 1200," 3 vol. (PhD diss., University of York, England, 1998); "Reading Augustine's *Confessiones* in Fourteenth-Century England: John de Grandisson's Fashioning of Text and Self," *Traditio* 52 (1997): 201–57; "Untangling the Thread of Internal Progress in a Benedictine Community: An Abridgement of Augustine's *Confessiones* from Medieval Norwich," in *The Medieval Reader: Reception and Cultural History in the Late Medieval Manuscript*, ed. Kathryn Kerby-Fulton and Maidie Hilmo (New York: AMS Press, 2001), 41–79; "Did Medieval English Women Read Augustine's *Confessiones*? Constructing Feminine Interiority and Literacy in the Eleventh and Twelfth Centuries," in *Learning and Literacy in Medieval England and Abroad*, ed. Sarah Rees Jones (Turnhout: Brepols, 2003), 69–96.

2. A classic example of both writing different things at different times and writing one thing and doing another is presented by Jerome, who in his *Contra Jovinian*, for instance, where he aimed to extol the virtues of a chaste lifestyle, wrote the most scathing things about women, while in other places he praised Paula and Eustochium and the other women whom he made his companions in

intellectual and theological studies. See Alcuin Blamires, ed., *Woman Defamed and Woman Defended: An Anthology of Medieval Texts* (Oxford: Clarendon Press, 1992), 64–74, for some relevant translated passages of his *Contra Jovinian,* and Elizabeth A. Clark, *Women in the Early Church* (Collegeville, Minn.: Liturgical Press, 1983), for many passages from Jerome's letters that express both his positive and not so positive views of women.

3. My own work on the way in which male readers of the *Confessiones* in the Middle Ages present both that text and their own imitative writings to women also suggests a relationship of greater equality between religious men and women based on their sharing of Augustinian ideas: see Olson, "Did Medieval English Women Read the *Confessiones*?"

4. See, for instance, his discussion and defense of his interpretation of Genesis in Book XII of the *Confessiones:* Lucas Verheijen, ed., *Sancti Augustini Confessionum Libri XIII,* Corpus Christianorum Series Latina 27 (Turnhout: Brepols, 1981).

■ ACKNOWLEDGMENTS ■

A book as long and complex as this one necessarily involves the efforts of many people and we would like to thank all of them. We are especially grateful to our many contributors for their wonderful essays, their willingness to participate in an innovative collection, and their patience in seeing it through the long processes of dialogue and publication. Diana Rutherford in the English Department at the University of Victoria has been a constant help with many aspects of the project, especially those of a technical nature, and we are also thankful to Shona Harrison for her assistance with early drafts, to Noelle King for her bibliographical work, and to Thea Todd for the index. The enthusiasm of Barbara Hanrahan at the Notre Dame Press has been invaluable, and we are particularly grateful to Carole Roos for all her careful work copyediting the manuscript. John Van Engen generously provided the funds for the cover illustration and other expensive aspects of publication, and both he and Bob Olson have unfailingly offered the essential but less tangible kinds of support that only true partners can give.

Reading, Writing, and Relationships in Dialogue

LINDA OLSON

Determining the literacy of past individuals and communities is a complex, often fraught project, and it too often seems that the more we learn, the more complicated the matter becomes, the more unstable the ground beneath our feet grows, and the more inadequate our pre-existing definitions and categories appear. I cannot here delve into the topic at great length; the essays that follow do that admirably well on their own. Yet some explanation of the problems, and what we can learn from them, seems in order. As a starting place (and there could be many) I will use the four levels of literacy outlined by David Bell in his important study of medieval nuns' libraries. "When speaking of Latin literacy," Bell writes,

> it is best to divide it into a number of levels. The first and simplest level is the ability to read a text without understanding it . . . ; the second level is to read and understand a common liturgical text; the third level involves reading and understanding non-liturgical texts or less common texts from the liturgy; and the fourth level is the ability to compose and write a text of one's own.[1]

This description seems to me extremely useful for reminding us that different people in the Middle Ages (as indeed now) would be literate in different ways and for different reasons, and hence for providing expansive ways of thinking about various possible medieval relationships with textual culture.

1

It distinguishes, for instance, between reading with understanding and reading without it. It reminds us that the presence and perhaps the use of a text in an individual's or community's collection need not imply what we moderns think of as functional literacy (simply pronouncing a text would not qualify, for instance), and then again, it might imply far more. It informs us that we need to consider unique types of literacy—like liturgical or devotional literacy[2]—in our understanding of what it might have meant to be a literate woman in the Middle Ages. It opens the door also to an endless string of diverse literacy possibilities. Think only of the potential range we might apply to the concept of "understanding" among the readers at the second and third of Bell's levels; of the difference it makes, for instance, if that reader understanding "a common liturgical text" on the second level simply grasps what the words say in a phrase or sentence, or if, on the other hand, she is familiar with the whole text and even with commentaries and interpretations which inform and enrich the liturgical text, even though she may not have physically read those or any additional texts herself. Each level is ambiguous and potentially expansive in this way, and we might also posit even at the first level a purely spiritual literacy—a direct line to what God means by the text—created through the affective experience of singing these texts devotionally with what the *Myroure of Oure Ladye* calls "entendaunce" (Schirmer). Once we begin to move in this way beyond a strict definition of medieval literacy based on reading Latin texts, then not only does the question of vernacular literacies of various levels arise, but also the issue of oral literacies, where speaking and hearing a text, even the ideas inherent in a text, are central.

Similarly, when we focus on writing as an aspect of literacy, as in Bell's fourth and highest level, "the ability to compose and write a text of one's own," a number of complications enter the picture at once. Two separate types of writing are referred to here—intellectual writing or the composition of texts, and physical writing or the copying of texts—and sometimes it is very difficult to know, based on extant evidence, where to draw the line between these two activities, and to whom we might properly assign responsibility for each when texts are the product, as they so often are, of collaborative efforts. Furthermore, the idea of writing in the Middle Ages could reach far beyond copying and composing to include such diverse activities as correcting, annotating, translating, collecting, excerpting, commenting, and abridging, to name only those which come to mind immediately. There are also frequent crossovers among these various categories of writing, each of which might vary significantly from individual to individual and might demonstrate an enormous range of familiarity with previous writings, with stylistic and rhetorical devices, with philosophical and theological concepts, with structural and narrative conventions, or not. Once again, the more the problem is considered, the more potentially diverse medieval literacy would appear to be, and the more hopelessly complex seems the effort to define and categorize the manifestations of literacy—the instances of reading and writing—we discover in the past.

The essays in *Voices in Dialogue* strongly suggest that these complications are far from being simply abstract or theoretical concerns. Indeed, the instances of reading and writing studied here reveal women who possessed and exercised various kinds and levels of literacy. Examples are too numerous to list, but we might readily compare the assumptions of Augustine about the abilities of his women correspondents not only in Latin comprehension, but also in theological interpretation (Conybeare and Vessey) with the careful and detailed instructions about reading for the Syon nuns in the English *Myroure of Oure Ladye* (Schirmer and Justice), and ultimately with the many and varying interpretations of female *ingenium*—women's ability to read and think and write—among authors of the Middle Ages (Blamires and Newman). We might lay beside the devotional and homiletic use of Latin literacy among the well-educated nuns of Shaftesbury (Morrow and Bell) and Admont (Beach and Van Engen) the more personal and secular manifestation of Latin proficiency in the woman's part of the *Epistolae duorum amantium* (Jaeger and Constable), which does indeed reveal "an astonishing degree and type of learning" (Constable), worthy of comparison with the writing, both monastic and secular, of Heloise. We might see both similarities and striking disparities among, say, the Syon nuns who owned a significant collection of vernacular writings in the fifteenth century (though their reading was not limited to the vernacular) and were encouraged by those writings to read and sing with understanding, even with interpretive freedom and clerical authority (Schirmer and Justice, Zieman and Fassler); Margery Kempe, who used a scribal assistant to transform her life into her English *Book*, but whose familiarity with textual culture suggests a wide range of readings in Latin and English (Watson and Riddy, Gertz-Robinson and Wallace); and Christine de Pizan, whose lively engagement through her texts with the literary circles and conventions of France is as fascinating as is her probable involvement in the production of manuscripts, including those of her own works (Blamires and Newman).[3] Indeed, how might Margery Kempe's writing of her *Book* with the help of her priestly scribe (Watson and Riddy) be related to Christine de Pizan's writing in relation to the predominantly male literary culture around her (Blamires and Newman)? The comparisons and contrasts, like the questions they raise, might easily continue, but I believe the message is already clear: the literate and authorial activities of the women discussed in *Voices in Dialogue* are as various and unique as the women themselves, and our concepts of literacy and authorship, reading and writing, seem, at times, hopelessly inadequate, as if our attempts at accurate definition, categorization, and generalization are curtailed by the complexities of reality as surely as they are limited by our incomplete records of that reality.

A closer look at two situations discussed in our dialogues will, I hope, clarify certain aspects of the problem, if they also necessarily complicate our understanding in the process. The first is that surrounding the composition of the *Epistolae duorum amantium*. I do not wish here to take up either side of the debate presented so energetically by Jaeger and Constable, but to point out instead the nature of the texts it is based upon. For we could hardly have a better example of the various processes of medieval writing, and the ways in which such complications can serve not to inform us about, but to distance us from, the original authors of the *Epistolae*—presumably a man and woman in both a romantic and intellectual relationship—and what they might have written. We cannot simply read the products of their hands. To mention only some of the possible stages of authorship here, these letters when first exchanged could well have been written on wax tablets and only copied onto vellum later, perhaps much later, perhaps only from memory, perhaps with a structural agenda in mind that never existed when the letters were first exchanged, perhaps by one of the original authors, perhaps not. Certainly they have been edited, abridged, and departicularized by their fifteenth-century Cistercian collector and excerpter, and now, through their recent republication and the heated debate (clarified in Jaeger's response) this has given rise to, they are undergoing a different form of manipulation—almost a kind of rewriting—as they are analyzed, debated, and authenticated (or not) in relation not only to the later monastic letters of Abelard and Heloise, which have themselves so recently passed through a similar process, but also to the events and chronology we have assigned to the lives of Abelard and Heloise, as well as to a number of learned preconceptions about women, learning, and the twelfth century that may or may not be right or even especially useful.

It is very difficult to find solid ground from which to argue for particular or certain authorship—even from which to define exactly what was originally authored—in such a situation. The essays by Jaeger and Constable present entirely valid approaches to the problem, but neither can hope to unravel completely the tangle of textual and historical problems highlighted by the *Epistolae*. The historical verification called for by Constable, for instance, is undoubtedly useful, and we might very much like to see a reference to Heloise's uncle Fulbert to assign the woman's part of the *Epistolae* to her, but if we did, would it mean that Heloise was certainly the author of the woman's letters, or rather that they were originally the product of a forger who was careful with detail and understood the mind of the historian? Similarly, the parallels of style and personality and historic events emphasized by Jaeger go a long way toward pointing us in the direction of authorial probabilities, but if, say, the man of the *Epistolae* did not sound an awful lot like Abelard, would it mean that Abelard did not write the man's letters, or that his personality, his perspective, even his style had undergone enormous changes between his earlier and later writings? The incomplete and complicated nature of the texts available to us makes such questions notoriously difficult to answer with accuracy and certainty, yet it also teaches us much about the ways in which texts were created and disseminated in the Middle Ages, about the convoluted and fragmented forms in which they come down to us, and about the choices we as historians and literary scholars make in reading and writing about them. There are several questions beyond original authorship that are well worth asking here.

My second example appears in the dialogue of Conybeare and Vessey, where an understanding of a high level of Latin literacy among Augustine's women correspondents is complicated in an upper-class culture which relegates the physical acts of reading and writing to slaves or paid professionals. What, then, is literacy? Or indeed authorship? Who might we call literate in that highly accomplished way indicated by Bell's fourth level? Those who dictate and conceive? Or those who write and construct? Or both? Can they even be separated, especially from our distant perspective? One particularly intriguing aspect of this compositional scenario is that a fair view must necessarily apply the same complications and hence the same questions and doubts discussed by Vessey in relation to women's literacy to male readers and writers of the time. Men, too, generally had slaves and professionals execute the physical acts of literacy—the reading and writing of texts. So even the literacy and authorship of someone like Augustine himself could be re-evaluated, and not unreasonably, from an entirely different perspective.[4] What if, for instance, we imagine him enjoying the benefits of an extremely accomplished *notarius* over a long period of time? We might easily attribute stylistic devices, rhetorical flourishes, even larger matters of structure and content to the one who physically wrote as readily as to the one who dictated—indeed, all too many of us would do it far more readily were it a woman's dictation we were discussing and a male scribe's record of that speech. Some might argue that it would have been virtually impossible in any case for a busy man like Augustine to worry about the structure and language of every sentence in his voluminous writings, and it is certainly possible to see those many instances where Augustine expresses different opinions on the same topic as evidence of changes in his *notarius,* rather than uncertainties or alterations in his thought. It is an argument I would not personally choose to pursue, yet it is as provocative as I expect it is unthinkable to most Augustinian scholars—as unthinkable as not applying these very kinds of questions and explanations and qualifications to women's literacy and authorship in the same period.

Here, then, the complications surrounding past literacies highlight not only the inadequate nature of our established terminology and paradigms when we strive to define and theorize upon a process with physical as well as intellectual, emotional, and even ethereal aspects which vary from individual to individual and may not have left adequate traces upon the historical record. They also illuminate for us how we as students of texts and writers of history, gathering our evidence and constructing our arguments, need to apply an even hand and eye to the men and women of the past. If we constantly make the women we study bear an extra "burden of proof" (Beach)—and there is no doubt that we do—then we should bring the same attitudes and questions to the men we study. Similarly, when we have the kind of evidence about women that would, if it were representative of male activities, present a convincing argument for high levels of literacy or attributions of authorship, then we should bring those same conclusions to bear upon the women.

An example from my own work on the English manuscripts of Augustine's *Confessiones* can be found in British Library MS Royal 5. C.V, a late thirteenth- or early fourteenth-century volume[5] in which Augustine's autobiography (among other works) has been provided with extensive contemporary marginal annotations which suggest a learned commentator and a sophisticated reading of the text. That alone makes MS Royal 5. C.V an interesting copy of the text, but the manuscript is especially relevant here because all other extant copies of the *Confessiones* with medieval English provenances are associated with male readers only. The single exception is this volume, which belonged to the Gilbertine house of canons and nuns at Sempringham. The conventional approach to such a manuscript would no doubt be to consider it the possession of the canons and of no use to the women, particularly since the volume was procured for the community by John de Glynton, a canon of the house and a master of Cambridge.[6] Yet Glynton also became a master of the Order, responsible for the education of its nuns as well as its canons, and his manuscript would, in fact, have been in the care of the nuns, for the Gilbertine *Institutes* specify that it is the precentress who is in charge of each community's books. In addition, we have every reason to believe that the nuns would have appreciated Augustine's text because Latin literacy was required of Gilbertine nuns and their daily tasks included reading, copying, and embellishing manuscripts.[7] There seems no reason, then, to exclude the Sempringham nuns as probable readers of the *Confessiones*, or, in fact, to see them as especially exceptional in so being. Goscelin of Saint Bertin in the late eleventh century clearly expects Eve to read the *Confessiones*, though no evidence of this exists beyond his *Liber Confortatorius*, and Christine de Pizan writing her *Book of the City of Ladies* and autobiographical *Vision* in the early fifteenth century certainly knows some form of both the *Confessiones* and the *City of God*.[8] Indeed, given the low survival rate of manuscripts from women's houses in the Middle Ages, it is more reasonable to see the instance of MS Royal 5. C.V as an indication that other medieval women might also have been readers of Augustine,[9] though more extensive manuscript evidence of this has not survived, than it is to view that lack of corroborative evidence as an indication that women did not read the text and thus as justification for ignoring or suppressing the positive evidence of MS Royal 5. C.V.[10] No one I have discussed this manuscript with has ever questioned whether the literate canons of the house could or would have read the book, though everything we know about Gilbertine communities suggests that the literate nuns of Sempringham might well have had even freer access to it.[11]

Scholarship that strives in this way for a more balanced way of looking at the texts of the past—that strives for some kind of equity of perspective with regard to gender—is in one way hopelessly idealistic because who can ever be completely equitable or objective? Yet in another way it urges us to examine the texts we study with our eyes newly open to the various roles of many potential participants, both male and female, in the composition, production, dissemination, reception, and revision of texts, and thus to the subtleties and complexities of the documents we study. The potential benefits of such a view are beautifully demonstrated by the dialogue of Alison Beach and John Van Engen, for Beach reveals how a number of the anonymous sermons and biblical commentaries written at the monastery of Admont in the twelfth century and long assigned exclusively to male authors should in fact be attributed to the nuns of the house, who worked as scribes, *notarii,* and authors for their community. It seems that the main reason why the strong evidence for female authorship has not been examined before is that no one wished to look for women authors (or indeed to analyze the complicated paleographical picture they have left us) and thus to gather and interpret the evidence with an eye to the possibility of their role, though once the evidence is placed before us, female authorship at different levels of involvement seems the inevitable conclusion for many of the Admont works. Even more fascinating in some ways than the strong probability of the Admont nuns as authors of their own sermons is the certainty of shared authorship between the nuns and monks, where dictation, drafting, correcting, and finalizing are completed in stages through various contributors, both male and female, of the physical and intellectual writing skills involved in authorship. It is the "collective achievement of the monastery's twelfth-century scholars and preachers, both male and female" (Beach), that stands out in Beach's study of the Admont manuscripts.[12] Though there may be a tendency to negate or minimize the role of each individual— particularly female ones—in group authorship of this kind, indeed even to suggest that the men are the real authors and the women only assistants, the scenario revealed by Beach suggests that the women members of this authorial network were not only active partners, but both the initiators and completers of textual projects. The implication is that textual production in the Middle Ages was not always "controlled largely by men" (Schirmer), and I expect that the more we look into the details of monastic authorship, the more we will discover that issues of gender did not in fact prevent active intellectual collaboration between the sexes.

Indeed, the more one reflects simply on the roles of *amanuenses* and scribes, *notarii* and *scriptoria* in ancient and medieval writing, on the very nature of the manuscripts that remain to us, the more one realizes that we can hardly dispense with this notion of "collective achievement" in thinking about the concept of authorship in Late Antiquity and the Middle Ages. When we focus particularly on women writers, this is all the more important, and not always because women did not have access to the physical and intellectual writing skills necessary to produce their own texts. Certainly we know that some women enjoyed that complete familiarity with textual culture indicated by Bell's fourth level of Latin literacy—what Conybeare calls "a high degree of literacy, in the sense of the ability to read and write good Latin." Heloise, whether she wrote the woman's part of the *Epistolae duorum amantium* or not, must be considered among these, as indeed must the nuns of Admont and the monastic author Gertrude the Great, who bore a wax tablet ready at her side and wrote in Latin both her own visionary and spiritual texts, and most probably (along with another nun) also the visions of her fellow nun Mechthild of Hackeborn, presumably from both notes and dictation.[13] Yet many women, like Mechthild, had others physically write their texts for them. Sometimes this must have been because of a lack of literacy skills, real or imagined, but in many instances (both with and without claims of textual incompetence) there are other important reasons why a woman author might have another physically record, even help structure, her text. Augustine's correspondents, with their scribal slaves (Vessey), are a case in point: here the issue is social class, and what we know is not that they could not write, but that they would have considered the physical act of so doing beneath them. The later medieval visionaries are another, and here it seems to be primarily an authoritative stamp of approval that is sought by women like Mechthild of Magdeburg, whom the Dominican friar Heinrich of Halle helped with the arrangement and presentation of her visions. His prologue reads more as a testimony to Mechthild's holy life, true visions, and proper spiritual progression than it does as an admission that she required a man to record her visions due to any lack in her own literate abilities.[14] It is a kind of authorization of orthodoxy that was rarely dispensed with even when it was women doing the physical writing for themselves or for other women, as indicated by the "Endorsement and Authorization" of the anonymous Helfta nun who wrote the first book of Gertrude's *Herald*.[15] Marguerite Porete's use of clerical responses as a preface to later copies of her *Mirror of Simple Souls* is another example, and one so blatantly, ironically, even dismissively defiant of the clerical authority she apparently seeks to secure that it suggests a clear understanding on her part of how it is the way in which readers view women and their writing that often determines not only what but exactly how a woman may write: freedom of thought and expression is, I suspect, far more the issue here than functional literacy.[16]

Certainly one gets the sense that Margery Kempe used her male *amanuensis* for reasons of authorization, shielding herself from dangerous modes of expression and the inclusion of questionable material as much as from the potentially harsh responses of readers. Yet the Proem to the *Book of Margery Kempe* also implies, though without specifically claiming any kind of illiteracy for "the creature" whose story it narrates,[17] that she needs someone to write her life and visions down for her, implying either an inability to shape letters on vellum, or perhaps not enough familiarity with literary conventions to feel secure constructing her own text. We can be no more precise about her motivations than we can be about the relative authorial roles of visionary and scribal priest. The possibilities and problems of authorship here are hashed out in the lively dialogue of Watson and Riddy, which not only offers a number of valuable insights on the composition of Margery's *Book*, but also demonstrates how our ability to identify and separate one "voice" from the other, assigning responsibility for particular words or sentences, thoughts or trends, chapters or structural dynamics to either Margery or her scribe, is as limited and fraught with difficulties as is the stance that the *Book of Margery Kempe* is a text which we should avoid questioning in terms of details of production and authorship because its mode of composition is simply too complex, or too caught up in the lived and irrecoverable experience of human exchange.

Leaving the fine lines of that debate to them, then, I would like to comment briefly on the way in which these two thoughtful essays suggested to me the *Book*'s use of the autobiographical mode I have reflected on so much in terms of Augustine's *Confessiones*. Both Watson and Riddy are agreed throughout their discussion that the *Book* is autobiographical, a text which strives to narrate the nature of a life (though the two may differ in their opinions as to whether the self so represented existed or not before its construction in text). The two also agree in claiming that Margery does not adhere to the "stage-by-stage ascent away from the carnal towards the spiritual" (Watson) which is characteristic of Augustine's influential autobiography. What struck me about this is how much of what they say about the *Book of Margery Kempe*—and space restraints here will keep me from going beyond points they have already raised—is in fact found in the *Confessiones* and the writings of those medieval individuals who use its story of spiritual progress as a model for their own "textualization of memory" (Riddy). Examples include the blurring of theological argument with the narration of a life in the *Book* (Watson); the way in which the *Book* records the tenacious, often uncertain searching of its subject in a text which makes enormous demands upon, even creates struggles of faith within, its readers (Watson); the muddled chronology presented by the *Book,* though it is precise about chronology in many places and there are good thematic reasons—reasons, I might add, related to the idea of spiritual progress—for its apparent vagaries (Watson); the struggle inherent in the *Book* as it refuses "vanity at the same time as raising its protagonist to such a height" (Watson); and finally, the way in which the *Book* equates confessing with the telling of Margery's life story (Riddy), and, more generally, makes dialogue with God the matter of autobiography. All of these qualities are intrinsic to Augustine's *Confessiones,* which is not to say that I disagree with Watson and Riddy and would have Margery adopting the Augustinian model wholesale, for no one who made use of it in the Middle Ages did that.[18] Indeed, transformation of the tradition adopted from the *Confessiones* is the norm—the very way of defining the self in relation to the self of Augustine—while the qualities listed above as manifest in the *Book of Margery Kempe* are among those much used by Augustine's readers.[19] It would take an entire dialogue to explore the many aspects of precisely what Margery and her scribe were doing with Augustine's autobiographical model in this first English autobiography of a woman, but it may be sufficient to point out here that the sophisticated use of Augustine's *Confessiones* by Margery and her *amanuensis* certainly suggests a high level of literacy in the authorship team—literacy traditionally considered Latin, patristic, monastic, and clerical. Yet, as Watson points out, the ideal of spiritual progress is hardly used in ways we might expect of a cleric, and I would not wish to assign this learning to one authorial partner or the other. Instead, the *Book*'s use of this sophisticated Latin tradition—like the theology Watson explores in the *Book;* like the theological arguments "usually discreetly buried in Latin scholastic discussions" but used by Julian of Norwich (Kerby-Fulton, "When Women Preached")—should give us pause to wonder about "how Latin actually did function in the middle of [a progressively] English culture;"[20] to wonder about "vernacular" literacies like those of the Syon nuns, the Bridgittine spiritual tradition Watson places Margery within; to question our "assumptions about the intellectual capacities of *illiterate* medieval women" (Watson, my emphasis); even to rethink academic preconceptions like the "cherished myth" of "Margery's illiteracy."[21]

The second thing I would like to emphasize from the dialogue of Watson and Riddy is closely related, for it is the degree to which the *Book of Margery Kempe* records in considerable detail and at various places in its narrative progression the processes and complications of its own production. Certainly it is a graphic example of Brian Stock's claim that "writing is not just the written, the product: it is whatever goes into the making of it" (quoted by Morrow), but it may be that one of the reasons why Margery's *Book* does this so explicitly is precisely because it is an autobiography. Writing about one's life—converting a life lived into a life textualized[22]—is, after all, a major life event, a self-generated record of the very self-understanding its narrative presents its subject in the process of seeking. This is particularly true when, as Watson points out in the case of Margery, the autobiographical subject knew that she would write her story long before she did and hence might have lived aspects of her life with its textualization in mind.[23] There is, then, a certain complicating authenticity to the *Book*'s efforts as an autobiography to represent "whatever goes into" its own "writing," an authenticity felt also in some of Margery's most intimate confessions of temptation, weakness, and doubt. This is to say that the record of shared authorship and its trials and challenges in the *Book of Margery Kempe,* like the progressions and regressions of Margery related by the text, like her vibrant sensuality and experiences of mystical union, like her theological speculations and evangelical ministry (Gertz-Robinson and Wallace, as well as Watson and Riddy), like her long arduous pilgrimages and days of simple survival under the burden of onerous spiritual gifts, is an essential part of her life record as a writing visionary living in the world. Writing Margery's text is as much of a struggle, it seems, as the other aspects of her life recorded in the *Book;* accordingly, writing is also redeeming, with the writing both Margery and her scribal priest do exceeding even prayer in God's esteem.[24] As Genelle Gertz-Robinson writes, "one might ultimately say that the *Book* makes heroic both the pursuit of education and the practice of such skills once they have been acquired," but in so doing, it also paints a complicated and realistic picture of the literacy and authorship of a late medieval woman.

The scenario of authorship in the *Book of Margery Kempe* that works so well both aesthetically as woman's autobiography and spiritually as part of a pious woman's life can be verified as an authentic record of authorial experience through other women studied in *Voices in Dialogue*. It is just this kind of complicated, shared process of authorship, with the various individuals playing different, often undefined and overlapping roles—composer, dictator, recorder, corrector, reviser, and so on—which often characterizes more "historical" evidence of women's writing, like that concerning Augustine's correspondents and Admont's nuns. There is little doubt that thinking about the writing and authorship of women in the past in ways that incorporate the wide potentials of such complicated authorial situations as well as the limitations they impose upon us as scholars does indeed tie something of a "Gordian knot of interpretive and historical problems" (Watson). Yet it can hardly be counterproductive if tying such a knot helps us develop "views that are more humanly and culturally rich, whether or not they satisfy the expectations of a grand narrative or the aspirations of our own age" (Van Engen). Indeed, we need to acknowledge such troublesome interpretive knots and ask questions that are more "concrete, more precise, better historically situated" (Van Engen); we need to delve deeply into the details of individual situations and entertain "a more complex range of stories" altogether (Van Engen); and we need to recreate in our writing and teaching a "more complicated" past based upon numerous "case by case studies."[25] For as Beach points out, only by accumulating a critical mass of evidence based upon careful and detailed studies of the lives and education, books and writings of individual women and women's communities, like her own into Admont's literate nuns, will the "paradigm shift" in our assumptions about women of the past be achieved on a larger scale. This must be an ongoing communal effort and indeed it is already well underway, with the essays collected in *Voices in Dialogue* making significant contributions and, like so much other recent work, indicating at least the general direction our "paradigm shift" might take.[26] The dialogues presented here on the whole support Bell's tentative conclusions that many religious women in the Middle Ages may have achieved a better education and a more accomplished form of literacy than hitherto believed; that "more women wrote more books" than the list of those clearly assigned to them can suggest.[27] That is to say, if we return again to Bell's four levels of Latin literacy, that there were more medieval women who could boast the fourth and highest level—"the ability to compose and write a text of one's own"—than scholars have assumed in the past.

Yet while giving more credit in this regard to women of the past, we should not forget that one of the most powerful and consistent messages voiced by the dialogues in this volume is that we must not isolate them in their reading and writing—that progress in our thinking about women's literacy and authorship from Late Antiquity through the Middle Ages must involve the essential element of human relationships. Many of the texts and individuals and scenarios studied by our contributors highlight the vital role played in textual production and reception by the bonds between people and the shared experience and active collaboration based upon and brought into being by those bonds. Several of the essays address these issues directly, drawing our attention to their importance. Riddy, for example, points out that the record of authorship we are given for the *Book of Margery Kempe*—and it applies to so many other instances of female authorship in the Middle Ages, like the nuns of Admont and Helfta—tends to make "a nonsense of our categories" for thinking and talking about writing and authorship. She urges instead that the Proem's record of the *Book*'s authoring describes "what some sociolinguists now call 'literacy events'." Inherently "embedded in sociability" and human relationships, "literacy events" are communal, though the community might be large or small, closely knit or spread at great distances, and are characterized as much by orality as literacy; as much by the emotional experiences of personal relationships— "affection, obligation, timorousness, reproachfulness, guilt and gratitude" (Riddy)—as by more overt textual activities. Though it is notoriously difficult, often completely impossible to determine the exact quality of, say, oral or emotional contributions, thinking in terms of shared "literacy events" prevents us from narrowing our perspectives in ways that simplify or obscure or negate some women's roles as writers and contributors to textual culture.

Conybeare and Vessey would have us take a similarly expansive view encompassing the "entire nexus of communication" which originally surrounded the "textual traces" of epistolary activity, and which, in the Middle Ages, as in the late antique world Conybeare explores in her study of Paulinus of Nola, "could include everything from supplementary notes, which have not survived, through gifts of one sort or another sent with the letter, to verbal messages brought by the letter-carriers."[28] In their dialogue there is also a clear extension of this perspective to wider issues of audience and dissemination. Vessey writes of Augustine's female correspondents as possessing what he calls a "functional 'literacy,'" which he defines as manifested in "their roles as initiators, facilitators, and sustainers of a set of discursive exchanges that typically involved the interpretation and dissemination of [complex] texts." This way of thinking about literate women in Late Antiquity is not intended by Vessey "to subordinate women (again) but to emphasize their substantial equality with men" in their influence and control over "the circuits of textual information." Thus their role remains central whether we see the women who shared letters with Augustine as sitting down to read and write texts themselves or contributing to the "circuits" through the more immediate literacy of others, whether we see this distancing from physical textuality as a choice or a necessity. Intimate networks of exchange become as important as individual readers and writers; intended audience and reading community are partakers along with authors and scribes in the production and circulation of texts. This is to say that we can further complicate our conceptions of reading and writing with authorial expectations of transmission "along a network of readers who share interests and vocabularies and practices" (Justice), as indeed with the actual responses of those readers at various stages of composition and dissemination.

It is precisely this sort of network or circuit of textual exchange that lies at the heart of the dialogue between Morrow and Bell. Through a close look at the twelfth-century Shaftesbury Psalter, Morrow reveals how the nuns of that house acted as participants in the networks of exchange—as indeed in other networks of monastic literacy at the time, like the production and circulation of mortuary rolls—which enabled the dissemination of the devotional texts of Anselm of Canterbury in the twelfth century. What Morrow argues for in our conception of Anselm's relationship with the nuns of Shaftesbury is a "mutually supportive colleagueship," in which it is possible to see the expected play of spiritual guidance and friendship, shared devotion and mutual affection, but also common interests, similar education and levels of literacy, equivalent social and institutional standing, and shared work of administrative and political dimensions. There is no doubt that this concept of collegiality is a useful one when applied to many of the situations presented in this volume, all the way from Augustine and his correspondents to Margery and her scribe, with instances of shared authorship being only the most obvious. It also works well to describe many aspects of the relationships women shared with men who are not studied here, like Jerome and his Christian friends, or Boniface and the nuns who forwarded his continental mission. The concept of collegiality does not, then, exclude women from serious consideration prior to the late eleventh century, as recent studies have suggested concepts of friendship and ennobling love did.[29] Collegiality also does not necessarily require the personal meeting of individuals, so it can exist between close intimate friends as between virtual strangers—the relationships shared by the contributors to this volume, for example, are as various as relationships can be, yet there is no doubt we are all colleagues. The concept of collegiality, then, rather than that of friendship so often used to describe the relationships of the past, but often inappropriately as Vessey suggests, may enable us to find a common denominator at the base of the bonds that the dialogues collected here have revealed among reading and writing men and women in Augustine's time, as in Margery's.

What I would like to do now is explore three different literate or textual relationships (one in some detail; the other two very briefly) both to test the applicability of mutually supportive collegiality and to delve a little further into a few of the circuits of exchange that involved women and have left us with textual records. The first and longest grows from the dialogue of Morrow and Bell, for the Shaftesbury Psalter with its pair of Anselmian prayers is only the tip of the iceberg when it comes to women's involvement in the circuits of textual exchange associated with Anselm's popular devotional writings. Anselm very deliberately passed his *Orationes sive Meditationes* along to women, just as he shared them with his monks,[30] and if we focus for a moment on the most important of his known female readers, Matilda of Tuscany (1046–1115), it is possible to catch a glimpse of a highly literate woman thoroughly involved in the reception and dissemination of texts which were influential in the most learned circles of the early twelfth century.

Although Matilda of Tuscany was not a nun, she was an extremely learned woman, as her biographer, the priest and monk Donizo of Canossa, informs us when he praises her for her learning, specifically for her composition of Latin letters, as well as her knowledge of German and French.[31] Anselm, like Augustine with his female correspondents, clearly knows this, expecting and assuming an accomplished level of literacy from her.[32] He recommends in the letter that accompanied his *Orationes sive Meditationes* that Matilda apply to his pieces a kind of reading which not only inspires personal devotion and self-reflection, but also requires "thoughtful meditation" and views them with an eye trained and insightful enough to use them as models for composing her own prayers.[33] The comments of both biographer and archbishop are in themselves striking testimonies to Matilda's literacy and potential authorship, yet even more fascinating is the extant evidence that demonstrates how the manuscript sent to Matilda in 1104 played a significant role in the medieval dissemination and textual traditions of Anselm's devotional writings.[34] I will focus my discussion here on only two manuscripts. The first is Admont, Stiftsbibliothek MS 289, which was reproduced in Salzburg around 1160 and is among several medieval copies of the *Orationes sive Meditationes* which represent the collection and order of Anselm's devotional texts just as they are thought to have appeared in Matilda's original copy.[35] It is an especially rare and accurate example of this Matildan recension because it is the earliest extant copy of the tradition and one of a very few copies which contain as a prologue Anselm's letter of readerly guidance to Matilda.[36] The second, Oxford, Bodleian Library MS Auct. D.2.6, was produced in England around the middle of the twelfth century, but it represents a post-Anselmian recension (though a relatively early one) of the devotional collection—that is, a recension in which prayers and meditations by contemporary and later authors working in Anselm's devotional mode have been added to the collection of pieces Anselm originally sent to Matilda.[37]

In both cases, then, Matilda's manuscript can be seen as inceptive, and in both cases one could also argue that Matilda's literate and devotional presence is grafted onto—even inscribed into—Anselm's *Orationes sive Meditationes*. In Admont MS 289, for instance, the retention of Anselm's epistolary advice to Matilda inscribes her as an important reader of the texts, while two illustrations of Matilda make her presence felt with the immediacy of the visual. The first is a full-page miniature which appears as a frontispiece before the Matildan prologue (figure 1). It features Matilda standing while Anselm, enthroned as archbishop, hands her a book, presumably the volume of *Orationes sive Meditationes* that was sent to her and copied (either directly or at some remove)

FIGURE 1. Matilda Receiving the Book from Anselm, in Admont MS 289, folio 1v. Reproduced by permission of Stift Admont.

ſcитат ṡ ſuffi cᶻɛ ʀ ɛ.

FIGURE 2. Matilda and Anselm Kneeling and Praying with Scrolls before Christ, in Admont MS 289, folio 2v. Reproduced by permission of Stift Admont.

to produce this manuscript.[38] The second appears at the head of the prayers themselves, particularly above *Oratio I Ad Deum,* and shows Anselm and Matilda kneeling on either side of Christ in Majesty, each with a scroll representing active prayer in hand, equal partners united in the act of devotion (figure 2).[39] In Bodleian MS Auct. D.2.6 the visual presence of Matilda is yet more frequent, with a female figure who has been convincingly identified as the descendant of the countess appearing several times.[40] In three instances she appears along with Anselm, as in the Admont volume, but with some significant variations. An initial S on folio 185v, for instance, depicts the scene in which Anselm as archbishop presents his book to Matilda, but she kneels before him rather than standing, and this scene occupies only the top half of the S; the bottom half records Anselm as abbot presenting his volume to his fellow monks (figure 3).[41] The other two miniatures depicting Anselm and Matilda position them before Christ: the one appearing on folio 191v is very similar to the illustration of the pair for *Oratio I* in the Admont manuscript, though in MS Auct. D.2.6 Christ places his hands on the couple's heads in a gesture of blessing (figure 4); the one appearing on folio 189v presents a new motif, with the couple standing at Christ's side much as Matilda stood by Anselm's side in the Admont frontispiece, though here no book is exchanged, but instead Christ points a finger at the two, both of whom hold hand to breast in a gesture of introspection and

FIGURE 3. Letter 'S' with Anselm, Matilda, and the Monks, in Oxford Bodleian Library MS Auct. D.2.6, folio 185v. Reproduced by permission of the Bodleian Library, University of Oxford.

penitence (figure 5).[42] There could hardly be a more compelling testimony to the shared participation of both men and women, Anselm and Matilda, in the learned textual networks—in the intellectual and spiritual circuits—that produced and exchanged and used devotional texts in the twelfth century and beyond.

But what of other women? Is there any evidence in our manuscripts to suggest the significant presence of a larger community of women readers to match the network of Benedictine monks who made use of Anselm's *Orationes sive Meditationes*? Indeed there

FIGURE 4. Anselm and Matilda Kneeling and Blessed by Christ, in Oxford Bodleian Library MS Auct. D.2.6, folio 191v. Reproduced by permission of the Bodleian Library, University of Oxford.

is, for both Admont MS 289 and MS Auct. D.2.6 belonged to communities of women in the Middle Ages. Admont MS 289 was made for a "Humilitas Abbatissa," perhaps Diemut, the abbess of Traunkirchen in Upper Austria, and depicts her kneeling in devotion with two of her nuns before an image of Paul rapt into heaven in the miniature adorning his prayer.[43] MS Auct. D.2.6, although we do not know its original place of production in England,[44] found its way to the Benedictine priory of nuns at Littlemore

FIGURE 5. Anselm and Matilda Standing beside Christ, in Oxford Bodleian Library MS Auct. D.2.6, folio 189v. Reproduced by permission of the Bodleian Library, University of Oxford.

during the thirteenth century, and it, too, emphasizes a female readership through its inclusion of several miniatures of Matilda alone, kneeling in devotion before Christ or the Virgin Mary, sometimes with a manuscript of Anselm's *Orationes sive Meditationes* in hand.[45] It is very difficult to believe that the significance of this illustrative tradition would have slipped by the literate nuns who encountered the manuscript, for as Bell points out, monastic reading habits of the time "would have seen the images as an integral part of the text"—indeed, the nuns (even those who could not read text) would probably have read "the images *as* text," in a meditative, even self-reflective way. Meditation upon the images of these two very different manuscripts would have suggested to their female readers that women, namely they themselves, were not only actively included in the learned Anselmian devotional network, but even prioritized as receivers and readers, disseminators and users of Anselm's devotional writings. The simple fact that such a manuscript existed in their library, that they were actually looking at it, would of course confirm this message.

Now, the precise origin of the illustrative tradition associated with the Matildan manuscripts of the *Orationes sive Meditationes* is unknown, but a couple of interesting possibilities present themselves. For one, it may be that this feminine illustrative tradition began in Italy with Matilda,[46] who thus inscribed herself into her manuscript as a devout reader of Anselm's writings. This possibility further highlights her essential role in shaping the textual circuits and hence the reading experience of others in her devotional network. Yet it is also possible that the illustrations began in England or France with Anselm himself, and were perhaps associated with a presentation copy made by the monks of Canterbury. This is the intriguing argument of Otto Pächt, who theorizes that the manuscript sent to Matilda by Anselm (in exile at Lyons at the time) was made in either England or France, but certainly illustrated by an English or English-trained artist. Thus the appearance of similar or related illustrations in later English manuscripts is explained, either because a duplicate of Matilda's manuscript was left behind in England or sent (or brought) there from Lyons.[47] This would mean that Anselm actually intended his devotions to be accompanied by illustrations of a woman receiving his texts beside—even before—his monks, and uttering them in devotion both by herself and along with their author. It is hardly an unreasonable suggestion given Anselm's efforts to disseminate his texts to women and make them a part of his readership. It is certainly possible that the manuscript Morrow suggests might have been sent by Anselm to Eulalia with the letter he writes her in 1104 (the same year he sends his works to Matilda) could have been a similar copy, and not only the source of Anselm's prayers in the Shaftesbury Psalter, but also at least one of the sources of the Matildan illustrations in England. Yet given the cooperative efforts of medieval "literacy events," there seems no reason to make the two origin scenarios for the Matildan illustrations mutually exclusive. It is quite possible, in fact, that Anselm and Matilda worked together (if at a distance much of the time), each of them controlling and enabling different aspects of the "circuits of textual information," each of them working to produce both text and illustrations for his *Orationes sive Meditationes*.

Whether we entertain this provocative possibility or not, however, Matilda's role in transmitting Anselm's devotional works, her presence both alone and with Anselm in the manuscript illustrations, the evidence that several manuscripts (like the Psalter discussed by Morrow and Bell) containing Anselm's pieces were available to and intended for women readers make it absolutely clear that women were not marginal members of this particular literate network, but were in fact very much in the forefront, sending and receiving its textual and devotional messages along with male literates. We need not create the circuit of exchange here to explain or justify or excuse a feminine participation that is somehow less significant or accomplished or real than the masculine, for it seems that Anselm's women readers have created the circuit themselves. Certainly I would call Matilda's involvement in Anselm's learned circle, and thus her relationship with Anselm, collegial, and given the central role of women in the network of Anselm's *Orationes sive Meditationes*, it is not even difficult to believe (unless we close our eyes to the evidence and adamantly refuse to do so without just cause) that some of Anselm's women readers followed the advice he gave Matilda and wrote their own devotional pieces. Anselm's devotional writings inspired numerous imitative works which were often circulated along with his pieces, and the majority of these remain anonymous, so it is entirely possible—dare I say probable considering the role of his women readers—that the authors of some of these prayers and meditations were in fact women. The manuscripts discussed above do not, of course, show Matilda and other women in the process of writing their own devotional pieces, but they also do not show Anselm and his monks doing so, though we know they did. Both men and women are shown, however, in the much more important readerly end-process of praying, whether the texts they use for this are Anselm's or their own, and women, much as they are spatially prioritized as the receivers of the *Orationes sive Meditationes*, are depicted more often than men.[48]

A somewhat distant parallel to this appearance of women in the manuscript tradition of Anselm can be seen in the involvement of women in the literary tradition of female *ingenium* discussed by Alcuin Blamires and Barbara Newman (my second example of collegial relationships). Here the dynamics of the literate network function primarily within texts, rather than, say, within manuscripts or within the *scriptorium*, yet it is clearly another way for authors to participate in an exchange of ideas and texts—a dialogue, if I may—with fellow authors, both contemporary and historical. Whatever notions of suppression we might attach to the literary canon explored by Blamires and Newman, we see in their dialogue women authors, from Hrotsvitha of Gandersheim in the tenth century, to the woman of the *Epistolae* in the twelfth, to Christine de Pizan in the fifteenth, involved in receiving and reconstructing the ideas of feminine intelligence and creativity they encountered in their own reading, as perhaps in their daily lives. Our evidence may not show as many women dealing with this topic as men, as indeed our evidence does not show as many women writing in the Middle Ages as men (though the balance is changing daily, of course), but those who do address the problem do not do so submissively, though their tone may be one of deference, as indeed is that of most medieval male authors when speaking of their own abilities.

Examples abound. Hrotsvitha uses the humble stance she adopts to write what she wishes, in the ways she wishes, using the sources she wishes, all the while dazzling her readers with her learning and rhetorical virtuosity in the very passages that construct "an extreme scenario of humility" (Blamires).[49] The woman in the *Epistolae* hardly negates her intelligence by playing it down; instead, as Blamires argues, she provides another example of "*ingenium* conspicuously manifesting itself even while it claims to be articulating its own ineptitude," and her "astonishing . . . learning" (Constable) comes across far more clearly than her humility. Though Christine de Pizan never creates the pretense of humility in her *Book of the City of Ladies*, she does reflect in its opening section upon the effect on readers like herself who encounter negative depictions of women in the literary tradition—on how stultifying such thinking can be.[50] Yet her "stupor" does not prevent her from reasoning the problem out, ambitiously rebuilding a salvation history for women (through a vernacular transformation of Augustine's *City of God*, which might usefully be compared to Margery's transformation of the *Confessiones*), and ultimately crediting women with sharper *ingenium* than men (Blamires). Christine's voice—defending, justifying, and celebrating women's natures and accomplishments—sounds always at the center of an active literary community; always it is working to inform and transform her readers, and often it is at its most penetrating and insightful when responding to the writing around her. The strong responses evoked by her writing on the *Romance of the Rose* alone stand as ample if "hostile" testimony to the seriousness with which her comments were considered by other literates of the time, even and especially by those who suggested in their diatribes against her that she was, in any case, unworthy to offer criticism.[51] When these women speak of their *ingenium*, then, they do not offer apologies as weaker members of a group, but lively dialogues, affirmations of ability, challenges to ideology—precisely the kind of work we might expect of literary colleagues.

It is consistent with the strong role these women play when participating in the literary networks they envision as they write that two of them inscribe their names into their texts. Hrotsvitha does so through a Latin play on her name (Old Saxon *Hrôthsuith*), which means "mighty voice" (*clamor validus* in Latin). Placing her *ego clamor validus* beside her "little genius" (*ingeniolum*) may suggest more bark than bite, but the echo of John the Baptist's *ego vox clamantis* clarifies her credentials.[52] The explicit authorial signature and "autobiographical persona" of Christine are discussed by Newman along with that of Marie de France, the latter of particular interest here because of the way in which she imagines a potentially hostile group of literate individuals around her who may be jealous and seek to steal her work. By suggesting that "many a clerc" would pay her the compliment, jaded though it is, of claiming her work as their own,[53] she provides us with an interesting view of the literate circles she moved within in the twelfth century. Though hers may not be a pleasant thought, it is certainly not the worry of someone who considered themselves a minor or untalented participant in textual culture. Her feminine name, her literary talent, and her successful participation in secular literate circles are thus brought to the attention of the reader with an immediacy that recalls how the Admont and Oxford manuscripts of Anselm's *Orationes sive Meditationes* focus the reader's attention on female participation in the devotional circuits of textual exchange and consumption. Since personalized salutations have not survived in the *Epistolae duorum amantium,* we can only imagine how the woman of the *Epistolae* would have inscribed her name into the texts she exchanged with her famous master, though some might see Heloise's sophisticated salutations as clues.

Thoughts of the *Epistolae* bring me to my third example—the relationship of Heloise and Abelard which so richly informs the dialogue of Jaeger and Constable (as indeed the wider debate) on the authorship of this fascinating and unique collection of letters. Certainly there are aspects of this relationship, as indeed of that we catch glimpses of in the *Epistolae,* that could be defined as collegial, but the relationship we see in the letters of Abelard and Heloise (and perhaps in the *Epistolae,* if it is one and the same) seems to burst beyond the boundaries of our definitions, encompassing, as it does, so many of the experiences and complications traditionally associated with both medieval and modern relationships. Is it an intellectual or a physical or a spiritual bond they share? Is it that of a student and teacher, a nun and monk, a wife and husband, or two lovers? It is all of these things and more, of course, and it rings true, for we experience similar complexities, though perhaps not all of us quite so many, in our daily interactions with each other. Clearly it is emotional, and it is also inherently textual, with Heloise's learning attracting Abelard as certainly as his did her, with the composition and exchange of letters punctuating their relationship from its erotic intellectual beginnings (whether we believe the *Epistolae* are those mentioned in Abelard's *Historia Calamitatum* or not) to its spiritual monastic conclusions. Of course, there is a certain redundancy in saying that such a relationship is textual since texts are ultimately what reconstruct it for us. But emphasizing the existence and exploring the role of relationships at the heart of textual production and reception—whether they be intimate letters or prayers, autobiographies or poems, visions or sermons, oral or written, Latin or vernacular—seems to come close to the heart of why we read and write in the first place. What is language after all—what is text—if not our means to share our ideas equally one with the other?

The dialogues collected here demonstrate that the relationships which produced texts from Late Antiquity through the Middle Ages are various and complicated, and still in need of considerable research and clarification. They remind us of the conceptual difficulties and problems of evidence we face even as they make their own contributions to our understanding of the "literacy events" and "textual networks" of the past. They exemplify the collegiality and the emotionalism of not only the texts we study, but also of historical research and scholarly writing. They present new and divergent perspectives and challenge more than one preconception about what people of the past did and read and wrote. In some small way *Voices in Dialogue* tries to begin what Vessey calls a "gender-blind" relationship, though not between Augustine and his fellow Christians, but between ourselves and the past. In this way it is hoped that we might find more women lost in textual circuits whose male participants are often well known to us, "create mental space" (Van Engen) for women among those men, and pay closer "attention to [the] words" (Newman) that women as well as men read and wrote and shared, as well as to the ways in which they read and wrote and shared them. Texts, it seems, formed a bond then, as they do now, that can indeed reach beyond distinctions of gender, perhaps even into an "inward space of critical judgment in which 'there is neither male nor female'" (Vessey), only shared thoughts and a "shared . . . drive for understanding and expression" (Van Engen). It is in this spirit—this hope—of historical equality and textual collegiality that we offer the dialogues in this volume.

Notes

I would like to thank the Social Sciences and Humanities Research Council of Canada for the funding and the English Department at the University of Victoria for the facilities to pursue some of the research presented here. I am most grateful to Diana Rutherford, Darlene Hollingsworth, and Sussi Arason in the English Department, who above and beyond the call of duty typed up research lost in a fire from burned papers as illegible as they were horrible to work with: their careful and generous work allowed some of that research to be used here. Finally, my thanks go out to Kathryn Kerby-Fulton for her thoughtful reading of this introduction certainly, but far more for the constant pleasure and support of her friendship through what have been rather unsettling years.

1. David Bell, *What Nuns Read: Books and Libraries in Medieval English Nunneries* (Kalamazoo, Mich.: Cistercian Publications, 1995), 60.

2. See, for instance, Margaret Aston's discussion of "devotional literacy" in *Lollards and Reformers: Images and Literacy in Late Medieval Religion* (London: Hambledon Press, 1984), 101–33; Katherine Zieman, "Reading, Singing and Understanding: Constructions of the Literacy of Women Religious in Late Medieval England," in *Learning and Literacy in Medieval England and Abroad,* ed. Sarah Rees-Jones (Turnhout: Brepols, 2003), 97–120; and Linda Olson, "Did Medieval English Women Read Augustine's *Confessiones*? Constructing Feminine Interiority and Literacy in the Eleventh and Twelfth Centuries," in *Learning and Literacy in Medieval England and Abroad,* ed. Sarah Rees Jones (Turnhout: Brepols, 2003), 69–96, where the use by women of both the *Confessiones* and the texts contemporary men write for them is seen by male authors as particularly devotional and affective in nature.

3. See Charity Cannon Willard, *Christine de Pizan: Her Life and Works* (New York: Persea Books, 1984), 44–48, for a discussion of Christine's possible associations with manuscripts of her own and other works.

4. We know that Augustine used a *notarius* in the normal course of his writing because he writes of his dilemma in the *Soliloquia* when he is troubled by the public nature of dictating to a *notarius* thoughts he feels deserve greater privacy. See *Saint Augustine: Soliloquies and Immortality of the Soul,* ed. and trans. Gerard Watson (Warminster: Aris and Phillips, 1990), 1:1: "*Ratio:* Ergo scribendum est. Sed quid agis, quod valetudo tua scribendi laborem recusat? Nec ista dictari debent: nam solitudinem meram desiderant."

5. On MS Royal 5. C.V, see G. F. Warner and J. P. Gilson, *British Museum: Catalogue of Western Manuscripts in the Old Royal and King's Collections*, vol. 1 (London: 1921), 108.

6. An early hand on folio 1v records that the manuscript was the "liber de domo de Sempringham ex impetratione Johannis de Glynton Canonici dicte domus." On Glynton, see A. B. Emden, *A Biographical Register of the University of Cambridge to 1500* (Cambridge: Cambridge University Press, 1963), 260.

7. See the discussions in B. Golding, *Gilbert of Sempringham and the Gilbertine Order c. 1130–c. 1300* (Oxford: Oxford University Press, 1995), 180 and 184–85, and Sharon K. Elkins, *Holy Women of Twelfth-Century England* (Chapel Hill and London: University of North Carolina Press, 1988), 139 and 142. Gilbertine libraries were situated in the nuns' quarters, with manuscripts being passed to the house's canons through a turning window.

8. For Eve, see Olson, "Did Medieval English Women Read the *Confessiones*?" For Christine's texts, see Earl Jeffrey Richards, trans., *The Book of the City of Ladies: Christine de Pizan* (New York: Persea Books, 1982); and Glenda K. McLeod, trans., *Christine de Pizan: Christine's Vision* (New York and London: Garland, 1993).

9. I have argued that the women whose male friends wrote *Confessiones*-style texts for them, like Eve of Wilton, Matilda of Tuscany, and Aelred of Rievaulx's sister, almost certainly were: see Olson, "Did Medieval English Women Read the *Confessiones*?"

10. It is worth noting here that Bell does not include the manuscripts from Gilbertine houses in his *What Nuns Read*, though they should certainly be considered among the books available to medieval English nuns.

11. The fact that Gilbertine nuns followed the Cistercian Rule can only have further motivated a relationship with the *Confessiones*, since Cistercian authors used Augustine's autobiography extensively: see Linda Olson, "Textual Construction of Monastic Interiority: Reading Augustine's *Confessiones* in England c. 1066–c. 1200" (PhD diss., University of York, England, 1998), especially vol. 2. The canons' adherence to Augustine's Rule would, of course, have had a similar effect.

12. "Collective achievement" among the literate members of monastic communities in the form of group authorship of textual projects was far from an unusual practice in monasteries of the eleventh and twelfth centuries. A very different example might be the Norman and Anglo-Norman histories (like the *Gesta* of the Norman dukes, Symeon of Durham's *Libellus de Exordio*, and the *Chronicle of John of Worcester*), in which the initial or main responsibility lay with a single individual, often the cantor or precentor in charge of the house's books, but the work was carried out by many, both contemporaries who acted as scribes and potential co-authors and later generations of writers, who continued the historic records. See the introductory discussions in Elisabeth M. C. van Houts, ed. and trans., *The Gesta Normannorum Ducum of William of Jumièges, Orderic Vitalis, and Robert of Torigni*, vol. 1 (Oxford: Clarendon, 1992); David Rollason, ed. and trans., *Symeon of Durham: Libellus de exordio atque Procursu istius hoc est Dunhelmensis Ecclesie* (Oxford: Clarendon, 2000); and P. McGurk, ed. and trans., *The Chronicle of John of Worcester*, vol. 3 (Oxford: Clarendon, 1998). Though these examples involve male authors only, it is only rational that any willing and capable literates in a community would be involved in such textual production, irregardless of gender, as they were, say, in the composition of the mortuary rolls that circulated among monastic houses (see Morrow and Bell). At Helfta in the thirteenth century, it is a community of women who are involved in the group authorship of visionary texts: see, for example, the discussion in chapter 5 of Caroline Walker

Bynum, *Jesus as Mother: Studies in the Spirituality of the High Middle Ages* (Berkeley and Los Angeles: University of California Press, 1982).

13. Gertrude is described as bearing a wax tablet at her side in the Prologue to the autobiographical second book of her *Herald*, where it enables her to record immediately with her own hand her experience of intimacy with God: see the translation by Alexandra Barratt of Books I and II, *Gertrude the Great: The Herald of God's Loving-Kindness* (Kalamazoo, Mich.: Cistercian Publications, 1991), 99. Books I and III–V of the *Herald* were written by at least one other Helfta nun, demonstrating that Gertrude was not the only one of the community's women who acted as the *amanuensis* and co-author of another. See the brief discussion of the collective authorship of the thirteenth-century Helfta texts by Walker Bynum, *Jesus as Mother*, 176–80.

14. See Frank Tobin, trans., *Mechthild of Magdeburg: The Flowing Light of the Godhead* (New York: Paulist Press, 1998), 31–33; Tobin (6–7) also discusses Heinrich's role in the production of Mechthild's text, emphasizing the way in which her confessor and spiritual guide "let Mechthild's text speak for itself."

15. Barratt, *Gertrude the Great*, 29–30.

16. The gist of the approbations offered by the three theologians (one a Franciscan, the second a Cistercian, and the third a master of theology in Paris) is that the *Mirror* is orthodox, but hard or nearly impossible to understand unless one shares the spiritual insight of its author, and thus that it should not be read by many. The preface appears in English and Latin versions of the *Mirror*. See Edmund Colledge, J. C. Marler, and Judith Grant, trans., *The Mirror of Simple Souls: Margaret Porette* (Notre Dame, Ind.: University of Notre Dame Press, 1999), where the approbations are translated on 180–81, and briefly discussed on xl–xli.

17. As Melissa Furrow, "Unscholarly Latinity and Margery Kempe," in *Doubt Wisely: Papers in Honour of E. G. Stanley*, ed. M. J. Toswell (London: Routledge, 1996), 240–51, at 245, points out, Margery could certainly read, for she is holding "hir boke in hir hand" when a beam from the roof of St. Margaret's church falls upon her, and Jesus tells her that he is equally pleased with her whether she reads or hears others reading to her ("redist er herist redyng"), both of which he equates with oral prayer and affective meditation ("preyist wyth þi mowth er thynkist wyth thyn hert"). See Sanford Brown Meech and Hope Emily Allen, eds., *The Book of Margery Kempe*, Early English Text Society *o.s.* 212 (London: Oxford University Press, 1940), chap. 9, p. 21, and chap. 88, p. 218.

18. See, for instance, Olson, "Textual Construction," for the many different uses and transformations of Augustine's autobiographical model among eleventh- and twelfth-century monks in England. A truly transformed *Confessiones* can be seen in the abridged fourteenth-century copy of the autobiography from Norwich Cathedral, where it may have been used to instruct novices in the spiritual life: see Linda Olson, "Untangling the Thread of Internal Progress in a Benedictine Community: An Abridgement of Augustine's *Confessiones* from Medieval Norwich," in *The Medieval Reader: Reception and Cultural History in the Late Medieval Manuscript*, ed. Kathryn Kerby-Fulton and Maidie Hilmo (New York: AMS Press, 2001), 41–79.

19. The principle of *confessio* upon which the *Confessiones* are structured, for instance, is one of the main qualities by which twelfth-century readers of the autobiography identified the affective genre of Augustine's text and explained its compelling quality. *Confessio* is discussed at length in the first volume of Olson, "Textual Construction," and some quotations from medieval authors on Augustine's confessional text are used in the opening pages of Olson, "Did Medieval English

Women Read the *Confessiones*?" *Conversio* is another Augustinian autobiographical principle much attended to by medieval readers and authors (see the second volume of "Textual Construction"), and though I do not have the space to discuss the matter here, the nature of conversion in Margery's *Book* also adopts and adapts certain Augustinian qualities.

20. Furrow, "Unscholarly Latinity," 250.

21. Josephine K. Tarvers, "The Alleged Illiteracy of Margery Kempe: A Reconsideration of the Evidence," *Medieval Perspectives* 11 (1996): 113–24, at 123.

22. For a discussion of the many levels of conversion in an autobiography like Augustine's see Geoffrey Galt Harpham, "Conversion and the Language of Autobiography," in *Studies in Auto-biography,* ed. James Olney (New York and Oxford: Oxford University Press, 1988), 42–50.

23. We all do this to some degree: think, for instance, of those times when we decide to do something not because we like the idea, but because it will look good on our *curricula vitae,* or professional autobiographical records. Indeed, the example of *curricula vitae* also highlights the way in which life is not only lived to create a pleasing textual format, but also reshaped to the same end.

24. See Meech and Allen, *Book of Margery Kempe,* chap. 88, p. 216: "Drede þe not, dowtyr, for as many bedys as þu woldist seyin I accepte hem as þow þu seydist hem, & þi stody þat þu stodiist for to do wrytyn þe grace þat I haue schewyd to þe plesith me ryght meche & he þat writith boþe. For, þow ȝe wer in þe chirche & wepte bothyn to-gedyr as sore as euyr þu dedist, ȝet xulde ȝe not plesyn me mor þan ȝe don wyth ȝowr writyng, for dowtyr, be þis boke many a man xal be turnyd to me & beleuyn þerin."

25. Furrow, "Unscholarly Latinity," 250. Similar changes in scholarly approaches are taking place in many areas of medieval history. An example far removed from the topics of literacy and authorship (and thus particularly interesting) can be found in recent archaeological studies of early medieval castles which are overturning with the complexity of their results wide-ranging assumptions about castle construction and development that have been held for nearly a century. See, for example, Philip Dixon and Pamela Marshall, "The Great Tower in the Twelfth Century: The Case of Norham Castle," *Archaeological Journal* 150 (1993): 410–32; and Robert Higham, "Timber Castles—A Reassessment," in *Anglo-Norman Castles,* ed. Robert Liddiard (Woodbridge: Boydell, 2003), 105–18.

26. I do not have the space to discuss the relevant scholarship here, but an excellent survey and bibliography of women's history, communities, and reading can be found in Jocelyn Wogan-Browne, "Analytical Survey 5: 'Reading Is Good Prayer': Recent Research on Female Reading Communities," *New Medieval Literatures* 5 (2001): 229–97.

27. Bell, *What Nuns Read,* 77–78.

28. Catherine Conybeare, *Paulinus Noster: Self and Symbols in the Letters of Paulinus of Nola* (Oxford: Oxford University Press, 2000), 19 (quoted from Vessey, p. 75).

29. See, for instance, Julian Haseldine, *Friendship in Medieval Europe* (Sutton, 1999), and Stephen Jaeger, *Ennobling Love: In Search of a Lost Sensibility* (Philadelphia: University of Pennsylvania Press, 1999), both of whom argue that women became true or full members of the relationships discussed only in the later Middle Ages.

30. Anselm sent his devotional works first to Adelaide, a daughter of William the Conqueror, who received seven of Anselm's pieces in c. 1072; and then to the influential countess, Matilda of Tuscany, who received the whole collection of *Orationes sive Meditationes* in 1104. See Olson, "Did Medieval English Women Read the *Confessiones*?" 90; and R. W. Southern, *Saint Anselm and His*

Biographer: A Study of Monastic Life and Thought, 1059–c. 1130 (Cambridge: Cambridge University Press, 1963), 37 and 42–43, and *Saint Anselm: A Portrait in a Landscape* (Cambridge and New York: Cambridge University Press, 1990), 92–93, 99, and 111–12.

31. See Joan Ferrante, *To the Glory of Her Sex: Women's Roles in the Composition of Medieval Texts* (Bloomington: Indiana University Press, 1997), 88 and 90, as indeed her whole discussion of Matilda and her biography on 85–90. See also Nora Duff, *Matilda of Tuscany, la gran donna d'Italia* (London: Methuen, 1909), 77–79, who notes how Matilda's pious mother Beatrice educated her and also describes how Matilda was trained in reading, warfare, hunting, and affairs of state. Mary E. Huddy, *Matilda, Countess of Tuscany* (London: John Long, 1906), 49–52, notes Matilda's early affinity for learning, especially literature and foreign languages; specifies Greek, Latin, French, and German as among the languages she was able to read and translate (106), and German, French, and Provençal as those she conversed in (278); and discusses Matilda's training in canon and civil law, as well as her "lengthy and laborious" letters, "written in a somewhat verbose and ponderous style, involving a thorough knowledge of Latin" (279).

32. It is a pleasant rarity that in Matilda of Tuscany we have corroboration between an author who wrote about her and an author who sent his works to her, for it suggests how seriously we might read similar praises and assumptions in cases where we have only one of the two to work from (like the praise of Heloise's learned accomplishments that come up in the Jaeger and Constable dialogue, though in that instance we also have her letters as confirmation, and the assumptions of Augustine about his women correspondents in the discussion of Conybeare and Vessey).

33. See Anselm's advice in the letter *Ad Mathildam* appended to the end of the *Prologus* in F. S. Schmitt, *S. Anselmi Cantuariensis Archiepiscopi Opera Omnia*, vol. 3 (Edinburgh: 1946), 4: "In quibus quamvis quaedam sint quae ad vestram personam non pertinent, omnes tamen volui mittere, ut, si cui placuerint, de hoc exemplari eas possit accipere. Quae quoniam ad excitandum legentis mentem ad dei amorem vel timorem seu ad suimet discussionem sunt editae, non sunt lengendae cursim vel velociter, sed paulatim cum intenta et morosa meditatione. Nec debet intendere lector quamlibet earum totam legere, sed tantum quantum ad excitandum affectum orandi, ad quod factae sunt, sentit sibi sufficere" (lines 4–11).

34. See, for instance, Southern, *Anselm and His Biographer*, 37, who notes that Matilda "was in a position to make the collection known, and a whole family of manuscripts in Austria and Italy has been shown to descend from her copy." Duff, *Matilda*, 79, writes of how Matilda collected manuscripts and encouraged the spread of learning; see also Huddy, *Matilda*, 106–107 and 278–79.

35. A. Wilmart, "Les prières envoyées par S. Anselme à la Comtesse Mathilde en 1104," *Revue Bénédictine* 41 (1929): 41–42, lists nine manuscripts in this Matildan tradition of the *Orationes sive Meditationes*.

36. See Wilmart, "Les prières envoyées à la Comtesse Mathilde," 38, and Schmitt, *Opera Anselmi*, 3:3–4.

37. See Southern, "St. Anselm and His English Pupils," in *Mediaeval and Renaissance Studies*, ed. Richard Hunt and Raymond Klibansky (London: Warburg Institute, 1943), 3–34, at 25; and Otto Pächt, "The Illustrations of St Anselm's Prayers and Meditations," *Journal of the Warburg and Courtauld Institutes* 19 (1956): 68–83, at 81. On the early monastic (and later) additions to Anselm's devotional collection, see also B. Ward, trans., *The Prayers and Meditations of St Anselm with the Proslogion* (Harmondsworth: Penguin, 1973), 278–86; Southern, *Anselm and His Biographer*, 35 and

42; Olson, "Textual Construction," 1:128–30. Schmitt's edition in Anselm's *Opera Omnia*, vol. 3, includes only those pieces now believed to be by Anselm himself, but the grand majority of the prayers and meditations by both Anselm and later writers can be found in J. P. Migne, ed., *Patrologiae Latinae Cursus Completus*, vol. 158 (1864), cols. 709–1016.

38. Folio 1v; see also Pächt, "Illustrations," p. 71 and plate 16a.

39. Folio 2v; see also Pächt, "Illustrations," p. 71 and plate 17a.

40. See the list of illustrations in Bodleian MS Auct. D.2.6 in C. M. Kauffmann, *Romanesque Manuscripts, 1066–1190*, vol. 3, *A Survey of Manuscripts Illuminated in the British Isles* (London: Harvey Miller, 1975), #75, p. 103.

41. Pächt, "Illustrations," 69–71, discusses this illustration; see also plate 16b. The presentation to his monks is an event depicted in a separate frontispiece in the Admont MS (plate 16d in Pächt; folio 2r), where it follows (or falls to the right of) that in which Anselm gives Matilda his book. It is interesting that Anselm is here shown giving scrolls to his monks, perhaps because they read his devotional pieces in progress or heard them read or prayed aloud in the first instance, while it is a book—the finished literary product—that Matilda receives.

42. See also Pächt, "Illustrations," p. 73 and plates 17c and 17e.

43. See Pächt, "Illustrations," p. 71 and plate 20b (folio 44v). As Alison Beach informs me, however, the precise provenance of MS 289 remains unclear.

44. Some of the problems associated with assigning an origin for MS Auct. D.2.6 are discussed in Pächt, "Illustrations," 69–70. I wonder if the problematic white robes depicted on the monks and clerics in MS Auct. D.2.6 (in figure 3, for example) might be explained not by the manuscript's origin, which they seem only to confuse, but by the manuscript tradition this copy lies within. MS Auct. D.2.6 presents a Bec-Canterbury recension of the *Orationes sive Meditationes* (see Kauffmann, *Romanesque Manuscripts*, 104), and it is possible that the white habits may have some (perhaps distant) relationship to the white habit that was worn at Bec and its dependent priories, a habit which perhaps as early as the time of Anselm set monks of these houses apart as a "distinctive brotherhood" or "congregation" within the larger Benedictine Order. On the white habit, see Sally N. Vaughn, *Anselm of Bec and Robert of Meulan: The Innocence of the Dove and the Wisdom of the Serpent* (Berkeley and Los Angeles: University of California Press, 1987), 75–76.

45. See folios 156r, 158v, 161r and 193v; Pächt, "Illustrations," plates 15a, 23b, 23e and 17b; and Kauffmann, *Romanesque Manuscripts*, plate 210. On folios 158v and 193v the figure appears praying with a book in her hand.

46. As Wilmart, "Les prières envoyées à la Comtesse Mathilde," 38 n. 1, suggests, arguing that "un exemplaire de luxe" commissioned by Matilda could have been responsible for the Admont illustrations, just as it led to the family of Matildan manuscripts of the *Orationes sive Meditationes*.

47. Pächt, "Illustrations," 76–82. Kauffmann, *Romanesque Manuscripts*, 104, points out how this argument is controversial, but also notes that "if this were the case, it would provide perhaps the earliest English example of a medieval text being illustrated during the author's lifetime." Since the white robes worn by the monks in MS Auct. D.2.6 may connect the illustrative tradition with Anselm and his monastic communities (see note 44 above), the argument seems a particularly probable and intriguing one.

48. Even though it is believed that MS Auct. D.2.6 was first produced by or for a community of religious men: see the discussion of the possibilities in Pächt, "Illustrations," 69–70.

49. See the translations and discussion in Peter Dronke, *Women Writers of the Middle Ages: A Critical Study of Texts from Perpetua (d. 203) to Marguerite Porete (d. 1310)* (Cambridge: Cambridge University Press, 1984), 55–83.

50. See the opening section of Richards, *City of Ladies*, 3–5.

51. See Willard, *Christine de Pizan*, 73–89, for a discussion of the literary debate known as the Quarrel of the Rose; and Joseph L. Baird and John R. Kane, *La Querelle de la Rose: Letters and Documents* (Chapel Hill: University of North Carolina, 1978), for translations of the relevant texts. An example of hostile testimony to the serious reception of Christine's ideas can be found in the words of Pierre Col, who writes in 1402, shortly after offering a lengthy and detailed response to Christine's criticisms of the *Romance of the Rose*, that "as a disciple of Meun, I have responded only once up to this time, although, granted, there was scarcely a need of it, because even to my limited understanding a single reading of your evasions is answer enough" (*Querelle*, 160).

52. See the discussion of this in Dronke, *Women Writers*, 70.

53. One might argue that the Gothic queen Amalasuintha is paid the compliment when she is captured and eliminated like a man in the plays for power that dominated leadership politics in early sixth-century Italy: see the discussion and letters in Marcelle Thiébaux, trans., *The Writings of Medieval Women: An Anthology*, 2nd ed. (New York and London: Garland, 1994), 71–84.

When Women Preached

An Introduction to Female Homiletic, Sacramental,
and Liturgical Roles in the Later Middle Ages

KATHRYN KERBY-FULTON

About half the essays in the present volume deal with the ways in which late medieval religious women—although hampered by severe official limitations—managed to appropriate to themselves a startling range of supposedly forbidden ecclesiastical roles. Recent scholarship has had a tendency to view these non-normative cases as transgressions against patriarchy or as bids for autonomy (both of body and spirit) in the modern feminist sense, and rightly so. But there are also other fruitful approaches, as the wide diversity in this volume will suggest. Moreover, the sheer amount of new evidence now being uncovered showing active ministry performed by women then *considered orthodox* asks us to rethink many of our starker binaries. The present essay is an attempt to set out some key issues in the larger cultural history of late medieval women's ministry, issues addressed in more specific studies by many of our contributors working in dialogue. What will interest us particularly here, then, is an introductory examination of the kinds of conditions under which, historically, women's spiritual leadership could extend to male-designated roles and *mixed* audiences. In the later Middle Ages this means, first of all, although not only, the study of female visionaries and their impact in opening up pastoral roles for women.

Just to remind us of our own historiographical moment, I would like to suggest briefly some reasons why these issues loom large for us now in the twenty-first century. First, despite its overwhelming popularity, vast amounts of material for the study of medieval women's culture are as yet inaccessible to most readers. This fact alone makes the work of many contributors to this volume important. To name but a few: Fiona Somerset assesses unpublished Latin disputations about the right of women to minister (consecrate the Eucharist, baptize, preach). Alfred Thomas provides a new translation of a Czech poem satirizing Wycliffite women preachers. Katherine Zieman contextualizes Birgitta of Sweden's achievement as a liturgist, a very rare form of composition for women. Alison Beach gives evidence of women's scribal, exegetical, and perhaps homiletic activities.

Second, heresy, seen as a form of female empowerment, has recently been much valorized in an academy understandably driven by contemporary concern for the marginalized, and by critique of hegemonies of all sorts, socio-political, aesthetic, and religious.[1] These have been vital to the study of women's history, and will remain so, but as scholars bump up against the inevitable limitations of exclusive reliance on such approaches, the essays in the present volume will be, we believe, especially helpful. These issues emerge explicitly, for instance, in the exchanges between Elizabeth Schirmer and Steven Justice, in which Schirmer notes that the supposedly all-powerful prohibitions of Arundel's anti-Wycliffite legislation did not in any way impede the vernacular reading habits of the nuns of Syon. Justice, in turn, shows that one of Schirmer's key texts, *The Chastising of God's Children,* placed very serious theological tools in ordinary women's hands. David Wallace's response to Genelle Gertz-Robinson's essay similarly focuses attention on the power of "ordinary" and widespread iconography of women preaching. Fiona Somerset's essay offers new doubts about the Wycliffite commitment to women's ministries, while my own response highlights burgeoning continental trends, both orthodox and otherwise, that were opening up daring possibilities for women.

Third, the recent high-profile decision of the Church of England to finally follow the lead of its affiliate churches abroad in ordaining women and the similar and on-going struggles of Roman Catholic women have sparked a new interest in medieval precedents. Somerset raises the first issue in relation to the topic of Walter Brut's 1391 advocacy of women's sacramental and preaching powers, and Margot Fassler raises it in relation to Hildegard of Bingen's and Birgitta of Sweden's freedom to compose liturgy as women. These points, however, hover in the background of all the essays on women's sacramental or performative roles, especially Genelle Gertz-Robinson's comparison of Kempe's skill in creating opportunities for "preaching" with that of the Reformation martyr, Anne Askew.

Finally, there has been a marked tendency in scholarship of late to divorce vernacular and Latin culture, carried out in the service of establishing a kind of "vernacular theology" (in Bernard McGinn's original formulation for European mysticism), especially in England.[2] While there is much to be said (and much has been said!) for the existence of kinds of vernacular theology, what is important about the exchanges in this volume is that, collectively, they help reposition our sense of vernacularity. Not all texts written by members of the laity were in the vernacular; not all women were wholly dependent on the vernacular, even in the later Middle Ages. Actual levels of literacy were unexpectedly diverse, as Linda Olson has already suggested. This topic is widely explored in the volume, by Zieman in relation to liturgical performance, Schirmer in relation to nuns' reading methods, Justice in relation to mixed gender audiences, and Somerset in relation to a *laicus litteratus* who wrote a "vernacular theology" in Latin. The essays, collectively, also serve to dispel the idea that there are hard and fast borders between Latin and English (or Anglo-Norman or Provençal or Czech) literacy. In fact, lay people crossed these regularly. Many of the late medieval women shown here as having negotiated or usurped the role of teaching, preaching, or sacramentalism, were, like literate laymen, able to cross boundaries.

But not always for the reasons modern scholarship wants to see. Fiona Somerset, for instance, reminds us that the anti-sacramental impulses of Wycliffites make their motives for encouraging female priestliness more dubious. Many women, however, did cross boundaries, and, again, sometimes for reasons that modern scholarship has been slow to notice. In fact, all the essays in this volume show, invoking a rich pluralism of archaeological methods, just how efficiently women negotiated the boundaries. Even satire on women teachers, such as Thomas discusses, is a "hostile source" which proves the case in spite of itself: if no women had been teaching, no one would bother to write satire. These essays, then, taken together, suggest a more complex world of possibilities for medieval women's ministries. With the help of both local and internationally powerful church officials, women assumed a variety of leadership roles: the Cistercians, the Franciscans, the Carthusians, and even occasionally the papacy, to name but a few institutions, played a sometimes unexpected part in opening possibilities for women. Some of the high points in the history of these possibilities and struggles I will try to sketch out below, using brief case histories that shed light upon, but do not replicate, the figures and texts our contributors explore in depth.

When Women Preached: Female Prophets in Pastoral Roles and Their Impact

Medieval clergy were well aware that women could be effective preachers. As Thomas of Chobham wrote in his *Manual for Confessors,*

> In imposing penance, it should always be enjoined upon women to be preachers [*predicatrices*] to their husbands, because no priest is able to soften [*emollire*] the heart of a man the way his wife can. For this reason, the sin of a man is often imputed to his wife if, through her negligence, he is not corrected. Even in the bedroom [*in cubiculo*], in the midst of their embraces, a wife should speak alluringly to her

husband [*inter medios amplexus virum suum blande alloqui*], and if he is hard and unmerciful, and oppressor of the poor, she should invite him to be merciful . . . if he is avaricious, she should arouse generosity in him, and she should secretly give alms from their common property, supplying the alms that he omits.[3]

Even in translation one can pick out the sexual metaphors that haunt the question of morally authoritative female speech, a topic Thomas and Elliott also engage below as they examine the alleged "seductiveness" of Czech women teachers. But, unpromising for women as this sort of innuendo sounds, male degeneracy was widely and theologically accepted as a valid precondition for female teaching[4]—and fortunately for medieval women, there was no shortage of male degeneracy about. Even the church fathers, often more strident in their misogyny than later medieval sources, were happy to invoke female aid in the face of such degeneracy. St. John Chrysostom, for instance, in his homily on Matthew 7, had this to say against men who visited the theatres to watch prostitutes swim naked in tanks of water:

> I want to hand you over to your own wives so that they may instruct you. According to the law of Paul, *you* ought to be the teachers, but since the order is overturned by sin, let us take even this other route.[5]

The right to teach outside the home, however, was—even when male degeneracy was reckoned to be rampant—harder to win approval for, and orthodox religious women laid claim to it with painstaking theological caution. When Julian of Norwich, for instance, wrote the first version of her earthshaking *Revelations of Divine Love*, she self-deprecatingly, but directly addressed the topic this way:

> *Botte* God forbede that ȝe schulde saye or take it so that I am a techere, for I meene nouȝt soo, no I mente nevere so. For I am a woman, leuede [unlearned], febille, and freylle. *Botte* I wate [know] wele this that I saye: I hafe it of the schewynge of hym that is souerayne techare. *Botte* sothelye [truly] charyte styrres me to telle ȝowe it, for I wolde God wared knawen and myn evyncrystene [peers] spede—as I wolded be myselfe—of the mare hatynge of synne and lovynge of God. *Botte* for I am a woman schulde I therfore leve that I schulde nouȝt tell ȝowe the goodenes of God—syne that I sawe in that same tyme that it is his wille that it be knawen? *And* that schalle ȝe welle see in the same matere that folowes aftyr, if it be welle and trewlye takyn [understood].[6] (emphasis added)

Setting aside as merely conventional her apology that she is "lewed, feeble, and frail," an apology used even by authoritative male writers, we can discern the elements of formal theological argument here. Note the incremental logic of the four "buts"[7] which carefully build the case: first, that her knowledge comes from divine revelation; second, that she is speaking out of charity for her fellow Christians; and (finally, and rhetorically well placed) that it would be absurd if she could not speak of the goodness of God simply because she is a woman. What the passage tells us is that, far from lacking in confidence, she is extremely well informed about the theological arguments supporting female teaching, or even preaching—arguments usually discreetly buried in Latin scholastic discussions, and not well advertised to the laity. For instance, Thomas Aquinas, one of the standard and most widely cited authorities on this subject, had given three "proofs" that a woman may use the "*gratia* of discourse" ("de gratia quae consistit in *sermone*").[8] In brief summary, these are:

(1) The verse in Proverbs 4:3–4 implying that Solomon had been taught by his mother ("Vnigenitus fui coram matre mea, et docebat me");

(2) Various biblical accounts of women who exercised the gift of prophecy including Miriam (Exod. 15:20), Deborah (Judges 4:4), Huldah (4 Kings 22:14), the daughters of Phillip (Acts 21:9) and "omnis mulier orans aut prophetans" (1 Cor. 11:5);

(3) The obligation, following 1 Peter 4:10, for those who have a gift of knowledge to use it for the benefit of others ("Unusquisque sicut accepit gratiam in alterutrum administrantes").

These three arguments were very closely followed by his contemporary Henry of Ghent, who added to the third argument that Mary and Martha had evangelized just as the Apostles had.[9]

Julian's justifications draw upon arguments similar to (2) and (3); moreover, her disclaimers suggest that she was aware of arguments similar to those Aquinas makes "*contra.*" He stresses that there is a distinction between the private and the public "sermo"— and it is the private that befits women (women are allowed to teach in the home, but normally only to children and other women). St. Paul, of course, had forbidden women to teach in church or assembly (1 Tim. 2:12 "Docere mulierem non permitto"), and Aquinas gives three reasons for this:

(1) The female sex is subject ("qui debet esse subditus"), following Genesis 3:16, and teaching belongs to those in authority;

(2) As Ecclesiasticus 9:11 says, a woman speaking can inflame the desires of men ("ad libidinem");

(3) Women are not sufficiently perfected in wisdom ("non sunt in sapientia perfectae").

To these standard arguments, dispassionately put in Aquinas, other theologians added more egregiously misogynist ones, like Humbert of Romans, who cites the folly that ensued from the teaching of the first woman, Eve, or Henry of Ghent, who stressed that not only teaching but *learning* is dangerous for women because "owing to the inadequacy of their natural talents [*debilitas ingenii*], instead of making progress in the mysteries of theology, they regress into heresy."[10] If Julian was aware of these more sensational misogynist assertions, she judiciously ignored them, concentrating instead on her theological right "to tell . . . of the goodness of God," and making a *de facto* claim for the gift of prophetic vision. This would immediately override Aquinas's objection number (3), and neatly out-maneuver his objection (1) by insisting that she teaches her "even-christens"— her peers—a deft reminder of the spiritual equality of men and women.

This juxtaposition of Julian with scholastic thinkers helps, I believe, to show how a clear-minded, purposeful woman might successfully dismantle supposedly fixed gender boundaries. However, in a surprising move that draws our attention to the host of historical issues this volume covers, Julian deleted this carefully worded passage when she revised this first text to create the longer version of the *Showings,* probably later in the 1390s, and likely before 1413. Scholars have struggled to explain why. Some have suggested that the deletion indicated a new self-confidence. Perhaps more important was the fact that between 1373 (when she tells us she had her first vision) and the 1390s (when she was working at revision), the discussion of a woman's right to teach was becoming both more high profile and more controversial. The rise of Wycliffism was one element, especially given the Wycliffite sympathy for notions of "a priesthood of all believers," and the trial of Walter Brut in 1391–33—all topics explored in this volume.[11] But in Julian's Norwich, Wycliffism was neither the primary temptation nor the primary concern that recent scholarship has tended to assume normative in England.[12]

In fact, there were concerns other than Lollardy being raised at the time that might have appeared just as or even more relevant to any English woman visionary. Just across the channel lay the source of much new and radical visionary and apocalyptic writing, both orthodox and otherwise, that was powerfully affecting the profile of women teachers. The Low Countries were home to the massive women's movement known as the Beguines, which allowed real autonomy to women, but had a checkered history by Julian's time of drawing inquisitorial suspicion for revelatory and mystical heresy (Franciscan Spiritualism, or Free Spiritism). Meanwhile, the new, impeccably orthodox *Devotio Moderna* movement, with its massive number of autonomous sisterhouses, was developing new active ministerial roles for women (including forms of preaching and confession). They, too, were drawing sporadic accusations from hostile inquisitors, raising the same concerns as they did with beguines. At home, English fears that Free Spiritism and other forms of unorthodox female religious thought would cross the channel begin to appear as early as the late 1380s.[13] Even more importantly, from roughly the death of Birgitta of Sweden (in 1373) onwards, fascination with and defensiveness about revelations by women began to emerge. In 1391 Birgitta was canonized amidst international controversy—a decision that would be revisited in the early fifteenth century amidst further high-profile controversy, and over against Lancastrian royal patronage of the Bridgittine abbey of Syon (on which see Schirmer and Zieman). In Bohemia the rising Hussite movement had already begun to implicate women in Wycliffism, but also in Free Spiritism and Joachism. In the present volume several essays contribute to a more detailed picture of these rival enthusiasms and concerns: Thomas's and Elliott's exchange on Hussite Wycliffism, Schirmer's and Justice's on Bridgittine reading and the limitations of Arundel's anti-Wycliffite legislation; Genelle Gertz-Robinson's and David Wallace's on both the actuality and the iconography of women's preaching up to and into the Reformation; and Fiona Somerset's and my own exchange on the relative conservatism of Lollardy in relation to the real elbow room for women created by various parallel continental movements.

In both England and on the continent, then, women's ministry was implicated in a wide range of new movements, literatures, and in some cases, heresies, during the fourteenth and fifteenth centuries.[14] Unlike Lollardy, these writings made extensive use of prophecy (or often, more specifically, reformist apocalypticism)—the one gift, as we have seen, which allowed women to preach and teach *publicly*. And, even, at times, to compose liturgy.

Reformist apocalypticism was a genre that had always been friendly to female prophetic thought, and even female preaching, ever since its inception in the twelfth century with the visions of Hildegard of Bingen.[15] But it was a genre that Wycliffite thinkers did not, on the whole, like or trust,[16] so perhaps it is no accident that the one Lollard intellectual known to have *actively* argued for the possibility that women might preach is also the one securely identifiable Lollard writer with any extensive knowledge of continental reformist apocalyptic thought. It was this tradition, I will suggest, that provided the most obvious available route to ministry for women between the twelfth and fifteenth centuries in a Church which otherwise tried its best to exclude them.

The Lollard intellectual in question was Walter Brut, a layman of remarkable learning, and in 1391–1393 the defendant in a high-profile trial before an unprecedentedly large and impressive team of theologians. More important than his case itself is what the new evidence presented later in this volume exposes about its intervention in an *already* widespread and on-going academic debate on women's ministry (discussed in several essays here).[17] Brut, like other medieval reformist thinkers, all of whom were fascinated with the early Church, seems to have been aware of its use of women in the diaconate (references to which had survived vestigially even in canon law until the twelfth century).[18] Building his case on the orthodox practice of allowing midwives to baptize in emergencies, he wrote that good women, along with good laymen, can even consecrate in cases of necessity:

> Since in baptism there is complete remission of sins, women absolve from sin those they baptize; hence women have the power of releasing from sin. But the powers of "binding and releasing" are interconnected, so women have the power to "bind and release" which is said to have been granted to priests. Therefore women do not seem to be excluded from Christian priesthood even though their power is restrained so long as others are ordained. . . . [19]

What the essays in this volume make clear, whether specifically in relation to this trial or more generally by uncovering other new evidence for contemporary female clericism, is that Brut does not necessarily represent the lunatic fringe. He was, rather, a single voice intervening in a larger, long-standing debate, which was still, in the late fourteenth century, quoting the thirteenth-century scholastics cited above and still harking back to twelfth-century claims of reformists like Hildegard of Bingen. So, for instance, the author of the anonymous disputation, *Utrum liceat mulieribus docere*, follows Aquinas's and Henry of Ghent's arguments very closely, and he concedes that, "Although women may not be allowed to teach in public, there are certain cases however where they are":

> . . . First, if it is granted to them as a special favour, as it was to women in the Old as well as the New Testament. . . . The second situation is when it is granted to women as a reproach to men who have become effeminate [*effeminati*]. It was for this reason that government of the people was granted to women, as appears in Judges 4 concerning Deborah. The third situation is when there is a great number of masses and only a small number of those administering. It was for this reason that it was granted to the women, Mary and Martha, to preach in public and to the four daughters of Phillip to prophesy in public. [20]

These two passages together are close in formulation not only to Aquinas and Henry, but to the views of Hildegard of Bingen, who had famously stressed that she lived in an "effeminate age" during which men had lost, through their corruption, the ability to teach. And so, she argued, it fell to women like herself to do so. [21] Since even Wyclif himself, after all, had been emphatic that women could not preach, [22] Brut's extensive testimony suggests a different set of influences. It indicates that he had encountered not only scholastic sources, but more of the continental reformist apocalyptic tradition than most of his contemporaries, and most likely Hildegard [23]—suggesting that it was his apocalypticism, not merely his Wycliffism, that prompted his campaign for women. This campaign, along with Julian's bid to teach, Margery's active ministry, and the liberalism of the Bridgittine and Carthusian projects themselves, all look much less unusual, as many essays here suggest, in the larger culture of turn of the century Europe. This culture shared with England one great inescapable international fact: the Great Schism. Church crisis had always, historically, benefited women with leadership aspirations. It forms, therefore, the backdrop to every essay on women's struggle for ministry here.

Historical Precedents for Female Ministry in the Mainstream Medieval Church

Indeed, the reformist apocalyptic tradition boasted an impressive array of women preachers, spiritual leaders, and even liturgists. I would like briefly to introduce the historical context in which some of the most important women, including those discussed in our volume, arose between the twelfth century and the late Middle Ages. These earlier women provide some of the key precedents for the major fourteenth-, fifteenth-, and sixteenth-century figures and texts this volume covers in rich detail, especially Birgitta of Sweden, *The Chastising of God's Children*, the Bridgittine *Mirror of Our Lady*, Margery Kempe, and Anne Askew. Three women in particular stand out for their enormous impact on and inspiration of women's ecclesiastical leadership. The first, Hildegard of Bingen, was the most brilliantly original and internationally known prophet of the twelfth century, a composer and activist in the Gregorian reformist tradition, influential even in dissenting traditions like English and Czech Wycliffism. Second, in the thirteenth century, Douceline de Digne was the founder of the southern European beguine movement, and the most highly revered Joachite female visionary.[24] Third, in the fourteenth century, the high-profile reformist prophetic preacher who castigated the papacy at the time of the Great Schism, Catherine of Siena, whose ministry was modeled on Birgitta of Sweden and is important to our understanding of both Margery Kempe and Syon Abbey.[25] All three of these women (and some of their prominent associates) preached in the formal sense of the word, that is, they delivered discourses to mixed audiences—not simply to other women. All three either wrote or performed liturgical or para-sacramental acts. All three were considered orthodox Christians in their day. Their cases can help to counterbalance the heavy emphasis on the heretical and the legendary that has been the focus of so much recent scholarship on women's ministry. Oddly enough, where we now need most to break new ground is in the study of *orthodoxy*— and what pluralism it might have tolerated, or even encouraged. And this is one of the strengths of the current volume.

Women preachers and religious leaders seem to have had more of a role in reformist apocalyptic thought, partly because of Hildegard's early influence. But it is worth noting that the other major thinker in the tradition, Joachim of Fiore, had made unusual use of positive female imagery in his biblical exegesis, giving leading roles in the development of

Salvation History to Old Testament women.[26] The popularity of Joachim and Hildegard in the centuries following their deaths was an important factor, because the fourth Lateran Council in 1215 laid a new emphasis on preaching to the laity, which, in the wake of further tightening and centralizing controls, gave women a weaker voice in all leadership roles after this time.[27] Other factors include, as we have seen with respect to Thomas Aquinas and even Henry of Ghent, the crucial loophole allowing a gifted woman the right to speak "by special grace." In the prophetic we have, then, a philogynist tradition—sometimes, to be sure, a suspect one, but its female exponents seem to have incurred much less censure than its male ones, and this factor alone deserves our attention.

Hildegard, of course, was the first great female preacher of the tradition—but it is not often realised that she did not begin preaching until she was sixty-one—that is, as Sabina Flanagan notes, when "her reputation had been well established by *Scivias* and her charismatic personality widely recognized."[28] These tours seem to have been conceived initially as trips to neighbouring monasteries, not only "to expound there the words God commanded," as her *Vita* says, but also sometimes, as she says herself of her fourth tour, "to settle their internal quarrels."[29] It is significant that she began preaching in monasteries. Permission to preach within a monastery was up to the abbot or abbess to grant and was therefore perhaps a freer space in many respects. The powerful Benedictine Order, throughout the Middle Ages, in fact, protected and fostered several fascinatingly radical writers and personalities.[30] But it appears that two things drew Hildegard's preaching tours outside of the monastic context: her campaign against the growing popularity of Cathar heretics (who allowed their own women the right to preach)[31] and the leadership crisis of the Church of her day (as emperor and pope fought for control of ecclesiastical powers). These problems were to be repeated throughout late medieval history, each time creating conditions under which women could rise to positions of leadership. In the present volume they especially account for the rise of Birgitta of Sweden, who was, like Hildegard, a prophetess to popes and a liturgist (see Zieman, Fassler, and Schirmer).

These factors drew Hildegard into a growing correspondence with political figures and clergy alike. Cologne, Trier, Metz, Wurzburg, and Bamberg are specially mentioned in her *Vita* as places where she preached to the "clergy and people," and letters from members of the cathedral clergy at Trier, Cologne, and Mainz suggest that she spoke in the cathedrals there, too.[32] We do not know exactly what oral form these sermons took—but, of course, we often do not know what oral form many medieval sermons took. Certainly in Hildegard's case we are often dependent on external evidence for the knowledge that certain of her letters were originally delivered as a sermons. This suggests, more broadly, that there was even more evidence for women preachers than has survived (a challenge explored in the current volume by Beach, Kerby-Fulton, and Gertz-Robinson). Sometimes we only know because a correspondent's letter survives, requesting a copy of the sermon Hildegard delivered, as in the case of her homily to the secular clergy of Cologne—whom she had lambasted in excruciating terms.[33] Cologne was a growing center of Cathar heresy, and Hildegard had laid the blame squarely on the shoulders of the local clergy:

> But your tongues are silent, failing to join in the mighty voice of the resounding trumpet of the Lord, for you do not love holy reason . . . on account of the waywardness of your own will. Thus the luminaries are missing from the firmament of God's justice in your utterances, as when the stars do not shine, for you are the night exhaling darkness, and you are . . . like a snake that hides in a cave after it has shed its skin, so you walk in filth like disgusting beasts [*uelut nudus coluber in cauernam se abscondit, sic uos fetidatem in uilitate pecorum intratis*].[34]

Although this might not seem the way to win friends and influence people, after Hildegard had delivered this sermon, Phillip, dean of the cathedral clergy at Cologne, writes to her:

> We want to inform you that after your recent visit to us at God's command when, through divine inspiration you revealed the words of life to us, we were greatly astonished that God works through such a fragile vessel, such a fragile sex, to display the great marvels of His secrets. *But "the spirit breatheth where he will"* [John 3:8]. . . . We further request that you commit to writing and send us those things that you said to us earlier in person. . . .[35] (emphasis added)

In fact, Phillip was no fool: what Hildegard had preached of the future, to judge from the text that survives, was strikingly original and alarmingly convincing. This was to be her best-known sermon, and, owing to its prophecy of a coming group of religious deceivers who would lead the people astray and beguile them to strip the monasteries of their wealth, the sermon was read right down to Wycliffite and Hussite times.[36] In fact, it was Phillip who later, as archbishop of Cologne, commissioned the *Vita* of Hildegard to be written—he apparently held no grudges and was only too happy to attach his name to a local rising star.

The passage from John 3:8 Phillip cites above seems to have been another "loophole" by which male clerics could understand, or choose to understand, female leadership. But it could be cited ironically. Arnold, archbishop of Mainz, who apparently resented Hildegard's sermons on pro-imperial grounds, also wrote to her that

> We know *"the Spirit breatheth where he will,"* distributing his gifts to each as he wishes . . . for if once he made plowman . . . into prophets, and caused an ass to speak [Num. 22:28ff], how can we be surprised if he teaches *you* with his inspiration [*si ille inspiratione* te *docet*]?[37]

Hildegard, who had no time for simoniac imperial appointees, responded by predict-ing his death—and he was indeed murdered by anti-imperial factions two years later.[38] But this episode suggests to us something about the complex political world in which Hildegard's gift for prophecy and her preaching operated—a world in which male clergy could be exiled or worse; a world in which being a woman was perhaps in some respects to her advantage. This we will see repeated in the lives of many women, includ-ing Douceline de Digne, Bloemardinne, Birgitta of Sweden, Catherine of Siena, and, in a more parochial way, Margery Kempe. Moreover, Hildegard was astute enough to know when to speak openly and when she could not (some of her sermons, including the one delivered at Mainz, are so steeped in obscure biblical and political allegory that even most of her contemporaries could not understand them—most, that is, outside of her immediate coterie).[39] Prominent in this group was especially Elizabeth of Schönau, with whom she shared a passionate missionary activism against the Cathars—against whom Elizabeth, too, got out and preached.[40] To Elizabeth she frankly confessed her sense of fear, which she conquered by an absolute conviction of her own instrumen-tality, as in her famous image of herself as God's trumpet: "Even I lie in the timidness of fear, occasionally resounding a little from the Living Light, like the small sound of a trumpet—whence may God help me to remain in His ministry."[41]

By the early thirteenth century it was getting harder for abbesses to preach out-side of their own convents—for example, in 1215 Pope Honorius III had to instruct the bishops of Burgos and Valences to stop certain abbesses from preaching.[42] But some-times good women preachers were even encouraged by the papacy, women like the Franciscan tertiary, Rose of Viterbo, whom the papacy invited to preach because she made so many converts.[43] We might note here that the Franciscans seem to have in-spired more women preachers than any other order from the thirteenth century on-wards, but even here the same pattern still holds: in general, women preachers seemed to emerge, and emerge unchallenged, particularly during periods of crisis of leader-ship. Such is the case, again, with Douceline de Digne: she emerged after a crisis that rocked the Franciscan Order, and the Church at large. Her brother Hugh of Digne was, according to the chronicler Salimbene, "one of the greatest clerks in the world and a great Joachite, a man of honest and most holy life, more than can be believed."[44] When he was silenced by a scandal that was not of his own making, Douceline seems to have carried on preaching his Joachite apocalypticism with extraordinary charisma—work which required subtle theological knowledge, the ability to speak sensitively under censorship, and the shield of ecstatic prophecy.

The 1254 scandal of the *Evangelium eternum* arose when a fanatical Franciscan claimed that writings of Joachim of Fiore would shortly supercede the New Testament, inaugurating the Third Age (the *tercius status,* that is, the "State" of the Holy Spirit in Joachim's trinitarian concept of history).[45] This scandal was to give a powerful impetus to anti-mendicantism, and with it—although this is not often realised—anti-beguinism, a fateful duo made most notorious perhaps in Jean de Meun's *Romance of the Rose*.[46] This is the scandal that left Joachite apocalypticism (even the orthodox kind preached by Hugh of Digne, and the saintly minister general of the Franciscan Order, John of Parma) to struggle under persistent suspicion, trailing various official condemnations ever after. That Douceline was intimate with these great Joachite thinkers is clear from the fact that when her brother died a year later, John of Parma himself came out of retirement to console her, and to encourage her: "Estai, filha, estai fermanens en so ques as ben comensat" (Stay, my daughter, stay faithful to that which you have begun).[47] After this event Douceline had a vision showing that her fledgling Southern beguine movement was under the special protection of the Trinity (an oblique reference to the central tenet of Joachite doctrine).[48] But Douceline's world, a hundred years on, was not as theologically free as Hildegard's, and it was getting tougher not just for women, but for alternative apocalypticisms generally, to win acceptance and tolerance. Douceline was a committed Joachite, devoted to radical Franciscan poverty—but as the century wore on, this was to become more and more dangerous, especially, though not only, for male clergy. This may account for why Douceline's preaching is as much or more performative, and indeed, para-liturgical in its nature, as it is homiletic (a feature we see in much thirteenth-century beguine writing, including those texts that reached England). Hildegard had both composed liturgy and preached on the authority of her claim to *private, prior* visionary experience. Douceline did both, but under the strengthened shield of now *simultaneous* ecstatic vision. Looking at foundational beguine figures like Douceline, we see the forerunners of and influences upon late medieval women in much more performative or "spectacle"-oriented roles (Catherine of Siena and Margery Kempe, for instance).

During this period Douceline was able to continue preaching Joachimism, not only to her women followers, but more widely still, likely because of her highly publicized gift for ecstatic visions, her reputation for sanctity, and, I would guess, the powerful following of aristocratic women she attracted.[49] These were highly educated women belonging to the upper strata of Provençal society, and in this she is like Hildegard, Birgitta, and various Hussite women: social class was a powerful enabler for medieval women seeking religious leadership roles (in this volume see, for instance, Morrow, Beach, Zieman, Thomas, and Elliott). Partly because of some especially graphic and unsettling passages in her *Vita,* Douceline has hitherto mainly attracted the attention of feminist scholars interested in issues surrounding the female body, and justly so.[50] But her ecstatic behaviour actually did give her both *homiletic* and *liturgical* empowerment of the sort normally open only to male clergy.[51] Whatever discomfort we as modern readers have with some of these episodes in her *Vita,* and those of similar beguines (like Marie d'Oignies or Christina Mirabilis), and those they influenced (like

Margery Kempe), it describes a powerful woman, able to out-preach and out-perform every cleric present.

Her preaching style we can gather from comments like this to her followers: "en l'amor de Crist est aissi acampadas, e Crist vos a liadas en la sieu caritat. Tut li autri sant orde an fort liam de regla; mai vos autras, sa dis, non est a plus liadas, mai sol a caritat." (You are gathered here together for the love of Christ, and He bound you to-gether in his love. All other holy orders are strictly bound by their rules, but you are bound by love alone)[52]—a conviction which suggests both why the beguines were so revered, and so suspect (one sees instantly parallels with Marguerite Porete's fateful style). Her sermons appear to have taken the form of "admonitiones" or "collationes"—that is, exhortations to disciples, interested laypeople, and sometimes clerics, espe-cially on feast days.[53] These terms were later used by adherents of the *Devotio Moderna*, whose women members, like the beguines, were also encouraged to give "charitable admonition and brotherly [or sisterly] correction."[54] We know too little, as yet, about *collationes*, but it is clear that in order to avoid the charge of usurping the official role of the ecclesiastical preacher, these lay preachers evolved a tradition of speaking from "*dicta*"—wise sayings among the Devout, or even vernacularized biblical or patristic quotations. Here again are the seeds of later developments, many discussed in this volume especially in relation to Brut, Kempe, and Askew (see Kerby-Fulton, Gertz-Robinson, and Wallace). In the lengthy Occitan *Vita* (or *Vida*) of Douceline, one can see the roots of much late medieval tradition in a mid-thirteenth-century southern be-guine, especially in her use of the "text" of a vision as a springboard for public discourse. The *Vita* traces how it is initially the preaching of her brother that attracts followers, but how, gradually, Douceline's discourses ("sanctas paraulas") emerge, then begin to be collected by followers.[55] The symbolism in her discourses engages the toughest and most sensitive of Joachite topics: the historical role of the Trinity, the coming age of the Holy Spirit, and also Franciscan poverty, increasingly dangerous subjects.[56] In fact, at one point it is through her intervention that the friars minor of Hyeres (who are ap-parently clinging to radical positions) are saved from, as they thought, certain death.[57] Her discourses seem to have evolved from a kind of extemporizing during ecstasy that uses Joachite doctrine obliquely and symbolically, such as when she is suddenly in-spired to chant a kind of closet Joachite liturgy of her own composition: "Nove Ihesu, nova Iherusalem, nova civitas sancti" (New Jesus, new Jerusalem, new city of the Holy). Whereupon the sisters would follow her in procession with lighted candles ("E totas am procession seguian la apres, am ciri abrazat").[58] This style of extemporizing she shares with another thirteenth-century woman, Mechthild of Hackeborn, who ranks importantly, along with Hildegard and Birgitta, as "liturgical" visionaries. For Douce-line this, in turn, becomes the "text" for a performative discourse, laden with visionary Joachite symbolism of the coming Third Age or Age of the Holy Spirit. Similarly, her extemporized vision of St. Francis, "sealed" with the seal of the Saviour (his stigmata), would have functioned as a tacit and daring reference to the Joachite belief that Francis was the angel of the sixth seal, an "alter Christus" (*La Vie*, 94–96). Her visions seem to have been ecstatically performative; indeed, as Joanne Ziegler has recently demonstrated in relation to Elizabeth of Spalbeek, only the modern equivalent of a trained liturgical dancer could perform some of the movements her *Vita* describes.[59] Her style, then, was a charismatic mixture of apocalyptic exegesis, dramatic performance, and liturgical extemporization—a formula for many women in generations to follow.[60]

At no time in the Middle Ages was it easy for a female liturgist to emerge with authority in this most hallowed of the medieval Church's creative expressions, as Zieman and Fassler suggest in the present volume, with respect to Birgitta of Sweden and Hildegard of Bingen. Medieval female liturgists especially, I would suggest, arose at moments of real Church crisis: Hildegard composes as the Church at large is torn by imperial factionalism and schism; Douceline composes and extemporizes out of the shards of once-powerful Franciscan apocalypticism, as her brother Spirituals go in fear of their lives; Birgitta composes as Rome seethes and popes cower in Avignon. Douceline's performative roles are sometimes even dramatically interactive: when the count of Artois comes to see her in ecstasy, he causes Franciscan friars to preach before her of St. Francis receiving the stigmata, but Douceline's "performance" upstaged the male preachers (*La Vie*, 92–94). It is just this kind of event that is played over and over in the lives of Kempe and Askew (see Watson, Riddy, Gertz-Robinson, and Wallace). It is this dramatic relaying of her visions before an assembled audience that her biographer, a beguine protégé, Phillipine de Porcelet stresses. Phillipine especially favours accounts of the vindication of Douceline over the learned males, and her correspondence with high-ranking political figures, such as Charles I, king of Sicily, "to whom she made known by writing the most secret and hidden things" (E li mandava motas cauzas secretas e rescostas) (*La Vie*, 156) and whom she admonished just as sternly as Hildegard did the princes of her day, and Birgitta the prelates of hers.[61] Douceline was held in the highest regard and never contravened orthodoxy, but hers was the generation just before the one that endured the most bloody censorship of Joachite ideas. By 1297, Boniface VIII "condemned the preaching of women who adopted habits of their own design and deceived simple souls," and by 1311, at the Council of Vienne, Clement V condemned "certain women commonly called Beguines."[62] These events likely explain why the redactor of Douceline's *Vita* working after 1311 toned down and apparently further camouflaged the overt Joachite references in the text.[63] This was the backdrop, ever more somber, against which fourteenth-century women would take up ministerial roles.

We have seen that there were two recognised occasions when female preaching was allowed, even by the most conservative theologians: when the woman had the gift of prophecy, that is, spoke on behalf of God, and when available males had somehow forfeited the right through corruption. It is astonishing how many times throughout the Middle Ages not that those conditions were met, but that they were *seen* to be met—in periods of schism, especially. We might today find the claim to a prophetic gift suspect, difficult of diagnosis. In the Middle Ages it is remarkable that the only woman who was executed by the Church for writings and public teachings was one who made only *indirect* claims[64] to a prophetic gift: the beguine, Marguerite Porete. Her radical dependence on Love, to the exclusion of all else, is close to Douceline's—but instead of subtly transforming difficult or suspect theology into symbolism (the strength of many of her fellow female teachers) Marguerite's verse Prologue pits the censors against her: "Theologians and other clerks, / you won't understand this book / —however bright your wits— / if you do not meet it humbly, / and in this way Love and Faith / make you surmount Reason: / they are the mistresses of Reason's house."[65] And she was politically unlucky, appearing on the scene in the wrong place at the right time.[66] Imitating Christ, she refused to speak at her own trial, and went to her death with dignity, taking much that we would like to know to the grave with her. But the *Mirror* (despite the threat of excommunication for ownership of it) was translated into four European languages, including Latin ("the highest accolade") and traveled incognito until the 1950s.[67] One of these languages was English, and it is truly remarkable that English women were entrusted with some of the more explosive texts of their day, including not only Porete's *Mirror,* but Ruysbroec's closely related attack on the Heresy of the Free Spirit, which appears in *The Chastising of God's Children.* As Justice's exchange with Schirmer in the present volume makes clear, cloistered women (certainly those at Syon, Barking, and even some of less formal vocation) were exposed to a range of Bridgittine and other "adult" religious works. Moreover, as my own response to Somerset suggests, *The Chastising* picks up Ruysbroec precisely because it is a part of a European tradition on volatile orthodoxy issues surrounding *women's* teaching.

Like Hildegard, Douceline, and Birgitta (whose story I leave here to Zieman and Schirmer), Catherine of Siena emerged as a public preacher during a period of crisis of leadership: the Great Schism. She had known all her life that she wanted to preach. As a child, Catherine wished to disguise herself as a male so that she could go on a preaching mission. She had all but given up on this dream by the time she reached adolescence, when God reminded her of it. Although she protested that she would not be listened to as a public preacher because she was a woman, her visionary experience repeatedly validated her sense of mission.[68] Though a Dominican tertiary, her real mentor was, like Douceline's, St. Francis. She was best known for having prophesied the Great Schism; in 1376 she tried to make peace between Florence and Gregory XI, and finally convinced the pope to return from Avignon to Rome. In 1378 she was living in Rome as Pope Urban VI's trusted advisor—this sort of spiritual friendship or "collegiality" being an important, often undervalued leadership role for women, explored in this volume in several essays

(Olson, Coneybeare, Vessey, Morrow, Jaeger, and Riddy). When the schism broke out between Urban and Clement VII, Catherine worked tirelessly—preaching and sending letters to both parties—to try to save the Church from disgrace. She used the spoken word (and the dictated word) as the main tool of her powerful missionary activism. After hearing Catherine preach, Raymond of Capua writes that Pope Urban VI said to the College of Cardinals (to quote the Caxton/de Worde translation): "This woman hath shamed us. She sholde rather be aferd than we by cause she is a woman yet in that we be aferde she is not aferd but conforted us wyth her good counseyls."[69]

Catherine was, by ordinary male clerical standards, fairly uneducated; the daughter of Sienese tradespeople, she had taught herself to read and write. For Catherine, Christ's female apostles (like Mary Magdalene, whom she calls "apostola") are models as current as they are unimpeachable; their knowledge and inspiration she understood to have originated in the experience of the Pentecost. As the exchange between Gertz-Robinson and Wallace here shows convincingly, the iconography of the Magdalene preaching was, like a range of other dynamic role models available to medieval women, surprisingly widespread. Catherine identified with the apostles personally—and it was to them that she turned to defend her preaching mission in the Sienese countryside to her own mother (who thought it disgraceful). She asks her mother to treat her with the same understanding that Mary showed her Son's Apostles after the Pentecost, "The disciples, who loved her without measure, actually leave joyfully and sustain every pain [of the separation] to give honour to God; and they go among tyrants, bearing many persecutions . . . you must know, dearest mother, that I, your miserable daughter, have not been put on earth for anything else."[70]

It was this sense of vocation which allowed her to intervene politically in a brutal world where, often, men could not have. I'd like to close with one of her more dramatic moments—an instance of ministry which is at once apocalyptic, political, visionary, and performative. Like Mary Magdalene at the cross of Christ, she fearlessly comforted a political prisoner through his final hours and even stood with him on the executioner's block, receiving his head into her own hands. At the prison, she tells him:

> "Take comfort, my sweet brother, for very soon we will arrive at the wedding. You shall go there bathed in the sweet blood of the Son of God. . . . And I will be waiting for you at the place of justice." . . . So I waited for him at the place . . . and I bent myself down, and reminded him of the blood of the Lamb. His mouth said nothing except "Jesus" and "Catherine." And while he was speaking, I received his head in my hands, closing my eyes in the divine goodness and saying, "I will."

At this point she has a vision of his soul received into "the open storehouse" of Christ's side:

He turned back, as does the bride when she had reached the door of her bride-groom, who turns back her glance and her head, bowing to one who has accom-panied her, and with that gesture makes a sign of her thanks. . . . When he was at rest, my soul so rested, in such a fragrance of blood, that I couldn't bear to remove from me the blood that had fallen on me from him. . . . And it seems to me that the first new stone has been put in place. . . . Now then, no more negligence, my sweet-est sons, because the blood is beginning to pour, and to receive the life.[71]

Catherine's role here is immensely complex: her gift for transforming hideous political brutality into a spiritual wedding, and a spiritual birth, is perhaps unparalleled. Cer-tainly she performed a role in this that it would have been difficult for a male, even a male cleric, to have played—and likely no male would have so naturally assumed a midwife's role, and posture, on the execution block. As Abelard had written to Heloise, extolling the role of the women at Christ's passion and resurrection: "the rams, or rather the very shepherds of the Lord's flock, flee: the ewes remain undaunted."[72] Cath-erine's "transcendent vision of the healing power of blood" is the vision of one who has found power in powerlessness—and who knows how to use it. It is also one of dozens of recorded instances in which medieval women visionaries found a way of per-forming the kind of sacramentalism they were officially debarred from performing in the Church.

This was heady stuff, and it did not always translate well outside of its immediate context (another thing we should remember about medieval female preaching—it was usually the charisma of the woman in question that carried the day). In England, for instance, Catherine's missionary evangelism was deliberately toned down in the trans-lation of her *Dialogo*, prepared for Syon,[73] and we can find a disturbing amount of bow-derlization in certain other female visionary texts translated for women and lay audi-ences. All this is true, and sobering, but several essays in this volume (Zieman's and Justice's especially) present new, more encouraging evidence to help complicate this picture, even for Syon, and elsewhere.

"Though constrained to hear, they heard"

This brings us to the fifteenth century, and so, in this volume, to Margery Kempe. Seen in the light of continental women's preaching traditions, Margery looks a good deal less unusual than she does in the insular world of vernacular English. She may have been exposed to continental apocalyptic thought via her Carmelite confidant, Alan of Lynn, but we do know that she had reformist impulses, and that she is well aware of her right as a woman to engage in *collationes* or *admonitiones* in contemporary conti-nental style. But she too often pushes beyond the safety of these traditions by quoting scripture in English. When Margery was hauled in before the archbishop of York for interrogation, they had this well-known interchange:

> Þan seyd þe Erchebischop to hir, "Þow schalt sweryn þat þu [ne] xalt techyn ne chalengyn þe pepil in my diocyse." "Nay, syr, I xal not sweryn," sche seyde, "for I xal spekyn of God & vndirnemyn [rebuke] hem þat sweryn gret othys wher-so-euyr I go vn-to þe tyme þat þe Pope & Holy Chirche hath ordeynde þat no man schal be so hardy to spekyn of God, for God al-mythy forbedith not, ser, þat we xal speke of hym." As-swyþe a gret clerke browt forth a boke & leyd Seynt Powyl for hys party ageyns her þat no woman xulde prechyn. Sche, answeryng þerto, seyde, "I preche not, ser, I come in no pulpytt. I vse but comownycacyon & good wordys, & þat wil I do whil I leue."[74]

Even though Margery was combating suspicion that she was a Lollard (knowledge of the gospel in the vernacular especially was, by this time, grounds for interrogation), we have to note that the archbishop heard her out, and that even he could not deny an informed woman the right to engage in *admonitiones*. Whatever status Margery had, and whatever the precise state of her literacy, she was theologically informed concerning her right to teach as a woman. The trial of Walter Brut a few decades before, and various concerns in the disputations related to it, tell us that these ideas were available to the educated laity. Genelle Gertz-Robinson's essay shows in marvelous detail how courageous women like Kempe and later, Anne Askew, negotiated theological and ecclesiastical hostilities on the strength of this knowledge to teach and preach publicly.

We, as modern scholars of medieval women, tend to be very hard on church authorities—the antagonists, most often, of our narratives. But, of course, we must also remember they were in a double bind every time a person claiming to be a visionary walked in the door (and they did walk in the door, and they were most often women). The crucial and sometimes striking thing, however, about medieval ecclesiastical officials is their surprising tolerance, however reluctant or short-lived, both for the prophetic impulse itself, and for the possibility that there could be a female saint around the next corner (points on which their tolerance exceeds our own). In the memorable words of Eric Colledge, speaking of Birgitta of Sweden's male audience at the papal curia, "Though constrained to hear, they heard."[75]

Notes

I would like to acknowledge the following people and institutions for support, encouragement, and constructive criticism on versions of this essay, originally written for the Colloquium of the Institute of Sacred Music, Yale University, at the kind invitation of Margot Fassler. Thanks are also due to Harold Coward and the Centre for the Study of Religion and Society, University of Victoria; Michael Curshmann and the Medieval Studies lecture series at Princeton University; Martin Aurell, for counsel on Douceline; Adnan Hussein, Mary Carruthers, and the Medieval Studies lecture series at New York University, and especially Jocelyn Wogan-Browne and Michele Mulchahey, for warm hospitality, enthusiasm, and learned advice on the occasion. Finally, my gratitude, as always, to Linda Olson, for wisdom and great good sense.

1. See the discussion of these issues in the Somerset and Kerby-Fulton exchange below. For a critique of this kind of approach more generally, see Steven Justice, "Inquisition, Speech and Writing: A Case from Late Medieval Norwich," *Representations* 48 (1994). Closely related to the Marxist view of Wycliffism is the "New Art History's" critique of high aestheticism, on which see Maidie Hilmo, *Images, Icons and Words: Illustrated English Literary Works from the Ruthwell Cross to the Ellesmere Chaucer* (Aldershot, U.K.: Ashgate, 2003). For a superb recent study of approaches to women's literary history, see Jocelyn Wogan-Browne, "Analytical Survey 5: 'Reading Is Good Prayer': Recent Research on Female Reading Communities," *New Medieval Literatures* 5 (2003): 229–97.

2. See Bernard McGinn, "Introduction: Meister Eckhart and the Beguines in the Context of Vernacular Theology," in *Meister Eckhart and the Beguine Mystics*, ed. B. McGinn (New York: Continuum, 1994), 1–14. See also McGinn, *The Flowering of Mysticism: Men and Women in the New Mysticism, 1200–1350* (New York: Crossroad, 1998), 4 and passim, for more recent discussion; and most recently, Fiona Somerset and Nicholas Watson, eds. *The Vulgar Tongue: Medieval and Postmedieval Vernacularity* (University Park: Penn State University Press, 2003).

3. "Mulierbus tamen semper in penitentia iniungendum est quod sint predicatrices virorum suorum. Nullus enim sacerdos ita potest cor viris emollire sicut potest uxor. Unde peccatum viri sepe mulieri imputatur si per eius negligentiam vir eius non emmendatur. Debet enim in cubiculo et inter medios amplexus virum suum blande alloqui, et si durus est et immisericors et oppressor pauperum, debet eum invitare ad misericordiam; si raptor est debet detestari rapinam; si avarus est, suscitet in eo largitatem, et occulte faciat eleemosynas de rebus communibus, et eleemosynas quas ille omittit, illa suppleat" (cited and translated by Sharon Farmer, "Persuasive Voices: Clerical Images of Medieval Wives," *Speculum* 61 [1986]: 517). Unattributed translations are my own.

4. The idea had been current at least since Hildegard of Bingen (for whom, see below), but for citations in the scholastic literature, see Alcuin Blamires and C. W. Marx, "Woman Not to Preach: A Disputation in British Library MS Harley 31," *Journal of Medieval Latin* 3 (1993): 34–63.

5. Translated by Elizabeth Clarke, *Women in the Early Church* (Wilmington, Del.: M. Glazier, 1983), 160.

6. Edmund Colledge and James Walsh, eds., *A Book of Showings to the Anchoress Julian of Norwich* (Toronto: Pontifical Institute of Mediaeval Studies, 1978), *Short Text*, 47.34–48.12.

7. I read this passage more positively than does Nicholas Watson in "The Composition of Julian of Norwich's *Revelation of Love*," *Speculum* 68 (1993): 637–83.

8. St. Thomas Aquinas, *Summa theologiae*, ed. Thomas Gillby et al., 61 vols. (London: Blackfriars, 1964–1980), vol. 45, trans. R. Potter (1970), IIa IIae, q. 177, art. 1, pp. 128–31 and art. 2, pp. 132–35; for excellent discussion see Blamires and Marx, "Woman Not to Preach," 40–41.

9. "[V]nde Maria, et Martha cum Apostolis genera linguarum acceperunt et publice sicut Apostoli docuisse et praedicasse leguntur" (Henry of Ghent's *Summa quaestionum ordinarium*,

Book 1, art. 11, q. 2, edited in Blamires and Marx, "Woman Not to Preach," 50–55, here 50, and note 52 on the development of the legend.)

10. Cited in Blamires and Marx from Henry of Ghent, *Summa in tres partes,* I:193–95, art. 12, q. 1, "Utrum mulier possit esse auditor sacrae scripturae," para. 5 (unedited). For Humbert of Romans, see *De eruditione praedicatorum,* in *Maxima bibliotheca veterum patrum,* vol. 25 (Lyons, 1677), 435, cited in Blamires and Marx, "Woman Not to Preach," 41. For the same idea in the church fathers, see Clarke, *Women in the Early Church,* 161.

11. On dating issues, and the rise of Wycliffism in relation to Julian, see Nicholas Watson, "The Composition."

12. See Norman Tanner, *The Church in Late Medieval Norwich* (Toronto: PIMS, 1984), 166; and see my essay in the present volume, "*Eciam Lollardi.*"

13. See "*Eciam Lollardi*" in the present volume.

14. See Robert Lerner, "Writing and Resistance among the Beguins of Languedoc and Catalonia," in *Heresy and Literacy, 1000–1530,* ed. Peter Biller and Anne Hudson (Cambridge: Cambridge University Press, 1994), 186–204; for Olivi's influence in England, see David Burr, *Olivi's Peaceable Kingdom* (Philadelphia: University of Pennsylvania Press, 1993), 255–59; for English concerns about misguided mysticisms and related issues, see J. P. H. Clark, "Walter Hilton and 'Liberty of the Spirit,'" *The Downside Review* 96 (1978): 61–78; and see my "*Eciam Lollardi*" below; for Hildegard of Bingen, see my "Prophecy and Suspicion: Closet Radicalism, Reformist Politics, and the Vogue for Hildegardiana in Ricardian England," *Speculum* 75 (2000): 318–41. For an Oxford case of disendowment condemnation in 1358, long prior to Wyclif and most likely associated with Franciscan Joachimism, see H. Anstey, ed., *Munimenta Academica,* Rolls Series 50, I.208–11. All of these are discussed in more detail in K. Kerby-Fulton, *Books under Suspicion: Censorship and Revelatory Theology in Late Medieval England* (Notre Dame, Ind.: University of Notre Dame Press, forthcoming).

15. See Kerby-Fulton, *Reformist Apocalypticism and Piers Plowman* (Cambridge: Cambridge University Press, 1990).

16. Kerby-Fulton, "Prophecy and Suspicion."

17. See Beverly Kienzle and Pamela Walker, eds., *Women Preachers and Prophets through Two Millennia of Christianity* (Berkeley: University of California Press, 1998), Larissa Taylor, *Soldiers of Christ: Preaching in Late Medieval and Reformation France* (New York: Oxford University Press, 1992), 176–78, and Katherine Ludwig Jansen, *The Making of the Magdalen: Preaching and Popular Devotion in the Later Middle Ages* (Princeton, N.J.: Princeton University Press, 2001), complete with many illustrations of Mary Magdalen preaching. In fact, at any given time, there were more women preaching throughout the later Middle Ages than we today realise, a factor which suggests that the sometimes panicked quality of official and academic attacks on female preaching did not arise in a vacuum.

18. Ida Raming, *The Exclusion of Women from the Priesthood,* trans. Norman R. Adams (Metuchen, N.J.: Scarecrow Press, 1976).

19. Translated by Alcuin Blamires et al., *Woman Defamed and Woman Defended: An Anthology of Medieval Texts* (Oxford: Clarendon Press, 1992), 251, from *Registrum Johannis Trefnant,* ed. W. W. Cupes (London, 1916), 258.

20. Translated by Blamires et al., *Woman Defamed,* 254–55 (on the complex and as yet imperfectly understood relation of this disputation to the Brut trial, see the Somerset and Kerby-Fulton exchange below); for the Latin text see Blamires and Marx, "Woman Not to Preach."

21. On Hildegard's "*tempus muliebre*" and the "womanish" weakness of the clergy, see, for instance, her *Prooemium vitae s. Disibodi*, ed. J. B. Pitra, vol. 8, *Analecta sacra* (Montecassino, 1882), 355, and various other passages, especially in the *Liber divinorum operum* (on which see Kerby-Fulton, *Reformist Apocalypticism*, 46–47), and Barbara Newman's "An Effeminate Age," in *Sister of Wisdom: St. Hildegard's Theology of the Feminine* (Berkeley: University of California Press, 1987), 238–49. I would point out that this was one of Hildegard's best-known concepts in the later Middle Ages, made famous in part by its inclusion in a much-consulted section of Vincent of Beauvais's *Speculum historiale*, 32:107. Reference to "effeminati" also appears briefly in Henry of Ghent's *Utrum mulier possit esse doctor*, in Blamires and Marx, "Woman Not to Preach," 51 n. 5. Wycliffites, of course, used the rhetoric of homosexuality as a common smear tactic, but other Wycliffites did not extend the argument in the unusual direction Hildegard had, that is, toward urging female ministry. Brut urges it on the grounds that "sancte virgines" have constantly done it (and by implication continue to do so), and especially when priests are afraid: "Si beati qui predicant et custodiunt verbus Dei, quoniam beacius est magis dare quam accipere" (Trefnant's *Registrum*, 345). This suggests to me that Brut's sources were a mix of the kind of academic disputational thought cited above, and the more philogynist continental apocalyptic tradition, most likely Hildegard.

22. Margaret Aston, "Lollard Women Preachers?" *Journal of Ecclesiastical History* 31 (1980): 441–61. For evidence that Langland's readers were interested in the female preachers the poem portrays, see Kerby-Fulton, "The Women Readers in Langland's Earliest Audience: Some Codicological Evidence," in *Learning and Literacy in Medieval England and Abroad*, ed. Sarah Rees Jones (Turnhout: Brepols, 2003), 121–34.

23. Kerby-Fulton, "Prophecy and Suspicion."

24. The primary source concerning her life is Phillipine de Porcelet, *La Vie de Sainte Douceline, fondatrice des beguines de Marseille*, ed. J. H. Albanes (Marseille: E. Camoin, 1879); see also Claude Carozzi, "Une Béguine Joachimite: Douceline, Soeur D'Hugues de Digne," *Franciscains d'Oc Les Spirituels ca 1280–1324*, Cahiers de Fanjeaux 10 (1989): 169–200; Martin Aurell I Cardona, *Une Famille de la Noblesse Provençale au Moyen Age: Les Porcelet* (Avignon: Aubanel, 1986); Geneviève Brunel-Lobrichon, "Images of Women and Imagined Trobairitz in the Béziers Chansonnier," in *The Voice of the Trobairitz: Perspectives on the Women Troubadors*, ed. William Paden (Philadelphia: University of Pennsylvania Press, 1989), 221 and 225. I would like to thank Martin Aurell for stimulating advice about Douceline.

25. On schism issues see Karen Scott, "'Io Catarina': Ecclesiastical Politics and Oral Culture in the Letters of Catherine of Siena," in *Dear Sister: Medieval Women and the Epistolary Genre*, ed. Karen Cherewatuk and Ulrike Wiethaus (Philadelphia: University of Pennsylvania Press, 1993).

26. Stephen Wessley, "Female Imagery: A Clue to the Role of Joachim's Order of Fiore," in *Women of the Medieval World*, ed. Julius Kirshner and Suzanne F. Wemple (New York: Blackwell, 1985), 161–78.

27. It is worth observing here that we can see this in the manuscript transmission of unusually forthright women prophetesses from before the end of the twelfth century. To take the example of Perpetua, it is therefore likely no accident that in England, as Thea Todd has discovered, manuscripts after 1200 tend not to contain the *Passio*. Another forthright twelfth-century woman, Elizabeth of Schönau, was not much copied in insular manuscripts after the twelfth century. Hildegard's, then, by the late fourteenth century, was a precious voice from the pre-Lateran past. Her sermons were preserved not as part of the growing corpus of women's mystical and visionary writing (a kind of writ-

ing which increasingly had to conform to certain ecclesiastical standards to gain approval). Rather, Hildegard's sermons survived as part of the rough and tough corpus of reformist polemic, and in the later Middle Ages, where she was not read by women so much as by men. On these matters see my "Hildegard and the Male Reader," in *Prophets Abroad: The Reception of Continental Holy Women in Late-Medieval England*, ed. Rosalynn Voaden (Cambridge: Brewer, 1996), 1–18. I would like to thank Thea Todd for allowing me to cite her unpublished findings on the manuscript transmission of Perpetua.

28. Flanagan, *Hildegard of Bingen: A Visionary Life* (London: Routledge, 1989), 173.

29. Cited in Flanagan, *Hildegard of Bingen*, 172, from Hildegard's *Vita*. This sounds a little like the traditional early medieval peacemaking roles for aristocratic and noble women; Hildegard was from a noble background, and her social class was an important factor in her freedom of activity.

30. See Kerby-Fulton, "Prophecy and Suspicion."

31. Peter Dronke, *Women Writers of the Middle Ages: A Critical Study of Texts from Perpetua (d. 203) to Marguerite Porete (d. 1310)* (Cambridge: Cambridge University Press, 1984), 228.

32. For discussion of her preaching tours, see Flanagan, *Hildegard of Bingen*, 172–75.

33. See the new edition in Konrad Bund, "Die 'Prophetin', ein Dichter und die Niederlassung der Bettelorden in Köln," *Mittellateinisches Jahrbuch* 23 (1988): 171–260.

34. Translated by Joseph Baird and R. K. Ehrman, *The Letters of Hildegard of Bingen*, 2 vols. (New York: Oxford University Press, 1994), 56, from L. Van Acker, *Hildegardensis Bingensis Epistolarium*, Corpus Christianorum Continuatio Mediaevalis 111 (Turnhout: Brepols, 1991), p. 36, lines 53–65 (from which my Latin insertions come).

35. Baird and Ehrman, *Letters of Hildegard of Bingen*, 55, trans. from *Epistolarium*, p. 33, lines 11–20.

36. Kerby-Fulton, "Prophecy and Suspicion," 322–33; Bund, "Die 'Prophetin,'" 180.

37. *Epistolarium*, p. 56, lines 4–8. Unattributed translations are my own.

38. On this letter, and the ecclesiastical politics surrounding Hildegard, see Kerby-Fulton, "'Smoke in the Vineyard': Prophet and Reformer," in *Voice of the Living Light: Hildegard of Bingen and Her World*, ed. Barbara Newman (Berkeley: University of California Press, 1998), 70–91.

39. For the Mainz letter, and her coterie, see Kerby-Fulton, "'Smoke in the Vineyard,'" 74–75.

40. On Elizabeth's anti-Cathar preaching, see Anne Clarke, *Elizabeth of Schönau: A Twelfth-Century Visionary* (Philadelphia: University of Pennsylvania Press, 1992).

41. Translated by Kerby-Fulton and Dyan Elliott, "Self-Image and the Visionary Role in Two Letters from the Correspondence of Elizabeth of Schönau and Hildegard of Bingen," in *On Pilgrimage: The Best of Vox Benedictina, 1984–1993*, ed. M. H. King (Toronto: Peregrina, 1994).

42. Taylor, *Soldiers of Christ*, 176.

43. Taylor, *Soldiers of Christ*, 176; Darleen Pryds, "Proclaiming Sanctity through Proscribed Acts: The Case of Rose of Viterbo," in *Women Preachers and Prophets through Two Millennia of Christianity*, ed. Beverly Kienzle and Pamela Walker (Berkeley: University of California Press, 1998), 159–72.

44. Joseph Baird et al., trans., *The Chronicle of Salimbene de Adam* (Binghamton, N.Y.: Medieval & Renaissance Texts & Studies, 1986), 561.

45. Marjorie Reeves, *The Influence of Prophecy in the Later Middle Ages* (Oxford: Oxford University Press, 1979; reprint Notre Dame, Ind.: University of Notre Dame Press, 1993), 59–61.

46. In the important characters of Faus Semblant (a friar) and Attenance Contrainte (a beguine).

47. Phillipine de Porcelet, *La Vie*, 136. All translations from this text are my own.

48. "Car per cert, sa dizia, tota li Trinitatz a cura d'aquest sant estament" (Porcelet, *La Vie*, 140).

49. Salimbene emphasizes the social status of these women in the passage cited above.

50. See, for instance, Caroline Bynum, *Holy Feast, Holy Fast* (Berkeley: University of California Press, 1987), 133–34, 174, 213 and passim.

51. For brief, but insightful comments, see Jo Ann McNamara, "De Quibusdam Mulieribus: Reading Women's History from Hostile Sources," in *Medieval Women and the Sources of Medieval History*, ed. Joel Rosenthal (Athens: University of Georgia Press, 1990), 238. See also Kathleen Garay and Madeleine Jeay, *The Life of Saint Douceline, a Beguine of Provence* (Cambridge: 2001), 131–34 especially on Douceline's preaching.

52. Porcelet, *La Vie*, 142; see also McNamara, "De Quibusdam Mulieribus," 238.

53. See Thom Mertens, "Collatio und Codex im Bereich der *Devotio moderna*," in *Der Codex im Gerbrauch*, ed. Christel Meier, Dagmar Hupper, and Hagen Keller (Munich: Wilhelm Fink, 1996), 163–82, discussed more fully in my "*Eciam Lollardi*" below, note 43.

54. Cited in John Van Engen, "Devout Communities and Inquisitorial Orders: The Legal Defense of the New Devout," in *Kirchenreform vom unten: Gerhart Zerbolt von Zutphen und die Brüder vom Gemeinsamen Leben*, ed. Nikolaus Staubach (Frankfurt, 2004).

55. Rather in the way that the *dicta* of the most revered among the *Devotio Moderna* were collected together, as in the origins of the *Imitatio Christi* of Thomas à Kempis. See Van Engen, "Devout Communities."

56. See Carozzi, "Une Béguine Joachimite."

57. Her text is especially important as a witness "d'une mentalité antérieure à celle des disciples d'Olieu," as Carozzi says, "Une Béguine Joachimite," 201.

58. Porcelet, *La Vie*, 114.

59. Joanna Ziegler, "The Blood and Sweat of Practicing Mysticism: Elizabeth of Spalbeek's Dance of Faith," Medieval Conference of the Northeast, Yale University, 14 October 2000. On Douceline's levitations to ecstatic practices, see Garay and Jeay, *The Life*, 131–32.

60. As this Good Friday exhortation suggests: "Fals mont, fals mont, can greu ponch ti ven desus! . . . Reculles vos, reculles vos, intras vos en la nau, que tot cant sera trobat defora sera perit." (False world, false world, what a great blow will come upon you! Come, come, enter into the nave [wordplay on 'ship'], all who are found outside will perish.) Then, even more emphatically, "Non auzes con crida, intras en la nau?" (Do you not hear the way he cries, 'Enter the ship'?) When the sisters ask her whether they will be in the ship, she replies with joy, "Veraiamens, sotz las alas de sant Frances, totas seres salvas" (Truly, under the wings of St. Francis you will all be saved) (Porcelet, *La Vie*, 108–10). For several other instances of Douceline's liturgical and exegetical extemporizing, see Carozzi, "Une Béguine Joachimite," 190–93.

61. See especially the scene in which she is interrogated by "un gran lector" of Marseilles (Porcelet, *La Vie*, 180), and several instances involving masters from Paris (88–90 and 118).

62. Ernest W. McDonnell, *The Beguines and Beghards in Medieval Culture* (New Brunswick, N.J.: Rutgers University Press, 1954), 374–75.

63. See Carozzi, "Une Béguine Joachimite," 194.

64. Porete did, however, make implicit claims to divine illumination.

65. Translated by Dronke, *Women Writers*, 224. There is a possibility that this Prologue did not originate with Marguerite, although it captures the tone of her book quite plausibly; see the introduction to Paul Verdeyen, *Margaretae Porete, Speculum Simplicium Animarum*, Corpus Christianorum Continuatio Mediaevalis 69 (Turnhout: Brepols, 1986), vii.

66. For the view that Porete suffered in an unwarranted way from the intersection of her trial with that of the Templars, see Robert Lerner, *The Heresy of the Free Spirit* (Berkeley: University of California Press, 1972).

67. See E. Colledge, "The Latin *Mirror of Simple Souls*," in *Langland, the Mystics and the Medieval English Religious Tradition: Essays in Honour of Stanley Hussey*, ed. H. Phillips (Cambridge: D. S. Brewer, 1990), 177–83.

68. Discussed at length in Elizabeth Petroff, *Medieval Women's Visionary Literature* (Oxford, 1986), 239.

69. From the translation of Raymond of Capua's original Latin printed by Caxton/de Worde, 1493. The full passage, interestingly abridged in the English, runs: "Haec muliercula nos confundit, mulierculam autem voco, non in contemputus eius, sed in expressionem sexus feminei, naturaliter fragilis & ad nostrem instructionem. Ista siquidem naturaliter timere deberet, etiam quando nos essemus bene sicuri: & tamen ubi nos formidamus, ipsa stat absque timore, suisque persuasionibus nos confortat" (cited in Karen Scott, "'Io Catarina,'" 95, from Raymond of Capua's *Legenda Major, Acta Sanctorum Aprilis*, vol. 3 [Antwerp, 1685], 927, col. 1). See Scott's note 24 on other instances of Catherine preaching to men. On the gender-related abridgements in the Caxton/de Worde edition, see Jane Chance, "St. Catherine of Siena in Late Medieval Britain," *Annali D'Italianistica* 13 (1995): 164–203. Connections between Urban's court and England account for some of the English favoritism towards Catherine, just as Birgitta's anti-French political prophecies won her an enthusiastic English audience; see E. Colledge, "Epistola solitarii ad reges: Alphonse of Pecha as Organizer of Birgittine and Urbanist Propaganda," *Mediaeval Studies* 43 (1956): 19–49.

70. "I discepoli che l'amavano smisuratamente, anco, con allegrezza si partono, sostenendone ogni pena per onore di Dio; e vanno fra i tiranni, sentendo le molte persecuzioni . . . Sappiate, carissima madre, che io miserabile figliuola, non son posta in terra per altro," from *Le Lettere di S. Caterian da Siena*, ed. Piero Misciatelli (Florence: Giunti, 1940), Letter 117, vol. 2, p. 185; trans. by Scott, "'Io Catarina,'" 112.

71. Translated by Petroff, *Medieval Woman's Visionary Literature*, 273–74.

72. Translated by Blamires et al., *Woman Defamed*, 247.

73. See Denise Despres, "Ecstatic Reading and Missionary Mysticism: *The Orcherd of Syon*," in Voaden, *Prophets Abroad*, 141–60.

74. *The Book of Margery Kempe*, ed. S. B. Meech and H. E. Allen, Early English Text Society *o.s.* 212 (Oxford: Oxford University Press, 1940), p. 125, lines 37–126, line 20, with omission. See Gertz-Robinson's essay for more detailed discussion, and Kerby-Fulton's on *collationes*.

75. Colledge, "Epistola solitarii," 49. See also Dyan Elliott, *Proving Woman: Female Spirituality and Inquisitional Culture in the Later Middle Ages* (Princeton, N.J.: Princeton University Press, 2004), which emerged while this book was in press.

ONE

Spaces between Letters

Augustine's Correspondence with Women

CATHERINE CONYBEARE

It is a source of some frustration that, amid the copious epistolographic remnants of Late Antiquity, almost no letters of undisputed female authorship survive. We know that such letters were written, for a remarkable number of letters responding to female addressees remains to us; and yet all we have is, as it were, the spaces between the letters of their male correspondents. My title intentionally echoes that of Paul Saenger's *magnum opus*,[1] for it is my contention here that if we work consciously to read these spaces between letters, the effect will be quite as transformative to our perceptions—if in a different way—as the reading of spaces between words.

In this instance, the spaces under consideration are those in the correspondence of St. Augustine. Some twenty letters to women survive among his collected letters, including several clustered together, undated and perhaps undatable, at the end of the collection.[2] From internal evidence, we know that he wrote many more. The remaining letters represent merely the tantalizing traces of an ongoing epistolary contact.

The process of reconstructing the other side of these epistolary exchanges is, of course, a delicate one. Letters in Late Antiquity were never what we know as private documents: techniques of distribution and the communitarian organization of households ensured that.[3] Moreover, many readers of Augustine—his letters and, more particularly, his treatises—find his language both to and about women coercive and stereotypical;[4] some have argued that "women" in his texts serve merely as a trope in a power struggle actually being played out between males.[5] The most extensive recent reading specifically of Augustine's letters to women is that of Kim Power, who insists that women were, to Augustine, not peers or friends, but merely "correspondents."[6] Yet what, exactly, does this tell us? Can the line between "friends" and "correspondents" be so clearly drawn? Perhaps this is why her sympathetic treatment of individual letters seems repeatedly to contend against her overall thesis, and in several places she emphasizes Augustine's recognition of the responsibility and authority of the women concerned.[7]

My own reading of Augustine's letters relies on the idea that in the spaces between them there may indeed be discerned some details of literate women and their intellectual lives.[8] Several arguments must be made from absence; much must be sifted out that seems to be superimposed by Augustine on his correspondents. But the net effect of reading the spaces—of recognizing these absences for what they are, silences once filled with women's writing, actions, opinions—prevents these women from disappearing into mere figures of rhetoric and restores to them some degree of historical particularity.[9]

Augustine was particularly skilled at adapting for his addressee the language and content of his letters, which makes him a good mediator for this type of study. However, Augustine himself is not my subject; in order to keep his agency as much in the background as possible, I have relegated to an appendix some observations on his use of gendered language and his tailoring of biblical quotation to female readers. An important further caveat should be mentioned here: it is very noticeable in dealing with Augustine's letters to women that when he is writing ostensibly to a husband and wife, it is in fact uniquely the husband that he addresses. The correspondence with the renowned aristocratic convert Paulinus of Nola and his wife Therasia is a case in point. Though much has been made of Augustine's praise of their spiritual marriage, it is based on only one passage:

> uidetur a legentibus ibi coniunx non dux ad mollitiem uiro suo, sed ad fortitudinem redux . . . quam in tuam unitatem redactam et redditam et spiritalibus tibi tanto firmioribus, quanto castioribus nexibus copulatam . . . resalutamus.[10]

> those reading there see a wife who does not lead her husband to indulgence, but rather leads him back to strength . . . ; we salute her, submissively received into unity with you, and bound to you by spiritual bonds as firm as they are chaste.

This is a touching testimony, but as the index to *Corpus Scriptorum Ecclesiasticorum Latinorum* (*CSEL*) says, "praeterea non memoratur nisi in inscriptionibus . . ." (otherwise she is not mentioned except in the superscriptions [to the letters]).[11] So too in the letter addressed to Armentarius and Paulina: the subject is a vow to preserve a chaste marriage taken by both parties, though it emerges towards the end both that the wife is the stronger and that it is the husband who is really being addressed. Augustine reiterates the strictures characteristic of him that such a vow must not be taken unless it is mutually felt:

> Una sola esse causa posset, qua te id, quod uouisti, non solum non hortaremur, uerum etiam prohiberemus implere, si forte tua coniux hoc tecum suscipere animi seu carnis infirmitate recusaret.[12]

> There could only be one ground on which I would not only not encourage you in what you have vowed, but actually forbid you to fulfil it, that is, if perhaps your wife refused to undertake it with you through weakness of mind or body.

But as it is, she is more prepared than he, and Augustine adds the goad: "si continentia uirtus est, sicuti est, cur ad eam sit promptior sexus infirmior, cum uirtus a uiro potius cognominata uideatur . . . ?" (if continence is a virtue—and it is—why is the weaker sex more ready for it, although virtue seems rather to get its name from the man [*uiro*]?). This extract fits well with the thesis of women used as rhetorical devices to shame men into action; and Letter 2* contains a very similar passage, in which Augustine goads a man to baptism through the example of his wife.[13] But the letter to Ecdicia, for example, shows that claims to mutuality are not necessarily hollow: "etiam si se ipse continere uoluisset et tu noluisses, debitum tibi reddere cogeretur . . ." (even if [your husband] had wished to remain chaste and you hadn't, he would have been obliged to do his conjugal duty by you).[14]

These snatches of information, if read as more than rhetoric, are of considerable interest; but it remains the case that, to distil much sense of the women, we must concentrate on letters to uniquely female addressees. And we may note that this is truly a process of distillation: of these addressees, we rarely have any but the slenderest biographical information, often not even that—most of these women do not even rate an entry in the standard *Prosopography of the Later Roman Empire*.[15] This makes the *argumentum ex silentio* the more complete.

■ ■ ■

It is revealing to consider not just what Augustine says in his letters to women, but what he takes for granted. First, he assumes in his female correspondents a high degree of literacy, in the sense of the ability to read and write good Latin. That this is taken for granted is shown above all in its absence: a letter is returned to Seleuciana:

> unde [Nouatiano] uideatur, quod inter apostolos baptizatos Petrus non fuerit baptizatus, ignoro et ideo exemplum epistulae tuae, ne forsitan tu non habeas, misi

tibi, in quo diligentius consideres ad ea me respondere, quae inueni in litteris tuis; si enim notarius non mendose excepit aut scripsit, nescio, quale cor habeat, qui, cum apostolos baptizatos dicat, Petrum baptizatum negat.[16]

I don't know where that Novatianist could have got the idea that, in the midst of apostles who were baptized, Peter might not have been baptized, and so I have sent you a copy of your letter, in case you don't have one, in which you may see with careful inspection that I am responding to what I found in your letter; if the copyist didn't mishear or take the dictation wrongly, I don't know what sort of judgement a person might have who says that Peter was not baptized although he says that the apostles were.

Yet despite his politely veiled doubts as to Seleuciana's grasp of theology, and even a later enquiry into the accuracy of her use of a preposition,[17] Augustine goes on to discuss in some detail both Peter's claims to baptism and the nature of the sacrament of baptism in general. There must be some hope that it is indeed the *notarius*, and not Seleuciana's comprehension, that is lacking.

Nowhere else does Augustine admit of such a suspicion when addressing female correspondents.[18] Frequent demands for letters in response to his own, especially in cases of anxiety about heresy, are made with no apparent doubt of their being answered.[19] When news reaches him that Demetrias has dedicated herself to virginity, it is the promptitude of the letter which he remarks on: he takes facility of composition for granted.[20] Ecdicia is a woman to whom we have no cause to attribute particular sophistication or learning, yet Augustine specifically recommends to her the delicate literary task of writing to her husband to seek his pardon for precipitating their current conjugal *impasse.*[21]

A particularly important series of instances of women's writing is seen in Letter 20*. First, there is an appeal to an extended correspondence with the receiver, Fabiola: Augustine asks her to bear with him, "patienter me tolera," as she knows that his letters are not usually as onerous as the one he is about to write.[22] The tone of the letter as a whole is of one addressing a close confidante: Augustine's exchanges with Fabiola (the only other surviving letter is Letter 267) seem to me to call into question the received wisdom that he had no female friends. (His relations with the household of Proba—which included Juliana and Demetrias—also bespeak a cordiality and closeness of involvement not normally attributed to him.[23]) In the complicated reversals of ecclesiastical politics which he goes on to confide to her, the letters of another woman, a landowner at Thogonoetum referred to only as *domina,* play a critical role. The partially defrocked Antoninus, a juvenile bishop by the ill-considered appointment of Augustine himself, has laid claim to an estate at Thogonoetum. To a crucial meeting with the ecclesiastical arbiter to settle Antoninus' vexed affairs, Augustine brings a letter from the *domina*, the lady of the manor, as proof of the proceedings: it forms the trump card in the investigation, and a second letter from her clarifies the situation still further (and duly enrages Antoninus). This is an astonishing instance of the power of a woman's writing, yet Augustine does not pause in his narration to remark upon it.[24]

As with writing, so with reading: women's ability and application are taken for granted. The directives assumed to be written for his sister's convent include a proviso that *codices* should only be made available to the nuns at fixed hours: clearly there was a demand for them, for the issue seems to be restricting their use, not furthering it.[25] Two of Augustine's letters to women are of considerable length, and one in particular, the *Liber de Videndo Deo* addressed to Paulina, contains without apology several chapters which are extraordinarily dense in language and concepts.[26] In another letter, the "studium sanctum" of Maxima pleases Augustine, and she is offered "laborum nostrorum opuscula," some little works of his refuting "diuersos errores" without any suggestion that she might prove unable to understand them.[27] That such a suggestion would, if necessary, have been made, we again know from the one instance in which Augustine doubts his correspondent's ability: his first extant letter to Italica is supported by a cover letter to Cyprianus, explaining the occasion for, and importance of, his exhortations.[28] Yet Italica cannot have been too inadequate, for we know that she wrote to Augustine at least four times.[29]

The second thing conspicuously taken for granted by Augustine is the freedom of movement of Christian women. Most striking is the letter of which two women, Galla and Simpliciola, are the bearers.[30]

> Honorabiles dei famulas et praecipua membra Christi, Gallam uiduam sancti propositi et eius filiam Simpliciolam uirginem . . . uenerationi tuae in Christi dilectione commendo et tamquam mea manu per hanc epistulam trado consolandas et in omnibus adiuuandas . . . .

> I commend to your Reverence, in the love of Christ, the honourable servants of God and outstanding limbs of Christ the saintly widow Galla and her daughter Simpliciola, a virgin; through this letter I present them to you as if with my own hand, to be cheered and helped in everything.

Once again, it is the lack of sense of anything out of the ordinary that is of interest: except for a mention of their relative merits in widowhood and virginity, the letter might just as well have been written to commend male bearers to its addressee.

Finally, there is just a hint that literary contact between women could be taken for granted as well. This extends beyond the obvious opportunities for contact within households—for example, between Juliana and her daughter Demetrias—to embrace a wider circulation of Augustine's letters among women. It is twice assumed in *De Videndo Deo* that Paulina will have read his shorter treatment of the same theme in his letter to Italica. This observation rests, of course, on the assumption that Paulina and Italica are not members of the same household; and, given that neither woman has been securely identified to date, this must remain merely an assumption.[31] That the evidence for such links might be extended with further study, however, is an intriguing possibility. Could women be using letters to create and sustain their own Christian communities just as men, *mutatis mutandis*, are doing?

■ ■ ■

One positive notion consistently emerges from Augustine's letters to women, a sense of the women's authority: their authority to speak, to write, to make decisions; their authority over others, and how to use it. These women seem to have possessed in a considerable degree a version of the Roman *auctoritas*—the sense that what one does carries weight and entails responsibility, a sense of one's own worth. Indeed, Christianity made this *auctoritas* available to them in a way that the sphere of Roman citizenship and political life, restricted exclusively to men of property, had not. Earlier, of course, such authority had been borrowed by laying claim to male qualities, even in some sense "becoming male"; one thinks of Perpetua's dream before she faces martyrdom, in which she expressly acquires the physical characteristics of a man.[32] But by the late fourth century, authority was being offered, if under restricted circumstances, to women *qua* women.[33] Attaching value to Christian women meant offering them autonomy in the sphere of action perceived as their monopoly, that of reproduction. Ambrose was all too capable of conjuring the subversive side of this, of demanding that committed virgins dissever themselves from family ties and expectations;[34] the positive version is perhaps epitomized in Letter 150, in which the young girl Demetrias can choose virginity as a way of appropriating the hereditary renown of her family: "virgines, quae sibi optant Aniciorum claritatem, eligant sanctitatem" (let those virgins who desire the glory of the Anicii for themselves make the choice of chastity). Emphasizing a rather different aspect of traditional womanhood, even the sad tale of Sapida shows how appropriation of Christian *mores* may strengthen a woman and lend her a degree of autonomy. When she asks Augustine to wear the tunic she made for her brother Timotheus, a deacon at Carthage who has recently died, he encourages her to turn to higher consolation:

> si enim, quia uestior, quoniam ille non potuit, ea ueste, quam fratri texueras, te aliquid consolatur, quanto debes amplius et certius consolari, quia, cui fuerat praeparata, incorruptibili indumento . . . uestitur![35]

for if it comforts you a little that I am wearing, since he could not, the garment which you wove for your brother, with how much more depth and security should it comfort you that he for whom it was made is clothed in an incorruptible covering!

It seems that this type of confidence, offered to women, gave rise to a certain rhetoric of women's freedom in Christianity. Thus, in Augustine's directions to the convent, he concludes that the nuns should observe his rules "non sicut ancillae sub lege sed sicut liberae sub gratia constitutae" (appointed not like maidservants under contract, but like free women under grace).[36] How literally such a behest might be interpreted is impossible to say, but it remains of interest that this is clearly an emotive image to use.[37]

One vivid form taken by this *auctoritas* is the responsibility of the women to ensure their orthodox belief, and the pains taken to make them feel its importance.[38] For example, when Proba, who has been recently widowed, asks for direction in prayer, Augustine teaches her both "qualiter ores" and "quid ores," both *how* to pray and what to say. She is expected to grasp the purpose of prayer,

> quod dominus et deus noster non uoluntatem nostram sibi uelit innotescere, quam non potest ignorare, sed exerceri in orationibus desiderium nostrum, quo possimus capere, quod praeparat dare.

> that our lord and God does not wish to be made aware of our will, which he can't fail to know, but for us to practise in our prayers the desire to be able to take what he is ready to give.

Above all, she must put aside wealth and family and pray "as if desolate."[39] That Proba takes seriously her responsibility to oversee her own religious development is made clear by Augustine's next letter to her: she has written to tell him of her meditations on the nature of the soul.[40] Letters to Italica and Juliana are both urgently concerned with making these women feel the error of heresy, and eradicating it from their belief.[41] The latter is prompted by the receipt of a book from the heretic Pelagius by Juliana's virgin daughter Demetrias: Pelagius is understood to have claimed that the spiritual riches of Demetrias' virginal state are due to herself alone. Augustine commands Juliana to scour the Pelagian book and report on its doctrine, which presupposes a grasp of the orthodox on her part. He also speculates on Demetrias' reception of the book:

> Et nos quidem de sanctae uirginis disciplina et humilitate christiana, in qua nutrita et educata est, hoc existimamus, quod, illa uerba cum legeret, si tamen legit, ingemuit et pectus humiliter tutudit ac fortassis et fleuit . . . .

Going by the education of the holy virgin, and the Christian humility in which she was nurtured and trained, I also think that, as she read those words—if indeed she did read them—she groaned aloud and humbly beat her breast, and perhaps even wept.

These women are expected to bear an unusually large burden of correct interpretation and appropriate response. Accordingly, Augustine takes Felicia's concern at scandals in the Church very seriously, but reminds her of the need to trust directly in God, not his fallible earthly representatives.[42] Not only, it seems, were women to claim *auctoritas,* but they were entitled to claim it as directly bestowed by God.

With so strong a sense in women of their responsibility to themselves, the responsibility owed to others by women naturally becomes an equally pressing issue. This, it seems to me, is the key to the letter to Ecdicia, customarily given a more negative reading.[43] In choosing her actions, she has to be brought to realize her responsibility to her husband and his spiritual development. She should also promote *concordia* for the sake of their son, "ut secundum tuam uoluntatem in dei possit nutriri et erudiri sapientia, necessaria illi est etiam uestra concordia" (your harmoniousness is necessary to him as well, so that he may be nurtured and educated, as you wish, in the wisdom of God). Augustine is at pains to say that he condemns Ecdicia's tactless means, not her worthy end:

> haec tibi scripsi, quoniam me consulendum putasti, non ut tuum rectum institutum sermone meo frangerem, sed quod te inordinate et incaute agente uiri tui factum dolerem.

> Since you thought I should be consulted, I have written these things to you, not in order to shatter your good resolution with my advice, but because I am grieved by what your husband has done through your rash and ill-considered action.

Responsibility, not just to husbands and sons, but to the wider household is a recurrent theme. Juliana feels obliged to make a statement, not only of her own belief, but of Christian *mores* in her entire household (note that this is one of the very few cases in which a woman's actual words are quoted):

> omnis . . . familia nostra adeo catholicam sequitur fidem, ut in nullam haeresim aliquando deuiauerit nec umquam lapsa sit, non dico in eas sectas, quae uix expiantur, sed nec in eas, quae paruos habere uidentur errores.[44]

> my entire household follows the catholic faith so precisely that it has never wandered or lapsed into any heresy—and I don't mean, into those sects which are almost unforgivable, but not even into those which seem to be only slightly erroneous.

One of the pleasant hopes that Augustine indulges at the time of Demetrias' commitment to virginity is that "imitentur eam multae famulae dominam ignobiles nobilem" (many humble maidservants might follow the example of their noble mistress).[45] Proba, too, is expected to set an example to her household.[46]

Fabiola once again proves quite exceptional. Augustine surrenders himself completely to her judgement in dealing with the renegade Antoninus:

> Audiat a te ista obsecro te et quanta tibi dominus dicenda donauerit non taceas homini, de cuius mentis cupio sanitate laetari. hanc enim prae illo aetatem geris, ut ei decenter exhibeas parentis affectum.

> Let him hear this from you, I beg you, and don't refrain from telling the man all the things which the Lord has prompted you to say, for I am longing to be gladdened by the health of his mind. For you are just so much older than him, that you may appropriately show him a parent's affection.

Women are expected, by Augustine at any rate, to take the initiative and make their own decisions. But after flattering Fabiola with reflections on her spiritual superiority, and reassuring her that she is indeed an appropriate choice for this difficult mission, Augustine at last says simply, "Per Christum te obsecro et per eius misericordiam et iudicium, ut adiuues me in hac causa et pro ipso et pro ecclesia" (Through Christ and his mercy and judgement, I beg you to help me in this situation, for his own sake and the Church's).[47] His appeal leaves no suggestion that Fabiola might not be *able* to help; he begs her to *choose* to help.

Further to the issue of women's *auctoritas,* it is striking that Augustine is willing to carry through his thoughts on interpretative multivalence and validity of individual opinion and apply them even to women.[48] This partly, of course, tells us about Augustine's own priorities, but also a little about the women who are prepared to take on such responsibility, or whose character and training make it even a possibility. His attitude during the complicated discussion in *De Videndo Deo* forms a good example. He warns Paulina near the beginning, "nolo auctoritatem meam sequaris" (I don't want you to follow my *auctoritas*), and concludes the work:

> Has sententias de re tanta uirorum tantorum non ob hoc interponere uolui, ut cuiusquam hominis sensum tamquam scripturae canonicae auctoritatem sequendum arbitreris, sed ut illi, qui aliter sapiunt, conentur mente uidere, quod uerum est . . . .[49]

> On such an important matter, I didn't want to put in the opinions of great men so that you would think that the interpretation of a mere human being should be

followed as if it were scriptural authority, but so that those who think differently should try to see inwardly what is true.

In the midst of the work, he invites Paulina to ponder the foundations for her knowledge, and points out that she is perfectly justified in doubting his interpretations (her reception of Scripture itself, however, is another matter).[50] Even in his letter to Florentina, who is so young and unsure of herself that her mother has written to Augustine on her behalf, he insists on making her responsible for her own opinions and interpretations. Throughout, he emphasizes his own inadequacy and his doubt that he will be able to answer her questions, and insists that her aim should be not to need an earthly teacher at all: "laborum periculorumque nostrorum singulare solacium est, cum ita proficitis, ut illo perueniatis, ubi nullius hominis doctoris egeatis" (there is a peculiar reward for our toil and risks: when you are so proficient that you reach the point at which you no longer need any man as teacher). If Florentina manages to learn anything worthwhile, "ille te docebit, qui est interioris hominis magister interior" (it is he who will teach you, the inward teacher of the inner self). Subversive doctrine for a young girl.[51]

■ ■ ■

Reading the spaces between these letters, then, does indeed yield some clues to women's literacy and its relationship with their power and authority in the wider world. The women need not be of the highest wealth and class: look at Ecdicia, Sapida, Florentina. But all, in the intersection of their literacy and their Christian faith, find scope for the exercise of certain skills and judgement; and Augustine, at least, does not doubt that with the help of the "magister interior" they may develop further.

Appendix

Augustine's Use of Gendered Vocabulary and Biblical Quotation in His Letters to Women

Augustine makes few concessions of language for his female correspondents. Letter 124, for example, which is directed to Albina, Pinian, and Melania is addressed to his "fratribus." At Letter 130.31 he asks for Proba's "orationes fraternae"; and examples could be multiplied. He often chooses honorific forms of address which do not reflect the woman's gender: so Proba is "sanctitas uestra" in Letter 150, and Fabiola is "eximietas tua" in Letter 20*.27 (both, one might add, extremely respectful titles). But he will also address women in elaborate phrases which do capture their gender: Proba is "domina insignis et merito inlustris et praestantissima filia" in Letter 131, and Felicia, being consoled about ecclesiastical scandals, is "domina merito suscipienda et in Christi membris honoranda filia" in Letter 208. (Perhaps in a related category comes the exhortation to Fabiola, in Letter 20*.28, to simulate the *consilia* of Antoninus' own mother in her attempt to make him see reason!)

It is of particular interest that Augustine takes the unusual step of justifying explicitly his use of male language to refer to both genders:

> neque enim ad solos uiros pertinet, quod scriptum est: Qui odit fratrem suum, homicida est, sed sexu masculino, quem deus primum fecit, etiam femineus praeceptum sexus accepit.[52]

> and the scripture "who hates his brother is a murderer" is not relevant only to men; the female sex received the precept along with the male, which God made first.

This forms part of the Rule for the convent. No wonder there has been hot debate about whether the male or female version of this Rule is the prior. Is the explanation testimony to Augustine's punctilio, or were there really women questioning whether the precept applied to them?

Notwithstanding his insistence on the universal applicability of masculine language, it is clear that Augustine takes particular pains to suit his choice of scriptural citation to a female reader. When he is providing guidelines for conjugal relations, he chooses to quote the passages of Paul which dwell upon reciprocity, rather than female subjection. In the letter to Ecdicia, it is 1 Corinthians 7:4, with its insistence on the power of husband and wife over each other's bodies, that forms the keynote (after all, it could have been Ephesians 5:22 and its *mulieres subditae!*).[53] Augustine uses 1 Corinthians 7:4 to emphasize reciprocity once again in his admonitory letter to Armentarius and Paulina (Letter 127.9). So too for personal *exempla:* not only does he choose biblical women, but he matches them as far as possible with his correspondent's situation. In Letter 130, the key text for the widowed Proba, who has asked for advice about prayer, is 1 Timothy 5:5–6:

> Quae autem uere uidua est, et desolata, speret in Deum, et instet obsecrationibus, et orationibus nocte ac die. Nam quae in deliciis est, uiuens mortua est.

> She who is truly a widow, and deserted, should trust in God, and apply herself night and day to prayers and entreaties. For she who lives in luxury is dead in life.

The parallelism with her situation hardly needs underlining. In the same letter, which is developed as an extended gloss on the Lord's Prayer, he also uses Luke 18:1–8, the parable of the persistent widow and the judge, and two Annas: the mother of Samuel

(1 Samuel 1:2–28), who illustrates "Deliver us from evil," and the widow Anna of Luke 2:37. By the time that Proba is exhorted "ora sicut uidua Christi" (Letter 130.29), she has a full notion of what might be meant by a "widow of Christ." In the more acerbic letter to Ecdicia, however, Augustine is particularly forceful on her premature appearance in widow's weeds: she should attire herself "non sicut Anna sed sicut Susanna," as befits her married state (Susanna is one of the women who serves Christ at Luke 8:3); and she is reminded of Esther, who considered her glorious robe "sicut pannus menstrualis" (Letter 262.9 and 10). Sara, wife of Abraham, is held up to Ecdicia as a model of conjugal obedience, *via* 1 Peter 3:5–6. Finally, Sapida is reassured that it is fitting to mourn the dead:

> nam et Martha et Maria, piae sorores et fideles, resurrecturum suum fratrem Lazarum flebant, quamuis eum tunc ad hanc uitam rediturum esse nescirent; et ipse dominus eundem, quem fuerat resuscitaturus, Lazarum fleuit . . . .[54]

> for Martha and Mary, who were dutiful and devoted sisters, also wept for their brother Lazarus, who was to rise again—although they didn't know then that he would return to this life; and even our Lord wept for Lazarus, whom he was about to revive.

Once again, the example is perfectly matched. Sapida too is a devoted sister, mourning her brother, and yet her consolation is to be greater than Martha and Mary's: their brother was resurrected back into *this* life (*ad hanc uitam*); Sapida, however, can look to the comfort of her brother's elevation to immortal life.

Notes

The kernel of this essay was originally given, as "Women's Letters and Lettered Women: The Evidence from St. Augustine," at the International Patristics Conference (Oxford, 1995); my thanks to all those who responded then with kind and constructive comments, especially to Kim Power. Thanks also to John Magee, for useful comments on an early version. The "dialogue" with Mark Vessey was initiated in a presentation at Villanova University in November 2000.

1. Paul Saenger, *Spaces between Words: The Origins of Silent Reading* (Stanford, Calif.: Stanford University Press, 1997).

2. The letters of Augustine are edited by Goldbacher in *Corpus Scriptorum Ecclesiasticorum Latinorum* (hereafter cited as *CSEL*) 34, 44, 57, and 58 (Vienna, 1895–1923), and by Divjak, *CSEL* 88 (Vienna, 1981). The Divjak letters, a recent discovery, are not numbered consecutively with Goldbacher's edition, and are conventionally designated by an asterisk. For a fuller discussion of the

transmission of Augustine's letters, see Vessey's response below, under the rubric of "The Survival of Augustine's Letters to Women."

3. See my *Paulinus Noster: Self and Symbols in the Letters of Paulinus of Nola* (Oxford: Oxford University Press, 2000), chaps. 1 and 2.

4. The extensive work of Elizabeth Clark on the subject is a case in point: examples are "'Adam's Only Companion': Augustine and the Early Christian Debate on Marriage," *Recherches Augustiniennes* 21 (1986): 139–62; "Devil's Gateway and Bride of Christ: Women in the Early Christian World," in *Ascetic Piety and Women's Faith: Essays on Late Ancient Christianity* (Lewiston, N.Y.: E. Mellen Press, 1986), 23–60; "Ascetic Renunciation and Feminine Advancement: A Paradox of Late Ancient Christianity," in *Ascetic Piety,* 175–208; "Vitiated Seeds and Holy Vessels: Augustine's Manichean Past," in *Ascetic Piety,* 291–349. Kari Børresen takes a more conciliatory view: see, for example, "In Defence of Augustine: How *Femina* Is *Homo,*" in *Collectanea Augustiniana: Mélanges T. J. van Bavel,* ed. B. Bruning, M. Lamberigts, and J. van Houtem, Bibliotheca Ephemeridum Theologicarum Lovanensium (Leuven: University Press, 1990), 1:279–96.

5. See, for example, Kate Cooper, "Insinuations of Womanly Influence: An Aspect of the Christianization of the Roman Aristocracy," *Journal of Roman Studies* 82 (1992): 150–64.

6. Kim Power, *Veiled Desire: Augustine's Writing on Women* (London: Darton, Longman, Todd, 1995), "Peers," 109; conclusion, 110: "From the evidence, one might say he has male friends and female correspondents." Power here is summing up a long tradition: see, for example, Gerald Bonner, "Augustine's Attitude to Women and *Amicitia,*" in *Homo Spiritalis: Festgabe für Luc Verheijen OSA,* ed. Cornelius Mayer (Würzburg: Augustinus-Verlag, 1987), 259–75, esp. 270; Clark, "'Adam's Only Companion'"; and even Peter Brown, *The Body and Society: Men, Women and Sexual Renunciation in Early Christianity* (New York: Columbia University Press, 1988), 396: "Compared with Jerome, Augustine moved in a monochrome, all-male world."

7. See Power's discussion of his relationship with Fabiola (*Veiled Desire,* 116–17), also treated here; and of Letters 252–55 (115).

8. In this I develop some pointers given by Jean Truax, who provides a more general reading of Augustine's works relating to women in "Augustine of Hippo: Defender of Women's Equality?" *Journal of Medieval History* 16 (1990): 279–99.

9. This is the trajectory envisaged in a recent article by Elizabeth Clark, who writes briskly: "stereotyping, naturalizing, universalising—three common ideological mechanisms through which the Church Fathers constructed 'woman.'" Yet, after surveying and exploring these mechanisms, she concludes that "we can infer *even from the representations of these women by male writers* that [this] gender ideology . . . did not result in their total silencing" (Clark, "Ideology, History, and the Construction of 'Woman' in Late Ancient Christianity," *Journal of Early Christian Studies* 2 [1994]: 155–84; quotes from 169 and 183 [my emphasis]).

10. Letter 27.2. All translations here are my own.

11. Paulinus of Nola reuses this passage of praise almost verbatim in a letter of his own (44.3): for a comparison of the passages, see Conybeare, *Paulinus Noster,* 82–83.

12. Letter 127.9; the next quotation is from the same section.

13. See especially Letter 2*.4: "non enim metuo te offendam, cum exemplo feminae ciuitatem dei te exhortor intrare: nam si res est difficilis, iam ibi est sexus infirmior, si autem facilis, nulla causa est, ut non ibi sit fortior."

14. Letter 262.2. It should be noted that this is one of the documents which Kate Cooper uses to support the opposite case; see "Insinuations of Womanly Influence," 159–60.

15. Exceptions are Proba, Juliana (*PLRE* I), and Demetrias (*PLRE* II), respectively grandmother, daughter-in-law, and granddaughter of the same family from the *gens Anicia* (on these three, there are relatively full entries); Fabiola (*PLRE* II) who also received Jerome Letter 76; and Italica (*PLRE* I) who also received a letter from Chrysostom (170). All, it seems, follow the pattern of moneyed, upper- (but not necessarily senatorial) class, influential women; but there is little further evidence.

16. Letter 265.1.

17. Letter 265.6.

18. Augustine is, however, as liable to blame his own lack of clarity as his reader's lack of intellect for a failure of understanding: as early as the preface to *De Genesi Contra Manichaeos* (387–88), he writes with humble approval of those who had criticized his earlier anti-Manichaean works as difficult or impossible for the uneducated to read: "Placuit enim mihi quorundam uere Christianorum sententia, qui cum sint eruditi liberalibus litteris, tamen alios libros nostros quos aduersus Manichaeos edidimus cum legissent, *uiderunt eos ab imperitioribus aut non aut difficile intellegi* et me beneuolentissime monuerunt, ut communem loquendi consuetudinem non desererem, si errores illos tam perniciosos ab animis etiam imperitorum expellere cogitarem."

19. See, for example, Letters 188.10 and 208.7.

20. Letter 150.

21. Letter 262.11.

22. Letter 20*.1.

23. See Letters 130, 131, 150, and 188. Power (*Veiled Desire*, 110) writes off Letter 267, to Fabiola, as lacking in warmth, but Augustine is here using exactly the language of affectionate friendship which he has learnt from Paulinus of Nola (see Conybeare, *Paulinus Noster*, chap. 6, esp. 141–45). This implies that ideas about Augustine's capacity for friendship with men *or* women must stand or fall together; or, as is implied in Vessey's Response here, to frame the question in terms of contemporary ideas of "friendship" at all may simply be inappropriate.

24. This sequence of events is described in Letter 20*.17–20. The *domina* plays an important role throughout the whole affair: she receives a petition from the *coloni*, the surrounding small farmers, in 10, and her rejection of Antoninus will end his chances in the region, in 14.

25. Letter 211.13: "codices certa hora singulis diebus petantur; extra horam quae petierint, non accipiant." This cannot, however, form conclusive evidence, as there is considerable debate about whether Augustine's Rule was first written for a community of men or of women: see George Lawless, *Augustine of Hippo and His Monastic Rule* (Oxford: Oxford University Press, 1987), 135–54.

26. Letter 130, to Proba on prayer, contains thirty-one paragraphs in the *CSEL* edition; *De Videndo Deo* contains fifty-four, of which the first eleven are a complicated epistemological exposition of Augustine's thoughts on the scope of and relationship between sense perception, mental perception ("mente conspicere"), and belief.

27. "Studium sanctum," Letter 264.1; "opuscula," Letter 264.3.

28. Letters 92 and 92A. The letter to Cyprianus may not indicate misgivings about Italica's reading, but merely Augustine's customary anxiety in the face of heresy.

29. Letter 99: "Tres epistulas tuae benignitatis acceperam, cum ista rescripsi . . . ." These three are to be added to the one to which Letter 92 responds.

30. Letter 212. Clark notes, in "Ascetic Renunciation and Feminine Advancement," that freedom to travel was one of the advantages gained by dedicated Christian women, as (germane to my previous section) was "praise for scholarship."

31. For the possible identities of Italica, and a general discussion of the difficulties of fourth/fifth century prosopography, see Peter Brown, "Aspects of the Christianization of the Roman Aristocracy," *Journal of Roman Studies* 51 (1961): 5–6.

32. James W. Halporn, ed., *Passio Sanctarum Perpetuae et Felicitatis* (Bryn Mawr, Penn.: Thomas Library, Bryn Mawr College, 1984), 10.7: "et expoliata sum et facta sum masculus." See the discussion of Karl Vogt, "'Devenir mâle', aspect d'une anthropologie chrétienne primitive," *Concilium* 202 (1985): 95–107.

33. Clark would, I think, find this too positive a reading of the Christian valorization of women: see especially her argument that friendship was only offered to women once they were considered to have attained through asceticism a "liminal," ungendered state, in "Friendship between the Sexes: Classical Theory and Christian Practice," in *Jerome, Chrysostom and Friends* (New York: E. Mellen Press, 1979), 35–106.

34. See Brown, *Body and Society*, 343–44.

35. Letter 263.4.

36. Letter 211.16; note also the pun on the *lex* of the Old Testament as opposed to the *gratia* of the New.

37. I have omitted from my discussion Albina and Melania, as represented in Letters 124 and 126, as it is abundantly apparent that, thanks to their social position and inordinate wealth, their *auctoritas* would have been considerable whatever the sphere in which they wished to exercise it. (Noted, with a rather different slant, by Clark, "Ascetic Renunciation and Feminine Advancement.") However, the obeisance of Augustine's letter to Albina, Letter 126, makes amusing reading.

38. Also noted, but with a negative interpretation, by Power, *Veiled Desire*, 127–28.

39. How to pray: Letter 130.9; purpose of prayer: 130.17; "as if desolate": 130.6–7.

40. Letter 131. Augustine begins as if in mid-conversation: "Est quidem ita, ut dicis, quod in corpore corruptibili anima constituta terrena quadam contagione constringitur . . . ."

41. Letters 92 and 188 respectively; the following quote from 188.9.

42. Letter 208, especially 6.

43. Letter 262; the following quotes both from 262.11. See Brown, *Body and Society*, 403–404, and Cooper, "Insinuations of Womanly Influence," 159–60, for readings very different from mine.

44. Letter 188.3.

45. Letter 150.

46. Letter 130.30. Here Proba's "nurus," her daughter-in-law, is singled out for special attention—the "nurus" being, of course, Juliana.

47. Letter 20*.28 and 33.

48. A clear statement on interpretative multivalence is to be found at *Confessions* XII.31 (42): "Ita cum alius dixerit: Hoc sensit, quod ego, et alius: Immo illud, quod ego, religiosius me arbitror dicere: Cur non utrumque potius, si utrumque uerum est, et si quid tertium et si quid quartum et si quid omnino aliud uerum quispiam in his uerbis uidet, cur non illa omnia uidisse credatur . . . ?"

49. Letter 147.2 and 54.

50. Letter 147.38 and 40.

51. Letter 266; quotation from 3. A similar ease with youthful choice is shown in Letter 3*, to Felix, concerning a widow who wishes to dedicate to God, in a spiritual barter, her own widowhood in lieu of the promise of her daughter's virginity. Augustine points out that the daughter's virginity is ultimately not the mother's to give away, and that the daughter must be allowed to choose her own course in life.

52. Letter 211.14.

53. The passages, respectively: "Mulier sui corporis potestatem non habet, sed vir. Similiter autem et vir sui corporis potestatem non habet, sed mulier"; and "Mulieres viris suis subditae sint, sicut Domino."

54. Letter 263.3.

■ ■ ■

Response to Catherine Conybeare

Women of Letters?

MARK VESSEY

Christian Literature in late antiquity allowed more space to women—as subjects, even if not as authors. Macrina, Gorgonia and Gregory Nazianzen's mother Nonna are balanced in the west by the two Melanias, the Elder and the Younger, as the subjects of Christian writing, and some "desert mothers" can be found in monastic literature; Therasia, the wife of Paulinus, and Augustine's mother Monica are known to us, at least indirectly, as are Jerome's friends Marcella, Paula and the rest, and Olympias, the loyal friend of John Chrysostom. Writings by women themselves are, however, few.[1]

In an earlier (oral) dialogue, the author of these words gently protested against my attempt to spirit away the female correspondents of a father of the Church. The women I would then have made vanish were friends of Jerome.[2] So it is pleasant now to do in writing what Jerome would never do for Augustine, and begin to sing a palinode.[3] Even if we only see them "indirectly"—and how else, at best, do we see their male counterparts?—the women whose names appear in the salutations of letters from Jerome, Augustine, and their sort make special claims on our historical attention. Not only do they survive as names—often with hints of social status, place of abode, and family connections—and thereby contribute to our expanding prosopographic database for Late Antiquity,[4] they do so in a discursive context that is particularly rich in opportunities for the modern interpreter.

More so than other kinds of writing, at least those affected by the conventions of classical rhetoric, letters imply reciprocity and exchange. The ideas of letter writing as conversation between absent persons and of the individual letter as "half a dialogue" are commonplaces of ancient epistolary theory.[5] Other literary genres—panegyric, say, or polemic—may also have an addressee who is expected to reply, but as a rule they do not presuppose the continuing (potential) reversibility of the poles of writer and reader that is the tacit, unquestioned postulate of epistolography. Even when a letter is written with a larger readership in view than its addressee(s), or when it is disseminated independently of any actual exchange, the implied "original" context may still be a factor in the responses of real readers, including in the first instance such persons as could have an interest in corresponding with the writer/author on their own behalf.

Thus, exceptionally, epistolary discourse—ancient no less than modern—points to the existence of a position for women between the otherwise exclusive locations of woman-as-author (rare) and woman-as-subject-of-male-author ("normal"): that of indirect object and putatively respondent subject of epistolography. At no time, of course, was this position reserved for women. Everything we know about late ancient Graeco-Roman culture indicates that in practice it was usually occupied by men. The actual division of the internal space of letters, as of any property, must be established case by case, according to the evidence. This is the task that Catherine Conybeare addresses and for which her reading of the substantive "spaces between letters" in Augustine's correspondence with women offers a methodological model. There are precedents for divinatory activity of this kind. The gaps in the dossiers of Augustine's correspondence with two of his most celebrated male contemporaries, Jerome of Bethlehem and Paulinus of Nola, have yielded to philological analysis.[6] Although no other group of Augustinian letters to and from a single correspondent compares with these for historical interest, the results of such work already suggest how much might be learned from a similarly attentive reading of other parts of his epistolary corpus. If further spur were needed, it should have been provided by the rediscovery in 1981 of twenty-seven Augustinian letters never before seen in print.[7] Only the appearance soon afterwards of an equally submerged series of the bishop's sermons can explain why so little progress has so far been made in this direction.[8]

It is not only Augustine's correspondence that is ripe for new reading. The total bulk of Greek and Latin epistolary texts extant from the period between 380 and 430 C.E., roughly the time of Augustine's own activity as a writer, far exceeds that from any previous half-century of Mediterranean history. Because it is possible to trace epistolary topoi which occur in all periods, and because letter-writers of Late Antiquity, Christian as well as "pagan," are fond of invoking classical models, it is easy to construe this phenomenon as just another symptom of a larger cultural revival which is sometimes called the "Theodosian Renaissance" and which broadly coincides with the "Golden Age of

the Church Fathers."⁹ In the past, scholars were content to refer to individual letters—
once they had been satisfactorily edited and, so far as possible, separately dated—for
the light they shed on events, personalities, careers, and the history of ideas and social
practices, without pausing to consider either the genre-specific features and functions
of the epistolary transaction, or the processes by which *collections* of letters began to
circulate. But the situation is changing. There are now signs of a growing interest on
the part of philologists and social historians alike in letters as constituents (as well as
documents) of late antique culture.¹⁰ Like other so-called renaissances, the cultural revival of the later fourth and early fifth centuries was in large part a collaborative and
contestatory work of writing.¹¹ Letters, we may assume, were among the means by which
it was brought about.

Conybeare's monographic study of the letters of Paulinus of Nola pioneers a style
of research that could usefully be extended to other bodies of epistolary writing from
this period.¹² Two of her working assumptions are particularly relevant to our inquiry.
The first concerns the object of research. Her primary interest, she explains, is in letters as "historical events."

> By speaking of letters as "historical events," I attempt to include far more than
> merely the textual traces of the correspondence: the letters of late antiquity, though
> abundant, are imperfectly and incompletely preserved; the superscriptions indi-
> cating recipients, which might be thought to be the most reliable indicators of
> their epistolary status, do not reliably survive. What must also be taken into ac-
> count is the entire nexus of communication which surrounded these textual traces,
> the written documents. This could include everything from supplementary notes,
> which have not survived, through gifts of one sort or another sent with the letter,
> to verbal messages brought by the letter-carriers. Indeed, I shall argue that what
> we refer to as a letter was often a relatively insignificant part of this more general
> and various communication. (19)

By reconceiving the letter as an event whose dimensions exceed the textual traces in our
manuscripts and printed editions, this definition already indicates the interstitial spaces
that are the focus of the present essay. The matter of defective superscriptions might
seem at first glance less germane, all the letters under discussion here having been chosen
because they survive with (more or less reliable) superscriptions showing them to have
been originally addressed to women. However, the reminder of the fragility of such
marks of original address can also be read as a hint to enlarge the definition of epistolary
"events" to include all possible after-events of the initial transmission-exchange. And it
suggests the relative openness of the position of implied or assumed indirect object of
epistolography in a society where "familiar" letters circulated at second and third hand.

A second major point concerns the long-term import of the letters in question. "The epistolary medium," Conybeare argues, "had especial significance, both historically and in the fourth century, for the creation and reinforcement of a sense of community within the Christian Church" (12). This general claim receives added emphasis in Paulinus's case because of his intense cultivation of the ideal of a broadly inclusive friendship among human beings that derives its force and meaning from their love of Christ. Here Conybeare confirms the deep affinity between Paulinus's thinking and Augustine's. She is also able to establish a close connection between this aspect of Christian theology and the practice of Christian letter writing as Paulinus understood it:

> We have already seen how letters were written for the eyes not just of those expressly addressed, but of the communities in which they lived and of anyone in the wider Christian community into whose hands the letter might fall. This extended implicit audience naturally both created and was created by an inclusive notion of *amicitia*. It is not that personal bonds of friendship (in a more traditional, exclusive and individuated style) cease to be important, but that *potential* bonds of friendship with the broader Christian community come to be considered as equally important. (80)

The blank or philologically unreliable superscriptions in surviving copies of Paulinus's letters to his friends are thus a graphic expression of the potential for wider Christian community that his letters hold out. "The ideal participants in Christian *amicitia* are . . . the whole community of the Christian Church. The question now arises: can *amicitia* include women as well as men?" (80). For Paulinus as for most other patristic writers of his time the answer seems to be no, unless a woman regenders herself by heroic feats of asceticism. The one obvious exception to this rule, Conybeare suggests, is a writer otherwise held largely accountable for the unjust treatment of women in western Christianity and in western society as a whole since the end of the Roman Empire: Augustine of Hippo.

The implications of Augustine's theological anthropology for his views on women's nature and status are nowadays well appreciated. After weighing the evidence of his writings in the light of recent feminist and other scholarship, E. Ann Matter concludes that

> Augustine's attitudes toward women are . . . as complex and contradictory as any of the major theological concepts with which he struggled in his long and eventful life. He certainly accepted the prevailing notions (both Christian and pagan) of his time: that women were subjected to men by the order of creation, and that women's embodiment was the specific focus of inferiority. However, he also maintained a certain type of spiritual equality between men and women, by virtue of the par-

ticipation of women in the category "human being" as defined by [i.e., with reference to] men. In this limited sense women are equally in the image of God, and are equally able to be in the divine presence in the resurrection.

She adds:

> Over the course of his life Augustine had a number of important relationships with women. After his conversion and renunciation of sexuality, and especially after the death of his mother, Augustine's relationships with women were more distant but still involved some extensive correspondence of pastoral care, especially with consecrated virgins and widows, and concern for the life of a house of monastic women in Hippo. This is a rich and varied legacy of attitudes about women for the Western Christian tradition.[13]

Unlike proponents of more heroically ascetical ideals of Christianity,[14] Augustine did not require women to become "as men" in order for him to treat them as his equals in the Christian society of this world. Rather, we could surmise, he dreamed of a society in which the bodily markers of femininity, signs of a difference construed by him and others as both functional and ontological, no longer signified in that way: one, in other words, that partly prefigured the society of the blessed in heaven. To the degree that such a ruse was imaginatively possible for a freeborn Roman male of his day and practically feasible for a Christian bishop, he may even be thought to have aimed in his own life at gender-blind social relationships.[15]

If we allow such a hypothesis, the potential importance of epistolography in Augustine's life from the time when his main theological convictions became settled (conservatively, c. 400) becomes clearer. "What God revealed to his understanding as he thought and prayed, he would teach in conversation to those who were present and in books to those who were not," wrote Possidius, his first biographer, of the newly converted Augustine.[16] As presbyter and later bishop of Hippo, the same writer records, Augustine was careful never to have a woman alone in his company.[17] Only at a distance, and by writing, could he henceforth hold anything like a sustained conversation with a member of the other sex. As disembodied but intelligible presences to each other, Augustine and his female correspondents might confer as though on the basis of their common, equal humanity and divinity-in-Christ, even if—as would often be the case—the subject of their conference was a question relating to sexual difference.[18] A space that only Monica could occupy in the conversations of Milan, Cassiciacum, and Ostia (at least as they are represented in the early dialogues and the *Confessions*) would thus be opened to women with opportunities to "write back" in a way that Monica never did.[19] Precious space for all parties . . . if it was real, and if it was taken!

The example of Monica raises an issue central to any consideration of the cultural significance of Augustine's correspondence with women: that of the educational attainments or, more precisely, the "literacy" of the women addressed. Women readers and writers aside, the word in quotation marks stands for a set of questions that have become more absorbing, if scarcely more tractable, in recent decades. The author of the best and most influential single study of Greek and Latin literacy in the ancient Mediterranean world, William V. Harris, has argued (1) that the "literate" population, on one definition, rarely exceeded 10 percent of the total, the majority of literate persons being male inhabitants of cities; (2) that rates and levels of literacy began to decline in most areas of the Roman Empire in Late Antiquity; and (3) that Christianity did little to arrest and much to accelerate the decline.[20] The second and third contentions are controversial: whatever the demonstrable state of affairs in, say, the seventh-century Latin West, late Roman historians remain suspicious of long narratives of "decline," and the question of the historical relations of Christianity and Roman or post-Roman literacy has been judged by many to require more circumspection. Not surprisingly, the evidence of Augustine—whose thoughts on Christian literary and textual culture, together with his practice as a writer, continue to engage specialists across disciplines—is cited by Harris at a critical juncture.

Considering the impact of Christianity as a "religion of the Book" in late Roman North Africa, Peter Brown once detected in Augustine's "vast correspondence" the signs of an attempt to install a new kind of Christian or "clerical" literacy, a literacy grounded in a more popular register of Latinity than the classical literary language, closer to the Latin of the Scriptures. "Behind Augustine's vast output in Hippo," he wrote, "we can sense the pressure of the need to extend this religious literacy as widely as possible."[21] Harris commends Brown for making a useful distinction between religious literacy and other kinds, but objects that his claim for Augustine

> runs up against the awkward fact that neither Augustine nor any other influential ecclesiastic ever even considered the problem of mass illiteracy—which is hardly suprising, since they had jettisoned the Greek cultural traditions which alone might have led them in that direction. For holy men and women the texts were of such importance that . . . monastic rules required the recruits to learn letters. Hence Christianity did lead to the instruction in reading (at least) of some people who would not otherwise have learned. But this effort, together with the struggle to maintain a literate clergy, exhausted the interest of the Christians in supporting literacy.[22]

While Brown may have overplayed the "democratizing" tendency in Augustine's projects of Christian education, Harris for his part appears to confuse the goal of mass literacy—which on his own admission, despite a classicist's nostalgia for abandoned Greek cultural traditions, does not announce itself before the modern industrial era—with that of a more expansive form of "religious literacy," however understood. That Augustine developed a fine sense of the textual resources and literate skills necessary or useful to the life of a Christian community like his own, and that this sense was significantly different from the common instinct of the late Roman "man of letters" which he also was, is apparent from such works of his as the *De doctrina christiana, Confessiones,* and *De catechizandis rudibus,* to name only the most programmatic. He recognized that the Christian community would be socially diverse. And he assumed, as a personal article of faith, that its various members and groups would cooperate. Forms of literacy proper to the clergy and those living under religious rule occupy an important place in his prescriptions for a biblically based Christian pedagogy, without ever becoming their exclusive focus. "Clerical" and "monastic" as the bishop's own literary persona may be said to be, in carefully qualified senses of those words, it is far from clear that these adjectives adequately characterize the sum of literary undertakings evoked by Possidius's *Life of Augustine* and its appended index of the saint's writings.[23]

Some of the works listed in that index, as we shall see, were addressed to women. What do such texts tell us about the kinds of (traditional) literacy that Augustine could take for granted among women of his acquaintance, and about the kinds of (Christian) literacy that he expected or asked of them? In an essay complementary to Harris's research on late ancient literacy and Brown's inquiry into the interactions of Christianity and local cultures, Keith Hopkins notes how Christian book-religion at once reconfigured the socially unifying and differentiating functions of ancient literary culture and was itself modified by literate practices:

> Sacred texts, exegetical commentaries, letters, written prayers, hymns, sermons, and decrees of church councils, all helped to integrate Christianity into a coherent if sub-divided body; it had a recognizable identity, forged and continually reforged by an argumentative network of writers and readers. The existence of Christian books and readers, emerging from a differentiated set of sub-cultures, and disseminated all over the Roman empire, deeply affected the nature of Christian religious teaching and experience. Literacy was not simply a passive technical skill; it was itself a cultural creation and a creator of culture.[24]

As an already visible subculture in late Roman society, the women of Augustine's correspondence may be thought to have had a role in the creation of a new Christian community and its culture(s).[25] It is the possibility of confirming and specifying their role that makes the project of reading these "spaces between letters" so engaging.

So what more can be read? As always, there is a danger of overreading texts that promise much yet remain partly opaque to the historian's gaze. In this case there is the additional risk that overreading will become overwriting. Rather than muffle the discussion now resumed among Augustine, his ancient (women) readers, and their modern counterparts by talking through it, I confine the remainder of this response to three extended glosses on my colleague's text. They concern the survival of Augustine's letters to women,[26] the literacy of his female correspondents, and the authority imputed to them (and others like them) in matters of the faith. If at times I emphasize elements of Augustine's agency that Catherine Conybeare has designedly kept "in the background," it will I hope be clear that I have no desire to reassert the bishop's property in texts that legally ceased to be his at the moment the letter-carrier left his door.[27]

The Survival of Augustine's Letters to Women

As Conybeare notes, several of the letters discussed here are to be found clustered together near the end of Augustine's collected correspondence (Letters 262–67). They are the letters to Ecdicia, Sapida, Maxima, Seleuciana, Florentina, and Fabiola. The impression of an epistolary subclass determined by gender of addressee is, however, largely a trick of modern editors. Since Augustine died before reviewing his letters and sermons as he had his "books" or major works (in the incomplete *Retractationes* or "Revisions"), we have no way of knowing for sure how he would have arranged his own correspondence. In the list published after his death by his disciple and biographer Possidius, which is organized partly by subject and partly by genre, some of the letters are grouped with treatises and sermons composed with particular adversaries in mind (pagans, Jews, Manichees, Donatists, etc.), while others appear in a class of "Miscellaneous Books, Sermons and Letters Written for the Benefit of All Devout Persons."[28] The rest—by far the greatest number—are placed in a separate category of "Letters," identified by addressee but not ordered according to any single or perspicuous principle. A few notable major clusters ("ten [letters] to Nebridius," "six to the holy Jerome," "eight to Paulinus") reflect deliberate arrangement and almost certainly an author's publishing initiative. Other, lesser clusterings may indicate no more than tidy filing, though dossier-style publication should not be excluded when there is reason to think it likely. The serial listing (*Indiculus* 44–47) of a letter to Proba "On Prayer to God" (now number 130), two other letters to the same (131 and another, not extant), a letter to Proba and Juliana "On the Veiling of Demetrias" (150), and one addressed to Juliana "On Holy Widowhood" (the epistolary treatise *De bono viduitatis*) can hardly be casual, given the status of the recipients and the highly charged atmosphere of the time in which these texts were composed, c. 411–14, in the aftermath of the "sack" of Rome. This instance aside, Possidius's placing of letters to female correspondents does not suggest any special discretion or discrimination.[29]

After Augustine's death his letters circulated as separate items or in small ensembles, only gradually being consolidated into the major collections known to us from the Carolingian and later periods, which in turn provided the basis for the first printed editions.[30] Not until the great edition of the *Opera omnia* by the French Benedictines of St. Maur in the late seventeenth century were all the known letters arranged systematically. The system then chosen was chronological and it gave rise to the numbering still in use (except for the asterisked "Divjak" letters which form a new series).[31] Letters that could not be dated with any precision were consigned by the Maurists to a class apart and numbered from 232, following the last datable letter (231). The apparent clustering of six letters to women at the end of the collected correspondence is thus an effect, first, of the absence of obvious chronological indices in those texts and, second, of a Benedictine sense of decorum.

This is not to say that the present distribution of letters to women in Augustine's corpus is necessarily without significance. All these letters were written by Augustine while he was bishop. That a somewhat higher proportion of them, relative to the letters to men, cannot now be more narrowly dated may be taken for a sign that the business on which he corresponded with women was, as a rule, less closely connected with major public events. Another, safer inference would be that Augustine the bishop could and did correspond with women at any and all times. With the exception of such conspicuously public and datable exchanges as those with Proba and Juliana, this was routine activity for him. Unlike Ambrose of Milan, most of whose "Letters" come down to us in a self-consciously monumental edition compiled late in life and consisting largely of material that was never meant for dispatch,[32] or Jerome of Bethlehem, who began publishing small collections of highly artificial letters (many of them addressed to women) as a way of advertising his abilities as a freelance Christian intellectual,[33] Augustine has left us a series of texts which are as close to "real" letters as we can normally expect to come for this period, short of digging in the sands for papyri. What difference might it have made to modern historiography if the Maurists had placed the "undatable" correspondence in the first section of the *opus epistolarum*? Less captivating than such premeditated and beguilingly gynocentric works as the *Life of Macrina*, the *Life of Melania*, Jerome's "Lives" of Paula and Marcella, or his own "Life of Monica," the ordinary run of letters that Augustine wrote to women now emerges as an oddly underexploited archive for "women's history."

The Literacy of Augustine's Female Correspondents

The women addressed in these letters appear to have possessed "a high degree of literacy, in the sense of the ability to read and write good Latin." Conybeare's definition is virtually classical. The *litteratus*, in a formula preserved by Suetonius, was one "able to speak or write on a given topic accurately, cleverly and expertly"; his ability to read at an equivalent level was taken for granted.[34] That a fair number of women in the upper echelons of late Roman society were able to read complex texts for themselves is widely allowed by contemporary scholarship.[35] Since girls did not usually attend school, reading skills would have to be learned at home. "When Augustine describes the ideal wife as 'litterata, vel quae abs te facile possit erudiri' ['literate or capable of being easily taught by you']," writes Harris, "the suspicion must be strong that he is thinking of basic literacy and implying that at his social level a woman of marriageable age (she would be very young by modern standards) might easily lack that qualification."[36] At least some of the women with whom Augustine corresponded were of higher status than his own, and all but one of the addressees of the extant letters were past the normal age of first marriage. Hence it is not altogether unlikely that they could read his letters for themselves. On the other hand, as Paul Saenger reminds us, the task of reading an extended text in *scriptura continua* was laborious enough for it to be regularly delegated to slaves or other "professionally" literate persons, whose presence in the households of most of Augustine's correspondents is as good as certain.[37] Even if these women could read, they would rarely have to, and it would always be easier and more natural for them to hear a text read aloud by another person, usually male.

A similar argument applies, with greater force, to women's "writing." First of all, no woman of means would expect to write a letter in her own hand, unless it were on an intimate topic—any more than Augustine or any male of comparable status would normally do so. Slaves or literate hired hands (*notarii*) were there to take dictation, to produce drafts for correction, and then to make fair copies. A few women of this period are known to have set their own hands to writing letters, but not to have produced texts of the quality of those that we are led to reconstruct in the spaces between Augustine's.[38] In most cases they would probably do no more than add an authenticating subscription, of the kind Augustine himself would append to a letter before dispatching it. A woman in Antiquity who qualified as *litterata* on Suetonius's definition—that is, who had the skills in literary composition that we associate with classical epistolography— would indeed be worthy of remark.[39] Is it merely an accident that the one surviving piece of artistic Latin by a female author of Late Antiquity consists of lines and half-lines composed by Virgil?[40] In a playful poem addressed to his secretary or *notarius*, the fourth-century poet Ausonius of Bordeaux jokes that the boy's hand kept outrunning his master's dictation: "God," he declaims, "has given you the gift of knowing in advance what I want to say."[41] The amanuenses of Augustine's female correspondents may not have been inspired, but it would have been a normal part of their job to give literate expression to their employers' concerns. Like the *domina* of Thogonoetum who plays a key role in the events narrated in Letter 20* to Fabiola, such women were used to dealing with documents in the administration of their households and estates,[42] and to having staff to handle them. For them no less than for the bishop, letter writing on matters of religion was part of the routine business of their social situation.[43]

It is in this broader domestic context of epistolography, I think, that we best interpret the hint of "secretarial" error in Letter 265 to Seleuciana. An anonymous individual, identified (by Seleuciana?) as a Novatianist, the name given to a sect that denied the efficacy of penitence for post-baptismal sin, had expressed opinions troubling enough to this female "servant of God" for her to wish to bring them to Augustine's attention. The logic of the offending person's position was not, however, entirely clear to the bishop. How could he claim, if in fact he did, both that "all Christ's apostles were baptized" and that Peter, though one of them, was not? And what exactly did he mean by saying that the apostles administered penitence "as a kind of baptism" (*pro baptismo*)? Eager to assist his correspondent in putting the alleged Novatianist right, Augustine is equally anxious not to confuse delicate issues. With the same documentary acuteness that he displays elsewhere, he feels his way back along the communication chain toward the original conversation with the supposed heretic, carefully checking each link. What has Seleuciana heard? What did she mean to report? Does her letter convey her intended sense? Her *notarius* has played a significant part in the transmission thus far, and will doubtless be involved in resolving the interpretive difficulties that now arise. Neither the woman's Latinity nor her theological acumen is directly in question. Having presented herself as an agent of orthodoxy in the African church, she is merely being held to the standard of communicative clarity that Augustine—with some years of experience in debates with another rigorist sect, the Donatists—already knew to be required in such cases.[44]

The cultural activity attributed to Maxima in Letter 264 is of the same order. She has reported on persons in her locality whom she suspects of holding a defective doctrine of the Incarnation. Once again, Augustine cannot be sure from the information received exactly what error, if any, is involved. While encouraging Maxima's vigilance and reiterating the orthodox position, he also asks that she send him copies of any texts circulated by these persons, so that he can compose a refutation in due form, if necessary. In the same breath, he suggests that she might like to provide herself for future reference with some of the anti-heretical works that he has already written. Let her send copyists to Hippo to transcribe them: "For it is God's will that you should do this most conveniently, who has furnished you with the wherewithal to do it."[45] Neither in this case nor Seleuciana's does anything further seem to have come of the matter, and we can only guess how the women responded. It is clear, nonetheless, that their willingness to engage in theological conversation, combined with their ability to sponsor the production and reproduction of texts, made them attractive allies for Augustine in the *mise-en-oeuvre* of Catholic doctrine.

A similar model of collaborative communication appears in the correspondence with Italica, an Italian woman of the highest rank. As he explains in his covering letter to the priest Cyprian, Augustine has used the opportunity of a letter of consolation on the death of Italica's husband to oppose the errors of those who hold that God can be seen with our ordinary bodily eyes. To her he writes, "If ever these people assault your ears, begin by reading this text [of mine] to them, and—if you don't mind—report their response to me in writing, as far as you can."[46] We should probably not imagine a noble Roman matron reciting a letter from the bishop of Hippo to a clique of recalcitrant anthropomorphites; Augustine himself is doubtful whether she will wish to take such a stand, and has a back-up plan already in mind.[47] What matters for him is that Italica is a woman of influence, well disposed toward him, who can serve as an intermediary for his teaching. Were she not genuinely alert to the kinds of issues he raises, and capable of grasping their importance, his strategy would make no sense. Its success, however, does not depend either on her reading his letters with her own bodily eye or on her redacting a report on the machinations of the opposing party. It is enough—indeed a great deal for his purpose—that she engage her name, her prestige, and the resources of her household in the verbal campaign that he is mounting. Fabiola's role in helping clear up the embarrassing business of Antoninus of Fussala would require more direct action on her part, but the model of collaboration envisaged by Letter 20* is essentially the same.[48]

In short, while one may hesitate to ascribe "the ability to read and write good Latin" *tout court* to all Augustine's female correspondents, it is still possible—indeed necessary—to credit them with a highly functional "literacy," according to a modified definition of that word. The literacy of these women, as a factor in the religious and cultural history of Late Antiquity, is, I suggest, to be measured less in terms of their personal skills in deciphering or composing complex texts than in relation to their roles as initiators, facilitators, and sustainers of a set of discursive exchanges that typically involved the interpretation and dissemination of such texts, and that contributed to the ideological and material formation of "orthodox" Christian society. Thus specified, the literacy of Augustine's women correspondents is of a kind also normal for men of their social rank, even if the latter, by virtue of the training prescribed for elite male citizens, had practical skills in the manipulation and composition of texts that were generally denied to women. To redefine elite women's literacy in this fashion is not to subordinate women (again) but to recognize their substantial equality with men in a vital area of late antique culture. The truly important difference of status, it may be, was not between "literate" elite men and "sub-literate" elite women but between those persons—male or female—whose means and position gave them the right to influence, if not control, the circuits of textual information, and those others—almost invariably male—whose most valuable asset was an ability "to speak or write on a given topic accurately, cleverly and expertly." In this perspective, the place of a career-*litteratus* like Augustine will appear closer to that of the *notarii* on whom both he and his correspondents depended for the conveyance of their ideas than to the elevated station of an Italica, Proba, or Melania.

The Doctrinal Authority of Women

While offering no support for the theory of Augustine's promotion of a Christian "low style," these letters to women nonetheless reinforce one's sense of his desire to extend a certain kind of "religious" literacy "as widely as possible" (Brown). As described above, that literacy is generically upper class, "religious" only in virtue of the content of the texts transmitted. If women participate in it, they do so not because of any proto-feminist intuition of Augustine's, arising from his Christian faith, but because he is a bishop with an interest in shaping public opinion, working through the usual networks of late Roman society. Does this mean that there is nothing potentially transformative for the cultural situation of women in Augustine's theology and pastoral practice? Not necessarily. Two of these letters are marvelously explicit on a point of capital importance for Augustine's theory of Christian teaching-and-learning, or what he elsewhere calls *doctrina christiana:* women, no less than men, have direct and personal access to the Truth spoken by Christ-the-teacher to the *homo interior* or "inner person." In drawing attention to this fact, Conybeare points to the most charmed of all the spaces marked out by Augustine's texts, one in which the terminal irrelevance of bodily markers of sexual difference and conventional signifiers of gender is anticipated in a dialogue of the soul.

Augustine's remarks on "seeing God" in Letter 92 to Italica caught the attention of a certain Paulina (called *clarissima* in some manuscripts, so presumably of patrician rank).[49] Possibly, as Conybeare suggests, this text and others were circulating among women. In responding to Paulina's request for an expanded treatment of the subject, Augustine evidently had the widest possible public in view. The epistolary treatise "On the Vision of God" (*De videndo deo*), now Letter 147, quickly gave offense to a male reader whose protests, reported by Bishop Fortunatianus of Sicca, called forth a sequel (Letter 148). In the order of his *Retractationes,* which enables us to date these works to c. 413–14, Augustine mentions that the two were bound together in a single codex in the library at Hippo.[50] Unusually, then, we have two virtually contemporary works of his on the same topic, addressed respectively to a man and a woman. If concessions were to be made to a less capable female readership, one might expect to notice them here. Does Augustine condescend? As Conybeare observes, the conversation in Letter 147 is as serious and demanding as ever. Even so, one detects signs of special care. Without writing down to Paulina, Augustine lays out a brief for the Christian reader as detailed and insistent as any he gave. If not as a woman, then certainly as a reader, and above all as a Christian reader looking faithfully forward to the vision of God, this female addressee carried a heavy burden of his hopes.

The topic was one of literally ultimate importance for Augustine. At the end of Letter 147 he postpones further discussion for a work that, in the event, would be Book 22 of the *City of God*, the last major theological discourse that he composed of his own free will. He writes now to Paulina, as he tells her, in the hope of obtaining divine help with a subject that exceeds his understanding. What value can his words have anyway? "Those who have learned from the Lord Jesus Christ to be meek and humble in heart, profit more from thinking and praying than from reading and hearing." Yet God may still have a use for his utterance. Therefore, he urges her,

> receive these words of [my] understanding according to [your] "inner person [*interiorem hominem*] which is renewed from day to day even as the outer fails" (2 Cor. 4:16). . . . Raise up [*erige*] the spirit of your mind, "which is renewed in knowledge after the image of him that created it," where Christ dwells in you by faith, "where there is neither Greek nor Jew, slave [nor] free, male [nor] female" (1 Col. 3:10–11), where you will not die even when you begin to be parted from your body, since you have not grown weak there even when full of years. Being raised up [*erecta*] in this inner part of you, attend and see what I have to say. I do not want you so to follow my authority that you feel bound to believe anything because it is said by me. No. Put your trust either in the canonical scriptures, if you cannot yet see how true something is [*si quid nondum quam sit verum vides*], or else in the truth that demonstrates inwardly, in order that you may see it clearly [*ut hoc plane videas*].[51]

The epistemology underlying this instruction was worked out by Augustine in the 390s and already informs the *Confessions*. It here acquires a massive additional charge by being applied in a context that at once emphasizes the question of gender and assimilates the apprehension of divine truth in the present life to the vision of God in the next. The scriptural certainty that Augustine is determined to uphold in this case is that the divine sight promised to the faithful lies in the future: "Blessed are the pure in heart for they *shall* see God" (Matt. 5:8). That future in its fullness, he will argue, awaits our resurrection bodies, but it is partly anticipated in the here-and-now, through Christ's dwelling in us by faith. To the idea of this pre-eschatological state of redemption or internal renewal Augustine attaches his distinctive anthropology of the divine image, based on St. Paul's idea of the *homo interior* or "inner person" (traditionally, of course, translated as "inward man"). He returns to the theme of Christ's daily renovation of the divine image in human beings later in the letter, to underline again the present possibilities of non-corporeal discernment, while also marking the huge difference that still separates such mental vision from the bodily vision of God that we may hope to enjoy when finally endowed with our spiritual bodies in heaven.[52]

It is a fine conceptual balance, on which much evidently depends for Augustine. Passages from Ambrose's commentary on Luke are pressed into service in support of it; Letter 148 will adduce more from other Greek and Latin fathers, making it one of Augustine's earliest sustained attempts at argument from "patristic" authority. But whereas the dissident *frater* for whose benefit that letter is intended appears in some danger of being bullied into submission,[53] Paulina and her kind are repeatedly urged not to let themselves be bamboozled by human authorities like the former bishop of Milan or the present bishop of Hippo,[54] and to test all opinions carefully in the "simplicity of [their] hearts." It is hard not to suspect Augustine of a hint of gender-bias in the framing of these directions. If there is a bias, however, it would seem precisely calculated to offset the normal expectation of female subservience to male authority in matters of doctrine, and thus consistent with the theory of an inward space of critical judgment in which "there is neither male nor female," accessible to a person whose social and grammatical gender nevertheless remains feminine (*erecta*). The simplicity that Augustine summons in Paulina is no *pis aller;* it is an exact pendant to the Christ-like humility that he seeks for himself, which ultimately makes all speech and writing between human beings superfluous. The most authentically Augustinian *sermo humilis* is a colloquy of the pure in heart.

Augustine's provision for this (woman) reader occurs in a text without initial salutation or epistolary topoi and supposes no theory of Christian *amicitia* beyond that implicit for him in the gospel commandment to love God and neighbor. The easy tone of the address to Paulina argues some confidence in her goodwill toward him, but there are few hints of familiarity. The author's concern for the reader's spiritual understanding is as impersonal as it is intense. "Friendship" may not, after all, be the ground on which Augustine's attitude to women stands most sharply revealed. Of all his letters, to men and women alike, none more poignantly sums up the values of his *doctrina christiana* than that sent, at the behest of her parents, to the young virgin Florentina (Letter 266). The Latin is simple and elegant, the tone mildly flattering but not ingratiating, the message plain and disabused. Many of the major tenets of the treatise to Paulina are recapitulated in miniature, with this difference: that a young woman is now encouraged to *begin* an epistolary conversation with a bishop—but only, like her elder, in order to cast beyond all human teachers, looking inward to the "inner teacher of the inner person" and forward to the place outside time where knowledge of God will be complete and no one will have anything more to teach or learn.[55] The letter is so short and full, the only way to add usefully to what Conybeare has written about it would be to quote it in its entirety.[56] It confirms in a few lines what the bishop's more voluminous writings lead one to expect and this new account of his letters to women makes harder to ignore: that the goal of Augustinian pedagogy is a communion of the human and divine that has no more use for distinctions of sex or gender (however these may manifest themselves in the bliss of eternity) than it will have for habits of literacy.

■ ■ ■

Like other utopias, this one can be shown to have its real sides. Although the goal was eschatological, the desire for it led Augustine to a present reckoning with the society of his time that had manifest consequences for the lives of women then and afterwards. We have seen that as a Catholic bishop intent on imposing uniform belief in core dogmas on a diverse population within and beyond his diocese, he took every opportunity to involve women in the diffusion of a Christian literacy. That literacy, as I have defined it here, differed from non-Christian text-based discourse chiefly in its content. While some of its "events" may have altered the social profile of individual women, households, or groups, and so affected the formation and differentiation of Christian community, it was not structurally disruptive of the status quo. (The related question of how the content of Christian teaching was affected by its passage through the circuits of late antique communication requires separate treatment.[57]) The more radical side of Augustine's partially realized utopianism appears in his advice to women on their comportment as readers—in the first instance, as readers of his own writings (letters and treatises). It is here that his potential contribution to a possibly emergent theory and practice of *Christian* literacy is most palpable. For whereas his approach to women as agents or transmitters of Christian literate knowledge seems to be largely conditioned by the cultural norms of his day, his attitude to them as potential creators—or, in terms of his own theology, divinely informed recipients—of that knowledge is distinctly original and constructive.

In the light of recent scholarship it would be careless, as well as pointless, to deny that "Augustine teaches that femaleness as such cannot be the image of God" or that the ideas on sexual difference that he inherited from Graeco-Roman culture "limited his ability to develop an anthropology in which women were perceived as the peers of men."[58] Nor would one lightly dispute that his writings on human sexuality, sin, and the body played a significant part in entrenching misogynistic attitudes and practices in the culture of western Christianity. But these are not Augustine's only legacies, and as historians we should not let our revulsion at what are now widely seen as unacceptable doctrines blind us to other impulses, some of them also affecting women in particular, that his written work may have transmitted to later ages. "Writing," after Althusser and Foucault, is often construed as an act amounting to a kind of violence against the person—

more particularly, the body—of another. The "writings" of Augustine and other hallowed fathers of the Church are certainly open to such a negative construction. When they write "on women," they may do so coercively, almost as if "writing" women transitively, treating them as objects of rhetorical—but not only rhetorical—invention and disposition. This can be the case even when they seemingly address themselves to women on the subject of women, the gesture of altruism concealing merely one more device of gendering subjection. The elision of the preposition "to" in epistolary "writing to" that is possible in American English creates a potent trope: Jerome *writes* Marcella, or Demetrias![59] Such "women" are mere figures of writing or the writer's (masculinist) thought. These unenchanted readings of the fathers are fully justified and form part of a vital revisionist trend in recent work on late ancient Christianity. Yet the difference between a direct and an indirect object of writing—in a word, the space of letters— should not be elided without a pause. Not all letters take the same direction, or the direction apparently intended by their authors, not even so-called "letters of direction."

What use might a young woman like Florentina make of the space for theological inquiry and conversation to which Augustine beckoned her? Even if Florentina herself made no use of it, what cues might the letter once sent to her give another female reader centuries later, say one who had been set on fire (or just incensed) by the same writer's *Confessions*? A colleague of mine recently invited the students in her first-year humanities course, who had also studied the *Confessions,* to reply on behalf of some of Augustine's correspondents to the letters he had addressed to them. The students apparently suffered no inhibitions. "Sapida," for one, complained that she had been misunderstood, and demanded the return of her brother's tunic! The experiment perhaps bears out the two modest but timely claims of Catherine Conybeare's essay: that some of Augustine's letters offer us a glimpse of the real world of fifth-century women, and that the correspondence concerns more than the man who appears as the author of its surviving part.[60] To adapt Averil Cameron's phrase: we might now allow more space to women in the Christian literature of Late Antiquity—as correspondents, as well as objects.

Notes

1. Averil Cameron, "Education and Literary Culture," in *The Late Empire, A.D. 337–425,* ed. Averil Cameron and Peter Garnsey, vol. 13 of *The Cambridge Ancient History* (Cambridge: Cambridge University Press, 1998), 665–707, at 702. As rare instances of women authors from this milieu Cameron names Egeria, who wrote an account of her pilgrimage to the Holy Land in the 380s, and Proba, composer of a Virgilian cento on the life of Christ around the same date if not earlier. These works are respectively nos. 2325 and 1480 in Eligius Dekkers, ed., *Clavis Patrum Latinorum,* 3rd ed. (Steenbrugge: Brepols, 1995), which, having listed the *Passion of Saints Perpetua and Felicitas* as a work dubiously attributed to Tertullian, offers no other case of a woman author among the

fathers before the sixth century. Laurie Douglass, "A New Look at the *Itinerarium Burdigalense*," *Journal of Early Christian Studies* 4 (1996): 313–33, argues for female authorship of a second fourth-century Latin pilgrimage narrative (with discussion by Susan Weingarten, *Journal of Early Christian Studies* 7 [1999]: 291–97). For two fifth-century Latin letters by Christians, whose language may indicate female authorship, see Virginia Burrus and Tracy Keefer, "Anonymous Spanish Correspondence; or the Letter of the 'She-ass,'" in *Religions of Late Antiquity in Practice*, ed. Richard Valantasis (Princeton, N.J.: Princeton University Press, 2000), 330–39.

2. "Jerome's Origen: The Making of a Christian Literary *Persona*," *Studia Patristica* 28, Papers Presented at the Eleventh International Conference on Patristic Studies, ed. Elizabeth A. Livingstone (Leuven: Peeters, 1993), 135–45, at 144: "[Marcella] is essentially Jerome's creature, attached to the documentary history of her time only by the slender thread of an alleged offer of marriage from a Roman senator, and even that anecdote occurs in a letter written by Jerome after her death, at a time when its veracity was unlikely to be challenged [Letter 127.2]." Marcella's rights have been reasserted by Silvia Letsch-Brunner, *Marcella—Discipula et Magistra: Auf den Spuren einer römischen Christin des 4. Jahrhunderts* (Berlin: Walter de Gruyter, 1998), and Philip Rousseau, "'Learned Women' and the Development of a Christian Culture in Late Antiquity," *Symbolae Osloenses* 70 (1995): 116–47, esp. 139–41. Jerome's relations with and representations of women have been subjects of intense scholarly interest over the past decade: see, inter alia, Christa Krumeich, *Hieronymus und die christlichen feminae clarissimae* (Bonn: Habelts Dissertationsdrucke, 1993); Patricia Cox Miller, *Dreams in Late Antiquity: Studies in the Imagination of a Culture* (Princeton, N.J.: Princeton University Press, 1994), 205–31 (Letter 22 to Eustochium); Barbara Feichtinger, *Apostolae apostolorum: Frauenaskese als Befreiung und Zwang bei Hieronymus* (Frankfurt am Main: Peter Lang, 1995); Patrick Laurence, *Jérôme et le nouveau modèle féminin: La conversion à la vie parfaite* (Paris: Institut d'Études Augustiniennes, 1997). Important for the study of Jerome's social milieu is Stefan Rebenich, *Hieronymus und sein Kreis: Prosopographische und sozialgeschichtliche Untersuchungen* (Stuttgart: Franz Steiner, 1992).

3. Augustine, Letter 40.70; 75.18 (= Jerome, Letter 112.18). At issue is Jerome's interpretation of Paul's reprimand of Peter in Gal. 2. This correspondence is the subject of two recent monographs: Ralph Hennings, *Der Briefwechsel zwischen Augustinus und Hieronymus und ihr Streit um den Kanon des Alten Testaments und die Auslegung von Gal. 2, 11–14* (Leiden: E. J. Brill, 1994) and Alfons Fürst, *Augustins Briefwechsel mit Hieronymus* (Münster in Westfalen: Aschendorff, 1999).

4. A. H. M. Jones, J. R. Martindale, and J. Morris, eds., *Prosopography of the Later Roman Empire*, 3 vols. (Cambridge: Cambridge University Press, 1971–92) (hereafter cited as *PLRE*); *Prosopographie chrétienne du Bas-Empire*, vol. 1 (Africa), ed. André Mandouze; vol. 2 (Italy), ed. Charles Pietri and Luce Pietri (Paris: CNRS, 1982–) (hereafter cited as *PCBE*).

5. Klaus Thraede, *Grundzüge griechische-römischer Brieftopik* (Munich: C. H. Beck, 1970), 22–23, 35–38, 162–65, 183–85; Abraham J. Malherbe, *Ancient Epistolary Theorists* (Atlanta, Ga.: Scholars Press, 1988), 12. The relations between Augustine's early practice of the dialogue and his experiments with the formal letter of friendship (notably Letters 1–20 to Nebridius and others) deserve study; see Brian Stock, *Augustine the Reader: Meditation, Self-Knowledge, and the Ethics of Interpretation* (Cambridge, Mass.: Harvard University Press, 1996), 125–37.

6. On Jerome see note 3 above. On Paulinus see Pierre Courcelle, *Les Confessions de saint Augustin dans la tradition littéraire: Antécédents et posterité* (Paris: Études Augustiniennes, 1963), 559–607, now with the chronology of Dennis E. Trout, *Paulinus of Nola: Life, Letters, and Poems* (Berkeley:

University of California Press, 1999), 290–92. In both cases the textual situation is made more favorable by the separate transmission of letters to or from Augustine assured by Jerome and Paulinus or their disciples.

7. Johannes Divjak, ed., *Epistolae [s. Augustini] ex duobus codicibus nuper in lucem prolatae,* Corpus Scriptorum Ecclesiasticorum Latinorum (hereafter cited as CSEL), vol. 88 (Vindobonae: Hoelder-Pichler-Tempsky, 1981). The full sequence of twenty-nine letters contains one of Augustine's that was already known and another, previously unknown, from Jerome to Aurelius of Carthage.

8. François Dolbeau, ed., *Augustin d'Hippone: Vingt-six sermons aux peuple d'Afrique* (Paris: Institut d'Études Augustiniennes, 1996). For the impact of both discoveries, see Peter Brown, *Augustine of Hippo: A Biography,* rev. ed. (Berkeley: University of California Press, 2000), 441–81.

9. For a critical appraisal of the evidence for one kind of "Theodosian Renaissance," see Alan Cameron, "The Latin Revival of the Fourth Century," in *Renaissances before the Renaissance: Cultural Revivals of Late Antiquity,* ed. Warren Treadgold (Stanford, Calif.: Stanford University Press, 1984), 42–58. A more neutral notion of the *saeculum Theodosianum,* applicable to the present subject, is outlined for the study of Latin Christian literary culture by Jacques Fontaine, "Société et culture chrétiennes sur l'aire circumpyrénéenne au siècle de Théodose," *Bulletin de littérature ecclésiastique* 75 (1974): 241–82, esp. 241–44, reprinted in his *Études sur la poésie latine tardive d'Ausone à Prudence* (Paris: Les Belles Lettres, 1980).

10. J. F. Matthews, "The Letters of Symmachus," in *Latin Literature of the Fourth Century,* ed. J. W. Binns (London: Routledge and Kegan Paul, 1974), 58–99, points in a new direction, followed by Philippe Bruggisser, *Symmaque ou le rituel épistolaire de l'amitié littéraire* (Fribourg: Éditions Universitaires, 1993). The epistolary corpora of all the major Greek and Latin fathers invite, and are beginning to receive, similar treatment. For orientation to materials, problems, and methods of research, see Paolo Cugusi, "L'epistolografia: Modelli e tipologie di communicazione," in *La circolazione del testo,* vol. 2 of *Lo spazio letterario di Roma antica,* ed. Guglielmo Cavallo et al. (Rome: Salerno Editrice, 1989), 379–419; Michaela Zelzer, "Die Briefliteratur," in *Spätantike,* ed. Lodewijk J. Engels and Heinz Hofmann, vol. 4 of *Neues Handbuch der Literaturwissenschaft* (Wiesbaden: AULA-Verlag, 1997), 321–53. For material aspects of Christian epistolary collections of the early centuries there is still much of value in J. de Ghellinck, *Introduction et compléments à l'étude de la patristique,* vol. 2 of *Patristique et Moyen Âge: Études d'histoire littéraire et doctrinale* (Gembloux: J. Duculot, 1947), 200–214.

11. Instructive comparisons are suggested by Lisa Jardine, *Erasmus, Man of Letters: The Construction of Charisma in Print* (Princeton, N.J.: Princeton University Press, 1993) and Carol Everhart Quillen, *Rereading the Renaissance: Petrarch, Augustine, and the Language of Humanism* (Ann Arbor: University of Michigan Press, 1998).

12. *Paulinus Noster: Self and Symbols in the Letters of Paulinus of Nola* (Oxford: Oxford University Press, 2000). Subsequent references appear parenthetically in the text.

13. E. Ann Matter, "Women," in *Augustine through the Ages: An Encyclopedia,* ed. Allan D. Fitzgerald et al. (Grand Rapids, Mich.: W. B. Eerdmans, 1999), 887–92, at 890; another version of this article appears as "Christ, God and Woman in the Thought of St Augustine," in *Augustine and His Critics: Essays in Honour of Gerald Bonner,* ed. Robert Dodaro and George Lawless (London: Routledge, 2000), 164–75.

14. Augustine's antipathy to the Christian version of classical (male) heroism is noted by Carole Straw, "Martyrdom and Christian Identity: Gregory the Great, Augustine, and Tradition," in

The Limits of Ancient Christianity: Essays on Late Antique Thought and Culture in Honor of R. A. Markus, ed. William E. Klingshirn and Mark Vessey (Ann Arbor: University of Michigan Press, 1999), enlarging on arguments made by Robert Markus, *The End of Ancient Christianity* (Cambridge: Cambridge University Press, 1990), esp. chaps. 4–5. Markus's analysis of the evolution of Augustine's thought through the 390s provides an essential context for perceiving the link between his view of human sexuality as the sign of fallen nature and his advocacy of a more communitarian and ecclesially oriented ascetic practice than was espoused by certain of his contemporaries (e.g., Jerome).

15. This, more decisively phrased, is essentially the conclusion reached by Jean A. Truax, "Augustine of Hippo: Defender of Women's Equality?" *Journal of Medieval History* 16 (1990): 279–99: "Unlike his modern critics, the Bishop of Hippo did not equate a woman's sexuality with her humanity, and he did not assume that an individual's sexuality was such an integral part of his or her personality that to renounce sexual relationships was to reject all members of the opposite sex as well. On the contrary, once the issue of sexuality had been set aside, Augustine found that new relationships were possible in which men and women were equal. Thus, while renouncing his own sexual nature, Augustine was still able to be a kind and considerate friend to the women of his Christian community" (296). Like Matter, Truax sets particular store by Augustine's correspondence with women.

16. Possidius, *Vita s. Augustini,* ed. A. A. R. Bastiaensen, in vol. 3 of *Vite dei santi,* ed. Christine Mohrmann (N.p.: Mondadori, 1975), 3.2. Unattributed translations are my own.

17. Possidius, *Vita s. Augustini,* 26.

18. At the theoretical limit, then, a female correspondent who shares with Augustine in a divinely given understanding of any subject—irrespective of whether that understanding is first given expression by him or by her—may be thought to constitute an *exception* to the rule, otherwise largely valid in Augustinian theology, that no woman "in her incarnate particularity can . . . possibly partake in that deep participation in the divinity described by Augustine in [passages such as *Conf.* 7.18.24]" (Matter, "Christ, God and Woman," 173). This possibility will be explored more fully below.

19. See Elizabeth A. Clark, "Rewriting Early Christian History: Augustine's Representation of Monica," in *Portraits of Spiritual Authority: Religious Power in Early Christianity, Byzantium and the Christian Orient,* ed. Jan Willem Drijvers and John W. Watt (Leiden: Brill, 1999), 3–23.

20. William V. Harris, *Ancient Literacy* (Cambridge, Mass.: Harvard University Press, 1989); the main discussion of Christianity and literacy occurs at 298–322. Notable responses to Harris and further contributions to the field include: *Literacy in the Roman World,* Supplementary Series of the *Journal of Roman Archaeology,* vol. 3, ed. J. H. Humphrey (Ann Arbor, 1991); Averil Cameron, *Christianity and the Rhetoric of Empire: The Development of Christian Discourse* (Berkeley: University of California Press, 1991); Alan K. Bowman and Greg Woolf, eds., *Literacy and Power in the Ancient World* (Cambridge: Cambridge University Press, 1994); Harry Y. Gamble, *Books and Readers in the Early Church: A History of Early Christian Texts* (New Haven, Conn.: Yale University Press, 1995); Elizabeth A. Clark, *Reading and Renunciation: Asceticism and Scripture in Early Christianity* (Princeton, N.J.: Princeton University Press, 1999), 45–69. For an assessment of Harris's work in the context of contemporary research on early medieval literacy and literary culture in the West, see my "Literacy and *Litteratura,* A.D. 200–800," *Studies in Medieval and Renaissance History* 13 (1992): 139–60.

21. Peter Brown, "Christianity and Local Culture in Late Roman Africa," *Journal of Roman Studies* 58 (1968): 85–95, reprinted in his *Religion and Society in the Age of Saint Augustine* (London:

Faber and Faber, 1972), 279–300, at 290. Already by 1968 the question of Augustine's role in the evolution of a distinctively "Christian" literacy was part of a complex historiographic legacy, as I have tried to show in "The Demise of the Christian Writer and the Remaking of 'Late Antiquity': From H.-I. Marrou's Saint Augustine (1938) to Peter Brown's Holy Man (1983)," *Journal of Early Christian Studies* 6 (1998): 377–411, esp. 395–403. The classic statement of Augustine's advocacy of a Christian *sermo humilis* is Erich Auerbach, *Literary Language and Its Public in Late Latin Antiquity and in the Middle Ages* (Princeton, N.J.: Princeton University Press, 1965), chap. 1, long overdue for reassessment; see also Michel Banniard, *Communication écrite et communication orale du IVe au IXe siècle en Occident latin* (Paris: Institut des Études Augustiniennes, 1992). In "The World of Late Antiquity Revisited," *Symbolae Osloenses* 72 (1997): 5–30, Brown himself stated that he "no longer regard[s] Christianity as the principal agent in the diffusion of a more adaptable form of classical culture to previously marginal groups and regions" (29).

22. Harris, *Ancient Literacy,* 320.

23. The *Indiculus* or *Elenchus* was edited by André Wilmart in *Miscellanea Agostiniana* (Rome: Tipografia Poliglotta Vaticana, 1930–31), 2:149–233. Numbers given for entries below refer to lines in the section for *Epistulae* in this edition (at 182–91).

24. Keith Hopkins, "Conquest by Book," in *Literacy in the Roman World,* Supplementary Series of the *Journal of Roman Archaeology,* vol. 3, ed. J. H. Humphrey (Ann Arbor, 1991), 148.

25. Cf. Rousseau, "'Learned Women.'"

26. Only his side of the correspondence survives. This is the normal situation with ancient epistolary texts. For explanations, see Emily A. Hemelrijk, *Matrona Docta: Educated Women in the Roman Élite from Cornelia to Julia Domna* (London: Routledge, 1999), 203–206.

27. According to de Ghellinck, "aux temps antiques, quand il s'agit de correspondances épistolaires, le droit de propriété, le *dominium,* passait au destinataire, sauf stipulation de l'auteur en sens opposé. C'était en un certain sens un don de l'auteur" (*Patristique et Moyen Âge,* 2:206).

28. The latter category includes "One Book to Paulina on the Vision of God," now counted as Letter 147. For the distinction between letter and epistolary treatise (*liber* or *libellus*), never clear-cut in this period, see Augustine, *Retractationes* 2.20, Corpus Christianorum, Series Latina (hereafter cited as CCSL), vol. 57 (Turnhout: Brepols, 1974), 106: "The first of these books is a letter, since its heading states who is writing to whom (*quis ad quem scribat*)."

29. Letters to Maxima (264) and Ecdicia (262) are listed one after the other (*Indiculus* 179–80), as are others to Florentina (266) and a certain Mariniana (none extant) (*Indiculus* 82–83). Letters to Albina (126) and to Albina, Pinianus, and Melania (124) appear in that order, slightly separated (*Indiculus* 152, 155). Others to Italica (92 and 99) and Seleuciana (265) appear severally (*Indiculus* 88, 171, 75). For two letters to Fabiola now known (267 and 20*), the list has just one (*Indiculus* 173). The names of Felicia (208), Galla and Simpliciola (212), and Sapida (263) are absent from the *Indiculus.* (Following Conybeare, I set aside letters to married couples.) Except in the rare cases where the *Indiculus* gives the subject-matter of a letter, all correlations with extant letters are necessarily hypothetical. Presumably both sides of all correspondence were archived at Hippo. However, the *Indiculus* was designed to take account only of Augustine's own writings; it was already in use before his death.

30. After Goldbacher's preface in CSEL 58 and the pioneering work of Donatien de Bruyne and Hans Lietzmann, see Johannes Divjak, "Zur Struktur Augustinischer Briefkorpora," in *Les lettres*

de saint Augustin découvertes par Johannes Divjak (Paris: Études Augustiniennes, 1983), 13–27, with fuller references, and "L'établissement de l'édition critique des 'Lettres' de saint Augustin par les Mauristes," in *Troisième centenaire de l'édition mauriste de saint Augustin* (Paris: Institut d'Études Augustiniennes, 1990), 203–13. Divjak ("L'établissement," 206–207) refers to a grouping of six "lettres aux femmes" in one of the early medieval corpora; apparently this comprised Letters 210 (to Felicitas, Rusticus, and the nuns at Hippo), 262 (to Ecdicia), 265 (Seleuciana), 92 (Italica) and two others; there is no suggestion that it was authorial.

31. Its first two divisions are respected by Goldbacher's edition: CSEL 34, part 1 (letters written before Augustine was made a bishop, none with female addressees), 34, part 2 (letters from the period 396 to 410, including those to Paulinus and Therasia and Italica). The remaining datable letters (numbered 124 to 231) formed the Maurists' third class, now split between CSEL 44 and 57.

32. See Michaela Zelzer's preface to CSEL 82, part 2. The only woman honored as an "addressee" in Ambrose's *Letters* is his sister, Marcellina.

33. In the autobiobibliographical last notice of his treatise *De viris illustribus* (392/3), Jerome mentions published volumes of letters "To Various Persons" and "To Marcella," as well as countless daily missives to Paula and Eustochium (by then resident with him in Bethlehem). The contents of these two volumes can be hypothetically reconstructed from his extant correspondence; see also note 2 above.

34. Suetonius, *De grammaticis*, 4.

35. See now especially Hemelrijk, *Matrona docta*, which makes incidental reference to late antique evidence.

36. Harris, *Ancient Literacy*, 314, citing Augustine, *Soliloquia* 1.10.17; cf. 309 for "a slender thread of testimony that girls sometimes went to school in the western provinces." Elaine Fantham, *Roman Literary Culture: From Cicero to Apuleius* (Baltimore: Johns Hopkins University Press, 1996), 247, recalls a Greek woman from the time of Nero, named Pamphile, who, having studied with her husband for thirteen years "since she was a child," attained the skill to compile a literary miscellany. See also Hemelrijk, *Matrona docta*, 31–36.

37. Paul Saenger, *Space between Words: The Origins of Silent Reading* (Stanford, Calif.: Stanford University Press, 1997), 11; Harris, *Ancient Literacy*, 249.

38. Harris, *Ancient Literacy*, 317, cites the papyrus archive of Aurelia Charite as evidence that "[i]n the period 325–350 a well-to-do woman in Hermoupolis [Egypt] could possess at least simple literacy." Her subscription, "follow[ing] the fluent cursive of the professional writer," appears on the document reproduced in Jane Rowlandson, ed., *Women and Society in Greek and Roman Egypt* (Cambridge: Cambridge University Press, 1998), 242. Fuller discussion by Raffaella Cribiore, "Windows on a Woman's World: Some Letters from Roman Egypt," in *Making Silence Speak: Women's Voices in Greek Literature and Society*, ed. André Lardinois and Laura McClure (Princeton, N.J.: Princeton University Press, 2001), 223–39, who makes the important point that "the fact that a letter was dictated to a scribe does not tell us anything about the literacy and writing ability of the sender" (229). On the separate class of female scribes, see Kim Haines-Eitzen, "'Girls Trained in Beautiful Writing': Female Scribes in Roman Antiquity and Early Christianity," *Journal of Early Christian Studies* 6 (1998): 629–46.

39. Hemelrijk, *Matrona Docta*, 188–203, reconstructs the epistolographic activity of elite women. Jerome, *Chronicon*, a. 336, records that "The daughter of the rhetor Nazarius achieved a

renown for eloquence equal to her father's"—but still she is not given a name! As with Pamphile (note 36 above), the family relationship explains the anomaly in this case. The epigraphic evidence relating to women's literary and rhetorical education in Augustine's milieu is usefully summarized by Konrad Vössing, *Schule und Bildung im Nordafrika der römischen Kaiserzeit* (Brussels: Collection Latomus, 1997), 476–79. It confirms that elite women could be seen to share the literary pursuits of their husbands but were excluded in principle from all public literary activity, and never praised in their memorials for eloquence (*facundia*). See also Janet Huskinson, "Women and Learning: Gender and Identity in Scenes of Intellectual Life on Late Roman Sarcophagi," in *Constructing Identities in Late Antiquity*, ed. Richard Miles (London: Routledge, 1999), 190–213. Vössing cites Augustine's correspondence extensively but makes no inferences about the literary culture of its female addressees.

40. Danuta Shanzer has argued (most recently in *Recherches Augustiniennes* 27 [1994]: 75–96) for the identity of the centonist Proba with Anicia Faltonia Proba, mother of Juliana and grandmother of Demetrias, and addressee of Augustine's Letters 130–31 and 150. The traditional attribution to Faltonia Betitia Proba (grandmother of Augustine's correspondent) remains in favor. For the family relationships, see the stemmata of the Anicii and Petronii at *PLRE* 1:1133, 1144.

41. Ausonius, "On His Stenographer" (*"In notarium"*).

42. Good evidence for this, for earlier periods, is the private rescripts addressed to women by Roman emperors: see Liselot Huchthausen, "Herkunft und ökonomische Stellung weiblicher Adressaten von Reskripten des *Codex Iustinianus* (2. und 3. Jh. u. Z.)," *Klio* 56 (1974): 199–228, and "Zu kaiserlichen Reskripten an weibliche Adressaten aus der Zeit Diokletians (284–305 u. Z.)," *Klio* 58 (1976): 55–85.

43. In the early sixth century, Caesarius of Arles would urge those who could not read the Scriptures for themselves to engage professional literates (*mercennarios litteratos*) to assist them, just as a merchant might hire such a person to assist him with his business transactions: Harris, *Ancient Literacy*, 316, with further discussion by Nicholas Horsfall, "Statistics or States of Mind?" in *Literacy in the Roman World*, Supplementary Series of the *Journal of Roman Archaeology*, vol. 3, ed. J. H. Humphrey (Ann Arbor, 1991), 73 f.; and William E. Klingshirn, *Caesarius of Arles: The Making of a Christian Community in Late Antique Gaul* (Cambridge: Cambridge University Press, 1994), 183–84. For similar arrangements attested in papyri, see Ann Ellis Hanson, "Ancient Illiteracy," in *Literacy in the Roman World*, 168–75.

44. Letter 265 is tentatively dated 408/409 in *PCBE* 1:1058.

45. Letter 264.3. Dated to 418 in *PCBE* 1:717, which would make it closely contemporary with the case of Leporius, a monk from Marseilles who was taken to task for a dualistic Christology by Augustine and who issued a retraction in the form of a *Libellus emendationis* (CPL 515), later integrated into the dossier of orthodox Latin Christology as understood after the Council of Ephesus (431). It is not clear where Maxima resided; Augustine refers only to *provinciam vestram* (1). The invitation to send scribes to copy theological works is found also in Jerome's correspondence, e.g., Letter 27* (Divjak) to Aurelius of Carthage.

46. Letter 92.6.

47. Letter 92A to Cyprian.

48. On this Fabiola, evidently a woman of high standing with a residence at Rome, possibly also the addressee of Letter 267, see Serge Lancel, "L'affaire d'Antoninus de Fussala," in *Les lettres*

de saint Augustin découvertes par Johannes Divjak (Paris: Études Augustiniennes, 1983), 278–79; *PCBE* 2.1:735–36.

49. It is not certain that she is the same Paulina who, with her husband Armentarius, received Augustine's Letter 127.

50. *Retractationes* 2.41 (CCSL 57:123).

51. Letter 147.2.

52. Letter 147.44.

53. Note esp. Letter 148.15. On the larger context of Augustine's controversial practice, see Eric Rebillard, "A New Style of Argument in Christian Polemic: Augustine and the Use of Patristic Citations," *Journal of Early Christian Studies* 8 (2000): 559–78. The interest attaching to his use of Ambrose in Letter 147 is remarked by Neil McLynn, "Ambrose of Milan," in *Augustine through the Ages*, ed. Allan D. Fitzgerald et al. (Grand Rapids, Mich.: W. B. Eerdmans, 1999), 17–19, at 18.

54. Letter 127.39; 54.

55. Letter 266.2; 4. For this trajectory in Augustine's thought, with special reference to the study of Scripture and an exclusive focus on his *male* interlocutors, see my "Conference and Confession: Literary Pragmatics in Augustine's 'Apologia contra Hieronymum,'" *Journal of Early Christian Studies* 1 (1993): 175–213.

56. It is translated by Sister Wilfrid Parsons in *Saint Augustine: Letters*, vol. 5 (New York: Fathers of the Church, 1956), 282–85. One can only blink at the omission of this and most of the other letters to women, including Letter 147 to Paulina, from the selection of Augustine's correspondence translated for the series of Nicene and Post-Nicene fathers.

57. Richard Lim, *Public Disputation, Power, and Social Order in Late Antiquity* (Berkeley: University of California Press, 1995) is an exemplary study. See also Cameron, *Christianity and the Rhetoric of Empire*, and "Christianity and Communication in the Fourth Century: The Problem of Diffusion," in *Aspects of the Fourth Century AD*, ed. H. W. Pleket and A. M. F. W. Verhoogt (Leiden: E. J. Brill, 1997), 24–42.

58. Kim Power, *Veiled Desire: Augustine's Writing on Women* (London: Darton, Longman and Todd, 1995), 168.

59. See Andrew S. Jacobs, "Writing Demetrias: Ascetic Logic in Ancient Christianity," *Church History* 69 (2000): 719–48, which builds on a valuable historiographical review by Elizabeth A. Clark, "The Lady Vanishes: Dilemmas of a Feminist Historian after the 'Linguistic Turn,'" *Church History* 67 (1998): 1–31. Another version of Clark's article, with fuller treatment of late antique material, appeared in *Journal of Early Christian Studies* 6 (1998): 413–30.

60. On all aspects of Augustine's epistolography, see now the article "Epistulae" by Johannes Divjak in *Augustinus-Lexicon*, ed. Cornelius Mayer et al., vol. 2, fasc. 5–6 (Basel: Schwabe, 2001), cols. 893–1057, which appeared after the present essay was completed.

TWO

Sharing Texts

Anselmian Prayers, a Nunnery's Psalter,
and the Role of Friendship

MARY JANE MORROW

Monastic service books preserve more than the textual tools for the work of the daily Office. The devotional books, like all medieval manuscripts, reflect the patrons who commissioned them, the craftsmen who produced them, and the readers who studied them. Therefore, the books may be viewed as the culminations of communities' exchanges of ideas, opinions, innovations, and the texts that supported them. Implicit in the process of book production was the necessity of institutional and personal relationships. As Brian Stock has observed, "Writing is not just the written, the product: it is whatever goes into the making of it. And all that this activity can tell us is relevant to an accounting of the past."[1] Thus, our studies of extant manuscripts have the potential to elucidate linkages among monastic communities and individuals, the professional and personal ties that influenced the composition, perpetuation, and even disuse of devotional texts. These thoughts underpin the following comments and questions regarding two prayer texts contained in a twelfth-century psalter that was owned from the time of its production by the English Benedictine nunnery, Shaftesbury.[2] These two prayers serve as a sort of textual window, an opening through which a segment of the nunnery's monastic literary community may be observed. The texts were composed by Anselm, archbishop of Canterbury from 1093 to 1109. The two prayers, one which addresses the Virgin Mary[3] and the other for use prior to the Eucharist,[4] represent the start and finish of Anselm's devotional compositions, the former completed no later than 1075 and the latter by 1104.[5] Their appearance in the Shaftesbury Psalter is striking for three reasons. First, there are several documented institutional and personal ties between the Shaftesbury community, its abbess, Eulalia, and Archbishop Anselm. Second, the prayers were written in the psalter for a female Latin reader. Third, these two prayer texts represent near contemporary copies, if the 1130 dating of the Shaftesbury Psalter is accurate, and therefore may be among the earliest extant copies produced in England.[6] These three points provide a basis for understanding how Shaftesbury's nuns may have acquired some of Anselm's devotional compositions. More broadly applied, these circumstances suggest conditions of textual exchange during the eleventh and twelfth centuries. I argue that devotional materials were shared among monastic and quasi-monastic women and men who perceived themselves as having similar social standing through recognition of shared work, common interests, and even friendship. Implicit in this exchange were participants' comprehension and appreciation of Latin devotional literature. While these relationships involved a minority of the European population, they were responsible for the circulation of devotional materials. In studying the conditions of these relationships and how texts were used within them, we may come to a better understanding of how and why certain medieval devotional texts survived.

The Shaftesbury Psalter, now British Library MS Lansdowne 383, was elegantly crafted for the kinds of worship prescribed by the Benedictine Rule, both the daily Office and private study. The book's handsome physical qualities and assemblage of distinctive texts reflect a process of careful, deliberate production. It contains a beautifully illustrated calendar, eight full-page illuminations depicting Jesus, Mary, and St. Michael, two of which feature a nun in adoration of Jesus.[7] Its texts include an occasional Office for the Holy Cross, the Gallican form of the Psalms, canticles, a litany, and creeds. The psalter also has forty-seven devotional prayers, which were placed immediately following the litany and creeds. The first forty-two prayers are in hierarchic order according to addressee from the Trinity to confessors. The final five prayers were for use in the Eucharist, which included Anselm's *Oratio ad accipiendum corpus domini et sanguinem*, and all are addressed to Jesus. Fourteen of the forty-seven prayers were copied into the psalter in expectation of a female Latin reader, noticeable either through first person singular verb forms (example: *quae suadente antiquo operata sum*)[8] or in nominative noun and adjective forms (example: *ego temeratrix immoderata*).[9] The prayers with feminine Latin word forms, including prayers for the Eucharist, are written in the same hand as the other portions of the manuscript and attest to the deliberate selection and acquisition of particular texts in the psalter's production.

Although there was no mandatory repertoire of texts for monastic use in Western Christendom during the eleventh and twelfth centuries, psalters generally contained the

FIGURE 1. Nun Adoring the Virgin, in British Library, MS Lansdowne 383, folio 165v. Reproduced by permission of the British Library.

FIGURE 2. Nun Adoring Christ, in British Library, MS Lansdowne 383, folio 14v. Reproduced by permission of the British Library.

kinds of materials found in the Shaftesbury Psalter. The texts of the Psalms, creeds, and canticles were fairly uniform from book to book and monastery to monastery.[10] There was, however, variation from community to community in the feast days recorded in calendars, saints commemorated in litanies, and devotional themes emphasized in prayers. These portions of a psalter allowed a monastic community to demonstrate two qualities. First, through the compilation of materials for the daily Office, the community affirmed its membership in the wider Benedictine community. Second, through the selection of specific observances, a community could assert its history, individual practices, and political affiliations.[11] At the time the Shaftesbury Psalter was produced, there were a variety of prayer texts in circulation that represented a range of liturgical and regional traditions and tastes, such as ninth-century Celtic confessions, tenth-century Carolingian compositions, and eleventh-century, hybrid Anglo-Gallican texts.[12] Anselm's prayers, in comparison, signaled a shift in contemporary prayer style, one marked by lengthy, deeply introspective expressions of contrition reminiscent of Augustine.[13]

The Shaftesbury Psalter's prayers reflect this range of traditions. For example, a prayer addressed to the Holy Spirit is derived from an early ninth-century Carolingian form.[14] A text likely of English origin addressed to a guardian angel dated from as early as the first quarter of the eleventh century.[15] One of the psalter's three prayers to the Virgin Mary was an eleventh-century composition of Maurillius, archbishop of Rouen, which was his rendition of the Carolingian-era prayer *Singularis meriti.*[16] Also there were contemporary compositions, such as Anselm's, that fostered extended meditation.[17] Thus, the psalter's collection indicated the nunnery's selection and acquisition of a variety of Latin prayer texts for female readers made possible through the community's inclusion in some manner in the monastic circuit of textual exchange. How each individual prayer text was acquired by the nunnery probably will never be known, but, by exploring the ties around the Anselmian prayers, we can gain insight into the kinds of social relationships and circumstances that fostered devotional texts' perpetuation among monastic communities.

As noted earlier, there was an on-going relationship between the Shaftesbury community and Archbishop Anselm. One testimony of this is found in a psalter that was produced before 1161, possibly for Henry of Blois, bishop of Winchester, and acquired by Shaftesbury in the thirteenth century, British Library MS Cotton Nero C.iv, commonly referred to as the Winchester Psalter.[18] Shaftesbury's acquisition of the psalter is confirmed by additions to the calendar of the occasions of King Edward the Martyr, the nunnery's patron saint, and an entry noting Anselm's attendance at the dedication of the nunnery's church (April 14). This archiepiscopal visit coincided with his correspondence with the nunnery's abbess, Eulalia, who served in that post from 1074 to 1106.

Anselm addressed three letters directly to Eulalia and her charges, one of which was written when he was in exile in Lyons.[19] Anselm's first letter to Eulalia was composed

c. 1094, which was within the first year of his accession to the archbishopric. In this let-ter he acknowledged the zealous spirit exercised in worship at the Shaftesbury commu-nity, and being ever the perfectionist, Anselm pushed the nuns for even greater devo-tional achievement through their conscientious attention to even the smallest detail in matters of thinking and speaking.[20] In closing, Anselm emphasized his need of the abbess's and monastery's support in light of his difficulties with King William II (Rufus):

> Oro, ut pro me oretis, et tanto attentius, quanto scitis me de dilectione vestra con-fidere; quoniam numquam cognovi me magis quam nunc orationibus indigere. Tam male enim sum in archepiscopatu, ut certe—si sine culpa dicere possum—malim de hac vita exire quam sic vivere.[21]

> I pray that you pray for me with even greater attention, for you know how much I trust in your love; since I know I have never been in need for prayers more than now. I am with such evil in the office of archbishop that, if I were able to say with-out sin, I would rather die than live in such a way.

Exiled in Lyons in 1104, Anselm wrote to Eulalia and her charges of his assurance of de-votion and affection for the nunnery. He also expressed his thanks for their requests for his continuing written communications so as to preserve his presence at Shaftes-bury while he was in exile.[22] Anselm's third letter to Eulalia and community, written upon his return to England in 1106, effusively thanked the women for their prayers and requested their continual prayerful support for his prosperity:

> Gratias ago religiosae dilectioni vestrae quia pro me orastis, quamdiu extra An-gliam fui in exilio, desiderantes reditum meum; nunc autem desiderantius rogo ut oretis, quatenus fructuosus sit reditus meus. Hoc volo, ut sciatis quia dilectio mea erga vos, ex quo vos cognovi, et vivit et perseverat, et quamdiu vivam, deo dante perseverabit.[23]

> I give thanks for your steadfast love while I was in exile out of England because you prayed for me, desiring my return. Now, moreover, I ask more earnestly that you pray for me in as much as my return may be fruitful. I wish that you know my love for you, as long as I have known you, both lives and abides, and as long as I live, God willing, will persevere.

That Anselm wrote to Eulalia was not extraordinary for the archbishop was a prodigious correspondent. What is interesting in Anselm's letters to Eulalia is the com-bination of features not routinely found in others: Anselm's admission of his frustration in the archbishopric early in his tenure, his consistent requests for supportive prayers, his reminders to Eulalia and her charges of his steadfast devotion to and respect for them, and an absence of episcopal reprimands. While the archbishop was appropriately encouraging in the nuns' devotional practices and clear in his affection for Eulalia, he did not write in stern admonition or for the sake of bureaucratic supervision.[24] Rather, his letters reflected a mutually supportive colleagueship, one in which he received as much encouragement and support as he gave to the abbess and her charges. His posture was as much grateful colleague as spiritual advisor, his acknowledgments respectfully conveyed within the hierarchal bonds culturally appropriate for an archbishop and an abbess. Whether the letters reveal more Anselm's personal affection or his political concerns is difficult to discern given the archbishop's contentious environment. Since Eulalia's background prior to her 1074 accession to the abbacy is unknown, it is possible that she and Anselm had crossed paths much earlier in their respective careers, and thus the letters of 1094–1106 reflect ties built over a much longer span of time. What is certain is that Anselm needed to cultivate and maintain the relationship with Shaftesbury during his conflicts with William II and Henry I. Shaftesbury was important to Anselm not merely because it was within his episcopal jurisdiction; Shaftesbury was a royally founded abbey, one of the monastic communities established and endowed by the venerable Anglo-Saxon king, Alfred the Great, c. 888. Shaftesbury's identity as a royally founded monastery was noted from its establishment by Alfred's biographer, Asser, and later reiterated by subsequent historical records, such as William of Malmesbury's *Gesta Regum Anglorum*.[25] Further Abbess Eulalia was mentioned specifically in some records, which given the nature of the citations, suggest that she must have held some degree of prominence in ecclesiastical and secular circles. The Winchester Annals, for example, marked her accession to the abbacy of Shaftesbury alongside notice of the peace accord between Edgar of Scotland and William II.[26] The abbess also was cited as recipient of land tenure grants from William II.[27] These notations reflected recognition of Eulalia's leadership of an abbey of royal foundation with continuing royal ties, a highly prized association and source of legitimacy surely sought by an archbishop buffeted by kings' demands and threats. Within this available information, Eulalia's and Anselm's colleagueship may be viewed as one begun out of administrative necessity that developed into a mutually supportive, politically important friendship.

The relationship between the abbess and the archbishop was not unique. Anselm maintained friendships with other women during his career, specifically lay women of aristocratic birth who adopted quasi-monastic modes of living. The formal posture of the relationships, as found in Anselm's letters to Eulalia, was that of male spiritual advisor to that of female suppliant.[28] Beneath this culturally crafted mantle, however, was an exchange of spiritual guidance and encouragement for political support and intercession, of which the most prominent examples were Anselm's friendships with Ida, countess of Boulogne, and Matilda, queen of England and spouse of Anselm's foe, Henry I.[29] During the course of some of these relationships Anselm shared his prayer compositions. Adelaide, the daughter of William I and ally of Roger of Beaumont, received early versions of seven of Anselm's prayers.[30] His most famous prayer recipient, Countess Matilda of Tuscany, received the entire corpus of prayers and meditations in 1104.[31] Matilda's prayer collection, as was Adelaide's, was accompanied with Anselm's instructions to read and study the prayers with the intent of provoking her mind to "either greater love or fear of God."[32] Adelaide and Countess Matilda were valuable political and social allies, and his gratitude for their friendship was expressed along with suggestions for enhancing their devotional practice. Even though he may have taken the stance of spiritual advisor with female associates, Anselm consistently acknowledged the importance of their support, especially during his bouts of political conflict.[33] For Anselm to share his compositions with Adelaide and Matilda implied that he was giving his works to friends whom he felt would read, use, and appreciate such devotional texts. Thus, it is plausible that Anselm would share his prayer texts with Abbess Eulalia because he did so with other female friends of long-standing, aristocratic women who, like Eulalia, took his part in times of political troubles and shared his fervor for devotional reading.

A specific exchange of prayer texts is not documented in the letters between Anselm and Eulalia. Anselm's letter of 1104 to Eulalia made mention of on-going communication between abbess and archbishop, but the prayer compositions were not noted specifically. Since this letter was written at the time that Anselm had his entire prayer collection sent to Countess Matilda, it is tempting to speculate that he made a similar gift to Eulalia. The appearance of Anselm's prayers in the Shaftesbury Psalter attests to the nunnery's familiarity with and acquisition of the texts c. 1130, but precisely how the nunnery's members learned of the texts, as well as the others that appear in the manuscript, is not directly documented. It is possible that the Shaftesbury Psalter's compiler's knowledge of the two prayers may have come through channels other than an exchange between Anselm and Eulalia. But, the recorded interactions between abbess and archbishop from 1094 to 1106, the political context of their relationship, and Anselm's documented manner of sharing prayer texts with female friends make the prayers' place in the nunnery's psalter more than coincidental.

In fact, the example of Eulalia and Anselm represents some qualities underpinning textual exchange among female and male monastics during the eleventh and twelfth centuries: mutual recognition of institutional and personal standing, educational accomplishment, and political influence. The fact of the abbess's and archbishop's friendship cannot affirm the sharing of the two prayer texts, but the tacit circumstances of their relationship prompt relevant speculation in two ways. First, the relationship suggests one mode of communication involved in the process of compilation and production of Shaftesbury's psalter, that being the acquisition of texts directly through collegial and personal ties. Second, the qualities represented in Anselm's and Eulalia's friendship can be used to apply new questions to the study of the development and perpetuation of monastic devotional and liturgical literature. That is, would the survival of some texts and the creation of new ones have been rooted in the recommendations given and decisions made in the course of friendships? Would texts be retained or discarded in light of their symbolic political associations? Were cultural expectations of religious women and men, as well as the posture of their relationships to divine authority, shaped and prescribed through the process of sharing reading materials? In the example of the Shaftesbury Psalter, the inclusion of the Anselmian compositions twenty-five years after the author's death may have been as much about assertion of the nunnery's reputation through association with a venerated archbishop as the retention of useful, or favored, devotional materials.

In addition to the Shaftesbury Psalter, other extant devotional and liturgical materials of the period suggest similar antecedents of literacy, social standing, and vocational experience in textual exchange.[34] One such example is the mortuary roll. A mortuary roll was a funeral register carried from one monastic community to another announcing the death of an abbess or abbot, in which each house would offer in writing prayers for the deceased and requests for prayers for their own deceased members.[35] The entry was an institutional autograph of sorts, an arena to demonstrate Latin literary prowess, scribal proficiency, and at its most essential, an indication of membership in the larger monastic community. Two early twelfth-century mortuary rolls, one for Abbess Matilda of St. Trinité, Caen, c. 1113, and another for Abbot Vital of Sauvigny, c. 1124, circulated among over 200 men's and women's monastic houses, as well as cathedrals, of northern France and England.[36] In focusing upon the English nunneries, those that participated in the rolls memorializing Abbess Matilda and Abbot Vital, which included Shaftesbury, were of royal foundation and association.[37] The majority of these were established by members of the Anglo-Saxon family of King Alfred, and all were tied in some manner to the Norman royal family of England. Those nunneries of non-royal affiliation and foundation were not included. Though the mortuary rolls represent a different sort of monastic devotional literature, the principle of inclusion is the same—religious institutions of similar standing that were considered members of a broad network.

These and other extant eleventh- and twelfth-century materials suggest that this specialized monastic literary community was broader than has been conjectured, one that was comprised of female and male participants. There are at least three reasons why exploration of the monastic literary community, at least for England, has not included nuns. First, few extant manuscripts are directly associated with English nunneries.[38] Second, nuns' Latin literacy, at least from the late Anglo-Saxon era, has been doubted.[39] Third, and related to the second, there has been general acceptance of male clerics' continuous mediation of Latin texts for religious women.[40] Thus, readily apparent reasons to explore textual exchange between female and male communities have been perceived as absent. Yet, it is in scrutinizing liturgical and devotional texts, as in this case of devotional prayers, speculating about texts' functions in their communities, and considering the social ties implicit in manuscript provenance and acquisition that the wider monastic community becomes visible.

Essential to the sharing of devotional reading materials was the assumption of literacy and the knowledge of how to use the texts appropriately. For this period in Western Europe, Latin was the language of those deemed literate.[41] Latin literacy was acquired by a very small segment of Western Europe's population, persons usually of economic and social standing with the means of acquiring education and affiliated in some manner with the Church.[42] The participants in textual exchange took for granted certain qualities held in common. For example, in the sharing of a prayer text, a donor assumed that its recipient could read and understand it as well as expect the recipient to know how to use it appropriately to deepen her or his relationship with God, whether that be in the daily Office or in private study. The conveyance of a text, as seen in Anselm's letters, carried its own representation of the donor-recipient relationship. As discussed here, the male spiritual advisor guided the subordinate female suppliant, but the directions assumed the woman's ability to read, understand, and apply correctly the materials herself. The letters portrayed the expected cultural hierarchy, but were grounded upon mutual appreciation of the literature in question. Thus, however the personal relationship was expressed explicitly in the process of sharing reading materials, the very act of exchange implied equally significant facets of monastic relationships and contemporary culture.

To illustrate the point regarding assumed literacy and comprehension, consider the relationship of Goscelin and Eve during the second half of the eleventh century.[43] Their friendship began at the royally founded English nunnery of Wilton; Eve was a nun and Goscelin served there in some teaching capacity. According to Goscelin's testimony in the *Liber Confortatorius*, his affectionate letter of instruction to Eve after her departure from Wilton, the two enjoyed a friendship at the nunnery based upon mutual appreciation of and pleasure in a wide array of devotional and patristic materials.[44] Goscelin maintained the mentor-protégé stance in the letter by advising Eve to deepen her spiritual meditation through contemplation of Scripture, Orosius's *History of the World*, Boethius's *Consolation of Philosophy*, and Augustine's *City of God*. Also he noted his appreciation for her gift of books to him earlier in their association. Eve's ability to read Latin texts and interpret them were not singled out, but took second place to Goscelin's position as spiritual advisor giving directives about emotional discipline and spiritual fervor. Yet the ability to share, read, and contemplate Latin devotional literature was an essential element of this friendship.

Goscelin's *Liber Confortatorius* and Anselm's letters are among the few extant materials in which the specific exchange of devotional texts is mentioned, ones from which to glean the multi-faceted meanings of sharing and using devotional texts.[45] While the questions here have focused upon the implications of Shaftesbury nunnery's acquisition of devotional prayers, similar questions should be applied to the monastic literature held by other royally founded and affiliated English nunneries.[46] For example, a finely crafted, early twelfth-century copy of Smaragdus's *Diadema Monarchorum*, autographed by an anonymous female scribe, was held at Nunnaminster.[47] Barking acquired a twelfth-century book of glosses of the Song of Songs and the Book of Lamentations in the early thirteenth century.[48] Elstow's Abbess Cecily de Chanville had produced for her c. 1192 a copy of Peter Comestor's *Historia Scholastica* and Richard of St. Victor's *Allegoriae in Vetus Testamentum*.[49] All of these works could have been applied in the routine of the Benedictine day, whether as part of the daily Office, chapter meeting, refectory reading, or private study. Further, these materials did not require an ordained clergyman for use, as would materials associated with Mass, confirmation, and ordination. That these kinds of reading materials survived from women's communities prompts speculation about the kinds of monastic literature that might have once existed in each house and the nature of the communities' and individuals' relationships though which acquisition was secured.

The monastic, Latin literate community of eleventh- and twelfth-century Europe was a clear minority of the population, but one that was grounded in the participation of both women and men of specific social, vocational, and educational experiences. Defining the kinds of relationships that developed between monastic men and women, both in terms of expectations and assumptions, will aid in understanding the transmission of their Latin literature. By using the example of Abbess Eulalia and Archbishop Anselm, the exploration of social relationships among female and male communities has potential to further our understanding of the development and perpetuation of certain devotional texts, make explicit the nature of the bonds that those texts represented, and broaden our understanding of the parameters of monastic friendships. These are many questions to pin onto a nunnery's copies of Anselmian prayers, but there is much to learn about the nature of monastic literary community from precious remnants of a valuable friendship.

Notes

The essay is based upon a paper presented at *Eius Dignitatis Cultores*, a symposium in honor of Professor Francis L. Newton upon the occasion of his retirement from Duke University's Department of Classical Studies, November 1999. The author wishes to thank David N. Bell and Thomas H. Bestul for their comments upon earlier versions of the essay.

1. Brian Stock, *Listening for the Text: On the Uses of the Past* (Philadelphia: University of Pennsylvania Press, 1995), 2.

2. Art historical studies have determined that the psalter was produced c. 1130–1140 as described by C. M. Kauffmann, *Romanesque Manuscripts, 1066–1190* (London: Harvey Miller, 1975), 82–84. Neil Ker indicated a general twelfth-century dating in *Medieval Libraries of Great Britain*, 2nd ed. (London: Offices of the Royal Historical Society, 1964), 177. A. G. Watson has determined that the manuscript was produced prior to 1173 through the absence of the feast of Becket in its calendar (*A Catalogue of Dated and Datable Manuscripts 700–1600 in the Department of Manuscripts, the British Library*, vol. 1 [London: The Library, 1979], 148, no. 850).

3. This particular prayer was the first of three Anselm composed, generally known as *Oratio ad Sanctum Mariam cum mens gravatur torpore* (F. S. Schmitt, ed., *Anselmi Opera Omnia*, vol. 3 [Edinburgh: T. Nelson, 1946], 13–14, no. 5).

4. *Oratio ad accipiendum corpus Domini et sanguinem* (Schmitt, *Anselmi Opera Omnia*, vol. 3, 10, no. 3). Benedicta Ward has viewed this prayer as the only one of Anselm's devotional prayer compositions suitable for the Mass. She did not assert that this was Anselm's intention, but speculated upon its eventual use in that fashion. Richard Southern's comments were along these lines. The psalter's copy of the prayer has been adapted for a female reader. See B. Ward, ed., *The Prayers and Meditations of St. Anselm* (New York: Penguin, 1973), 30; R. Southern, *Saint Anselm: A Portrait in a Landscape* (Cambridge: Cambridge University Press, 1990), 11.

5. Southern, *Saint Anselm*, 106–11.

6. There are eleven extant twelfth-century manuscripts of English origin known to contain copies of some of Anselm's nineteen prayers. By the fourteenth century, Anselm's prayers were being circulated as a collection along with prayers composed in imitation of the Anselmian style. Until André Wilmart's study of the manuscript traditions, these imitations were considered genuine Anselmian compositions. Two of these Pseudo-Anselmian texts are contained in the Shaftesbury Psalter as described in note 17 below. See A. Wilmart, *Auteurs Spirituels et Textes Dévots du Moyen Age Latin* (Paris: Bloud and Gay, 1932). Also see J. F. Cottier's recent work on the Anselmian apocrypha's development in "Le Recueil Apocryphe des Orationes sive Meditationes des Saint Anselme: Sa Formation et sa Réception en Angelterre et en France au XIIᵉ Siècle," in *Anselm: Aosta, Bec and Canterbury*, ed. D. E. Lunscombe and G. R. Evans (Sheffield: Sheffield Academic Press, 1996), 282–95. Thomas Bestul has studied several of the twelfth-century manuscripts that contain Anselmian texts including the following: "A Note on the Contents of the Anselm Manuscript, Bodleian Library, Laud misc. 508," *Manuscripta* 21 (1977): 167–70; "The Verdun Anselm, Ralph of Battle, and the Formation of the Anselmian Apocrypha," *Revue Bénédictine* 87 (1977): 383–89; "The Collection of Anselm's Prayers in British Library MS Cotton Vespasian D.xxvi," *Medium Aevum* 47 (1987): 1–5; "British Library MS Arundel 60 and the Anselmian Apocrypha," *Scriptorium* 35 (1981): 271–75.

7. The iconography of the illuminations has been noted in studies of the English Romanesque style, such as M. A. Farley and F. Wormald, "Three Related Romanesque Manuscripts," *The Art Bulletin* 22 (1940): 157–61; Kauffmann, *Romanesque Manuscripts*, 82–84. The illuminations that include the image of the nun are found on fols. 14v and 165v, the nun's image in the former seemingly added as an afterthought and the latter clearly original to the illumination's design.

8. London, British Library MS Lansdowne 383, fol. 170r, Prayer to St. Peter.

9. London, British Library MS Lansdowne 383, fol. 172r, Prayer to St. Lambert.

10. Philip Pulsiano has studied the widespread use of the Gallican version of the Psalms in England from the tenth century and beyond ("Psalter," in *The Liturgical Books of Anglo-Saxon England*, ed. R. W. Pfaff [Kalamazoo: Medieval Institute Publications, Western Michigan University, 1995], 61–85).

11. For further articulation and application of these principles, see Margot Fassler's study of the implementation of the sequence during the twelfth century at the Abbey of St. Victor, *Gothic Song: Victorine Sequences and Augustinian Reform in Twelfth-Century Paris* (Cambridge: Cambridge University Press, 1993), esp. part 4, pp. 187–240. Also, see R. W. Pfaff's evaluation of the Eadwine Calendar, Cambridge Trinity Coll. MS R 17.1 and its implications for the Canterbury community (*The Eadwine Psalter: Text, Image and Monastic Culture in Twelfth-Century Canterbury* [London: Modern Humanities Research Association, 1992], 62–87).

12. To date there is no comprehensive study of medieval liturgical prayer. Thomas Bestul has written on a variety of aspects of prayer development in later Anglo-Saxon/early Norman England in "Continental Sources of Devotional Writing," in *Sources of Anglo-Saxon Culture*, ed. Paul Szarmach (Kalamazoo: Medieval Institute Publications, Western Michigan University, 1986), 103–19; "The Collection of Private Prayers in the 'Portiforium' of Wulfstan of Worcester and the 'Orationes sive Meditationes' of Anselm of Canterbury," in Raymonde Foreville et al., *Spicilegium Beccense II: Les mutations socio-culturelles au tournant des XIᵉ–XIIᵉ siècle* (Paris: Editions du Centre National de la Recherche Scientifique, 1984), 355–64; and "St. Anselm and the Continuity of Anglo-Saxon Devotional Traditions," *Annuale Mediaevale* 18 (1977): 20–41.

13. There are varying interpretations about the innovativeness of Anselm's compositional style. Southern provides syntactical and stylistic analysis of Anselm's work in comparison to Augustine. He emphasizes Anselm's advanced, focused introspection inspired by, but not in direct imitation of Augustine (Southern, *Saint Anselm*, 71–86). Bestul links Anselm's style to an evolution in the intensity of earlier Anglo-Saxon prayer forms ("St. Anselm and the Continuity of Anglo-Saxon Devotional Traditions"). In the comparative context of late eleventh- and early twelfth-century prayers, Anselm's writings encouraged prolonged meditation through the suppliant's psychological scourging of the soul. The expressions did not dwell on carnal or bodily sin as found in Anglo-Saxon prayers, but, in a manner of speaking, sought the obverse superlative of being the most wretched of sinners.

14. Fol. 53v. The earliest known analogue is contained in *Liber Parisinus*, as edited by André Wilmart, *Precum Libelli quattor aevi karolini* (Rome, 1940), 37.

15. Fol. 169v. The earliest known analogue for the prayer is found in London, BL MS Titus D.xxvi, commonly referred to as *Aelfwine's Prayerbook*, ed. Beate Günzel, Henry Bradshaw Society 108 (Rochester, N.Y.: Boydell and Brewer, 1993), 128, no. 47.

16. The prayer begins fol. 166v, but the folio containing the conclusion has been excised. Archbishop Maurillius was an advisor to and friend of Anselm's, but there has been no evidence of Maurillius's direct influence upon Anselm's compositions according to Thomas Bestul as quoted in Theme III, Discussion in *Spicilegium Beccense II*, 411; Southern, *Saint Anselm*, 31, 183, 267.

17. Two of the Shaftesbury Psalter's prayer texts, *Salva sancta crux* (fol. 156) and *Ave glorisissima omnium lignorum* (fol. 156v), are now identified as part of the Anselmian Apocrypha. These are among the earliest known copies of the prayers. The prayers are edited in the *Patrologia Latina*'s corpus of Anselmian prayers, vol. 158, nos. 45 and 42, respectively. For the former, see A. Wilmart,

"Prières Mediévales pour l'Adoration de la Croix," *Ephemerides Liturgicae* 46 (1932): 22–65, esp. 61 n. 4; and the latter, A. Wilmart, "La Tradition des Prières de Saint Anselm," *Review Bénédictine* 36 (1924): 52–71, esp. 67. Three other prayers with no known analogues are also distinctly different from tenth- and eleventh-century styles and more closely resemble the Anselmian texts. These are prayers to St. Peter (fols. 170r–171v), St. Lambert (introduction excised, fol. 172r–173r), and an unusual version of *Ave Maria gratia plena* (fol. 166), which is discussed by Henri Barré, *Prières Anciennes de l'Occident a la Mère du saveur* (Paris: P. Lethielleux, 1963), 283–64 and edited by E. Beck, "A Twelfth Century Salvation of Our Lady," *Downside Review* 42 (1924): 185–86.

18. The manuscript's production date and Shaftesbury acquisition are detailed in K. E. Haney, *Winchester Psalter: An Iconographic Study* (Leicester: Leicester University Press, 1986), 7–8.

19. In his letter c. 1099 written from Lyons to Hugh, archdeacon of Canterbury, Anselm instructed that his greetings and blessings be conveyed to Eulalia as well as the abbesses of the English nunneries of Wilton and Nunnaminster (Winchester). See Schmitt, *Anselmi Opera Omnia*, vol. 4, 102–103, no. 208.

20. Anselm used this comment frequently in his letter to his spiritual and episcopal advisees, such as to the quasi-monastic lay women Rodbert, Seith, and Edith (Schmitt, *Anselmi Opera Omnia*, vol. 4, 134–35, no. 230); the monks of St. Werburgh, Chester (Schmitt, *Anselmi Opera Omnia*, vol. 4, 136–38, no. 231); and the monks of Canterbury (Schmitt, *Anselmi Opera Omnia*, vol. 4, 210–11, no. 291).

21. Schmitt, *Anselmi Opera Omnia*, vol. 4, 67, no. 183.

22. Schmitt, *Anselmi Opera Omnia*, vol. 5, 274, no. 337.

23. Schmitt, *Anselmi Opera Omnia*, vol. 5, 347–48, no. 403.

24. The contrast is noticeable in comparison with Anselm's letters to Athletis, abbess of Romsey, regarding the community's veneration of a deceased, locally prominent gentryman (Schmitt, *Anselmi Opera Omnia*, vol. 4, 144–45, no. 237) and Matilda, abbess of Wilton, regarding her attitude in her reporting relationship to the bishop of Salisbury (Schmitt, *Anselmi Opera Omnia*, vol. 4, 69–71, no. 185).

25. Regarding the translation and burial of King Edward the Martyr at Shaftesbury, William of Malmesbury noted "certe apud Scestoniam splendidum regiae sanctitudinis refulgurat speculum; quoniam illius meritis deputatur quod eo loci multus devotarum Deo feminarum chorus, claritate religionis terras istas irradians, etiam ipsa perstringit sidera" (certainly the splendid mirror of royal sanctity glitters at Shaftesbury; since it is considered that there in that place of great merit is a chorus of women devoted to God, illuminating that land with splendor of religion, even extending up to the stars themselves) (*Gesta Regum Anglorum*, Rolls Series 90, pt. 1, 184–85).

26. *Annales monastici Anglorum*, Rolls Series 36, pt. 2 (1865), 30.

27. While feudal tenure is not the focus here, it is important to consider the various social relationships nunneries fostered through land donations, which would have shaped the houses' standing and political influence in their respective regions. Kathleen Cooke's investigation of Shaftesbury's donations c. 1086–1122 suggests that the nunnery's aristocratic legacy may have been one of several reasons Anglo-Norman landholders of minor aristocratic standing sought to place their daughters in this community. Regarding Shaftesbury's feudal ties, see K. Cooke, "Donors and Daughters: Shaftesbury Abbey's Benefactors, Endowment, and Nuns, c. 1086–1130," *Anglo-Norman Studies* 12 (1989): 29–45, and Ann Williams, "The Knights of Shaftesbury Abbey," *Anglo-Norman Studies* 8 (1985): 214–37.

28. Joan Ferrante has examined the topoi exchanged in women's and men's letters during the medieval period and the pragmatic relationships that were enveloped by the language. Ferrante's discussion reveals that no matter the topic at hand there is a consistent hierarchic posture in correspondence, a clear identification of the experienced superior and aspiring and admiring subordinate. This was not strictly a male-female phenomenon, but was carried out, for example, in the letters between Hildegard of Bingen and Elizabeth of Schönau. See Ferrante's description and assessment of these letters in *To the Glory of Her Sex: Women's Roles in the Composition of Medieval Texts* (Bloomington: Indiana University Press, 1997), esp. 18–26.

29. Sally N. Vaughn examines the political advantages of Anselm's friendships with women, especially emphasizing his long-standing relationship with Ida, countess of Boulogne, who after the death of her second husband, Eustace, informally pursued monastic practice at the family-patronized monastery of St. Vaast ("St. Anselm and Women," *Haskins Society Journal* 2 [1990]: 83–93).

30. Adelaide requested from Anselm his favorite Psalms excerpts c. 1072, at which time he was serving as prior of the monastery of Bec. The monastery was near the geographical center of Roger of Beaumont's barony, and Adelaide's tie to Roger must have been known to Anselm. In fulfilling Adelaide's request, Anselm sent along his compositions. In an accompanying letter, he especially recommended her meditation on the prayers to Sts. Stephen and Mary Magdalene, calling himself "servus et amicus animae vestrae" (as the servant and friend of your soul) (Schmitt, *Anselmi Opera Omnia*, vol. 3, 113–14, no. 10; Southern, *Saint Anselm*, 92–93, 99).

31. The earliest surviving copy of Matilda's collection is Admont, Stiftsbibliothek MS 289. See Southern, *Saint Anselm*, 111–12.

32. "ad excitandam legentis mentem ad dei amorem vel timorem" (Schmitt, *Anselmi Opera Omnia*, vol. 3, 4).

33. A copy of Countess Matilda's formal intercession with Pope Paschal II on Anselm's behalf was kept among the archbisop's personal letters (Schmitt, *Anselmi Opera Omnia*, vol. 5, 289–90, no. 350). Queen Matilda's letters of support also were preserved by Anselm. The sixteen letters exchanged between them provides full display of the conditions of friendship (Schmitt, *Anselmi Opera Omnia*, vol. 4, nos. 242, 243, 246, 288, 296; vol. 5, nos. 317, 320, 321, 329, 346, 347, 384, 385, 395, 400, 406).

34. There are numerous prayer collections contained in eleventh-century service books that feature both masculine and feminine Latin word forms, some of these original and some additions. The use of these books and the acquisition of their texts is open for speculation since the majority of these texts are firmly associated in origin with a male monastic house and/or abbot, such as British Library Cotton MS Titus D.xxvi and MS Titus D.xxvii (Abbot Aelfwine of New Minster c. xi), Cambridge, Corpus Christi College MS 391 (Abbot Wulfstan of Worcester C. xi^{med}) and Vatican Library, Regina MS 12 (Bury St. Edmunds c. xi^{med}). A prayerbook of similar configuration, British Library Cotton MS Galba A.xiv, has been linked to the Benedictine nunnery of Nunnaminster, Winchester. See Beate Günzel, *Aelfwine's Prayerbook;* Anselm Hughes, ed., *The Portiforium of Saint Wulfstan*, vols. 1 and 2 (London: Henry Bradshaw Society, 1958, 1960); A. Wilmart, "The Prayers of the Bury Psalter," *Downside Review* 48 (1930), 118–216; and B. J. Muir, ed., *A Pre-Conquest Prayer-Book*, Henry Bradshaw Society 103 (1988).

35. Jean DuFour, "Les rouleaux des morts," in *Codicologica*, vol. 3 (Leiden: E. J. Brill, 1980), 96–102.

36. Both rolls are printed in L. Delisle, *Rouleau des Morts du IXe au XVe siecle*, Société de l'Histoire de France, no. 135 (Paris, 1866), 177–279. The author wishes to thank Professor Daniel Sheerin

for sharing his unpublished paper, "Sisters in the Literary Agon: Female Religious in the Mortuary Rolls" presented at University of North Carolina at Chapel Hill, November 1995.

37. The other English nunneries included in the rolls were Amesbury, Barking, Malling, Nunnaminster, Romsey, Stratford at Bow, Wherwell, and Wilton. All but Malling and Stratford at Bow were royally founded communities. Stratford at Bow and Malling were established by William, bishop of London and advisor to William I, and Gundulf, bishop of Rochester and advisor to William II, respectively. Gundulf's mother retired to St. Trinité, which may have been another reason for Malling's inclusion in the Matilda Roll.

38. All of the known extant manuscripts linked to English nunneries are listed and described in David N. Bell, *What Nuns Read: Books and Libraries in Medieval English Nunneries* (Kalamazoo: Cistercian Publications, 1995), 103–217.

39. Bell surveys the debate on this topic and notes reasons to reconsider evidence for Latin literacy among several nunneries, especially Barking (Bell, *What Nuns Read*, 61–69, 57–96).

40. To date there is no study of the role of clerics in the royally founded English nunneries prior to 1200. The presumption of ordained clerics' association with and the nature of their roles in nunneries often is cited from A. H. Thompson's assertion regarding the work of male clerics in nunneries in the later Middle Ages, "there is no reason to doubt that the arrangements which existed in later days were of early origin" ("Double Monasteries and the Male Element in Nunneries" in *The Ministry of Women: A Report by a Committee Appointed by His Grace the Lord Archbishop of Canterbury* [London: Society for Promoting Christian Knowledge, 1919], 145–64, esp. 150).

41. The meaning of literacy in England shifted during the course of the eleventh century. In general, during the tenth and first half of the eleventh century, Anglo-Saxon English was used frequently in conjunction with Latin in monastic liturgical books. The use of Anglo-Saxon in monastic books ceased after William of Normandy's conquest of England in 1066. David Dumville has studied the relationship of the two languages in liturgical materials in *Liturgy and the Ecclesiastical History of Late Anglo-Saxon England: Four Studies* (Woodbridge: Boydell Press, 1992), 127–32.

42. This generalization glosses over the important nuances in numerous scholarly studies of the precise meanings and implications of literacy, as found, for example, in Franz Baüml, "Varieties and Consequences of Literacy and Illiteracy," *Speculum* 55 (1980): 237–65; Brian Stock, *The Implications of Literacy: Written Language and Models of Interpretation in the Eleventh and Twelfth Centuries* (Princeton, N.J.: Princeton University Press, 1983); Michael Clanchy, *From Memory to Written Record: England 1066–1307*, 2nd ed. (Oxford: Oxford University Press, 1993); and Martine Irvine, *The Making of Textual Culture: Grammatica and Literary Theory, 350–1100* (Cambridge: Cambridge University Press, 1994).

43. For an examination of the relationship of advisor and recluse, see Gopa Roy, "'Sharpen your mind with the whetstone of books': The Female Recluse in Goscelin's *Liber Confortatorius*, Aelred of Rievaulx's *De Institutione Inclusarum*, and the *Ancrene Wisse*," in *Women, the Book, and the Godly*, ed. L. Smith and J. Taylor (Oxford: D. S. Brewer, 1995), 113–22.

44. Goscelin, *Liber Confortatorius*, ed. C. H. Talbot, *Studia Anselmia* 37, 1–117, esp. 39, 81.

45. For the thirteenth century, the words of Gilbert of Sempringham regarding nuns' relationships with Latin reading materials addressed these same issues, if obversely. See Brian Golding, *Gilbert of Sempringham and the Gilbertine Order, c. 1130–1300* (Oxford: Oxford University Press, 1995), 183–86.

46. These issues are addressed in my "The Literary Culture of English Benedictine Nuns, c. 1000–1250" (PhD diss., Duke University, 1999).

47. P. R. Robinson, "A Twelfth-Century *Scriptrix* from Nunnaminster," in *Of the Making of Books: Medieval Manuscripts, Their Scribes, and Readers,* ed. P. R. Robinson and R. Zim (Aldershot: Scolar Press, 1997), 73–93.

48. Bell, *What Nuns Read,* 11–12, no. 12.

49. Ibid., 137, no. 1.

A Token of Friendship? Anselmian Prayers and a Nunnery's Psalter

Response to Mary Jane Morrow:
Where Do We Go from Here?

DAVID N. BELL

In this interesting and important essay, Mary Jane Morrow presents a wide-ranging discussion centred on two Anselmian prayers which appear in the Shaftesbury Psalter. She sees these prayers as providing important material for an "exploration of social relationships among female and male communities," and such an exploration, in turn, "has potential to further our understanding of the development and perpetuation of certain devotional texts, make explicit the nature of the bonds that those texts represented, and broaden our understanding of the parameters of monastic friendships" (p. 107). This is a tall order (as the author herself admits), and we must remember that the friendship of Anselm of Canterbury and Eulalia of Shaftesbury was a friendship of two remarkable individuals and cannot be regarded as normative. It *was* a monastic friendship, certainly, and we have evidence of other similar monastic friendships (one need think only of the letters of Hildegard of Bingen), but the monasticism might be seen as ancillary to the friendship. Matilda of Tuscany was not a nun. Nor need we be wholly convinced by Morrow's observation that Anselm wrote to Eulalia as much as a "grateful colleague as spiritual advisor" (p. 103). "Grateful colleague" might be taking things a little too far.

But the fact of the prayers remains, and interesting prayers they are. Morrow rightly draws attention to the way they signal a shift in prayer style and in this she is in agree-

ment with Sir Richard Southern and Sister Benedicta Ward. The former wrote the Foreword to the latter's poetical and popular translation of Anselm's authentic prayers and
meditations.[1]

From both a literary and a theological point of view, Anselm's prayers were remarkable productions. They are written in an intricate, rhymed prose, sometimes too
precious for our modern taste, and some of them reflect the new theology which would
become such an important part of the twelfth-century renaissance. Not all the prayers,
however, contain novel ideas, and the two sent by Anselm to Eulalia are, in fact, more conservative than others. Whether this is significant or not we cannot say. The prayer before
communion has its antecedents in earlier compositions (the *preces* of Ratherius of Verona[2]
come immediately to mind) and Sister Benedicta may have emphasized its originality a
little too much. She speaks of it as "personal and ardent, and at the same time scriptural
and theological,"[3] and observes that in this it differs from earlier prayers of this nature. It
may be *more* personal and ardent than earlier examples, that is true, but the difference is
a matter of degree rather than kind. The same is true of the Marian prayer. That sent to
Eulalia is the first of three that Anselm wrote and it is the third, not the first, which is the
most startling. But if we look back to the work of Odo and Odilo of Cluny (especially the
latter), we see the same heartfelt devotion and the same sense of sinfulness and humility
which is so apparent in Anselm.[4] Once again, the difference is a difference in degree.

As to how his prayers should be read, Anselm neither was nor intended to be original. The purpose of the prayers, he tells us, is

> ad excitandam legentis mentem ad dei amorem vel timorem, seu ad suimet discus-
> sionem editae sunt, non sunt legendae in tumultu, sed in quiete, nec cursim et ve-
> lociter, sed paulatim cum intenta et morosa meditatione.[5]

> to awake the reader's mind to the love or fear of God, or to self-examination. They
> are not to be read in a turmoil, but quietly, not in haste and hurry, but little by little,
> with attentive and careful meditation.

This is no more (and no less) than the old, traditional, Benedictine concept of
lectio, meditatio, and *oratio.*[6] It is grounded in Gregory the Great and may be paralleled
in a number of writers, not least the Venerable Bede, a good English author, and the
universally read encyclopedist Isidore of Seville.[7] Anselm resurrects the old idea and
certainly introduces it to a wider audience—Matilda, as we have said, was not a nun—
but he does not invent it. If anyone invented it, it might have been the Psalmist. Nor is
Anselm original in his "deeply introspective expressions of contrition" mentioned by
Morrow on p. 101. He is here Gregory the Great *redivivus.* As Sister Benedicta has said,
Anselm's clear and independent mind

gave new life to traditional teaching, and carried it through into a new age. He prayed in the tradition of the Fathers, but he gave this received teaching expression in the concepts and language of his times, with the result that the later outpouring of devotion to the humanity of the Saviour had its roots in the tradition of the church.[8]

Anselm's instructions on how his prayers were to be read leads us to a second point: just how *were* they read? It is not uncommon these days to hear the question "How would a medieval woman have read this book?" The answers vary widely—wildly, even—for between the medieval and modern mentality there is fixed a great gulf, and crossing it demands an intimate familiarity with medieval culture which few possess. But if we restrict ourselves to twelfth-century religious women, we can, perhaps, provide at least two out of a number of answers to the question. First, a nun would have read the Anselmian prayers for transformation, not information, and she would have read them in the communal and liturgical context of the *opus Dei*. Second, the way in which she would have read them would have been affected by the way in which they appear in the Shaftesbury Psalter. Let us consider these two points in a little more detail.

Few manuscripts have been traced to the Shaftesbury library, no catalogue has survived, and save for a couple of minor bequests, I have found no other information relating to either books or book-room. In my own study compiled in 1995, I listed and described no more than seven volumes from the house, though this tells us nothing of whether the library itself was large or small.[9] Two intriguing hints from press-marks of two books belonging to the Augustinian priory of Campsey in the south of England imply that nuns' libraries might have been very much larger than we have hitherto thought.[10]

Of these seven manuscripts, five are liturgical (there is one book of hours and four psalters), and the other two contain Middle English devotional treatises, most of them well known.[11] Save for specialists in medieval liturgy (who are not numerous), there is a tendency for modern scholars to concentrate on the Middle English material. This is understandable, not least because few modern scholars are also monks or nuns belonging to contemplative orders, and do not always appreciate that twelfth-century monastic spirituality was not primarily individualistic and private, but communal and liturgical. The matter was clearly explained in the 1930s by Mother Bernard Payne, later abbess of the Cistercian abbey of Stapehill. Her book is not well known and that is a pity; it contains an admirable and accurate account of the essential features of Benedictine/Cistercian spirituality. The liturgy, she wrote,

is essentially a collective, social prayer. It would be difficult to exaggerate the importance of this as a factor in the work of sanctification. During those hours when she is engaged in the "Work of God," the choral Office, the religious is not praying as a mere individual; she is praying in and with the entire Mystical Body of Christ, both those members of it who are still on earth, and those already in eternity, and the entire Mystical Body is praying in and through her. It is easy to see how such a prayer, rightly understood, emancipates the soul from the little world of its own individual spiritual life, introducing it into the incomparably vaster and fuller life of the Church; again, how it demands the sacrifice of egoism in entire self-devotion to the community act of praising God. We are far removed here from sentimental pietism.[12]

Having had some experience of modern contemplative communities, I can vouch for the truth of her description. It is not idealized. But it was, in a sense, even more true for contemplative communities in the twelfth century when the idea of privacy hardly existed, the discovery of the person (rather than the individual)[13] had not been fully achieved, and life in general was communal life. The essential business of both monks and nuns was precisely this "work of sanctification"—a work carried out individually within community—and the fact that there were plenty of monks and nuns who were true neither to their vocation nor their Rule is irrelevant. Monks and nuns did not, in theory, enter contemplative orders to perfect their theology or have easy access to books; and when they read, they did not read as we do today. *Lectio,* as Anselm makes quite clear, is not speed reading.

> It is not the rapid perusal of one spiritual treatise after another, but the attentive rumination of the sacred texts, allowing the Word of God to sink deep into the soul—a kind of spiritual communion with the Divine Word hidden beneath the written text. Such reading is in itself a meditation.[14]

In other words, the Benedictine quest for God was, at heart, communal, collective, meditative, and liturgical, and this, as we have said, is sometimes forgotten by secular scholars. It can also lead to misunderstanding. In 1396, for example, the library of the Cistercian abbey of Meaux in the north of England possessed a large and varied collection of manuscripts. The catalogue, compiled by its abbot, Thomas of Burton, survives and has been edited.[15] There are 363 entries, but since many of the entries refer to more than one work (manuscript 49, for example, contained more than twenty separate treatises[16]), the actual number of works represented is very many more. There were works on theology, spirituality, sermons, grammar, rhetoric, law, classics, history, literature, and medicine. But how many writers did Meaux produce? Hardly any. Apart from Thomas of Burton, the only writer I know of to come from the house was Alan of Meaux who wrote some mediocre verses on Susanna.[17] The academic response to this might be to suggest that the library was obviously not used and that the monks were obviously uninterested in learning. The monastic response might be unmitigated delight:

a Cistercian monk's business was not to write books—he did not have to publish or perish—it was "the work of sanctification." And what does one need for that? Let us return to the Shaftesbury Psalter.

The Shaftesbury Psalter is not, of course, just a psalter, and Abbess Elizabeth Shelford's exquisite early sixteenth-century Book of Hours from the same abbey is not just a book of hours.[18] They are, in fact, compact libraries of selected devotional material, and, together with the *lectio* of one book a year which the Rule of St Benedict requires,[19] they offer all that any nun or monk would need in their quest for salvation. The Shaftesbury Psalter does indeed contain a psalter, just as Elizabeth Shelford's Book of Hours contains the Hours of the Virgin, but both contain much else, not least a series of prayers. In the Shaftesbury Psalter the Anselmian compositions are only two out of a series of forty-seven prayers. In another way, however, the two manuscripts are significantly different. The Psalter reflects a more communal spirituality than that of the Hours, for the setting of the prayers in the former remains collective and liturgical, whereas the devotions in the latter are essentially individual and private. The psalter was "the prayer book *par excellence*"[20] of an earlier age which, as we have said, was itself more communal, and the transition from the one to the other reflects a fundamental change in the nature of medieval piety which it is not our business to examine in this brief response. But one thing is certain: it is this later, personal, private, individualistic spirituality which is of more interest to our personal, private, and individualistic modern society.

The collection of texts in the Shaftesbury Psalter would offer to any religious a solid and, indeed, comprehensive basis for the "work of sanctification." But there is more to it than that. The Psalter is illuminated. There are six full-page miniatures before the text of the Psalms and two after it. The case of London, BL, Cotton Nero C.iv—the so-called Winchester Psalter, which soon passed into the possession of Shaftesbury—is even more dramatic: it opens with no less than thirty-eight magnificent full-page miniatures.[21] These are not just pretty pictures and they are not only "art." One of the problems faced in modern academe is that of ever-increasing specialization. There are historians of art and there are historians of literature, and it is sometimes said that art historians do not read and literary historians do not look. This may, perhaps, be somewhat of an exaggeration, but it remains a fact that, at scholarly gatherings, the two groups tend to hold their own distinct sessions, and more interaction between them would be of great benefit to both.

Be that as it may, the unknown abbess who commissioned the Shaftesbury Psalter[22] would have seen the images as an integral part of the text. More than that: she would have seen the images *as* text.[23] Not only do the illuminations support and embellish the text, but discursive meditation on the images may be just as rewarding as ruminative reading of the text itself. Consider, for example, the miniature of the Tree of Jesse (which is very similar to the same subject in the Winchester Psalter).[24] Not only does it tell the whole complex story of the Incarnation, but the depictions of the biblical figures are mini-biographies of the figures themselves. Both the story and the biographies could easily have been read by any nun whose participation in the liturgy and the *opus Dei,* day after day and year after year, had provided her with the keys to a comprehensive understanding of what lay before her. *Lectio divina,* in other words, is not confined to the written word.

There is still more to be said. We asked earlier how a Shaftesbury nun would have read her Psalter, and we replied that one of the ways in which she would have read it would certainly have been affected by the way in which the material actually appears in the book itself. We are speaking here of the importance of the *mise en page.* Scholars began to devote attention to this very important question in the 1970s, but a major step forward was taken in 1990 with the publication of *Mise en page et mise en texte du livre manuscrit* edited by Henri-Jean Martin and Jean Vézin.[25] The tradition continues with Lesley M. Smith's recently published *Masters of the Sacred Page: Manuscripts of Theology in the Latin West to 1274,*[26] but we still have a long way to go. In this matter, modern scholars, used to their dreary pages of solid text, can profit much from discussion with publishers of newspapers; and approaching a medieval manuscript as a newspaper can often be more rewarding than approaching it as no more than a repository of textual information.[27] Much, obviously, depends on the nature and purpose of the manuscript, but twelfth-century liturgical/devotional volumes like the Shaftesbury Psalter lose much of their meaning in the regularized typescript of modern editions.

In a few texts, the *mise en page* is everything. I am thinking especially of the treatise *In honorem sanctae crucis* of Rabanus Maurus with its extraordinary visual gymnastics. Certain sentences are arranged in the form of a cross, so that when we read them we are actually crossing ourselves with our eyes.[28] The same tradition continued into the seventeenth century with the poems of George Herbert: his poem on the altar is actually in the form of an altar.[29] These, admittedly, are extremes, but in 1979 N. R. Ker provided an instructive example of the importance of presentation by comparing two manuscripts of Jerome's commentary on Habakkuk.[30] A fragment from Christ Church, Canterbury is almost certainly a direct copy of another manuscript from Canterbury, but the scribe of the former adopted a layout quite different from that of his exemplar, and the impact, accordingly, is also quite different.

In the case of psalters like the Shaftesbury Psalter, the layout of the page will often indicate to the reader how the page is to be read—in this brief response, we cannot enter into details—and the actual position of the prayers on the page (since we are talking here of prayers), the nature and quality of their initials and script, their order and so on, can be of major consequence. For too long scholars have concentrated on the textual content alone.

Format is also of significance in another form of monastic literature to which Morrow justly calls our attention: the mortuary roll. This, as the author says, was a sort of institutional autograph, "an arena to demonstrate Latin literary prowess, scribal proficiency, and, at its most essential, an indication of membership in the larger monastic community" (p. 105). This is true. Morrow introduces two early twelfth-century examples to support her case: the mortuary roll for Abbess Matilda of Sainte-Trinité de Caen (which unfortunately exists only in a seventeenth-century copy), and that for Abbot Vitalis of Savigny. Equally interesting for England are the mortuary rolls for Lucy, prioress of Castle Hedingham,[31] and Amphelisa, prioress of Higham.[32] Both are thirteenth century, but the later date is irrelevant. They reflect precisely the same tradition. The mortuary roll of Lucy begins with three illuminations which, again, are an integral part of the text and not merely attractive embellishments, and it contains replies from 122 houses. The mortuary roll of Amphelisa contains replies from no less than 372 houses. This second roll was the subject of a study by C. E. Sayle at the beginning of the twentieth century,[33] but that was a hundred years ago, and palaeography, codicology, and art history have all moved on since then. In fact, a palaeographical examination of the various replies is of the greatest interest, and it is surprising that these important documents have not received more attention.

But let us return to the format: why a roll? Why not a mortuary codex or booklet? M. T. Clanchy has drawn attention to the nature of rolls and the problems surrounding their nomenclature and use, and he observes that "the roll was the most convenient format for conveying a message or letter in parchment."[34] He then goes on to discuss the same two mortuary rolls as are mentioned by Morrow, but adds that "despite the use of rolls for monastic obituaries, there was a prejudice against them," partly (perhaps) because of an association with Judaism, but certainly because they were not particularly convenient to use.[35] Indeed they are not. A letter is one thing, but the mortuary roll of Amphelisa is over thirty-seven feet long. If you were one of the last houses to sign it, you had to unroll some thirty-six feet of parchment, and that cannot be considered overwhelmingly convenient. So why the roll?

The reason, I would suggest, is that the roll represented monastic continuity. The nature of what Morrow rightly calls "the larger monastic community" unrolls—literally— before one's eyes. There is no page-break; there is no discontinuity. Entry is linked to entry as house is linked to house, and the mortuary roll may be seen as a physical symbol of the wide-ranging and interconnected Benedictine community. The Order unfolds, house by house, and the roll unrolled—all twelve yards or so—is a dramatic representation of the size and power of the Order it encapsulates. I may add at this point that in my own study of the books and libraries of medieval nuns, I should have placed more emphasis on the inscriptions in mortuary rolls in support of my call for a re-evaluation of the literacy of women religious in the Middle Ages.

That Abbess Eulalia could read and appreciate Anselm's prayers cannot be doubted. Nor was that any small achievement: Anselm's Latin can be convoluted. How many other members of her community could do the same thing is impossible to say. Rather more, probably, than we think, but Shaftesbury was a rich and noble house, and the education—or, more precisely, the possibility of education—of daughters of rich families was very different from the non-education of the young women who might have found their way to Lambley or Nunburnholme or Fosse or Grimsby or any other of a dozen small, poor, and politically insignificant nunneries. But this was also true of the men's houses. Too often we are presented with the black-and-white contrast of literate men as opposed to illiterate women, but an examination of the records of episcopal visitations reveals, in (too) many places, crass ignorance on the part of both parties.[36] Nor was it restricted to England and the Middle Ages. After his visitations of the French Cistercian abbey of Reigny (near Auxerre in northern Burgundy) in 1600 and 1608, the abbot of Clairvaux observed that many of the monks could not even understand the Mass, and instructed the prior of the house to explain it to them in French.[37]

There were also women who could write at Shaftesbury. The mortuary roll for Abbot Vitalis, happily available in facsimile,[38] has a well-written entry from the abbey, and there are no grounds whatever for ascribing that entry to a chaplain—save by prior assumption. Unfortunately, as Morrow says, the precise role of male clerics in women's houses before 1200 is unclear, and projecting backwards from later information (of which there is a good deal) is an untrustworthy occupation.

The Shaftesbury Psalter, with its prayers, its texts, its illuminations, its *mise en page*, its overall unity, is a great achievement, not just as a twelfth-century manuscript, but as a source of twelfth-century spirituality. But, like other liturgical/devotional material from the same period, it must be approached holistically. The two Anselmian prayers which are the subject of Morrow's study are important not only because of their early date and their testimony to a particular friendship, but also because, as Sister Benedicta Ward rightly says, they contain

> a unique combination of theological veracity and personal ardour that has value at any time. They are ultimately prayers that are meant to be prayed; that is, they are ways to come to God, preparations for that silence of soul which is prayer.[39]

And that, after all, was what the Benedictine life was all about.

Notes

1. Benedicta Ward, trans., *The Prayers and Meditations of St Anselm*, with a foreword by R. W. Southern (Harmondsworth: Penguin Books, 1973), 10–11, 19–20.

2. Ratherius of Verona, "*Exhortatio et preces,*" *Patrologia Latina* 136: 443–50. I find his first prayer before communion—445C–7B—every bit as moving as that of Anselm.

3. Ward, *Prayers and Meditations*, 30.

4. See Jean Leclercq, François Vandenbroucke, and Louis Bouyer, *The Spirituality of the Middle Ages* (London: Burns and Oates, 1968), 122, and the important articles cited there in notes 145–51.

5. F. S. Schmitt, ed., *Sancti Anselmi Opera Omnia* (1946; reprint, Stuttgart, 1984), 3:3.

6. For a brief account, see Leclercq et al., *Spirituality of the Middle Ages*, 62–67. There is an extensive literature on the subject.

7. The relevant citations can be found in ibid., 65–66.

8. Ward, *Prayers and Meditations*, 81–82.

9. David N. Bell, *What Nuns Read: Books and Libraries in Medieval English Nunneries* (Kalamazoo, Mich.: Cistercian Publications, 1995), 163–67.

10. See ibid., 41–42.

11. They are all listed in ibid., 164–65, nos. 2–3.

12. *La Trappe in England. Chronicles of an Unknown Monastery*, by A Religious of Holy Cross Abbey, Stapehill, Dorset [Mother Bernard Payne] (London: Burns, Oates, and Washbourne, 1937), 188.

13. See Giles Constable, *The Reformation of the Twelfth Century* (Cambridge: Cambridge University Press, 1996), 293.

14. *La Trappe in England*, 195 (with minor amendments).

15. David N. Bell, ed., *The Libraries of the Cistercians, Gilbertines and Premonstratensians* (London: British Library in Association with the British Academy, 1992), 34–82.

16. See ibid., 41.

17. See Richard Sharpe, *A Handlist of the Latin Writers of Great Britain and Ireland before 1540* (Turnhout: Brepols, 1997), 33, no. 76. Alan died sometime after 1212. For Thomas of Burton, who died in 1437, see ibid., 647, no. 1716.

18. For Elizabeth Shelford's Hours, see Bell, *What Nuns Read*, 163–64, no. 1.

19. *Regula S. Benedicti* 48.15–16; Bell, *What Nuns Read*, 41–42.

20. Ward, *Prayers and Meditations*, 36.

21. See Francis Wormald, *The Winchester Psalter* (London: Harvey Miller, 1973).

22. Claus M. Kauffmann, *Romanesque Manuscripts, 1066–1190* (London: Harvey Miller, 1975), 83, suggests Emma, but that is not certain.

23. See, for example, the collected papers in Margaret M. Manion and Bernard J. Muir, eds., *Medieval Texts and Images. Studies of Manuscripts from the Middle Ages* (Philadelphia: Harwood Academy Press, 1991), especially Vera F. Vines's "Reading Medieval Images: Two Miniatures in a Fifteenth-century Missal" (127–38). Vincent Gillespie speaks of "Medieval Hypertext" ("Medieval Hypertext: Image and Text from York Minster," in *Of the Making of Books. Medieval Manuscripts, Their Scribes and Readers. Essays presented to M. B. Parkes*, ed. Pamela R. Robinson and Rivkah Zim [Aldershot, England: Scolar Press, 1997], 206–29). Insightful comments may also be found in Miriam Gill's "The Role of Images in Monastic Education: The Evidence from Wall Painting in Late Medieval England," in *Medieval Monastic Education*, ed. George Ferzoco and Carolyn Muessig (Leicester: Leicester University Press, 2000), 117–35. One could now present an extensive bibliography on this important subject.

24. Fol. 15. See Kauffmann, *Romanesque Manuscripts*, p. 83 and Plate 133.

25. Published in Paris by Éditions du Cercle de la Librairie-Promodis.

26. Published by the University of Notre Dame Press in May 2001.

27. To read Maurice Mouillaud and Jean-François Tétu, *Le Journal quotidien: événement, mise en page, illustration, titres, citations, faire savoir, faire croire* (Lyon [c. 1989]), with manuscripts in mind is an illuminating experience.

28. See Michel Perrin, ed., *Rabani Mauri In Honorem Sanctae Crucis,* Corpus Christianorum Continuatio Mediaevalis 100 (Turnhout: Brepols, 1997), especially pp. CXVIII–CXX, 34–41.

29. The poem beginning "A broken altar, Lord, thy servant reares."

30. Neil R. Ker, "Copying an Exemplar: Two Manuscripts of Jerome on Habakkuk," in *Miscellanea codicologica F. Masai dicata MCMLXXIX,* ed. Pierre Cockshaw et al. (Gand: E. Story-Scientia S. P. R. L., 1979), 1:203–10.

31. London, BL, Egerton 2849; Bell, *What Nuns Read,* 128.

32. Cambridge, St John's College, 271; Bell, *What Nuns Read,* 142.

33. Charles E. Sayle, "The Mortuary Roll of the Abbess of Lillechurch, Kent," in *Proceedings of the Cambridge Antiquarian Society,* vol. 10 (1901–1904): 383–409. Lillechurch and Higham are different names for the same place.

34. M. T. Clanchy, *From Memory to Written Record: England 1066–1307,* 2nd ed. (Oxford: Oxford University Press, 1993), 139.

35. Ibid., 140–41.

36. See Bell, *What Nuns Read,* 64–65.

37. Auxerre, *Archives départementales de l'Yonne,* H.1568.

38. Léopold Delisle, *Rouleau mortuaire du b. Vital, abbé de Savigni, contenant 207 titres écrits en 1122–1123 dans différentes églises de France et d'Angleterre* (Paris, 1901).

39. Ward, *Prayers and Meditations,* 82.

THREE

Epistolae duorum amantium and the Ascription to Heloise and Abelard

C. STEPHEN JAEGER

A set of 113 love letters, abridged, copied, and entitled *Ex epistolis duorum amantium* by a Cistercian monk of Clairvaux, Johannes de Vepria, in the late fifteenth century, enjoyed total obscurity in the libraries of Clairvaux and Troyes until the German medieval Latinist Dieter Schaller noticed them in 1967 and passed to his student, Ewald Könsgen, the task of editing them. Könsgen's edition appeared with an extensive apparatus in 1974 with the title *Epistolae duorum amantium: Briefe Abaelards und Heloises?*[1] The small flame of Könsgen's subtitle flickered pale against the bonfire set under the corpus of personal and monastic writings of Abelard and Heloise two years before by John Benton, stoked again by Benton and Fiorella Prosperetti Ercoli in 1975, and at last all but extinguished in 1980 by the same man who had set it.[2] The reviews of Könsgen's edition left the same question mark in place that he had put there.[3] No one rushed in to remove it. Peter Dronke, the strongest defender of the authenticity of Heloise's personal and monastic letters, withheld judgment on a possible ascription of the *Epistolae* to the young Abelard and Heloise.[4]

In 1999 Constant Mews published a study of the letters confidently arguing that the collection indeed excerpts the authentic letters exchanged by Abelard and Heloise from the early years of their love affair, c. 1115–1117.[5] Mews himself and his publisher considered his studies conclusive and announced them as such.[6] Mews's arguments have been accepted by John O. Ward and Neville Chiavaroli (Mews's co-translator) and shored up in a dense study of rhetorical aspects of the *Epistolae*.[7]

A great deal remains to be learned about these letters and their authors from a close reading and comparison with other comparable Latin love letters. This study explores the character of the two authors, their literary styles, and their educational backgrounds. The results strengthen the ascription to Heloise and Abelard and point out what is gained for understanding the education of the young Heloise when the letters of the woman are recognized as products of her pen. I begin by summarizing some of the information that is to be gleaned about the writers and the context of their letters.

There is a lack of specifics that is typical of medieval love letters.[8] Though they may once have teemed with facts and details that would have allowed us to identify their writers beyond question, Johannes de Vepria was compiling a collection of model letters, and he probably omitted precisely passages with time- and place-bound contents. We can get some idea because he marked his own elisions. For instance, the woman writes (M 45)[9] that she would far rather discuss in person "all that I now convey by letter." An elision mark follows, after which the text resumes with generalities.[10] "All that I now convey" is lost, but we can still infer some details of the identities and circumstances of the writers as they emerge from the text of the letters:

1. They live in a city (*urbs nostra*)[11] in France, possibly Paris. He praises her as "distinguished in our city." He calls her "Gem of all Gaul" (*gemma tocius Gallie*), which, Könsgen argues, means Francia, the Île de France.[12] The "pigheadedness of the French" (*cervicositas Francigenarum*) yields to him,[13] she claims, and may indicate by the formulation that the man is not himself French.[14]

2. The man is a teacher so famous that not only do the stiff-necked French yield to him, but "the haughtiness of all the world rises in respect before him."[15] In a later letter the woman foresees the very mountaintops bowing down before him as part of God's own plan.[16] The woman is his adoring student. Her greatest joys have flowed to her through the wealth of his philosophy.[17] She might often have despaired of her own studies, if the "magisterial skill" of his instruction had not recalled her to the path.[18] As a result of some grand success against a rival, the man displaces his predecessor as *magister*, and crowds of students bask in his brightening light.[19]

3. The woman clearly is not just his student, but exceptional, indeed, famous or at least widely known and admired in her own right. He addresses her as "alone among the girls of our age as a disciple of philosophy, the only one on whom fortune has bestowed all the gifts of the manifold virtues, the only attractive one, the only gracious one. . . ."[20] Shortly after this salutation he launches into praise of her talent: "I am astonished at your genius. . . . Your mind, your eloquent speech have begun to grow, beyond the custom of your age and your sex,

to virile strength."[21] Because of her talents and virtues, "all people magnify you above all others, they raise you up to the heights, so that from there you can shine forth like a lamp and be revered by all."[22] He confesses that he is not her equal, because she surpasses him in the very things in which he ought to excel. And later he claims that he would have no eloquence were it not for her.[23]

4. Because of the man's position the love affair makes them vulnerable. They are beset by envy and intrigues; they are at pains from beginning to end to ward off dangers,[24] which at various points shake their relationship.

Some other features of the letters give us a closer fix on the character of the collection. One of the clear and still unquestioned findings of Könsgen is that the letters were actually written by two people, who remain throughout the correspondence the same *mulier* and *vir,* and that the letters were actually exchanged. That is, they were not the product of a single author creating a fictional romance as, say, a school exercise or a set of sample letters.[25] Könsgen demonstrates this from consistent differences in the salutations, the vocabulary, and the style of the two, which could not be the result of a conscious attempt of a single author to distinguish the man's from the woman's letters and which prove they could not have been written originally as exemplary letters, though Johannes de Vepria put them to that use.

The letters contain a number of comments which remain obscure to the reader but clearly were intelligible to the recipient. This feature of the collection, no less than their dual authorship, seems to me to rule out the possibility of a literary fiction, an epistolary novel, a collection of letters composed as pattern letters or as a reminiscence of the love affair of Abelard and Heloise. I will quote these private references extensively here, tedious as that might be, since their frequency is good evidence of the private character of some of the communications:

- V 47 consists of a greeting, a farewell, and sandwiched between them the heated lines: "Ill-fated night, hateful sleep, cursed sloth of mine!"[26] The exclamation refers to nothing detectable in the letters which precede, and there are no elision marks.
- V 41: Likewise, a greeting, a farewell, and the statement, "I have no guidance for you; do what you will"[27]—unexplained by the context, clearly answering a request from the woman that does not appear in the preceding letters.
- V 54: After an elision mark, at the end of a longer letter: "Let those whom we cannot keep with us depart; that will be a good plan."[28] Likewise, no context.
- V 59: "A pressing matter hindered me and set its left foot against my desire. I am guilty; I forced you to sin."[29] Apart from the greeting, this is the entire letter; there is no farewell.

- V 67: (No salutation, the letter begins with leave-taking.) "Farewell my sweetest woman, and give your beloved your permission."[30] The reason for the requested permission is unexplained.
- In V 75 the man apologizes (after an elision by de Vepria) for a wounding remark: "O foolish promise, O words too rash and indiscreet."[31] Nothing in the preceding letters prepares for it, and nothing remaining in V 75 after de Vepria's edit suggests what the remark may have been.
- M 84: "I shall repay you for your prologue which you composed for me. . . ." Nothing explains what this "prologue" might have been.[32]

These passages are inconsistent with a claim of narrative coherence or display composition. Nor are they consistent with any evident editorial policy of de Vepria. Some follow elisions, some are the entire communication of the letter, but others are embedded in longer letters. Also none of these remarks has to do with the fluctuations of the love affair; they are not poses and postures of lovers struck in a single, isolated moment. (There are many such passages in the letters which could be construed as display pieces, though without context.) The remarks quoted above are all directed to events and circumstances of everyday life which certainly would never have been conceived by an author or composer of dictamenal letters and would have been eliminated at once by an editor. What they show clearly is that another frame of reference intrudes into that of the epistolary "narrative": the experiences of the writers. The only intended reader is the recipient, and he or she is fully informed about what needs forgiveness, what advice is referred to, what friends or enemies are to depart, what prologue is to be repaid. The statements show the letters—at the minimum, these parts of them—as private communications, not fictional narratives or coherently composed pattern letters.[33]

On the dating of the letters, Könsgen places them tentatively in the early twelfth century on the basis of themes and motifs popular in that period.[34] The letters offer no straightforward ground for dating, and Kindermann has challenged Könsgen's arguments for a dating in the twelfth century.[35] However, Constant Mews argues in a recent article that the use of rhyme-prose and cursus locates them in the early twelfth century.[36] Also Ward and Chiavaroli place them convincingly, first, within a crux in the development of rhetoric and school training which occurred in the early twelfth century, and, second, within a trend in the representation of love and friendship in the late eleventh and early twelfth century.[37] I will add some observations to their comments later.

It should be stressed that the letters are remarkable and unique documents, in their revelation of personality, in their poetic and prose styles, and in the apparent closeness to experience. It is true, as both Könsgen and Dronke fretted in pondering the question of authorship, that other exchanges of love letters and poems between masters and female students, or clerics and nuns, offer parallels to the cast of characters of the *Epistolae*.

There are for instance the love letter/poems either written or collected by Marbod of Rennes at the end of the eleventh century; the exchange of love letter/poems between Baudri of Bourgueil and various learned nuns at the turn of the eleventh to the twelfth century (and in one case a letter which purports to be a love letter answering Baudri's); the Regensburg Love Songs from c. 1106; or the Tegernsee love letters compiled as instructional texts in *ars dictaminis* in the later twelfth century.[38] A comparative reading sets our letters clearly apart. Furthermore, their scope is unique among medieval letters and letter collections: a personal correspondence sustained over 113 letters. Finally, the development of character and "narrative" observable in the corpus of letters also distinguishes them from any other medieval love letters.

In the course of the letters a "story" of the love affair emerges in its general lines, though not in detail. They were exchanged over the course of one year at least, perhaps two. Their arrangement can be sequential, one letter often answering the previous directly; situations are addressed, developed, resolved. But many are not locatable in a sequence of events or of topics treated. Since we have no idea what kind of source Johannes de Vepria worked from,[39] there is no way of knowing whether all the letters and poems are in the sequence of his source. Nonetheless in the *Epistolae* we can follow the course of a relationship, watch its waxing and waning.

The man is initially drawn to the woman by her beauty, her nobility, her fine manners, and especially her learning: "I am amazed at your genius. . . . I chose you among many thousands because of your countless virtues. . . . Your mind, your eloquent speech. . . ."[40] He also finds in her comfort and consolation for the tribulations of his public life:

> I chose you . . . for no other benefit than that I might find rest in you, or that you might be comfort for all my miseries, so that your beauty alone of all good things in the world might restore me and make me forget all sorrows. You are my fill when hungry, my refreshment when thirsty, my rest when weary, my warmth when cold . . . indeed in all my intemperance, you are my most wholesome and true temperance.[41]

She is attracted by his good looks and his poetry: "Glory of young men, companion of poets, how handsome you are. . . ."[42] Overwhelmed by his erudition and his high standing, she subjects herself completely to his will and his instruction. But their love affair is clandestine and dangerous. It begins with passion, abandon, high intensity—and with bravado directed towards enemies—but is soon troubled, hindered, eventually nearly destroyed, by dangers and complications suffered by both the man and the woman. These seem largely to consist in discovery and exposure. Some unexplained crisis leads to the woman's decisively ending their writings and their relationship in *Ep.* 60.

She feels utterly betrayed and abandoned; she heaps reproaches on him. There follows an apparent reconciliation, but the woman's later letters often reproach him for his coldness and disloyalty. His later letters turn cool and even banal, compared with the earlier.[43] Towards the end of the correspondence, they live closer together than before; their closeness makes visits possible and salutations in their letters unnecessary.[44] The mood changes again. Their final seventeen letters are among the warmest in the collection. Whatever the reason for the correspondence breaking off with the man's poem V 113, it is not revealed in these letters.[45] Such is the course of this love as the sparse indications in the letters allow us to reconstruct it.

One of the most striking features of the correspondence is that two distinct personalities emerge. A prominent feature of the man is his rashness and impulsiveness. He cannot contain himself, as he himself puts it: "se dilectus tuus continere non potuit [. . .]" (V 6, p. 192); "me continere non potui [. . .]" (V 17, p. 200). She evidently is aware of this fault and corrects it mildly: "remember that thoughtful delay is better than imprudent haste";[46] and again more brusquely: "No one ought to live and prosper for the good who does not know how to love and to govern his love affairs."[47] But while his caution may grow, his headlong impetuosity continues from beginning to end. He begs her to come to him, otherwise he'll wither, and he wants her to know how he seethes with desire: "Ask the messenger what I did after I wrote this letter. On the spot I assuredly threw myself onto the bed out of impatience. Farewell." The gesture is that of a spoiled child, the attention he calls to it that of a vain and self-aware peacock.[48]

"Impatience" is another term he applies to himself: he desires her "with an impatience such as can scarcely be expressed or believed."[49] Also prominent is "rashness" (*preceps*).[50] Closely related to this self-characterization is his tendency to berate his own weakness and stupidity. He is grateful that she has forgiven him for "all the wrongs which I, stupidly and thoughtlessly and with a mind too impetuous and too weak to resist my sorrows, inflicted on my most beloved without any consideration."[51] He berates himself for a broken promise: "So foolish a promise, words too impetuous and ill considered, a remark made by one apparently out of his mind or drunk."[52] Again he begs her forgiveness for words that angered her: it was impulse, not reason that made him speak thus.[53] Having apparently lost her for good, he berates and pities himself: "Nothing is more serious than a fool favored by fortune. . . . I'm paying the price for my stupidity."[54] His final poem contains a telling line: "Forgive me what I've said. I do not love patiently."[55] The fact that the line is a quotation of *Heroides* 19.4, Hero to Leander, gives depth and resonance, especially in view of the fact that the impatience of those two lovers cost them their lives.

Rash impulsiveness may be a fool's vice, but it is also that of a man with an overswollen ego. It is hard to put any other construction on exclamations like the following: "You ought not to wonder if twisted jealousy turns its eyes towards a friendship so distinguished and so harmonious as ours."[56] "I believe and confidently assert that there is no mortal, no relative, no friend whom you would prefer to me, or to speak more boldly, whom you would compare with me."[57] "Farewell, and make sure that you compare no mortal with me."[58] "Radiant be your night, let nothing be lacking besides me / But lacking me, my lovely, think that you lack everything."[59] "Never has this glory befallen any other woman that she be worthy of my song."[60]

While rash, impatient, and vain, he is also a famous and successful teacher—not a good combination, especially in light of the lurking envy and the snares that rivals clearly are laying for him. As early as *Ep.* 28 the danger of their relationship becomes apparent, and the man faces it with the headlong rashness typical of him:

> Let's give to those who envy us plenty of cause for it! May they slowly shrivel up at the thought of our overflowing wealth. Put the very sea between us, and it could not separate us! I shall always love you. . . . Therefore let them backbite, let them drag us down, let them gnaw, let them waste away inside, let our happiness cause them bitterness; you will still be my life. . . .[61]

Bold words, but bluster, as it turns out. The pose, "Let's really give them something to envy!" requires a certain mindset, and it would seem to be consonant with the way Abelard described his youthful foolishness in the *Historia calamitatum:* "I began to think myself the only philosopher in the world with nothing to fear from anyone. And so I yielded to the lusts of the flesh."[62] The man who said, "Let them drag us down!" likewise must have considered himself invulnerable, or pretended to to impress his lover. It seems probable that this brusk challenge to the envious was provoked by some event, a discovery of the affair perhaps. In any case the woman replies immediately in fear: "Since I've thrown all else to the winds, I take refuge under your wings. . . . I can scarcely utter these sad words: Farewell."[63]

If these hints might make us concerned about the good judgment of this academic adventurer, his hyperbole in swearing eternal love also puts his firmness as a lover somewhat in question: "Let them place the very sea between us; it will not separate us. I will always love you";[64] "If I crossed the sea . . . ; if I climbed the Alps in bitterest cold, or risked my life searching for you in the midst of fire, I'd count all this as nothing."[65]

Yet hardly have danger and hindrances smaller than fire, sea, and mountains risen up, when caution, coldness, and distance come over him. He suggests more letters and less visits because "the envy of evil men" prevents them from being together (V 54, p. 236). Three letters later she complains about not having enjoyed *intima confabulacio* with him for a long time (M 57, p. 238); a chill enters her tone, and in M 60 she breaks off the correspondence, feeling deceived and betrayed. Her next letter (M 62), though still complaining of his neglect, offers a reconciliation and calls for happier tones in their writings, a plea she herself answers in M 66, a jubilant celebration of the man's victory over a rival. Her complaints of neglect and betrayal resume in M 69. The only cause for his wavering in his love appears to be external threats. Nowhere is it suggested in the letters that another woman is behind what she calls his "infidelity" (*infidelitas*), though in a string of references to the *Heroides* the woman once compares herself to the nymph Oenone abandoned by Paris for Helen of Troy (M 45). What is clear is that discovery and the threat of discovery took the edge off his boldness; his career outweighed his love when put to the test.[66] He is a man who overreaches himself, or at least whose bravery reveals itself as bravado in a crisis. Like the cowardly lion he can strut and preen himself on his courage until danger arises; and like the player queen in *Hamlet*, his seething, volcanic claims of loyalty prove empty when tested. It seems likely that he took in his horns and claws to protect his blossoming career. Whatever the cause and the implications for his character, we know that his words and actions wounded his lover deeply and nearly destroyed the relationship.

The man alternates in his moods between bravado and self-deprecation, and this seems to me consistent with a hot-headed and egotistical character who does not hold up well in critical situations. His own words spoken when he thought he was losing her are a motto for his posture in this affair: "Nichil insipiente fortunato gravius est" (V 106, p. 282): "There's nothing more serious than a fool favored by fortune."

Against this we can set as the woman's epigraph her own words, "Non sum harundo vento agitata" (M 88, p. 270): "I'm no reed shaken by the wind." Her firmness in facing dangers and suffering is in stark contrast to his vacillation: "Whether you want it or not, in my heart I shall remain loyal to you."[67] Her protestations of loyalty increase as the crises in the affair multiply, and this is perhaps the best indicator of how seriously we can take her claim. Even if his love fails, she says, hers is permanent: "Whether you want it or not, you are and always will be mine; never will my vow to you be changed, nor will I turn my mind from you."[68] She contrasts his vacillations with her constancy, clearly to stiffen his backbone, but at the same time suggesting that she did indeed maintain firmness in facing external dangers when he did not: "never can the perfect devotion of my love be extinguished by any troubles that arise."[69] "No external event will avail to obliterate the memory of you, which I have bound to my heart by a golden chain."[70] "I shall remain faithful to you, stable, unchangeable, and unwavering. . . . I would never leave you unless compelled to and driven out by force. I am no reed shaken by the wind. Nor shall any tribulation or allurement take me from you."[71] The salutation of a late letter reads, "To [him] the ship in danger, lacking the anchor of loyalty, she whom the winds that blow your infidelity do not move."[72]

While she regularly accuses him of breaking faith, he never accuses her of it. One passage suggests that she recognized constancy as a trait of her own character, not a momentary posture brought on by circumstance: "I give you the most precious thing I own: myself namely, firm in loyalty and affection, stable in love, and never wavering."[73] This shows her many vows of loyalty-come-what-may as not just a rebuke to her weak-kneed lover, but also an assertion of what she values most ("the most precious thing I own") in herself.

She also shows consistently, from her earliest to her last letters, a tendency to abase herself before the man, mainly in the context of studies, but not only. She considers herself far beneath him, and apologizes for her wretched, incapable genius, so threadbare in comparison with his brilliance:

> Although I wanted to write back to you, the magnitude of the task, being beyond my powers, drove me back. . . . The burning feeling of my spirit longed to do so, but the weakness of my dried-up talent refused.[74]

> When I too reflect in my mind's eye what love is and what it can do, given the similarity of our characters and our studies . . . my thoughts bring me to repay your love with my own and to obey you in all things.[75]

> It is very rash of me to send studied phrases to you, because even someone perfectly learned . . . would not be capable of painting a portrait of eloquence florid enough to justly deserve being seen by so great a teacher—certainly not I who am hardly apt for trifles. . . .[76]

> To you through whose marks of nobility the light of wisdom shines forth miraculously . . . she who is totally barren of skill.[77]

These are formulas of humility, topoi, and as such open to the Curtian fallacy that they mean nothing. But they represent at least a consistent characterization of the woman. She not only places herself beneath him, but also vows complete obedience and self-subjection:[78] "my thoughts bring me to repay your love with my own and to obey you in all things."[79] "Since I've thrown all else to the winds, I take refuge beneath your wings; I submit in all things wholeheartedly to your authority."[80] "I send you this unadorned letter as proof of how devotedly I submit myself to your instructions in all matters."[81]

Now it is in odd contrast with these protestations that the woman's style in both prose and poetry is clearly and demonstrably more learned, more elegant, more classical, more complex, and more richly allusive than that of the man. This is one of the insights that we can book on the side of fact in judging this dossier. The woman is the more versatile stylist and shows greater literary learning than the man. The man himself agrees: "I am inferior to you in every way, because you surpass me even where I seemed to surpass you. Your genius, your eloquence, have begun to grow beyond the custom of your years and sex, to virile strength."[82] While this may be the urge stirring in every lover's breast to submit to his beloved as the instrument of some higher power to which he is in thrall (so, at least, says Goethe in the "Marienbad Elegy"), still, his judgment of his own inferiority in *facundia* also corresponds with what we can learn from stylistic analysis of the letters.[83]

The differences in their poetic styles are prominent and easily locatable. Both are accomplished verse makers. While both quote classical and biblical works extensively,[84] hers not only quote widely, but build on formal elements at home in the learned traditions of cathedral schools and royal courts. This is especially clear in her acclamation hymn (M 66), which deserves a longer analysis.

The poem is her most polished and elaborate. It congratulates her lover on some great success as *doctor* and *magister*. It is composed with the manneristic formality of Carolingian panegyric, still alive in Germany and France in the eleventh century, to which it adds a touch of preciosity consistent with the mannerist style of eleventh-century school poetry.[85] She invokes Clio to assist her undertaking with a "happy omen" (*omine felici*); she calls on all musical instruments to sound forth with the auspicious breezes of Jove. Her lover's victory is evoked in the image of sunlight chasing away the dark:

> Lo day approaches and night seeks an escape;
> Lo day has arrived and night withdraws in confusion.
> Behold how the throng of the clergy shines radiant in the light of the master,
> And the splendor of the doctor drives out the night of his predecessor.[86]

The poetess then ushers in the muses to sing individual acclaims: Clio: "Hail Flower of the clergy forever!" Urania: "Let him live magnified by virtues!" While Urania "ornaments" him with "manners" (*mores*), Polyhymnia (Polimnia) is to give him honor. Erato is to wish him bodily happiness in this world, but also joy in the world to follow. Finally all the muses sing in unison: "Salve, vive, vige!"

Any educated member of the clergy will have recognized the type of the acclamation hymn,[87] sung in varying voices or choruses on occasions like coronations, the inauguration of a bishop, the arrival of a king or bishop in a town, or simply on any celebratory occasion, like the birth of a child. They are formulated insistently in the imperative or optative, calling down divine blessings.[88] They ordinarily involve triadic hails, such as "feliciter, feliciter, feliciter"; or "Vincas, valeas! Multis annis imperes!" or "Omnes cantemus: multis feliciter annis / Rex vivat, valeat, vincat. . . ."[89] The resonance with the choric hails of the muses at the end of M 66 is evident: "Salve, vive, vige!" The imperial, ceremonial forms amalgamated comfortably with panegyric,[90] which made the form available for a wide variety of occasions and personalities quite apart from the arrival of the emperor.

A poem with intent, formal structure, and classicistic frame similar to M 66 is Wipo's "Tetralogus."[91] The chaplain of Henry III composed this poem for the German emperor in 1040. The four voices of this "tetralogue" are the Poet himself, the Muses, the Law, and Grace. The poet begins, invokes the muses, and asks them to sing the praises of Henry; he, Wipo, will write down what they dictate. The muses then sing blessings and praise. Henry rules as the "friend of virtues," second only to Christ. There are sixteen lines of hails in the form, "Rex Heinrice, Deo regum carissimus esto!" They who gave words to Virgil and Ovid (i.e., the muses) will arrange praise through all times for Henry. Great honors are due to him, and after this life, "a portion of heaven." (Cf. M 66, 18–20: "Dic et nunc Erato: 'felix sit corpore mundo. / Felix sit mundo sed gaudens postque secundo / Quo sibimet grati gaudent sine fine beati.'")[92] A wise creator sought out Henry as the vessel of virtues: "Forma, genus, probitas concordant omnia regi." More hails: "Salve, certa quies populorum . . . / Salve, pax orbis. . . ."

Serlo of Bayeux, a Norman poet active from the late eleventh to the early twelfth century, with ties to the poetesses of Le Ronceray, wrote a poem of congratulation to his patron, Bishop Odo of Bayeux, on the occasion of his release in 1087 from the imprisonment which his half-brother, William the Conqueror, had imposed on him five years previous.[93] It is close to M 66 in its imagery. The poem begins with the wish that Odo will join the citizens of heaven when this life has reached its term. Odo now restores light to a happy world and commands the clouds of sadness to depart. "The new sun has risen, the ancient horror has flowed [sic: *fluxit*] from the sky; black night departs, and serene light returns. . . . Upon your arrival, O father, the enemy and the black angel flees. Those two yield, driven out by your strength. . . . The mountains rejoice, the forests too, the rivers and fountains; the chorus sings in harmony. Let the voice of the poets ring out, celebrating this blessed father, let the lyre sound forth with miraculous art, singing of this man":[94]

Sol novus illuxit, vetus horror ab aere fluxit,
  Nox nigra discedit, luxque serena redit . . .
Te veniente pater, fugit hostis et angelus ater;
  Cedunt ista duo pulsa vigore tuo . . .
Exultant montes, silvae quoque, flumina, fontes,
  Tanto pastori concinat ordo chori.
Vox resonet vatum, patrem celebrando beatum,
  Huncque canens mira personet arte lyra.

The milieux of these two poems are significant: one from imperial circles, the second from a cathedral canon. It is clear that the author of the poem in *Ep.* 66 commands the neo-classical idiom of the humanist poetic traditions of German and French cathedral schools. The poem in M 66, "Omine felici," is quite at home in these traditions, the only remarkable thing being that this poetic celebration of a promotion in the schools is, as far as we can tell, purely private. In any case, it is a display of considerable mastery of topoi widely practiced in humanistic Latin poetry of celebration in the early twelfth century and before. Another poem of praise by the woman (M 73) is similarly based on earlier panegyric conventions still current in Germany and France in the eleventh century.[95]

In a song of lament (M 69), she sends the complaint of an abandoned lover to the man in the conceit, borrowed from Ovid's "Tristia" and popular in Carolingian times, that she issues instructions to her letter/poem telling it what it should say to the recipient. In short the woman's taste in composition and form is distinct and locatable.

The man's poems are in contrast yeomanly products of verse making; the sentiments are often compelling and moving. They are more original, i.e., not governed by learned traditions alive in contemporary culture. They show no traces of the manneristic learned verse of the old-style cathedral schools. The language of V tends to be plain and the metaphors repetitive. There are enough sun and stars images to sate even readers very patient with trite metaphors. Her language tends to be inventive and original,[96] her metaphors ingenious. His are all love poems (20, 38a, 38c, 87, 108, 113); she has two love poems (38b, 82); the others are poems of celebration (66), praise (73), and complaint (69). He makes no use of the kind of learned forms which she commands. His poem 38c hovers between routine and banal:

> Vite causa mei, tu clemens esto fideli
> Cuncta mee vite quoniam spes permanet in te.
> Diligo te tantum non possum dicere quantum
> Hec michi lux nox est, sine te michi vivere mors est
> Sic valeas vivas sic cuncta nocentia vincas,
> Ut volo ceu posco ceu totis viribus opto.

> You who are my reason for living, be kind to me who am faithful.
> Since all my life's hope resides in you.
> I love you so much, I cannot say how much.
> This daylight is night to me, and to live without you is death.
> Thus thrive, live, thus conquer all harm,
> As I wish or rather demand or rather desire with all my might.

A line like "Diligo te tantum non possum dicere quantum" may thrill a girl by its sentiment, but surely not by its form. It is the work of a schoolboy or apprentice poet, a line carpentered with all the sophistication of two sticks nailed together. It vies for ordinariness with the final line with its string of intensifying verbs: "ut volo ceu posco ceu totis viribus opto." The man's poems never call on techniques of assonance and musical language other than the internal rhyme of leonine hexameters.[97] By contrast, consider the woman's lines (M 82, p. 262):

> Suppositi terre lapides velut igne liquescunt
> Cum quibus imposita liquitur igne pyra
> Sic nostrum late corpus vanescit amore [. . .]

> Stones placed on the earth turn molten as though ignited
> When a pyre set over them is consumed in flames.
> Thus also our body is wholly consumed in love. . . .

Hers are elegiac couplets, certainly a common meter in the eleventh and twelfth centuries, but for modern ears more elegant than the slightly wooden leonine hexameters. The lines are, however, clearly more ornate and mannered. The sound repetitions create a rich lyricism and internal tension (*l*apides-*l*iquescunt; liqu*e*scunt-*c*um *qu*ibus-liq*ui*tur; lique*sc*unt-*sic* no*str*um-vane*sc*it) for which one searches in vain in his lines. Also the sophistication of the metaphor is evident as soon as one tries to puzzle out its logic.[98] It suggests a physical union so complete and ecstatic that the single body into which two are transformed vanishes and is scattered abroad (*late vanescit*) like ashes in the wind. The "flames of love" may be a trite metaphor, but the idea of fusion, consumption, and dispersion is a sophisticated variation on it.

Heloise admired the poetic skill of Peter Abelard, and the woman of the *Epistolae* admired that of her lover. If a very different kind of poetic talent is apparent in the man's verses, it may be that the woman (and Heloise) responded positively to a plainer style, less overladen, less weighted by learned freight, than her own. Such a taste in poetic style would correspond to a trend in which the mannerism of school poetry gave way to a new naturalism around the turn of the eleventh to the twelfth century.[99] What appears to us (to me at least) as the pitter-pattery quality of lines like "Diligo te tantum, non possum dicere quantum," may have struck some readers in the twelfth century, cloyed with the baroque excesses of a poetry modeled on Martianus Capella, as a new and refreshing naiveté, as in the folk-song simplicity of Goethe's "O Maedchen, Maedchen, wie liebe ich dich, / Wie blinkt dein Auge, wie liebst du mich!" after the overladen and empty conventionality of early eighteenth-century anacreontic love poetry. But whatever aesthetic judgment any reader may bring to bear on the poems of M and V, the fact of their distinctness of style and learnedness remains. They are from two different cultural realms.

It is in their prose, however, where the stylistic difference between the two shows most clearly. Here too she adapts more sophisticated forms than he does. For instance, she constructs imaginary dialogues modeled on Boethius. In one passage her "emotions" (*animi affectus*) and her "genius" (*ingenium*) hold speeches; the two personifications give her conflicting advice (M 23, pp. 204–206). In another an allegorical woman, presumably Lady Philosophy, makes reproaches to her; she responds, but her response is not transmitted (M 107, p. 282). There is nothing comparable in the man's letters.

His are scholastic; hers are rhetorical. There are few passages with rhyme and rhythm in the man's letters; there are many in the woman's. Compare this passage from her Letter 84:

> te solum dilexi, diligendo quesivi, querendo inveni, inveniendo amavi, amando optavi, optando omnibus in corde meo preposui [. . . .] Velis, nolis, semper meus es et eris, nunquam erga te meum mutatur votum neque a te animum abstraho totum. In te quod quesivi habeo, quod optavi teneo, quod amavi amplexata sum [. . . .]

with this from his answer, Letter 85: "Si verba dilecti tui notare perspicaciter velis, aperte notare potes dulcissima quod [. . .] " (If you will note carefully the words of your beloved, you can clearly note, O sweetest one, that . . .). The repetition, *notare–notare*, is awkwardness, not rhetoric. It shows how little the man is concerned with elegance and ornament of language. Or take this bit of learned instruction by the man, which combines the language of dialectics (the universals controversy) with a definition of Love:[100]

> Est igitur amor vis quedam anime non per se existens [. . .] et cum altero idem effici volens ut de duabus diversis voluntatibus unum quid indifferenter efficiatur. . . . Scias quia licet res universalis sit amor, ita tamen in angustum contractus est ut [. . . .] (V 24, p. 208)

> Love, then, is a certain force of the soul which does not exist in itself. . . . It wants to be made identical with the other so that from two diverse wills a non-differential reification [*unum quid indifferenter*] results.[101]

The man's conscious striving for dialectical panache is especially evident comparing a line of his definition with its Ciceronian source: *De amicitia* 81: "ut efficiat paene unum ex duobus"; M 24: "ut de duabus diversis voluntatibus unum quid indifferenter efficiatur." Both sentences say the same thing; the first is elegant, the second heavy (*unum quid indifferenter* is scholar's argot; cf. the plainness of the Ciceronian *unum ex duobus*). While the woman also tries her hand at professorial jargon,[102] she strives regularly for rhetorical effect.[103] Her lines are richly overladen with allusions and quotations;[104] and while the man is prone to adapt classical authors, he avoids the woman's more showy allusiveness.[105]

These stylistic differences are consonant with another distinction between the two writers: their ethical vocabulary. She speaks the language of the old cathedral school learning.[106] Her ethical language *and her style* are both clearly locatable in the context of the humanistic curriculum which was still practiced in the old-fashioned schools of France and Germany in the eleventh and early twelfth century, but which was swiftly losing in competition with the newer, more fashionable schools of dialectic in Paris. John O. Ward placed his rhetorical studies of the *Epistolae* in this educational crux, and a look at the woman's ethical vocabulary adds weight to his observation. This is to my mind the strongest argument for the dating of the *Epistolae* in the early twelfth century. She praises her lover as "tantus magister, magister moribus, magister virtutibus" (M 49). This is praise that was highly regarded and crucial to the conception of education in the eleventh century,[107] which combined "letters and manners," *litterae et mores.*[108] But the new Paris masters of the twelfth century would have taken such praise as assigning them to the old school. If for instance I were to praise my teacher as a truly great positivist and an outstanding member of the Historical School, it would be fine praise in a certain context of the history of methodology. But if the audience were deconstructionists, postmodernists, and new historians, the praise might understandably be taken as mockery. In fact given the new contentiousness of the Paris schools, in which this man may well have participated, "master of manners and virtues" had to be an ill-fitting term. Certainly Peter Abelard might have felt the term ill-suited him. It is worth mentioning that she does not say *magister morum,* which implies what he teaches, a curriculum; *magister moribus* says that because of, or in respect to, his *mores* he is a master. This term and others the woman uses fell out of fashion in the schools in the course of the twelfth century, disappeared altogether in the thirteenth and fourteenth, and reappeared in Renaissance humanism.[109]

The ornate language of cathedral school ethics is abundant in her letters. In her hymn of laud to the successful *magister,* she appeals to the Muse Urania, "Vivat virtutibus auctus." And to Polyhymnia: "Moribus hunc ornes et honore" (M 66, p. 246). She writes to him in a later letter: "I wish you to be well, clothed with the beauty of the virtues, girt about with the gems of Sophia, endowed with decorousness of manners, decorated with the ornament of all composedness."[110] Again, straight out of the cathedral schools, truly old hat in the new Parisian schools. The old humanistic curriculum in "letters and manners" cultivated an ideal of the eloquent, well-mannered man, elegant and composed in appearance and bearing, sweet-flowing in speech. It represents a renewal or continuation of ideals of the orator's education from Antiquity and adapted an ethical vocabulary enriched with the traditions of late Latin and Carolingian panegyric. Like these traditions, it cultivated an ideal of the beautiful appearance as a visible manifestation of inner virtues (Greek, *kalos kai agathos,* Latin, *decor*). The woman states this ideal in praising her lover: "Rarely do we find anyone on these shifting seas so composed in his good fortune, so perfect in virtue, whose body does not show some flaw as a source of deep embarrassment, except you and you alone who through all things and in all things remain virtuous."[111] The idea is that virtue registers along the whole range of his being from his body to his mind.

The man's use of this vocabulary is infrequent, pale, far less locatable in a specific context. Her "probity and merits," he says, give him inexhaustible matter to praise (V 14, p. 198); he has chosen her from many thousands for her virtues, among which he includes *ingenium,* eloquence, humility, affability, dignity, and temperance (V 50, p. 232), a routine listing of commonplace virtues, as one might expect for a new master of philosophy called upon to use the language of the virtues but whose interests are not in traditional rhetoric and ethics. The passages lack any overlay of classical and patristic metaphors of virtues as ornamentation (clothed, girded, ornamented, gems of virtue or wisdom), in which the woman's language is rich.

We can conclude (with Ward and Chiavaroli) from the style and the ethical language of the two that the woman's education is that of the humanistic cathedral schools, but we can also say more generally, of the learned Christian traditions richly intermixed with the language and concepts of classical Latin learning. Given her skill in poetry, she would seem well placed among the women who emerge into short-lived poetic fame at the end of the eleventh century.[112] Ward and Chiavaroli, accepting the identification of M with Heloise, take Heloise's move from Argenteuil to Paris as a move between two phases of European education—old humanism and early scholasticism. The results for Heloise, they argue, were tragedy both in love and learning. The latter consists in the failure of an older mode of thought in its confrontation with the new.[113] But in identifying the context for the learning of the young Heloise, an important avenue of study opens. Michael Clanchy suggested plausibly that Heloise's mastery of pagan philosophy and literature had an important influence on Abelard.[114] We know that Heloise's style, learning, and consequent fame did not come from Abelard, but were acquired prior to her move to Paris.[115] If the woman correspondent of the *Epistolae duorum amantium* is indeed Heloise, then we have in these letters an extraordinary wealth of material on the style, thought, and education of the young scholar-philosopher-poetess. Constant Mews has marked out some directions in which the study of Heloise in her pre-Abelard phase at Argenteuil can lead,[116] and while it may be possible to identify some of the works which established the fame of the young Heloise, the educational context from which her works arose is an equally promising subject. If the "M" of the *Epistolae* was not Heloise, then we have nonetheless a priceless set of writings from a woman educated in the old-style humanism of the turn of the century.

Closely related to the intellectual/literary divide separating the two lovers is the difference in the way they talk about love: the woman is a Ciceronian/Christian; the man Ovidian, and while that trenchant formulation overrides an occasional blending of the two great authorities on love,[117] it holds true for the critical passages on love. The two lovers philosophize on the subject. "You often ask me what love is," he writes. Then follows his definition. Love is "a force of the soul." It has no existence in itself. That is, it is not a "universal" in the Realist sense of a thing existing outside of those who experience it. It flows over into the beloved constantly "with appetite and desire"; it wants otherness transformed into sameness "so that from two different wills a single thing without distinction is created."[118] While the definition is based on Ciceronian reminiscences presented in the jargon of the universals controversy,[119] the element of *appetitus* and *desiderium* constantly flowing over into the beloved is foreign to the highly spiritualized friendship of Cicero, who spoke only of the uniting of souls. The man leaves his definition quite open to the union of bodies along with souls. His admission that love may be a *res universalis* is more a witticism than a serious philosophical definition;[120] it plays on the possibility of two individuals monopolizing a universal force: though love may be a universal thing, it has taken up its abode exclusively in us. More important is that their love is "all-encompassing, well tended, and sincere" (*integrum, invigilatum, sincerum*), and he returns to the Ciceronian ideal of unanimity: "We approve of the same things, we disapprove of the same things, we feel the same in all things." But while the man's "philosophical" definition of love is based on the Ciceronian ideal of like-mindedness, he never mentions the thought central to Cicero, that friendship is love of virtue in another person from which the selflessness of true friendship derives, and he suggests a sensuous element foreign to *De amicitia*.

Sensuality, however, is the dominant of his other letters and poems. There is a compulsiveness or drivenness in many of his letters which we discussed earlier, and it seems that she is at pains to temper his impulses.[121] There is powerful longing and desire in both, but he confesses himself incapable of reining in his desires. That becomes her job. His words can be explicitly sexual.[122] This is most evident in the poem which ends the collection, V 113. It is also the closest to Ovid of any of his poems or letters.[123] Some excerpts:[124]

> The man whom your beauty does not move is no man, but a stone.
>> Nor can I be a stone since I am deeply moved.
> Poets have striven to depict the body of Venus
>> [An omission mark]
> But could they fashion your equal? Of course not.
>> For your beauty surpasses even the goddesses themselves.
> Should I go on or be silent? By your permission, I will speak [. . .]
> What are those parts like that your clothing conceals? My mind finds no rest.
>> When they enter my thoughts, I wish to caress them.
> But fortune and shame and that which I fear most—
>> People's murmuring gossip—hinder my desires [. . .]
>> [An omission mark]
> Forgive me, for Love dictates what I'm compelled to write.
>> Forgive such a confession, for I admit that I do not love patiently.
> You have conquered me, whom no woman could conquer.
>> Thus I burn more strongly, this being my first love,

For never before has its flame penetrated my innards.
    Any earlier love was tepid.
You alone make me eloquent; such glory has befallen no woman
    That she be worthy of my song.

The poem is saturated by the Ovidian strain: he is driven by the force that conquers all, that no one can resist; it overrides reason and good sense; it is guided by impulse, and a man under its spell is as one drunken or demented (cf. V 75, p. 254). The talents and beauty of his beloved may be what aroused his love, but it is far from being gratified in contemplation, cultivation of virtue, restraint, and discipline. The thought of her body captivates him, leaves him no rest, makes him want—not to admire the soul it expresses or to ask about the source of divine beauty—but rather to caress it.

She shares his sensuality (though the expression is never so explicit), but not his impetuosity. We have already seen the tempering effect that from beginning to end he claims as one of the most important benefits of her love (n. 41 above). In her ideas on love, Ciceronian theory registers in a remarkably pure form. Her *Ep.* 49 is a showpiece of love theory based on Cicero's *De amicitia.* Her precepts are, briefly summarized: The firmest friendship is that based on the goodness, the virtue, and the intimate love of the partner. Those who love their lovers for their possessions will soon lose them. She loves him on one compulsion only: his "most excellent virtue," not wealth. Virtue requires no material benefits, in fact it requires nothing other than virtue itself. Virtue is like a governing force over all the dangers of love: it "reins in lusts, keeps loves in check, moderates joys and eradicates sorrows." She has found in the man himself (i.e., in nothing outside of him—not his fame or his wealth) the reason that she loves him, and what she has found in him is "summum et omnium prestantissimum bonum." Not wealth, high dignities, or anything that worldly people lust after can separate her from him.[125]

It is not necessary to document the Ciceronian provenance of these ideas.[126] Any educated contemporary would recognize their source. Her lover certainly does. His immediate response is, "I am amazed at your genius [*ingenium*]. You discuss the rules of friendship so subtly that you seem—not to have read Tully—but to have given those precepts to Tully himself!"[127] The Ciceronianism informing this letter is clearest in the "purity" of the love posited: it is unmotivated by anything other than the mind, soul, and virtue of the lover. She restates her "pure love" in verse:

If I could have all that Caesar ever owned,
Such wealth would be of no use to me.
I will never have joys except those given by you.[128]

The turn of thought will recur prominently in Heloise's first letter to Abelard.

Taking M 49 and V 113 as paradigmatic statements, we can confirm that her sentiments and language are Ciceronian, his Ovidian. In this distinction too, a clear historical trend registers. Just as humanist cathedral schools were giving way to schools of dialectic, a long-standing aristocratic social tradition of Ciceronian love and friendship—blended with the language of love and friendship from the Song of Songs, the Psalms, and gospels—was meeting, opposing, being absorbed into, a new, far more sensual Ovidian strain.[129] As is generally recognized, the twelfth century belonged to Ovid. Not so commonly credited was the authority of Cicero on love and friendship in the earlier Middle Ages and still strongly in the twelfth century.[130] The Ciceronian strain was borne in the earlier Middle Ages by cults of friendship that could emerge at worldly courts, or in clerical and monastic communities.[131] Its distinguishing features are the highly spiritualized character of its discourse (*honestum*, not *utile;* distant love, physical presence not necessary for genuine love), its all-male exclusivity, and its definition of love and friendship as "the love of virtue in another man." Perhaps one of the most remarkable moments in the history of sensibilities and social forms is the point in the late eleventh century when women were admitted to the exclusive male social game of ennobling love and friendship. The most noteworthy documents of this change are the Latin epic *Ruodlieb,* the Regensburg love songs, and *Ep.* 49 from the *Epistolae duorum amantium.* The persona of the woman in that letter collection is the more remarkable for combining the highly spiritual, chaste language and conceptions of Ciceronian friendship with a far more sensual strain.[132] In her love language as in her learning, she forges a bold and original amalgamation of old and new.

■ ■ ■

So, are these the "lost love letters of Abelard and Heloise"? Let me survey some of the results of my readings and those of Könsgen, Mews, and Ward-Chiavaroli.

There are no quick and easy means of falsifying the ascription to Abelard and Heloise, no obvious anachronisms that set the letters in a time other than the early twelfth century, and there is much that argues for that dating. There are also no glaring inconsistencies in the events or the characterization of man and woman that would eliminate Abelard and Heloise as the authors, no comments like, "since your father and mother disapprove," or "perhaps I'll accept the bishopric of York." What we learn about these two lovers is consistent with what we know of Heloise and Abelard from the *Historia* and personal writings.

Conversely there is no single statement or observation in the letters that pins down the ascription with absolute certainly, no reference to "Uncle Fulbert" or "my old teacher, Roscelinus, now my enemy." But there is a great deal that commends the ascription. Könsgen observed, cautiously, that this pair of lovers was "*like* Abelard and Heloise" (p. 103). After Mews's, Ward's, and my studies of the letters, they look even more like them. A telling congruence between Heloise and the *mulier* of *Epistolae* has to do with the literary fame of *mulier*. Not only does V stress M's literary skill, evident in her letters, but he makes clear that she has, already before knowing him, reached heights of poetic accomplishment and was acknowledged for it—and similarly Heloise. As V praises M as "*the only disciple* of philosophy among all the girls of our age, *the only one* on whom fortune has conferred totally the gifts of all the virtues" (V 50), so Abelard holds up Heloise as "*the only woman* of this time" skilled in the three biblical languages.[133] In the *Epistolae duorum amantium*: "*sola . . . etatis nostre*"; and in Abelard's *Ep.* 9: "*sola* hoc tempore."

Likewise, the woman of the *Epistolae* has "reached the pinnacle, arrived at the highest point."[134] Abelard praises Heloise for being "supreme in her mastery of letters."[135] Some anonymous verses on Heloise written around the time of her taking the veil (presumably 1118/19) echo this theme. The poet claims that Heloise's learning had set her "above all other girls."[136] Peter the Venerable says virtually the same: "I heard that you . . . gave supreme effort to the study of letters and secular learning . . . that you surpassed all women and bested nearly all men."[137]

Conceivably such talent could have remained known only to her teacher, her lover, and a circle of admirers. After all, the identity of the learned women authors of the Regensburg love songs remains totally obscure. But those who comment on the learning of M and of Heloise agree that this was not the case: they/she won fame and notoriety through learning: "Do not all magnify you above all others, do they not raise you up to the heights, whence like a candelabra you may shine forth and be revered by all?"[138] and "You have made yourself distinguished in our city."[139] In the same way Heloise had made herself "most renowned throughout the realm" by her knowledge of letters.[140] Hugo Metellus wrote to Heloise praising her fame, which "reverberates through the void"; he too proclaims her victory over the female sex in literary skill;[141] and Peter the Venerable had hardly finished adolescence when the fame of her "honest and laudable studies" reached him, telling him how she "surpassed all women and bested nearly all men" in her literary studies (see above, n. 137).

Striking as they are, such correspondences do not by themselves establish the identity of M and Heloise conclusively. Literary skill of women was growing rapidly— at least being celebrated in marked contrast to earlier periods—at the beginning of the twelfth century, but it was still sufficiently rare a phenomenon that Hildebert of Lavardin could praise Muriel, a nun of the convent of Le Ronceray in Angers in comparable terms. He says that while ancient times enjoyed ten Sibyls, the present age has only one and so is not altogether lacking a "virgin poetess." The cultured words that flow from

Muriel's mouth surpass all that the ancients wrote, he goes on; only gods are superior to her. "Both sexes are astonished at your eloquence."[142] But such extravagant praise is not conventional in praise of literate women. Baudri is generous with his praise of women for their poetry and learning, but nowhere does he use anything like the phrase, "alone among the women of our time," or "renowned through the whole kingdom" (or even town).[143]

Our *mulier* is highly skilled in prose and poetry, learned in the classical tradition and the Bible. The women of the Regensburg Songs and the Lady Constance in her long, learned, and ornate letter-poem to Baudri master their classical mythology and Ovid, but none of them has the range of the woman of the *Epistolae*: Ovid, Terence, Cicero, Boethius, the Bible, and Jerome. And the same can be said of Heloise.

Our author uses rare words and neologisms, and Hugo Metellus praised Heloise for this very skill. That praise does not apply to any other female Latin poets writing in the period known to me.

The congruence of the man with Peter Abelard is also striking: his bravado, ego, rashness, foolishness, his provoking and succumbing to opposition, all have their counterparts in the character and destiny of Abelard as recorded in the *Historia calamitatum*. V writes prose and poetry in a style that cultivates plainness, avoids rhythm and rhyme in prose, and favors a kind of technical, commentary-style vocabulary. Abelard not only writes a plain, unrhetorical style in all his works from earliest to latest, but states outright, in the prefatory letter to his sermons, hymns, and sequences for the Paraclete, his preference for plainness and rejection of rhetoric, which he represents not as a default setting in a writer not capable of stylistic complexity, but rather *as an ideal of style:*

> . . . I insist on plainness of exposition, not cultivated eloquence, the literal sense, not the ornament of rhetoric. And perhaps a pure rather than an ornate style of writing is all the more accommodated to the understanding of the unsophisticated the more straightforward it is. And depending on the auditors, even the rusticity of uncultivated language will be itself a form of urbane ornament, and simple understanding [will be] a kind of child-like delicacy of taste.[144]

The man of the *Epistolae* shares in common with Abelard his high standing as a teacher and philosopher/poet. He also shares his involvement in conflict. Our male author faced stiff-necked French opposition and universal haughtiness, and both bowed to him. The same can be said, in the short run, of pre-castration Abelard. The rivalry of our author and his victory as magister is a telling detail (see M 66). He drives out his predecessor ("noctem fugat prioris"—see above and n. 86).

A rivalry ends in the victory of one master and the "retreat" of his predecessor. This was an unusual event for the old-style cathedral schools up to the late eleventh century.

It is true that studies were in a process of fast transformation after about 1060, and masters of the "old learning" were withdrawing from the schools or retiring either for lack of students or for their inability or unwillingness to enter into the new discourses.[145] The nature of the older cathedral schools, where the bishop's monopoly on teaching in the diocese gave him strict control over studies, shielded cathedral schoolmasters from the threat of losing their position to a more gifted rival.[146] The displacement of a master under circumstances described by Abelard and by M 66 was not an everyday event. Paris is the most likely city for such an event to take place. Abelard could shake William of Champeaux loose from his chair at Notre Dame, but his challenge to Anselm of Laon did not have the same result—on the contrary, the results were ultimately dire for Abelard.[147] One did not with impunity challenge masters at these schools where student-teacher relations were based on reverence and authority.[148] Walter of Mortagne is a case in point. He challenged the teaching of Master Alberich of Rheims, whose classes he visited as tutor of Hugh, future abbot of Marchiennes. Forced out of Rheims, Walter set up a school at St. Remi of Rheims, was forbidden to teach there also by Master Alberich, and was forced out of the diocese.[149] A scuffle between the young Wolfgang of Regensburg and his master at the cathedral school of Wuerzburg, though a century and a half earlier, is also instructive. This brilliant young student challenged his teacher, Stefan of Novara, by producing a commentary on Martianus Capella superior to that of the master. Stefan then began what Wolfgang's biographer regarded as a campaign of harassment, which ultimately forced Wolfgang out of the school. He had to find an alternate route to a bishopric and sainthood.[150]

Paris in the early twelfth century was a very different place. R. W. Southern described the first half of the twelfth century at the Parisian schools as a period "when there was a wide opportunity for individual enterprise and for ruthless competition, which was never again so uncontrolled."[151] John of Salisbury's *Metalogicon* depicts the Paris schools as contentious and nasty. In the rough and tumble of the new schools William of Conches lost his position, so did Richard the Bishop.[152] Yet even in the more open atmosphere of Paris, where the bishop's monopoly was less rigorously enforced than in more static communities, and where swift expansion encouraged independent schools presided over by a single master,[153] the displacement of one in rivalry with another is a rarity. However, there are three instances of such an event. Peter Abelard reported all of them, and in all of them he was the successful rival. William of Champeaux lost popularity as teacher at Notre Dame of Paris as a result of Abelard's success: "my reputation for dialectic began to spread, with the result that the fame of my old fellow-students and even that of the master himself [William] gradually declined and came to an end."[154] William's successor as master at Notre Dame ceded his position to Abelard: "Even William's successor as head of the Paris school offered me his chair so that he could join the others as my pupil, in the place where his master and mine had won fame."[155] And his successor, hand-picked by William as a rival of Abelard, ultimately also steps down: "He [William] had filled my place there by one of my rivals. . . . He had previously had a few pupils of a sort . . . but . . . he lost them all and had to retire from keeping a school."[156] Again the master's chair, which Abelard clearly regarded as his personal property, is vacated and its former holder also "retreats" to the monastic life. Abelard took over the position, probably c. 1114, after a stay in Brittany upon his mother's conversion and his later studies with Anselm of Laon had intervened.[157] He represents the demise of his rivals as determined by his own success: "ita in arte dialectica nomen meum dilatari coepit, ut . . . ipsius magistri fama contracta paulatim exstingueretur." As Abelard's fame expanded, that of the rival master contracted in the same degree. That is how the author of M 66 depicts the advent and transfiguration of her lover and the departure of his rival: the one determines the other.

Does the poem M 66 celebrate one or all of these events? If Heloise was the author, then the date seems not to coincide precisely with the love affair, normally taken to have begun in 1115. Still we also must not rule out Heloise as the author and Abelard's rise to the chair of Notre Dame as the occasion on the basis of dates. We have no idea how long Abelard's stay in Brittany was, nor how long he studied with Anselm of Laon, nor indeed, when the affair with Heloise began. It is plausible that the poem harks back to the demise of any one of Abelard's three rivals for the chair of Notre Dame—or of all three lumped into one—and celebrates his resumption of the chair in Paris some time after 1114. The departure of the rival need not be simultaneous with the accession of the victorious master, though the poem seems to contract the two events into a single one. Also we cannot assume that the poem was written immediately upon Abelard's ascent to the teaching position at Notre Dame. A poem of celebration does not have to be written simultaneous with the events it celebrates. Petrus Riga's poem celebrating the birth of Philip Augustus was written as many as six years after the event it celebrates.[158]

While the dating and sequence of events must remain uncertain, the wording of the poem is unambiguous: it celebrates the departure, "in confusion," of the new master's predecessor: "En lux advenit, nox et confusa recedit / . . . / Splendor doctoris noctem fugat <at>que *prioris*." At least we can say that the event celebrated in the poem M 66 has a close counterpart in events in the life of Peter Abelard.

Furthermore the relationship which develops between the man and the woman is strikingly congruent with that of Abelard and Heloise as registered in the *Historia* and letters: she the awestruck student, he the self-intoxicated master; she steadfastly loyal and tenacious in her love;[159] he vacillating, driven partly by sensuality, partly by ego, partly by love. The woman of the *Epistolae* obeys her teacher-lover in all things: "[our near identity of character and intellectual pursuits encourages me] to obey you in all things" (M 25); "I submit to your authority in all things" (M 29); and "I send you these unadorned letters, showing thereby how devotedly I subject myself in all things to your commands" (M 71); and Heloise says of her relation to Abelard: "I have fulfilled all that you commanded me . . . completely. . . . I would have willingly perished at your command . . . at your command I immediately changed not only my habit, but also my mind . . .";[160] "I believed that the more I humbled myself on your account, the more gratitude I should win from you . . .";[161] "I submit all to your scrutiny, yield to your testimony in all things";[162] "I carried out everything for your sake and continue up to the present moment in complete obedience to you";[163] and "I have feared to offend you rather than God, and tried to please you more than him."[164] For both writers of the *Epistolae* this is their first love, and Abelard says the same for his love of Heloise.[165]

The recurrent stress on the theme of envy and persecution in the *Epistolae* and the writings by and relating to Abelard is worth noting.[166] While it is true that many students, teachers, and lovers may have suffered envy and persecution in Paris in the early twelfth century, the persistence of the theme in these two bodies of texts is striking.

The woman of the *Epistolae* claimed to love with a selfless, unwavering love:

> The friendship of those who love each other for wealth or pleasures, I believe, cannot be long lasting, because those material things for whose sake they love each other seem to have no permanence. Whence it happens that, their riches or their lust exhausted, their love will vanish at the same time, since they love each other for possessions, not possessions for the sake of each other. But my love for you is very different. It was not the useless burdens of wealth which compelled me to love you, but only your most excellent virtue. . . .[167]

Heloise says very much the same of her love for Abelard:

> God knows I never sought anything in you except yourself; I wanted simply you, nothing of yours. I looked for no marriage-bond, no marriage portion, and it was not my own pleasures and wishes I sought to gratify . . . but yours.[168]

The woman says that she would not exchange the joys she receives from her lover for Caesar's wealth (M 82, p. 260), and Heloise says she would rather be Abelard's mistress or whore than the wife of Augustus with unending reign over the whole world.[169] Abelard said that in the turmoil of the love affair, he neglected his lectures, putting his mind to love songs more than to philosophy: "As my interest and concentration flagged, my lectures lacked all inspiration and were merely repetitive."[170] The man says, "I direct my words to others; to you I direct my thoughts [intentions]. I often stumble in my words because my mind is estranged from them."[171] Finally, they share concepts with Abelard and Heloise, not only "pure love," but the ethic of inwardness that will find its expression in Abelard's *Ethica*.[172]

No single instance of these inner-textual correspondences is decisive in proving that Heloise and Abelard were the authors of the *Epistolae,* but the accumulated weight of evidence makes for a strong argument in favor of the ascription. This testimony is strengthened to the point of virtual certainty by the three areas of historical-cultural context of the early twelfth century in which the *Epistolae* are situated: (1) the conflu- ence of old, humanistic cathedral school learning with its ornate, classicistic style and its freight of ethical ideals, and the new trend to early scholastic philosophy with its es- chewing of ornate language, its penchant for jargon, and its combative style; (2) a series of changes in schoolmasters at the school of Notre Dame of Paris in the years 1114–1116, in which the first successor of William of Champeaux yielded his position to Peter Abe- lard, the second retired for lack of students, and Peter Abelard eventually took over; (3) the amalgamating of the two major trends in the representation of love and friend- ship in the Middle Ages: a spiritualized Ciceronian friendship and a sensual Ovidian love. These considerations and others from style justify ruling out a dating of these let- ters later than the early twelfth century.

It is hard to account for the "fit" of these letters with Abelard and Heloise other than assuming their authorship. To reject the ascription requires positing either fraud, fiction, and forgery of a highly refined, essentially non-medieval kind—or another pair of learned French lovers who write, think, behave, and are just as famous and contro- versial as Abelard and Heloise. The nature of the letters and the conditions of medieval forgery and of fictive, model letters exclude the first,[173] and I know of no candidates for the second.

Notes

1. Ewald Könsgen, *Epistolae duorum amantium: Briefe Abaelards und Heloises?* (Leiden and Cologne: Brill, 1974); hereafter Könsgen. The manuscript is Troyes BM 1452. For description and history of the text, see Könsgen, xx–xxxiii. Könsgen can find no trace of Johannes de Vepria's source for the love letters. It remains unknown.

2. John F. Benton, "Fraud, Fiction and Borrowing in the Correspondence of Abelard and Heloise," in *Pierre Abélard–Pierre le Vénérable: Les courants philosophiques, littéraires et artistiques en occident au milieu du XIIe siècle. Abbaye de Cluny, 2 au 9 juillet 1972,* Colloques internationaux du CNRS 546 (Paris: Editions du CNRS, 1975), 469–512; John F. Benton and Fiorella Prosperetti Ercoli, "The Style of the *Historia Calamitatum:* A Preliminary Test of the Authenticity of the Correspon- dence Attributed to Abelard and Heloise," *Viator* 6 (1975): 59–86. Benton's "recantation": "A Reconsideration of the Authenticity of the Correspondence of Abelard and Heloise," in *Petrus Abaelardus (1079–1142): Person, Werk und Wirkung,* ed. Rudolf Thomas et al., Trierer Theologische Studien 38 (Trier: Paulinus Verlag, 1980), 41–52. Benton's final study of the subject was "The Cor- respondence of Abelard and Heloise," published posthumously in *Faelschungen im Mittelalter: In- ternationaler Kongress der Monumenta Germaniae Historica Muenchen, 16–19. September 1986. Teil V:*

Fingierte Briefe; Froemmigkeit und Faelschung; Realienfaelschungen, Monumenta Germaniae historica Schriften 33.5 (Hannover: Hahn, 1988), 95–120. For a recent survey of the authenticity question see John Marenbon, "Authenticity Revisited," in *Listening to Heloise: The Voice of a Twelfth-Century Woman,* ed. Bonnie Wheeler (New York: St. Martins, 2000), 19–33. No questions raised by Benton, or indeed, by the 150 years of scholarship during which these texts have been under scrutiny, remain that cast doubt on the *Historia calamitatum,* the personal and monastic letters, as genuine works by and documentation on the lives and thought of Heloise and Peter Abelard. The question of who might have edited the corpus of texts in the form in which they appear in the Manuscript Troyes BM 802 is little more than a reminiscence of the authenticity squabble. Martin Irvine confirms the unanimous ascription to Abelard and Heloise from the medieval manuscript tradition. See "Heloise and the Gendering of the Literate Subject," in *Criticism and Dissent in the Middle Ages,* ed. Rita Copeland (Cambridge: Cambridge University Press, 1996), 87–114, esp. 88 and n. 5. Irvine speaks of a "hermeneutics of suspicion" produced by "bogus medievalism and rank prejudice," which originally cast doubt on the ascription. For a trenchant criticism of the inauthenticators, sensible observations on the authorship, and an argument for authenticity from the manuscript tradition, see Barbara Newman, "Authority, Authenticity, and the Repression of Heloise," *Journal of Medieval and Renaissance Studies* 22 (1992): 121–57, reprinted in her *From Virile Woman to WomanChrist: Studies in Medieval Religion and Literature* (Philadelphia: University of Pennsylvania Press, 1995), 46–75. For the manuscript tradition, see Newman, "Authority, Authenticity," 131–33.

    3. E.g., Anke Paravicini in *Francia* 4 (1976): 844; H. Silvestre in *Scriptorium* 31 (1977): 130; A. Pattin in *Tijdschrift voor filosofie* 41 (1979): 521; Arnulf Stefenelli in *Zeitschrift für romanische Philologie* 93 (1977): 118. A review article by Udo Kindermann ("Abaelards Liebesbriefe," *Euphorion* 70 [1976]: 287–95) draws the line at the concession of a "striking" resemblance of the letter writers with Abelard and Heloise, "Doch weiter sollte man in der Tat nicht gehen" (292), since that same situation was well known in the fifteenth century. Kindermann also questions Könsgen's arguments for a dating in the early twelfth century. His conclusion: "es kann absolut nicht als nachgewiesen gelten, dass sie echtes Gut des Abaelard und der Heloise darstellen" (293). However, the main point of Kindermann's balanced review is not to deny the ascription of the letters to Abelard and Heloise (a point which he leaves open, or rather, unproven), but rather to criticize the uncritical acceptance of their "authenticity" by Therese Latzke in her edition of the love songs from the Ripoll collection.

    4. Peter Dronke, "Abelard and Heloise in Medieval Testimonies," in *Intellectuals and Poets in Medieval Europe,* Storia e Letteratura 183 (Rome: Edizioni di storia e letteratura, 1992), 270–72 (originally published as the twenty-sixth W. P. Ker Memorial Lecture, University of Glasgow Press, 1976); also Dronke, *Women Writers of the Middle Ages: A Critical Study of Texts from Perpetua (d. 203) to Marguerite Porete (d. 1310)* (Cambridge: Cambridge University Press, 1984), 92–97.

    5. Constant J. Mews with translations by Neville Chiavaroli and Mews, *The Lost Love Letters of Heloise and Abelard: Perceptions of Dialogue in Twelfth-Century France* (New York: St. Martins, 1999). The book includes Könsgen's edition of the Latin texts with translations by Neville Chiavaroli and Mews on facing pages. See also Mews, "Philosophical Themes in the *Epistolae duorum amantium:* The First Letters of Heloise and Abelard," in *Listening to Heloise,* ed. Bonnie Wheeler (New York: St. Martins Press, 2000), 35–52.

    6. The publisher distributed a press release declaring, "Scholar proves letters lost for eight centuries to be those of famous lovers Heloise and Abelard."

7. John O. Ward and Neville Chiavaroli, "The Young Heloise and Latin Rhetoric: Some Preliminary Comments on the 'Lost' Love Letters and Their Significance," in *Listening to Heloise,* ed. Bonnie Wheeler (New York: St. Martins Press, 2000), 53–119. See also the review of Mews's book by Michael Clanchy in *Times Literary Supplement,* 25 February 2000. Clanchy accepts the ascription to Heloise and Abelard. Also Barbara Newman in her review of Mews and Chiavaroli in the Bryn Mawr Medieval Review (e-mail book review list) and Chrysogonus Waddel, "Heloise and the Abbey of the Paraclete," in *The Making of Christian Communities in Late Antiquity and the Middle Ages,* ed. Mark Williams (London: Anthem Press, 2002).

8. See Ward and Chiavaroli, "The Young Heloise," 73.

9. I cite the Latin text with page numbers from the Mews and Chiavaroli edition. I have consulted their translation but have used my own unless otherwise noted. Where I cite or adapt the Chiavaroli and Mews translation I indicate it with "trans. C-M" and the page number. I cite the letters as Könsgen and Mews do: M 45 = Letter 45, from the woman; V 113 = Letter 113, from the man. The designations M for *mulier* and V for *vir* are those of Johannes de Vepria. The fifteenth-century editor's deletion marks appear in Könsgen's editions as "....."; I place my own ellipsis in brackets: [. . .].

10. M 45, p. 224: "quicquid nunc per litteras, totum tecum per corporalem conferrem presenciam.... Te discedente tecum discessi spiritu et mente [. . . .]"

11. V 113, p. 288: "Forma genus mores per que pariuntur honores / Urbi te nostre conspicuam faciunt."

12. M 89, p. 272. Könsgen, *Epistolae duorum amantium,* 91. Mews strengthens the argument for Isle de France/Paris, *Lost Love Letters,* 25 and n. 77.

13. M 49, p. 228: "magistro tanto [. . .] cui jure cedit francigena cervicositas [. . . .]"

14. Though Könsgen's claim (p. 91) from this phrase that V is not himself from France seems a bit weak.

15. M 49, p. 228: "cui jure cedit francigena cervicositas, et simul assurgit tocius mundi superciliositas [. . . .]"

16. M 112, p. 286: "Quamvis futurum sit, tamen iam tibi moncium cacumina supplicare conspicio. Nec dubito, quin in te impleatur hoc quod opto divino consilio." Cf. Gen. 8:5.

17. M 23, p. 206: "Scio quidem et fateor ex philosophie tue diviciis maximam michi fluxisse et fluere copiam gaudiorum [. . . .]"

18. M 76, p. 256: "Vere fateor dilectissime quod multociens ut pecus ignavum via subsisterem, nisi magisterialis institucionis tui sollercia, me prono digressam assidue revocaret tramite."

19. M 66, p. 246: "Ecce manus cleri splendescit luce magistri."

20. V 50, p. 230: "Soli inter omnes etatis nostre puellas philosophie discipule, soli in quam omnes virtutum multiplicium dotes integre fortuna conclusit, soli speciose, soli graciose [. . . .]"

21. V 50, p. 232: "Tuum admiror ingenium [. . . .] Ingenium tuum, facundia tua, ultra etatem et sexum tuum iam virile in robur se incipit extendere."

22. V 50, p. 232: "Nonne te super omnes magnificant, nonne te in excelso collocant? Ut inde quasi de candelabro luceas et omnibus spectabilis fias?"

23. V 113, p. 288: "Facundum me sola facis [. . . .]"

24. V 28, p. 214: "Nec mirari debes si in nostram tam insignem, tam aptam amiciciam prava emulacio suos obliquat oculos [. . .]"; V 54, p. 236: [We will have to forego each other's presence and make do with letters for a while] "cum edax malorum hominum invidia nos pro libito nostro iungi

non patitur"; M 69, p. 248: "Hos rogo ne versus oculus legat invidiosus / Hosque sciant nolo pectora plena dolo"; M 81, p. 260: "Vale tu, et illi pereant qui nos disiungere temptant"; V 85, p. 264: "Ignis noster [. . .] invidos et insidiantes decipiat [. . .]"; V 101, p. 278: "Cautius te modo alloquor si notare vis, cautius aggredior, pudor se amori contemperat [. . .] ut [. . .] famam que de nobis orta est paulatim attenuemus."

25. Könsgen, 78–84. Könsgen estimates that even allowing for chance and the selectivity of an editor making elisions, the differences in their practices of quotation are decisive in establishing dual authorship (84).

26. V 47, p. 226: "[. . .] O noctem infaustam, o dormitationem odiosam, o execrabilem desidiam meam. Vale etc. [. . . .]"

27. V 41, p. 222: "Ego preceptum in te non habeo, fac quod vis."

28. V 54, p. 236: ". . . Abire permittamus, quos retinere non possumus. Bonum inde consilium erit." It may have had a context which de Vepria effaced by his elision, but then why retain a phrase which his elision rendered meaningless?

29. V 59, p. 240: "Causa necessaria obstitit, que meo desiderio pedem sinistrum opposuit. Ego nocens sum qui te peccare coegi."

30. V 67, p. 248: "Vale dulcissima mea, et tuam licenciam dilecto tuo concede." He is departing on a trip, evidently, and this may suggest he is requesting "license" to depart, though it is not made explicit.

31. V 75, p. 254: ". . . O stulta promissio, o vox nimium preceps et temeraria [. . . .]"

32. M 84, p. 264: "Prologum tuum quem composuisti michi, cum graciarum actione, cum amoris servitute recompensabo tibi."

33. There are no such illogical inclusions in the twenty-nine pattern letters in Latin edited by Ernstpeter Ruhe, *De amasio ad amasiam: Zur Gattungsgeschichte des mittelalterlichen Liebesbriefes*, Beitraege zur romanischen Philologie des Mittelalters 10 (Munich: Fink, 1975), 299–342. All the letters he includes are logically composed from beginning to end to demonstrate usable phrases in love letters. They are also flat and banal in the extreme. Most of them contain signals of the "sampling" purpose of the letter, e.g., varied formulas separated by "vel." None of these, or any in Ruhe's study, extend an epistolary dialogue beyond a single exchange.

34. Könsgen, 93–97: the favoring of Ovid in quotations and allusions; three reminiscences, if not quotations, of Marbod of Rennes (significantly, all in the woman's verse); the personification of Natura creating beautiful human beings like a sculptor or artist; the prominence of Fortuna; various phrases and formulations popular in the twelfth century (95); the treatment of friendship. Könsgen's conclusion: "Was wir an Einzelheiten aus den Briefen ermitteln konnten, spricht am ehesten dafuer, die Entstehung der Briefe in der ersten Haelfte des 12. Jahrhunderts anzunehmen" (97).

35. Kindermann, "Abaelards Liebesbriefe," 292–93.

36. Constant J. Mews, "Hugh Metel, Heloise, and Peter Abelard: The Letters of an Augustinian Canon and the Challenge of Innovation in Twelfth-Century Lorraine," *Viator* 32 (2001): 81–82.

37. Ward and Chiavaroli, "Young Heloise," 55–57.

38. See Dronke, *Women Writers*, 84–106, esp. 92–97; Mews, *Lost Love Letters*, 87–114. The Regensburg songs were exchanged between the teacher (perhaps more than one) and a number of female students. Some of them are clearly intended as compositional exercises. The collection has, accordingly, a very different character from the *Epistolae*, a private correspondence between lover and beloved.

39. On the transmission of the *Epistolae,* see Könsgen, ix–xxxiii; Mews, *Lost Love Letters,* 3–27.

40. V 50, p. 232: "Tuum admiror ingenium [. . .] ego te inter multa milia ob innumeras virtutes tuas elegi [. . . .] Ingenium tuum, facundia tua [. . . .]"

41. V 50, p. 232: "ego te [. . .] elegi nullum veraciter ob aliud commodum nisi ut in te quiescerem, nisi ut omnium miseriarum michi lenimen esses, ut de terrenis bonis omnibus, sola tua venustas me reficeret et omnium dolorum oblivisci faceret. Tu michi in fame saturitas, tu in siti refectio, tu in lassitudine quies [. . .] tu demum in omni intemperie saluberrima michi et vera temperies." (Chiavaroli and Mews translate "intemperies"-"temperies" as "storms"-"calm"—also correct. But "intemperance" is consistent with his self-characterization as rash. See below, notes 48 and 50.) "Comfort in tribulations" is a persistent motif of the man's letters (see Könsgen, 81): V 2, p. 190: "lassate mentis unico solamini [. . .]"; V 8, p. 194: "Vale o requies mea"; V 28, p. 214: "mea in angustiis recreacio [. . .]"; V 31, p. 214: "in omni egritudine unico remedio suo"; V 45, p. 224: "Nam quociens fortuna deposuit, tue dulcedinis consolacio me restituit"; V 47, p. 226: "Vale sola refectio mea [. . .] unica quies mea"; V 105, p. 280: "Summo lassorum animorum solamini [. . . .]"

42. M 21, p. 202: "O decus juvenum, consors poetarum, quam decorus aspectu [. . . .]"

43. For instance the greetings to V 68: "Dulcissime dulcissimus: quicquid dulcius excogitari potest"; V 70: "Expectato desiderio suo et semper expectando: quicquid boni desiderari vel expectari potest. Vale" (that is the entire letter); V 75: "Unice suavitati sue: quicquid in vita suavissimum reperiri potest"; V 77: "Gaudio suo: gaudium et leticiam." A woman in love could be pardoned for expecting more effort and ingenuity from her lover than what is offered by his various *quicquid*'s. Also the consistency of form in letters sent so close together seems more lack of inspiration than elegance. The formula, "quicquid . . ." is a convenient replacement for thought, like our "*all* good wishes." Cf. the letter of Count Stephen of Blois to his wife in 1097 cited by Mews, "Philosophical Themes," 39: "Stephanus . . . Adelae, dulcissimae amicae, uxori suae, quicquid mens sua melius aut benignius excogitare potest." The woman can use this formula, but cf. the elaborate, highly learned, and allusive salutation to M 45, ending with "et quicquid in eorum dulcedinis comprehenditur ambitu." See the examples of formulaic use of "quicquid" in love-letter writing in Ruhe, *De amasio ad amasiam,* 299.

44. M 109, p. 284: "Quia uterque nostrum alter alterius conspectui modo in momento presentari valet, littere nostre salutacione non indigent." *Sic,* curious though the thought is. One might have expected, "make letters unnecessary." Clearly their proximity does not replace their letters, only their salutations.

45. Mews's reading of the development of the relationship is off the mark in important points. Reading M 112 and 112a very much against their grain, he suggests that she has become pregnant, and since she "no longer wishes to speak to him" she ends the affair content with the child she has received from the lover she no longer needs (Mews, *Lost Love Letters,* 141–42). Mews also reads the man's intensely passionate and sensual poem, V 113, as breaking off their relations, the man proclaiming himself a victim of the snares of sensual passion. Nothing in this poem or in the last letters justifies either reading. They do not represent the "Breakdown of a Relationship" (22), but one of its highpoints.

46. M 34, p. 216: "Vale et premeditare quod melius est provida dilacio quam incauta mentis festinatio."

47. M 48, p. 226: "Nemo debet vivere, nec in bono crescere, qui nescit diligere, et amores regere."

48. V 37, p. 218: "Interroga nuncium quid egi postquam litteras perscripsi: ilico certe in lectum pre inpatiencia me conieci. Vale." It is not easy to construe this letter as rising genuinely from an experienced moment without drawing such inferences about the man's self-awareness. Did he actually instruct the messenger to wait while he threw himself on the bed, then reclaimed the letter/ wax tablet to make a postscript, so that his thrashing about would not go unappreciated? Or did the messenger simply wait around for whatever reason, and so allow him to add the postscript? Or did the man write the letter, then instruct the messenger to tell her about his thrashing whether or not he had performed it in the unlikely sequence of the letter? However, any of these scenarios is at least as likely as that the whole letter is a fiction, a product of some writer's imagination who did not experience any of it. In any case, the point is that a rash, impatient, and impetuous personality emerges from the man's letters, and that holds true, whatever the background to this letter.

49. V 46, p. 224: "quod cum quanta desidero impatiencia, quanta vix dici vel credi potest." Cf. V 37, p. 218: "in lectum pre inpatiencia me conieci"; V 113, p. 288, line 20: "Da veniam fasso, non patienter amo."

50. V 74, p. 254: "mente nimis precipiti"; V 75, p. 254: "nimium preceps."

51. V 74, p. 254 (trans. C-M, 255): "cum oblivisci vis omnis iniurie, quam ego stultus et improvidus mente nimis precipiti, et nimium molli ad resistendum doloribus sine omni deliberacione dilectissime mee intuli."

52. V 75, p. 254 (trans. C-M, 255): "O stulta promissio, o vox nimium preceps et temeraria, o dictum hominis qui vel amens vel ebrius aperte videatur."

53. V 87, p. 268, lines 35–37: "Non hoc consilio, non hoc egi racione. / Qui male consuluit, impetus ipse fuit."

54. V 106, p. 282: "Nichil insipiente fortunato gravius est [. . . .] Ego precium ob stulticiam fero [. . . .]"

55. V 113, p. 288, line 20: "Non patienter amo."

56. V 28, p. 214: "Nec mirari debes si in nostram tam insignem, tam aptam amiciciam prava emulacio suos obliquat oculos [. . . .]"

57. V 50, p. 232 (trans. C-M, 233): "Ego credo et confidenter affirmo quod nemo sit mortalium non cognatus non amicus, quem michi anteponas, et ut audacius dicam quem michi conferas."

58. V 72, p. 252: "Vale et ut neminem mortalium michi compares, diligenter observa [. . . .]"

59. V 111, p. 284: "Lucida nox tua sit, preter me nil tibi desit; / Dum me pulcra cares defore cuncta putes."

60. V 113, p. 288, lines 25–26: "[. . .] hec gloria nulli / Contigit, ut fuerit carmine digna meo."

61. V 28 (trans. C-M, p. 214): "Qui nobis invident, utinam invidendi longa eis materia detur et utinam nostris opimis rebus diu marcescant quandoquidem ita volunt. Me a te separare, ipsum si nos mare interluat, non potest; ego te semper amabo [. . . .] Rodant ergo detrahant, mordeant, in seipsis liquescant, nostra bona suam amaritudinem faciant; tu tamen mea eris vita, meus spiritus [. . . .]"

62. *Historia calamitatum* cited here from the edition by Jacques Monfrin, *Abélard: Historia calamitatum: Texte critique avec une introduction* (Paris: J. Vrin, 1959) and from the translation by Betty Radice, *The Letters of Abelard and Heloise* (Harmondsworth: Penguin, 1974). Here, HC M 252–56 (= ed. Monfrin, lines 252–56), trans. Radice, p. 65: "Sed quoniam prosperitas stultos semper inflat . . . cum jam me solum in mundo superesse philosophum estimarem nec ullam ulterius inquietationem formidarem, frena libidini<s> cepi laxare." It is curious that in Abelard's Palm Sunday sermon for

the Paraclete, he explained Christ's motive in allowing himself to be honored by crowds on this day as giving his enemies greater cause to envy and hate him: "eo amplius invidiam perversorum contra se commovit, ut quod jamdudum voluerant, perficere maturarent, et ab eo daretur facultas . . ." (*PL* 178, 435D); and again, "Ut autem majori incitarentur invidia, qui de morte Domini jam tractabant . . . tantum sibi honoris hodie permisit exhiberi, quantum nulli regum legimus exhibitum" (436A). Peter Abelard clearly understood the mechanism of "giving those who envy us plenty of cause." But then so did the Christian tradition of commentary on Palm Sunday. See the *Glossa ordinaria* on Matt. 21:10, *Biblia sacra cum glossa ordinaria* (Antwerp, 1617), 5.345 and 942 (on Luke 19:37).

63. M 29, p. 214: "Omnibus omissis sub alas tuas confugio [. . . .] Dicere vix possum tristia verba."

64. V 28, p. 214: "Me a te separare, ipsum si nos mare interluat, non potest; ego te semper amabo [. . . .]"

65. V 75, p. 254: "Si mare in spe talis boni transeam, exiguus labor est, si Alpes in asperrimo frigore transcendam, vel si de medio igne cum vite discrimine te petam, in omnibus his nichil fecisse videbor."

66. Similarly, Ward and Chiavaroli ("Young Heloise," 92): "It is possible that Abelard 'took fright' when their affair became known, causing Heloise to write letter 60." She had noticed early on that the fluctuations of his fortunes determine the mood of their relations: "sicut res tue se habent, noster variatur animus [. . .]" (M 25, p. 210).

67. M 38b, p. 218: "Nolis atque velis tibi corde manebo fidelis."

68. M 84, p. 264: "Velis, nolis, semper meus es et eris, nunquam erga te meum mutatur votum neque a te animum abstraho totum."

69. M 49, p. 228: "quia indefective caritatis dulcedinisque stimulus in tue dilectionis amorem me, licet eciam tibi foret ingratum, quod absit <inpulit>, invenit erga te mee dilectionis fervens affectio, ut nunquam potest aliqua interveniente molestia perfecta excludi devocio."

70. M 55, p. 236: "Ita nulla extrinsecus accidentia aliqua racione poterunt obsolere tui memoriale, quod cordi meo adnexui aureo vinculamine."

71. M 88, p. 270: "Tecum permanebo fida, stabilis, immutabilis, et non flexibilis [. . .] nunquam a te nisi vi coacta et penitus expulsa, recederem. Non sum harundo vento agitata, neque me a te movebit asperitas ulla, nec alicuius rei mollicia."

72. M 95, p. 274: "Navi periclitanti, et anchoram fidei non habenti, illa quam non movent ventosa que tue infidelitati sunt congrua."

73. M 102, p. 278: "Quod preciocissimum habeo, tibi do, scilicet meipsam, in fide et dilectione firmam, in amore tuo stabilem, et nunquam mutabilem."

74. M 23 (trans. C-M, p. 204): "Cum vellem tibi rescribere, reiecit me impar viribus meis rei magnitudo [. . . .] Voluit animi fervens affectus, renuitque aridi defectus ingenii."

75. M 25, p. 210: "Quid sit amor, vel quid possit naturali intuitu ego quoque perspiciens morum nostrorum studiorumque similitudine [. . .] conciliat perspecta vicissitudinem amandi tibi rependere et in omnibus obedire."

76. M 49 (trans. C-M, p. 228): "Magne temeritatis est litteratorie tibi verba dirigere, quia cuique litteratissimo et ad unguem usque perducto [. . .] non sufficit tam floridum eloquencie vultum depingere, ut iure tanti magistri mereatur conspectui apparere, nedum michi, que vix videor disposita ad queque levia [. . . .] Cf. M 53, p. 234: "Sapiencie lumine per nobilitatis insignis

mirabiliter prefulgenti [. . .] [she who is] tocius expers pericie." M 71, p. 250: "has inornatas litteras tibi mitto, earum probans indicio quam devote in omnibus me tuis preceptis subicio." M 79, pp. 258–60: "Scio enim et fateor pro singulis quibusque tuis beneficiis quod grates persolvere nullatenus sufficio animi vel corporis officio [. . . .] Tuus honor meum geminasse videretur si usque ad finem fatalem nos conversari liceret pariter. Nunc autem satius eligo mortis terminari periculo, quam vivens dulcifluo tui aspectus privari gaudio [. . .]" (mortis terminari periculo = to die; cf. Mews and Chiavaroli: to be confined by the threat of death). M 84: "pro te mori non differo." M 112, p. 286: "Cum ergo tanti beneficii meritis dignam rependere vicem nullatenus valeam, tamen disiderio desidero indeficienter tuo vacare studio."

77. M 53, p. 234: "Sapience lumine per nobilitatis insignia mirabiliter prefulgenti [. . .] tocius expers pericie [. . . .]"

78. This consistent characterization of the woman as serving, subjugating herself, I believe places the letters in sharp contrast to the Regensburg letters, the Tegernsee letters, and the letter attributed to Lady Constance supposedly written to Baudri. In all of the latter cases the women correspondents tend to take on superior and dominating positions vis-à-vis the master, to become the master's teachers, especially clear in the Regensburg songs. See C. Stephen Jaeger, *Ennobling Love: In Search of a Lost Sensibility* (Philadelphia: University of Pennsylvania Press, 1999), 74–78, 94–99, 101–103. In the case of the Baudri-Constance exchange the checking, correcting, and dominating position of the woman is all the more striking if the author of both letters was Baudri. I am skeptical of Jean-Yves Tilliete's claim that Baudri wrote the letter ascribed to Constance. See his "Hermès amoureux, ou les métamorphoses de la chimère: réflexions sur les *carmina* 200 et 201 de Baudri de Bourgueil," *Mélanges de l'Ecole Francaise de Rome: Moyen Age* 104 (1992): 121–61, here 136–44. On this point see Gerald Bond, *The Loving Subject: Desire, Eloquence, and Power in Romanesque France* (Philadelphia: University of Pennsylvania Press, 1995), 229 n. 71.

79. M 25, p. 210: "tibi [. . .] in omnibus obedire."

80. M 29, p. 214: "Omnibus omissis sub alas tuas confugio, tue dicioni me suppono obnixe tibi per omnia subsequendo."

81. M 71 (trans. C-M, p. 250): "has inornatas litteras tibi mitto, earum probans indicio quam devote in omnibus me tuis preceptis subicio."

82. V 50, p. 232: "Tibi [. . .] omnibus modis impar sum, quia in hoc eciam me excedis, ubi ego videbar excedere. Ingenium tuum, facundia tua, ultra etatem et sexum tuum iam virile in robur se incipit extendere." Is this posture perhaps good pedagogy when a male teacher receives poems from a female student? A poem in the Regensburg songs from a master to his (female) student also protests the master's inferiority: "Iam non est tutum contendere carmine tecum! / . . . / Longe precellis, longe me carmine vincis. / Victum me fateor tandemque manus dare cogor" (Nr. XXVIII, ed. Dronke, *Medieval Latin and the Rise of the European Love-Lyric*, 2nd ed. [Oxford: Oxford University Press, 1968], 431). Cf. also Baudri of Bourgueil to the poetess Emma, clearly a teacher of poetry for the women of Le Ronceray, Angers (Baudri wishes to sign up as a disciple of hers), Carmen 139, lines 17–18, ed. Hilbert, p. 192; Serlo of Bayeux, to Muriel, also of Le Ronceray, who says he hesitates to disturb a place so fecund of poetry as their town with his own pedestrian verse, since theirs are far better (ed. Thomas Wright, ed., *Anglo-Latin Satirical Poets and Epigrammatists of the Twelfth Century*, Rolls Series 59 [London, 1872; rpt. 1964], 233).

83. See Könsgen, 81–82, on rhyme and rhythm in the two authors (the woman regularly uses both; the man never, or only by chance). Also Mews, *Lost Love Letters*, 118–20.

84. On the use of classical and biblical quotations, Könsgen, 82–83, and Ward and Chiavaroli, "Young Heloise," 68–70. Könsgen's inventory of quotations produces the following table:

	Ovid	Boethius	Jerome	Virgil	Terence	Vulgate
V	34	1	0	4	5	28
M	18	8	8	8	1	70

Cicero, Horace, and the Song of Songs are quoted by both more or less equally.

85. For instance, her command to Clio, "Carmine sis comens tabulas et suavia promens." Könsgen (67) identifies Ovidian reminiscences in the poem.

86. M 66, p. 246, lines 5–8:

En lux adventat, nox et discedere temptat.
En lux advenit, nox et confusa recedit.
Ecce manus cleri splendescit luce magistri.
Splendor doctoris noctem fugat <at>que prioris.

87. On the development of the acclamation hymn from the *adventus* ceremony of Late Antiquity, see Sabine G. MacCormack, *Art and Ceremony in Late Antiquity* (Berkeley: University of California Press, 1981), esp. 17–89. Also Ernst Kantorowicz, *Laudes Regiae: A Study in Liturgical Acclamations and Mediaeval Ruler Worship* (Berkeley and Los Angeles: University of California Press, 1958). On the "Christus vincit, Christus regnat, Christus imperat" formula, *Laudes Regiae*, 21–32. The *adventus* ceremony and associated texts and hymns are incidental to Michael McCormick's study, *Eternal Victory: Triumphal Rulership in Late Antiquity, Byzantium and the Early Medieval West* (Cambridge: Cambridge University Press, 1986), but he cites much material relevant to the topic, esp. 362–75.

88. See for instance the Reims acclamations for the seating of a bishop, *PL* 138, 901A ff. The language of sun and daylight supplanting dark night is conventional for the advent of a new age or ruler or bishop. See MacCormack, *Art and Ceremony*, 21 and 282 n. 21, pp. 35–37 and Plate 13, on the image of the rising sun in the frieze on the arch of Constantine celebrating Constantine's triumphal entry into Rome in 312. Also below on Odo of Bayeux. Cf. the poem by Petrus Riga celebrating the birth of Philip Augustus (it dates c. 1165–1171): "Nox . . . suam perdit lumine victa vicem. / Nox erat, ecce dies, media de nocte diescit; / Lucent cuncta, diem lux numerosa facit. Nox et adest et abest, toti jubar imperat urbi, / . . . / Nocturnoque stupent sidera lesa die. / Urbs adeo nituit quod nil ibi noctis in ipsa / Nocte fuit, lucem, res nova! fama parit . . ." ("Versus de gaudio filii regis Quando fuit natus," lines 21–30). See the edition and commentary by William Chester Jordan, "*Quando fuit natus:* Interpreting the Birth of Philip Augustus," in *The Work of Jacques LeGoff and the Challenges of Medieval History*, ed. Miri Rubin (New York: Boydell, 1997), 171–88, here 186–87. Könsgen associates the form with christological hymns, which may well share the image of light supplanting dark, but M 66 derives from a very different tradition. On the transference of the sun imagery from imperial *adventus* to Christ, see MacCormack, *Art and Ceremony*, 66, 172.

89. Kantorowicz, *Laudes Regiae*, 25.

90. Cf. Theodulf's hymn on the arrival of Louis the Pious in Arles, Monumenta Germaniae historica Poetae 1. 529; Sedulius Scotus on Bishop Franco of Liège, *Sedulli Scoti Carmina*, ed. I. Meyers, Corpus Christianorum Continuatio Mediaevalis 117 (Turnholt: Brepols, 1991), p. 37, Carm. 18; also on the arrival of Lothar in Xanten, p. 47, Carm. 24.

91. See Max Manitius, *Geschichte der lateinischen Literatur des Mittelalters*, 2.321–22. The text of the "Tetralogus": *Die Werke Wipos*, 3rd ed., ed. Harry Breslau, Monumenta Germaniae historica Script. rer. Germ. in us. Schol. (Hannover and Leipzig: Hahn, 1915), 76–86.

92. The turn of thought is virtually obligatory in acclamation hymns. Kantorowicz refers to this motif as "the interlacing of eternal and present rulership which was indispensable to the acclamations of the times" (i.e., late Carolingian).

93. On Serlo see Manitius, *Geschichte der lateinischen Literatur*, 3.869–72; and Kindermann in *Lexikon des Mittelalters*, 7.1788–89.

94. *Anglo-Latin Satirical Poets and Epigrammatists*, 2:254. The translation aims at reproducing the clumsiness and ungrammaticality of the original.

95. M 73, p. 252. Some comments on the opening lines:

Flos juvenilis ave, lux et decus imperiale,
Imperiale decus, flos juvenilis ave.
Cum te plasmavit, sat te natura beavit
Viribus interius, laudibus exterius [. . . .]

Imperiale decus: cf. Hrotsvit of Gandersheim, poem to Emperor Otto I, *PL* 137, 1152A: "Et licet imperii teneas decus Octaviani / . . . / Dicatur sceptri *decus imperiale* secundi." Pope Gregory VII, Registrum, Part 1, Bk. 2, *PL* 148, *Ep.* 44 to Judith Queen of the Hungarians (1075): "Praeterea multum te commendat nobis tua praeclara et inclyta fama, quod in tam tenera aetate . . . generis tui gloriam decorasti: quippe quae in excelso nata imperio nihil in actibus et in habitudine tua nisi *decus imperiale* hactenus demonstrasti." (For further references, see Könsgen, 41 n. 1.) Könsgen believes there is a reminiscence of Marbod of Rennes in the line "Cum te plasmavit, sat te natura beavit." Cf. Marbod, Carm. 24, *PL* 171, 1660: "Praestat habere palam quo te natura beavit." A search for "natura beavit" on the *Patrologia Latina* database produces only two hits: the passage from Marbod and another from Alan of Lille.

96. On her neologisms and unusual formulations, see Mews, *Lost Love Letters*, 129–31 and Ward and Chiavaroli, "Young Heloise," 84.

97. His poem V 87 is remarkable as a versifying of prose. Apart from the sun and light metaphor developed in lines 11–16, the poem has no lyric quality other than meter and hardly any rhetorical features. Consider the one other exception, the lines 19–22 (p. 268), which extend an anaphora over three verses:

[Lacking your heavenly eyes I am bereft of everything]
Sic dici possum felicior omnibus esse,
  Sic dici possum nil habuisse boni,
Sic igitur verum, quod diximus ante, probatur,
  Qualiter annalis hec mora transierit.

Thus I can be said to be the happiest of men,
  Thus I can be said to have had nothing good,
Thus therefore it is proven true what we said earlier,
  About how this year has passed.

The repetition ("Sic dici possum") is heavy and its predicates anticlimactic and contradictory ("the happiest of men"—why? The point is his desolation; "bereft of everything good"). The scholastic thump sounds once more ("Thus therefore it is proven true . . ."). Otherwise the diction and communication of the poem could be turned into prose with no sense of violating the prose usage common elsewhere in his letters. But the prosaic character of the verse may have been seen by writer and recipient as lucidity and simplicity, not poetastery.

98. See Dronke's commentary, *Women Writers*, 96–97. He finds the lines "enigmatic" and notes their "wistful, moving qualities." I am skeptical that the love ecstasy suggested in the lines indicates inexperience in love (Dronke, 97); rather the opposite. Mews finds an illusion to "Dido immolating herself in her love for Aeneas" in the lines (*Lost Love Letters*, 112). Ward and Chiavaroli also point to the allusion to Dido and Aeneas, detect another to Orpheus and Eurydice, and a third to Deucalion and Pyrrha creating a new race after the flood by sowing stones, which liquefy and become human ("Young Heloise," 93).

99. See Bond, *Loving Subject*, 70–98, chap. 3, "Natural Poetics: Marbod at Angers and the Promotion of Eloquence"; and Jaeger, *Envy of Angels: Cathedral Schools and Social Ideals in Medieval Europe, 950–1200* (Philadelphia: University of Pennsylvania Press, 1994), 162–64. On Abelard's idealizing of stylistic plainness, below, p. 145 and note 144.

100. See Mews's commentary on the philosophical vocabulary, *Lost Love Letters*, 124–28.

101. My translation admittedly goes a little far in inventing a clunky phrase. But it does capture the atmosphere if not the precise meaning of the Latin. "A single thing without distinction" is more literal, but misses the philosophical panache of *unum quid* and *indifferenter*.

102. Sometimes elegantly and cryptically. Cf. the greeting to M 21: "Dilecto suo speciali et ex ipsius experimento rei esse quod est." It is untranslatable: "To her special beloved and, from direct knowledge of the thing itself, the essence that is." (Cf. C-M, 203: "To her beloved, special from experience of the reality itself: the being which she is.") *Esse quod est* is a technical term common in Trinitarian theology, therefore it is unlikely she is referring to herself but rather to her lover. (Cf. William of St. Thierry, *PL* 180, 263B: "et habet uterque, tam filius quam spiritus sanctus esse quod est. . . ." The phrase produces 273 hits in the *Patrologia Latina* database.) Heideggerian German can come closer than English: "Esse quod est" = "das Wesen, das west," or "das seiende Sein." Cf. also the greeting to M 86: "pars anime eius individua [. . .]," a witty word-play (on "individual" and "undivided") and oxymoron (a part can only be the product of division) that takes up his greeting from the previous letter: "to the best part of his body, undivided love." On the language of individuality, see Mews, *Lost Love Letters*, 120–24. On this formulation, Mews, "Philosophical Themes," 41, with reference to an occurrence in St. Anselm. It is a witty play on language well known in letters of friendship. Cf. John of Salisbury's letter 111 to Peter of Celle: their friendship is an *insecabilis unitas;* he aspires to nothing that might divide it, leaving Nature herself astonished (*The Letters of John of Salisbury: Volume One, The Early Letters [1153–1161]*, ed. W. J. Millor and H. E. Butler, rev. C. N. L. Brooke [London: Thomas Nelson, 1955], 181).

103. Ward's and Chiavaroli's study of the cursus patterns in sentence endings concluded that both writers use them infrequently and without an apparent mastery of the forms. See "Young Heloise," 78–80.

104. Cf. the greeting to M 27: "Oculo suo Bezelielis spiritum, trium crinium fortitudinem, patris pacis formam, Idide profunditatem." See Mews's elucidation, *Lost Love Letters*, 18, 138.

105. This corresponds closely with Peter Dronke's observations on the prose style of Heloise and Abelard in the private letters: *Women Writers*, 114 ff. See also his essay, "Heloise's *Problemata* and Letters: Some Questions of Form and Content," in his *Intellectuals and Poets in Medieval Europe*,

295–322, and 302: "not only is Heloise's writing a product of high artistic nurture, but we can see how it was enhanced by one of the most modern and most unusual stylistic currents of her day." This applies to cursus patterns in her writings, of which there is no consistent use in the letters of M. But Dronke shows the influence of Albertus Samaritanus as decisive in Heloise's use of cursus, and his tract did not begin to circulate until 1115. The common point is that both M and Heloise are sensitive to learned trends in style, while V and Abelard are more or less indifferent to them.

106. See Jaeger, *Envy of Angels*, 36–179.

107. Cf. the usage in Marbod, *Vita licinii, PL* 171, 1495D: "Prorsus in professione discipuli *morum magister* factus erat." And *Vita Gualterii, PL* 171, 1567C: "Interea sub professione discipuli, *morum quoddam magisterium* exercebat...."

108. See Jaeger, *Envy of Angels*, 49–52 and passim.

109. See my article, "Der Magister in der Moralphilosophie des Mittelalters und der Renaissance," in *Entzauberung der Welt: Deutsche Literatur 1200–1500*, ed. J. Poag (Tübingen: A. Francke, 1989), 119–31.

110. M 109, p. 284: "Cupio te tamen esse salvum, virtutum decore indutum, sophie gemmis circumtectum, morum honestate preditum, omnisque composicionis ornatu decoratum."

111. M 88, p. 270: "Raro quenquam invenimus in hoc salo tam composite felicitatis, tam perfecte virtutis, quin corpus eius non bene politum, deesse sibi peniteat multum, nisi tu solus, qui per omnia et in omnibus extas virtuosus."

112. See Gabriela Signori, "Muriel and the Others ... or Poems as Pledges of Friendship," in *Friendship in Medieval Europe*, ed. Julian Haseldine (Stroud: Sutton, 1999), 199–212; Dronke, *Women Writers*, 84–106.

113. Ward and Chiavaroli, "Young Heloise," 58–59: "Whatever the great project that drew her to the intellectual foyer of Paris in the early twelfth century, it came unstuck; the intellectual partnership with Abelard ... died.... With the demise of Heloise's great project comes also the deaththroes of the oral/ethical/intellectual vitality that marked the prescholastic age. A world recognizable to us is born, a world in which women are marginalized or banished from an intellectual milieu that is increasingly patriarchal, increasingly textual."

114. M. T. Clanchy, *Abelard: A Medieval Life* (Oxford and Cambridge, Mass.: Blackwell, 1997), 169–72. Dronke had also questioned the dominance of the "master" over the pupil in stylistic matters in *Women Writers*, 111–12.

115. Hence arguments that Abelard wrote the letters ascribed to Heloise are unconvincing. See also Newman, "Authority, Authenticity," 148–51.

116. Mews, *Lost Love Letters*, esp. 161–72. Mews is overly eager to ascribe to Heloise writings that derive from that same education. The poem "Laudis honor, probitatis amor, gentilis honestas" (see *Lost Love Letters*, 164–69), by a poetess who has been ill-treated (for her poetry and her learning, she claims) at the hands of an unnamed powerful man, may be from the educational milieu of Heloise, but little in it argues for her authorship.

117. She compares herself at one point with heroines from Ovid's *Heroides* (M 45), while he builds a philosophical definition of love around a Ciceronian precept (V 24). Könsgen distinguishes the two postures as "Amor spiritualis" and "Amor carnalis" (88–91). Mews distinguishes the language of love, *amor, dilectio,* and *caritas* (*Lost Love Letters*, 16–18, 136–38). See also Irvine, "Heloise and the Gendering."

118. V 24, p. 208: "Est igitur amor vis quedam anime non per se existens nec seipsa contenta, sed semper cum quodam appetitu et desiderio se in alterum transfundens et cum altero idem effici volens, ut de duabus diversis voluntatibus unum quid indifferenter efficiatur. . . ."

119. Cicero, *De amicitia* 20: "omnium divinarum humanarumque rerum cum benevolentia et caritate consensio"; ibid. 81: "cuius animum ita cum suo misceat, ut efficiat paene unum ex duobus."

120. See Mews, *Lost Love Letters*, 127.

121. Cf. M 48, p. 226: "Nemo debet vivere, nec in bono crescere qui nescit diligere et amores regere"; and she commends the kind of love based on virtue since "cupiditates omnes refrenat, amores reprimit, gaudia temperat [. . .]" (M 49, p. 228). He values, among other of her virtues, her "temperance" (V 50, p. 232). See also above, p. 129 and note 41.

122. V 26, p. 212: "O quam fecundum suavitatis pectus tuum, o quam integra venustate prefulges, o corpus succi plenissimum, o ineffabilis odor tuus, profer quod latet, revela quod habes absconditum [. . .] quia nichil actum credo, dum aliquid restare video." (So long as anything remains to be done, I believe I've done nothing.) It sounds like Abelard's confession of eager sexual experimentation: "Nullus a cupidis intermissus est gradus amoris, et si quid insolitum amor excogitare potuit, est additum" (HC M 342–44).

123. Könsgen identifies seventeen quotations from Ovid in its thirty-two lines. Overall in his letters he quotes Ovid thirty-four times. Half of the quotations are concentrated in the thirty-two lines of this poem.

124. V 113, p. 288:

Non homo sed lapis est quem non tua forma movebit.
    Credo quod moveor, nec lapis esse queo.
Cur fuit Veneris effingere membra poetis
    . . . . .
Sed tibi num finxere pares? Non estimo certe
    Exuperat veras nam tua forma deas.
Eloquar an sileam? Si sit tua gracia dicam . . .
Qualia sunt que veste tegis? Vix mente quiesco.
    Que palpasse volo cum subeunt animo.
Sed fortuna pudorque meis dulcissima votis
    Obstant et populi murmura que timeo [. . .]
    . . . . .
[. . .] Da veniam quia dictat amor que scribere cogor
    Da veniam fasso, non patienter amo.
Tu me vicisti, potuit quem vincere nulla.
    Fortius hinc uror, est quia primus amor,
Nam non ante meas penetravit flamma medullas.
    Si quis amor fuerat ante fui tepidus.
Facundum me sola facis, hec gloria nulli
    Contigit, ut fuerit carmine digna meo.

125. M 49, pp. 226–28: "Nosti o maxima pars anime mee multos multis se ex causis diligere, sed nullam eorum tam firmam fore amiciciam quam que ex probitate atque virtute, et ex intima

dilectione proveniat. Nam qui ob divicias vel voluptates sese diligere videntur, eorum nullomodo diuturnam arbitror amiciciam, cum res ipse propter quas diligunt, nullam videantur diurturnitatem habere [. . . .] Nec me ignava opum pondera [. . .] te diligere compulerunt, sed sola excellentissima virtus, penes quam omnis honestatis, tociusque prosperitatis causa consistit. Illa quidem est que sibi sufficiens, nullius indiga, cupiditates omnes refrenat, amores reprimit, gaudia temperat, dolores extirpat; que [. . .] nichil se melius reperire valet. Habeo sane repertum in te, unde te diligam, summum scilicet atque omnium prestantissimum bonum [. . . .] Crede igitur michi o desiderabilis non opes non dignitates non omnia que sectatores huius seculi concupiscunt, poterunt me a tui dilectione secernere."

126. See Könsgen's annotations, 25–26.

127. V 50, p. 232: "Tuum admiror ingenium, que tam subtiliter de amicicie legibus argumentaris ut non Tullium legisse, sed ipsi Tullio precepta dedisse videaris."

128. M 82, p. 260: "Si quicquid Cesar unquam possedit haberem, / Prodessent tante nil michi divitie. / Gaudia non unquam te nisi dante feram."

129. See Bond, *Loving Subject.* Also his earlier article, " 'Iocus amoris': The Poetry of Baudri of Bourgueil and the Formation of the Ovidian Subculture," *Traditio* 42 (1986): 143–93. Also Jaeger, *Ennobling Love,* esp. 36–53, and Ward and Chiavaroli, "Young Heloise," 57.

130. See Jaeger, *Ennobling Love,* passim, and Jan Ziolkowski, "Twelfth-Century Understandings and Adaptations of Ancient Friendship," in *Mediaeval Antiquity,* ed. Andries Welkenhuysen et al., Mediaevalia Lovaniensia Series 1, Studia 24 (Louvain: Louvain University Press, 1995), 59–81.

131. The idea of a characteristically "monastic" friendship prior to the late eleventh century requires revision. The best overview and guide to sources is Brian McGuire, *Friendship and Community: The Monastic Experience, 350–1250,* Cistercian Studies Series 95 (Kalamazoo, Mich.: Cistercian Publications, 1988), who however interprets many sources from secular courts and cathedral communities as "monastic." McGuire's article, "Heloise and the Consolation of Friendship," in *Listening to Heloise,* ed. Bonnie Wheeler (New York: St Martin's Press, 2000), 303–21, is concerned with the interweaving of consolation and spiritual friendship in the monastic letters of Abelard and Heloise.

132. See Jaeger, *Ennobling Love,* 157–73. Also Martin Irvine, "Heloise and the Gendering," 96–101, on Heloise's combining the classical notions of *amicitia* with sensual love and religious devotion.

133. Abelard, *Ep.* 9 to the nuns of the Paraclete on the study of letters (*Peter Abelard, Letters IX–XIV: An Edition with an Introduction,* ed. L. J. Engels [Groningen: Rijksuniversiteit, 1983], 233 [*PL* 178, 333B]): "Magisterium habetis in matre [i.e., Heloise] quod ad omnia vobis sufficere, tam ad exemplum scilicet virtutum quam ad doctrinam litterarum, potest, que non solum Latine, verum eciam tam Ebraice quam Grece non expers litterature, *sola hoc tempore* illam trium linguarum adepta periciam videtur . . ." (my emphasis).

134. V 50, p. 232: "in ulteriora semper profectum, si proficere potest que ad summum pervenit."

135. HC M 284–85: "per habundantiam litterarum erat suprema."

136. Edited and discussed in Dronke, "Abelard and Heloise in Medieval Testimonies," 280: "Damnosum [erat] tenere minus or<r>endeque puelle, / Quam facies multis, quam philosophia puellis / Pretulerat cunctis, qua sola Gallia pollet." Dronke's translation: "[to take the veil] was destructive for a tender and not at all matronly girl—she whose face had set her above many, whose philosophy had set her above all other girls, she through whom alone Gaul has worth."

137. Peter the Venerable, *Ep.* 115 to Heloise, ed. Constable, 1.303: "Necdum plene metas adolescentiae excesseram . . . quando nomen . . . honestorum tamen et laudabilium studiorum tuorum michi fama innotuit. Audiebam tunc temporis, mulierem licet necdum saeculi nexibus expeditam, litteratoriae scientiae quod perrarum est, et studio licet saecularis sapientiae, *summam operam* dare . . . tu, illo efferendo studio tuo, et *mulieres omnes evicisti,* et pene viros universos superasti." Mews has ignored Peter's extravagant praise of her learning and literary skill in claiming that his words show the "suppression of Heloise" as learned woman ("Hugh Metel, Heloise, and Peter Abelard").

138. V 50, p. 232. See note 22 above.

139. V 113, p. 288. See note 11 above.

140. HC M 288: "[litteratoria scientia] in toto regno nominatissimam fecerat."

141. Hugo Metellus, *Ep.* 16 to Heloise, *Sacrae Antiquitatis Monumenta,* ed. Charles-Louis Hugo (Saint-Die: Joseph Charlot, 1731), 2:348–49 (quoted in Mews, *Lost Love Letters,* 350 n. 56): "Fama sonans per inane volans apud nos sonuit, quae digna sonitu de vobis, nobis intonuit. Foemineum enim sexum vos excessisse nobis notificavit." See Mews, "Hugh Metel, Heloise, and Peter Abelard."

142. Hildebert, *Carmina Minora,* ed. A. B. Scott, (Leipzig: Teubner, 1969), 17, #26: "Tempora prisca decem se iactavere sibillis, / et vestri sexus gloria multa fuit. / unius ingenio presentia secula gaudent, / et non ex toto virgine vate carent. / . . . / stupet eloquio sexus uterque tuo." On Muriel and the circle of nun poetesses at Le Ronceray, see Gabriela Signori, "Muriel and the Others"; Dronke, *Women Writers,* 84–106; Bond, *Loving Subject,* 141–43.

143. Carm. (ed. Hilbert) nos. 137, 139, 142, 153, 200. Writing to the same Muriel, the nun-poetess praised by Hildebert, he says that he had known of her earlier through *fama,* now through personal colloquies. He now knows how many of her talents "jealous fame" had hidden. Her compositions have "placed her in the company of the famous poets."

144. To Heloise, *PL* 178, 379: "expositionis insisto planitiem, non eloquentiae compositionem: sensum litterae, non ornatum rhetoricae. Ac fortasse pura minus quam ornata locutio quanto planior fuerit, tanto simplicium intelligentiae commodior erit; et pro qualitate auditorum ipsa inculti sermonis rusticitas quaedam erit ornatus urbanitas, et quoddam condimentum saporis parvulorum intelligentia facilis."

145. Goswin of Mainz, writing in c. 1065, laments that the advent of a new type of wandering scholar, disputatious and contentious, encouraged the retirement of a number of old masters. See Jaeger, *Envy of Angels,* 217–36 ("Old Learning against New") and 368 (the letter of Goswin, retirement of old masters).

146. So did the support of a master's students, who had important interests invested in the prestige and personal authority of the master.

147. John of Salisbury reports that Anselm and Ralph of Laon turned aside the onslaughts of the "Cornificians" and that no attack on them remained unpunished ("quos nemo laceravit impune") (*Metalogicon,* 1.5, ed. J. B. Hall, Corpus Christianorum Continuatio Mediaevalis 98 [Turnholt: Brepols, 1991], 21, lines 30–35). See Clanchy, *Abelard,* 71–74, for a discussion of the politics of Abelard's foray into Laon and of "the foundations of a master's power."

148. When some students at the cathedral school of Worms wrote a poem in the 1030s that seemed potentially insulting to a master of the school of Würzburg they caused a huge flap, documented in a poem of the Würzburg students written in retaliation. The "culprits" faced harsh penalties. See Jaeger, *Envy of Angels,* 66–74. Wibald of Stablo could still complain in the mid-twelfth

century that students love their masters more than the truth in their "sentences," and he sees one school competing with another, not in defense of the truth, but "in hate or love" of individual masters (*Ep.* 167, *Wibaldi Epistolae*, ed. Philipp Jaffé, Bibliotheca rerum Germanicarum 1: Monumenta Corbeiensia [1864; rpt., Aalen: Scientia, 1964], 277).

149. See Emil Lèsne, *Les écoles de la fin du VIIIe siècle à la fin du XIIe siècle*, vol. 5, *Histoire de la propriété ecclésiastique en France* (Lille: Faculté Catholique, 1940), 287. Also R. W. Southern, "The Schools of Paris and Chartres," in *Renaissance and Renewal in the Twelfth Century*, ed. Robert Benson and Giles Constable (Cambridge, Mass.: Harvard University Press, 1982), 117–18.

150. See Jaeger, *Envy of Angels*, 64–65.

151. Southern, "Schools of Paris and Chartres," 115. Also Clanchy, *Abelard*, 75.

152. Jaeger, *Envy of Angels*, 240.

153. See Southern, "Schools of Paris and Chartres," 120–21.

154. HC M 58–61 (trans. Radice, 59): "ita in arte dialetica nomen meum dilatari cepit, ut non solum condiscipulorum meorum, verum etiam ipsius magistri fama contracta paulatim extingueretur."

155. HC M 104–108 (trans. Radice, 60): "et ipse qui in scolis Parisiace sedis magistro successerat nostro locum mihi suum offerret, ut ibidem cum ceteris nostro se traderet magisterio ubi antea suus ille et noster magister floruerat."

156. HC M 128, 137–41 (trans. Radice, 61): "locum nostrum ab emulo nostro fecerat occupari. . . . Ille quippe antea aliquos habebat qualescunque discipulos. . . . Postquam autem magister advenit, omnes penitus amisit; et sic a regimine scolarum cessare compulsus est."

157. The only firm dates are William of Champeaux's conversion in 1108 and his election as bishop of Châlons in 1113. The resignation of his first successor in favor of Abelard occurred some time after 1108. The demise of the next successor must have happened several years later, some time between 1110 and 1112. After the rival's demise Abelard returned to Brittany, then back to France to study theology with Anselm of Laon, then returned to Paris, probably not before 1114, and resumed "his" duties as master of Notre Dame of Paris, during which time the affair with Heloise ran its course. On the dating see Robert-Henri Bautier, "Paris au temps d'Abélard," in *Abélard en son temps: Actes du colloque international organisé à l'occasion du 9e centenaire de la naissance de Pierre Abélard* (Paris: Les belles lettres, 1981), 53–55.

158. See Jordan, "*Quando fuit natus*," 171–72.

159. This steadfast loyalty is the point of departure for Peter von Moos's most searching analysis of the correspondence, "Die Bekehrung Heloises," *Mittellateinisches Jahrbuch* 11 (1976): 95–125, here 95: "[through all controversy] eines scheint festzustehen: Heloise gilt unangefochten als eine Frau von ungewoehnlicher Gefuehlskonstanz . . . sie ist also sich selbst und ihrer ungluecklichen Liebe nie untreu geworden. Solches duerfte zum gesicherten Wissen der Mediaevistik gehoeren." Von Moos's article argues against projecting this loyalty to Abelard beyond her conversion, not against the claim of an earlier persistent loyalty.

160. Heloise, *Ep.* 1, ed. Muckle, 70: "universa quae jusseris . . . impleverim . . . me ipsam pro jussu tuo perdere sustinerem . . . ad tuam statim jussionem tam habitum ipsa quam animum immutarem. . . ."

161. Heloise, *Ep.* 1, ed. Muckle, 71 (trans. Radice, 113): "ut, quo me videlicet pro te amplius humiliarem, ampliorem apud te consequerer gratiam. . . ."

162. Heloise, *Ep.* 1, ed. Muckle, 72 (trans. Radice, 116): "Tuo examini cuncta committo, tuo per omnia cedo testimonio. . . ."

163. Heloise, *Ep.* 1, ed. Muckle, 72 (trans. Radice, 116): "omnia propter te compleverim nunc in tuo maxime perseverans obsequio."

164. Heloise, *Ep.* 3, ed. Muckle, 81 (trans. Radice, 134): "te magis adhuc offendere quam Deum vereor; tibi placere amplius quam ipsi appeto." Also *Ep.* 3, ed. Muckle, p. 82: "tibi per omnia placere studeo." Abelard confirms the formulation and the sentiment by appropriating her own words in his response: "Quae cum mihi per omnia placere, sicut profiteris, studeas, . . . ut mihi summopere placeas, hanc depone . . ." (Abelard, *Ep.* 4, ed. Muckle, p. 87).

165. M calls him "a novice" in love (M 98, p. 276: "Tyroni et amantium dulcissimo"). He states outright (quoting Ovid, *Metamorphoses*, 1.452), "This is my first love, For the flame of love has never before penetrated my innards" (Tu me vicisti, potuit quem vincere nulla. / Fortius hinc uror, est quia primus amor, / Nam non ante meas penetravit flamma medullas"—V 113, p. 288). Abelard says in the *Historia:* ". . . I began to relax the reins of desire, I who previously had lived most chastely" (frena libidini<s> cepi laxare, qui antea vixeram continentissime—HC M 256–57); "I had always held myself aloof from unclean association with prostitutes, and constant application to my studies had prevented me from frequenting the society of gentlewomen" (Quia igitur scortorum immunditiam semper abhorrebam et ab excessu et frequentatione nobilium feminarum studii scolaris assiduitate revocabar nec laicarum conversationem multum noveram . . .—HC M 272–78, trans. Radice, 66); Abelard's "previous reputation for continence" relieved Fulbert of any suspicion ("duo erant, quae eum [Fulbert] maxime a turpi suspicione revocabant, amor videlicet neptis et continentie mee fama preterita"—HC M 329–31); "We entered on each joy the more eagerly for our previous inexperience" (Et quo minus ista fueramus experti gaudia [i.e., amoris], ardentius illis insistebamus, et minus in fastidium vertebantur—HC M 344–46, trans. Radice, 68). Charges of lechery and womanizing directed against Abelard may cast some doubt on his claim of previous chastity (see John Marenbon, *The Philosophy of Peter Abelard* [Cambridge: Cambridge University Press, 1997], 14–15), but far more likely is that these are scurrilous claims of rivals delighting in Abelard's fall and heaping abuse on him, deserved or not.

166. For relevant passages in the *Epistolae*, see notes 24, 61, and 62 above. In writings by and about Abelard: HC M 43–44: "quo amplius fama extendebatur nostra, aliena in me succensa est invidia"; HC M 108–10: "Paucis itaque diebus ibi me studium dialectice regente, quanta invidia tabescere, quanto dolore estuare ceperit magister noster non est facile exprimere"; HC M 188–91: "quanto manifestius ejus me persequebatur invidia tanto mihi auctoritatis amplius conferebat . . ."; HC M 679–80: "[my school flourished; others shrank.] Unde maxime magistrorum invidiam atque odium adversum me concitavi . . ."; HC M 932–34: "et legatus coram omnibus invidiam Francorum super hoc maxime detestaretur"; HC M 1239–41: "Sicque me Francorum invidia ad Occidentem sicut Jheronymum Romanorum expulit ad Orientem"; and an epitaph of Abelard, *PL* 178, 104D: "Invidit mors ipsa tibi, qui causa fuisti / Omnibus invidiae. . . ."

167. M 49, pp. 226–28. See note 125 above.

168. See above, p. 142. Heloise, *Ep.* 1, ed. Muckle, 70–71 (trans. Radice, 113): "Nihil unquam, Deus scit, in te nisi te requisivi, te pure, non tua concupiscens. Non matrimonii foedera, non dotes aliquas expectavi, non denique meas voluptates aut voluntates, sed tuas . . . adimplere studui. . . ."

169. Heloise, *Ep.* 1, ed. Muckle, 71: "Deum testem invoco, si me Augustus universo praesidens mundo matrimonii honore dignaretur, totumque mihi orbem confirmaret in perpetuo praesidendum, carius mihi et dignius videretur tua dici meretrix quam illius imperatrix."

170. HC M 349–56 (trans. Radice, 68): "Tediosum mihi vehementer erat ad scolas procedere vel in eis morari; pariter et laboriosum, cum nocturnas amori vigilias et diurnas studio conservarem. Quem etiam ita negligentem et tepidum lectio tunc habebat, ut jam nihil ex ingenio sed ex usu cuncta proferrem. . . ."

171. V 22, p. 204: "Ad alios verba, ad te intencionem dirigo. Sepe in verbis cado, quia cogitacio mea ab eis extranea est."

172. See Mews, *Lost Love Letters*, 131–35.

173. What John Benton stated, in an essay published posthumously, modifying his original skepticism of the *Historia* and letters should serve as a caution against theories of fictional composition, forgery, and fraud that resist large bodies of inner-textual evidence: ". . . I can no longer believe, as I did in 1972, that any medieval forger could write an extended work using so many of Abelard's favorite phrases and quotations, and most certainly that a thirteenth century forger could avoid any clearly demonstrable anachronisms. . . . I consider all the errors and distortions can be attributable to Abelard himself" ("The Correspondence of Abelard and Heloise," 98 n. 6).

■ ■ ■

The Authorship of
the *Epistolae duorum amantium*

A Reconsideration

GILES CONSTABLE

Abelard wrote in the *Historia calamitatum* that when he was first attracted to Heloise, and hoped to seduce her, he already knew of her love and knowledge of letters and hoped "that we would be able to be together by mediating writing even when we were apart, that many things could be written more boldly than spoken, and could thus always take part in pleasant speeches." Heloise lived with her uncle the canon Fulbert, who wanted Abelard to teach his niece, and not long afterwards he moved into Fulbert's house. "We were first joined under one roof, and later in spirit. Under the guise of teaching, therefore, we were entirely free for love." Abelard consequently neglected his studies and lectures, and if he composed anything, "They were love songs, not the secrets of philosophy."[1] Abelard and Heloise were separated after Fulbert discovered the affair, but they continued to see each other. When Heloise became pregnant, Abelard sent her to his sister in Brittany, where she gave birth to their son Astrolabe. They then secretly returned to Paris and were married. "And we soon withdrew separately in secret, and subsequently we saw each other only rarely and privately, greatly hiding what we had done."[2] Years later, looking backwards, Heloise wrote to Abelard that "When you at one time sought me for shameful pleasures, you visited me with frequent letters, [and] by your many songs you placed your Heloise in the mouth of everyone."[3]

These passages show that Abelard and Heloise exchanged a number of letters during the course of their love-affair. These letters were presumed to be lost until 1974, when Ewald Könsgen published 113 letters and poems (some of them abbreviated) from MS Troyes, Bibliothèque municipale, 1452, under the title *Epistolae duorum amantium. Briefe Abaelards und Heloises?*[4] In his introduction, Könsgen argued, among other things, that the letters dated from the early twelfth century and were written by two writers, identified in the manuscript as V(ir) and M(ulier), of whom the man was a well-known teacher and writer and the woman was well educated, and whom Könsgen tentatively (as the question mark in his title shows) identified as Abelard and Heloise.

Könsgen's book attracted comparatively little attention at the time it appeared. It was reviewed, so far as I know, in only seven journals, none of them in England or the United States.[5] The reviewers for most part accepted Könsgen's argument that the letters were authentic in the sense that they were written by two correspondents over a period of time and were not form letters or a literary fiction. They were less convinced about the date or authorship. One reviewer wrote that "The dating is the weak point in the argument for the authorship of Abelard and Heloise,"[6] and another that "The evidence for a 'probable' dating in the first half of the twelfth century . . . is either uncertain . . . or too summarily handled."[7] The views of other scholars, who did not review the book, varied. Terese Latzki enthusiastically accepted the attribution to Abelard and Heloise and referred to Könsgen's edition as sensational.[8] Peter Dronke, writing in 1976, questioned the attribution, though he accepted that the letters were written in the early twelfth century and were "genuine letters and not from a rhetorical *ars dictandi.*"

> For all their individual touches, these letters take their place within a specific tradition, one that we can follow at Regensburg in Bavaria and Le Ronceray on the Loire in the late eleventh century, and again in Bavaria, at Tegernsee, in the early twelfth.[9]

Kindermann wrote that there was no proof that the letters were by Abelard and Heloise and suggested that they may have been written later, after the story of Abelard and Heloise became known.[10] Jolivet likewise stressed, "The question-mark of the subtitle has all its strength."[11]

There the matter rested, with occasional references by other scholars, notably the translations by Etienne Wolff of sixty-one of the letters,[12] until 1999, when Constant Mews, in his book *The Lost Love Letters of Heloise and Abelard*, sought to remove Könsgen's question mark and to show, primarily on the basis of style and content, that Abelard and Heloise were indeed the authors of these letters (which will be referred to here as the early or "love" letters as distinct from the late or "monastic" letters). "The close interconnections between their correspondence [both the early and the late letters] and their other writings," Mews maintained, "leaves no doubt that Abelard and

Heloise did write the correspondence attributed to them."[13] C. Stephen Jaeger likewise argues in the essay in this volume that "To reject the ascription requires positing either fraud, fiction, and forgery of a highly refined, essentially non-medieval kind—or another pair of learned French lovers who write, think, behave, and are just as famous and controversial as Abelard and Heloise."[14] Between them Mews and Jaeger, in spite of some differences, brought a wealth of learning and ingenuity to strengthen Könsgen's case for attributing the letters to Abelard and Heloise. In particular they analyzed the differences in style, vocabulary, and ideas between the two writers and examined the themes and motifs that were current in the early twelfth century. They showed that the letters could have been written by Abelard and Heloise, although they found no positive evidence that they were.

Mews's volume met with a mixed reception. Some scholars, including Barbara Newman, declared themselves convinced by his arguments.[15] Others expressed reservations. Werner Robl in a long internet article argued that the letters were both real letters and a literary fiction and that in spite of many parallels with the works of Abelard and Heloise they offer no firm evidence for their authorship.[16] Peter von Moos went further, calling the "sensation" of the letters' discovery a "soap-bubble" and suggesting that they may be subsequent reconstructions, put together perhaps on the basis of genuine originals but incorporating fictional elements and memories of spoken words.[17] In these discussions there is a tendency for literary scholars to present arguments based on style and vocabulary and for historians to look for factual proof, such as a reference to Fulbert or your uncle, which would put the matter beyond reasonable doubt. There is no clear division, however, and scholarly views and personal convictions, including the desire to hear a distinctive voice of Heloise, are sometimes mingled.

Since the letters are not attributed to Abelard or Heloise in the text or in the manuscript, or presumably in the exemplar, they cannot (as Jaeger says) be called a fraud, forgery, or hoax in the usual sense of these terms, unless the writers were subtle enough to foresee that future scholars might attribute the letters to Abelard and Heloise on the basis of style and content, without any concrete details. The fact that the letters are not forgeries, however, does not prove that they are "real," "authentic," or "genuine" in the sense that they contain the words of the writers at the time they were written, either by Abelard and Heloise or by another pair of lovers, real or fictional. Most medieval letters were to some extent revised after they were written (or dictated) and before they were incorporated into the collections in which they survive. Many were used in formularies and handbooks of letter writing, or *dictamen*, which include letters and epistolary exercises that are authentic in their own way. Some derive from genuine letters. Others, though fictional in the sense that they were not sent to another person, are part of a recognized genre and often derived from and served (both then and now) as a basis for letters that were actually sent and received. Mews himself said that the letters can be read as a novel,[18] and Ward and Chiavaroli that the literary training of the writers led to "a blurring of fiction and reality."[19]

The dating of the letters poses some problems for the proponents of their attribution to Abelard and Heloise. According to the accepted chronology of their lives, they must have been written in 1116–17, when their love affair was at its height and when they were both living in the house of Heloise's uncle Fulbert.[20] Ward and Chiavaroli, while maintaining that most of the letters were written "during a single year,"[21] date the collection to around "1116 to 1118" but also divide it into two groups, of which they date the second (*Epp.* 87–113) to "the period after Heloise's removal to Argenteuil" and even as late as 1129.[22] The question is of importance for the chronology of the life of Heloise, who is commonly thought to have been born around 1100 and to have acquired her learning at Argenteuil, where she retired after the affair with Abelard and presumably, therefore, after these letters were written.[23] The letters certainly show an astonishing degree and type of learning, verging at times on pedantry, for a girl of sixteen or seventeen.[24] Mews therefore pushed back the date of her birth, and Ward and Chiavaroli suggested that she was in her "late teens, mid-twenties perhaps,"[25] which would make her closer in age to Abelard (who was born about 1079) than is generally assumed and very old for even a trusting uncle to have taken a grown man into his home as her tutor.

The text-history of the letters also poses problems. The *Ex epistolis duorum amantium* form the final signature (fols. 159r–167v) of the Troyes manuscript, which was completed in the second half of the fifteenth century by a monk (later prior) of Clairvaux named Johannes de Vepria (La Voire or La Woevre, near Verdun).[26] The other works in the manuscript, mostly letters and some of them excerpts, are by Cassiodorus, Cicero, Sidonius Apollinaris, Ennodius, Cyprian, Transmundus (a papal notary and monk of Clairvaux who died after 1216), John of Limoges (who died in the mid-thirteenth century), Carolus Virulus (who died in 1493), and the English historian William of Malmesbury.[27] Johannes de Vepria gave no indication of the sources from which he derived the texts either in this manuscript or in another collection of *Deflorationes* (MS Troyes, Bibl. mun., 2471), which includes excerpts from the works of Petrarch, Homer, Virgil, Ovid, Tibullus, and Sidonius Apollinaris.[28] Since no other manuscript of the works of at least one of these authors is listed in the 1521 catalogue of the library at Clairvaux, de Vepria apparently made use of other libraries.[29] The title *Ex epistolis duorum amantium* is ambiguous, since it may mean that he made a selection from the letters that he had before him, that he abbreviated all or some of them, or that they were already excerpted. In the manuscript the divisions in the text are marked by a faint sloping line (represented by a vertical line in Könsgen's edition) and the omissions by two faint sloping lines.[30] To judge from the indications in the printed editions, about one third of the letters are abbreviated and two thirds of them are complete, including a few long letters, such as *Ep.* 49 (67 lines in Mews's edition).[31] It is an error, therefore, to say that the collection, in spite of the title, is made up entirely of excerpts or to assume that all the letters were abbreviated in order to exclude passages that might have given explicit clues to their authorship, provenance, or date.[32]

It is hard to know Johannes de Vepria's principles of selection and abbreviation. It would be interesting to study his excerpts from works of which the full texts are known, but for the *Epistolae* this is impossible, unless a complete manuscript comes to light. His primary interests, to judge from MS 1452, seem to have been epistolary. Ward and Chiavaroli remarked on "de Vepria's interest in dictamen rather than love letters per se" and called his collection "an advanced resource book for dictamenal and epistolary purposes."[33] This view is supported by his inclusion of the works of Transmundus and John of Limoges, who were masters of letter writing, and perhaps also of the *Epistolae*, if they were, as Mews put it, "as much an exercise in the art of composition as a genuine communication of ideas."[34] The Cistercians were interested in letter writing and made some significant contributions to the literature of dictamen, but they would hardly have had any use for these letters, which chart the course of a passionate love affair. It may be that Johannes's concern with the art of letter writing overtook his practical concerns and that he succumbed to the interest of the letters as works of literature.

It is not known how the letters were preserved between the time they were written and the second half of the fifteenth century, when they came to the attention of Johannes de Vepria. Among the suggestions that have been made are that de Vepria found them at the Paraclete or that they were given to Bernard of Clairvaux either by Heloise or (which seems unlikely) by her uncle Fulbert to use as ammunition against Abelard.[35] Since original letters of the twelfth century are of the utmost rarity, and large collections of originals unknown, it is almost certain that, like most medieval letters which have survived, they were gathered and copied at the time they were written or not long afterwards.[36] Even so, the preservation of such an extensive correspondence between two individuals is, so far as I know, unique for the eleventh and twelfth centuries.[37] A few short exchanges of letters are known, and many examples of individual letters and replies, but no other sustained one-on-one correspondences except for those attributed to Abelard and Heloise.[38]

This raises the question of how the letters were written and collected, presuming that they are by Abelard and Heloise. Like most letters at that time, they were probably first taken down on wax tablets and later copied onto parchment.[39] In one letter the man asked to be allowed to keep the woman's tablets so that he could write many things (*Ep.* 14). At least one of them was apparently sealed,[40] but it was unusual for writers of relatively modest social position to seal personal letters at that time, and a letter of this type, of which the authenticity was presumably not in doubt to the recipient, would have required a seal only if it was written on parchment, in the interests of secrecy. The letter was then given to a messenger, who carried it to the recipient and sometimes also delivered an oral message. At the end of *Ep.* 37 the man wrote "Ask the messenger what I did after I wrote the letter: I at once really threw myself onto the bed out of impatience." This passage, whether it was written before or after (as the writer claims) the letter was written, as Jaeger points out,[41] shows that it was less spontaneous than might appear at first sight. One or the other of the correspondents—scholars seem to have assumed it was the woman (i.e., Heloise) but it may have been the man— either kept copies of their letters (which would have been unusual outside the context of a chancery) or recovered the originals and copied them, or had them copied, into a volume which served as the basis, either directly or indirectly, of the collection in which Johannes de Vepria found the letters.[42]

Both Abelard and Heloise knew how to write. Heloise, as a student, may have been accustomed to preparing wax tablets and parchment, but Abelard presumably had these tasks done for him. Even texts they wrote themselves were later transcribed onto parchment by professionals. The writing of the volume in which the *Epistolae* were gathered was doubtless also the work of a professional scribe. Medieval love letters are extremely rare,[43] and private letters in the modern sense of the term hardly existed, which is why confidential messages were so often (and so frustratingly, from the modern point of view) entrusted to the mouth of a messenger. Scholars must therefore abandon the distinction between "public" and "private" letters,[44] since all medieval letters had a measure of publicity, from the moment they were written until their delivery, frequently by word of mouth before more than one person.

It is unclear why Abelard and Heloise should have written to each other so frequently and at such great length at a time when they were allegedly living under the same roof and seeing each other every day. The *Epistolae* may have been written earlier or later. Heloise in the passage cited above referred to "the frequent letters" written by Abelard at the time he sought her out "for shameful purposes." This sounds like the time before he moved into Fulbert's house or after they returned from Britanny, when their meetings were comparatively rare. In *Ep.* 54 the man wrote that "It is not absurd that from time to time, as now, we visit each other and a letter takes the place of bodily presence, since the consuming envy of evil men does not allow us to be joined in the way we wish."[45]

A possible solution to this difficulty is that the letters were re-written or even reconstructed after the lovers returned to Paris, or later, on the basis either of memory or of fragmentary drafts. Some time ago I wrote of the monastic correspondence, "Even if the letters are genuine in the sense that they were written by Abelard and Heloise, and sent between them, they were revised into a literary work which was intended to be read in its entirety as a retrospective narrative."[46] The same may be true of the love letters. They should not be read as if they were modern letters or spontaneous expressions of private feelings.[47] The learned references, elegant vocabulary, and elaborate variation, especially in the salutations, all smell of the lamp rather than of urgent passion.[48] Most lovers occasionally repeat the same terms in addressing their beloved, but here every salutation is different and often flat, as if searching for variety rather than an expression of real feeling.[49] This apparent lack of spontaneity would be explained, as would some of the practical scribal and epistolary questions, if the letters were later reconstructions of what Abelard and Heloise wrote (or thought they should have written) at the height of their love affair. It would also be explained if they were written by two other writers who were perhaps (though not necessarily) familiar with the circumstances of the lives of Abelard and Heloise and who composed the letters either for their own amusement or for the instruction of others, perhaps as a classroom exercise.

This impression is confirmed by some of the contents, such as the use by the man in *Ep.* 22 of the sun/moon image.

> Since the moon is made darker the closer [it is] to the sun, I am more on fire the more I am brought to you [and] the closer I am to you, and I am so inflamed, as you yourself have often noticed, that when I am next to you I am completely on fire [and] am totally burned down to the marrow.

The image here apparently means that as the moon derives its fire (and light) from the sun, and is seen less clearly the closer it is to the sun, so the writer of the letter burns more brightly the closer he is to his beloved. The sun/moon image was used in many ways in the Middle Ages. In the Bible the sun was compared to a holy man (constancy) and the moon to a fool (changeability), and St. Paul's reference to the "lights of the world" was commonly taken to mean the sun and the moon.[50] William of Conches, writing about 1125, cited the view of those who held that "Greater splendor appears in it [the moon] the further it is from the sun; lesser, when it is closer."[51] The sun and the moon were often compared to the secular and ecclesiastical powers,[52] most famously by Innocent III in his well-known letter of 1198, of which the first version argued (as Leonard Boyle put it) that "As the strength of the moon's light depends upon its proximity to the sun, so the *regalis potestas* depends upon the *pontificalis auctoritas,*" and the second that "The farther away the moon is from the sun the more it appears to shine in its own right, the nearer it approaches the more it is overshadowed."[53] The use of the image in *Ep.* 22 resembles that by Innocent III in that it argued from the relative positions of the sun and moon. It depends more on the heat of the sun than its brightness, but it also says that the moon is darker the closer it is to the sun. It is one of the earliest appearances of this image, if not the earliest, in a non-political context.

Many of the scholars who have studied the *Epistolae* clearly hope that they are by Abelard and Heloise, and there is an element of wishful thinking in their arguments. Heloise in particular has achieved something of a mythic status as a romantic heroine. Henry Adams wrote over a hundred years ago that Heloise "was, by French standards, worth at least a dozen Abelards."[54] The reaction to any perceived criticism therefore tends to be emotional. Anyone who attended the conference on Abelard and Peter the

Venerable held at Cluny in 1972 will remember the response by René Louis, who at that time was almost blind and spoke from memory, to the doubts raised by John Benton concerning the monastic letters.[55] To question their authenticity was for Louis not only to insult a long series of distinguished French scholars but also, and worse, to dishonor France and French womanhood. Mews expressed a similar view when he said that to argue that Abelard wrote all the letters "is to silence the voice of Heloise" and that those who question his attribution of the early letters "reflect an unwillingness to accept that such a gifted and independently minded woman could have existed in twelfth-century France."[56]

Scholars should not allow themselves to be intimidated by accusations of this sort if they doubt the attribution to Heloise or even that the letters labeled "M" were necessarily written by a woman. Nor should they lose sight of the interest of the letters apart from their authorship, like a work of art of which the only value lies in the name or names attached to it. Even if they were not written by Abelard and Heloise, it would not subtract significantly from their interest, since they add comparatively little to what is already known about Abelard and Heloise. Indeed, the attribution is based almost entirely on knowledge derived from works more firmly attributed to them. In any case, the *Epistolae* are of value in themselves. Scholars may differ regarding their authorship, date, style, and quality,[57] but they are without question a remarkable addition to the corpus of medieval love letters.

Notes

An expanded version of this article was published under the title "Sur l'attribution des *Epistolae duorum amantium*" in the *Académie des Inscriptions et Belles-Lettres: Comptes Rendus*, 2001: 1679–93. Since writing this essay, I have read three contributions arguing against the attribution to Abelard and Heloise: (1) a review of *Listening to Heloise* (cited in note 15) by Peter Dronke, suggesting that the female writer's literary formation was in Bavaria and that she was a *magistra* in her own right, (2) a long article by Peter von Moos, "Die *Epistolae duorum amantium* und die säkulare Religion der Liebe," *Studi medievali*, 3 S, 44 (2003): 1–115, saying the letters are the work of a single author writing in the late Middle Ages (probably fourteenth century) and that they are either "a bravura literary performance of early humanistic epistolary art" or "a reworking of a writing-exercise of a school of late *Ars dictaminis*," and (3) Jan M. Ziolkowski, "Lost and Found, or Lost and Not Yet Found? The Ascription of the Lost Love Letters of Heloise and Abelard" (forthcoming).

    1. J. T. Muckle, ed., "Abelard's Letter of Consolation to a Friend," *Mediaeval Studies* 12 (1950): 183–84. In the first excerpt "together" is literally "to be present to each other."

    2. Ibid., 189.

    3. J. T. Muckle, ed., "The Personal Letters between Abelard and Heloise," *Mediaeval Studies* 15 (1953): 73.

4. Ewald Könsgen, *Epistolae duorum amantium. Briefe Abaelards und Heloises?* Mittellateinische Studien und Texte 8 (Leiden: Brill, 1974). *Ep.* 38 is divided into three parts (38a, 38b, 38c) and *Ep.* 112 into two (112, 112a), making a total of 116 numbered letters.

5. *Deutsches Archiv* 32 (1976): 266–67 (Gabriel Silagi); *Cahiers de civilisation médiévale* 19 (1976): 181–82 (Edward Little); *Francia* 4 (1976): 844–47 (Anke Paravicini); *Scriptorium* 31 (1977): 130–31 (Hubert Silvestre); *Zeitschrift für romanische Philologie* 93 (1977): 118–19 (Arnulf Stefenelli); and *Maia: Rivista di letterature classiche* 33 (1981): 245–56 (Gioachino Chiarini), to which can be added the brief notice by A. Pattin, in *Tijdschrift voor filosofie* 41 (1979): 521.

6. Paravicini, in *Francia*, 846, who said that "The subtitle raises claims that Könsgen from the beginning was not ready to fulfil" (847).

7. Stefenelli, in *Zeitschrift für romanische Philologie*, 118.

8. Therese Latzke, "Die Carmina erotica der Ripollsammlung," *Mittellateinisches Jahrbuch* 10 (1975): 144–45.

9. Peter Dronke, *Abelard and Heloise in Medieval Testimonies*, W. P. Ker Memorial Lecture 26 (Glasgow: University of Glasgow Press, 1976), 25. See his *Medieval Latin and the Rise of European Love-Lyric*, 2nd ed. (Oxford: Oxford University Press, 1968), 2:422–47 and 472–82; and *Women Writers of the Middle Ages: A Critical Study of Texts from Perpetua (d. 203) to Marguerite Porete (d. 1310)* (Cambridge: Cambridge University Press, 1984), 92–97, where he expressed further doubts.

10. Udo Kindermann, "Abaelards Liebesbriefe," *Euphorion* 70 (1976): 292–94. I wrote that "There is no sure evidence of their authorship" in my *Letters and Letter-Collections*, Typologie des sources du moyen âge occidental 17 (Turnhout: Brepols, 1976), 34 n. 100.

11. Jean Jolivet, "Abélard entre chien et loup," *Cahiers de civilisation médiévale* 20 (1977): 312 n. 20. While nothing proved that the letters were not written by Abelard and Heloise, Jolivet said, nothing proved that they were. Jean Leclercq, *Monks and Love in Twelfth-Century France* (Oxford: Oxford University Press, 1979), 79–81, said (without further evidence) that the *Epistolae* were "written somewhere between the Île de France and the region of Clairvaux, in the second half of the twelfth century, and, more precisely, between 1183 and 1185" (thus excluding the authorship of Abelard and Heloise) and calling them "an amusement between lettered persons." See also Rüdiger Schnell, *Causa amoris*, Bibliotheca Germanica 27 (Bern: Francke Verlag, 1985), 21, 154, and 166.

12. *La lettre d'amour au moyen age*, trans. Etienne Wolff (Paris: NiL éditions, 1996). Like previous scholars, Wolff considered the letters an authentic correspondence between two individualized lovers but said that since there were no concrete indications of when or where they were written, the attribution to Abelard and Heloise remained a supposition. See also Rolf Köhn, "Dimensionen und Funktionen des Öffentlichen und Privaten in der mittelalterlichen Korrespondenz," in *Das Öffentliche und Private in der Vormoderne*, ed. Gert Melville and Peter von Moos, Norm und Struktur 10 (Cologne, Weimar, and Vienna: Böhlan Verlag 1998), 337, saying that the authenticity of the *Epistolae* was problematical.

13. Constant J. Mews, *The Lost Love Letters of Heloise and Abelard: Perceptions of Dialogue in Twelfth-Century France* (New York: St. Martin's Press, 1999), 55; see 143: "These letters must have been written by Abelard and Heloise." But he expressed some hesitation on 74 and 119.

14. Cited here as Jaeger, "*Epistolae.*" See also his *Ennobling Love: In Search of a Lost Sensibility* (Philadelphia: University of Pennsylvania Press, 1999), 160–64 and 226–29.

15. See the reviews by Barbara Newman on the internet *Medieval Review* (dated 1999) and by Michael Clanchy in the *Times Literary Supplement*, 25 February 2000; John O. Ward and

Neville Chiavaroli, "The Young Heloise and Latin Rhetoric: Some Preliminary Comments on the 'Lost' Love Letters and Their Significance," in *Listening to Heloise: The Voice of a Twelfth-Century Woman*, ed. Bonnie Wheeler (New York: St. Martin's Press, 2000), 53–119; Chrysogonus Waddell, "Heloise and the Abbey of the Paraclete," in *The Making of Christian Communities in Late Antiquity and the Middle Ages*, ed. Mark Williams (forthcoming); and Anne Lester, "Une autre voix d'Héloïse? La femme dans les 'Epistolae duorum amantium,'" in *Très sage Héloïse* (La Vie en Champagne, H. S., 2001), 22–25. Jacques Verger, "Abélard et Héloïse d'apres les sources historiques," in *Héloïse et Abélard: Entre passion, raison et religion*, ed. Lise Grenier (Cluny, 2001), 31–38, considered the attribution to Abelard and Heloise uncertain and that "the strictly biographical interest of these letters is in any case limited."

    16. Werner Robl, "*Epistolae duorum amantium*—Authentische Liebesbriefe Héloïsa's und Abaelard's?" (internet article dated April 2000).

    17. Peter von Moos, "Abaelard, Heloise und Paraklet: ein Kloster nach Mass," in *Individualität und Religiosentum*, ed. Gert Melville (forthcoming).

    18. Constant J. Mews, "Philosophical Themes in the *Epistolae duorum amantium:* The First Letters of Heloise and Abelard," in *Listening to Heloise: The Voice of a Twelfth-Century Woman*, ed. Bonnie Wheeler (New York: St. Martin's Press, 2000), 48. See also Mews, *Letters*, 14.

    19. Ward and Chiavaroli, "Young Heloise," 67. Cf. Morgan Powell, "Listening to Heloise at the Paraclete: Of Scholarly Diversion and a Woman's 'Conversion,'" in *Listening to Heloise: The Voice of a Twelfth-Century Woman*, ed. Bonnie Wheeler (New York: St. Martin's Press, 2000), 257, where he called the correspondence "history's first epistolary novel, whether fact or fiction" and "something of a medieval *unicum*."

    20. Jaeger dates them c. 1115–1117. Silvestre, in *Scriptorium*, 130–31, said the correspondence lasted at least a year, and Lester, "Autre voix," 24, dated it 1116–1117/18. See also Constant J. Mews, *Peter Abelard*, Authors of the Middle Ages 5 (Brookfield, Vt.: Variorum, 1995), 12, and Mews, "Philosophical Themes," 37, and Wheeler in the introduction to *Listening to Heloise*, xviii.

    21. Ward and Chiavaroli, "Young Heloise," 81.

    22. Ibid., 62, 66, and 95. See also note 32 below.

    23. Deidre Stone, "Heloise: *La très sage* Abbess of the Paraclete," in *Illumined by God: Essays on Medieval Monastic Women from Tjurunga*, ed. Kym Harris (Croydon, Vic., 2000), 29 n. 12, and 31.

    24. Peter the Venerable, who was born in 1092 or 1094, said that he had heard of Heloise's honest and praiseworthy studies while he was still a young man (*The Letters of Peter the Venerable*, ed. Giles Constable, Harvard Historical Studies 78 [Cambridge, Mass.: Harvard University Press, 1967], 1:303; *Ep.* 115).

    25. Mews, *Letters*, 32, and "Philosophical Themes," 37; Ward and Chiavaroli, "Young Heloise," 58. Robl, "*Epistolae*" suggested c. 23.

    26. On Johannes de Vepria, who lived from 1445/50 to 1517/19, see Könsgen, *Epistolae*, xx–xxxviii, who estimated that he was about twenty-five years old at the time he completed this manuscript, and Mews, *Letters*, 8–11.

    27. The manuscript is listed in the catalogue of the library of Clairvaux compiled by Mathurin de Cangey about 1521 (MS Troyes, Bibl. mun., 2616) under the title *Deflorationes bone. manu Joannis de Vepria scripte*, with the number o b XIII: see André Vernet, *La bibliothèque de l'abbaye de Clairvaux du XIIe au XVIIIe siècle*, I, Documents, études et répertoires publiés par l'Institut de recherche et d'histoire des textes (Paris, 1979), 545, no. 1432; cf. 483, no. 822b (T c IIII).

    28. Vernet, *Bibliothèque*, 528, no. 1310a.

29. It is not therefore certain, as most scholars have assumed, that the manuscript from which he took the *Epistolae* was at Clairvaux, unless (which is highly improbable) he destroyed or otherwise disposed of a manuscript in the library at Clairvaux after making his excerpts.

30. Könsgen, *Epistolae*, xxviii–xxix, and Mews, *Letters*, 182–83. These indications are inconsistent, and the divisions and omissions in the manuscript are not entirely clear in the printed editions. Neither Könsgen nor Mews, for instance, indicate the omission sign after the title, which is clearly visible even in the reproductions of the first page. The punctuation is also changed.

31. Lester, "Autre voix," 23, suggested that the increasing proportion of entire letters after *Ep.* 20 may be owing to the beauty of the language.

32. Ward and Chiavaroli, "Young Heloise," 83, said the de Vepria collection "contains only some of the letters exchanged by Abelard and Heloise at different times, and most have been expurgated and deprived of unequivocal references to events of their lives."

33. Ibid., 71 and 99.

34. Mews, *Letters*, 14. In his *Abelard*, 41, Mews said that the collection showed "the humanist interest at Clairvaux in the late fifteenth century."

35. Bernard certainly never alluded to them: Robl, "*Epistolae,*" 21–22.

36. Constable, *Letters*, 56–62. See also Kohn, "Dimensionen," 331 and 339–48, and Mary Garrison, "'Send More Socks': On Mentality and the Preservation Context of Medieval Letters," in *New Approaches to Medieval Communication*, ed. Marco Mostert (Turnhout: Brepols, 1999), 74: "The most fundamental feature of medieval Latin letters is that they were almost without exception intentionally preserved through recopying into manuscripts, usually letter-collections or miscellanies."

37. See Richard W. Southern, "The Letters of Abelard and Heloise," in his *Medieval Humanism and Other Studies* (Oxford: Oxford University Press, 1970), 87, and Mary McLaughlin, *Heloise and the Paraclete* (forthcoming), calling the monastic letters "unique among contemporary letter-collections."

38. The monastic letters, which were well known in the later Middle Ages, may have inspired imitators.

39. Constable, *Letters*, 44–45; Elisabeth Lalou, "Les tablettes de cire médiévales," *Bibliothèque de l'Ecole des Chartres* 147 (1989): 123–40, who said that "Le parchemin était done trop cher pour qu'on l'employât pour le brouillon. La cire était le brouillon idéal" (134); and the two articles by Richard and Mary Rouse, "Wax Tablets," *Language and Communication* 9 (1989): 175–91, and "The Vocabulary of Wax Tablets," *Harvard Library Bulletin* n.s. 1.3 (1990): 12–19. See also Silvestre, in *Scriptorium*, 131; Wolff, *Lettre*, 26; and Garrison, "Send More Socks," 78–80.

40. The man wrote at the end of the poem (*Ep.* 38a) sent with *Ep.* 37, "facio finem concludens ista sigillo": Könsgen, *Epistolae*, 20, and Mews, *Letters*, 218, where "seal" may refer to a kiss or some other personal mark rather than a conventional seal. See also the reference to *signaculum* in *Ep.* 16: Könsgen, *Epistolae*, 7, and Mews, *Letters*, 198. Abelard apparently had a seal in 1118: see Paravicini, in *Francia*, 846.

41. Jaeger, "*Epistolae,*" n. 48.

42. Christopher Baswell drew my attention to the reading Oluna for Clinia in *Ep.* 45 (Könsgen, *Epistolae*, 24, var. a; Mews, *Letters*, 224, var. h), which suggests that de Vepria had difficulty with the minims in his exemplar, which had Clinia.

43. Garrison, "Send More Socks," 95–99.

44. J. de Ghellinck, *L'essor de la littérature latine au XIIe siècle*, Museum Lessianum—Section historique 4–5 (Brussels, 1946), 1:111; Jean Leclercq, "Les lettres familières d'un moine du Bec,"

Analecta monastica, vol. 2, Studia Anselmiana 31 (Rome: Libreria vaticana, 1953), 145; Köhn, "Dimensionen," 319–26; and Powell, "Listening to Heloise," 280 n. 14.

45. Könsgen, *Epistolae,* 31, and Mews, *Letters,* 236, where (following a suggestion of Christopher Baswell) I have emended "uel" (which makes no sense in the context) to "ut" in the phrase "aliquando uel sic."

46. Giles Constable, "Forged Letters in the Middle Ages," in *Fälschungen im Mittelalter. Internationaler Kongress der Monumenta Germaniae historica. München, 16.–19. September. 1986.* Monumenta Germaniae historica Schriften 33 (Hanover: Hahnsche Buchhandlung, 1988–90), 5:25.

47. Von Moos, "Abaelard," 6 and n. 23.

48. Jaeger, "*Epistolae,*" 137 and 138, says that the woman's letters were more "weighted by learned freight" than the man's and that "Her lines are richly overladen with allusions and quotations."

49. Wolff, *Lettre,* 118; Ward and Chiavaroli, "Young Heloise," 73 and 75; and Robl, "*Epistolae,*" 33.

50. Eccles. 27:12 and Phil. 2:15.

51. William of Conches, *Philosophia,* II, xv, 69, ed. Gregor Maurach (Pretoria: University of South Africa, 1980), 67.

52. See Ernst Bernheim, *Mittelalterliche Zeitanschauungen in ihrem Einfluss auf Politik und Geschichtschreibung,* I. *Die Zeitanschauungen* (Tübingen: J. C. B. Mohr, 1918), 154; Percy Ernst Schramm, *Kaiser, Rom und Renovatio,* Studien der Bibliothek Warburg 17 (Leipzig: B. G. Teubner, 1929), 1:124 n. 5; and Othmar Hageneder, "Das Sonne-Mond-Gleichnis bei Innocenz III," *Mitteilungen des Instituts für österreichische Geschichtsforschung* 65 (1957): 340–68, who concentrated on Innocent III but included (346–47 n. 36) references to some earlier uses of the simile.

53. Othmar Hageneder and Anton Haidacher, ed., *Die Register Innocenz' III., 1. Pontifikatsjahr. 1198/99,* Publikationen der Abteilung fur historische Studien des österreichischen Kulturinstituts in Rom, II, 1 (Graz: H. Böhlaus Nachf, 1964), 600. See the review by Leonard Boyle in *Speculum* 42 (1967): 155–56.

54. Henry Adams, *Mont-Saint-Michel and Chartres* (Boston and New York: Houghton Mifflin, 1936), 284. See John Marenbon, "Authenticity Revisited," in *Listening to Heloise: The Voice of a Twelfth-Century Woman,* ed. Bonnie Wheeler (New York: St. Martin's Press, 2000), 22, and Powell, "Listening to Heloise," 259, who remarked on the tendency of scholars "to suppress the voice of the abbess in favor of that of the passionate lover."

55. See *Pierre Abélard–Pierre le Vénérable. Les courants philosophiques, littéraires et artistiques en Occident au milieu du XIIe siècle. Abbaye de Cluny, 2 au 9 juillet 1972,* Colloques internationaux du Centre national de la recherché scientifique 546 (Paris: Editions du Centre national de la recherché scientifique, 1975), 75. Louis's talk (of which the text was not printed) was given in the church of St-Marcel-lez-Chalon.

56. Mews, *Letters,* 116 and 170. Cf. Barbara Newman, "Authority, Authenticity, and the Repression of Heloise," *Journal of Medieval and Renaissance Studies* 22 (1992): 121–58.

57. For some they are of relatively little interest and importance, whereas for others they are a major literary discovery. On the style, cf. the views of Jaeger, "*Epistolae,*" 133–38 and Newman, in *Medieval Review,* who referred to "the shimmering beauty, intensity, and intellectual excitement of the original [Latin] letters." Most of the reviewers of Könsgen's edition such as Little were not particularly impressed by the literary style of the letters.

■ ■ ■

A Reply to Giles Constable

C. STEPHEN JAEGER

Giles Constable's gentlemanly skepticism is a brake on a vehicle which is moving slightly above the speed limit. His "Reconsideration" is not a refutation or a reply to the arguments in favor of ascribing the *Epistolae duorum amantium* to Heloise and Abelard. His purpose is to slow down Constant Mews and others, like me, who have accepted Mews's finding, prematurely he believes. He does not present evidence or substantial arguments against the ascription of the *Epistolae* to Abelard and Heloise; he just issues a gentle cautioning.[1]

As Constable says, no "positive evidence" identifies and locates the *Epistolae duorum amantium* with certainty. That means, no signatures, no clearly locatable details of the identity of the authors.

Constable implies two categories of evidence: "positive evidence," that is, "factual proof, such as a reference to Fulbert or your uncle, which would put the matter beyond a reasonable doubt,"[2] on the one hand, and textual analysis (style, vocabulary, ideas, themes, and motifs) on the other. Mews, Könsgen, and Jaeger have produced "arguments," but not proof, says Constable. He does not concern himself with the weight or flimsiness of those arguments. One could read the "Reconsideration" with no sense that those arguments might range on a scale from "highly probable" to "possible" to "improbable" to "false." This unconcern implies that proof is not available through this second means, as though stylistic and innertextual arguments simply did not play in the same league with "positive evidence."

If theoretical scientists applied such a rigorous standard of proof and put aside every theory which could not be proven with "certain evidence," they would eliminate one of the most fruitful modes of discovery. Where absolute certainty is not available in any question—in laboratories, courts of law, or the study of the past—proof turns to a scale of probability: theses are advanced for testing, verifying or falsifying. There is a point where "highly probable" moves close enough to "certain" that the texts affected can reliably be treated according to the close-to-proven premises, at least until those are overturned. "Explanatory power," the strength, simplicity, and "elegance" of arguments become measures of the validity of theses. This second line of "proof" is especially important in the corpus of writings of Abelard and Heloise—now held in dubious suspicion for nearly 200 years, objections to authenticity repeatedly overturned—lest that rich and important body of writings become the Jarndyce and Jarndyce of medieval scholarship.

While "positive evidence" is lacking in the case of the *Epistolae*, we have a large number of texts available for analysis, works of self-revelation so remarkable (whoever the "selves" may be) as to fall outside of the framework of medieval conventions. We have a large collection (there is no such thing) of private love letters (there is no such thing),[3] documents, in other words, that the conventions and traditions of medieval epistolography would seem to exclude. What shall we do? Rule the *Epistolae duorum amantium* out of bounds as an *adynaton* of Medieval Studies? Find some other medieval textual tradition to whose conventions they do conform? Or come to terms with them as a unique set of documents? Obviously, the latter. The result may even be a broadening of our conceptions of medieval epistolography.

Searching and scrupulous analyses of the texts have to be the starting point. If anything has emerged from the authenticity controversy of the 1970s and 1980s, it is that careful and broadly comparative textual analysis is the best method of authentication or falsification when absolute factual proof is either altogether lacking or present but placed in question by the suspicion of forgery, borrowing, interpolation, or literary imitation.[4]

Careful literary and stylistic analysis can be a perfectly valid method for providing proof of Abelard and Heloise's authorship—or proof that they had nothing to do with the letters. Dronke and Janson, for instance, succeeded in dating the *Historia calamitatum* and personal letters in the early twelfth century by analysis of the cursus patterns. Their "arguments" lay to rest decisively the thesis of a thirteenth-century forgery.[5] It would be quixotic to insist on more "positive evidence" of dating or to rule out the stylistic evidence by a hierarchy of "Beweiskraft" with facts at the top and style at the bottom. Von Moos's article, "Post festum," is a concentrated case for the practical superiority of stylistic analysis to historical fact in judging the Abelard-Heloise correspondence.[6] It is possible to authenticate the *Epistolae duorum amantium* as writings of Abelard and Heloise—or to falsify them as such.[7] We are not operating outside of a framework of critical proof in turning to textual analysis (style, vocabulary, ideas, themes, and motifs).

Falsification is the first order of proof, preferable to verifiability, since a hundred confirming parallel examples adduced to verify a hypothesis mean nothing in the face of a single example which falsifies it. If a claim cannot be falsified, it can also not be verified.

Here is a criterion of falsification for many of my arguments in "The Ascription": Könsgen shows persuasively that these letters are the products of two different authors. If that claim can be proven false, I will certainly "reconsider." Dual authorship of the *Epistolae* is generally accepted, though Constable argues that it is improbable because medieval epistolographic conventions would seem to rule out 113 letters composed by two correspondents and exchanged privately. But they exist nonetheless and it is no more possible to deny dual authorship on the basis of epistolographic considerations than it is to deny the existence of the *Epistolae* duorum *amantium* themselves on those grounds.

The claim of dual authorship is strengthened by Ward and Chiavaroli's and my observations of two different styles, two distinct personalities, two modes of conceiving love, and two different ethical vocabularies in the letters—considerations which tighten the weave of the argument that would have to be unwoven if the *Epistolae* are to be regarded, say, as a collection of pattern letters, a school exercise, or a literary imitation of Abelard and Heloise.

The idea that these are pattern letters or a literary imitation is rendered at best highly improbable by the extensive nature of the collection, by the dual authorship, and by the many passages with no context in the letters but a context in the private dealings of the correspondents (see "*Epistolae* and the Ascription," pp. 127–28). An author of a memoir or an epistolary dialogue might have allowed himself a slip or two, some incoherent utterance made perhaps to give the aura of immediacy and experience to his literary creations (but did anyone in the Middle Ages accept incoherent utterances as establishing immediacy of experience, and even if they did, did immediacy of experience count for anyone as a quality of letters that made them appear "genuinely experienced"? I doubt it.) An editor of pattern letters or even of reminiscences on the lives of two lovers would almost certainly have removed any and all such utterances. But there are too many of them in the body of texts to make an argument for extensive editorial or authorial oversight. The fact that Johannes de Vepria did not remove them suggests either lazy habits of editing or respect for the received text, interest in its contents and character. It is unthinkable that he would himself have composed a whole string of incoherent passages, or that he would have allowed them to stand, if he regarded his purpose solely as presenting a collection of pattern letters.

There is, moreover, also a large body of evidence in the letters pointing to Abelard and Heloise as the authors. The way to confute the evidence produced by Mews, Ward-Chiavaroli, and me is to challenge it and show our errors of analysis. The points of congruence between the *Epistolae* and Heloise and Abelard are not produced by wishful thinking, foredrawn conclusions, or a romantic desire to restore "the voice of Heloise." They are there in the texts of the letters, and those skeptical of the ascription would be on firmer ground if they would direct their critical gaze to the texts[8] rather than to my—or Mews's or Barbara Newman's or Michael Clanchy's—hidden motives and intentions, a realm into which they do not possess reliable insight.

The nature of their transmission (a fifteenth-century copy, no original manuscript preserved) coupled with the lack of concrete factual evidence of authorship of the *Epistolae* will necessarily generate hypotheses about the origins of these letters.[9] Constable's "Reconsideration" mentions several:[10]

- Constable had proposed for the eight "monastic" letters that "even if the letters are genuine in the sense that they were written by Abelard and Heloise, and sent between them, they were revised into a literary work which was intended to be read in its entirety as a retrospective narrative," and, he says, the same may be true of the *Epistolae duorum amantium;*
- Another possibility: [the composed character and the scribal and epistolary peculiarities may be explained if the letters were] "re-written or even reconstructed after the lovers returned to Paris, or later, on the basis either of memory or of fragmentary drafts";
- or "if they were written by two other writers who were perhaps (though not necessarily) familiar with the circumstances of the lives of Abelard and Heloise and who composed the letters either for their own amusement or for the instruction of others, perhaps as a classroom exercise" (pp. 172–73);
- or "they may be subsequent reconstructions, put together perhaps on the basis of genuine originals but incorporating fictional elements and memories of spoken words" (p. 169 with reference to von Moos).[11]

These suggestions bring us perilously near to Benton's and Silvestre's discredited reconstructions. They are hypotheses based not on the text of the letters, but rather on current knowledge of medieval epistolography and letter conventions, like "epicycles" conceived to rescue the Ptolemaic system of planetary motion, whenever observation threatened to overturn the theory. As to the idea that Abelard or Heloise may have reworked earlier letters: these letters seem pretty much unreworked. Those longer letters with discursive and philosophical content may come in the orbit of this explanation (which by no means places them out of the orbit of Heloise and Abelard—just the contrary), but the incoherent ones do not. If Constable's suggestion (Abelard and/or Heloise reworked their own early letters) were true, however, then we would be far closer to accepting the origins of these letters in the actual experiences of Abelard and Heloise (neither of whom presumably would have created fiction out of whole cloth when reconstructing their own love affair. They would have "reconstructed" their love affair; not a fiction of it, however romanticized or demonized it may have become through the fog of memory and the tug of circumstance after the affair). Likewise, if the *Epistolae* were a compilation work by someone close to Abelard and Heloise,[12] close enough to accomplish this striking counterfeit of their characters, styles, modes of feeling and expression—then his compilation work would be of considerable historical value. But this notion also seems more like an "epicycle" than a valid thesis. The qualities that link this correspondence to Heloise and Abelard are more simply explained as written by them than by some other person who knew them well. No one questions the presence of two distinct voices in these letters. Why is it necessary or useful to conjure a third?

Lowest in probability is the suggestion of two authors creating a fictional correspondence either for amusement or as a school exercise, one perhaps assigned by a teacher ("You take Abelard; you take Heloise"), and so creating two distinct individual styles and two distinct characters. No such thing exists, to my knowledge, either in Antiquity or the Middle Ages. Hypotheses have strength from explaining facts and resolving apparent contradictions, from "rescuing the phenomena." This hypothesis explains only how the letters might have originated with two authors but without Abelard and Heloise. It shows what follows when an anomaly is forced to fit the currently dominant knowledge of epistolography. We know for certain that Abelard and Heloise exchanged, at least claimed to have exchanged, many love letters in the heyday of their affair. That possibility exists as a reality, at least as a real concept of twelfth-century lovers. Two students (both presumably male) composing a historicized fictional dialogue does not exist as a reality or a concept. Add to the non-existence of the compositional mode the fact that the results of this hypothetical collaboration turn out to have many similarities, obvious and subtle, to the life, thought, and literary style of Heloise and Abelard—and this hypothesis falls on the scale of probability to "highly unlikely." One does not need either wishful thinking or a romantic desire for the "voice of Heloise" to judge it far more likely that Abelard and Heloise actually wrote and exchanged these letters and that they are transmitted (by whatever route) more or less as composed. The current knowledge of medieval epistolography must not be made into a straitjacket to torture the *Epistolae* until they conform.

The study of these letters has just begun. Let us hope that others engage in the discussion and that it proceeds in reasoned debate. I would also urge Peter von Moos to engage not by polemics, but by publishing the considerations that have set him so vehemently against the thesis of authorship by Abelard and Heloise.[13] If the line of argument begun by Mews is a soap bubble, then it will be easy to burst.

A truce is in order and particularly a moratorium on accusations of hidden motives, corrupted judgment, opinions nurtured by romantic desires. The probability that the *Epistolae duorum amantium* were written by Heloise and Abelard is high. Anyone who doubts it should disprove it.

Notes

1. Peter von Moos takes up a skeptical position far more vehemently in a forthcoming study of the collaboration of Heloise and Abelard at the Paraclete ("Abaelard, Heloise und ihr Paraklet: ein Kloster nach Mass, Zugleich eine Streitschrift gegen die ewige Wiederkehr hermeneutischer Naivitaet," in *Individualitaet und Religiosentum*, ed. Gert Melville). He begins with a heated polemic against "hermeneutic naiveté" in the post-Benton era of the "authenticity question." His polemic is directed especially against a "confidence, virtually void of any critical sense, in the ascription of anonymous sources," and he means by that Mews's book and its reception. He signals that Giles Constable's "Authorship . . . A Reconsideration" will put an end to the confidence in the ascription of the *Epistolae* (". . . Giles Constable [wird] demnaechst der erwaehnten Zuschreibungs-Zuversicht den Boden entziehen"—n. 14). But Constable's "Reconsideration" certainly does not fulfill that prophecy, and I doubt that Constable himself would make that claim for it. Von Moos sees himself as arguing against a decadence of scholarship and corruption of judgment. He believes that the ascription of the *Epistolae* to Abelard and Heloise is motivated by wishful thinking, a feminist research agenda, an appetite for scholarly sensations, and the conspiring of a sentimental desire for "the voice of Heloise" with "hermeneutic naiveté." He lashes out at those who disagree with him: Dronke is "obsessive" in his romanticism; Marenbon's distinction of arguments from evidence and arguments not from evidence is "manichaean"; Barbara Newman's "shallow but brilliantly written" article is borne by an "ideological subsystem," and her brand of medieval studies shows a "disinclination to history of spirituality," one connected with a "decline in education on the history of Christianity." The ascription of the *Epistolae* to Abelard and Heloise is a pack of "wild speculations," their positive reception by Mews's reviewers "shrill" (with a suggestion of hyped by charlatans—"marktschreierisch"). The whole line of argument in favor of the ascription is a "soap bubble," inflated by the romantic hopes and the femininist agenda of its proponents. He also brings no arguments against the ascription to Abelard and Heloise.

2. It should be said that concrete references such as the ones Constable mentions are useless for authentication if there is any suspicion of literary imitation (or forgery, not at issue here), since the creators of epistolary fictions (like forgers) also want to authenticate their handiwork. See the methodological considerations in my study, "The Prologue to the 'Historia calamitatum' and the Authenticity Question," *Euphorion* 74 (1980): 1–15.

3. Constable, "Reconsideration," p. 172: "private letters in the modern sense of the term hardly existed. . . . Scholars must therefore abandon the distinction between 'public' and 'private' letters, since all medieval letters had a measure of publicity, from the moment they were written until their delivery, frequently by word of mouth before more than one person."

4. As von Moos argued in 1980: "precisely [thorough textual interpretations] are in my opinion the most important methodological instrument of a rigorous critical approach to authenticity . . ." ("Post Festum: Was kommt nach der Authentizitaetsdebatte ueber die Briefe Abaelards und Heloises?" in *Petrus Abaelardus [1079–1142]: Person, Werk und Wirkung*, ed. Rudolf Thomas et al., Trierer Theologische Studien 38 [Trier: Paulinus, 1980], 79).

5. Janson, "Schools of Cursus in the Twelfth Century and the *Letters* of Heloise and Abelard," in *Retorica e poetica tra I secoli XII e XIV*, ed. C. Leonardi and E. Menestò (Florence: Scandicci, 1988), 171–200; Dronke, "Heloise's *Problemata* and *Letters*: Some Questions of Form and Content," in

Petrus Abaelardus, ed. Thomas, 53–73, reprinted in his *Intellectuals and Poets in Medieval Europe* (Rome: Edizioni di Storia e Letteratura, 1992), 295–322; also the refinement of his and Janson's earlier comments on cursus patterns in "Heloise, Abelard, and Some Recent Discussions," *Intellectuals and Poets*, 323–42, esp. 333–42. See also John Marenbon, *The Philosophy of Peter Abelard* (Cambridge: Cambridge University Press, 1997), 84.

6. Von Moos, "Post festum," 79, points to the case of Chrysogonus Waddell making plausible beyond any doubt that the *Historia* and letters arose at the same time as the Paraclete by connecting the prayers in Abelard's Letter 3 to the form of the daily collects of the Paraclete liturgy. Von Moos comments: "for Benton's change of mind [i.e., the recanting of his forgery thesis] apparently it was not the weakness of his historical evidence of contradictions—which could be dismissed relatively easily—but rather the strength of a single, small correspondence turned up by literary analysis."

7. Constable also assumes that the proponents of Abelard and Heloise as authors of the *Epistolae* have made no effort to test and falsify their own findings, but have put forward only what will confirm their foredrawn conclusions.

8. Werner Robl, a doctor and amateur medievalist, has posted an extensive study of the *Epistolae* on a website (http://www.abaelard.de/abaelard/575epist.htm), which has the great advantage of presenting arguments for and against the ascription to Abelard and Heloise based on extensive citation and analysis of the texts. He concludes, "May the letters remain for us what they in fact are: highly readable but in the final analysis anonymous masterpieces of the medieval art of the letter." There is useful material in Robl's study, but his attempt to show distinct contradictions between the *Epistolae* and genuine works of Abelard and Heloise is not persuasive. His parallels and contrasts are often imprecise. He draws overly strong conclusions from weak evidence and occasionally quotes out of context.

9. The same was true, for instance, of the Paston Letters, some 780 letters and documents, comprising the business and private letters of generations of an English family from the fifteenth to the seventeenth century. The manuscripts disappeared for about a century, and this provoked forgery theories. Their reappearance in 1889 put such theories to rest. See the article by Norman Davis, "Paston Letters," in *Dictionary of the Middle Ages*, 9.448–52.

10. Constable has his eye only on the artificial, composed character of the letters, "Reconsideration," pp. 172–73: "They should not be read as if they were . . . spontaneous expressions of private feelings. The learned references, elegant vocabulary, and elaborate variation, especially in the salutations, all smell of the lamp rather than of urgent passion." But the rhetorical, learned aspects by no means rule out or even argue against direct, unedited authorship by Abelard and Heloise. To my mind they confirm it.

11. Von Moos, "Ein Kloster nach Mass": "[we] are equally justified in regarding the present work as a reworking of available materials from various periods and as a fictional epistolary dialogue conceived in one stroke with the help of these materials."

12. Von Moos suggests Berengar of Poitiers as a possible candidate, in "Ein Kloster nach Mass."

13. Since I wrote these comments, Peter von Moos has completed a new study of the *Epistolae* displaying vast erudition: "Die *Epistolae duorum amantium* und die 'säkulare Religion der Liebe': Methodenkritische Vorüberlegungen zu einem einmaligen Werk mittellateinischer Briefliteratur." The study appeared in *Studi Medievali* 44 (2003). It is in large part a study of the rhetorical and topical elements of the *Epistolae*. He analyzes central motifs of the letters in a tradition of love literature

ranging from Antiquity to the Renaissance and tries, unsuccessfully, I believe, to show influence from Aelred of Rievaulx and Peter of Blois. He does not come to firm conclusions about the authorship and date of the letters, but he does urge two hypotheses of their origins: "Die in Frankreich oder Italien entstandenen Briefe sind entweder die Überarbeitung von Stilübungen (nicht Musterbriefen) einer Schule der späten *Ars dictaminis* oder eine literarische Bravourleistung frühhumanistischer Briefkunst." The work is a valuable study of the intellectual and rhetorical tradition of the love letters, but his attempt to refute the ascription to Abelard and Heloise (which he dismisses as "dilettantish") is far from conclusive, and his arguments for a dating in the fourteenth century, for influence of "dolce stil nuovo" and humanism, are forced. In the framework of the present exchange it must be said that an immensely learned specialist on medieval Latin love literature and intellectual traditions has not come to conclusive results on the dating, authorship, or circumstances of composition of this unique collection of texts. Authorship by Abelard and Heloise remains to my mind the most probable of the theses yet put forward.

Listening for the Voices of
Admont's Twelfth-Century Nuns

ALISON I. BEACH

Between 1715 and 1717, Bernard Pez (d. 1735), an Austrian historian and monk of Melk, traveled across Austria, Bavaria, and Swabia with the Maurists as his model, searching the libraries of Benedictine monasteries for the writings of the Order's authors. When he arrived at Admont—a community set on the banks of the Enns River in the Austrian province of Steiermark—Pez made an exciting discovery.[1] In Admont's library he found twelve manuscripts containing more than 250 original biblical commentaries and sermons. Many of these texts were the work of Irimbert (d. 1176), who would serve as abbot from 1172 to 1176.[2] The majority, however, were written anonymously. This did not stop Pez from printing them in his *Thesaurus anecdotorum novissimus* under the name of Godfrey, who was abbot from 1137 until his death in 1165.[3] But there is no evidence, either medieval or modern, in the manuscripts or elsewhere, that Godfrey wrote these or any other texts. For Pez, it seems, the simplest explanation was that the anonymous sermons were the work of the monastery's most visible twelfth-century *man*—a high-profile and long-lived abbot who also had the attraction of being prolific Irimbert's older brother. When Jacques-Paul Migne (d. 1875) reprinted Pez's version of the sermons in the *Patrologia Latina* in 1874, he retained Pez's attribution to Godfrey. Recent scholars have noted the tenuous, even non-existent, connection between Godfrey and the sermons.[4]

If not Godfrey, then who wrote these unattributed homilies? This question draws us into the fascinating world of twelfth-century Admont, where both men and women participated in, and contributed to, the community's vigorous intellectual life. There, in schools patterned after those at the reform monastery of Hirsau, students—both male and female—were trained in the liberal arts. While some students learned only the basics, others moved on to more advanced training in scriptural interpretation and dictamen (the art of formal letter writing). At the center of all of this literate activity were two busy and prolific scriptoria—one staffed by nuns, the other monks—which produced the manuscripts needed for all aspects of community life: liturgical books, the books of the Hebrew Bible and the New Testament, patristic and medieval theology and biblical commentary, saints' lives, canon law collections, and texts for individual devotional reading.

Although men and women were strictly segregated, a spirit of cooperation is evident both in written accounts of life at the monastery and in the manuscripts that survive from the period. In the scriptoria, teams of scribes—as many as six at a time—worked together to produce books, carefully coordinating script and parchment for uniformity.[5] In the women's chapter house, nuns took dictation as Irimbert preached, and together they transformed his spoken word into a written text. As other sermons were written, scribes copied them into individual booklets that would later be bound into manuscripts, which, thanks to careful coordination of parchment, ruling, and script, had a remarkably unified appearance. This tendency toward collective effort at Admont, either emerging from or reflecting a strong sense of community and common purpose, tends to obscure the accomplishments of individuals. While the group worked to record and edit a new sermon, the identity of its author could recede into obscurity. The community, it seems, was not interested in telling us who wrote individual sermons. Some questions, however, are hard to ignore: was it the nuns? Can we add any more examples to the relatively short list of texts written by medieval women?

Several scholars have mentioned the possibility that some of the Admont sermons were written by nuns, and a considerable amount of evidence points in their direction.[6] Women first entered the religious life at Admont during the first half of the twelfth century, following the introduction there of the customs of the Hirsau Reform. Irimbert tells us that the women conducted their own daily chapter meetings, where the *magistra,* as the head of a female community associated with the Hirsau Reform was called, was in charge. The women generally relied upon a monk to appear at the window of their chapter house—allegedly their only point of contact with the outside world—to deliver the daily sermon. On important feast days, Irimbert explains, when the monks were occupied with their own rituals, one of the nuns would preach. Some, he tells us, were highly experienced students of scripture.[7]

Irimbert knew what he was talking about: he had a special familiarity with their intellectual abilities through their collaborative work. It was the nuns, Irimbert suggests, who initiated this effort during the 1140s by secretly taking down his words as he preached to them on Ruth and Judges 19–21. Soon their idea was out in the open, and two women were assigned to assist him full-time.[8] The nuns took dictation on parchment or wax tablets, and then drafted successive versions of the text. Because Admont's nuns were strictly cloistered, we must imagine that they passed a working copy of the text out of their enclosure for delivery to the men's house where Irimbert read it over, made or requested corrections and additions, and returned it to the nuns. These men and women knew how to work together as a group to get the job done, in spite of the rules that required that the two sides of the community be physically separate.

This interaction is evident in the four surviving recensions of Irimbert's *Commentary on the Book of Ruth:* Vorau MS 193, Admont MS 650, Admont MS 682, and Admont MS 17. Vorau 193 (f. 186r–214v) was the first copy the nuns made from their notes, taken in dictation as Irimbert preached. This earliest version of the commentary contains the hand of three nun-scribes who shared the work of copying the main text. At least three hands—two of which are not identifiable as female scribes and therefore possibly scribes in the men's workshop—made corrections in the margins and on stubs of parchment that were bound into the manuscript. One corrector dominates the margins, and his (or less likely, her) corrections are taken up seamlessly into subsequent recensions of the text. A second corrector dominates the stubs, and these corrections, too, appear in all three later recensions. Except for Irmingart, who was the main scribe of the Ruth text and who copied a section of text on the last stub in the manuscript (f. 211r), the identity of the correctors is not known. It is possible that one of these was Irimbert, or that one or more were male scribes working for Irimbert in the monks' scriptorium.

The two intermediate recensions of the text, Admont MS 650 and MS 682, show the same group of female scribes at work on the text, with corrections made in the margins by a number of other hands, including the primary marginal corrector of Vorau 193. Both of these copies contain fewer marginal corrections and stub additions than Vorau 193, probably a reflection of a later stage in the textual editing. The two are similar in size and format, and the textual differences between them are not great. It is possible that one copy was produced for the nuns' library, and one for the monks'. Admont 650 evidently belonged to the monks and Admont 682 to the nuns. The variants in Admont 17, the final version of the commentary copied by the nuns, generally follow the corrected text in Admont 682, suggesting that MS 682 was the nuns' primary exemplar. Patterns of copying and correcting clearly show both ongoing work on the text and the nuns' continued involvement in the process.

The manuscripts do not reveal, however, the extent to which the text reflects the exegetical voice or voices of the nuns, and to what extent it reflects Irimbert's exegetical voice. In the process of taking dictation and creating a working draft of the commentary, the scribes must have made editorial decisions—we cannot expect their rendering of the sermon to be a verbatim representation of what was actually spoken.[9] As they heard Irimbert speak, they made choices—either consciously or unconsciously—about what to write down, how to write it down, and what to omit. It is clear that there was an active process of modification and correction taking place, though, and it seems that the nuns should get credit, if not for co-authorship, then for helping to give the text its literary shape and Irimbert his exegetical voice.

But did the nuns write any of the anonymous sermons themselves? They certainly had the intellectual skills, thanks to their internal school and its focus on training in biblical exegesis, as well as the experience they must have gained working with Irimbert. They had materials, skilled labor, and a workshop at their disposal. They also had access to a resource essential for the research and study required for writing sermons and commentaries: a good library. The nuns' book collection was tended by an in-house librarian, whose title was important enough to warrant mention in the house necrology by the beginning of the thirteenth century.[10] The librarian was in charge of an impressive library, which included biblical texts, patristic and medieval homilies, service books, saints' lives, and collections like the *Miracles of the Blessed Virgin* for spiritual edification and guidance. An even larger selection could be found right across the way in the monks' quarters.[11] The men's library was especially strong in patristic and medieval theology and biblical interpretation, including a particularly impressive collection of the works of Augustine, Bernard of Clairvaux, and Rupert of Deutz. A late medieval notation in Admont MS 232, a collection of patristic and medieval homilies, states that the monks had borrowed the book from the women's library, and it may be that the nuns had similar borrowing privileges. There is no evidence of any restriction on women's reading material.

A closer look at the nuns' library suggests still more about the origins of the anonymous homilies. Significantly, it was the nuns, not the monks, who seem to have owned Admont MS 58, MS 62, MS 63, MS 73, and MS 455, the carefully produced volumes containing the final recensions of the Admont sermons. Further, paleographical analysis suggests that these volumes were products of the nuns' scriptorium. All five volumes contain sermons for Sundays, and two, Admont MS 58 and MS 62, contain homilies for feast days—the days on which Irimbert tells us the nuns themselves preached.

Images in two of these volumes strengthen the connection between these manuscripts and the nuns. In MS 62 (folio 2r) a nun appears above the arch framing the table of sermon *incipits* (see figure 1). The nun, wearing a monastic habit (painted in blue and red), gazes straight out at the reader. Her facial features are not stylized: this appears to be the portrait of a woman, with large eyes, an oval face, broad nose, and small mouth. She holds a large book upright against her chest, her left hand supporting its weight, and her right hand raised. The distance between her right hand and the book is unclear. The artist may have intended to show the nun's hand resting on the book, or perhaps lifted in a gesture of preaching. Is this an image asserting the nuns' ownership of the book or some closer connection between the woman and the text? A

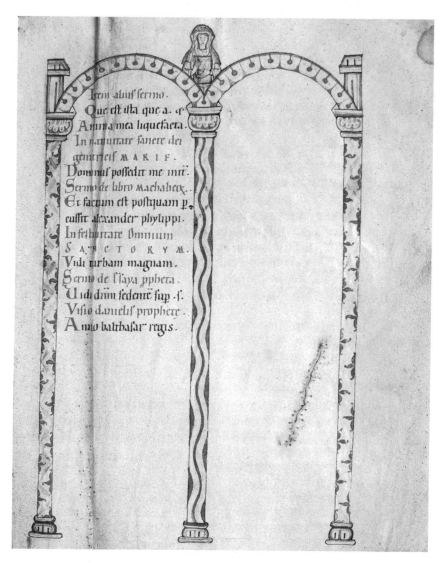

FIGURE 1. Nun Preaching, in Admont MS 62, folio 2r. Reproduced by permission of Stift Admont.

parallel image in Admont 58 (folio 1v) is equally intriguing (see figure 2). Here another nun appears above the arch framing the table of contents. This second woman wears the same head covering as the first, and the sleeves of her habit extend beyond the folds of an outer garment. Her face, which is similar to that of the nun in the first image with its large eyes and broad nose, is turned slightly away from the reader. Cradled in her right arm is a book (perhaps MS 58 itself, or a copy of the Bible) not much wider than her

FIGURE 2. Nun Holding a Book, in Admont MS 58, folio 1v. Reproduced by permission of Stift Admont.

hand, and her left hand is raised. This nun is clearly preaching. If we compare this with an image of Irimbert in Admont 17 (p. 471)—one that can certainly be interpreted as an author's portrait—we see a similar gesture: Irimbert stands, replacing the letter I in the opening line of his commentary on Ruth. In his left arm he holds a book, and his right hand is raised in a gesture of preaching or teaching. There is no doubt that Irimbert was the author of the text associated with the image. The juxtaposition of the image of the preaching nun in MS 58 and the sermons contained in that volume clearly suggest some connection between the two.

Two other books owned by the nuns show that they were serious enough about their biblical studies to reach out to regional experts when their questions exceeded their own expertise and that of the local monks. Admont MS 579, a copy of Honorius Augustodunensis' *Hexameron* and *Sign of Saint Mary*, contains a copy of a letter written by the theologian Gerhoch of Reichersberg (d. 1169) to the Admont nuns. A second copy is preserved in one of the nuns' liturgical books (Admont MS 602). In the letter, Gerhoch indicates that he is replying to a letter from the nuns, which is now lost, in which they solicited his interpretation of Psalm 50.[12] Gerhoch wrote another letter between 1145 and 1169, this time explaining the image of the centurion in Matthew 8:5–13. Here he refers to the women who had made the inquiry only as "his beloved sisters in Christ," but these may well have been Admont's nuns.[13]

Although the letters of exegetical inquiry to which Gerhoch referred have not survived, other letters written by the women are preserved in the remnants of a late twelfth-century copybook recently discovered in the monastery's archives. It is in these letters that we hear most clearly the exegetical voices of the nuns, and it may be possible to establish an intellectual and spiritual connection between them and the anonymous sermons.[14] In several cases, the writer of a letter introduces a biblical image, and then uses this core image, sometimes quite subtly, to make a rhetorical point. In one letter, a woman writes to a kinsman who has left the monastery and failed to make his promised return:

> I know, and it grieves me to know, that I do not have a faithful kinsman in you, but rather a reedy stick, useless and worthless that if a man leans on it, it shall pierce his hand. (Isa. 36:6).

This image serves to illustrate vividly that he is a source of harm rather than of help, but it may also have evoked a wider spiritual meaning for the sender and the recipient. Among the anonymous homilies preserved at Admont is one that explicates this particular chapter of Isaiah, setting forth a moral interpretation in which the story of Hezekiah and the king of the Assyrians becomes a story of perseverance in the religious life in the face of the temptations of the flesh and the pull of the world.[15] The reedy stick (*baculum*) in this moral reading is the "strict discipline of the spiritual life."[16] Fasting, vigils, and flagellation are practices that produce proximate pain, but that lead to joy as a reward in eternity.[17] It is the devil, in the guise of the king of the Assyrians and his messengers, who whispers into the ear of the person living the spiritual life that the pain and striving brought on by the *baculum* are in vain—a whispering that causes many to despair and, presumably, to leave the monastery with unfulfilled promises to return.[18] "But inasmuch as you have made your faith vain and you cared little to fulfill your promises, I grieve more for you than for me because you have lost the favor and love of the entire congregation." But here it is her kinsman who is this woman's *baculum*. Perhaps he is the source of her proximate pain, which having been endured will prove spiritually beneficial. Whether the writer or the monk-deserter were aware of this particular homily on Isaiah—either reading it or hearing it preached—is unclear. In any case, the *baculum* provides a powerful central biblical image that suited the rhetorical purposes of the letter. In their letters, the nuns made sophisticated use of biblical imagery, not simply citing passages, but also using particular images to frame and to motivate entire letters.

In another case, the writer introduces the image of the Canaanite woman who appears in the gospels of Matthew (Matt. 15:22–28) and Mark (Mark 7:24–30) and begs Jesus to cast out the demons that are plaguing her daughter. The author, who makes an impassioned plea for the return of her daughter who has been abandoned with strangers, returns to this image several times as she uses its power to make her point to the recipient:

> Carrying her in my arms, therefore, I have recourse to you, lord father, and throwing myself down, I place her before the feet of your lordship, and I wail and cry out in the place of and in the voice of the Canaanite woman: Lord, have mercy on my little daughter.

She transfers herself, via biblical reference, into the presence of the addressee, the archbishop of Salzburg, speaking "in the place and voice," of this other panic-stricken mother. The writer thus uses an image from the Bible as a vehicle through which she could "visit" a person outside the monastery.

This tendency toward epistolary visitation suggests another possible intellectual and spiritual connection between the nuns and the anonymous sermons. Alf Härdelin has pointed out the persistence of the idea of visitation (*visitatio*) in the anonymous homilies, and he considers this to be one of the "fundamental structures of that reform centre's spiritual thought."[19] He cites the example of a sermon on Luke 19:41–47, in which the preacher discusses Jesus' *visible*, physical visit to Jerusalem and then uses this image to signify Jesus' ongoing, *invisible*, approach to the individual soul. Härdelin notes the presence within the sermons of many different "modes" in which God is said to approach God's people.[20] There is a possible parallel here between the concept of visitation in the sermons and the kind of epistolary visitation that the nuns attempt. To be sure, there are also significant differences. The visiting that takes place in the sermons and commentaries is primarily theological: God approaches the faithful through a kind of mystical visitation. In the letters, it is the woman who appears to the recipient, not in a theological sense, but arguably in a mystical, or at least spiritual one. It may be that the possibility of spiritual visitation was appealing to a group of cloistered women, for whom physical visitation was out of the question. Neither of these parallels proves that the women wrote the anonymous sermons preserved at Admont, but they do reflect the nuns' engagement in biblical exegesis, both passively in the form of hearing or reading exegetical sermon-commentaries and actively in the form of their own biblically framed letters. These women clearly had the intellectual skills and the resources to write their own sermons, and patterns of scribal activity and book ownership suggest that they did.

Another possibility must not be overlooked: Irimbert himself may have written some of the anonymous sermons. Stephan Borgehammar, who has worked extensively on Irimbert's exegesis, notes that while the language of the sermons tends to be more florid, there are strong stylistic similarities between his commentaries and the anonymous sermons. Both emphasize sound and rhythm, and both follow the model of the formal classical homily, which was considerably outmoded by the twelfth century.[21] The close connection between Irimbert and the nuns, and particularly the nuns' intense familiarity with his style and methods, could well account for these similarities. Irimbert himself seems to have patterned his exegetical method after that of Gregory the Great, and the nuns may have consciously followed the model of the monk who was their teacher and collaborator.

The most plausible answer may be the one suggested by Alf Härdelin, that Admont's anonymous sermons and commentaries were "collective works."[22] Although sharing a similar style that could suggest that they are the work of a single author, they represent the collective achievement of the monastery's twelfth-century scholars and preachers, both male and female—I imagine this as a kind of parallel to the highly developed, regular bookhand used by the community's scribes. Just as this uniformity makes the identification of individual scribes difficult, the teaching and use of a common exegetical style complicates our ability to discern individual authors among the sermons and, as John Van Engen points out in this dialogue, we must not assume that the nuns learned exegesis from Irimbert: perhaps they learned from one another. Van Engen is also correct to say that the next step must be to look within the sermons themselves for distinctive voices, and emphases, and images. Admont's collaborative spirit, though, tends to blur the voices of individuals and blend their achievements. We may never know which individuals wrote these sermons, perhaps because we were never meant to know more than that they were the work of Admont.

Assigning authorship of an anonymous medieval text to any author—male or female—is a difficult business, but attributing texts to medieval women is particularly difficult even, as in the case of Heloise and her letters to Abelard, when the writer appears to have identified herself. The suggestion of female authorship is often countered with myriad, sometimes quite complex, counter-possibilities.[23] *A priori* assumptions about what women did or did not do during the Middle Ages move into the foreground and can define the boundaries of the debate. Perhaps the work was written by a man claiming to be a woman—perhaps a bored and clever monk-scribe. Perhaps a school master instructed a male student to write in the voice of a woman. This tendency to doubt the possibility of female authorship led nineteenth-century historian Wilhelm Preger (d. 1889) to suggest that Hildegard of Bingen was not a woman, but a female *persona* dreamed up and given life by an inventive medieval monk.[24] Another nineteenth-century German historian, Joseph von Aschbach (d. 1882), claimed that humanist Conrad Celtes (d. 1508) forged—rather than discovered—the work of the tenth-century German playwright Hrotsvitha of Gandersheim in order to glorify Germanic culture. Von Aschbach based this assertion on his assumption that no woman would have had access to the education necessary to write the works in question.[25] Frequently when I speak about my own work on female scribes, a member of the audience will suggest that a copyist who identified herself as Sophia, or another as Diemut, might in reality have been a man using a feminine pen name (i.e., the personification of wisdom or humility: "Wisdom wrote this" rather than "Sophia wrote this").

To be sure, all of these suggestions are viable on some level: Sophia *could* have been a monk, and Heloise's letters *might* have been written by a man. But such hypotheses violate the logical principle of Ockham's razor, which states that the simplest theory should be given investigative priority. Begin with the most straightforward explanation, and move into more complex alternatives only as simpler explanations fail. Perhaps more importantly, they demonstrate the power exerted by a historian's assumptions about the lives of medieval women as he or she evaluates new evidence. Scholars attempting to identify female authors frequently bump up against the intellectual barriers erected by such assumptions, and therefore must shoulder a double burden of proof. First he or she must prove that a woman *could* have behaved or worked in ways that contradict long-held suppositions about women's intellectual activities. This can be difficult to do when individual cases of "atypical" activity are dismissed as exceptions or as too unusual—too far outside the accepted paradigm—to be taken at face value. Patterns of skepticism and rejection based on *a priori* assumptions prevent the accumulation of the critical mass of evidence required for a paradigm shift.

For Admont, the evidence is clear: learned nuns, experience with scriptural exegesis, excellent library resources, an active scriptorium, images of preaching nuns in books of sermons copied by and owned by nuns. Women wrote some—and possibly many—of the anonymous sermons from twelfth-century Admont. The burden of proof is on those who, in the face of such evidence, would argue otherwise.

Notes

1. Admont was founded in 1074 by Archbishop Gebhard of Salzburg as a Benedictine monastery for men, and the community has been in continuous operation since that time. For a general history, see Jakob Wichner, *Geschichte des Benediktinerstiftes Admont*, 4 vols. (Admont, 1874); and Rudolf List, *Stift Admont. 1074–1974. Festschrift zur 900-Jahrfeier* (Reid im Innkreis: O. O. Landesverl, 1974). On the nuns' community, see Jakob Wichner, "Das ehemalige Nonnenkloster O. S. B. zu Admont," *Wissenschaftliche Studien und Mittheilungen aus dem Benediktiner-Orden* 2 (1881): 75–84 and 288–319.

2. A monk who may have been raised at Admont from boyhood, Irimbert was charged with preaching to the community's nuns. Standing at the window of their enclosure, their only point of regular contact with the outside world, he would deliver regular sermons. Irimbert left Admont in 1147 to serve, briefly and unsuccessfully, as abbot of Seeon, and then transferred to the monastery of St. Georgen am Längsee, where he again was given the job of preaching to the nuns. It was at St. Georgen in 1151 that he began to compose a series of sermon-commentaries on the Books of Kings,

which he continued and completed at Admont after his return there at the end of the same year. Irimbert was especially active between 1151 and 1153, completing his work on Kings, a long commentary on the Book of Joshua, and a shorter one on Judges 1–18. These commentaries appear in their final form in two carefully executed, large format volumes: Admont MS 16 (1–4 Kings) and MS 17 (Joshua, Judges, and Ruth). Earlier, still evolving, versions of these works appear also in three smaller, less elegant volumes—Admont MS 650, MS 651, and MS 682—where they are bound together with numerous anonymous sermons.

3. Bernard Pez, *Thesaurus anecdotorum novissimus,* 6 vols. (Augsburg, 1721–1729).

4. Fritz Peter Knapp, *Die Literatur des Früh- und Hochmittlealters in den Bistümern Passau, Salzburg, Brixen, und Trient von Anfängen bis zum Jahre 1273,* Geschichte der Literatur in Österreich von den Anfängen bis zur Gegenwart 1, ed. Herbert Zeman (Graz, 1994), 75–77.

5. Alison I. Beach, "Claustration and Collaboration between the Sexes in the Twelfth-Century Scriptorium," in *Monks and Nuns, Saints and Outcasts: Religion in Medieval Society,* ed. Sharon Farmer and Barbara H. Rosenwein (Ithaca, N.Y.: Cornell University Press, 2000), 66–67.

6. Alf Härdelin, "God's Visiting: A Basic Theme in the Homilies Ascribed to Godfrey of Admont," in *Munkarnas Och Mystikernas Medeltid: Tjugofyra kapitel om teologi, spiritualitet och kultur,* Opuscula selecta 1 (Skelleftea: Artos, 1996), 213 n. 9. See also Karl Brunner, "Quae est ista, quae ascendit per desertum. Aspekte des Selbstverständisses geistlicher Frauen im 12. Jahrhundert," *Mitteilungen des Instituts für Österreichische Geschichtsforschung* 107 (1999): 271–310, and Stephan Borgehammar, "Who Wrote the Admont Sermon Corpus—Gottfried the Abbott, His Brother Irimbert, or the Nuns?" in *De l'homélie au sermon: Histoire de la prédication médiévale,* ed. Jacqueline Hamesse and Xavier Hermand (Louvain-La-Neuve, 1993), 47–51, at 49, where he suggests that the nuns might have given some of the sermons their literary form.

7. "They hold chapter themselves each day, with the *magistra* or her representative presiding. On feast days, when the abbot is not able to come to them, there are persons among them able to give the sermon. Indeed, they are exceedingly literate and wonderfully trained in the knowledge of sacred Scripture" (Capitulum suum inter se quotidie habent, Magistra vel ejus Vicaria praesidente. Et in festis diebus, cum Abbas ad eas non poterit venire, sunt inter eas personae ad verbum exhortationis faciendum dispositae. Valde quippe sunt litteratae, and in scientia sacrae scripturae mirabiliter exercitatae) (Bernard Pez, ed., *Bibliotheca ascetica antiquo-nova,* 8 vols. [Regensburg, 1725] 8:460).

8. "difficultate earundem sororum utrimque recreatus sum liberalitate, ut duas michi sorores ab omni occupatione liberas deputarent, que a me dicta in tabulis excipi potuissent" (Johann Wilhelm Braun, "Irimbert von Admont," *Frümittelalterliche Studien* 7 [1973]: 320).

9. See Nicole Beriou, *La prédication de Ranulphe de la Houblonnière: Sermons aux clercs et aux simple gens à Paris au XIIIe siècle,* 2 vols. (Paris: Etudes augustiniennes, 1987), 1:59–64, for a discussion of the interaction between speaker and hearer in creating a written record of an orally delivered sermon.

10. *Adlheit m.n.c. armaria.* Monumenta Germaniae historica, Necrologia Germaniae 2, 297.

11. As the library is preserved today, it contains the consolidated collections of both the women and the men. Once maintained as two separate libraries, the nuns' books were handed over to the monks following the closing of the women's community in the sixteenth century. Admont's twelfth-century library was exceptionally large: over 200 books are today preserved in the monastery's

library, many of which were copied at Admont. By comparing two late medieval book lists from the monks' library with the most up-to-date catalog, it is possible to identify surviving volumes that belonged to the men. Surviving books that were not owned by the men—and there are forty-seven of these—may have belonged to the women. See Alison I. Beach, *Women as Scribes: Book Production and Monastic Reform in Twelfth-Century Bavaria* (Cambridge: Cambridge University Press, 2004).

12. Gerhoch, Letter 27, *Patrologia Latina* 193, Col. 607C/D; Damien Van Den Eynde, *L'Oeuvre Littéraire de Géroch de Reichersberg*, Spicilegium Pontificii Athenaei Antoniani 11 (Rome, 1957), 198–99; Peter Classen, *Gerhoch von Reichersberg. Eine Biographie* (Wiesbaden: F. Steiner, 1960), 404.

13. Classen, *Gerhoch,* 404–405 and Van Den Eynde, *L'Oeuvre,* 288. Van Den Eynde suggests Reichersberg (p. 288), while Classen suggests Admont.

14. Alison I. Beach, "Voices from a Distant Land: Fragments of a Nuns' Twelfth-Century Letter Collection," *Speculum* 77, no. 1 (January 2002).

15. *Patrologia Latina* 174, col. 72D–82A.

16. *Patrologia Latina* 174, col. 76C.

17. *Patrologia Latina* 174, col. 76B.

18. *Patrologia Latina* 174, col. 77A–77B.

19. Härdelin, "God's Visiting," 212.

20. Ibid., 203–205.

21. Borgehammar, "Admont Sermon Corpus," 8.

22. Härdelin, "God's Visiting," 213 n. 9.

23. I am thinking here in particular of the recent controversy surrounding Constant Mews's recent work, *The Lost Love Letters of Heloise and Abelard: Perceptions of Dialogue in Twelfth-Century France* (New York: St. Martin's Press, 1999).

24. Barbara Newman, *Voice of the Living Light: Hildegard of Bingen and Her World* (Berkeley: University of California Press, 1998), 1.

25. Larissa Bonfante, trans., *The Plays of Hrotswitha of Gandersheim* (Oak Park, Ill.: Bolchazy-Carducci, 1986), x.

■ ■ ■

The Voices of Women in
Twelfth-Century Europe

JOHN VAN ENGEN

Alison Beach offers us a startling image of literary life at Admont in the mid-twelfth century: cloistered women taking down sermon notes in Latin, transforming corrected notes into polished homilies, transcribing biblical commentaries expertly on parchment, even preaching and teaching themselves on feastdays and Sundays. These literate women, working together in community, also with monks in adjoining wings of their monastic complex, cooperated so fully that individual contributors to a given commentary or sermon have become impossible to sort out in the finished whole. Beach's work, in this essay and in her book on women scribes,[1] challenges us to rethink on two fronts. She shows what a close reading of texts, more especially of codices, can yield. She has recovered the work of these women from folio volumes that remained on site, more or less, for the past eight hundred years, their existence and contents known since the eighteenth century, the books themselves accessible to scholars (in situ or on film) for a generation or two. But no one before, it seems, read them closely enough—more importantly, with historical imagination enough—to see what their form and content might have to tell us about the lives of those who first produced them. It requires patience, also skill, to see in these folio pages, in their variants, corrections, and scripts, the possible lives and purposes of their scribes, that is, the women who first wrote them out. Beach's act of scholarly "seeing" goes to the heart of the way medievalists have practiced their craft for a generation or two now, and it poses a question: Is it truly possible to gain from these codices and scripts, from the material remains of a departed

199

culture, the living voices of human beings, even women living in cloister and under silence? Beach's work further reminds us that a small opening, a mere crack in the door, can sometimes illumine a whole room, even a whole landscape. Hence a second question, not methodological but interpretive: What is it we see in that room, in that landscape? Is it what we expected to see? Or, to turn the metaphor from sight to sound, what do we hear in these texts? Is this a voice we expected to hear?

Twelfth-century Europe stands out in accounts of the Middle Ages as few other periods do. For many post-war interpreters, the years between about 1050 and 1200 marked *the* turning-point in European history, the "renaissance" or "reformation" or "take-off" from which Old Europe sprang, its social structures and cultural paradigms "modernized" and finally obliterated only by violent revolution, industrialization, and two wars. Whatever the truth in this grand narrative[2] (a story-line that continues to fascinate, with newer work asking about the psychology and culture of those who found themselves on the other side of the year 1000), historians have worried more of late about those who got left behind or shunted aside. What of those who failed to fit in or keep step? What of "dissenters" who took innovation in other directions or failed to innovate at all? What of Jews who refused to convert or take their "place"? What of peasants whose labors made possible the leisure of these innovators? This grand narrative, accepted or contested, implicitly or explicitly invoked, has turned the twelfth century into an interpretive hinge, a point of "swing" from an earlier time into the openings and energies that created "Old Europe" (1150–1750). Studies of nearly every conceivable topic pivot on the changes wrought during these two or three generations. Those studying the "main story" focus upon religious reform, a revitalized culture, intellectual renewal, institutional and economic consolidation. The reverse story comes largely built in, crying for attention: a tale of margins, of oppression or suppression, of subordination— in short, of others forced into resistance or subversion. The one mirrors the other, almost requires the other, with elements of truth in both: in the language of one mirror-image, for instance, a "reforming" and a "persecuting" Church.

Scholars have only begun to ask seriously about the place of women in this world of renaissance and reformation.[3] Could their aspirations and labors enter into the making of a new society, new culture, new Church, new intellectual life, new literary life? Or did new structures only subordinate and "veil" them all the more effectively, in image or in practice? Most accounts of women in twelfth-century Europe have adopted, consciously or not, versions of the mirror images already noted: ameliorating notions suggested by enhanced possibilities for expression in culture (romance, lyric) and religion (Fontevraux, early Prémontré, Marian devotion), countered by equally forceful moves to exclude them (new orders, universities), reduce them to icons (Mary, the untouchable beloved), or allow them to act in ways only extraordinary (prophets, visionaries) or subversive (Eve, temptress). The evidence is multiple and ambiguous. Women, too, joined in the yearning for new forms of religious life and expression, as fully as men, so fully that already two generations ago Herbert Grundmann spoke of a "women's movement" (*Frauenbewegung*) as central to the impulses of this age.[4] But women were also driven away from the new orders as troublesome, burdensome, or seductive. Some women (Matilda of Tuscany, Eleanor of Aquitaine) acted as important players and patrons in the political and ecclesiastical battles of this era; others were made to serve as marriage pawns in familial and political bargaining. Women, by their persons and in their writings, transformed the literary culture of this era. But the understanding of that, too, is ambiguous. In the practice of "*amicitia,*" an ancient and complex web of love, virtue, personal bonds, and literary expression, the move by women into public roles during this period, Stephen Jaeger argues, unsettled inherited notions of male desire as being "channeled" into virtue, and thus becoming "ennobling."[5] As objects of potent desire, idealizing or erotic, women, too easily and too often, were drained of personality or humanity to become mere figures in the new literary culture, Latin and vernacular. All the evidence need not be reviewed here.[6] The tension within and between these narrative-interpretive lines speaks for itself, as in discrepant approaches to an expanding Marian cult: Does this Virgin Mother represent the emptying-out of real women in the world or even in religious life? Or was she, as "co-sufferer" and "mother," the indispensable companion of the incarnate God, and thus an immanent cultural presence?[7]

Marie d'Oignies (d. 1216) in the diocese of Liège and Elizabeth of Marburg (d. 1224) in north-central Germany lived inventive religious lives in the same years as the layman Francis of Assisi (d. 1226) and the cleric Dominic Guzman (d. 1221). Marie would serve subsequently as the exemplar for tens of thousands of beguines, Elizabeth for hospice workers. Yet we think of Marie and Elizabeth altogether differently than we do of Francis or Dominic. Why? Because the forms of expression and influence open then to women were different? True, but Francis and Dominic, as persons, also represented vastly different cases. Because the women's followers were not institutionalized and empowered in the same ways? Agreed, and important; but the followers of Francis famously fell into horrific competing factions, and not all of them gained institutional recognition, some actively silenced or suppressed. Or is it because long ago we came to think of the men and their orders as the central story? Still, beguines gained approvals and Franciscans suffered condemnations; Elizabeth entered the *Golden Legend* along with Francis and Dominic. In short, interpretive pressures continue to descend upon these historical figures, almost unawares. Even Swanson's recent account refers to the "oddity" of Heloise, the "problematic" nature of Hildegard, and only to Marie de France as possessing her own authorial voice.[8] She wrote in the vernacular and for court audiences, cultural and social forms with recognized stories. Or is it that for women at court we have a recognizable, if still contested, historical narrative?

Twelfth-century phenomena, whether historical, literary, or religious (that, too, dominated by polarities such as monastic vs. scholastic theology), deserve a more complex range of stories, not all headed in one of two directions, not always predictable. We need views that are more humanly and culturally rich, whether or not they satisfy the expectations of a grand narrative or the aspirations of our own age. Recent scholars have sought to uncover more middle ground, more negotiation, between "popular" and "clerical" expressions of religion, even between the rigidities of "orthodoxy" and "dissent," with attention to specific instances and to variations regionally and temporally. The same holds for encounters between Jews and Christians during this period of upheaval. They could be horrifically violent, but not all were, as Beryl Smalley pointed out long ago. They took on a wide range, with fears, suspicions, interests, borrowings, and curiosity evident on both sides.[9] The lines were not always neat. Historians have been tempted to make the lines neat, or at least neater, with respect to the roles and images of women in this era, in part by placing them, so to speak, outside the lines. Nearly every woman author—Heloise, Hildegard of Bingen, Elizabeth of Schönau, Marie de France, to name the most prominent—ends up looking "odd," in a special category or with their authorship contested, their roles "contained" in the lines, often with equal strictness, whether in the extraordinary or the marginal. For all the work these past fifty years on twelfth-century religion and thought, a Heloise or Hildegard or Elizabeth has hardly entered the main story, is always the exception. That is an outrage. But it is a reverse mistake, in my view, to focus on them exclusively, make them inhabit the special space of a visionary or some other apart cultural category, central or marginal. Are these our only choices? Must the voices of twelfth-century women be heard not at all, or as totally other? What happens if we include them?

Let us listen for a moment to the one author said nearly to escape these constraints. In one of her remarkable Lais, *Le Fresne*, Marie sets up a plot involving separated twins. To do so, she creates a mother with striking attitudes and an unmistakable voice. This woman, upon learning that her neighbor has borne twin sons, lashes out in spite and jealousy: Never has a woman borne two sons at once except by the "doing" of two men! This echoed a common folkloric motif. For this outburst, so blatantly "dishonoring" of the neighboring knight, her husband rebuked her. As rumors of it spread, she faced more anger ("Mult en fu la dame haïe") from women who heard the story ("Tutes les femmes ki l'oïrent, / povres e riches, l'en haïrent"). Later this woman herself bore twins, daughters, and she nearly went mad. She perceived herself as losing all esteem and honor among her neighbors ("Ja mes pres ne honur n'avrai"), knowing henceforth only scorn, shame, dishonor ("hunie sui"). So she resolved to kill one of the infants to preserve her own honor. As Marie puts the daring thought in the distraught mother's mouth: she would rather try to make amends with God hereafter than suffer such dishonor now ("Mielz le vueil vers Deu amender / que mei hunir ne vergunder!").

Her chambermaids, however, persuaded her that infanticide was not a light matter. A maid then proposed that they deposit one child at the gate of a monastery—and so the plot moves forward.[10]

This is a remarkable scene, of Marie's own creation, vivid in what it represents, much of it going beyond the strict requirements of plot: rivalry and jealousy among women and men in a local society, turning in part on the production of children, male and female, and attendant personal honor; one noblewoman's instinctive turn to abandonment in a moment of trouble, her impulse even to infanticide; and her overtly more immediate passion for honor in this world than for making right with God in the next. Should we hear in these lines the voices of twelfth-century aristocratic women, of lives caught in personal and social turmoil and captured here in inner expression? Do we do justice to Marie and the women of her society if we take these lines only as playful lyrics, as twitting some untouchable sacralities and unthinkable attitudes? A distraught new mother, faced with trouble and dishonor, chooses life in the world for herself and has her child removed to a cloister—this is a literary motif, a rich one in fact.[11] It could also be a social reality and an awful personal dilemma.

The nuns of Admont sprang from largely the same social class as Marie, in the same era, and would have instinctively resonated, I suspect, with the sentiments and difficulties in her courtly poem. One of them had, it seems, faced a comparable dilemma and chosen the cloister for herself. The same nuns who shared in the work of preparing commentaries and sermons also—this we know owing to another of Beach's findings—wrote letters on occasion, some to inquire about intellectual matters like exegesis, others more personal in nature. Nineteen of the latter survive because the parchment on which they were copied served nearly two centuries later as the outer wrapper for an annual wine account book. One (#14) deserves note by way of comparison with Marie's *Le Fresne*. This nun, apparently, left behind a child on entering the cloister, whatever her circumstances, and was now pleading by letter for human contact, some minimal occasion for sight and touch. "I remember, lord bishop," she writes, "nor could I possibly forget, my own little orphan whom I carried in my womb and nourished with my breasts and whom I caused to be exiled with me and without counsel or forethought left with strangers." She begs for the means now to offer her little daughter some little gift, even through a barred window.[12] We cannot know what lies behind this letter, nor whether the copy is complete, but we cannot miss its particularity and pathos. She had left, she claims, all her relatives and acquaintances and "for love of the heavenly fatherland" found shelter under the bishop's "wings." Perhaps she was widowed young and put at social risk, or perhaps with child under circumstances adjudged scandalous. In any case, she had chosen for the cloister and for heavenly honor, and now pined for her child— and so petitioned the bishop by letter. She found her way to written expression, in part, through a web of scriptural language, the words that informed her scribal and prayer life—as Beach draws out in this essay. But first of all: a cloistered nun second-guessing a decision she had made in crisis. That is a voice we must hear.

Letters are an incomparably rich source, arguably the central medium for twelfth-century culture and society; yet, despite a generation of hard work, difficult to interpret historically and literarily. They were in fact both history and literature, the means for getting work done, political, cultural, or personal, and done at the same time in a decidedly and self-consciously rhetorical manner. Some are short and relatively personal (as are most by these nuns at Admont), some lengthy and essayistic (famous pieces by Peter Damian, Bernard of Clairvaux, and others), all the rhetorical means to assure social and cultural communication in this age.[13] Women authors have suffered, it turns out, from precisely this ambivalence between history and literature, their work nearly always reduced to rhetoric rather than life, even their rhetoric credited to clerical "handlers" or "impersonators." We may concede that women in distress, abandoning their children, appear often enough (think of the mother of Guibert of Nogent) to become a literary figure, almost a trope. But is that a reason to deny the authentic voice of this nun with her subsequent aching sense of loss? In Hildegard's correspondence a noblewoman appears, sent all the way from Burgundy by sympathetic Cistercian abbots for help with a contrasting problem, failure to produce an heir, in the hope that Hildegard's prayers could prove powerful, or her medical and personal advice helpful.[14] We must consider why, generally speaking, we are readier to reduce to literary trope a nun's writing or imagination than we are a cleric's. Unless we ban all this to the fictive imagination and leave twelfth-century women trapped in literary categories partly of our own making, we must stretch our sense of the historic possibilities, which Beach's work is now helping us to do.

Think about the nuns at Admont in terms of what we know about Hildegard of Bingen. She, too, was of the gentry class and a cloistered nun, committed to the religious life since childhood. She took an interest in exegesis and preaching, and generated her own. She directed the production of manuscripts, some of which still exist. She wrote letters far and wide, some four hundred still preserved. She knew much about the social, moral, and sexual mores of her time, more than our images of cloistered nuns would ordinarily warrant. We, owing to our present interest in Hildegard and her amazing texts, have begun to imagine the possibility of nuns at Admont also making commentaries and sermons. But interpretively and historically, I submit, it is the other way round. Because in the twelfth century there were engaged and thoughtful and even literate women at courts and especially in monastic houses, a truly exceptional talent like Hildegard could eventually emerge, one who rises above all the unsung figures like the nuns of Admont. In their time, I would insist, Abelard and Bernard were equally extraordinary. They become intelligible only if we presume, as they did, hundreds of cleric-students and monks around them, doing what they did, in less brilliant, even entirely unknown, ways. Beach's findings, that is, help us grasp Hildegard better, not the other way round. She received, and responded to, queries about all sorts of matters, also from bishops and masters, including a request for help in the exegesis of thirty-eight disputed biblical passages.[15] The nuns of Admont, for their part, addressed letters with questions, chiefly about exegesis, to at least two of the leading figures in their region (both men). The abbess of Rupertsberg addressed a large number of her letters to female correspondents, usually nuns, who had written to her for help or for spiritual guidance. The language of their letters was as rhetorically sophisticated as Hildegard's own, if not more so, more indebted to the stylistic techniques of the schools. They looked to Hildegard as someone who could advise them in trust and understood their concerns, whether they wrote as heads of houses, as people with secret sins and troubled consciences, or as ordinary religious given to a life anchored in text-based prayers. This world of women's cloisters was a relatively small one, and elitist—but that takes nothing from its social reality and cultural powers.

Against all odds Hildegard managed to found, establish, and privilege her own religious house, and locate it at the confluence of the two most heavily traveled rivers in her region[16]—the equivalent in our day of building at the intersection of two major interstate routes. She self-consciously set herself up as consultant to the whole of Christian society, best attested by her letters, a first collection of which she dispatched from the Rupertsberg a year or two after she had settled there.[17] She self-consciously sought approval for her writings from Bernard of Clairvaux, the most renowned monk of her day, as well as from her bishop and the pope. When it was not directly forthcoming— contrary to the standard historical accounts—she invented that approval and forged ahead with her writing and her consulting.[18] It was her *fama*, her spreading fame, that brought people of all ranks from across Europe to her person, either in their own person or through the letters of consultation they sent her. And it was her letters in return— often moving in directions quite independent of the wishes or predilections of the petitioners—that established her powers as a teacher, a spiritual guide, and a prophet. In historical practice men set her apart for reasons both negative and positive: to keep her out of their business as school masters, monastic leaders, church prelates, but also to take advantage of her supposed unmediated access to God for prayer, for guidance, for prophecy. She understood these expectations well, and exploited them, and insisted upon participating. To be sure, her letters go out as the work of "a poor little woman," or alternatively as a mere vessel through whom the "Living Light" speaks. To what degree this arose from experience and conviction, to what degree as a rhetorical ploy in a culture where she could not speak as a master or a priest, this we can never finally know. Readers will have differing intuitions. But her position in that society, her voice, her writings, were no less central, no less mainstream, than that of a Bernard or any famous master—who, in their own times, were equally contested and denounced.

If we made women's voices a part of the scene, interacting with other voices, male and female—with gendered constraints, to be sure, but interacting nonetheless—how might we come to think differently about the upheavals and cultural energies at work in this "twelfth century"? Our questions, first, must be concrete, more precise, better historically situated. Social distinctions affected women fully as much as men, maybe more so. Could women's voices be heard in the public world of deeds or in writing mostly, or even exclusively, if they stood in the ranks of a narrow elite? Prior to the twelfth century nearly all women's religious houses, and they were few enough, served the socially privileged, often those with high political connections. A sudden expansion in numbers, but also in social classes, proved part of the problem during the twelfth century. Those who could be fit in with that older social elite, or enjoyed its patronage, fared better in many ways than their newer counterparts—this possibly one real contrast with the world of men (and especially clerics) in the twelfth century. As the nuns of Admont came largely from socially privileged origins, so Hildegard and Heloise and Marie came from families of standing, if not the absolute highest ranks. Hildegard, the most recent introductory study suggests, is also best understood as a "conservative revolutionary."[19]

Those social privileges could extend to education. Think of Hrotsvitha writing Latin plays on the strength of her remarkable knowledge of the classics, also the laywoman Ava writing religious epics in her native German. Opportunities to learn Latin or to cultivate lyric and song, also to participate in high-level decision making, were socially conditioned realities, perhaps especially for women. Within this privileged space, they could learn and get help with learning, could compose and get help with composing, sometimes surpassing their lay male relatives, especially at court or in cultured association with religious houses. The new and more open culture of the urban schools was less open to them, but Heloise in particular, and Hildegard too, knew much about the issues under discussion there, and we must take care not to make the divide absolute. The nuns of Admont were intrigued by exegesis, as were Hildegard and Heloise, as were the schoolmen at Laon and Paris. In the thirteenth century the women who made their own way in vernacular expressions of great religious power—a Hadewijch or a Mechthild—still presumed privilege, often courtly backgrounds, it seems, but not generally the same milieu of utter privilege that had made possible extended Latin learning. Beach's findings alert us to much work that remains, and help us begin to consider a variety of social and cultural distinctions.

So what then of the older assumption, going back in part to Grundmann, that women's voices could be heard in matters religious and intellectual only if they expressed themselves in the vernacular? This assumption, perhaps an opening at first, and even still, has nonetheless effectively marginalized women writers who might use Latin, especially in the twelfth century, even a Hildegard—also among modern interpreters who have trouble imagining women expressing themselves authentically in Latin. Certainly, women began to express themselves in the vernacular during the twelfth century, more in court circles like Marie's, as with the "trobaritz," but in religious circles too, like Ava in southern Germany. Hildegard's is an especially complex and controverted case, though I incline toward those who believe that she in some significant measure produced and controlled the Latin prose and poetry that went out in her name. Anne Clark has written a balanced analysis with respect to the visions of Elizabeth of Schönau, and Bernard McGinn has encouraged us to think of these women as engaged in "conversation" with their clerical helpers/handlers, even if that conversation, doubtless, knew pressure and manipulation.[20] It makes all the difference what we imagine possible. If we agree that, at Admont, at the very least, the nuns and some of the monks worked together to generate these sermons and biblical commentaries, to take down, correct, and write out Latin texts, can we further imagine these same women sufficiently in control of Latin to shape their own language and express their own thoughts? In the somewhat rarefied world of a privileged cloister, it was possible, I believe, and did happen. Beach employs passages from the letters, in her contribution here, to suggest that the biblical tongue was not just one of abstruse learning but also could serve for personal expression.

So could women's voices be heard, third, only if they spoke as visionaries? Or, could they be heard in letters and in exegesis and in sermons as well? While the extant evidence concerning twelfth-century women is relatively sparse, as was doubtless the original production, work in these genres must be recognized for what it is. Women did express themselves in letters, as Joan Ferrante has reminded us, not only as seers but as intellectual inquirers, as correspondents, as persons of social responsibility, a Matilda in Tuscany, or as the lady of an estate or castle whose husband had gone off to war or on crusade. Women also did "preach," as several contributions to this volume remind us, and that already in the twelfth century.[21] Women, as noted, took an interest in exegesis: Abelard responded to requests from Heloise and her community, as Hildegard responded to queries about exegetical conundra from monks and masters. In the materials produced at Admont, sermons and especially commentaries, a hermeneutic of suspicion might better be applied, as Beach intimates, to the monk, Irimbert, than to the nuns. In the prologue to his commentary on the Second Book of Kings, his first effort, he goes on at some length about his inadequacy, about being called to this task against his will by his abbot, and so on—only to note how quickly he completed it, with nearly exact dates. Then he acknowledges that he had first spoken to the Sisters about this material years earlier ("ante annos aliquot a me audierant"), and they had made copies of these talks for themselves, he supposedly unawares ("que, me nesciente, ipse in membranis exceperant"). More, his zeal for this work gained great stimulation from their interest and endeavors ("per quod etiam studium meum valde prouocauerant"). More still, he now inserted their material, as they prepared it, into his finished commentary.[22] In the prologue to the fourth book he confides that it was the "prayers" of the Sisters that had kept him at it, with two of them set free to take down his talks on wax tablets and transform those into written codices.[23] So who did the real work, drove the exegetical conversation forward, composed the Latin text passed down to us? It is the presumptuous and falsely modest Irimbert that we would do well to regard with a real measure of suspicion.

There was a kind of reply to the heady Irimbert, I would suggest, and it may be found in the images Beach has found and reproduced. At the head of these commentaries and sermons women are depicted in the same position as the monastic leader. What does it mean? Patron of the book? Scribe? Author? Teacher? Preacher? The gesture of the right hand certainly suggests preaching or teaching, reading at the very least. Who made the illumination? Who allowed or authorized them? Were they in place before the monks saw, if they did? We must imagine, I suggest, an atmosphere of collaboration, and yet one with monks probably reluctant to concede entirely the gendered authority that was ordinarily theirs. So comparable illuminations of this sort, for any to see who took the book down from the shelf, represented a telling act, approved or unapproved, an open declaration on the women's part or a coded message.

About the exegetical work itself: The Book of Kings was not standard reading matter, though it could form part of a full year's cycle of scriptural reading if that were actively carried out. Someone was intrigued by these stories, and wondered what they meant for religious; someone kept Irimbert at it, even the elaborate process of preparing finished texts. He had most to lose if he confessed how much this initiative owed not just to the work and interest of these women, but to their questions and their writing, their curiosity about the meaning of this "active" or "worldly" biblical book. Indeed they had their own quite particular questions, as did the schoolmen. They were intrigued by the book of Ruth (also not standard teaching matter), no less by the gruesome story, just before it, in Judges 19, of a woman estranged and then abused, her husband calling for vengeance by sending parts of her body to all Israel, with dire consequences. This world of estrangement, rape, vengeance: this was a world they had left behind, as had Ruth, and yet doubtless knew about, and they could legitimately wonder why it should appear as part of the Sacred Writings, what its meaning could be for them. The leisure and material support which their interests, reflection, and learning presumed, also in a sense the social confidence this work and collaboration seems to exude, was probably found in relatively few places, not, on the whole, among those families whose daughters streamed to the new religious houses or later to the beguines. It is worth recalling here Hildegard's comments about Richardis, the nun companion who had helped her in some undetermined way with the writing of *Scivias*, then was pulled away by her highly aristocratic family to be made an abbess elsewhere.

In a letter of lament Hildegard, feeling orphaned, gives expression to what it is she misses, the character of this companion, her love for Richardis's nobility of *mores* (the meaning here, I think, at once spiritual and social), her wisdom (which points toward her joint contribution to their learning or writing), her chastity, her soul or spirit, and indeed her very being, her whole life ("Amaui nobilitatem morum tuorum et sapientiam et castitatem et tuam animam et omnem uitam tuam").[24] This array of virtues, and this sense of deep spiritual and social and personal companionship, must have cohered among the nuns at Admont as well as they worked together on the production of these commentaries and sermons in grand folio codices.

So, then, finally, did women share in the intellectual energies so evident in this era? If we allow that leading figures were always exceptional, whether men or women, the issue turns more on possibilities for the ranks of potential followers and fellow contributors, equivalent to all the new students and new monks we invoke or imagine. We must create mental space for these nuns at Admont, for the women correspondents in Hildegard's letters, for the nuns who joined Heloise at the Paraclete, for the laywomen who would have enjoyed Ava's or Marie's poetry. They were there, if, doubtless, in smaller numbers and in the face of greater obstacles. They appear to have shared this drive for understanding and expression, especially for understanding texts, then found in so many university men and cloistered monks, animating so much of their oral or written production. Common to both men and women was a powerful sense that the Sacred Text especially is not sufficiently grasped if it is only the source of mumbled prayers or readings, where the performance is all or most all. They wanted to grasp the text itself, in the strength of their own minds and spirits, in their own way and with their own purposes, as did the university men who turned Scripture into the textbook for theology. Their aim was to enter into these texts, not just hear them read out to them, not just copy them out for preservation between embossed covers as a kind of sacred hieroglyphics. The nuns at Admont had access to biblical commentaries by recent luminaries like Rupert of Deutz and Hugh of St. Victor. The image that emerges of these nuns at Admont, with their transcriptions, their own preaching and teaching, then their correcting and copying, is not just that of scribes busy about the hard manual labor of inscribing parchment for posterity and to please Irimbert's vanity. They were eager to think about these texts and to preserve fair copies of their understanding for future nuns. Hence the letters to experts beyond the cloister on difficult passages. Some of the results may look fairly prosaic, or standard, for those who know twelfth-century exegesis, but the intellectual labor behind it, the honest curiosity, in my view, is unmistakable and to be registered. Beach is right to insist, with respect to intellectual cooperation, that the burden of proof lies with those who would deny it.

So what should we say about the women of Admont and these marvelous codices? Whatever deference to Irimbert's authority as priest and preacher they may have shown, their active participation and collaboration, and his grateful use of their help, hints that he owed far more to them than his prologues begin to suggest. Beach argues, from iconography, from the customary, even the codices, that on occasion one or more of the leading women also preached, even on feastdays. The inevitable final question is this: Do some sermons have a distinctive voice, a distinctive set of emphases or of imagery? This would require yet another approach, at once exegetical and literary, with a sensitive ear, one that Beach did not undertake here (except by way of occasional hints), and one I could not undertake without a full reading of all the materials myself. In its final written form the voices are blended; so paleography or codicology alone will not answer that question. Further, if there was genuine intellectual and spiritual interaction, if the scribal hands were so finely trained that it is nearly impossible at times to distinguish one from another, including a man's from a woman's, may we not assume that exegesis, the import of the gospel of the day, also might yield remarkably similar-sounding themes, built upon common readings (especially of Gregory the Great)? Must the voices be distinct? Did not Irimbert and the abbot learn from the women, as they did from the men? How should we listen for individual voices in a close, cloistered community of lifelong religious? Is it even possible? Was it even desired? These are fundamental questions that Beach's groundbreaking work challenges us to begin to tackle.

Notes

1. Alison I. Beach, *Women as Scribes: Monastic Reform and Book Production in Twelfth-Century Bavaria* (Cambridge: Cambridge University Press, 2001).

2. The most recent attempt at a synthetic account acknowledges the reality of historical change and as well the difficulty of interpreting it; hence this concluding sentence: "even if consensus is lacking on what the twelfth-century renaissance actually was, there is understanding and appreciation of the different approaches to a phenomenon which is often at the same time intriguing and infuriating, and which was of profound significance for the intellectual and cultural development of western Europe" (R. N. Swanson, *The Twelfth-Century Renaissance* [Manchester, 1999], 213). The significant synthetic effort by Giles Constable (*The Reformation of the Twelfth Century* [Cambridge: Cambridge University Press, 1996]) is bolder in its concluding claims: "The reformation of the twelfth century was a watershed in the history of the church and of Christian society as well as of monasticism and religious life. It involved a passionate reexamination of what it meant to be a Christian in a world where the traditional links between people and between the individual and God were loosened" (325, 328). More recently still, in a challenge to sixteenth-century Reformation historians, Constantin Fasolt has suggested that theirs was only the "second act" in European history, the first coming in the twelfth century: "Europäische Geschichte, zweiter Akt: Die Reformation," in *Die deutsche Reformation zwischen Spätmittelalter und Früher Neuzeit,* Schriften des Historischen Kollegs, Kolloquien 50 (Munich: R. Oldenbourg, 2001), 231–50.

3. This question has now been posed by Swanson, *Twelfth-Century Renaissance,* 188–206.

4. Herbert Grundmann, *Religious Movements in the Middle Ages*, trans. Steven Rowan (Notre Dame, Ind.: University of Notre Dame Press, 1995). Attempts to render this insight in more concrete and nuanced ways have only begun; see now, for instance, Franz J. Felten, "'*Novi esse uolunt . . . deserentes bene contritam uiam*' Hildegard von Bingen und Reformbewegungen im religiösen Leben ihrer Zeit," in *Im Angesicht Gottes suche der Mensch sich selbst: Hildegard von Bingen (1098–1179)*, ed. Rainer Berndt (Berlin, 2001), 28–30, with further studies noted there.

5. C. Stephen Jaeger, *Ennobling Love: In Search of a Lost Sensibility* (Philadelphia: University of Pennsylvania Press, 1999), 82–106.

6. I cite, representatively, Peter Dronke, *Women Writers of the Middle Ages: A Critical Study of Texts from Perpetua (d. 203) to Marguerite Porete (d. 1310)* (Cambridge: Cambridge University Press, 1984); Joan Ferrante, *To the Glory of Her Sex: Women's Roles in the Composition of Medieval Texts* (Bloomington: Indiana University Press, 1997); Barbara Newman, *From Virile Woman to WomanChrist: Studies in Medieval Religion and Literature* (Philadelphia: University of Pennsylvania Press, 1995), esp. 19–45, "Flaws in the Golden Bowl: Gender and Spiritual Formation in the Twelfth Century"; and Peggy Shine Gold, *The Lady and the Virgin: Image, Attitude, and Experience in Twelfth-Century France* (Chicago: University of Chicago Press, 1985).

7. See now, for these images, Rachel Fulton, *From Judgment to Passion: Devotion to Christ and the Virgin Mary, 800–1200* (New York: Columbia University Press, 2003).

8. Swanson, *Twelfth-Century Renaissance*, 195, 197.

9. This at least is the general approach found in the essays recently edited by Michael Signer and myself, *Jews and Christians in Twelfth-Century Europe* (Notre Dame, Ind.: University of Notre Dame Press, 2001).

10. Marie, *Le Fraisne*, lines 25–120, cited here from *Lais de Marie de France*, ed. Karl Warnke and Laurence Harf-Lancner (Paris, 1990), 88–94.

11. Barbara Newman, "'Crueel Corage': Child Sacrifice and the Maternal Martyr in Hagiography and Romance," in Barbara Newman, *From Virile Woman to WomanChrist: Studies in Medieval Religion and Literature* (Philadelphia: University of Pennsylvania Press, 1995), 76–107.

12. For the Latin text, see Alison Beach, "Voices from a Distant Land: Fragments of a Twelfth-Century Nuns' Letter Collection," *Speculum* 77 (2002): 34–54, here 53.

13. I have addressed this in two previous essays: "Letters, Schools, and Written Culture in the Eleventh and Twelfth Centuries," in *Dialektik und Rhetorik im frühen und hohen Mittelalter*, ed. Johannes Fried, Schriften des historischen Kollegs, Kolloquien 27 (Munich: R. Oldenbourg, 1997), 97–132; and "Letters and the Public *Persona* of Hildegard of Bingen," in *Hildegard von Bingen in ihrem historischen Umfeld*, ed. Alfred Haverkamp (Mainz: P. von Zabern, 2000), 375–418.

14. Hildegard, *Epistolarium* LXX, ed. Van Acker, Corpus Christianorum Continuatio Mediaevalis 91, 153.

15. Anne Clark Bartlett, "Commentary, Polemic, and Prophecy in Hildegard of Bingen's Solutiones triginta octo questionum" *Viator* 23 (1992): 153–65.

16. For the location, and Hildegard in context, see now Alfred Haverkamp, "Hildegard von Disibodenberg-Bingen: Von der Peripherie zum Zentrum," in *Hildegard von Bingen in ihrem historischen Umfeld* (Mainz: P. von Zabern, 2000), 15–70. For her acts as founding abbess, see my "Abbess: 'Mother and Teacher,'" in *Voices of the Living Light*, ed. Barbara Newman (Berkeley: University of California Press, 1998), 30–51.

17. For Hildegard's letters as a way into her public life and public roles, see my "Letters and the Public *Persona* of Hildegard," 375–418. It is possible to improve upon what I said there, summarizing the transmission of her letters, by consulting the introduction to the just-completed third volume of Hildegard's letters.

18. Ibid., 379–92 for the details of this argument.

19. Thus Felten (note 4 above), 84, in his concluding sentence: "könnte man in Hildegard eher eine 'konservative Revolutionärin' als eine 'Traditionalistin' sehen." If it is not an anachronistic label, as Felten himself notes, it fits, I think, quite well.

20. Anne L. Clark, *Elisabeth of Schönau: A Twelfth-Century Visionary* (Philadelphia: University of Pennsylvania Press, 1992). See as well the various essays on this subject gathered in Catherine Mooney, ed., *Gendered Voices: Medieval Saints and Their Interpreters* (Philadelphia: University of Pennsylvania Press, 1999).

21. See, for instance, Michel Lauers, "Expérience béguinale et récit hagiographique," *Journal des Savants* (1989): 61–103.

22. Johan Wilhelm Braun, "Irimbert von Admont," *Frühmittelalterliche Studien* 7 (1973): 318–19.

23. Ibid., 320.

24. Hildegard, *Epistolarium* LXIV, ed. Van Acker, Corpus Christianorum Continuatio Mediaevalis 91, 147.

Women and Creative Intelligence in Medieval Thought

ALCUIN BLAMIRES

Before Christine de Pizan, medieval women did not write much about their own creative intelligence. However, Hrotsvitha of Gandersheim in the tenth century is a major, early, and self-conscious exception. In the prefatory and other discourses accompanying her writings she invokes *ingenium,* the key Latin term for creative talent. She also insists that while the faculty of creative intellect is allegedly slack in women, it is conferred in order that it should be utilized, even by women.[1] The present analysis will seek to disclose not just the explicit challenges that women had to overcome (and the arguments available to them) in affirming and using their own inventive intelligence, but also the subtler effects of a masculine culture's attempts to discredit that intelligence. It will not be possible or desirable to restrict our discussion to literary creativity. In fact, in the Middle Ages, a somewhat surprising range of considerations proves to be enmeshed with the concept of inventiveness. As we shall see, the subject draws into itself seemingly dissociated topics such as magic and the myth of the Golden Age.

Hrotsvitha clearly knows her own intellectual powers. Like any creature with the capacity to learn, she points out, she potentially has knowledge of the arts and is moreover a recipient of a divine gift of "penetrating imaginative insight" (*perspicax . . . ingenium*). The question—she pretends to wonder—is whether she may have failed to achieve knowledge in actuality, or may have failed to cultivate her *ingenium* adequately, so that it "lags" (*torpet*) through her slothful inertia. Hrotsvitha is conspicuously adapting the conventional medieval rhetoric of writerly modesty to an extreme scenario of humility, one befitting a woman writer. Hence her strategy in two of her prefaces of claiming only minuscule intelligence, using the diminutive *ingeniolum*. Hence, too, an ostentatiously self-abasing posture as a paltry little woman (*muliercula*), full of gratitude that certain intellectuals of her acquaintance are prepared to say they have found in her a knowledge of the arts more subtle than might be expected from a merely womanly intelligence (*muliebre ingenium*). Hence, finally, the neat paradox she offers, that God the "bestower" of *ingenium* will be all the more praised through whatever contribution she has managed to patch together, precisely because "women's understanding is held to be more retarded."[2]

Peter Dronke has rightly drawn attention to the confident tone of professional banter in all this, though Hrotsvitha's knowing engagement with the rooted prejudices of masculine culture is perhaps not best served by his description of her strategy as "literary coquetry."[3] Just how rooted were the prejudices concerning female creative intelligence will be worth demonstrating from their reappearance in two other works, one a woman's voice presumed to be of the twelfth century and the other, later in the Middle Ages, a work by Boccaccio.

The woman's words are those inscribed by the monk Johannes de Vepria at Clairvaux in the anthology of epistolary writings he compiled in 1471, which includes snatches and sometimes whole copies of letters written by, or as if by, a pair of lovers. It is now strongly argued by Constant Mews that these are the "lost" letters of Abelard and Heloise, that is, the letters written during their courtship.[4] In *Ep.* 5 in the collection, the woman skillfully begs God the "Giver of human talent" (*humani ingenii . . . dator*) to fill her with skill in philosophical art sufficient for her to write as she would wish to her lover.[5] In *Ep.* 23 she eruditely professes that the weakness of her "dried-up talent" (*aridi defectus ingenii*) subverts her capacity to write to him; she goes on to maintain that her own intellect reproaches her with rushing naively ahead forgetful of her "cold" physiology and the brutish "sluggishness" which characterizes her.[6] We are of course back in the realms of *ingenium* conspicuously manifesting itself even while it claims to be articulating its own ineptitude. Later the man's voice allows himself to be duly impressed by the intelligence she has demonstrated in her analysis of friendship—impressed, at least, so far as to affirm in the classic pseudo-complimentary trope of the central Middle Ages that her *ingenium* and eloquence are attaining towards "manly strength."[7]

The Abelard-Heloise correspondence as previously known to us attends to Abelard's controversially creative talent rather than to Heloise's.[8] By contrast the woman's letters in the exchange reproduced by Johannes de Vepria (further letters by Heloise, according to Mews) manifest no less than Hrotsvitha's a consciousness of formidable female creative capacity that is nevertheless prepared to express itself through the sanctioned forms of gendered modesty. The man's (Abelard's?) response to this is a touch patronizing, a touch complacent so far as his partner's *ingenium* is concerned, though nevertheless forthright in addressing her as sole "disciple of philosophy" among the young women of the age.[9]

With Boccaccio in the fourteenth century we hear the tone of patronization again in the *De mulieribus claris,* even amid the pro-feminine gestures which abound there.[10] This compilation "On Famous Women" is particularly relevant to the present chapter because it expressly celebrates many women for their creative talents. Boccaccio's the-oretical position is that creative intelligence is available without regard to gender be-cause "intellects suitable for different undertakings" (*apta rebus variis ingenia*) are given to everyone alike. Yet there is an important rider: such potential may become produc-tive through *studium,* but alternatively it may "grow torpid through sloth."[11] Boccaccio makes it clear that he thinks women are more handicapped because in order to apply their intellect studiously they have to battle, more than men, against indolence or slug-gishness. He seems unsure whether to ascribe this alleged "sluggishness of mind" (*tar-dum ingenium*) in women to nature or to social conditioning.[12] Either way he offsets his acknowledgments of creativity in women with that insinuating vocabulary of inertia which we saw Hrotsvitha pointedly bandying about—the verb *torpere,* the adjective *tardus.* Admiring the skills of the Greek painter Irene, for instance, he cannot resist adding that such notable *ingenium* is usually "very tardy" in women.[13]

Later we shall observe that there was a quasi-scientific rationale for this gender asymmetry where the creative intellect was concerned. For the moment, it should be clear already that *ingenium* and its vernacular derivatives will be likely to loom large in any medieval discussion of creative talent. Boccaccio himself helps us to see a definitive association between creativity and *ingenium,* for he declares that "nothing new has been discovered by anyone without its proving the power of his intellect."[14] The word is hard to translate, however. Even in the short space of a few pages on Hrotsvitha, Dronke vari-ously renders it "imagination," "imaginative genius," "genius," and "imaginative in-sight."[15] Guarino's translation of the *De mulieribus claris* opens up a wider thesaurus for *ingenium* including "mind," "intelligence," "wisdom," "ingenuity," "talent," "intellect," and "genius" (though never "imagination"), of which "intellect" and "mind" are the most frequent. It will be necessary to explore the slipperiness of the concept, especially in its vernacular derivatives, in order to clarify what sort of creative intellect women were most credited with. The topic will prove to be entangled with moral imperatives about utiliza-tion of skills on the one hand, and anxieties about the propriety of improving material civilization on the other. The question of women's creative talent, it will here be argued, straddles important fault-lines in late medieval thought.

One reason for the chameleon aspect of *ingenium* is that it can encompass so many different kinds of discovery or innovative application, from the techno-creative to the aesthetic and cognitive. In Boccaccio you never know what kind is coming next. He writes that *ingenium* is successively shown in women's invention of (or in some instances, special expertise in) the plow, the Egyptian alphabet, cultivation of flax and hemp, weaving, prophetic writing, the Latin language, divination by fire, the battle-ax, cotton combing, new poetic forms, painting, philosophical critique, poetic composition, Heliconian verse, and the cento. In short, invention crisscrosses the domains of the material and the speculative even though medieval culture hypothetically separated them. According to Deguilleville's *Pilgrimage of the Life of Man* (to cite a representative fourteenth-century example of that separation) the distinction ought to be between a "school" of Nature covering all creative *craftes*, and an analytical "school" of Science in which things are not "made" so much as investigated and judged. (It is worth staying with this text for a moment. We discover there that Lady Sapience is the president or "maistresse" of both schools. When Aristotle is thrust forward by Nature to dispute with Sapience concerning the unnaturalness of eucharistic bread, the philosopher eventually has to acknowledge her intellectual genius. He describes her as a woman with "engyn so subtil" because she has used analogies of broken mirrors, the heart, and the memory to demonstrate that the part can accommodate a greater whole, and therefore that the concept of plenitude-within-division which characterizes eucharistic bread is not an offense to nature.[16] That the passage credits a female personification with inventive intelligence is interesting, and Barbara Newman will show in her response to this essay what positive implications may reside in such personification. That the subtle *ingenium* in question should be characterized as a sort of expertise in quantum physics is also— it will turn out—significant.)

When Christine de Pizan adapts the *De mulieribus* in her *City of Ladies* she imposes order on Boccaccio's inchoate sequence by invoking a binary model like that which Deguilleville uses.[17] Reason tells Christine that many great *sciences et ars* have been discovered through women's creative intelligence and subtlety (*"par engin et soutiveté de femmes"*), both in "the theoretical sciences which are expressed through the written word, and in the technical crafts which take the form of manual tasks and trades."[18] Yet what Deguilleville and Christine try to keep asunder, the cognitive and the practical, become everywhere blurred in the concept of *engin* itself. Over twenty years ago the meanings of this word were the subject of a useful chapter in Robert Hanning's book *The Individual in Twelfth-Century Romance*.[19] He showed how the major meanings of *ingenium* in classical Latin ("innate quality, talent, genius") broadened in medieval Latin and thence in its vernacular derivatives, acquiring a range of significance including "imagination," "artfulness," "contrivance," and hence "trickery," too.

Although I believe with Hanning that latent derogatory connotations inhered more in Old French/Middle English *engin/engyn* than in the Latin *ingenium*, the vernacular word nevertheless retained substantial positive as well as negative meanings. A glance at Chaucer's usage shows this. For the Parson, *subtil engyn* is one of the natural "goodes" of the soul alongside wit, understanding, and memory (X.453).[20] The narrator of the *House of Fame* confirms the word's latent association with literary creativity when he summons Thought to deploy "engyn and myght" in order to help articulate his dream (*HF* 528). Such inventiveness becomes less respectable, however, in the idiom of Pandarus when he warns Troilus of the outcry there would be if it were known that Pandarus had cajoled his niece into a liaison "thorugh myn engyn" (*TC* III.274).

Hanning sums up *engin* as the "shaping of the human environment to one's advantage by the gifts of the mind," but such shaping can be illusionistic or manipulative and therefore in the one word are linked together, he suggests, "contradictory judgments on witty or ingenious problem-solving behavior and its physical embodiment in artifacts."[21] The most characteristic occurrences of *engin* in medieval narrative involve ingenious contrivances, whether mechanisms or stratagems (that is, whether intricate locks or intricate deceits), phenomena that in modern cognates of the key term we would probably ascribe to "ingenuity" rather than "genius."

Two instances of technological ingenuity may help at this point. An *engin* or *gyn* can be the cleverly designed artifact itself—a "gadget" as we might now call it. One splendid example is found in Chaucer's *Squire's Tale,* where a visitor stuns the royal court of Cambyuskan by arriving with a mechanical brass flying horse. The visitor remarks that its creator "koude ful many a gyn," that is, had wide experience of mechanical devices (V.128). Eventually the visitor confides that, to make the horse-machine fly, it is just a matter of flicking a switch in its ear ("trilling a pin," V.316, 321, 328): "For therin lith th'effect of al the gyn"—the key to the whole device (V.322).

Chaucer presents a mixture of scientific, historical, and superstitious reactions prompted in the court crowd by the sight of this equine jump-jet. The horse cannot be moved by any of the people's own "engineering" resources ("For noon engyn of wyndas or polyve," V.184). They gauge and admire its proportions, but mutter about its potential as a means of political treachery (a new Trojan Horse) or as an outright manifestation of "Fairye" or as a juggler's illusionistic "apparence" (V.192, 201, 209, 218). Towards their speculation, the Squire-narrator maintains an attitude of condescension. He alleges that the public awe results from bafflement before things that are fashioned *moore subtilly* than an uninformed person can comprehend (V.199–205, 221–23), even though it is obvious that the people are applying plausible theories to the phenomenon. Chaucer's tone is difficult to judge. Perhaps there is satire on the Squire for wanting at the same time to parade knowledge yet appear to be aristocratically aloof from technical matters.[22] Perhaps the public desire to explain the ingenious horse represents a kind of demystifying of the exotic, against which the Squire tries to protect his romance.[23] Yet there remains the possibility that the condescension owes something to a personal and traditionalist authorial distaste in Chaucer himself for material contrivances in themselves.

A second instance goes further in disclosing an atmosphere of suspicion that surrounds *engin.* This time it is a case of a woman's creative intelligence—that of Melior, the heroine in the romance of *Partonope*. The sole child of an emperor, she has been educated by "grette clerkes" the better to be able to govern in the future. She describes how the power of her intellect, subtly trained in "wysdome," has been manifested in feats of spatial manipulation—in fact the sorts of triumphant compressions and expansions which we have already seen associated with "subtil engyn" in the case of Dame Sapience lecturing Aristotle. Melior could make her chamber seem a mile broad and was able to fill it with a whole tournament. The fifteenth-century English poem follows the twelfth-century French version of the romance in partly associating what it calls Melior's *crafte of experimentes* with a hint of the occult—in the remark that she accomplished the feats "by craft of nygromauncye and such gynne"—and partly associating it with knowledge and cleverness conferred by God; *savoir* and *sens* in the French, *connynge* and *wytte* in the English.[24]

The pedagogical background to Melior's expertise is only belatedly disclosed to the reader and to Partonope, the knight whom she has brought to her land as prospective partner. Partonope's knowledge of her *ingenium* is at first confined to the lavish ornamental and architectural contrivances that characterize her city when he enters it. The walls there are surmounted by animated golden eagle statuary made "by crafte and goode engyne" (919); a bed is somehow hung in a chamber by "good engyne" (1135); and Melior relates how at her design the city rises upon caves "made by goode engyne" in the rock (2165).[25]

The repeated modifier in "*goode* engyne" is instructive in two ways. In one way it may signal a fifteenth-century desire to disambiguate a concept whose valence, positive or negative, was felt to be too uncertain when it remained unmodified. (*Malengyn* is a disambiguation in the opposite direction, used in the same century by Malory.[26]) In another way, I suspect, the repeated qualifier is part of a narratorial campaign to try to "disinfect" Melior's exceptional *ingenium*—to reassure readers that despite any appearances or presumptions to the contrary she is deploying her intellect benevolently and is not the demonic, illusionist, succubus-like figure preying on the soul that Partonope's mother and advisers back home make her out to be. In other words the narrative plays out medieval anxieties about feats imagined to be within the extreme reach of *ingenium* which might be sufficiently problematic if associated with clerks, but which were even more deeply insidious if associated with women. Spatial ingenuity is registered as awe-inspiring in Chaucer's *Franklin's Tale* when a clerk of Orleans is able to contain whole vistas, including jousting knights, in his study (V.1189–1208)—but this clerk's ingenuity is called into question as magic and illusion (1202, 1292).[27] Even the lesser ingeniousness that animates birds made of gold and jewels is open to suspicion elsewhere. In *Mandeville's Travels* the narrator marvels over such contrivances at the Great Khan's court and wonders whether they are produced "by craft or be nygromancye." He settles for a scientific explanation because with the Khan are the world's "moste sotyle men in all sciences and in alle craftes."[28] But the *Partonope* story multiplies the anxiety in that the exponent is a woman. After all, the arbiters of medieval culture (as we should now remind ourselves) predetermined that a woman's intellect, if not dormant, was productive chiefly in errant, devious, and pragmatic ways.

Certain medieval scholastics, such as Henry of Ghent in the thirteenth century, took deficiency of female intellect (*debilitas ingenii muliebris*) as axiomatic, though not without attributing a lack of *ingenium* also to some men.[29] In understanding how such views justified themselves we need recourse to the humoral theory whereby—as Alexandra Barratt summarizes it—"women's 'cold and damp' constitution was held to be inhospitable to intellectual activity."[30] When physiology was invoked to address questions (that is, to rationalize answers) about relative male/female intellectual capacities, factors such as "humidity" and "softness" were thought critical. Particularly relevant to the modeling of female *ingenium* are some insinuations in a discussion of the relative moral educability of men and women. Albertus Magnus deals with this in one of his *Quaestiones de animalibus*. The *quaestio* has justly been noticed by contributors to medieval gender studies such as Joan Cadden and Clarissa Atkinson, as well as by a Chaucerian, David Burnley, in whose work I first came across it.[31]

The title of the *quaestio* is "Whether the male is more apt at learning good behavior than the female." Although *ingenium* is not expressly at issue, the allied faculty of "prudence" is. The basis is that people cannot usefully be taught if they are deficient in prudence—that is, in the capacity to direct the intelligence towards beneficial aims by an exercise of *providentia*.[32] The difficulty for Albertus here was that Aristotle had seemed to believe that women have more prudence than men. Albertus's predictable move to dissociate women from prudential educability is to allege that female "humidity" prevents women from *retaining* what their minds receive. They learn ephemerally, as it were. There follows cant about female "inconstancy," "slipperiness," and "always seeking novelties." He then goes on to assert outright that women cannot be more "apt at learning" than men because their "cold" constitutions make their minds less acute.[33] A similar view is expressed by the fourteenth-century authority Johannes Buridanus writing on Aristotle's *Politics*. As a result of the greater "fluxibility" of a woman's "phlegmatic material" her intellect allegedly has less staying-power and is subject to "varying perturbation."[34]

Albertus concludes that women exercise only a cheap and worldly-wise version of prudence, one that really requires another name. It is a tell-tale shift in terminology. "Strictly speaking a woman is not more prudent than a man, rather she is more astute (*astutior*), a quality that tends not to good but to evil."[35] Burnley's note on this includes an interesting gloss on "astuteness" by the fourteenth-century Parisian theologian Gerson: "*astutia* is distinct from good counsel in its tendency, *for it is a vice of the intellect teaching one to discover* [invenire] *comfortable means towards evil ends.*"[36] Thus astuteness, which Albertus genders female, emerges as a sort of debased creative intellect which seeks easy new ways of achieving objectives of a morally dubious kind.

There is a powerful convergence between astuteness and *engin,* in the more pejorative sense of that word. The chief dictionary definitions for *astutia* are "dexterity," "adroitness," "craftiness," "archness." Astuteness is at best a worldly exercise of intellection. One would not have to go far to confirm that it deals in the wisdom of this world, not God's, for that is the distinction conspicuously urged in 1 Corinthians 3:19, a famous passage where Paul says that the "wisdom" of the world is "folly" before God, and that the merely worldly wise are recognized by their astuteness. Even worse, astuteness is the quality by which it is suggested in 2 Corinthians 11:3 that the serpent seduced Eve.[37] Astuteness is, according to Albertus's prejudiced theory, what women fall into by default: a short-term use of intellection at best and a materialistic perversion of prudence at worst. It is in effect *engin* devoted dubiously to material advantage.

Now, "womanly astuteness" is an expression readily thrown about by Boccaccio in the *De mulieribus.* It is with womanly astuteness (though the details remain unexplained) that Opis saves her children from death at Saturn's hands. It is through "women's astuteness" that Iole binds Hercules in dotage to herself, and in the same mode Flora contrives her own fame by naming the Roman people her heirs.[38] The most revealing instance is, however, the case of Dido. Here, for Boccaccio, are two conspicuous examples of *astutia.* In the first, it is with calculated (*excogitata*) astuteness that Dido makes it appear that she has ditched her dead husband's treasure at sea by throwing sand-filled chests overboard. As for the more famous creative idea whereby after coming ashore in Africa she engineers the space for a whole city out of what an ox-hide will encompass, by slitting the hide into threadlike strips, Boccaccio is moved to outright exclamation: *O mulieris astutia!*[39]

The present importance of the Dido example is that it demonstrates the synonymy between *astutia* and *engin.* In the twelfth-century *Roman d'Enéas,* the episode of the ox-hide had been taken to be an exemplification of *engin.* Dido asks "par grant engin" whether the North African prince will sell whatever land an ox-hide will enclose. The prince, not wary of her ingenuity, agrees.[40] If Hanning is right, in this instance (and therefore by analogy I would suppose in Boccaccio's Dido's *astutia*) the cleverness shown amounts to "readiness to take advantage of a situation, problem solving, manipulation of others."[41] Given the combination of ruse and foresight, we might think of it as an ambivalent example of "creative" intelligence rather in the same sense in which we nowadays speak of "creative accountancy."

This evidence suggests that one writer's *engin* can be another writer's *astutia,* and that what the words share is (by the fourteenth century, at least) something gendered feminine. Yet there is a third writer's view of Dido's creativity to be considered: namely the view of Christine de Pizan, who complicates the picture not by re-instituting *engin* in this narrative, but by decisively upgrading the quality displayed and calling it "prudence." For Christine—or at least for Christine's character Reason—Dido becomes a supreme epitome of prudence because she fulfills the prudential criteria of "weighing up carefully what you wish to do and working out how to do it."[42]

Insofar as Christine is reacting to Boccaccio's Dido, she is working this up from not more than a couple of hints in his account, one of which is the qualifier *excogitata* attached as we have seen to Dido's "astuteness," and the other of which is the suggestion that Dido may have fled her homeland "because she planned it herself . . ." (*ex proprio mentis sue consilio*).[43] Christine eliminates the insinuation of "astuteness" and insists instead that prudence is manifest in Dido's actions—she first "considered," and then "steeled herself to put her plans into effect."[44] The ox-hide idea becomes in this view not a symptom of female wiliness but evidence of *sçavoir et grant prudence.* Only from the perspective of those selling her the land is there any imputation of trickery, since they are said to be amazed by her "cunning ruse" (*a cautelle et scens de ceste femme*).[45]

It will be useful to dwell upon Christine's resistance to the Boccaccian model of womanly astuteness, and on her own explorations of *engin,* since this will lead us into a debate about material betterment which complicates medieval perspectives on the creative intellect. Christine proves to have conducted quite a systematic campaign to upgrade the relevant Boccaccian heroines from astuteness to prudence. Opis saved the lives of her children through wise cunning (*saige cautelle*), not astuteness, and was honored for her "prudent behavior."[46] Penelope was "wise and prudent" rather than astute in her handling of the unwanted suitors.[47]

Christine's tacit campaign in this respect is consistent with her view that women are *not* creatures of slushy or humidly impressionable intellect, unable to sustain thought and plan properly ahead. As though with scholastic and physiological opinion in mind, she carefully repeats that women have abundant retentive power. God, she insists, has made women's minds sharp enough to learn, understand, and "retain" any form of knowledge. Doubtless the verb *retenir* is repeatedly used with polemical intent to undermine all that cant about humid fluxibility.[48] It is the corrective to Boccaccio's worry about the stamina of female *ingenium.* Christine does also sense how the allegation of flux can be turned into an advantage, for she suggests that as a compensation for relatively slighter physique women may display a beneficial mental agility: they have minds potentially more *delivre* or more nimble than men's when they apply themselves.[49] But it is more characteristic of her, both in the *City of Ladies* and elsewhere, to make a stand on behalf of women's prudential capacity, a capacity for thorough foresight. Hence the marked emphasis on Dido carefully considering what she needed to do.

The idiom of that statement is worth incidental mention. Dido took counsel with herself (*prist en soy . . . avis*) about her plan. By contrast we might recall from Chaucer's poetry what seems to be a stereotype of quick-witted but perhaps implicitly stop-gap feminine resourcefulness. When the love of Troilus and Criseyde is threatened by the Trojan decision to exchange Criseyde for Antenor, Pandarus suggests to her that her wits may somehow solve the problem, for "Women ben wise in short avysement" (*TC* IV.936). She seems to accept this construction of herself, since not long afterwards we find her putting her ideas to Troilus as "a womman . . . avysed *sodeynly*" (IV.1261–62, my emphasis). Subsequently, amid her isolation in the Greek camp she diagnoses a deficiency in this womanly talent for emergency problem solving (or astuteness?). She theorizes that she has always understood past and present but has lacked foresight, the third component of *prudentia.*[50]

Precisely because such gender constructions as these questioned women's posses- sion of extensive foresight, Christine de Pizan has to insist on a "prudential" dimen- sion in women's creative intellects. Equally, and in a way more boldly, Christine has to insist on the social beneficiality—the *wise* foresight—of the products of that creative intellect. The significance of this requires investigation in the last part of this essay.

As we saw earlier, Boccaccio's famous women range from those who have applied their *ingenium* in literary innovation to those who have applied it in the discovery of technological improvements in such areas as agriculture, cloth manufacture, even trans- port. Christine follows him in dwelling on the *soultiveté d'engin* manifest not only in cog- nitive developments but in practical inventions of all sorts. However, Boccaccio professes to find himself in a quandary so far as the fundamental propriety of the techno-creative impetus is concerned. Contemplating the invention of the plow and thence of crop cul- tivation by Ceres, he introduces a quasi-scholastic debate on the effects of civilization, claiming that whether the application of *ingenium* to such ends is to be praised or con- demned is open to question.[51] On the one hand are the improvements to life—better nourishment and a transformation from barbarous existence in the woods to the or- derliness of farming and urban culture, things apparently good in themselves. On the other hand agricultural progress, by luring humanity from its Golden Age of nut-eating austerity in the wild, has ushered in the disadvantages of indulgence, land ownership, greed, and enmity. The *inventio* (the "finding out") of agriculture is in this view also the uncovering of vices hitherto dormant.

In a flash, we can sense how the devotion of the creative intellect (in Hanning's phrase) to "shaping the human environment to one's advantage by the gifts of the mind," could strike a negative chord for those trained up on Ovidian Golden Age rheto- ric.[52] The creative impulse, indeed, stood in a complicated relationship with the Golden Age myth and with post-Golden Age human circumstances. Jean de Meun acknowl- edges this in a part of Genius's "sermon" near the end of the *Roman de la Rose,* where Genius speaks of the degeneration of the world under Jupiter's reign.[53] Prior to that reign, people "foraged together for the good things that came to them spontaneously" in a golden dawn of socialism (20,095–96, p. 310). But Jupiter inaugurated an era gov- erned by the edict that everyone (particularly himself) should devote themselves to liv- ing comfortably and aiming at delight (20,065–84, pp. 309–10). He set an example by inventing animal traps and falconry to catch more tasty food, and by concocting gourmet sauces to go with it, but he also gratuitously *withheld* communal resources—such as fire—so that people had to find ways of generating them. The result of prioritizing and privatizing individual human comfort was deprivation for the many who could not attain it. And this, says Genius, was "the beginning of the arts." The creative impulse is galvanized by material hardship: "men's ingenuity is stimulated when they encounter hardship" (*li mal les angins esmeuvent*).[54]

As Jean de Meun indicates, the exercise of creative ingenuity so as to ameliorate one's immediate environment is something of a materialist enterprise, a focus on worldly rather than other-worldly objectives. In fact, as the reader will perhaps by now have noticed, it is disconcertingly close to Gerson's negative definition of *astutia*. And since we know that "astuteness" is gendered feminine by Boccaccio, there is perhaps a latent misogyny in Boccaccio's expression of philosophical doubt concerning the pragmatic application of *ingenium* by the likes of Ceres. The gendering of astuteness as feminine and the link Boccaccio observes between women and improvements to material life threaten to circumscribe women in a realm of wily pragmatism. This belongs to that classic strategy of sexual differentiation which proposes (as Nina Auerbach reminds us) that "women are . . . deficient in the capacity for abstraction" and that "woman's bent may be for the 'practical' rather than for 'general principles.'"[55]

Christine de Pizan's answer to all such doubt and insinuation is to affirm unreservedly the creative talents (the *engin*) of women in every category of endeavor noted by Boccaccio—and to insist absolutely on the "necessity" of women's discoveries in the material domain. In the *Cité des Dames* she represents herself as asking Reason whether women have been able to discover previously unknown arts and sciences through the exercise of subtle *engin*. Reason responds by telling of the "marvellous" *engin* of Carmentis in inventing Latin, the very language of culture itself, then of the great *excellence en engin* of Minerva, who invented wool making, the production of oil from olives, cart building, and the forging of armor.[56]

Christine goes on to challenge received hierarchies lest they contribute to a demotion of women's inventiveness. On the one hand she finds that we can attribute the very basis of literary culture to a woman's (Carmentis's) creativity. On the other, such practical discoveries as how to spin thread and produce cloth "have all benefited humankind enormously, despite the fact that some men scorn women for performing such activities."[57] Minerva's practical inventions were "vital" things (*choses neccessaires*). It is women like Minerva, Ceres, and Isis who introduced the amenities of daily existence.[58] The achievements of Aristotle and the philosophers pale in their value to humankind compared with what the ingenuity (*sçavoir*) of such women has achieved.[59]

The Golden Age topos (and Aristotle) are incidental casualties of Christine's repositioning on the question of invention here. She throws out of the window any notion that invention has been the mother of abuse. Boccaccio's doubts are put in their place on the doctrinally sound basis that things discovered are the gift of God; the users, not the discoveries, are to be blamed for any abuse.[60] It is quite refreshing to find the negative clichés of Golden-Age thinking so decisively scotched in the interests of an inclusive view of the benefits of feminine inventiveness. By contrast, the receptivity of Chaucer to Golden-Age nostalgia is perhaps symptomatic of a temperament inhospitable to the kind of defiant move that becomes necessary to the rehabilitation of feminine *engin* in Christine.[61]

This also is a reminder that since the assertions about women and creative intellect by Boccaccio and Christine are produced in contexts which expressly aim to celebrate women and which are moreover tightly related to each other, it might be objected that they are not representative. Yet they are not alone. They are joined, for instance, by someone as unlikely and traditionalist as John Gower. In his *Confessio Amantis* Gower has various uses of *engin* in its pejorative sense of "trick" (by association with "Falssemblant" for example),[62] but he also uses the term without embarrassment to describe women's creative talents in a discourse on the "uses of labor" in Book 4 of the *Confessio*. Here Gower produces a catalogue of achievements brought forth by the industriousness of former times—another sort of golden age myth in fact—and names names, though somewhat eccentrically, for in the standard edition of Gower there is uncertainty as to where some of the material comes from. Among other men Jubal is commended for inventing music, Zenzis for painting, Prometheus for sculpture, Tubal for forging, Jadahel for nets and fishing, Saturn for tilling and coins.[63] In the list are women. Minerva invented wool making, "Delbora" found out how to work flax: "Tho wommen were of great engyn" (IV.2,435–38). And among the Italians "Carmente made of hire engin / The ferste lettres of Latin" (2,637–38).

The context of this passage is analysis of the sin of Sloth. For Gower, *ingenium* (as he writes in an accompanying Latin gloss), and equally the *engin* of the women-inventors, is a crucial antidote to Sloth. Whatever talent is given to anyone is to be actively used for the common benefit, not left unused in idleness, with no fruition. The reminiscences of other voices that we have rehearsed in this essay, from Hrotsvitha on, are so telling that it is worth presenting the gloss in full:

> Here he speaks against the indolent, and most especially against those who possess creative talent together with excellent foresight, yet wallow without producing the fruit of any achievement. And he puts forward the example of the industry of our predecessors who, to the enlightenment and benefit of the whole human race, originally invented crafts and sciences by their persistent toil and study, with the help of divine grace.[64]

The vocabulary of effort rather than torpidity, of social utility, and of the proper deployment of divine gifts is now familiar.

Interestingly, while the focus of the gloss is on *ingenium,* Gower's English text uses the cognate *engin* only to describe the women's inventiveness, not that of any of the men. (The passage generally repeats the formula that the men "first found" this or "first made" that; otherwise there is only a generalized reference to the production of metal "Thurgh mannes wit and goddes grace" [2452].) Unless this is a coincidence it may imply a predisposition to associate the word *engin* with women because of the connotations of wiliness latent in the vernacular term. That would leave us with the irony that women's reputation in the Middle Ages for astuteness may sometimes have facilitated their being credited with inventiveness of a more profound sort. Conversely as we have seen in the case of Melior, a deeply educated woman's capacity for inventiveness might create an aura of suspicion, suspicion that she would inevitably deflect her intellect into occult and destructive channels. Morgan le Fay comes to mind as the epitome of such *engin.*

When we draw the threads of this analysis together, we see that the concept of the creative intellect is located at a point of stress in the medieval value system, where opposing impulses meet. That would be so of men as well as women—but it is aggravated in the case of women.

One impulse that we have seen expressed several times urges that creative talents are to be actively deployed, both because creative industriousness should benefit society and because it is an antidote to personal inertia and the sin of sloth. So far as writing was concerned these were powerful validations of literary endeavor, ones that were used time and time again. Women may be said to have needed such validation more acutely than men in that their intellectual authority was doubted *a priori.* However, for women there was a complication when it came to literary diligence: they were not *expected* to cultivate a dynamic literary creativity because they were anyway stereotyped as having only sluggish intelligence. At the same time (paradoxically!) they were attributed with a considerable mental dexterity labeled as "astuteness."

A second impulse was the genuine awe and excitement which people felt in the presence of creative invention. This we saw acknowledged (though not unreservedly) in *The Squire's Tale.* However, where it is a case of "scientific" female ingeniousness as manifested by Melior, there seems to be a distinct accretion of anxiety, as though the female intellect could not be trusted to engage in such ingenuity without slipping towards illicit magic. The associations between astuteness and *engin,* and between *engin* and trickery, leave women of ingenuity exposed to such doubts. (For this reason we may recall our earlier example and wonder whether, when Aristotle remarks on the "subtil engyn" of Lady Sapience in Deguilleville's text, Deguilleville means that the pagan philosopher is trying to insult her, not commend her.)

The third impulse, implicit in the Pauline and Albertan disparagement of astuteness, confines itself to technological inventiveness. This type of *ingenium* is rendered suspect on the grounds that devoting oneself to improvement of material life is a deflection from spiritual ends towards hedonistic ones. Jean de Meun roots *engin* in the desire to escape personal privation; so *engin* is compromisingly linked with materialism and fosters a degeneration from pristine austerity. Women, to whom *astutia* especially belongs according to two of the writers we have looked at, seem to be thereby prone to this materialistic exercise of the intelligence.

Prejudice conspired with semantics in these ways to leave women straddling faultlines of medieval culture more uncomfortably than men, so far as the inventive faculty was concerned. Yet, an affirmation that women possessed *ingenium* of the highest order and should use it was available if parts of the discourse were emphasized, and others jettisoned. Inventiveness was a "gift" not confined to one sex or the other, as women themselves (from Hrotsvitha to Christine de Pizan) insisted, and when one had a gift like that, ethical and biblical authority enjoined one to use it. As for the mistrust of ingenuity evinced by bucolic nostalgia, where would we be (as Christine de Pizan and John Gower both observe) without the inventions of past genius?[65] In any case, the tenacity of traditions about figures such as Minerva and Carmenta and the ways in which they are deployed by Christine and Gower prove that the creative intelligence of women remained an open matter in the Middle Ages.

Notes

It is a pleasure to acknowledge the stimulus of the UK Gender and Medieval Studies group, for whose conference on "Gender and Creativity" (Oxford, January 1998) organized by Lesley Smith and Jane Taylor a first version of this essay was developed. Its consolidation was furthered by the invitation to present it at the 2000 conference of the Medieval Association of the Pacific at the University of Victoria, for which I am especially indebted to Elizabeth Archibald.

1. The prefaces to Hrotsvitha's legends and to her plays, and the letter "Ad Fautores" linked with the latter, are investigated in a subtle discussion by Peter Dronke, whose translations I use and to which I am much indebted, in *Women Writers of the Middle Ages: A Critical Study of Texts from Perpetua (d. 203) to Marguerite Porete (d. 1310)* (Cambridge: Cambridge University Press, 1984), 65–67, 69–73, and 73–75. For the Latin text see *Hrotsvithae Opera*, ed. Hélène Homeyer (Munich: Schöningh, 1970), 37–39, 233–34, 235–37.

2. "et largitor ingenii tanto amplius in me iure laudaretur, quanto muliebris sensus tardior esse creditur" (Homeyer, *Hrotsvithae Opera*, 236).

3. Dronke, *Women Writers*, 72.

4. Constant Mews, *The Lost Letters of Heloise and Abelard* (Basingstoke and London: Macmillan, 1999), 1–177, passim. I use the edition and translation of the letters provided by Mews (with Neville Chiavaroli) on 179–289.

5. Mews, *Lost Letters*, 192–93.

6. "Respice pectus tuum brutum et frigidum, . . . et tantum crassi aeris segnicie turgidum" (Mews, *Lost Letters*, 206–207).

7. *Ep.* 50, Mews, *Lost Letters,* 232–33.

8. On Abelard's self-representation in the *Historia calamitatum* of his creative *ingenium* as opposed to the conventional *usus* of the schools, see R. W. Hanning, *The Individual in Twelfth-Century Romance* (New Haven and London: Yale University Press, 1977), 21–31.

9. *Ep.* 50, Mews, *Lost Letters,* 230–31.

10. Giovanni Boccaccio, *De mulieribus claris,* ed. Vittorio Zaccaria, vol. 10, *Tutte le opere di Giovanni Boccaccio,* ed. Vittore Branca (Verona: Mondadori, 1970); and *Concerning Famous Women,* trans. Guido A. Guarino (London: Allen and Unwin, 1964). There are discrepancies between the chapter numbers in these. In order to avoid confusion, further citations will identify chapter and page number separately for edition and translation in the notes.

11. Zaccaria, xviii, 90–92; Guarino, xvii, 39.

12. The deficiency is attributed to nature in the Preface: Zaccaria, Proemio, 24; Guarino, Preface, xxxvii. It is more ambiguously a *torpor* associated with womanly occupations in the chapter on Proba: Zaccaria, xcvii, 394–96; Guarino, xcv, 220.

13. Zaccaria, lix, 244; Guarino, lvii, 131.

14. "Nil enim novi . . . ab aliquo compertum est, quod non sit ingentis ingenii argumentum," from the chapter on Pamphile: Zaccaria, xliv, 184; Guarino, xlii, 95.

15. Dronke, *Women Writers,* 65–75.

16. *The Pilgrimage of the Lyfe of the Manhode,* ed. Avril Henry, vol. 1, Early English Text Society *o.s.* 288 (London: Oxford University Press, 1985), 37–43, 42. This is an anonymous prose translation of the first recension of Guillaume de Deguilleville's early fourteenth-century *Le Pèlerinage de vie humaine,* ed. J. J. Stürzinger for the Roxburghe Club (London: Nichols and Sons, 1893), in which Aristotle likewise commends Sapience "Qui l'engin avez si soutil" (line 3220).

17. I use Maureen C. Curnow, "The *Livre de la cité des dames* of Christine de Pisan: A Critical Edition" (PhD diss., Vanderbilt University, 1975), available in two volumes through Xerox University Microfilms, Ann Arbor; and *The Book of the City of Ladies,* trans. Rosalind Brown-Grant (Harmondsworth: Penguin, 1999). Quotations will be identified in the notes with reference to Curnow's page numbers and Brown-Grant's book/chapter numbers and page numbers. Christine's text is self-consciously in dialogue with Boccaccio's. Although Curnow argues strenuously (138–47) that Christine's immediate source is a 1401 French translation of Boccaccio attributed to Laurent de Premierfait, it seems to me that she works with both the Latin and the French at her elbow. Moreover the points at which she diverges from both versions prove more interesting than the points at which she specifically echoes the wording of the French.

18. Curnow, 735; Brown-Grant, I.33, p. 64.

19. Chap. 3, "'Engin' in Twelfth-Century Courtly Texts," 105–38.

20. *The Riverside Chaucer,* ed. Larry D. Benson (Boston, Mass.: Houghton Mifflin, 1987), *Canterbury Tales,* X.453. All subsequent Chaucer references are to this edition. For the Second Nun *engyn* is similarly a category of thought, one of a trinity which includes *memorie* and *intellect* (VIII.339).

21. Hanning, *Individual in Twelfth-Century Romance,* 107–108.

22. Robert P. Miller, "Chaucer's Rhetorical Rendition of Mind: *The Squire's Tale,*" in *Chaucer and the Craft of Fiction,* ed. Leigh A. Arrathoon (Rochester, Mich.: Solaris Press, 1986), 219–40, at 231–36.

23. John M. Fyler, "Domesticating the Exotic in the *Squire's Tale,*" *Journal of English Literary History* 55 (1988): 1–26, at 3–6. See also Paul Strohm's view that the Squire, "knowing the tradition

within which such marvels occur (romance, rather than 'gestes' or old science), knows how they are to be taken" (*Social Chaucer* [Cambridge, Mass.: Harvard University Press, 1989], 170).

24. *The Middle English Versions of Partonope of Blois*, ed. A. Trampe Bödtker, Early English Text Society *e.s.* 109 (London: Trübner, 1912), lines 5,913–91, and *Partonopeu de Blois: A French Romance of the Twelfth Century*, ed. Joseph Gildea, 2 vols. (Villanova, Penn.: Villanova University Press, 1967), lines 4,586–672.

25. In the OF, the animated images are made "par grant savoir" but are Moorish productions. The emphasis on "good engyne" appears to be the ME writer's idea. At 4,665–67 in the OF *engin* is collocated with a word for "fraud" when Melior claims knowledge of "totes les ars, / Et tos engiens et tos baras."

26. For example, Bors comments on Guinevere's role in the "Poisoned Apple" episode that "for good love she bade us to dyner and nat for no male engyne" (*Malory: Works*, ed. Eugène Vinaver [Oxford: Oxford University Press, 1977], Bk. XVIII, p. 617; see also XVIII, p. 638, and XX, p. 677). The expression is largely a fifteenth-century phenomenon in English.

27. Some readers have nevertheless found this clerk a sympathetic figure, even a kind of surrogate poet (Paul G. Ruggiers, *The Art of the Canterbury Tales* [Madison, Wisc.: University of Wisconsin Press, 1965], 235). In *The Reeve's Tale* Symkyn refers with open sarcasm to the spatial inventiveness of clerks (I.4122–26); however, it is simple ingenuity of a different order which enables them to maneuver within his cramped quarters.

28. *Mandeville's Travels*, ed. M. C. Seymour (Oxford: Clarendon Press, 1967), 157. A bird is part of the gadgetry recorded by the thirteenth-century designer Villard de Honnecourt in his sketchbook (J. B. A. Lassus, *Album de Villard de Honnecourt* [Paris: Imprimerie Impériale, 1858], fol. 9r [Pl. XVI and p. 91]): the glosses among the designs draw attention to *engins* on two further pages, fol. 23r (Pl. XLIV and p. 175) and fol. 30r (Pl. LVIII and p. 203).

29. See Alcuin Blamires, "The Limits of Bible Study for Medieval Women," in *Women, the Book and the Godly*, ed. Lesley Smith and Jane H. M. Taylor (Cambridge: D. S. Brewer, 1995), 1–12, at 7 and 9.

30. Alexandra Barratt, *Women's Writing in Middle English* (London: Longman, 1992), 30 n. 11.

31. Albertus Magnus, *Opera omnia*, xii, *Quaestiones super de animalibus*, ed. Ephrem Filthaut, O.P. (Aschendorff: Monasterii Westfalorum, 1955), XV. Q. 11, "utrum mas habilior sit ad mores quam femina" (265–66); Joan Cadden, *Meanings of Sex Difference in the Middle Ages* (Cambridge: Cambridge University Press, 1993), 158; Clarissa Atkinson, *The Oldest Vocation: Christian Motherhood in the Middle Ages* (Ithaca, N.Y.: Cornell University Press, 1991), 36–37; and David Burnley, "Criseyde's Heart and the Weakness of Women," *Studia Neophilologica* 54 (1982): 25–38, at 33–35.

32. Burnley, "Criseyde's Heart," 31 n. 12, citing Cicero, *De inventione* II.53, dividing *prudentia* into "memoria," "intelligentia," and "providentia."

33. "quia propter frigiditatem complexionis in muliere debilitantur vires sensitivae, quia est peioris tactus, et per consequens est debilioris intellectus" (Albertus Magnus, *Opera*, xii, 266).

34. "intellectus mulierum variatur propter fluxibilitatem materiae fleumaticae. Unde est varia perturbatio intellectus" (*Quaestiones in octo libros politicorum Aristotelis* [Oxford: William Turner, 1640], III. Q. 5, p. 124).

35. "mulier non est prudentior quam mas proprie loquendo sed est astutior. Unde prudentia sonat in bonum et astutia in malum" (Albertus Magnus, *Opera*, xii, 266).

36. (My emphasis.) "Astutia opponitur eubuliae quoad finem intentum; et est vitium intellectuale docens invenire accommoda media ad finem malum" (Burnley, "Criseyde's Heart," 34 n. 19).

37. Respectively "Sapientia enim huius mundi, stultitia est apud Deum. Scriptum est enim: Comprehendam sapientes in astutia eorum," and "Timeo autem ne sicut serpens Evam seduxit astutia sua . . ." (*Biblia Sacra iuxta Vulgatam Clementinam*, ed. Alberto Colunga, O.P., and Laurentio Turrado, 8th ed. [Madrid: Biblioteca de Autores Cristianos, 1985]).

38. Respectively Zaccaria, iii, 38; xxiii, 100; and lxiv, 258; and Guarino, iii, 8; xxi, 46; and lxii, 140 (though *astus* is substituted for *astutia* in the third of these instances). Penelope in particular is credited with *astutia* in her tactics for delaying her suitors during Ulysses's absence: given the feminine gendering of the concept, it is exceptional that Boccaccio then also attributes to *astutia* Ulysses' disguise as a pauper on his return (Zaccaria, xl, 162–64; Guarino, xxxviii, 82).

39. Zaccaria, xlii, 170–72; Guarino, xl, 87–88.

40. *Eneas*, ed. J.-J. Salverda de Grave (Paris: Champion, 1929), 393, and "qui de l'engin ne se garda," 398.

41. Hanning, *Individual in Twelfth-Century Romance*, 108.

42. Curnow, 768; Brown-Grant, I.46, p. 82.

43. Zaccaria, xlii, 170; Guarino, xl, 86.

44. Curnow, 770; Brown-Grant, I.46, p. 83.

45. Curnow, 773; Brown-Grant, I.46, p. 84. Christine does not owe these changes to the French translation of the *De mulieribus*, which follows Boccaccio's vocabulary in the expressions "par grande astuce" and "O tant fut grande lastuce de la dite dame!" (Giovanni Boccaccio, *Le liure de Jehan Bocasse De la louenge et vertu des nobles et cleres dames*, trans. Laurent de Premierfait [Paris: Vérard, 1493], ch. xliii).

46. Curnow, 776; Brown-Grant, I.47, p. 86. *Des nobles et cleres dames* attributes the action of Opis to "son astuce," ch. iv.

47. Curnow, 881; Brown-Grant, II.41, p. 144. Again Christine is independent of the French translation as well as Boccaccio's Latin, since in *Des nobles et cleres dames*, ch. xli, it is "par son astuce" and "par subtille . . . inuencion" that Penelope sustains her independence.

48. Curnow, 762; Brown-Grant, I.43, p. 78: the retentive faculty is also ascribed to Carmenta (Curnow, 747; Brown-Grant, I.37, p. 70); and to Sempronia (Curnow, 760; Brown-Grant, I.42, p. 77).

49. "l'entendement plus a delivre et plus agu" (Curnow, 721; Brown-Grant, I.27, p. 57).

50. "Prudence, allas, oon of thyne eyen thre / Me lakked alwey . . . / On tyme ypassed wel remembred me, / And present tyme ek koud ich wel ise, / But future tyme, er I was in the snare, / Koude I nat sen" (*TC* V.744–49). Although Prudence, too, can be gendered feminine as in the *Tale of Melibee*, the notion of *engin* as a characteristically feminine facility for thinking on one's feet is found in the plots of Chaucerian and continental fabliaux. Lesley Johnson describes it as women's "striking ability to turn a dangerous situation . . . to their advantage," citing the narrator's admiration for the wife's *engien* in *Le Dit dou Pliçon* ("Women on Top: Antifeminism in the Fabliau?" *Modern Language Review* 78 [1983]: 298–307, at 299–300). Caxton elaborates this gendering thus: "verily hit cometh of nature oftentymes to women to gyve counceyll shortly and unavysedly to thynges that ben in doute or perillous and nedeth hasty remedye" (*Caxton's Game and Playe of Chesse, 1474, A Verbatim Reprint*, intro. William E. A. Axon [London: Elliot Stock, 1883], III.4, p. 115). See further B. J. Whiting, *Proverbs, Sentences, and Proverbial Phrases from English Writings Mainly before 1500* (Cambridge, Mass.: Harvard University Press, 1968), W531, "Women are wise in short advisement." Boccaccio himself offers some examples of ready female wit (*ingegno*) in the stories of the sixth and seventh days in the *Decameron*.

51. "Harum edepol ingenium utrum laudem an execrer nescio" (Zaccaria, v, 44; Guarino, v, 12).

52. For the precedent in Ovid see *Metamorphoses*, I.89–112. On the Golden Age tradition see Arthur O. Lovejoy and George Boas, *Primitivism and Related Ideas in Antiquity* (Baltimore, Md.: Johns Hopkins University Press, 1935), 23–102, and Ernst Robert Curtius, *European Literature and the Latin Middle Ages*, trans. Willard Trask (New York: Pantheon, 1953), 106–27.

53. Guillaume de Lorris and Jean de Meun, *Le Roman de la Rose*, ed. Felix Lecoy, 3 vols. (Paris: Champion, 1965–70), 20,053–190; *The Romance of the Rose*, trans. Frances Horgan (Oxford: Oxford University Press, 1994), 309–11. Further references in the text are to Lecoy's line numbers and Horgan's page numbers.

54. "Ainsinc sunt arz avant venues / Car toutes choses sunt vaincues / Par travaill, par povreté dure, / Par quoi les genz sunt en grant cure; / Car li mal les angins esmeuvent / Par les angoisses qu'il i trevent" (20,145–50, p. 311). Doubtless a proverb lurks here (cf. "necessity is the mother of invention") but I have not discovered an Old French equivalent. There is another meditation on the Golden Age by Ami at 8,325–424 (pp. 129–30). The passages are discussed by Paul B. Milan, "The Golden Age and the Political Theory of Jean de Meun: A Myth in *Rose* Scholarship," *Symposium* 23 (1969): 137–49.

55. These suppositions (which draw on phraseology in John Stuart Mill's *The Subjection of Women*) constitute a "pervasive nineteenth-century stereotype" according to Nina Auerbach, *Woman and the Demon* (Cambridge, Mass.: Harvard University Press, 1982), 54–55.

56. Curnow, 734–43; Brown-Grant, I.33–34, pp. 64–67.

57. Curnow, 753; Brown-Grant, I.39, p. 73.

58. Curnow, 750; Brown-Grant, I.38, p. 72.

59. Curnow, 752; Brown-Grant, I.38, p. 73.

60. Curnow, 754; Brown-Grant, I.39, p. 74. For Christine's reaction to Boccaccio's position see further Rosalind Brown-Grant, "Décadence ou Progrès? Christine de Pizan, Boccace et la question de l'âge d'or," *Revue des Langues Romaines* 92 (1988): 295–306, and the important section "Perspectives on History: Progress Versus Decline," in her *Christine de Pizan and the Moral Defence of Women* (Cambridge: Cambridge University Press, 1999), 154–63.

61. See Chaucer's poem "Aetas prima" (entitled "The Former Age" in modern editions), which draws on Boethius, *De consolatione philosophiae*, II. m. 5, Ovid, and perhaps Virgil's Fourth Eclogue, as well as the *Roman de la Rose*.

62. *The English Works of John Gower*, ed. G. C. Macaulay, Early English Text Society *e.s.* 81–82 (London: Oxford University Press, 1900–01), *Confessio Amantis*, II.1956. The verb *enginen* signifies "to deceive" at I.1101 and II.2116.

63. Macaulay (*English Works of John Gower*, p. 508, n. to IV.2396 ff.) is mystified by some names in the catalogue, but finds parallels in Godfrey of Viterbo, *Pantheon*.

64. The *Confessio* sidegloss reads: "Hic loquitur contra ociosos quoscumque, et maxime contra istos, qui excellentia prudencie ingenium habentes absque fructu operum torpescunt. Et ponit exemplum de diligencia predecessorum, qui ad tocius humani generis doctrinam et auxilium suis continuis laboris et studiis, gracia mediante diuina, artes et sciencias primitus inuenerunt."

65. "For we, whiche are now alyve, / Of hem that besi whylom were, / Als wel in Scole as elleswhere, / Mowe every day ensample take, / That if it were now to make / Thing which that thei ferst founden oute, / It scholde noght be broght aboute" (*Confessio* IV. 2,346–52).

More Thoughts on Medieval Women's Intelligence

Denied, Projected, Embodied

BARBARA NEWMAN

Let me respond to Alcuin Blamires's lucid account of medieval women and creative intelligence with three questions that can both extend his inquiry and define its limits. First, why does Blamires's discussion of female creativity in medieval thought necessarily exclude almost all the women writers known to us between Hrotsvitha in the tenth century and Christine de Pizan in the fifteenth? Second, given medieval clerics' reluctance to acknowledge the mental capacities of women, why were they so infatuated with wisdom goddesses that they not only revived classical and biblical exemplars, but invented a whole new pantheon of female deities to personify precisely those abilities women were said to lack? And finally, in light of medieval culture's well-known tendency to link women with embodiment, how might the pragmatic quality men ascribed to female intelligence be connected to the production and care of bodies?

Medieval Women and the Suppression of Agency

Twenty years ago Joanna Russ published a delicious book entitled *How to Suppress Women's Writing*.[1] In it she skewered the strategies honed by generations of critics to dismiss women writers and secure the literary canon as an all-male preserve. Faced with any text purportedly authored by a woman, the critic could choose among a variety of options: denial of agency, pollution of agency, false categorizing, isolation, and many more. He could argue that she didn't actually write it—some man did. Or she didn't write it—it wrote itself. Or she wrote it, all right—but she shouldn't have. Or she wrote it—but it makes no sense. Or she wrote it and it's not bad, for a woman—but there's only one of it. And so forth.

Although Russ did not include medieval women among her examples of suppressed authorship, the period would have yielded a rich harvest. Marie de France, for example, knew how easily her work could be appropriated by the "envious," whom she attacks at the beginning of her *Lais.* Even more explicit is her poetic signature at the end of the *Fables:*

> Me numerai pur remembrance:
> Marie ai num, si sui de France.
> Put cel estre que clerc plusur
> Prendreient sur eus mun labur.
> Ne voil que nul sur li le die!
> E il fet que fol ki sei ublie![2]

> I'll give my name, for memory:
> I am from France, my name's Marie.
> And it may hap that many a clerk
> Will claim as his what is my work.
> But such pronouncements I want not!
> It's folly to become forgot!

Christine de Pizan took still greater pains to sign her books with her trademark "je, Christine," imbuing them so thoroughly with her autobiographical persona that it is hard to imagine how her authorship could have been effaced. Yet even so, when several of her works were translated into English in the fifteenth and sixteenth centuries, they were ascribed to various male translators, to "doctours of the most excellent in clerge [at] the nobyl Vniuersyte off Paris," and even to Geoffrey Chaucer. "Dame Christine" meanwhile dwindled to the status of a noble patroness who had commissioned clerics to compile books for her.[3]

Male appropriation of female authorship has, of course, bedeviled women's literary history from Antiquity to the present. One special variant of "she didn't write it" enjoyed exceptional currency in the Middle Ages, namely the claim that "she didn't write it—God did." That particular denial of agency explains why Alcuin Blamires's narrative about women and creative intelligence in medieval thought conspicuously omits most of the now-celebrated medieval women who wrote. It was not Blamires, of course, who denied them the dignity of authorship, but the women themselves—mystics and visionaries all. "Creative intelligence" was precisely what such women, not to mention their hagiographers and scribes, did *not* want to claim, for their paradoxical authority stemmed precisely from the belief that inspired women, having neither the right nor the ability to speak for themselves, had by necessity to speak for God. Or, as they would have said, God chose to speak through *them* so that men, whether they would or no, were compelled to listen.[4]

To be fair, male writers also denied their own literary merits, especially in the "humility prologues" that were *de rigueur* in religious texts. For every Abelard or Dante, sure of his place among the Olympians, dozens of meek monks and flattering courtiers bewailed their unworthiness and laid all credit at the feet of beneficent patrons. But the stakes were lower, for a male writer without talent risked little more than an undistinguished career, while a woman—talented or not—could scarcely be permitted to exercise her *ingenium* at all unless compelled by divine command. Humanistic writers such as Hrotsvitha and Heloise, highly self-conscious about their own gifts and the odds against them, must be seen as exceptions even among the exceptions. Far more often, it was the denial not only of superior talent, but of any agency whatsoever that gave a woman writer her best chance at legitimation.

Since the tropes used to authorize medieval women's charismatic writing are well known, one example may serve for many. Shortly before 1300, the Dominican lector Heinrich honored Mechthild of Magdeburg, the great German poet and visionary, by the supreme compliment of translating her *Flowing Light of the Godhead* into Latin.[5] But before circulating the text, he added a prologue that employed virtually every distancing strategy known to the age. First there was the act of translation itself, which, by elevating Mechthild's words from her own "primitive tongue" into the Church's universal language, rendered her book safe for male readers (and incidentally toned down its prophetic critique of the clergy). Second, Heinrich justified the anomaly of female authorship by reminding readers that often "almighty God has chosen what is weak in the world to confound what is stronger" (1 Cor. 1:27), that is, he has granted men victory and enlightenment through miracles performed in the "fragile sex."[6] Third, Heinrich suppressed the name of Mechthild, "the woman through whom this writing was made public," commending only her humble and virtuous life, her "sincere devotion and dove-like simplicity." Finally, as an absolute guarantee of the book's authority and worth, he asserted its true provenance: "Its author is the Father, Son, and Holy Spirit."[7]

Such double-edged responses to the female prophet and visionary afforded her a high-risk, high-gain strategy, so long as she was willing to be no more and no less than the mask of God—or, in Hildegard of Bingen's words, "the voice of the Living Light." If a woman's claims to divine revelation were accepted, she could attain not only a literary voice and a reputation for holiness, but also considerable authority in return for her effacement of agency. Yet even widely admired mystical writers seldom gained recognition as saints or became subjects of sacred biography. In fact, there is remarkably little overlap between holy women who wrote and those who were written about: no one bothered to write a *vita* of Hadewijch, Mechthild of Magdeburg, Angela of Foligno, Marguerite Porete, or Julian of Norwich. It is as if a woman's active engagement with the word—even God's word—were too dangerous to let her life be upheld as a model for imitation.[8]

For women mystics who failed to win credibility, the stakes were high—and no stake ever cast a longer shadow than the one at which Joan of Arc was burned in 1431. Although the peasant Maid was no writer, she belongs in this company because her followers ascribed to her a most unusual and unfeminine brand of *ingenium*—strategic military genius. At her rehabilitation trial, witnesses testified that while Joan may have been "simple and innocent," she displayed exceptional skill in the art of war. The knight Thibault d'Armagnac said that in battle "she behaved like the most experienced captain in all the world, one who had been educated in warfare for an entire lifetime." The duke of Alençon agreed, adding that the Pucelle "held herself magnificently . . . especially in the setting up of artillery." But it was on the basis of her revelations, not her military prowess, that Joan would be first condemned and then canonized. Her supporters were certain she was a prophet sent from heaven, and her enemies equally sure it was the devil who led her.[9] The warrior maid, no less than the mystical poet, stood or fell in men's sight by the grace of God, not by her own intelligence or skill.

Even female achievements of a less spectacular kind were hard for men to credit. By 1200, for example, Latin literacy among nuns had become the exception rather than the rule, but since they continued to chant the Divine Office in Latin, many must have acquired at least a passive command of the language. Hagiographers, however, apparently found it easier to believe that God granted saintly nuns an infused knowledge of Latin than to imagine them learning it themselves. Hence the topos of miraculous literacy—another consequence of the entrenched belief that any wisdom displayed by women, given the innate weakness of their minds, must have a supernatural source. St. Umiltà of Faenza (1226–1310) was officially taught to read only after she astonished her religious sisters by a demonstration of miraculous literacy, or perhaps inspired preaching, in the refectory one day.[10] Birgitta of Sweden began the study of Latin in her forties at the Virgin Mary's command; in addition to a living teacher she had the assistance of a "native speaker," the martyr St. Agnes, who appeared to her in visions.[11] Conversely, a woman's unexpected Latinity could be taken as a symptom of demonic possession. St. Norbert of Xanten (d. 1134) once exorcised a girl whose demon mocked him by reciting the Song of Songs from beginning to end in Latin.[12] Another female demoniac, according to Caesarius of Heisterbach, claimed that the devil is bound in hell with "three words of the Mass" which she could easily locate in a missal, despite her supposed illiteracy.[13] In short, since it was as "unnatural" for a woman to know Latin as it was for her to write, one who confounded male expectations had to be inspired by either God or the devil.[14] Even in the realm of romance, as Blamires has shown, a heroine as brilliant as Melior might be suspected of magic. Confronted by women of unusual intelligence or skill, medieval men resorted to supernatural explanations because they knew such capacities lay beyond the limited female ken.

Weak-Minded Women and Strong-Minded Goddesses

It was a strange blend of reverence and misogyny that surrounded exceptional women in the Middle Ages, exalting some of them as mouthpieces for God while denying their agency and mystifying their intelligence. This divine propensity for speaking through feminine voices also had repercussions on the purely symbolic level. In his *Pèlerinage de la vie humaine,* as Blamires notes, Guillaume de Deguilleville staged a debate between Dame Sapience and Aristotle (himself the protégé of Dame Nature) in which the goddess of wisdom carries off the victory. This text is by no means unusual, for Deguilleville's Sapience is one of countless allegorical goddesses who haunt the pages of medieval literature—teaching, preaching, debating, exhorting, and generally speaking with the voice of Wisdom and Truth.[15] At the turn of the sixth century the mother of them all, Lady Philosophy, had released Boethius from his prison of self-pity through her salutary doctrine on the workings of fortune, providence, and free will, in a work so resoundingly successful that English monarchs from King Alfred to Queen Elizabeth would be among its translators. In other late antique works no less beloved of medieval writers, more goddesses are exalted: Prudentius's *Psychomachia* ends with the triumphant enthronement of Sapientia in her temple, while Martianus Capella's fabulously popular *Marriage of Philology and Mercury* recounts the apotheosis of Philology, or human learning, divinized by a celestial marriage and dowered by her bridesmaids, the seven liberal arts. Around 1150, when the poet Bernard Silvestris of Tours wished to write a cosmological epic, he exchanged Genesis for Plato's *Timaeus* and ascribed the cosmos to the creative intelligence of two goddesses, *ingeniosa* Noys (also called Minerva) and *sollers* Natura. Later in the epic, these deities turn their hands and minds to the creation of man with the help of two more goddesses, Urania and Physis, who personify the knowledge of celestial and terrestrial mysteries.[16]

What can we make of the fact that Wisdom and her allies, including the arts and Muses, were so often personified as women? It will not do to blame Latin grammar,[17] for the feminine gender of abstract nouns did not in itself mandate the trope of personification, nor can it explain the appeal of wisdom goddesses to generations of medieval readers and writers, who kept inventing more and more of them. The power of tradition in a conservative culture may account in some measure for the goddesses' longevity, but scholars have been too ready to dismiss them as instances of mere "personification allegory," a genre that remained in critical disfavor for most of the twentieth century.[18] While it would be foolish to claim that allegorical goddesses as such "empowered women," their ubiquity suggests at the very least that medieval authors did not find it intrinsically ridiculous to place valued doctrine in the mouth of an authoritative female teacher. But why would they have used women to personify the very qualities women were so often said to lack—powers such as abstract thought, wide-ranging erudition, philosophical discipline, and reason triumphantly conquering passion?

One speculative answer is that, in the vogue for wisdom goddesses, we see a classic instance of the return of the repressed. Denied or mystified at the level of empirical reality, women's intelligence returns, enveloped in a numinous aura, at the level of the symbolic. Indeed, it is often in a dream that the male narrator, having regressed to childlike ignorance and helplessness, encounters his divine interlocutor.[19] And often his goddess/teacher is also a mother, carrying the full weight of maternal authority, as if to compensate for the loss of the real mother from whom boys were commonly parted at the age of seven. The allure of these maternal teachers—awesome, austerely wise, radiant, severe—represents the apotheosis of the mother who, in real life, was barely trusted with the teaching of very young children. Even the demythologized goddess Carmentis, credited by Boccaccio, Christine de Pizan, and John Gower with inventing the Latin alphabet, projects onto the mythic past the literate mother's responsibility for teaching her children their ABC.[20] It is no wonder that Christine exults with special pride in the achievements of Carmentis, for this divine woman is made to stand at the origin not just of the "mother tongue," but of that very language "thanks to which [men] consider themselves so lofty and honored."[21] Christian art acknowledged the same maternal responsibility in the favorite late medieval image of St. Anne teaching the Virgin to read, thus opening to Mary the mysteries of Scripture that she would herself fulfill.[22] In this way the teaching authority that medieval culture refused to grant women on earth was restored to them in heaven. The supreme example may be "Mater Ecclesia," the goddess who personified the male magisterium itself, perhaps best known to English readers in the guise of Langland's Lady Holicherche.

Wisdom goddesses, no matter how pervasive and compelling their literary presence, probably did not improve the average cleric's opinion of female intelligence, but there is ample evidence that women found validation in such goddesses. Even on a comic level, wives could apparently use the feminine gender of Muses and Virtues as a debating point in the mundane battle of the sexes. In *Il Corbaccio*, Boccaccio's most misogynistic text, he has a husband's ghost remark that women, "when they wish to exalt themselves far above men, say that all good things are of the feminine gender: the stars, planets, Muses, virtues, and riches."[23] True, the Virtues may be female, concedes this scurrilous woman-hater, but unlike their flesh-and-blood counterparts, they at least do not piss.

More seriously, many female authors used allegorical goddesses to legitimize their own writing. In their adaptations of the goddess tradition, we see the denial of their own agency so often required of them counterbalanced by the representation of divine agency and intelligence as female. Hildegard ascribed many of her revelations, including her autobiographical memoir, to the voice of Sapientia, and she compensated for the clericalism of her ecclesiology by developing the figure of Mater Ecclesia into a goddess of unprecedented mythic grandeur.[24] Hadewijch, Mechthild of Magdeburg, and Marguerite Porete all submerged their own identities, and sometimes that of their divine Beloved, in the potent voice of Lady Love (Frau Minne, Dame Amour).[25] Julian of Norwich, who had included a standard apologia for herself as "a woman, ignorant, feeble, and frail," in the original short text of her *Showings*,[26] felt confident enough to remove it more than twenty years later when she wrote the longer version, in which she taught that "as truly as God is our Father, so truly is God our Mother."[27] Christine de Pizan invented her own wisdom goddess, Othéa, early in her career, and relied heavily on such figures as Dame Nature and the Sibyl throughout her writing life. By the time she penned her *City of Ladies* she was ready to rehabilitate not only the history of women, but also the goddess Reason, whom she rescued from the misogynist clutches of Jean de Meun to reinvent her as the chief eulogist of women's creative intelligence.

Minding the Body

Of all the allegorical goddesses invented in the Middle Ages, one in particular captured the cultural imagination and continued to shape ideas of "the feminine" well into the twentieth century. That divinity was Natura, daughter of God and *vicaria* in charge of procreation, whose dominion over the realm of sexuality made her gender conspicuous. Unlike the sapiential goddesses in the lineage of Lady Philosophy, her concern lay with the engendering of bodies. Yet Natura was never represented simply as a fertility goddess or primordial Great Mother, for intelligence and skill are ascribed to her: her creativity is always mediated by images of craft. In his twelfth-century tour de force, *The Complaint of Nature*, Alan of Lille devised the influential portrait of "Nature at her forge," tirelessly hammering out the shapes of birds, beasts, and babies on her anvil: Jean de Meun perpetuated the conceit, which became a favorite with illustrators.[28] Christine de Pizan, ever the revisionist, apparently found this image too phallic and replaced Nature the blacksmith with Nature the bakerwoman, substituting an oven and a set of waffle-irons for the hammer and anvil of Alan's goddess.[29] But whether Natura toiled in a smithy or a kitchen, her labor was represented as at once sexual and artisanal.

The goddess thus linked the ostensibly masculine activity of imposing form on matter with the primary creative act of women: bringing new bodies into the world.

Blamires has argued persuasively that, when medieval men did acknowledge the intellect of women, they tied it more closely to pragmatic and material ends—which in turn are readily linked to the body. This should not be surprising, given the deep cultural associations that bound the feminine to flesh, matter, and sexuality. In fact, the primary arts of civilization ascribed to women often had to do with the care of bodies and might be regarded as an extension of the maternal role to cultural history: just as women were responsible on a daily basis for the preparation of food and clothing, they were said to have invented agriculture, gardening, animal husbandry, and the textile arts at the dawn of time. Just as the myth of Natura acknowledges women's role in the production of bodies, the euhemerized myths of Isis, Ceres, and Minerva acknowledge their cultural work in the care and feeding of bodies.

One special case of "embodied" creative intelligence is the art of healing bodies. Medieval women provided routine health care in their capacities as wet nurses, midwives, village herbalists, and monastic infirmarians, while a handful of learned women in the later Middle Ages practiced medicine professionally, with or without permission. Such real-life practitioners were sometimes prosecuted by university-trained physicians jealous of their prerogatives.[30] But there was another, less threatening realm in which the female healer was indispensable, for romance literature credits women with exceptional skill in binding wounds, gathering medicinal herbs, concocting salves and potions, identifying poisons, and even curing insanity. Here, too, there is a catch: the *ingenium* of the female healer could be ascribed to almost anything except her intelligence. If a saintly woman performed cures, they were of course miraculous—even in the case of Hildegard of Bingen, the one pre-modern woman who wrote prodigiously on theoretical and practical medicine. Hildegard's *Vita* never mentions these writings and ascribes to her only supernatural healings, not medical ones.[31] When a romance heroine performed cures, on the other hand, a poet might praise her medical skill, but he would leave no doubt that her love and beauty, if not her magic, accomplished the deeper healing.

The topos of the eroticized female healer is ubiquitous in romance. In Chrétien de Troyes's *Yvain*, for example, the hero's madness is cured by a damsel with a magic salve that "Morgan the Wise" had sent to her mistress. But Chrétien, in a titillating comic scene, shows the damsel wasting the whole box of precious ointment by using it as massage oil, for she cannot bear to take her hands off Yvain's naked, slumbering body.[32] In *Silence,* a thirteenth-century romance ascribed to Heldris of Cornwall, the heroine Eufemie is "the wisest doctor in the land," so she has no trouble curing her knight's infirmity, caused by the venom of a dragon he has slain. But even as she heals, she simultaneously renews his symptoms with lovesickness.[33] This stock episode conflates the woman's practical skill in medicine with the lover's standard plea that his lady must be his "physician," since her body or love is the only "medicine" that can heal his otherwise-fatal affliction. Behind the incident in *Silence* lies a similar episode in *Tristan*, the most famous romance to employ the motif. In Gottfried von Strassburg's version of the tale, both Isolde the Fair and her mother, Queen Isolde of Ireland, are represented as skilled physicians. The elder Isolde is "versed in herbs of many kinds, in the virtues of all plants, and in the art of medicine":[34] she alone can heal Tristan—and does so without knowing him—after he has been wounded in the act of slaying her own brother. She heals him a second time, still not recognizing him as her mortal enemy, when he has been poisoned by a dragon's tongue. But if the "prudent" queen twice unwittingly saves Tristan, she also unwittingly brews his destruction in the form of the love philtre that will go tragically astray. The third and last time that Tristan incurs a poisoned wound, he must die, since, because of his own infidelity, Isolde the Fair is unable to reach him in time with her life-saving medicine.

The eroticizing of the female physician has an obvious utility for romance plots, but it also provides a way of defusing the physical intimacy of the doctor-patient relationship, which men must have found especially humiliating when they were compelled to endure the ministrations of a woman. From this perspective, Marie de France's lai of *The Two Lovers* may offer a sly comment on the standard romance treatment of women doctors. In this folkloric lai, an obstructive father will not allow his daughter to marry until one of her suitors is able to carry her up a mountain in his arms. As soon as the daughter falls in love, she sends her chosen youth to Salerno to procure a strength potion from her aunt there, who is "an expert on medicines."[35] This potion can be read as a demythologized counterpart of Tristan and Isolde's love philtre. But when the hero actually faces his ordeal, he refuses the drink out of misplaced romanticism and carries the princess unaided, only to drop dead on the mountaintop. *The Two Lovers* may or may not be parodic, as Robert Hanning and Joan Ferrante argue, but it does seem to vindicate feminine pragmatism against courtly male idealism. By locating her skilled physician in Salerno, the leading medical school of the day, Marie distances her from the beloved lady and thus de-eroticizes the female practitioner. The princess herself, ever the pragmatist, contributes to the hero's endeavor by fasting to make herself lighter. But her lover, in his eleventh-hour refusal of the potion, also refuses the common sense of his beloved, opting for a tragic and romantic death in lieu of a practical happy ending.

By a curious twist of fate, the one historical Salernitan woman whose name has come down to us, the empiric and medical writer Trota, had by the late Middle Ages become hopelessly enmeshed in the web of romanticized female medicine. Her own brief treatise on women's health was swallowed up within a much larger compendium, called the *Trotula* after its putative author, and the *Trotula* materials in turn converged with a different line of texts purporting to reveal the anatomical and sexual "secrets of women" to prurient men.[36] In this way "Trotula" herself came to be constructed as an authority on female sexuality, a woman who had been "very beautiful in her youth" but lived to be old, cunning, and all too knowledgeable about women's ways—rather like Jean de Meun's old procuress, "la Vieille," or her English descendant, the Wife of Bath. In fact, as the Wife tells us, Trotula was one of the two female authors (along with Heloise) represented in her husband Jankyn's *Book of Wikked Wyves*.[37] This is what Joanna Russ would call "pollution of agency" with a vengeance.

Given Trotula's posthumous reputation, as Monica Green has shown, it is no wonder that Christine de Pizan left her and all women healers outside the gates of her *City of Ladies*.[38] Instead she included the legend of Novella, daughter of a law professor at Bologna "not quite sixty years ago," who is supposed to have lectured from time to time in her father's stead. But when she did so, she drew a curtain before her face "to prevent her beauty from distracting the concentration of her audience"—or as we might now say, to deflect the male gaze in the hope that her students might finally pay attention to her words.[39]

Notes

1. Joanna Russ, *How to Suppress Women's Writing* (Austin: University of Texas Press, 1983).

2. Marie de France, *Fables*, ed. and trans. Harriet Spiegel (Toronto: University of Toronto Press, 1987), 256–57.

3. Jennifer Summit, *Lost Property: The Woman Writer and English Literary History, 1380–1589* (Chicago: University of Chicago Press, 2000), 61–107, esp. 73–76.

4. The bibliography on medieval religious women as writers is enormous, but see for example Peter Dronke, *Women Writers of the Middle Ages: A Critical Study of Texts from Perpetua (d. 203) to Marguerite Porete (d. 1310)* (Cambridge: Cambridge University Press, 1984); Ulrike Wiethaus, ed., *Maps of Flesh and Light: The Religious Experience of Medieval Women Mystics* (Syracuse, N.Y.: Syracuse University Press, 1993); Edward P. Nolan, *Cry Out and Write: A Feminine Poetics of Revelation* (New York: Continuum, 1994); Elizabeth Petroff, *Body and Soul: Essays on Medieval Women and Mysticism* (New York: Oxford University Press, 1994); Barbara Newman, *From Virile Woman to WomanChrist: Studies in Medieval Religion and Literature* (Philadelphia: University of Pennsylvania Press, 1995); Joan Ferrante, *To the Glory of Her Sex: Women's Roles in the Composition of Medieval Texts* (Bloomington: Indiana University Press, 1997); Catherine M. Mooney, ed., *Gendered Voices: Medieval Saints and Their Interpreters* (Philadelphia: University of Pennsylvania Press, 1999); Rosalynn Voaden, *God's Words, Women's Voices: The Discernment of Spirits in the Writing of Late-Medieval Women Visionaries* (York: York Medieval Press, 1999).

5. Mechthild von Magdeburg, *Das fliessende Licht der Gottheit*, ed. Hans Neumann, 2 vols. (Munich: Artemis, 1990, 1993); Latin translation, *Lux divinitatis fluens in corda veritatis*, ed. Louis Paquelin, vol. 2, *Revelationes Gertrudianae ac Mechtildianae* (Paris: Oudin, 1877). I quote from Brother Heinrich's prologue to the Latin version in Frank Tobin's translation, *The Flowing Light of the Godhead*

(New York: Paulist, 1998), 31–33. This Heinrich, as Tobin points out, cannot have been the Heinrich of Halle who was Mechthild's longtime confessor and editor, as he had died before the Latin translation was made.

6. This argument, pioneered by Hrotsvitha and Hildegard, would have a long run especially among male apologists for female achievement. See Barbara Newman, *Sister of Wisdom: St. Hildegard's Theology of the Feminine* (Berkeley: University of California Press, 1987), 255–57, and Alcuin Blamires, *The Case for Women in Medieval Culture* (Oxford: Clarendon, 1997), 132–37.

7. On Mechthild's medieval and postmedieval reception, see now Sara S. Poor, *Mechthild of Magdeburg and Her Book: Gender and the Making of Textual Authority* (Philadelphia: University of Pennsylvania Press, 2004).

8. It is interesting that the few holy women for whom we have both writings and *vitae* include the three prophets who were most politically active: Hildegard of Bingen, Catherine of Siena, and Birgitta of Sweden. Also exceptional were Gertrude the Great and Mechthild of Hackeborn, who collaborated in writing each other's lives and visions at the monastery of Helfta, where the women's unusually high level of Latinity made clerical mediation unnecessary.

9. Kelly DeVries, "A Woman as Leader of Men: Joan of Arc's Military Career," in *Fresh Verdicts on Joan of Arc*, ed. Bonnie Wheeler and Charles T. Wood (New York: Garland, 1996), 3–18, 9.

10. *Vita* I.6, trans. Elizabeth Petroff in *Consolation of the Blessed* (New York: Alta Gaia, 1979), 124.

11. *Vita* 66, trans. Albert Ryle Kezel in *Birgitta of Sweden: Life and Selected Revelations*, ed. Marguerite Tjader Harris (New York: Paulist, 1990), 92, 247.

12. *Vita S. Norberti* 45–47, AA. SS. June, tom. 1 (Paris, 1867), 821–22; Penelope Doob, *Nebuchadnezzar's Children: Conventions of Madness in Middle English Literature* (New Haven, Conn.: Yale University Press, 1974), 42–44.

13. Caesarius of Heisterbach, *Dialogus miraculorum* 5.13, ed. Joseph Strange, 2 vols. (Cologne, 1851), 1:292. Miraculous Latinity remained an important criterion for possession in the early modern era as well. See Daniel P. Walker, *Unclean Spirits: Possession and Exorcism in France and England in the Late Sixteenth and Early Seventeenth Centuries* (Philadelphia: University of Pennsylvania Press, 1981), 12.

14. For more on female saints and demoniacs see Barbara Newman, "Possessed by the Spirit: Devout Women, Demoniacs, and the Apostolic Life in the Thirteenth Century," *Speculum* 73 (1998): 733–70; Peter Dinzelbacher, *Heilige oder Hexen? Schicksale auffälliger Frauen in Mittelalter und Frühneuzeit* (Zurich: Artemis and Winkler, 1995).

15. Barbara Newman, *God and the Goddesses: Vision, Poetry, and Belief in the Middle Ages* (Philadelphia: University of Pennsylvania Press, 2003); Joan Ferrante, *Woman as Image in Medieval Literature from the Twelfth Century to Dante* (New York: Columbia University Press, 1975). On visual allegory see Marina Warner, *Monuments and Maidens: The Allegory of the Female Form* (New York: Atheneum, 1985).

16. Bernardus Silvestris, *Cosmographia*, ed. Peter Dronke (Leiden: Brill, 1978); trans. Winthrop Wetherbee (New York: Columbia University Press, 1973). The world-creating Noys praises her own *ingenium*: "Ecce mundus, operis mei excogitata subtilitas, gloriosa constructio, . . . quem ad eternam ydeam ingeniosa circumtuli" (*Microcosmus* 1, Dronke p. 121). Nature's ingenuity (*sollertia*) is of a sexier kind: "Format et effingit sollers Natura liquorem, / Ut simili genesis ore reducat avos" (*Microcosmus* 14, Dronke p. 154).

17. Morton Bloomfield, "A Grammatical Approach to Personification Allegory," *Modern Philology* 60 (1963): 161–71.

18. Recent attempts to rehabilitate allegory, long disdained as the inferior cousin of symbolism, include Walter Haug, ed., *Formen und Funktionen der Allegorie* (Stuttgart: Metzler, 1979); Maureen Quilligan, *The Language of Allegory: Defining the Genre* (Ithaca, N.Y.: Cornell University Press, 1979); Stephen Greenblatt, ed., *Allegory and Representation* (Baltimore, Md.: Johns Hopkins, 1981); Carolynn Van Dyke, *The Fiction of Truth: Structure and Meaning in Narrative and Dramatic Allegory* (Ithaca, N.Y.: Cornell University Press, 1985); Jon Whitman, *Allegory: The Dynamics of an Ancient and Medieval Technique* (Cambridge, Mass.: Harvard University Press, 1987); and James Paxson, *The Poetics of Personification* (Cambridge: Cambridge University Press, 1994).

19. Paul Piehler has remarked that "the manifestation of goddesses in transcendent landscapes . . . constitutes the central psychic experience in medieval allegory" (*The Visionary Landscape: A Study in Medieval Allegory* [London: Edward Arnold, 1971], 15).

20. Susan Groag Bell, "Medieval Women Book Owners: Arbiters of Lay Piety and Ambassadors of Culture," *Signs* 7 (1982): 742–68. See also Marie Denley, "Elementary Teaching Techniques and Middle English Religious Didactic Writing," in *Langland, the Mystics and the Medieval English Religious Tradition,* ed. Helen Phillips (Cambridge: D. S. Brewer, 1990), 223–41.

21. Christine de Pizan, *Le Livre de la Cité des Dames* I.38.4, ed. E. J. Richards, *La Città delle Dame* (Milan: Luni Editrice, 1998), 184; trans. E. J. Richards, *The Book of the City of Ladies* (New York: Persea Books, 1982), 80. In I.33.2 Christine says of Carmentis's discovery of Latin grammar that "nothing more worthy in the world was ever invented"; in I.37.1 she asks, "Where was there ever a man who did more good?"

22. Pamela Sheingorn, "'The Wise Mother': The Image of Saint Anne Teaching the Virgin Mary," *Gesta* 32 (1993): 69–80; Wendy Scase, "St Anne and the Education of the Virgin: Literary and Artistic Traditions and Their Implications," in *England in the Fourteenth Century,* ed. Nicholas Rogers (Stamford, U.K.: Paul Watkins, 1993), 81–96.

23. Giovanni Boccaccio, *The Corbaccio,* trans. Anthony Cassell (Urbana: University of Illinois Press, 1975), 32.

24. Newman, *Sister of Wisdom.*

25. Barbara Newman, "*La mystique courtoise:* Thirteenth-Century Beguines and the Art of Love," in *From Virile Woman to WomanChrist: Studies in Medieval Religion and Literature* (Philadelphia: University of Pennsylvania Press, 1995), 137–67; Bernard McGinn, *The Flowering of Mysticism: Men and Women in the New Mysticism (1200–1350)* (New York: Crossroad, 1998), 199–265.

26. "Botte god for bede that ye schulde saye or take it so that I am a techere for I meene nought soo, no I mente nevere so. For I am a womann, leued, febille & freyll" (*The Shewings of Julian of Norwich,* Short Text, chap. 6; ed. Georgia Ronan Crampton [Kalamazoo, Mich.: Medieval Institute Publications, 1993], 207).

27. "I saw and understod that the hey myte of the Trinite is our fader, and the depe wisdam of the Trinite is our Moder, and the grete love of the Trinite is our Lord; and al this have we in kynd and in our substantial makyng. . . . As veryly as God is our fader, as verily God is our Moder; and that shewid He in all" (*Shewings,* Long Text, chaps. 58–59; Crampton, *Shewings of Julian of Norwich,* 121–22).

28. Alan of Lille, *De planctu Naturae* VIII, prose 4, ed. Nikolaus Häring, *Studi medievali* ser. 3, 19:2 (1978): 797–879; trans. James Sheridan, *The Plaint of Nature* (Toronto: Pontifical Institute,

1980), 146. Cf. Jean de Meun, *Roman de la Rose*, lines 15,891–921, ed. Daniel Poirion (Paris: Garnier-Flammarion, 1974), 428–29.

29. Christine de Pizan, *Lavision-Christine* I.1–3, ed. Sister Mary Louis Towner (Washington, D.C.: Catholic University of America, 1932), 73–75; trans. Renate Blumenfeld-Kosinski in *The Selected Writings of Christine de Pizan* (New York: Norton, 1997), 175–77. A similar version of Nature appears in the romance of *Silence*, ed. and trans. Sarah Roche-Mahdi (East Lansing, Mich.: Colleagues Press, 1992), 84–93.

30. Margaret Wade Labarge, *A Small Sound of the Trumpet: Women in Medieval Life* (Boston: Beacon Press, 1986), 169–94.

31. Hildegard's medical works are now available in English: *Physica*, trans. Priscilla Throop (Rochester, Vt.: Healing Arts Press, 1998); *On Natural Philosophy and Medicine* (an abridged translation of *Cause et cure*), trans. Margret Berger (Cambridge: D. S. Brewer, 1999). For her *Vita* see Anna Silvas, ed. and trans., *Jutta and Hildegard: The Biographical Sources* (Turnhout: Brepols, 1998), 135–210.

32. Chrétien de Troyes, *Yvain, or the Knight with the Lion*, trans. Ruth Harwood Cline (Athens: University of Georgia Press, 1975), 83–84.

33. *Silence*, 28–31. Of Eufemie it is said, "El païs n'a si sage mie" (line 594). On lovesickness as a physical affliction, see Mary Wack, *Lovesickness in the Middle Ages: The* Viaticum *and Its Commentaries* (Philadelphia: University of Pennsylvania Press, 1990).

34. Gottfried von Strassburg, *Tristan*, trans. A. T. Hatto (Harmondsworth: Penguin, 1960), 134.

35. "En Salerne ai une parente, / Riche femme, mut ad grant rente. / Plus de trente anz i ad esté; / L'art de phisike ad tant usé / Que mut et saive de mescines" (*Deus Amanz*, lines 103–107, in *Les Lais de Marie de France*, ed. Jean Rychner [Paris: Champion, 1973], 96). For English, see *The Lais of Marie de France*, trans. Robert Hanning and Joan Ferrante (Durham, N.C.: Labyrinth Press, 1978), 126–33. See also the commentary by Hanning and Ferrante, 133–36.

36. On this genre see Karma Lochrie, *Covert Operations: The Medieval Uses of Secrecy* (Philadelphia: University of Pennsylvania Press, 1999). For the original corpus see Monica Green, ed. and trans., *The Trotula: A Medieval Compendium of Women's Medicine* (Philadelphia: University of Pennsylvania Press, 2001).

37. Wife of Bath's Prologue, lines 669–85, in *The Riverside Chaucer*, ed. Larry Benson (Boston: Houghton Mifflin, 1987), 114.

38. Monica Green, "'Traittié tout de mençonges': The *Secrés des dames*, 'Trotula,' and Attitudes toward Women's Medicine in Fourteenth- and Early-Fifteenth-Century France," in *Christine de Pizan and the Categories of Difference*, ed. Marilynn Desmond (Minneapolis: University of Minnesota Press, 1998), 146–78.

39. *Livre de la Cité des Dames* II.36.3, ed. Richards, *La Città delle Dame*, 316; Richards, *Book of the City of Ladies*, 154.

Eciam Mulier

Women in Lollardy and the Problem of Sources

FIONA SOMERSET

It scarcely seems worth asking what anti-Wycliffites thought about women's learning: the arguments, as we might expect, are so familiar.[1] The consequences of women's exposure to argument are described, for example, by Roger Dymmok in his 1395 *Liber contra duodecim errores et hereses Lollardorum:*

> Et sic per hunc modum lasciuiam necessariam affirmant, continenciam impossibilem predicant, et contra diuinum preceptum illam esse allegant. Quibus uersutis argumentis plenis fallaciis et decepcionibus animas simplices et indoctas mulierum intendunt decipere ac terrere, ne continenciam perpetuam seruare quouismodo proponant, ut sic facilius eis abuti ualeant ad libitum . . . .[2]

> And so in this way [Lollards] affirm that lasciviousness is necessary, and preach that continence is impossible, and allege that it is contrary to divine precept. With such crafty arguments, full of fallacies and deceptions, they intend to deceive and terrorize the simple, untaught souls of women, so that the women will in no way aim to remain continent, and in this way they will more easily be able to abuse them at will.

If poor, simple women make the mistake of even listening to heretical arguments (which of course when addressed to them will focus on assailing their sexual mores rather than on any more abstract theological issue), then they will be dissuaded from chastity, and seduced, by ill-intentioned deceivers. The female grotesques in the Bodleian Library manuscript of Dymmok's *Liber* provide an excellent—if unintentional—illustration of the place women hold in arguments such as Dymmok's.[3] Leering, grimacing, or vacant-eyed, they look outward from the text's margins; and the text itself is at least equally incapable of looking them squarely in the eye, unable as it is to refer to them without lurching into the commonplaces of misogyny. Any genuine evaluation of women's capacity for learning is always foreclosed—glancing toward the grotesques—by remarks on either their seductibility or their seductiveness.

Yet in time, as the movement grows in reputation, anti-Wycliffite polemic against women ceases merely to dismiss them as untaught. Hoccleve's 1415 "Remonstrance against Oldcastle" is often cited:

> Somme wommen eek, thogh hir wit be thynne,
> Wole argumentes make in holy writ.
> Lewed calates, sittith down and spynne
> And kakele of sumwhat elles, for your wit
> Is al to feeble to despute of it.
> To clerkes grete apparteneth þat aart;
> The knowleche of þat God hath fro yow shit;
> Stynte and leue of, for right sclendre is your paart.[4]

Women are by nature incapable of any useful contribution to men's weighty arguments: rather than meddling with the Bible they should employ their feeble wits in domestic affairs. Regardless of how much Hoccleve's argument relies on spurious claims about female stupidity, however, it *is* dissuasive. Behind it lurks the fear that women *are* attempting to participate in theological argument.

Is this fear groundless, merely the product of a tendency to figure the laity as female in order to align conventional misogyny with apprehensions about lay learning? Or did any women find through Lollardy, as writers like Hoccleve seem to have feared they might, access to kinds of learning and even to spiritual roles that had previously been reserved to men? Some accounts, encouraged by discomfiture such as Hoccleve's, have given us a rather optimistic view of the available evidence.[5] But Shannon McSheffrey's comprehensive analysis of fifteenth- and sixteenth-century Lollard communities paints a generally depressing picture, showing that "[m]ale and female members of [Lollard] communities played roles that reflected rather than overrode late medieval gender expectations. . . . The sect affirmed in theory and practice the norm of the male-dominated family, where women were restricted to roles that kept them close to the domestic center and where men were the public leaders."[6] Far from leading to the abandonment of conventional mores, as anti-Wycliffite polemicists suggest, Lollardy seems in the main to have reinforced them, and with them an abiding conviction of women's subordination. Still, while it was almost unheard of for Lollard women to attain prominence as scholars, teachers, or spiritual leaders over men as well as women in their communities, some of the case evidence suggests that nonetheless some Lollard women do seem to have managed to attain unusual learning, and even perhaps some limited recognition as instructors of women and children.[7]

It might seem surprising, however, that there were not more such women, and that they did not attain more prominence. Women were, of course, throughout the later Middle Ages barred from attending university or being ordained as clerics. Yet some women from time to time in the Middle Ages found ways to circumvent these exclusions and negotiate for themselves a high level of education, a role in public affairs and/or as a spiritual advisor, and if not status as priests, some sort of control over sanctity; for other women, the rule, influence, or even the famous example of such women could lead to increased opportunities.[8] McSheffrey is surely right to point out that scholarship has on some occasions been too eager to equate heresy with hopes for social reform of every kind,[9] but especially when we consider Wycliffism's expressed investment in communicating to the laity just the sorts of academic learning women were excluded from achieving through official institutional channels, and the movement's rejection of the institutional priesthood and praise of the capacities of virtuous laity, it seems puzzling that no Lollard variety of a woman like Margery Kempe has ever been unearthed.[10]

We might attempt to blame this on the available evidence. Our picture of women's activities within Lollardy is strongly colored by what orthodox prosecutors expected to find. As McSheffrey has shown, prosecutors, unlike polemicists, seem often to have assumed that women were very unlikely to become involved in heresy except at the instigation of their menfolk; and male Lollards themselves often seem to disregard or downplay their women's capacities.[11] If there is any hope of finding positive evaluations of women's capacities in Wycliffism and suggesting that they had a positive impact on women's lives, perhaps our best source will be the writings of the same sort of educated Wycliffite polemicists who argue for lay theological education in more general terms.

However, not many Wycliffite polemicists have a lot to say about women—although some of them do address themselves to both men and women, and some of those who do not may in fact be considering women within the terms of a determinedly universalist mode of address.[12] So it is that the extensive theoretical defense of women's capacities by one rather unusual Wycliffite, Walter Brut, has received considerable attention. Margaret Aston has discussed Brut's arguments at length in an article which suggests that perhaps some Lollard women did perform priestly functions or take on clerical roles.[13] Aston is far too scrupulous a historian to suggest that Walter Brut's defense of women is evidence that Lollard women were priests, but she does seem to think that Brut's claims provide circumstantial support. Alcuin Blamires, Karen Pratt, and C. W. Marx have also tried to suggest that Brut's defense of women has real implications: they have selectively translated parts of the debate over women that surrounded Brut's trial in order to suggest that it provides firm evidence for support of women's ordination in the fourteenth century, of a kind that they suggest should influence the debate in the twentieth century.[14]

In my view, however, both Walter Brut's claims for women's capacities and the responses to them need to be reconsidered. They do not provide us with straightforward statements of fact, but neither are they straightforward statements of aspiration. Rather than providing any sort of evidence for support of women's learning, what they can do is help us to understand why Lollardy was never a hospitable ground for the growth of extraordinary learning among women. The tradition of argument in which this debate is conducted entirely excludes, and continues to exclude, women's participation: just as in the Bodleian Library manuscript of Dymmok's *Liber*, there are no women readers here.

Although Brut's arguments, even if labeled heretical, can be placed within the mainstream tradition of writing about women, it should be acknowledged that he was a rather unusual Lollard, with rather unusual views; and that the response to his heresy (and especially his comments on women) was also somewhat unusual.[15] Our best source of information on Brut is the detailed account of his trial for heresy in the register of Bishop Trefnant, though further evidence of his notoriety is provided by the list of his heretical propositions copied into British Library MS Royal 10 D X, a fragment of a response to his reply by William Woodford in Bibliothèque Nationale MS lat. 3381, and four anonymous disputations (of which one refers to him by name, another refers to "Lollardos" and refutes the same list of arguments as the first, and the others appear with the first two and refer to other arguments with some resemblance to Brut's) in British Library MSS Harley 31 and Royal 7 B III.[16] The academicism, and the volume, of the response to Brut is more of the sort we would expect to find in the case of a university heresiarch like Wyclif himself than that of a layman for whom there is no record of attendance at university: for his trial Trefnant assembled twenty-two experts for the occasion from as far away as Cambridge, and consulted at least one more, William Woodford in London.[17] The reply in Latin to the accusations against him that Brut was required to write certainly justifies the attention he received: it occupies seventy-four pages in the printed edition and gives evidence of fluent facility in written Latin and a broad-ranging education which includes knowledge of idioms of university argumentation (if Brut did not attend university, he studied with someone who did) as well as enough idiosyncratic knowledge to suggest that Brut read widely on his own.[18]

Brut's views on women occupy a relatively short portion of his reply, where they are woven into a broader discussion of the Eucharist and the priesthood in which women are the primary subject for only two pages.[19] But women were obviously more prominent in the minds of at least some of those who accused and responded to Brut: in the broad paper trail left by his trial, no responses to his views ignore what he says about women, while some responses are largely devoted to this issue. Among the initial series of charges against Brut to which he had to reply, his views on women are the subject of the first: "Item prefatus Walterus Brut asseruit palam, etc., quod quilibet Christianus eciam mulier extra peccatum existens potest conficere corpus Christi ita bene sicut sacerdos" (The aforementioned Walter Brut asserted openly, etc., that any Christian, even a woman, who is not in sin, can consecrate the body of Christ as well as a priest) (279). Among the thirty-seven conclusions drawn from Brut's reply and condemned as heretical, number 30 refers to his views on women (361–65; 364). In the two responses to Brut by the Cambridge doctors William Colvyll and John Neuton included in the register (though perhaps incompletely or in summary form, since not all the conclusions are answered and not all points are fully explained) the question of women's capacities appears in the second. Their treatment of women is imbricated with concerns about the priesthood and the Eucharist just as it is in Brut's reply, and receives little individual treatment (indeed, Aston has suggested that the register may here refer to a lengthier treatment elsewhere[20]) but nonetheless the doctors' response does occupy a full page (382–83). Of the four anonymous disputations, three are mainly concerned with women, giving a much-expanded account of both the positive and negative sides of the case, while the fourth, which addresses the closely related issue of lay priesthood, has its arguments incorporated into the disputation on women that it is paired with in two manuscripts.[21]

In examining the disputations I will focus mainly on the two disputations on women that debate women's ability to consecrate the Eucharist, *Utrum mulieres sint ministri ydonei ad conficiendum eukaristie* (which attributes to Brut a list of ten arguments which clearly rely extensively upon his reply) and *Utrum mulieres conficiunt vel conficere possunt* (which attributes to "Lollardos" the first disputation's first nine arguments, as well as two other arguments, both found in the first two conclusions of the first disputation but not attributed there to Brut). The third disputation on women, *Utrum liceat mulieribus docere viros publice congregatos,* is related to Brut's defense of women only tangentially: Brut touches on the question (as we will see) where he bases one of his arguments for why women can consecrate on their ability to preach.[22] Although this disputation may well have been written and/or collected in Harley 31 in association with Brut's case, as Blamires and Marx suggest in their edition of the text, its arguments have little to do with Brut's views.[23] It is not clear whether Brut himself was responsible for the expansions of his views presented in the disputations, although he could have been; material related to his reply appears in further objections to the responses to his arguments as well as in the arguments themselves, sometimes in exact quotation, so one must grant at least that whoever prepared the positive side of the case was extensively familiar with Brut's arguments.[24] Even if the expanded list of positive arguments is itself viewed as a response to Brut in another form rather than his own contribution to these determinations, it provides us with a framework within which we can pick out particular issues and draw out similarities between both the refutations of these arguments, the arguments themselves, and the reply by Brut from which they stem.

Even though this is very important for our understanding of how the university world responded to this well-schooled layman, the way in which the conclusions attributed to Brut or "Lollardos" are presented within the scholastic disputational setting in which they appear has never been described. The first disputation, *Utrum mulieres sint ministri ydonei ad conficiendum eukaristie* (D1) places the proposition and ten arguments it attributes to Brut within a larger frame. After an initial list of twelve arguments in support of the proposition that gives the disputation its title and a short (indeed it looks summarized) *ad oppositum* (196v–197), three conclusions are argued in detail: these are "Satanas neminem efficit ydoneum ad conficiendum eukaristie sacramentum" (Satan renders no one fit to consecrate the Eucharist) (197–98); "Nullus sexuum requiritur ad sacerdocium" (Neither gender is required for priesthood) (198–99); and "Mulieres possunt esse sacerdotes de potencia dei absoluta; dicere tamen assertiue aliquem mulierem esse sacerdotem sumendo sacerdotem pro illo qui habet potestatem suis verbis datam ad corpus christi conficiendum est hereticum" (Women are capable of being priests through God's absolute power, but to say assertively that any woman is a priest, taking "priest" as he who has the power of consecrating the Eucharist through his words, is heretical) (199–204v). After the third conclusion, the initial twelve arguments that supported the opening proposition are briefly answered (204v–205).

D1's tone remains abstract, speculative, and politely academic until Brut's ideas are brought into the argument in the third conclusion, where they are not given initially, but are embedded as a loose response (in no way point-by-point) to thirteen proofs of the proposition which are given at the outset (199–201v). These thirteen proofs are never properly answered, though the writer retorts at one point that Brut would have to answer them if he wanted to be taken seriously by educated as well as vulgar listeners.[25] D1 presents Brut's repeated concession that women, although *able* to perform the sacraments, should desist from doing so when male priests are available, far more clearly than Brut's reply itself. Whereas the concession is a repeated afterthought in Brut's reply whose intended impact on the main argument remains unclear, in D1 the concession frames the arguments, appearing as an initial proviso and in the final summing-up. Brut's arguments are answered by a lengthy preamble (in which an extensive distinction on the meanings of "posse" attempts a comprehensive answer to Brut's concession) followed by nine counterarguments (one covers Brut's seventh and eighth arguments together), some of which include further objections attributed to Brut and responded to in the second person in the manner of an embedded dialogue. The preamble in particular is strongly worded: Brut is repeatedly censured, and threatened, for breaking academic decorum by teaching dubious conclusions to the laity, as here:

> ... Tunc pari racione qua docet laicis quod mulieres possunt conficere, habet docere laicos et eis publice predicare quod mulieres possunt matrimonium contrahere cum patribus suis et filiis propriis et quod deo consecrata sancta[26] monialis potest contrahere matrimonium cum religioso professo; et quod mulieres possunt facere solem et lunam, eleuare montem maximum et illum in mare proicere; quod quelibet mulier potest deum concipere et parere, genus humanum reducere, et totum primum mundum adnichilare, cecos illuminare, facere surdos audire et mutos loqui. Et talis predicatoris lingua meretur amputari. (202r–v)

> Then by the same argument by which he teaches lay people that women can consecrate, he has to teach lay people and preach to them publicly that women can contract matrimony with their fathers and their own sons, and that a nun consecrated to God can do so with a professed religious. Also, that women can make the sun and moon, raise the highest mountain and throw it in the sea, and that any woman can conceive and give birth to God, unmake the human race, annihilate the whole creation, give light to the blind, and make the deaf hear and the mute speak. The tongue of such a preacher deserves to be cut out.

Along with the threat to Brut here, we can see the usual slippage to misogyny. Women's learning leads us to sexual licentiousness, and thence to blasphemy: if women could consecrate, then by the same argument they would commit incest and every other unspeakable act—and we're allowing this man to teach this to the laity? But this usual slippage has not, of course, newly emerged. It is prominent in the first two conclusions of the first disputation, and in the second disputation as well.

In the second disputation (D2), the affirmative arguments attributed to the Lollards are similarly preceded by thirteen arguments that the question never answers; several of these are very like arguments among the thirteen given at the start of the first disputation's third conclusion (218–19). The discussion similarly becomes more venomous in tone once Lollards have been mentioned. Most of the arguments attributed to Brut in D1 are treated more fully here, and are often better explained on both the positive and negative sides, though sometimes the issues treated more fully here are not ones that Brut discussed in his written reply. A schematic comparison of the conclusions made in each disputation will clarify:

Disputation 1 (D1)	Disputation 2 (D2)
1) women can baptize in cases of necessity; therefore they can consecrate the Eucharist	1) similar
2) women can and frequently have preached; therefore etc.	2) similar
	3) a woman gestated, nourished, and suckled Christ's body, therefore etc.
	4) to consecrate is no more than to turn bread into flesh and wine to blood—but a woman can do this by her nutritive power, therefore etc.
	5) a woman "consecrates" the body of Christ by conceiving, whether with a man or the Holy Spirit, therefore etc.
3) since women are able to have jurisdiction, they can bind and loose, which follows from their ability to create form	6) the jurisdiction point on its own; note that on the left, 3 presupposes absent arguments based on women's ability to conceive
4) since women confer the Holy Spirit when they baptize, therefore etc.	7) similar
5) since women participate in marriage by giving consent, thus conferring grace, therefore etc.	8) similar
6) since God makes the Eucharist at the request of a bad priest, why not at that of a good woman, especially since Jesus made water into wine at the request of Mary in the New Testament	9) similar
7) and likewise, he raised Lazarus at the request of Mary and Martha	10) similar
8) and likewise, he left the image of his face on linen for Veronica	11) similar
9) Pope Joan ruled for two years, conferred holy orders, and exercised all other papal powers; even if it is argued that all her actions are null and void, how do we know which priests and bishops might have been ordained by her or might proceed from those who were; but if her actions hold good, why cannot women now consecrate the Eucharist	12) similar, with objection and response embedded
10) even if only priests can make sacrifices, that is not a good reason for why women cannot consecrate because the Eucharist is not a sacrifice, but the memorial of one; otherwise Christ would be daily crucified	
	13) a bishop conferring holy orders can do so upon female and male souls in just the same way
	14) there were female priests in the past

Arguments 3, 4, and 5 in D2 (209v) address in detail the implications of women's ability to conceive. That helps to make sense of the end of D1's argument 3, which mentions conception in an aside, but both may be drawing on another source than Brut, who in his reply never cites women's ability to conceive as an argument for women's ability to create the body and blood of Christ.

Among the arguments in D1, only 3 differs considerably from Brut's reply: Brut's reply argues only on the basis of women's ability to bind and loose and thus to perform the sacrament of confession, where 3 mentions women's capacities for conception and jurisdiction. This one marked difference in content points, however, to a larger difference in emphasis. The main emphasis in Brut's reply, throughout his discussion of women, is upon the sacraments: he places D1's arguments in the order 1, 2, 3, 4, 5, 9, 6, 7, 8, as a survey (based in comparisons with the Old and New Testaments and with established church practice) of baptism, preaching, confession, matrimony, holy orders, extreme unction, then the Eucharist.[27] In keeping with this emphasis, the overall drift of Brut's argument in his reply often seems less feminist than anti-sacramental. Brut's keynote point in his reply after all, corresponding to D1 10 but in the reply appearing just before the focused discussion of women begins, is that even if only priests can make sacrifices, the Eucharist is not a sacrifice, but the memorial of one.[28] In reply to the first charge against him, that "quilibet Christianus eciam mulier extra peccatum existens potest conficere corpus Christi ita bene sicut sacerdos" (any Christian, even a woman, who is not in sin, can consecrate the body of Christ as well as a priest),[29] Brut wants to emphasize not that women can *also* perform the sacraments, just as well as men, but rather that *even* a woman is perfectly capable of performing the sacraments—*eciam mulier* in another sense—because the sacraments are far less intrinsically reserved to a special brethren of priests than the accretions of established church tradition would have us believe.

Brut does, however, include among the sacramental arguments in his reply one point about women's preaching. This point alone attributes to women a capacity that Brut, and Lollards in general, value highly. Here alone Brut abandons the qualifications— "secundum tradiciones ecclesie Romane" and the like—that elsewhere litter his accounts of sacramental sanctity. Here, too, Brut's repeated concession that women, while capable of performing the offices of priesthood, should not do so when there are men available seems to reach a kind of crisis—and this is no coincidence. In his defense of women's preaching, Brut insists that although Paul did not *permit* women to preach or to rule over men, nonetheless Paul did not say that women were *unable* to preach or to rule: "Quod tamen non possunt docere neque in virum dominari non dicit Paulus, nec ego audeo affirmare, cum mulieres, sancte virgines, constanter predicarunt verbum Die et multos ad fidem converterunt sacerdotibus tunc non audientibus loqui verbum" (But Paul does not say that they are *unable* to teach or to rule men, nor do I dare to affirm it, since women, holy virgins, have constantly preached the word of God and converted many to faith, while priests did not dare to say a word) (345; my emphasis). Brut does not specify which holy virgins he might be referring to here, whether recent or more distant, but his strategy is startlingly unusual, for himself or any Lollard. Here he rejects biblical authority in favor of later church tradition, saving himself from direct contradiction of Paul's meaning only through a rather specious distinction between "permittere" and "posse."

Even though it contravenes Brut's stated principle that only arguments from reason and sacred scripture will convince him—a principle affirmed in Brut's reply, referred to by both disputations and also frequently stated by other Wycliffites[30]—this argument on preaching is one that Brut has to make. Preaching, in contrast with all the sacramental cases where Brut concedes that women should not perform the task where there are priests ordained for the purpose, is a sacerdotal office which Brut considers truly essential, and which he thinks the established priesthood are not performing adequately. Thus, this is the one place where Brut wants to assert, against his repeated provisos, that women *have* stepped in as substitutes in cases where male priests have not performed an essential function—even though his approval leads him into contradiction of Paul's dictum. Ironically, the reply to the "Lollard" conclusions in D2 would agree with Brut here—although only because it considers preaching less, rather than more, important than the sacraments. D2's reply answers Brut's second argument by denying that women can ordinarily preach, because of the peril of their seductive powers, but giving three unusual cases in which women have been permitted to preach, of which the second is "in contumeliam virorum qui effeminati erant" (to the shame of effeminate men)—note the anti-female bias implicit here: women can only preach when men are even worse, *more* feminine, than they are (221).[31] We may suppose that Brut and the disputant of D2 would disagree on when such cases may arise, but there is no way to tell: neither makes any reference to examples in his own time.

Brut's one other argument from historical precedent is of a rather different sort. When near the end of his sacramental survey he adduces Pope Joan as an example of a woman who performed the sacraments, he makes no effort to show that her case fits with his proviso that no qualified men should have been available to take her place, nor even to suggest that she was exemplary. Thus Brut's argument here has puzzled and disappointed scholars who have read him as a defender of women:

et an mulieres possint conferre ordines videamus de Johanne, pontifice Romanorum, existente in sexu muliebri, Romanam ecclesiam amplius quam duobus annis gubernante, et conferente ipso tempore diversis diversos ordines et alia operante Romani pontificis statui pertinencia. Si omnia huiusmodi eius facta sint cassa et vana, dubium est nobis an qui nunc existunt pontifices et sacerdotes sunt legitime ordinati et an sacramenta ministrent, ignoramus enim an qui nunc ordinantur processerunt ab hiis quos ipsa ordinavit. Si facta eius vera erant, quare nunc bone mulieres non possunt sacramenta ministrare cum ipsa fornicaria talia ministravit? (346)

As to whether women can confer orders, let us consider Joan, pope of the Romans, of the female sex, who governed the Roman Church for more than two years, during this period conferring a variety of orders on a whole range of people as well as doing the other things that pertain to the status of the Roman pope. If all her actions are null and void, we are now in doubt as to whether popes, archbishops, bishops and priests now are legitimately ordained, and whether they may administer the sacraments, for we do not know whether those who are now ordained are descended from those she ordained. But if her actions were real, why are good women now not able to administer the sacraments, since that whore did so?

The response in D2 (very similar to D1's response, but clearer and better organized) seems (or pretends) in its final peroration to share these modern readers' surprise, even while it pruriently details Joan's sexual corruption:

Si aliqua mulier vmquam erat sacerdos vel esse posset secundum legem dei ordinatam, illa Johannes . . . que pretendebat se esse sacerdotem et summum pontificem, fuerat sacerdos et episcopus summus, quia ad sacros ordines iuit et putatiue recepit et putatiue consecrata fuit propter excellenciam litterature et ingenii in episcopum et in papam. Sed ipsa non fuerat episcopus vel sacerdos, in cuius signum deus eam reprobauit et maliciam suam detexit, faciendo eam parere in publica processione in strata publica inter ecclesiam Collocenses[32] et ecclesiam Sancti Clementis dum tendere vellet ad ecclesiam Lateranensem. Quam viam dominus papa semper eundo declinat in detestacionem sceleris illius et quia ibidem illa miserima sepelitur. Nec in cathologo summorum pontificum ponitur neque reperitur— hoc Martinus in cronica sua. Et quam deus reprobauit et ad sui confusionem detexit et eam a tota ecclesia dei reprobandam esse docuit et omnia facta sua officium sacerdotale concernencia adnullauit. Miror ergo quomodo Lollardi hanc historiam pro se audeant allegare per quam oppositum propositi eorum a deo et vniuersali declaratur. (222r–v)

If any woman ever was a priest, or could be by God's ordained law, then that Joan, . . . pretending herself priest and pope, was a priest and the highest bishop, because she proceeded to holy orders, and supposedly received them and was consecrated as bishop and pope, because of her excellence in learning and intellectual ability. But she was neither priest nor bishop, and as a sign of this God censured her and revealed her bad character by making her give birth in a public procession, right in the street between the Collocene church and the church of St. Clement, while she was on her way to the Lateran church. The pope always avoids this street, in detestation of her crime and because she is buried there. Nor is she found in the catalogue of popes—so says Martin in his chronicle. Thus God censured and revealed her, to her downfall, and taught that she should be censured by the whole Church of God, and annulled all her actions that involved sacerdotal office. I am astonished therefore that the Lollards dare to argue their side using this story, through which the opposite of their argument is made clear by God and all humanity.

At this point the disputant of D2 has dealt already (to his own satisfaction, if not ours) with the real substance of Brut's argument: he has asserted that Pope Joan's nonsacerdotal actions (such as conferring benefices) did hold true, but that all her sacerdotal actions (which in her two-year reign must have been few in any case) were profane and false, and must have been repeated again by men after she was discredited, since any priests and bishops she had ordained or consecrated would have *known* that they were not really priests and bishops yet. Now, the disputant can afford to return to the main argument and point out that Pope Joan is a very ineffective example for proving that women can be priests. He would be right if that were Brut's intention. Joan is far too easy a target, given the reputation that has been attributed to her: she is an idea example for proving the case that women are immured in their physicality and over-susceptible to corruption—and indeed, her legend was probably invented for that purpose.[33]

However, if we look more closely at Brut's treatment of Pope Joan in his reply, we can see that this passage demonstrates not Brut's ineptitude in defending women, but rather his lack of interest in mounting any effective defense of women's capacities. Brut distances himself from this "Roman pope" and her operations even while linking her actions to members of the Church in the present day; his skepticism about sacramental theology and the established Church in general is prominent. Plainly his aim is to cast the Church's embarrassment over Joan in its teeth and force it to swallow her, by arguing that it must do so through the logic of its own sacramental theology of ordination if it wants to maintain the validity of the sacraments in the present day. Brut is quite happy to revile Joan in order to reinforce his argument; to suggest that he leaves himself open to counterargument on the basis of Joan's morals is to miss the point.

Pope Joan, at least by the report of D1 and D2 (for Brut does not comment on her intellect or education) is an educated paragon of just the kind that Lollardy did not produce. Brut's treatment of her, which epitomizes his treatment of women in general, helps to show why: the opinions of women expressed by a learned Lollard differ from the mainstream just as little, it seems, as Shannon McSheffrey has shown us that those of a Lollard paterfamilias do. While Brut himself is an example of the sort of layman for whom Lollardy provided a hospitable educational environment, his views on women help to demonstrate why Lollardy was not hospitable to women's learning.

The negativity of this conclusion may seem unproductive. On the contrary, I think that recognizing and insisting on women's complete absence from the academic debate opens up more interesting possibilities than those provided by the attempts to claim they were included. McSheffrey's *Gender and Heresy* has examined what heresy trials from later on in the history of the movement can tell us about women's and men's activities and attitudes. The academic debates supply an earlier perspective on educated elite male attitudes of the sort held by persecutors and educated Lollards alike. This is what men thought about women when theorizing in their absence. The possible impact of these attitudes on women's lives as academic discourse began to be made accessible to new readers; the ways these attitudes may have combined or clashed with the methods of more practical-minded disseminators of heresy; how these attitudes may have affected the sorts of Lollard husbands, brothers, and sons who would later discourage or downplay their womenfolk's learning: all these topics have yet to be considered.

Notes

1. Rita Copeland's article "Why Women Can't Read: Medieval Hermeneutics, Statutory Law, and the Lollardy Heresy Trials," in *Representing Women: Law, Literature, and Feminism*, ed. Susan Sage Heinzelman and Zipporah Batshaw Wiseman (Durham, N.C., and London: Duke University Press, 1994), 253–86, is largely devoted to placing what anti-Wycliffites thought about women's reading in a larger context—though see note 5 below. On the more novel question of what the opponents of Hussitism and Wycliffism in Bohemia thought about women's learning in Wycliffism, see Alfred Thomas in this volume. While the answers are no more unexpected than those for anti-Wycliffites in England, this comparative literary perspective helps to underline their very conventionality.

2. Roger Dymmok, *Liber contra duodecim errores et hereses Lollardorum* (London: Wyclif Society, 1922), 275, lines 19–26. This and all following translations are my own.

3. See Oxford, Bodleian Library, Lat. th. e 30, for example on fols. 15v, 19, 21v, 42, 51, 52, 77, 80, 121, 139, 141. Nearly all of the marginal figures are women (apart from those on fols. 76, 136v); all figures are depicted from the neck up looking away from the text. For notes on the ownership of this manuscript see Fiona Somerset, *Clerical Discourse and Lay Audience in Late Medieval England* (Cambridge: Cambridge University Press, 1998), 111 and n. 17; for brief descriptions see the unpublished accessions catalogue in the Bodleian Library, *Checklist of Medieval Western Manuscripts Acquired 1916–*, vol. 3, or Otto Pacht and J. J. G. Alexander, *Illuminated Manuscripts in the Bodleian Library Oxford*, 3 vols. (Oxford: Clarendon Press, 1973), iii, no. 778.

4. "The Remonstrance against Oldcastle," in *Selections from Hoccleve*, ed. M. C. Seymour (Oxford: Clarendon Press, 1981), pp. 60–74, lines 145–52.

5. Margaret Aston for example cites part of the Hoccleve passage I quote in "Lollard Women Priests?" *Journal of Ecclesiastical History* 31 (1980): 441–61; reprinted with additional notes in Margaret Aston, *Lollards and Reformers: Images and Literacy in Late Medieval Religion* (London: Hambledon Press, 1984), 49–70, 51. Rita Copeland, "Why Women Can't Read," 270–80, puts a sanguine cast on trial evidence, drawing partly on Claire Cross, "'Great Reasoners in Scripture': The Activities of Women Lollards, 1380–1530," in *Medieval Women Studies in Church History Subsidia* 1, ed. Derek Brewer (Oxford: Blackwell, 1978), 359–80. To a lesser extent Anne Hudson also endorses Cross's arguments: see *The Premature Reformation: Wycliffite Texts and Lollard History* (Oxford: Clarendon Press, 1988), 136–37.

6. Shannon McSheffrey, *Gender and Heresy: Women and Men in Lollard Communities, 1420–1530* (Philadelphia: University of Pennsylvania Press, 1995), 4.

7. See McSheffrey's discussion of women permitted only restricted roles in "Prominent Women in Lollardy," *Gender and Heresy,* 109–24. Alice Rowley from Coventry is McSheffrey's single example of a woman who influenced men as well as women—largely because she was wife of the former mayor in Coventry, where women (very unusually) had some degree of autonomy because they held women-only conventicles (123–24). See also pp. 55–61, where McSheffrey disputes Claire Cross's claim that women gained authority by memorizing sections of the Bible, suggesting that while some Lollard women were literate and a few evidently had extraordinary powers of memory, nonetheless it seems very unlikely that they attained leadership roles through this skill, especially since several of the reported cases refer to children.

8. A great deal of scholarship on medieval women, of course, has focused on women who achieved prominence in these sorts of ways; other newer scholarship has begun to focus on less well-known women and their roles in their communities. For essays on both more and less well-known women see, for example, Karen Cherewatuk and Ulrike Wiethaus, eds., *Dear Sister: Medieval Women and the Epistolary Genre* (Philadelphia: University of Pennsylvania Press, 1993) and Diane Watt, ed., *Medieval Women in Their Communities* (Cardiffe and Toronto: University of Wales Press and University of Toronto Press, 1997).

9. For McSheffrey's comments on the tendency to associate heterodoxy and egalitarianism, and especially opportunities for women, see *Gender and Heresy,* 2–3.

10. On Margery's use of the rhetoric and mechanisms of dissent created by the Lollards and their opponents, see Ruth Shklar [Nissé], "Cobham's Daughter: *The Book of Margery Kempe* and the Power of Heterodox Thinking," *Modern Language Quarterly* 56, no. 3 (September 1995): 277–304. Despite the frequency with which the accusation was leveled, however, Margery was certainly not a Lollard.

11. McSheffrey, *Gender and Heresy,* 110–18.

12. These arguments have been made by Katherine Little, "Reading Women into Lollardy," paper delivered at the 34th International Congress on Medieval Studies, Kalamazoo, Mich., 1999.

13. Aston, "Lollard Women Priests?" 52–59.

14. Alcuin Blamires, ed., with Karen Pratt, and C. W. Marx, *Woman Defamed and Woman Defended: An Anthology of Medieval Texts* (Oxford: Clarendon Press, 1992), 250–60. It is significant, I think, that this book was published right in the middle of the sometimes vehement debate that preceded the ordination of women in the Anglican Church in England, and one must applaud the authors' conviction as well as the scope of their investigations. In addition to the general misrepresentation of tone in the section devoted to Brut, the translated excerpts ascribe to Brut in part A

arguments that were made in a disputation only very indirectly related to his statements on women (*Woman Defamed,* 251–52; see also below); and in part B, parts of the first disputation on the Eucharist that are in no way associated with Brut in the MS, and bear no resemblance to his reply (*Woman Defamed,* 255–57). Blamires's and Marx's later edition of the tangentially related disputation that addresses the issue of women's preaching is more cautious in its claims: see Alcuin Blamires and C. W. Marx, "Woman Not to Preach: A Disputation in British Library MS Harley 31," *The Journal of Medieval Latin* 3 (1993): 34–63.

15. The fullest and most recent account of Brut's heretical career is Anne Hudson, "*Laicus litteratus:* The Paradox of Lollardy," in *Heresy and Literacy, 1000–1530,* ed. Peter Biller and Anne Hudson (Cambridge: Cambridge University Press, 1994), 222–36. The best previous account of Brut's views on women is Aston, "Lollard Women Priests?" 52–59. For a detailed reassessment of the place of Brut's views on the Eucharist in relation to the broader debate see David Aers, "Walter Brut's Theology of the Sacrament of the Altar," in *Lollards and Their Influence in Late Medieval England,* ed. Fiona Somerset, Jill C. Havens, and Derrick G. Pitard, (Woodbridge, Suffolk: Boydell and Brewer, 2003), 115–26.

16. The Trefnant register is published as W. W. Capes, ed., *Registrum Johannis Trefnant* (London: Canterbury and York Society, 1916); materials relevant to Brut appear on pp. 278–394 and will be cited parenthetically. On the list of Brut's heretical propositions in London, British Library MS Royal 10 D X, fols. 312r–v, see Aston, "Lollard Women Priests?" 53 n. 16. On the Woodford reply in Paris, Bibliothèque Nationale MS lat. 3381, fols. 115–124v, see Hudson, "*Laicus litteratus,*" 223 and n. 6. In the order mentioned above the four disputations are *Utrum mulieres sint ministri ydonei ad conficiendum eukaristie, Utrum mulieres conficiunt vel conficere possunt, Utrum liceat mulieribus docere viros publice congregatos,* and *Utrum quilibet laicus iustus sit sacerdos noue legis.* The first appears in London, British Library MS Harley 31, fols. 196v–205; the second in Harley 31, fols. 218–23 and also in London, British Library MS Royal 7 B III, fols. 2–4v; the third in Harley 31, fols. 194v–6, the fourth in Harley 31, fols. 216–18 and Royal 7 B III, fols. 1–2; they will be cited by folio from Harley 31. For all transcriptions, abbreviations will be silently expanded; medieval spellings will be retained, but modern punctuation and capitalization supplied. On the disputations see also Hudson, "*Laicus litteratus,*" 224 and nn. 7–8.

17. On the response to Brut see also Hudson, "*Laicus litteratus,*" 223–24.

18. Brut's reply appears on pp. 285–358 of *Trefnant.* Hudson gives details of the extent of Brut's learning in "*Laicus litteratus,*" 225–58, though this assessment is my own.

19. See *Trefnant,* pp. 341–50; and for the section focused on women, pp. 345–47.

20. Aston, "Lollard Women Priests?" 54. See also Hudson, "*Laicus litteratus,*" 223 and n. 5.

21. On the four disputations see note 16 above. The fourth disputation's arguments against lay priesthood are all cited as support for the negative side of the second disputation, in its first argument against the proposition (fol. 218).

22. For more on how this disputation is related to the eucharistic disputations, see below. note 31.

23. Blamires and Marx, "Woman Not to Preach," 38–39.

24. Hudson details some quotations from the register in "*Laicus litteratus,*" 224 n. 7.

25. "Tales proposiciones communiter in vulgari sunt intellecte; ipse habet respondere ad illa 13a argumenta in contrarium facta." (Such propositions are commonly understood among the vulgar; but he [Brut] would have to respond to those thirteen arguments made to the contrary) (202v).

26. sancta] *sancti* (italics indicate the expanded abbreviation).

27. Compare *Trefnant*, 345–47, with Harley 31, 201v–202.

28. In Brut's reply this point is made on pp. 344–45, after women have first been mentioned on 341, but before they become the focus on 345–47. In D1, the point is revised so that it makes specific reference to women and presented as the tenth conclusion, where it seems more of an after-thought, and does not have the same anti-sacramental weight (202). In D2 the point does not appear.

29. See above, *Trefnant*, 279.

30. See Brut's reply, *Trefnant*, 286; D1 204r (in answer to argument 8); D2 219r (in the eleventh argument given at the outset). For several examples elsewhere in Lollard writing and more explanation of the pairing, see Somerset, *Clerical Discourse*, 180–83 and n. 9.

31. This argument also appears in the disputation on women's preaching *Utrum liceat mulieribus docere viros publice congregatos*, as its third conclusion, asserted but not subjected to debate (Blamires and Marx, "Woman Not to Preach," 62). The close resemblance between the two disputations' versions of this three-point argument hints at some overlap of influence, though it need not be one occasioned by Brut's trial. Blamires and Marx point out that the effeminacy point also appears (though not as one of three possibilities) in Henry of Ghent, whose text they reprint in their article (cf. Blamires and Marx, "Woman Not to Preach," 54).

32. This phantom church is apparently a misunderstanding of Martinus's reference to the Coliseum; Higden's account of Pope Joan correctly identifies the Coliseum, but it seems confusion has arisen here.

33. Pope Joan's legend appears to have originated in the thirteenth century and was not officially discredited until the sixteenth century, although the disputant of D1 does seem to have his doubts about the story's veracity. Versions of the story available in England and likely to have influenced Brut's knowledge include Martin of Troppau's popular chronicle of popes and emperors, printed as *Martini Oppaviansis Chronicon pontificum et imperatorum*, ed. L. Weiland, vol. 22 of *Monumenta Germaniae Historica Scriptores*, ed. G. H. Pertz (Hanover, 1872), 377–475, 428; Ranulph Higden's citation of Martin in his *Polychronicon*, 9 vols., ed. C. Babington and J. R. Lumby (London, 1865–86), 5:332; or a translation and updating of Martin such as those printed in *The Chronicles of Rome: An Edition of the Middle English "Chronicle of Popes and Emperors" and "The Lollard Chronicle,"* ed. Dan Embree (Woodbridge, Suffolk: Boydell, 1999), 88 and 196, 124 and 227.

Permission from the British Library for quotations from British Library MS Harley 31 in this article is gratefully acknowledged.

■ ■ ■

Eciam Lollardi

Some Further Thoughts on Fiona Somerset's "Eciam Mulier:
Women in Lollardy and the Problem of Sources"

KATHRYN KERBY-FULTON

Et tamen beatus Thomas, Secunda Secunde questio clxxvii, determinat
quod mulieribus licitum sit uia ammonicionis et familiaris collocutionis
alios instruere, ammonere seu exhortari. Unde patet quod non requiritur
quod sit superior uel litteratus qui alium debet ammonere.
— *Gerhard Zerboldt van Zutphen*

The records of Walter Brut's trial (1391–93) before Bishop Trefnant are among the
most extraordinary Lollardy has left us. As Fiona Somerset quite rightly says, Brut was
"rather an unusual Lollard with rather unusual views." In fact, he was, as I will argue,
a great deal *more* than a Lollard. As I have already suggested in this volume, many of
his ideas look far less unusual in a context of continental apocalypticism and other alternative theologies from abroad.[1] I believe Trefnant knew that, and, as I will further
suggest, he knew exactly where to go for advice on *non*-Wycliffite dissent in England
when he set up his formidable panel of experts to examine the *laicus litteratus.*[2]

Although I have no wish to alter Somerset's cogent portrait of the Harley 31 disputations on women in priestly roles and their relation to Brut's opinions, I would like

to open up a wide angle lens onto it. The larger picture here is late medieval European intellectual history, and only it, I believe, can help us with one of the great remaining puzzles of the Harley disputations, that is, that they provide striking evidence of discussion much larger than the trial of Walter Brut alone could have sparked. Modern scholars of the English tradition have tended lately to fixate on Lollardy as England's only dissent preoccupation, and, with respect to women, as English Christianity's only window of opportunity for religious empowerment. The tendency has too often been to treat both issues in an insular vacuum rather than as part of a larger fourteenth-century European trend towards challenges to the Church, especially, though not only, from the Great Schism onwards.[3] Various kinds of reformist dissent and speculative theology in general, and women's movements in particular, all played high-profile roles in these challenges. To divorce England and Wycliffism from these is to tell only part of the story, and to deprive ourselves of knowledge that English medieval thinkers took for granted.

Both Blamires and Marx's[4] and Somerset's articles on the Harley sources have made it clear that they reflect an on-going scholastic debate of some sort—one into which Brut's trial apparently intruded itself as something of a sideshow. This reading makes sense to me, because the *Frauenfrage* was already under heated discussion in international academic circles, and so in England, too, for reasons often distinct from Wycliffism.[5] Among the interesting English references to beguines, for example, is a comment made by Adam Usk, one of the many theologians brought in to examine Brut. Usk would later write to a correspondent in Rome expressing anxiety that an Old Testament disempowerment of the clergy through corruption would subsequently repeat itself in the New Testament period on account of the schism in the priesthood caused by Lollards and beguines ("scisma Lollardensibus atque Begwinis operantibus").[6] Medieval England, we so often forget, was part of medieval Europe.

Both Fiona Somerset and Anne Hudson have remarked on the oddity that such a powerful panel of theologians was brought in to respond to Brut, and from as far afield as Cambridge. This, in itself, I would argue, is a clue to non-Wycliffite concerns in the case of Brut's trial. Adam Usk's knowledge of international issues, canon and civil law, and continental apocalypticism must have been complimented by that of the recently recanted Nicholas Hereford's, also on the examining board.[7] There is, moreover, the involvement of high-profile Cambridge theologians.[8] In the 1390s Cambridge, about one third the size of Oxford, was still a very regional university, drawing especially upon East Anglia and nearby areas. But several Cambridge and Cambridge-trained theologians during this decade were engaged in a campaign for orthodoxy and moderation on at least three fronts: against Lollardy, against infiltration of Heresy of the Free Spirit (sometimes connected to Joachimism), and against the excesses of Rollean and other forms of "enthusiasm."[9] It was also from Cambridge that England's primary native interpreter of Olivian apocalypticism had come (although Olivi was not unknown at Oxford).[10] English clergy, especially in the Cambridge and East Anglian areas, were acutely aware, then (being geographically on the front lines), of *non*-Lollard dissent and other developments on the continent in relation to women.

As I will suggest, several of the non-orthodox or unusual ideas raised both by Brut and by the Harley disputants about female teaching and female sacramental capacities smack more of Free Spirit and other continental doctrines—both orthodox and otherwise—than they do of Lollardy. Moreover Brut's apocalypticism is distinctively continental, drawing upon philogynist traditions as diverse as Hildegardian and perhaps even Olivian beguinism—the latter, of course, closely tied to the poverty and disendowment controversies of the Franciscan Spirituals, but under severe persecution in fourteenth-century France.[11] Brut had argued, as I mentioned in my Introduction above, several points that are technically orthodox but more commonly cited by or in support of women on the continent, such as, for instance, his suggestion (or that of the *Utrum liceat* author) that women may come forward and preach on the strength of prophetic gifts when men are *effeminati;* or Brut's insistence that "*sancte virgines*" have "*constanter*" preached and converted when men have dared not speak.[12] In addition, and with much less orthodoxy, he casts doubt on the opinions of biblical authors, and even the apostles[13]—an extremely un-Lollard willingness to challenge scriptural authority very like the radical apocalypticism of the Olivian beguines.[14]

The Harley sources and the Brut trial, then, are even more fascinating than we have previously thought. They show English scholars in contact with new continental ideas, and wrestling academically and publicly with a new threat—one that took them far beyond the concerns of even Lollardy—*eciam Lollardi.* These *quaestiones*—if one reads against the grain of their disputational misogyny—also put forward very searching *pro* reasons for female leadership, and this, in itself, is instructive as further evidence of the possibility of alternative and radical viewpoints at the time. I would argue, these sources underline that Lollardy was not the *only* issue that concerned ecclesiastical authorities in the 1390s, nor was misogyny the only conceptual category available to the medieval Church when confronted with the prospect of female priestliness. That the English authorities were an edgy lot in 1391—concerned about Lollardy, and invoking misogyny far too often in shrill anti-Lollard polemic—I readily agree, and Somerset's demonstration of instances of both could not be finer. But if Lollardy and misogyny are all we are looking for, then that is all we tend to see. There is more, much more, on the table here.

The first thing to examine is the range and orthodoxy of *other* materials and influences encouraging women to assume clerical roles in Brut's time. Julian of Norwich, to take an obviously non-Wycliffite writer, also cited the same theology of female teaching, at least in her Short Text, to support her right to do so.[15] It is important for us to remember that just a channel crossing away from Julian's Norwich, women were being *encouraged* to engage in a form of public teaching.[16] Writing in or not long after 1395,

Gerhard Zerboldt of Zutphen, one of the most brilliant apologists and canon lawyers of the *Devotio Moderna* movement, seized upon the same passage in Aquinas that Brut had, and argued it into a licence for the Sisters of the New Devout to give *admonitiones* and even *collationes*—that is, "admonitions" and even informal sermons or reflections. The licence to do so was wrested from a train of logic that began with the observation that admonitions were open to all Christians to give, and ended, cleverly, with the assertion that women could therefore "alios instruere, ammonere seu exhortari," as the quotation from Gerhard that heads this essay makes clear.[17] Gerhard was justifying actual and continuing practice, and the fact that the movement had, in many cities, several sisterhouses for every house of the brothers, suggests that this life was an attractive and empowering one for women. Moreover, the literature of the movement was reaching England from its inception,[18] along with evidence of other continental influences that encouraged women's leadership in one form or another. Some of these were far less orthodox than the Devout, and all were aimed at religious or semi-religious women. This is why, I believe, Lollardy is only of passing and peripheral concern, for instance, to the author of *The Chastising of God's Children*, who thought it much more important to disseminate to his women readers Ruysbroec's attack on heresy of the Free Spirit. This attack was freshly available in England in a Latin translation of Ruysbroec's *Die Geestelike Brulocht* done by the founder of the *Devotio Moderna*, Gerhard Grote. *The Chastising* expends two full chapters translating Ruysbroec's arguments, distilled from his opposition to two enormously influential women teachers of his day, Bloemardinne of Brussels and Marguerite Porete.[19] *The Chastising* also takes up validation issues with respect to another body of literature encouraging women's leadership, the internationally famous Bridgittine *Revelations*. (Birgitta was canonized amidst controversy the same year as Brut's trial began, in 1391.) Other sources of alternative ideas about women's roles wafting across the channel came from orthodox beguine literature, speculative mysticism, and "heretical" groups like the Free Spirit, Olivian beguinism, and more. The historically identifiable women who assumed leadership roles in association with these influences, like the literature that made these roles possible, run the gamut of the orthodox-heterodox scale. It is in this sense I think that we need to be prepared to see texts like the Harley *quaestiones*, both those that clearly respond to Brut and those which appear to deal with issues independent of his trial, as evidence of growing English awareness of the plurality of perspectives on women's priestliness.

One of the great difficulties in the Harley sources is to distinguish the rhetoric of polemic from statements that can actually tell us something about day-to-day functioning attitudes towards women, whether among orthodox thinkers or among Lollards. In response to Somerset's initial question, then, I would suggest that it *is* worth asking what even anti-Wycliffites thought about women's capacity for learning.[20] It seems important to remember here that what comes across to us now as a barrage of patronizing misogyny regarding women's theological incapacities was, at the very least, a category resorted to on *both* sides of the polemic. Dymmock's invocation of the specter of poor, unlearned women ("animas simplices et indoctas mulierum") falling prey to the rhetoric of the Lollards is, I would point out, actually reversed thunder: its source is anti-mendicant polemic—a polemic that the Wycliffites themselves used against the friars in spades.[21] The trope (and here, for once these days, we have something that does deserve to be called a trope!) originates in 2 Timothy 3:5–6, which describes a group of religious hypocrites ("habentes speciem quidem pietatis") that will arise in the last days, leading astray the faithful, and especially penetrating houses to "lead captive weak women laden with sins, who are led away with diverse desires" (captivas ducunt mulierculas oneratas peccatis, quae ducuntur variis desideriis). These verses had been used persistently against the friars ever since William of St. Amour famously volleyed them at the Paris mendicants in the 1250s.[22] Ironically, William's inspiration came in large part from the writings of a woman he admired: they originated in Hildegard of Bingen's letter to the Cologne clergy, and which in both genuine and pseudonymous renditions was attributed to her in Wycliffite manuscripts.[23] But, I would point out, the Dominicans, faced with the rise of Lollardy and with its tendency to proselytize women, had begun (gleefully, one imagines) to reverse the trope.[24] There is intriguing codicological evidence of this that can actually be related to Dymmock: a Dominican-owned copy of Hildegard's prophecies, Bodleian Library Digby 32, contains annotations from the late fourteenth century, denouncing Hildegard's pseudo-prophets as "Lollardi." In the margin beside Hildegard's prophecy that they will seduce women doctrinally ("et eas in errorem suum ducunt"), and afterwards sexually ("postea eisdem feminis secreta luxuria commiscebuntur"), the Dominican annotator has written triumphantly, "Ecce quomodo lollardi seducent mulieres" (Behold how the Lollards will lead away [or seduce] women). What is especially interesting about Dymmock is that he was a Dominican in the London house in which his fellow friar, John Blackwell, who made these annotations, ended his career sometime before 1412.[25]

What this indicates is that we have to be careful about taking polemical clichés at face value as evidence of what anti-Wycliffites *really* thought about women—because apparently Wycliffites, at least in their anti-mendicant polemic, thought exactly the same as their opponents. But fortunately the story does not end here. What we have learned from scholars of anti-mendicant literature like John Fleming and Penn Szittya—that is, that this polemic bears more relation to *exegesis* than to life—is every bit as relevant to polemical misogyny. Here it seems to me we have important evidence for why, as Somerset quite rightly points out, "not many Wycliffite polemicists have a lot to say about women." Not a lot, at least, that transcends the hothouse world of exegetically based polemic.

The reason, I believe, is that the real revolution was going on elsewhere. In saying this I am making a different point than scholars like Aers and McSheffrey, who have repeatedly registered disappointment in not finding Lollardy to be the locus they had hoped for social reform, or indeed, for Aers, a socially "progressive" Christianity.[26] Lollards, I am sure, would be surprised by such expectations. They believed themselves to be engaging in *religious reform*, which is an entirely different project, and—it is too easy to forget this—largely a conservatizing one.[27] Within this mandate I believe, with Somerset, that Lollard women did play more roles than we can now document. But my point here, rather, is this: for documentable gender-role-breaking activity that allowed women to assume publicly certain kinds of preaching, teaching, and "priestly" functions one has to look to a range of other, often *orthodox* influences. These include: speculative mysticism, apocalypticism, and most especially visionary vocation (often conducted under the protective auspices or encouragement of certain religious orders or of high social class), not to mention various continental *Frauenbewegungen*. English women do not seem to have had as large a share in these possibilities as some others, and this is sad, but speculative mysticism, along with visionary vocation, gave Julian her platform, just as visionary vocation did Margery Kempe. Various continental models were widely available via diverse media to English readers and church-goers, from the *Revelations* of St. Birgitta to the iconography of Mary Magdalene, Martha, Cecilia, and other female saints preaching in religious art.[28]

Thomas Aquinas, even Henry of Ghent, and others whom the Harley sources follow closely had been unwilling to shut down the important loophole of a woman's right to preach "by special grace": "Non licet mulieri viros docere, *nisi speciali gratia* praedita."[29] For these men there were too many important precedents, biblical, hagiographical, and contemporary, to close down the option completely.[30] By Brut's time there were even more powerful instances—in women like Birgitta of Sweden and Catherine of Siena with massive international reputations for wielding power at the very apex of the medieval Church, where popes in exile or schism had heeded their teachings.[31] Moreover, high social class (the most long-standing means to religious power for medieval women) or, alternatively, membership in a movement like the *Devotio Moderna* also provided some opportunities for females to assume semi-pastoral roles, such as giving *collationes* or hearing confession.[32] Certain religious orders, too, provided wider opportunities to women. Franciscans like Eustache de Arras, writing about 1263, had argued that Paul's injunction against women teaching (1 Cor. 14:34) applied only to married women, not to virgins[33]—and under the encouragement of the Franciscan Order, a small but significant number of women did preach or teach without censure.[34] Under the auspices of other orders, most especially the Cistericans in the Low Countries and, in late medieval England, the Carthusians, women instructed men regularly via the written page. Ironically, Wycliffites were largely (with the exception of Brut and few others) close-minded about all these forms of spirituality by the early 1380s.[35]

This, I would suggest, is a deeply significant reason why Lollardy never proved "fertile ground," in Somerset's phrase, for women's learning or for women's high-profile leadership. Although I would not, with McSheffrey, so fully despair of the glimpse Aston and Cross have given us of women active as oral biblical instructors in the home and the conventicle, perhaps even sporadically experimenting with assuming sacramental roles,[36] I would point out this: Wycliffism was, for all its startling theological radicalism on certain points, deeply reactionary on others. This comes across especially in relation to Wyclif's own negative attitudes towards alternative spiritualities and revelatory theology[37]—areas in which, we must remember, the Church at large actually provided more flexibility on women's leadership than Wycliffism did.[38]

What is especially important for us to realise is that it is in response to precisely these largely continental phenomena that the academic tradition drawn upon by both Walter Brut and the Harley disputations on women's preaching and sacramentalism was originally developed. Henry of Ghent and Thomas Aquinas, whose writings the Harley disputants use, did not themselves tackle these issues as merely academic exercises. Nor, then, should we assume the English disputants did. Blamires and Marx wondered whether the Harley material just represents the kind of *pro* and *contra* thought available in the scholarly tradition to be invoked whenever need be.[39] It is an astute observation, and, I believe, partially right, but it is important to note that the development of these arguments happened in relation to actual history.

Henry of Ghent flourished in the generation that witnessed the first real tensions with respect to teaching and preaching beguines. He writes his scholarship from the minority standpoint of a secular, and, originating from Ghent, a large center of beguinism. Henry, in what can too easily appear to us today as simply abstract misogyny, says in one of his *contra* positions that it can be dangerous for women even to attend lectures.[40] But despite the "academic" nature of Henry's project, there is an element here of the secular's concern with actual pastoral care. Beguines *did* attend lectures in Henry's time, and in large numbers.[41] Many of Henry's more liberal-minded scholarly colleagues were actively engaged in delivering these lectures[42]—and in this respect we have to realise that Henry represents a conservative, if not downright reactionary, perspective. More importantly, some women of the "semi-religious" vocation represented by beguines and Sisters of the New Devout gave lectures and sermons, or at least *collationes,* some of which survive.[43] Henry's much younger contemporary, Ruysbroec, for instance, also a secular, attacked the orthodoxy of the influential beguine lecturer, Bloemardinne. Even though Ruysbroec lived in a more repressive generation for beguines than Henry's own, that is, after the Council of Vienne, Bloemardinne was so influential that he only dared attack her after her death. Ruysbroec's biographer writes:

> Such was the popular esteem of [Bloemardinne] that it was imagined that whenever she appeared before the altar to receive the Holy Communion she walked between two rows of Seraphim. Since she had written much on the spirit of freedom [*de spiritu libertatis*] and on the most abominable venereal love, which she called

seraphic, she was revered by many followers as the founder of a new doctrine. Indeed when teaching and writing she sat on a silver seat which, it is said, was offered after her death to the duchess of Brabant because of her admiration for her ideas. . . . I can affirm from my personal experience that these writings, though excessively baleful, have such an aspect of truth that no one can perceive in them any seed of heresy *save with the grace and assistance of Him who teaches all truth.*[44] (my emphasis)

This last idea was so worrying that where it appears in Ruysbroec's *Brulocht*, the passage was suppressed by the author of *The Chastising*. Bloemardinne's ideas were, from what we can now gauge, heresy of the Free Spirit in tendency, and Ruysbroec also attacked, in lucid detail, the ideas of the more famous *beguine clergesse*, Marguerite Porete, as set out in her *Mirror*.

Speculative theology of the sophistication these two women engaged in was to a significant degree the gift of Dominican ministry to the beguines.[45] Thomas Aquinas was a Dominican and would have been well aware that the ministry had become controversial in certain respects. Moreover, Henry of Ghent and Thomas Aquinas both taught at Paris during the 1270s, the period, that is, of Bishop Tempier's condemnations and attempts to shut down certain kinds of theological speculation (Aquinas's own among them).[46] It does not seem unusual in this context that such men would be wrestling with issues of what we would today call, in broad terms, intellectual freedom. If we think Paris academics were remote from these issues in relation to actual historical women of their time, we need to think again. Witness, for instance, the letter of support that Godfrey of Fontaines, who had written an important *quodlibet* on academic freedom in the wake of the Tempier condemnations, provided for Marguerite Porete's book.[47]

To be fair, then, to both Henry and Thomas—and as a modern woman this is not easy—there *is* some genuine wrestling. (More genuine in Thomas than in Henry, I believe.) Neither produces the result we would wish, but at the same time we should not forget that even Henry (*eciam* Henry!) is unwilling to shut down the possibility of female instrumentality, and this is significant. There is—by later English standards—an openness in their work to the possibility of legitimate female prophetic vocation, and this even though both men were historically positioned to see rising tensions about the large and sophisticated male teaching ministry to beguines and female tertiaries. Their misogyny, especially Henry's, is cause for modern regret, but the potential for prophetic authenticity among women preachers must have outweighed *even* this, and even for scholastics (a group not noted for enthusiasm about visionary experience generally).[48] As I have suggested in my introduction in the present volume, the celebrated women preachers of the 1250s (like the beguine, Douceline de Digne, who preached before nobility, and the Franciscan tertiary, Rose of Viterbo, who preached by papal command), had given way, by the time that Henry and Thomas are writing, to growing concern about the orthodoxy of preaching and teaching women religious. This nervousness is evident in the withdrawal of male tutelage on the part of some religious orders, the harassment of beguine communities, the growing persecution of Olivian beguinism in the south of France, and the development of a literary satire of preaching beguines.[49] One thinks here of the flight of Mechthild of Magdeburg from the beguinage to the safety of Dominican-protected Helfta at about 1270, or of the cautiously censuring redaction of the *Vita* of Douceline between 1297 and 1310[50]—and of a host of events leading up to the decrees of the Council of Vienne, and the horrific death of Marguerite Porete in 1310. The culmination of all these events, of course, is the now infamous papal decree forged at Vienne in 1311, *Cum de quibusdam mulieribus:*

> There are certain women, commonly called beguines who, although they promise no one obedience and neither renounce property nor live in accordance with an approved rule, . . . nevertheless wear a so-called beguine habit, and cling to certain religious to whom they are drawn by special preference. It has been repeatedly and reliably reported to us that some of them, as if possessed with madness, dispute and preach about the Highest Trinity and divine essence and in respect to the articles of faith and the sacraments of the Church spread opinions that are contradictory to the Catholic faith. . . . Therefore, we believe we must . . . prohibit forever their status. . . . Moreover, the aforesaid regulars who are said to promote these women . . . are strictly forbidden on pain of excommunication . . . to offer such sectarians any counsel, aid or favor.[51]

Even this, however, did not shut down the preaching of women. We have already mentioned the case of Bloemardinne that so troubled Ruysbroec, and in his attack on her teachings and on Porete's, we have yet another text which, along with Birgitta's *Revelations,* had reached England and was actively disseminated at the time of Brut's trial. Both these, in fact, reached not just the Latin literate, but English readers—and here we might note, large numbers of *women* readers as well—in the form of *The Chastising of God's Children.*[52] This accounts in part for why the clarion note of alarm about heresy sounded in *The Chastising* is not about Lollardy, but rather about Free Spiritism, and about *revelatory theology*—both strongly associated with women (semi-)religious:

> Now longe I haue taried зou to shew зou . . . hou sum men walken to ferre out fro our louyng lord, . . . hou sum wiþ her errours bien taken wiþ wikked spirites, and *hou sum in* [disseit][53] *after her desire han reuelacions. Many mo* I miзt shew to make зou be war of hem, as of sum þat now holden plainli, and nat зit opinli, but priueli for drede, aзens confessions and fastynges, aзens worshippyng of ymages, and shortli,

as men seien, aȝens al states and degrees and þe lawe and þe ordynaunce of hooli chirche. But al þese I leeue, because it nediþ nat greteli, for I trowe *heere bien rehersid þo þat bien most in our knowyng to be dred.* (*Chastising* 144.21–145.10; my emphasis)

Although Robert Lerner has read this passage as proof that the author mistook Ruysbroec's description of Free Spiritism for Lollardy, this is grammatically, as well as interpretively, impossible, given the coherence of the author's account.[54] The syntax alone makes it clear that Lollards are "sum" among the "many mo" he *could* name, but that "it nediþ nat greteli," because the ones he has already spoken of are the ones "*most in our knowyng to be dred*" (most in our [present] knowledge to be feared).

This passage comes from a paragraph at the end of Chapter 12 which, as Bazire and Colledge pointed out, has no counterpart in Ruysbroec's Dutch, and which makes clear that what the writer has been concerned to show is "hou manye perels and disceites fallen and haue falle *to goostli lyuers*" (145.15–16), that is, to contemplatives. I might add that the paragraph also has no counterpart in Gerhard Grote's Latin version, the translation of Ruysbroec from which the *Chastising* author worked (which Bazire and Colledge did not know). The English author composed it to set out a clear hierarchy of heresies and spiritual dangers to be avoided, among which Free Spiritism and delusory revelations far outrun Lollardy.[55] But what is especially striking about the English author is his (or, less likely, her) marked tendency to suppress Ruysbroec's more continental trust in divine illumination in the discernment of spirits:

> Dese machmen qualijcke bekinnen, en ware een mensche die verlicht ware ende onderscheet hadde der gheeste ende [der] godlijcker waerheit. (These people can hardly be recognized except by one who would be enlightened and would have the discernment of spirits and of divine truth.)[56]

In Grote's Latin translation this runs,

> Hii homines non sunt bene cognoscibiles nisi per hominem illuminatum et per eum qui spirituum haberet discretionem et diuine ueritatis.[57]

In *The Chastising* the whole sentence disappears, though the material immediately before and after it follows Grote's Ruysbroec closely. The more dicey aspects of *discretio*, like having to depend upon divine illumination in order to detect the validity of a *claim* to divine illumination, were a minefield for ecclesiastical authorities in the prosecution of heresy. Certainly the *Chastising* author wants no truck with them, preferring to urge his women readers to recognise false opinions empirically. It was perhaps in part for this reason that *The Chastising* was attributed to Walter Hilton,[58] that pillar of commonsense orthodoxy on the spiritual life. Hilton's close associations with Cambridge theologians (including visitors from the continent) give solid evidence of a concerted and intelligent campaign against Free Spiritism in the 1380s and 1390s.[59]

And this, I would argue, is why Trefnant went as far afield as Cambridge to get theologians (and not just any theologians) to respond to Brut.[60] For help with ordinary Wycliffite examination, he need not have looked farther than nearby Oxford, but it must have been immediately apparent to Trefnant that many of Brut's ideas did not fit the Wycliffite template.[61] Even though I think we tend to overestimate the extent to which that profile had wholly solidified by 1391, still Brut's alternative ideas on apocalypticism and on women must have tipped Trefnant off to the fact that he was dealing with continental influences.[62] Clark has documented Hilton's associations with Cambridge theologians active in the mid-1380s and 1390s against what they called "Liberty of Spirit." To his evidence I would like to add another dimension: Cambridge also had a history of dealing with Olivian apocalypticism, not to mention connections with theologians of East Anglia empathetic both to it and to women visionaries. Alan of Lynn (1348–1423), for instance, later confidant to Margery Kempe, took the trouble to index former Cambridge lector Henry of Costesy's Apocalypse commentary.[63] Alan also indexed Birgitta's *Revelations* (a copy of which survives in Lincoln College, Oxford, MS 69).[64] Henry of Costesy had been cited to Avignon along with three other Cambridge Franciscan lectors during the witchhunts of John XXII, but his Apocalypse commentary, laced with Olivianism as it was, continued to be widely copied and read, especially locally, as Alan's indexing project indicates.[65] And here it is important to stress that we cannot draw hard and fast lines, and neither could Trefnant: it was entirely possible for orthodox theologians to support women's ministry when that ministry was shielded by a claim to special grace.[66] On this point local culture and jurisdiction made a great deal of difference. East Anglia, we know, nurtured women visionaries. Alan of Lynn did so for Margery, and must have thought her gifts of a similar nature to Birgitta's, to whom he was devoted.

These factors go some way toward explaining the evidence in Harley that there was already a wider and on-going debate within the academic community, a debate into which Brut's trial suddenly intruded itself. With the benefit of 600 years of hindsight, Lollardy looms large and formalized for us now in a way that it could not have in 1391. To the academics writing in Harley, Brut's ideas appear somewhat clumsy but not uninteresting academically, and certainly not as unheard of. Somerset very helpfully lifts out the ambiguity of tone in one remark from *Utrum mulieres sint ministri* in which the author sets out what Brut must do to be taken seriously by the academic establishment: "Tales proposiciones communiter in vulagri sunt intellecte; ipse habet respondere ad illa argumenta in contrariaum facta" (Such propositions are commonly understood among the vulgar; but he [Brut] would have to respond to those thirteen arguments made to the contrary).[67] But, to adopt Blamires and Marx's metaphor, neither the *pro* nor the *contra* arguments in any of these sources are just tilting at straw targets. And Trefnant knew that Brut's arguments were not straw targets either. He knew that in other ecclesiastical environments these ideas had given and continued to give women and their clerical supporters some real room to maneuver. He judged, I would suggest, that his diocese could, at his historical moment, ill afford the potential risks of such liberality, or, better, what Norman Tanner has called "leftwing orthodoxy."[68] But he wanted to show that it had been duly considered.

What the treatises in Harley show is that every conceivable stone had been turned. They address issues parallel to and even broader than those Brut raised, and in the safety of academic Latin, ponder much more daring ones than the *laicus litteratus* did. Some of the ideas in *Utrum mulieres conficiunt* (Somerset's D2) on a woman's ability to consecrate based on her ability to conceive perhaps stem from Olivian beguinism, which by the very early fourteenth century had developed ideas of a priesthood of all believers, and among whom women played important roles. They, too, were anti-sacramentalist (only marriage, one of their most prominent female visionaries believed, would survive in the coming Age of the Holy Spirit).[69] Or, perhaps, Free Spiritism: its relative indifference to, if not contempt for sacraments, and fascination with bridal nuptualism and alternative sexual ideas may well have combined to evoke the unique ideas pondered in *Utrum mulieres conficiunt.*[70] These are only possibilities. What is beyond doubt, however, is that Olivian or Free Spirit ideas *do* appear mixed in with Wycliffite ones in certain English inquisitorial contexts.[71] Somerset's point that the Harley disputations show us why Lollardy was never very hospitable ground for women's learning is well taken, but with scholastic argument the cup can be, and remain, half full at the same time as it is half empty. These disputations do show us, I believe, that encounters with the rise of articulate women in the recent historical past had pushed academics to develop some very careful responses, and to allow explicitly for exceptional women. What the Harley sources give us a window on is further and compelling evidence of what Brut's trial has always indicated: that in his hands English Wycliffism had lost its purity, and certainly its Englishness.

Notes

I would like to thank Anne Hudson, Steve Justice, Fiona Somerset, and Linda Olson for reading this piece with care and enthusiasm, and, as always, John Van Engen, for his learning and generosity.

1. On Brut's apocalypticism, see my introduction to the present volume, "When Women Preached." Brut, himself, of course, was not English but Welsh, and the Welsh had a special fascination with prophecy, both political and religious, native and continental. See, for instance, the introduction to *The Chronicle of Adam Usk, 1377–1421,* ed. C. Given-Wilson (Oxford: Clarendon Press,

1997), "Portents and Prophecies," and "Dreams, Fortune, and History," lxvii–lxxix. For an example of the type of manuscript in which readers like Brut, or his compatriot, Usk, would have found this kind of mix of prophecy, see the discussions of National Library of Wales, MS Peniarth 50, in K. Kerby-Fulton and E. Randolph Daniel, "English Joachimism, 1300–1500: The Columbinus Prophecy," in *Il profetismo gioachimita tra Quattrocento e Cinquecento*, ed. G. L. Potestà (Fiore: Atti del III Congresso Internazionale di Studi Gioachimiti, 1989), esp. 324–26.

2. For a discussion of this designation of Brut, see Anne Hudson, "*Laicus litteratus:* The Paradox of Lollardy," in *Heresy and Literacy, 1000–1530*, ed. Peter Biller and Anne Hudson (Cambridge: Cambridge University Press, 1994), 222–36.

3. See John Van Engen, "The Church in the Fifteenth Century," in *Handbook of European History, 1400–1600*, ed. Thomas A. Brady, Heiko Oberman, and James D. Tracey (Leiden: Brill, 1994), 305–28.

4. Alcuin Blamires and C. W. Marx, "Woman Not to Preach: A Disputation in MS Harley 31," *Journal of Medieval Latin* 3 (1993): 34–63.

5. For an introductory history, see Ernest W. McDonnell, "Social Origins: The *Frauenfrage,*" in his *The Beguines and Beghards in Medieval Culture* (New York: Octagon, 1969), 81–101.

6. For Adam's apocalyptic sense of Old and New Testament concordances and the ceasing of the "three miracles" of priesthood on account of corruption, see his *Chronicon* for 1402, "Quare sicut ueteris testamenti uenalitate sacerdocium corrumpente tria cessarunt miracula . . ." (Given-Wilson, *Chronicle of Adam Usk,* 160); he later returned to the same theme in a letter to William Swan, "utriusque et templi sequitur confusio in nouo testamento inter Romam et Constanciam ac in sacerdocio subsequens scisma Lollardensibus atque Begwinis operantibus" (ibid., lxxvii).

7. For Hereford's history abroad, and the theory that he was the author of the *Opus Arduum,* see Anne Hudson, "A Neglected Wycliffite Text," in *Lollards and Their Books* (London: Hambledon, 1985), 43–66; for discussion of the continental apocalypticism of the *Opus,* see Curtis Bostick, *The Antichrist and the Lollards* (Leiden: Brill, 1998), chap. 4.

8. Two of the Cambridge theologians were William Colvyll, chancellor of the university, and his successor, John de Necton. See Richard Sharpe, *A Handlist of the Latin Writers of Great Britain and Ireland before 1540* (Turnhout: Brepols, 1997), 760.

9. See J. P. H. Clark, "Late Fourteenth-Century Cambridge Theology and the English Contemplative Tradition," in *The Medieval Mystical Tradition in England,* vol. 5 (Cambridge: Brewer, 1992), 1–16. See also my *Books under Suspicion: Censorship and Revelatory Theology in Late Medieval England* (Notre Dame, Ind.: University of Notre Dame Press, forthcoming).

10. Peter Olivi was a Franciscan Joachite thinker and spiritual leader of the beguines in southern France. Henry of Costesy (Costesy is in East Anglia) had been a Franciscan lector at Cambridge and wrote an Apocalypse commentary in the Joachite and Olivian tradition. He was cited to Avignon on charges of heresy in 1330, but apparently cleared. His commentary, by far his most popular work, was surprisingly well disseminated: fourteen copies are known or attested (see Sharpe, *Handlist,* 166). On Henry see David Burr, *Olivi's Peaceable Kingdom: A Reading of the Apocalypse Commentary* (Philadelphia: University of Pennsylvania Press, 1993), 255–61; and Clark, "Late Fourteenth-Century Cambridge Theology," 13. Copies of Olivi's works were confiscated from Oxford in or by 1389. See Hudson, "A Neglected Wycliffite Text," 54.

11. See "When Women Preached." On the beguines of southern France, see Gordon Leff, *Heresy in the Later Middle Ages* (Manchester: Manchester University Press, 1967), 195–229. See also

Ruth Nissé's important article, "Prophetic Nations," *New Medieval Literatures* 4 (2001): 95–115, on Brut and the Franciscan Spiritual writer, John of Rupescissa.

12. See "When Women Preached," note 21, for more detailed discussion. The first point goes back to Hildegard, although it also appears in Henry of Ghent ("in virorum contumeliam, quia effeminati facti erant" [Blamires and Marx, "Woman Not to Preach," 54]). Brut's extensive knowledge of continental apocalypticism gives his very positive usage of it a very different colour than Henry's. For Brut's full text, see the *Registrum Johannis Trefnant,* ed. W.W. Capes (London, 1916), esp. here 345. We do not know whether it was Brut's trial that prompted *Utrum liceat* or not, but we do know that the reference to the "effeminati" occurs in a second Harley disputation, one much more closely linked to Brut's trial than *Utrum liceat.* Furthermore, we know that in Brut's own handwritten testimony he makes reference to "Mulieres, sancte virgines, constanter predicarunt verbum Dei et multos ad fidem converterunt sacerdotibus tunc non audientibus loqui verbum" (*Trefnant,* 345).

13. "Nullius vero magistri, Cristo excepto, nudis verbis simpliciter credam nisi ipsa fundare poterint in veritate experiencie aut scripture quoniam in sanctis apostolis a Cristo electis inventus est error ex testimonio scripture sacre, quoniam et Paulus fatetur se reprehendisse Petrum quia reprehensibilis erat, ad Gal. Ii. In sanctis doctoribus preteritis inventus est error . . ." (*Trefnant,* 286).

14. For this evidence, see Leff, *Heresy,* 1:197.

15. See "When Women Preached."

16. For this information I am indebted to John Van Engen, and to his essay "Devout Communities and Inquisitorial Orders: The Legal Defense of the New Devout," in *Kirchenreform von unten: Gerhart Zerbolt von Zutphen und die Brüder vom Gemeinsamen Leben,* ed. Nikolaus Staubach (Frankfurt, 2002), 44–101.

17. Albert Hyma, "Het traktaat 'Super modo vivendi devotorum hominum simul commorantium' door Gerard Zerbolt van Zutphen," *Archief voor de geschiedenis van het Aartsbisdom Utrecht* 52 (1926): 46–56, here 48.

18. On the spread of *Devotio Moderna* literature in England, see *The Chastising of God's Children,* ed. Joyce Bazire and E. Colledge (Oxford: Blackwell, 1957); Wolfgang Riehle, *The Middle English Mystics* (London: Routledge), 22–23; and Michael G. Sargent, "The Transmission by the English Carthusians of Some Late Medieval Spiritual Writings," *Journal of Ecclesiastical History* 27 (1976): 225–42.

19. See Robert Lerner, *The Heresy of the Free Spirit in the Later Middle Ages* (Berkeley: University of California Press, 1972), 191–94. Ruysbroec's attack in each case was, so far as we know, upon doctrine, not gender.

20. Or, at least, what *non*-Wycliffites thought. We might remember, for instance, that Julian of Norwich herself would fit this category.

21. See Penn Szittya, *The Antifraternal Tradition in Medieval Literature* (Princeton, N.J.: Princeton University Press, 1986), esp. 218, for Wycliffite works using 2 Tim. 3:6, and also 152–53 and 170, for Wyclif's use of the 3:1–9 passage generally.

22. William's *De periculis novissimorum temporum,* ed. E. Brown, in appendix to O. Gratius, *Fasciculus rerum expetendarum* (London, 1690), 18–41, pretends to be a long exegetical commentary on 2 Tim. 3:1–8, giving forty signs for distinguishing true from false apostles (that is, for telling secular pastors from friars), and a further eight signs that the End Times are nigh. These verses from 2 Tim. 3 had in fact been used earlier in history to castigate the Waldensian heretics and the beghards. See R. E. Lerner, "Vagabonds and Little Women: The Medieval Netherlandish Dramatic Fragment

'De Truwanten,'" *Modern Philology* 65 (1968): 301–306; James Doyne Dawson, "William of St. Amour and the Apostolic Tradition," *Mediaeval Studies* 40 (1978): 223–38.

23. For the Wycliffite interest in Hildegard, see Kerby-Fulton, "Prophecy and Suspicion: Closet Radicalism, Reformist Politics, and the Vogue for Hildegardiana in Ricardian England," *Speculum* 75 (2000): 318–41. William refers appreciatively to Hildegard's Cologne prophecy when he is elucidating the fact that the pseudo-prophets will penetrate homes "et captivas ducunt mulierculas" (2 Tim. 6). He appeals to the authority of Hildegard's prophecy to show that among these new pseudo-apostles, spiritual seduction of women goes hand in hand with physical seduction, or, at the very least, acts as a cover for it: "quia licet ab initio forte per simulationem hypocrisis videantur habere spiritualem fa-miliaritatem cum illis, in fine tamen cum eis plerumque incestuose commiscentur" (*Collectiones*, in William of St. Amour, *Opera omnia* [Constance, 1632], 196); on this passage see Szyitta, *Antifraternal Tradition*, 59. The passage he is alluding to in Hildegard's Cologne letter runs: "Et hoc modo feminas sibi contrahunt, et eas in errorem suum ducunt. Unde etiam ipsi in superbia tumentis animi dicent: 'Omnes superavimus'. Qui tamen postea eisdem feminis secreta luxuria commiscebuntur, et ita iniquitas et secta eorum denudabitur." Citations from Hildegard are from the full edition of the Co-logne letter in Konrad Bund, "Die 'Prophetin,' ein Dichter und die Niederlassung der Bettelorden in Köln," *Mittellateinisches Jahrbuch* 23 (1988): 171–260; 250, lines 175–78.

24. "Hildegard and the Male Reader: A Study in Insular Reception," in *Prophets Abroad: The Reception of Continental Holy Women in Late-Medieval England*, ed. Rosalynn Voaden (Cambridge: Brewer, 1996), 1–18, esp. 17–18.

25. I have identified Blackwell as Hand 3 in Digby 32. See Kerby-Fulton, "Prophecy and Sus-picion," 323 and 340.

26. Shannon McSheffrey, *Gender and Heresy: Women and Men in Lollard Communities* (Phila-delphia: University of Pennsylvania Press, 1995); David Aers, "Wyclif and Poverty," paper presented at the Lollard Society session, International Medieval Congress, Kalamazoo, Mich., Western Michi-gan University, May 2001, and his *Faith, Ethics, and Church: Writing in England 1360–1409* (Wood-bridge, U.K.: 2000).

27. On fundamental notions of reform for the Middle Ages, see Gerhart B. Ladner, *The Idea of Reform: Its Impact on Christian Thought and Action in the Age of the Fathers* (New York: Harper and Row, 1967).

28. Roberto Rusconi, "Women's Sermons at the End of the Middle Ages: Texts from the Blessed and Images of the Saints," in *Women Preachers and Prophets through Two Millennia of Christianity*, ed. Beverly Kienzle and Pamela Walker (Berkeley: University of California Press, 1998), 173–98.

29. The quotation comes from the final conclusion of Henry of Ghent's *Summa quaestionum ordinarium*, Book 1, art. 11, q. 2, "Utrum mulier possit esse doctor, seu doctrix huius scientiae" (Blamires and Marx, "Woman Not to Preach," 55). The conclusion is positioned so as to be defini-tive, and override the previous two conclusions in special cases.

30. On the widespread use of images of Mary Magdalene and other saints preaching in con-temporary medieval dress, see Rusconi, "Women's Sermons," and in the present volume see the il-lustration in David Wallace's essay below.

31. For brief but contextualized comments on Birgitta and Catherine see Rusconi, "Women's Sermons," 186–87. See also my "When Women Preached."

32. See Van Engen, "Devout Communities."

33. For the text, see Jean Leclercq, "Le magistère du prédicateur au XIIIe siècle," *Archives d'Histoire doctrinale et littéraire du Moyen Age* 15 (1946): 105–47; 121; and see Nicole Bériou, "The Right of Women to Give Religious Instruction in the Thirteenth Century," in Kienzle and Walker, *Women Preachers and Prophets,* 138.

34. In addition to Rose of Viterbo, Umilita of Faenzà, Douceline de Digne, and others with more formal Franciscan connections, even women such as Catherine of Siena, officially a Dominican tertiary, were in fact more profoundly affected by Franciscan openness to alternative positions for women. (See "When Women Preached.") I would like to thank John Fleming for his advice on this subject.

35. The author of the *Opus arduum* is one of the few other Wycliffites who shows openness to prophetic thought. See Curtis Bostick, *Antichrist and the Lollards,* chap. 4.

36. M. Aston, "Lollard Women Priests?" *Journal of Ecclesiastical History* 31 (1980): 441–61; Claire Cross, "'Great Reasoners in Scripture': The Activities of Women Lollards, 1380–1530," *Studies in Church History Subsidia* 1 (1978): 359–80.

37. On Wyclif's own views, see Kerby-Fulton, "Prophecy and Suspicion."

38. See Norman Tanner, *The Church in Late Medieval Norwich* (Toronto: PIMS, 1984), 166, who remarks of Norwich that "an important reason for the [city's] lack of interest in Lollardy was that the religion provided by the local Church was sufficiently . . . tolerant towards what might be called the left wing of orthodoxy, as to cater for the tastes of most citizens." Norwich was obviously not alone in this.

39. Blamires and Marx, "Woman Not to Preach," 38.

40. In Henry's "Utrum mulier possit esse audior sacrae scripturae," in his *Summa in tres partes,* 1:193–95, art. 12, q. 1, para. 5, cited in Blamires and Marx, "Woman Not to Preach." The text is not yet edited.

41. See the chapter on "The Preachers and Beguine Spirituality," in McDonnell's *The Beguines,* 341–61.

42. McDonnell catalogues the distinguished preachers who participated, including Geoffrey of Beaulieu, confessor and biographer to Louis IX, recorded as preaching for the beguines of Paris in the early 1270s. Much of our information comes from the famous collection of Pierre de Limoges.

43. The collection of Pierre de Limoges, for example, contains fragments of two homilies by the mistress of the Paris beguinage. See McDonnell, *The Beguines,* 343, and for the New Devout, see Thom Mertens, "Collatio und Codex im Bereich der *Devotio moderna,*" in *Der Codex im Gerbrauch,* ed. Christel Meier, Dagmar Hupper, and Hagen Keller (Munich: Wilhelm Fink, 1996), 163–82.

44. "Erat in oppido Bruxellensi eo tempore . . . mulier quaedam perversi dogmatis, dicta vulgariter Bloemardinne, tantae famae et opinionis ut etaim tempore sacrae communionis, quando videlicet ad aram accederet, inter duos gradi seraphim crederetur. Haec multa scribens de spiritu libertatis et nefandissimo amore venereo, quem et seraphicum appellabat, tanquam inventrix novae doctrinae a multis suae opinionis discipulis venerabatur. Sedebat quippe docens et scribens in sede argentea: quae quidem sedes, ob suae opinionis redolentiam, post ejus obitum ducissae Brabantiae fuisse dicitur praesentata. . . . Expertus enim de testimonio, quod scripta illa nefandissima taliter fuere prima facie veritatis specie supervestita, quod nemo possit erroris deprehendere seminarium, nisi per Illius gratiam et auxilium qui docet omnem veritatem" (cited in McDonnell, *The Beguines,* 494–95, from *Analecta Bollandiana* [Paris-Brussels, 1882], 4:286).

45. McDonnell, *The Beguines*, 341–61.

46. See J. M. M. H. Thijssen, *Censure and Heresy at the University of Paris, 1200–1400* (Philadelphia: University of Pennsylvania Press, 1998).

47. See the discussion of Godfrey as approbator by Kent Emery in his introduction to *The Mirror of Simple Souls*, trans. Edmund Colledge, J. C. Marler, and Judith Grant (Notre Dame, Ind.: University of Notre Dame Press, 1999), x.

48. See Kerby-Fulton, "Prophecy and Suspicion."

49. See Renate Blumenfeld-Kosinski, "Satirical Views of the Beguines in Northern French Literature," in *New Trends in Feminine Spirituality: The Holy Women of Liège and Their Impact*, ed. J. Dor and Jocelyn Wogan-Browne (Turnhout: Brepols, 1998), 1–14.

50. For bibliography and further discussion, see my "When Women Preached."

51. Translated by McDonnell, *The Beguines*, 524, from Fredericq, *Corpus documentorum Inquisitionis Haereticae pravitatis Neerlandicae*, I, 167–68, no. 171.

52. Ed. Joyce Bazire and E. Colledge (Oxford: Blackwell, 1957). On textual matters see also G. B. de Soer, "The Relationship of the Latin Versions of Ruysbroeck's 'Die Geestelike Brulocht' to 'The Chastising of God's Children,'" *Mediaeval Studies* 21 (1959): 128–46.

53. I have emended this reading, following the logic of Bazire and Colledge's own doubts about their reading here. All manuscripts except one read "disseit" and the word is used again in the same context at 145:15–16. See Bazire and Colledge's textual 145 n. 3.

54. See Lerner, *Free Spirit*, 195–99.

55. For further discussion of this passage in the context of the *Chastising* author's often confident attitudes towards his readers, see Steven Justice's perceptive essay in the present volume. The *Chastising* author's work as a "professional reader" on behalf of his audience is an extremely complex subject; on such see Kerby-Fulton, *Books under Suspicion*.

56. Jan Van Ruusbroec, *Die Geestelike Brulocht*, ed. J. Alaerts, Corpus Christianorum Continuatio Mediaevalis 103 (Turnhout: Brepols, 1988), p. 561: b2499–2501.

57. *Gerardi Magni Opera Omnia: Ioannis Rusbroachii, Ornatus Spiritualis Desponsationis*, ed. Rijcklof Hofman, Corpus Christianorum Continuatio Mediaevalis 172 (Turnhout: Brepols, 2000), p. 203: 32–39–41.

58. See Sargent, "The Transmission by the English," 228–29.

59. See especially J. P. H. Clark, "Walter Hilton and the 'Liberty of Spirit,'" *Downside Review* 96 (1978): 61–78; and Clark's "Late Fourteenth-Century Cambridge Theology." One of Hilton's more interesting associations with continental faculty visiting Cambridge appears in his translation of Luis de Fontibus's *Eight Chapters on Perfection*, which deals, among other things, with Free Spiritism. Luis was present in Cambridge in 1383, and perhaps again sometime between 1391–94 (see Clark, "Late Fourteenth-Century Cambridge Theology," 5–6). On Hilton and Free Spiritism see also Steven Justice's essay in the present volume.

60. Two, as mentioned above, were the chancellor and his successor.

61. See Hudson, "The Examination of Lollards," in *Lollards and Their Books*, 125–40.

62. In 1389, books by Olivi had been confiscated at Oxford (see note 10 above). Trefnant or his advisors may have suspected Olivian beguinism, partly because of the philogynist slant of Brut's "priesthood of all believers" position.

63. See note 10 above on Henry.

64. Fols. 197r–233v. On Henry's Cambridge career, see Clark, "Late Fourteenth-Century Cambridge Theology," 13.

65. For the substantial list of extant and attested manuscripts of his Apocalypse commentary, see Sharpe, *Handlist*, 166.

66. As we see, for instance, with Godfrey's startling support of Porete.

67. Harley 31, fol. 202v.

68. Tanner, *Church in Late Medieval Norwich*, 166.

69. See Leff, *Heresy*, 195–230, on the beliefs of the Olivian beguines and on Na Prous Boneta. Her testimony can be found in translation in Elizabeth Petroff, ed., *Medieval Women's Visionary Literature* (Oxford: Oxford University Press, 1986), 284–90.

70. See Leff, *Heresy*, 313–15.

71. The best study to date mentioning Free Spirit contamination of Lollardy is Anne Hudson, "A Lollard Mass," in *Lollards and Their Books*, 111–24. Hudson also mentions cases of unmixed Free Spiritism in England. For the Joachite connections, see Kerby-Fulton, "Prophecy and Suspicion."

SEVEN

The Wycliffite Woman

Reading Women in Fifteenth-Century Bohemia

ALFRED THOMAS

One of the most original and witty works in medieval Czech literature is the Catholic satire known as *Viklefice* (*The Wycliffite Woman*), a copy of which survives in an early fifteenth-century manuscript in the library of the south Bohemian town of Třeboň (MS A 7, leaf 155).[1] Both the form *Viklefice* and its variant *Viklefka*, which occurs several times in the same text, are derived from the proper name of the Oxford theologian John Wyclif (1330?–1384)[2] whose works were widely disseminated in and around the University of Prague (founded 1348). In fact, several important Wyclif manuscripts are extant only in Prague, having been copied by Czech students at Oxford and brought back to Bohemia. By the early fifteenth century some of these works had been translated or adapted into Czech, for example, Jacobellus de Stříbro's version of the *Dialogus* (1415), the *Trialogus,* and *De Civili Dominio* which were translated at much the same time.[3]

Writing more than sixty years ago, the Czech scholar Jan Vilikovský maintained that *The Wycliffite Woman* was aimed at the female followers of Wyclif or at least those Bohemian women who were associated with his heretical teachings.[4] In this essay I shall question this assumption and suggest that the poem does not necessarily reflect the experience of real women in a direct fashion, as Vilikovský asserts, but rather mediates between standard clerical anti-feminist rhetoric and the specific social reality of fifteenth-century Bohemian women. In this sense, the poem can serve as a paradigm of the general difficulty of "reading women" in the Middle Ages, that is to say, of differentiating between women as objects of male writing and as reading subjects in their

280 VOICES IN DIALOGUE

own right. This problem is as acute for the Bohemian context as it is for England or anywhere else in the early fifteenth century. Almost all the available sources concerning female literacy involve men writing specifically for a female audience of listeners (such as John Hus or Thomas of Štítné) or secondhand accounts of women as readers and writers (such as *The Little Books*, a work purportedly written in Czech by an anonymous woman defending Hus against the Antichrist).[5] It has recently been shown that Queen Sophie's letters to the anti-pope John XXIII and the College of Cardinals protesting against the prohibition of Wyclif's books in Bohemia were probably student exercises in the *ars dictaminis* rather than direct products of female authorship. Ironically, the only extant evidence we have of women readers and writers in fifteenth-century Bohemia are the letters of two Catholic noblewomen, Agnes and Perchta of Rožmberk.[6]

Ultimately, then, widespread evidence of women as readers of heretical texts is hard to come by. In making the claim that the female readership of such texts says more about orthodox fantasies about wayward women than it does about real women, I argue that the conventional view of Hussitism as a refuge for independent-minded women readers is probably exaggerated and may in part derive from a Protestant bias in Czech historiography. One can trace it from the nineteenth-century writings of František Palacký through T. G. Masaryk's influential view that the true meaning of Czech history has been its unchanging commitment to the humanist values of truth, tolerance, and democracy. Typical of this teleological view of Czech history is Anna Císařová-Kolářová's pioneering study *Woman in the Hussite Movement* (1915).[7] In claiming that Hussitism appealed to all Bohemian women, regardless of rank, her monograph perhaps tells us more about twentieth-century notions of nationalism than it does about the real conditions of late medieval religious life. Close attention to the available medieval sources suggests that the situation of Bohemian women was altogether more complicated than has often been assumed and that it is not so easy to generalize about female lay literacy. For one thing, what does "literacy" actually amount to in a pre-modern culture in which private reading was far less common than group listening, and group listening less common than "visual literacy"? As in England at about the same time, it seems that the majority of Bohemian women were largely accustomed to listening rather than reading (whether in large or small groups) and were strongly attracted to the traditional veneration of holy images.[8] Moreover, the Hussites certainly did not hold a monopoly on writing and preaching for the female laity. The Bohemian Dominicans had been writing specifically for women (whether as nuns or layfolk, in Latin and the vernacular) since the thirteenth century and continued to do so until the Hussite wars put an end to their activities.

I begin a more detailed consideration of these questions by providing a complete and new rhymed translation of *The Wycliffite Woman* with a literal prose translation in the appendix.

The Wycliffite Woman: Text

Harken to this wondrous tale
of how a squire, young and hale,
was summoned by a Wycliffite
to visit her quite late at night
and study everything that's right.   5

She told the scholar: "Come to me,
but do so very quietly.
Then I will teach you what is true,
and if you follow what I do,
I'll show the gospels, Old and New."   10

The young lord said without delay:
"I'll come to your house straight away."
Ever anxious to be better,
he promised faithfully to let her
teach him Scripture to the letter.   15

Eager now to be his keeper,
the Wycliffite urged him deeper:
"Come to me without a sound
when there is no one far around
and I'll disclose what I have found."   20

Whereupon she said good-bye
with certain knowledge he'd comply.
And sure enough, when all was dead,
he came to her with furtive tread
on Sunday after each had fed.   25

"Welcome, my most beloved guest,"
so she cried with joy and zest,
"For whom my soul has deeply yearned,
for whom my heart has fiercely burned!
Come in and hear what I have learned."   30

"Please sit down and rest a bit,
while I reveal the Holy Writ.

As you will pretty soon discern,
Holy Scripture's your concern:
it's up to you to try and learn."   35

Here the wench revealed the Book
to the boy's delighted look:
two lovely chapters round and bare,
each one delicious like a pear,
and in his eyes so very fair.   40

The eager youth stood up and cried:
"Just give them here, my precious bride!"
And out he took his scholar's quill
and studied Scripture to his fill
until the sun rose past the hill.   45

And when he glimpsed the light of day,
the boy prepared to slip away.
But now the woman grasped his sleeve,
and said: "Before you take your leave,
there're still the matins, I believe."   50

How joyous was their parting song
as well befits this courtly throng

.   .   .   .

.   .   .   .

ascending to the treble clef.   55

And when the matins had been sung
they said farewell with joyful tongue.
In the love they each other bore
there was no anger that I saw
but more bliss than the night before.   60

And therefore, pages fair and bold,
take courage from the tale I've told.
If you should wish to find the light
you must consult a Wycliffite
and study with her every night.   65

For no one knows the Book as well—
from Genesis to Daniel;
the Song of Songs she can recite.
A priest is not so erudite!
So serve her like a faithful knight.   70

Her expositions, sweet and clear,
resound like music in your ear.
Whoever serves this learned wife
will never know the pain of strife.
God make her fruitful all her life!   75

The Wycliffite Woman: Context

The Wycliffite Woman was composed in a society in which orthodoxy was already on the defensive and heresy in the ascendancy. In distinction to the early years of Lancastrian rule in England, the situation in Bohemia was highly unstable. Four years after Hus's execution at Constance in 1415, the death of King Wenceslas IV (r. 1378–1419) ushered in a seventeen-year interregnum in which the Hussite reformers would control the reins of government and manage to repel and defeat successive papal and imperial armies sent to eradicate the Bohemian heresy. Within Bohemia itself, Catholic churches were being sacked and razed to the ground and monasteries plundered, while clerics—both secular and monastic—lost their livelihoods and sometimes even their lives.

A Czech poem of lament, extant in a manuscript from the Rajhrad Monastery, expresses this situation very eloquently.[9] Written from the standpoint of a dispossessed cleric (perhaps a monk of the Rajhrad Monastery itself), this text utilizes the genre of complaint literature to show how the Catholics had become outsiders, their parishes robbed and burnt by "Wycliffites" (*Viklefuov,* line 5). The anonymous author reserves special censure for those women (lines 45–46) who have led men to adopt such heretical ideas in the first place. Clearly the sentiments of this poem are rooted in bitter experience and considerable suffering, although misogynistic fantasy intrudes by unreasonably blaming women for the catastrophe that has been visited upon the land.

The Wycliffite Woman belongs to the same tradition of blaming women for a difficult political situation. Yet its tone is much more tongue-in-cheek and witty. It takes the form of a mock-courtly dawn poem in which a female follower of the English reformer lures a young squire to her house under cover of darkness to seduce him with vernacular readings from the Scriptures. Cleverly subverting the *loci communes* of the *aubade* in which the lover secretly visits his lady at sunset and leaves her shortly before dawn, the satire consists of a series of double-entendres which equate lay learning with female promiscuity and illicit scriptural readings with casual sex. The anonymous author is here drawing upon and conflating two genres which were especially popular in fourteenth- and early fifteenth-century Latin and vernacular rhymed verse: the anti-feminist satire, exemplified by the poem "The Beguines," and the courtly love lyric such as the Czech "Radiant Day."[10] That our anonymous author is evidently at home with the conventions of the love lyric is made clear by formulaic lines such as "so serve her like a faithful knight" (70) as well as its dialogic alternation between a woman and a student which parodies the Bohemian Latin lyric "Filia, si vox tua" and its Czech variant "Dear Scholar" in which a virgin (*virgo*) and a cleric (*clericus*) express their illicit love for each other.[11]

In the course of the poem, which takes place on a "holiday such as this" (probably the sabbath), the female follower of Wyclif assumes the false role of preacher and priest, displaying her lovely white breasts in a gesture reminiscent of the sacerdotal ritual of revealing the open gospels or raising the Host to the congregation during the celebration of the Mass. To all intents and purposes, then, the poem would appear to be a standard anti-feminist satire on the audacious desire of religious women to usurp the roles of preacher and priest, functions denied them by St. Paul himself and given elaborate doctrinal justification in Catholic writings dating back to Peter Lombard's *Libri Sententiarum*, which around 1223/7 had been established as the dominant textbook in the Parisian faculty of theology.[12] Like those writings, our satire draws upon an equally long-standing trope of the text as a body and the association of erroneous teachings with the sinful snares of the female body and preaching with prostitution, which culminated in orthodox polemics against the Waldensian heresy of the twelfth and thirteenth centuries.[13] The association between the female and the heretical became particularly acute in late fourteenth- and early fifteenth-century Bohemia and England, where reformist women were frequently associated by the authorities with the desire to preach and even usurp the role of the priest, as the official deposition of the Lollard Walter Brut in October 1393 makes clear.[14]

This association has its origins in the biblical myth of the Garden of Eden in which Eve attracts Adam with the forbidden fruit of the Tree of Knowledge, a detail that finds an explicit parallel in the pear-like breasts which the Wycliffite Woman offers to the young lad. Complicating this straightforward assessment of the Czech poem as an anti-feminist tract is the deployment of the love lyric as the generic vehicle of the satire. If the Wycliffite Woman's active agency as a seducer of men and as a reader of the Bible is a parody of normative gender behavior, it equally parodies the passive status of the lady expecting the arrival of her lover-knight in the lyric. Although she awaits the young man at home, it is made clear at the opening of the poem that the Wycliffite Woman instigates the visit. Underlining the visitor's passive role is the term *panic* (unmarried young lord). Its frequent attestation in the poem (six times) suggests that the author wishes to emphasize the passive, "feminized" status of the male visitor. The same word is used by the female speaker in the Czech religious lyric "A Bundle of Myrrh"—a paraphrase of chapter three of the Song of Songs—to refer to the beloved whom she seeks at midnight (line 27). Here the speaker of the poem is identified with the female-associated Soul (*anima*) in quest of her virginal Bridegroom Christ:

Arising I will go and seek him,
I will ask for him for whom my heart faints,
saying: beloved,
my love,
show me your face, little falcon.[15]

Such affective language is mimicked by the Wycliffite Woman when she greets her visitor:

"Welcome, my most beloved guest,"
so she cried with joy and zest,
"For whom my soul has deeply yearned,
for whom my heart has fiercely burned!
Come in and hear what I have learned."

These lines also parody the eucharistic Czech "Prayer of Kunhuta" (c. 1290), written for the private devotions of Princess Kunhuta, abbess of the St. George Convent at the Prague Castle, in which the Soul welcomes the beloved Christ as he descends in the form of the Host at the Mass:

Welcome, almighty king,
In all places all-seeing,
All penitents loving,
Eternal life giving![16]

The satirical function of *The Wycliffite Woman* was far from unique in fifteenth-century Bohemia. For example, the beginning of the Gospel of St. Matthew is given an explicit parodic form in an anti-Hussite Latin satire from the early fifteenth century and popularly known as *The Wycliffite Mass*.[17] The list enumerates the most prominent academic followers of the Hussite heresy in Bohemia and concludes with the regret that the errors have now spread from the literati (those with a knowledge of Latin) to the laity and the hope that their eyes will be illuminated with the truth.[18]

Although religious parody was meant to generate a humorous reaction, it would also seem to signal anxiety about the unstable relation of orthodoxy to heresy in early fifteenth-century Bohemia. Concerns about appropriate religious and gender roles are exemplified by the Wycliffite Woman assuming the active role of the priest in the Mass, and, by implication, the authority of Christ himself. This suggestion is reinforced by the fact that the "service" she performs takes place on a Sunday. It is because she appears to usurp the authority of Christ and his Church in this way that the Wycliffite Woman becomes synonymous with the name of Wyclif, which had become a byword in Bohemia for heretical teachings on a whole range of doctrinal issues from the sacramental problem of the Eucharist to the disputed authority of the pope and his bishops. The poem's conflation of Wyclif's reputation for heretical teachings and the conventional association of wayward women with sexual promiscuity is, of course, part of its satirical *pointe* in equating old ideas about gender with new ideas about heresy.

By the time of Hus's exile from Prague (1412) Wycliffism and Hussitism had become more or less synonymous in Bohemia. Hus himself seems to have taken a special interest in the spiritual welfare of his female congregation. While in exile he even wrote a work in Czech specifically for his female followers at the Bethlehem Chapel, *The Daughter,* so named since each of its ten chapters begins with the words of the bridal psalm 44:11 "Audi filia" (Listen, my daughter):

> Audi filia et vide et inclina aurem tuam et obliviscere populi tui et domus patris tui et concupiscet rex decorem tuum quia ipse est dominus tuus.

> Listen, my daughter, hear my words and consider them: forget your own people and your father's house: and, when the king desires your beauty, remember that he is your lord.[19]

The wording of the psalm is significant here in inviting the female addressee to forget her family and prepare herself for her impending marriage. In the same way, Hus's tract addresses the daughters of the Bohemian gentry and aristocracy who had left their fathers' households and chosen to live together in the service of their celestial husband, Christ. The reference in the psalm to the king desiring the daughter's beauty inevitably recalls the erotic content of *The Wycliffite Woman,* thus reinforcing its topicality as an anti-heretical satire. But more significant still is the fact that Hus's invocation of the bridal psalm was not original at all but derived from orthodox tradition. The biblical verses were familiar from the liturgy for the Assumption of the Blessed Virgin Mary and also evoked the Presentation of the Virgin in the Temple, the archetypal scene of monastic enclosure for women.

A good visual example of the latter is the *Buch der Ersetzung* by the fifteenth-century German Dominican Johannes Meyer, which was transcribed and illustrated by nuns at the Dominican Katharinenkloster in Nuremberg shortly after 1455.[20] The full-page drawing of the friar high in his pulpit and the enclosed sisters in miniature below him in many ways parallels the familiar image of Hus preaching to the laity at the Bethlehem Chapel from the *Jena Codex*, a manuscript compiled about fifty years later than the *Buch der Ersetzung*. The crucial point here is that Hus's use of the verses from the bridal psalm does not offer a unique or unprecedented case of writing for women but partakes of a long-standing orthodox tradition. The language of initiation into monastic enclosure has simply been appropriated for lay purposes. This would explain the ironic reference in *The Wycliffite Woman* to the young man's desire to join the lady's "order" (*zákon*, line 15).

Although the Hussite deployment of the official liturgy is being mocked in *The Wycliffite Woman*, the rhetorical affinity between the monastic and lay spheres must have caused considerable alarm for the Catholic authorities, since the heretics were seen to be stealing the initiative in appealing to the laity with the language of traditional devotion. This was a particular concern for the Dominicans, one of whose principal aims, since the foundation of their Order, had been to wrest female members of the urban laity from the clutches of heretical preaching and bring them back into the orthodox fold.

Just as Hus's rhetorical practice was unoriginal, so was his habit of addressing the female laity in Czech neither novel nor revolutionary. Since the second half of the fourteenth century the Czech language had been deployed to serve both the needs of the church authorities and their critics. The verse *Life of Saint Procopius* (c. 1350s) and the verse *Life of Saint Catherine* (c. 1360–75), both written in Czech, exemplify this struggle for the hearts and minds of the laity. The latter, in particular, would have appealed to a female audience on account of the courtly setting and affective imagery it employs. By the 1370s the competition for the devotion of the laity had moved into the pulpit with the Dominican friar John Milíč of Kroměříž preaching his reformist sermons in German and Czech from the Church of St. Giles in Prague. His virulent attacks on the concupiscence of the Church paved the way for the more radical sermons of Hus and his followers in the next century.

On the whole, the religious split at the University of Prague (of which Hus became rector) was divided along ethnic and linguistic lines: the German masters aligned themselves with orthodoxy, while the Czech students identified with Wycliffite heresy. One celebrated marginal comment to a Wyclif manuscript copied by Hus in 1398 reads: "Germans haha; out—out!"[21] And, indeed, following the royal decree of Kutná Hora in 1409, which gave an effective majority vote to the *nacio bohemica* in the administration of the University of Prague, most German masters and students left the city, eventually to found a new university at Leipzig.[22]

In Bohemia Wyclif was perceived as an advocate of the use of the vernacular, probably because of the so-called Wyclif Bible. As Anne Hudson reminds us, it was John Hus who made the claim that Wyclif translated the whole Bible into English (*per Anglicos dicitur*), although the charge was rarely made by Wyclif's own countrymen.[23] Thus the anonymous poet of *The Wycliffite Woman* was probably equating the name of

Wyclif not only with dangerous heretical ideas but also with the reading of the vernacular Bible. Having enticed the squire to her house, the Wycliffite Woman refers specifically to reading the Bible.

To what extent was this fear of women reading and disputing Holy Scripture an imaginary anxiety on the part of men in authority and to what extent was it rooted in social reality? By the beginning of the fifteenth century, female lay access to the Bible and other religious works was no longer limited to the immediate royal family, an illustrious tradition represented by the *Passional of Kunhuta* (early fourteenth century) and Anne of Bohemia's apparent possession of the New Testament in Czech, German, and Latin, an astonishing case of female lay literacy that Wyclif mentions in his *De Triplici Vinculo Amoris* and which his Lollard followers were quick to exploit to justify their own desire to read the Scriptures in English.[24] The connection between Wyclif and Queen Anne has led English scholars to regard the latter as the "grandmother of the English Reformation."[25] This claim patently ignores the queen's immaculate orthodox credentials and erroneously assumes that female lay literacy was automatically reformist. In fact, there is a great deal of evidence that female lay literacy in Bohemia was not limited to the followers of John Hus. Perhaps the most vocal female correspondent in fifteenth-century Bohemia was the Catholic noblewoman Perchta of Rožmberk, who corresponded with her father and brothers as a way of making public her unhappy arranged marriage with the Moravian magnate John of Lichtenstein.[26]

At the same time, however, it cannot be denied that certain aristocratic Bohemian women *were* attracted to the teachings of Wyclif and Hus. One such woman was Agnes, daughter of the prolific lay writer and nobleman Thomas of Štítné, who translated devotional works from Latin for the benefit of his family and his immediate circle in the south of Bohemia. After her father's death in 1401, Agnes of Štítné left her provincial home and went to live in Prague where she became an adherent of the Hussite reform movement and a frequent visitor to the Bethlehem Chapel, founded in 1393 for the purpose of preaching in the Czech language and by this time a hotbed of heretical ideas.

It was perhaps the activities of such women as Agnes of Štítné that the anonymous author of *The Wycliffite Woman* had in mind in his depiction of a virago not content to play the passive role of lady in the dawn poem but bent upon assuming the active role of preacher and even the sacerdotal function. Whether Bohemian women of the reformist persuasion ever went thus far or were encouraged to do so by their male leaders is a moot point. Certainly, there is very little evidence to support such an audacious claim in either England or Bohemia.[27] It is more likely that even high-born Bohemian women of the reformist persuasion were expected to play a passive role as listeners rather than as readers or preachers by their conservative-minded brethren. Hus's own writings suggest that his social views on class and gender were conventional as his famous letter "To His Friends in Bohemia" from prison in Constance, dated 10 June 1415, clearly demonstrates.[28] Even his benevolent work *The Daughter* insists on traditional notions of monastic obedience to authority and assumes that women's natural tendency is to be sinful. Moreover, if we look at representations of women in the fifteenth-century Hussite *Jena Codex*, women feature in polarized positive *and* negative terms as the eager listeners of Hus's sermons in the Bethlehem Chapel and as the lascivious entourage of a corrupt and sinful pope.

That Hus's female supporters were playing a less active role than their Catholic critics attributed to them tells us, I suspect, as much about orthodox male fantasies projected onto women as it does about the actual status of historical women. After all, the association of preaching with prostitution, as personified by Mary Magdalene who allegedly preached of Christ's resurrection to his disciples, was itself a product of traditional Catholic teaching.[29] Ironically, it was the most fervently anti-heretical spokesmen of this tradition, the Dominican friars, who idealized the Magdalene as the *apostolorum apostola* in one breath and excoriated women preachers in the next. In his *De eruditione praedicatorum*, the Dominican sermon-writer Humbert of Romans (d. 1277) provides four reasons why women should not preach, one of them being that, in doing so, they provoke lust. Seen in this light, the scene of seduction played out between the male virgin and the Wycliffite Woman may be regarded as a fantasy originating in the male, clerical imagination. Since many Czech texts of orthodox devotion had been written by Dominicans in the fourteenth century—including the parable of Christ-as-Knight *De strenuo milite* by the court theologian Kolda of Koldice—it is not inconceivable that *The Wycliffite Woman* is the work of a mendicant friar eager to appropriate the genre of social satire in the larger fight against the heretics.

By the late fourteenth and early fifteenth centuries, as Anne Hudson has shown with respect to English at this period, writing in the vernacular was becoming the most effective way of enjoining the support of the laity in the struggle against the heretical ideas of the Lollards.[30] Among such devotional works are Nicholas Love's *Mirror of the Blessed Jesus Christ*, a loose adaptation of the pseudo-Bonaventuran *Meditationes Vitae Christi*, which was officially endorsed by Archbishop Arundel for use against the Lollard movement, and the Middle English Pseudo-Augustinian *Soliloquies* (dated between 1365 and 1425) which has an anti-Wycliffite commentary attached to it.[31]

Yet even orthodox works that purported to ignore Wycliffite ideas altogether sometimes seem to blur the distinction between "orthodox" and "heretical." One such example is the late fourteenth-century Middle English *Book to a Mother*, which, in the words of Anne Clark Bartlett and Thomas Bestul, "weaves together strands of virulent clerical antifeminism against a generous, even remarkable validation of the female intellect."[32] It is at such moments that this scrupulously orthodox text begins to read like an apology for women's right to read the Bible: "And you can better learn Holy Writ than can any Master of Divinity who loves God less than you do; for whoever loves God best understands Holy Writ best."[33] When the Wycliffite Woman lures the young lord to her house, it is precisely this privileged female access to the ultimate understanding of Holy

Writ that she repeatedly invokes in lines 10, 20, and 31. If our Czech poem is a parody, it would also appear to be mimicking orthodox as well as heterodox sentiments about women's right to read—and ability to comprehend—the Scriptures.

Another aspect of *The Wycliffite Woman* that mediates between the orthodox anti-feminism and social reality is the setting of the lady's home as a secret place to hold illicit services and as a house of ill repute in which the Wycliffite Woman is simultaneously a madame procuress and a prostitute seductress. By 1415 there were at least eighteen lay houses in Prague where beguines gathered together for a life of prayer and good works.[34] As the Czech satirical poem "The Beguines" makes clear, such women were held in great suspicion by orthodox writers and were believed to be readers of the vernacular Bible, an association that dates back to the early fourteenth century when the beghards and beguines of Languedoc and Catalonia were exposed to works written in the local languages of the region.[35] The author of this satire makes the point that these women are argumentative, gossipy, and have no Latin.[36]

The proverbial equation of women with gossip is important for an understanding of the seduction of the young man in *The Wycliffite Woman*, especially when the lady insists that he come to her house "very quietly" (line 7) and after dark when no one is around (line 19). Here again there is a convergence between the deviant practice of women (gossip) and the orthodox practice of priests who hear confession. Seen in this light, the Wycliffite Woman's secretive invitation to the young lord assumes a parodic resemblance to the sacrament of the sinner going to church to make confession. As Karma Lochrie puts it in her book *Covert Operations:* "Confession and gossip are closer in nature than the medieval church would have liked, in spite of the elaborate system of regulations it devised for the sacrament following the Fourth Lateran Council."[37]

When Agnes of Štítné moved to Prague in the fall of 1401, she established a household next to the Bethlehem Chapel for herself and other unmarried young ladies of the reformist persuasion. However, the idea of worshipping and reading religious texts in a domestic space was hardly initiated by heretics. In early fifteenth-century Bohemia there was obviously no need for the reformers to conceal their beliefs behind closed doors, as the frequent attendance of Agnes of Štítné and her lay sisters at the Bethlehem Chapel demonstrates. In fact, the idea of worshipping in secret has its origins in the words of Jesus in the Sermon on the Mount (Matt. 6:6):

> Tu autem cum orabis intra in cubiculum tuum et cluso ostio tuo ora Patrem tuum in abscondito et Pater tuus qui videt in abscondito reddet tibi.

> But when you pray, go into a room by yourself, shut the door, and pray to your Father who is there in the secret place; and your Father who sees what is secret will reward you.[38]

This scriptural precedent became a topos deeply embedded in the most orthodox of medieval saints' lives. For example, the fourteenth-century Czech *Life of St. Catherine of Alexandria*—a text scrupulously orthodox in tone and content—depicts the eponymous virgin-martyr locking herself into her private chamber and praying before an image of the Virgin Mary and the Christ child at the instigation of her hermit-counselor:

> This is a painting of the young Lord, whom I told you about with His mother. Take the picture and go home with your mother. When you are in your room lock yourself in and kneel humbly before this picture, raise your eyes to heaven and earnestly request this dear lovely, most radiant and gracious virgin reveal her son to you.[39]

Having complied with the hermit's advice, Catherine weeps copiously before the image in her chamber and eventually falls asleep, whereupon she has a vision of her celestial bridegroom, Jesus, who is described as a "beautiful" courtly lover and sings to her "in an appealing, sweet, precious voice":[40]

> Welcome, my most precious one! Welcome, my lovely bride! Come here to me, little face that I have chosen, my dear little dove.[41]

This feminized description of Jesus and his sung epithalamium (with its obvious echo of the Song of Songs) recalls the portrayal and greeting of the Wycliffite Woman. In this sense, the entire poem can be seen as a parodic inversion of the traditional monastic ritual of enclosure with the Wycliffite Woman playing the part of the Bridegroom Christ and her young visitor cast in the role of the celestial Bride. Moreover, the eucharistic association of the Wycliffite Woman's welcome to her beloved visitor would reinforce the parody of monastic practice. Significant in this connection is the well-known Hussite insistence on communicating in both kinds (*sub utraque specie*) and their reverence for the chalice. Although *The Wycliffite Woman* is parodying the heretics' appropriation of liturgical and monastic language in this instance, the parody itself signals authorial anxiety at the dangerous proximity of Hussite to orthodox discourse.

Another way in which *The Wycliffite Woman* elicits anxiety is the spectral threat of the "priest's wife," the repressed tradition in the early Church of allowing priests to marry. Dyan Elliott has discussed how the desire of the Church during the eleventh century to broaden the gap between the clergy and the laity resulted in the "erasure of the female," a process whereby sacerdotal wives were banished to the margins of society.[42] Elliott goes on to show how subsequent *vitae* of married saints struggled to discredit their spouses. In some cases, priests' wives were elided altogether, a good example being the fourteenth-century Czech prose *Life of St. Procopius,* the work of an anonymous Dominican friar writing at the behest of Emperor Charles IV.

The historical Procopius, founder and abbot of the Monastery of St. John and the Virgin Mary on the Sázava River, had been a married nobleman with a son. All of these aspects are excluded in the prose account of his life with the saint emerging as a poor celibate preacher, an ideal role-model for the mendicant orders. However, the pre-reformist verse life of the same saint, written around the middle of the fourteenth century, includes a direct reference to the abbot's son and thus tacitly alludes to his marital status.

In early fifteenth-century Bohemia (and England) there was increasing clamor in reformist circles for the reinstatement of married clergy. The eponymous Wycliffite Woman can be seen as an embodiment of this clamor as well as a reincarnation of ancient ecclesiastical fears for the preservation of the priest's unique authority over—and superiority to—the laity.

As Dyan Elliott has persuasively argued, the repressed motif of the "priest's wife" returned to haunt the late medieval Church in the Freudian "splitting" of women into good and bad polarities.[43] The good imago was personified as the Virgin Mary while the bad imago became increasingly identified with the female desecrator or thief of the Host, a denigrated role that was often conflated with the misconduct of witches and Jews. We have a crucial example of this female splitting in the representation of the Wycliffite Woman. When she offers her bare breasts to her young visitor, her gesture echoes the Marian function of lactation as well as the sinful invitation to commit fornication: the roles of the intercessor Mary and the seductress Eve are skillfully conflated in the same gesture.

As we suggested earlier, the proffering of the round white breasts to the young lad can also be seen as a mock-sacerdotal gesture of elevating the Host at the Mass. The anxiety about women denigrating the Host was related to the fear of Jews desecrating the eucharistic wafer. One way to explain this conflation of women with Jews is in the Freudian terms of projective inversion: male Christian doubts about the truth of transubstantiation are repressed by being attributed to the "Other" (women and Jews). An illustrative example of the use of parodic inversion to vilify Jews is the *Passio judaeorum secundum Johannes rusticus quadratus* (The Passion of the Jews According to John the Stocky Peasant), which concerns an alleged Host desecration in Prague in 1389.[44] The *passio* is a narrative in scriptural language evoking Christ's Passion. In the *Passio judaeorum* the genre assumes the form of a parody with the Jewish children of Prague cast as monstrous Christ killers and their elders as Pharisees: a Jewish boy throws a stone at a monstrance as it is being carried by a priest though the streets near the Jewish Quarter. This alleged incident provided the instigation for the wholesale persecution of Prague Jews, many of whom were murdered and/or lost their properties and livelihood in the ensuing disturbances.[45] The trope of parodic inversion deployed by the *Passion judaeorum* and *The Wycliffite Woman* recalls the vilification of women, Jews, and Germans in the Latin-Czech play *Unguentarius* (c. 1320–40s).[46] Although the use of parody was an indicator of ecclesiastical anxieties, it was by the same token an effective discursive tool to generate hatred of Jews, heretics, and women.

If *The Wycliffite Woman* may be said to mediate in an ambiguous fashion between clerical fears and heretical practices, it may also be said to mark a diachronic transition from high and late medieval connections between female sexuality and heresy to early modern associations of witchcraft with demonology. According to Dyan Elliott in her discussion of pollution, sexuality, and demonology in the Middle Ages, "woman's reproductive capacity rendered her additionally ripe for uncanny insemination.[47]

In the widely disseminated clerical stories of demonic offspring, women become the bodily agents of diabolical reproduction (the "demon seed") which usually takes place at night while the female victim is dreaming. An interesting variant on this theme is Marie de France's well-known courtly lai of *Yonec* about a beautiful young woman trapped in a sterile marriage. Elliott delineates this supernatural tale in the following way: "In her loneliness, she [the lady] fantasizes about the perfect lover, whereupon a huge bird flies through her window and promptly transforms itself into a handsome knight" (lines 91–115).[48] Although Marie's lai is subversive of clerical misogyny in presenting the fantasy in valorized terms, it resembles *The Wycliffite Woman* in conflating a clerical exemplum about the "demon seed" with a courtly narrative of illicit love and reveals the extent to which such master-plots could be recycled to serve the ideological interests of the author.

In the case of *The Wycliffite Woman*, the clerical motif of the "demon seed" is made explicit in the mock-aspiration in the final line of the poem that God should make female heretics fruitful. The point about this tongue-in-cheek conclusion is that it betrays deep-rooted clerical fears and fantasies of sinful women giving birth to monstrous offspring, fears that also animate the aforementioned *Wycliffite Mass* in which Wyclif is the progenitor of a long succession of Bohemian heretics. If this parodic inversion of Christ's descent from King David equates Wyclif with Antichrist, it also associates the English heresiarch's teachings with out-of-control female sexuality and procreation.

These misogynistic examples should suffice to make it clear that the wayward practices with which female heretics were identified did not necessarily derive from social reality but just as likely originated in orthodox writings. Discussing the literalism that the authorities condemned in the Englishwoman Margery Baxter, Rita Copeland makes the same crucial point with respect to anti-Wycliffite writings in England: "But the literalism that marks her hermeneutic as heretical is in essence the same literalism that the late medieval church encouraged in the form of affective devotion to images of Christ's life."[49]

As we have seen, *The Wycliffite Woman* fails to distinguish clearly between orthodox fantasies about women and the heretical practices of real women. Thus it complicates those very oppositions (men-women, orthodoxy-heresy) upon which its claim to truth is based. This begs the question: why does our anonymous author choose the courtly love lyric as the principal vehicle of his satire? What does its deployment in the ideological battle against Wycliffites tell us about the relationship between the court and the church in the early fifteenth century? After all, in the fourteenth century, many scrupulously orthodox texts, including several written in Czech, had employed courtly forms and motifs to make their religious message more palatable to an aristocratic audience, a good example being the aforementioned verse *Life of St. Catherine*, in which the virgin-martyr and her celestial spouse, Christ, are compared with the courtly lovers Tristan and Isolde.

Ever since the late thirteenth century, courtly and religious discourses had intermingled in Latin, German, and Czech texts composed in the Bohemian lands. German love poetry (*Minnesang*) and devotional Marian verse flourished at the court of Wenceslas II (1271–1305); and the Latin parable *De strenuo milite* and the Czech "Prayer of Kunhuta," both of which interweave courtly and religious motifs, were composed for the same king's sister in her capacity as abbess of the Benedictine Convent of St. George at the Prague Castle. This pro-courtly trend continued through the reigns of John of Luxembourg and Charles IV. But after the latter's death in 1378, the harmonious fusion of clerical and courtly discourses began to break down, a process that reflects the larger political and religious divisions in the reign of Charles's son, Wenceslas IV. Significantly, Wenceslas's second wife, Queen Sophie, became an enthusiastic adherent of the religious reform movement and appointed Hus as her personal confessor.[50] Sophie was also an enthusiastic reader: among her posthumous effects were discovered one book in German and ten in Czech, including a psalter, a copy of the satirical *Decalogue*, and a romance of the life of Alexander the Great.[51]

With this change in the religious complexion of the court, the traditionally close relationship between the church and the court was replaced by conflict and discord. Although this situation was instigated by the Schism of 1378, it was exacerbated by the new king's weak and vacillating policies. Largely due to Queen Sophie's influence, King Wenceslas supported the pro-reform party headed by Hus until the breakdown in civil order forced him to change sides and exile Hus from Prague in 1412. Although she was an adherent of Hus's teachings, which were generally critical of courtly activities like dancing and gambling, Sophie was not averse to the secular pleasures of courtly life. The German Bible commissioned by Wenceslas IV in the 1390s (hence known as the *Wenzelbibel*) is full of marginal courtly motifs such as lovers' knots and scenes of court life, in which the king is shown being bathed by his wife, depicted as a scantily clad bath attendant. In spite of scholars' attempts to explain these curiously mannerist and intimate images in the metaphorical terms of spiritual purification, their sexual explicitness and secular worldliness hardly seem appropriate as marginal illustrations of the Bible.[52] The curious juxtaposition of sacred text and secular imagery helps to provide the cultural context within which to read the strange fusion of anti-reformist and anti-courtly elements in *The Wycliffite Woman*.

The fact that courtly culture had previously served the ideological interests of orthodox writers in reinforcing orthodox female piety would explain the skill with which our anonymous author was able to deploy the love lyric as a weapon against the heretical opposition at the court. The alignment of the court with Hus and the reform party would also shed light on the reference to the court (*dvór*) in verse two of the eleventh strophe of the poem in connection with the singing of the *Te Deum* ("as befits that court"). The transformation of the love lyric from affective religious poem to satire implies a concomitant shift in the implied audience. Whereas the verse *Life of St. Catherine* was probably written for a court audience sympathetic to orthodox teachings, *The Wycliffite Woman* was more likely aimed at a non-courtly audience with the intention of inflicting as much damage as possible on the reformist elements which dominated it. This would explain the ironic apostrophe at the beginning of the thirteenth strophe to "fair pages" (*nádobné panoše*). Regarded in this light, the Wycliffite Woman might even be seen as a veiled allusion to Queen Sophie herself and her young lover, a reference to her malleable and apparently licentious husband Wenceslas IV.

Since the high Middle Ages clerical writers had traditionally attacked the excesses of court life and were especially troubled by the way courtly dress seemed to obliterate the distinctions between conventional gender roles. Knights were condemned for dressing in too feminine a fashion while ladies were mocked for following suit. As E. Jane Burns points out with regard to the attack on female courtly fashion by the French Dominican Gilles of Orleans in a sermon he delivered in 1273, clerical opprobrium could result in the absurd conclusion that women are simultaneously "too knightly and too seductive."[53] In *The Wycliffite Woman* we encounter a similar world turned topsy-turvy in which the lady seems to have assumed the traditional knightly role and the knight has become passively female. We can glimpse a similar disparagement of knightly pursuits in the boorish figures of Dietrich von Bern and his followers in the late fourteenth-century Czech version of the minstrel epic *Laurin*.[54] The risible figure of the eponymous dwarf-king Laurin may well have been intended as a satirical reference to Wenceslas IV, who at the time was engaged in a series of protracted military struggles with his disaffected magnates. The ending of the epic, in which the dwarf-king is vanquished and imprisoned by Dietrich and his fellow knights, would reinforce this parallel since Wenceslas more than once became the prisoner of his own victorious nobles.

In the fourteenth century, satirical literature had tended to function as a tool appropriated by those who perceived themselves in the margins of society to attack those at the center of power. The Catholic establishment had tended to harness genres such as the love lyric and the chivalric romance to instruct a courtly (and partially female) audience. Now the situation was reversed: the Catholics were no longer in the ascendancy at court and accordingly resorted to more popular broadsides to get their message across to a larger, non-courtly audience. The love lyric had now become a weapon to attack the court establishment rather than flatter it. As we have seen, the parodic deployment of the courtly love lyric in the name of anti-feminist clerical orthodoxy reverses the generic representation of the lady as passive and the knight as active by presenting the former as a sexual predator and the latter as her hapless victim. At the same time, the lady becomes a dangerous heretic whose ideas lead her young novice astray. In deploying the love lyric as an anti-feminist *and* anti-Wycliffite satire, the Catholic author has managed to target both the court and the heretical elements within it. His success in doing so is, however, an ironic testimony to the failure of orthodoxy and the success of the reform party in early fifteenth-century Bohemia.

Appendix: Literal Prose Translation of *The Wycliffite Woman*

It happened once upon a time,
Perhaps on such a holiday as this,
that a Wycliffite Woman
invited a young lord to her house,
wishing to teach him the true faith.   5

She said: "For Jesus' sake,
Come to me very quietly!
I wish to teach you the faith,
And if you want to listen,
I will reveal the Scriptures to you."   10

The lad answered the Wycliffite Woman
And looked at her lovingly,
Saying: "I am glad to do all
If you wish to teach me
And join your order."   15

The Wycliffite said: "Look at me,
My young lad, come to me
When all is still,
When no one is about and
I'll reveal the Holy Scriptures."   20

Without delay the lad
Did as she commanded.

After dinner on Sunday,
When the time was right,
He came to her quietly.   25

Eagerly the lady said:
"Welcome, my dear guest,
whom I have so long desired,
for whom my soul has yearned!
Please come in,   30

And sit with me for a while.
I wish to expostulate on the Scriptures,
And also the reading of the Bible.
You will find plenty
To keep you busy."   35

Here the hag laid out
Two chapters of the Bible,
Pretty and very round;
They were like pears
And also very white.   40

The lad said without fear:
"Give them here, my dear."
He began to examine the Bible
And interpret the chapters
From evening till dawn.   45

And when it began to grow light,
The lad was about to leave.
But the Wycliffite grabbed him
And said: "you must stay
And perform matins with me."   50

They began to sing a Te Deum
As befits that court.
. . . .
. . . .
and started to descant.   55

When they had finished the morning Mass,
They embraced each other nicely
In God's love and grace.
There was no anger
That I could detect.   60

Well, you young lords,
And you fair pages,
Who wish to join the order,
You must ask the beguines
And learn from them.   65

They are versed in the gospels,
The Book of Kings and Solomon,
And the Psalms of David
More than most priests.
You should serve them gladly.   70

They have sweet expositions,
Complete, and without fault.
Whoever lets himself be used by them
Will be very happy.
God grant them fecundity!   75

Notes

I would like to thank Miri Rubin, Fiona Somerset, and especially Dyan Elliott for their perceptive comments on an earlier version of this essay.

1. *Staročeská lyrika*, ed. Jan Vilikovský (Prague: Melantrich, 1940), 120–22.

2. For Wyclif's life and times, see K. B. McFarlane, *John Wycliffe and the Beginnings of Nonconformity* (London: English Universities Press, 1952).

3. See Maurice Keen, "The Influence of Wyclif," in *Wyclif in His Times*, ed. Anthony Kenny (Oxford: Oxford University Press, 1985), 127–45, 140. See also František Šmahel, "Doctor Evangelicus super omnes evangelistas: Wyclif's Fortunes in Hussite Bohemia," *Bulletin of the Institute for Historical Research* 43 (1970): 16–34, at 21.

4. Vilikovský, *Staroceská lyrika*, 191–92. For more up-to-date scholarship, see Jana Nechutová, "Ženy v Husově okolí. K protiženským satirám husitské doby," in *Jan Hus: Mezi epochami, národy a konfesemi*, ed. Jan Blahoslav Lášek (Prague, 1995), 68–73.

5. For more details of these secondhand claims, see Alfred Thomas, *Anne's Bohemia: Czech Literature and Society, 1310–1420*, Medieval Studies at Minnesota, vol. 13 (Minneapolis and London: University of Minnesota Press, 1998), 46–47.

6. For doubts about the authenticity of Queen Sophie's letters, see Božena Kopičková and Anežka Vidmanová, *Listy na Husovu obranu z let 1410–1412: Konec jedné legendy?* (Prague: Karolinum, 1999). See also John Klassen, *Warring Maidens, Captive Wives, and Hussite Maidens: Women and Men at War and at Peace in Fifteenth-Century Bohemia* (Boulder, Colo.: East European Monographs, 1999), 260 n. 24. For the Latin documents in question, see *Documenta Mag. Joannis Hus*, ed. František Palacký (Prague, 1869), 411–12, 413, 423, 424–25. See also *The Letters of the Rožmberk Sisters: Noblewomen in Fifteenth-Century Bohemia*, trans. John M. Klassen (Cambridge: D. S. Brewer, 2001).

7. Anna Císařová-Kolářová, *Zena v hnutí husitském* (Prague, 1915).

8. Although mediated through satirical male writing, it is worth citing the account of peasant women dropping to their knees and kissing the holy images of the cleric in *The Dispute between the Groom and the Scholar* (c. 1380). See *Staročeské satiry Hradeckého rukopisu a Smilovy školy*, ed. Josef Hrabák (Prague: Nakl, 1962), 122 (lines 255–62). See also Thomas, *Anne's Bohemia*, 146. For the importance of non-scriptural religion to lower-class woman in England, see Shannon McSheffrey, *Gender and Heresy: Women and Men in Lollard Communities, 1420–1530* (Philadelphia: University of Pennsylvania Press, 1995), 138. For the problem of defining "reading" in the later Middle Ages, see Joyce Coleman, *Public Reading and the Reading Public in Late Medieval England and France* (Cambridge: Cambridge University Press, 1996).

9. Vilikovský, *Staročeská lyrika*, 123–24.

10. Ibid., 118–19 and 58–60 (respectively).

11. Ibid., 68–69 (for the text of the Czech poem) and 83–84 (for information about the manuscript and the Latin source).

12. See A. J. Minnis "De impedimento sexus: Women's Bodies and Medieval Impediments to Sexual Ordination," in *Medieval Theology and the Natural Body*, ed. Peter Biller and A. J. Minnis, York Studies in Medieval Theology, vol. 1 (York: York Medieval Press, 1997), 109–39 (110 ff.)

13. See Beverly Mayne Kienze, "The Prostitute-Preacher: Patterns of Polemic against Medieval Waldensian Women Preachers," in *Women Preachers and Prophets through Two Millennia of Christianity*, ed. Beverly Mayne Kienzle and Pamela J. Walker (Berkeley: University of California Press, 1998), 99–113. For the clerical trope of the text as body, see *The Book and the Body*, ed. Dolores Warwick Frese and Katherine O'Brien O'Keeffe (Notre Dame, Ind.: University of Notre Dame Press, 1997).

14. Margaret Aston, *Lollards and Reformers: Images and Literacy in Late Medieval England* (London: Hambledon Press, 1984), 52. For more information concerning the alleged right of women to preach in the transcripts of Walter Brut's trial in 1391, see *Woman Defamed and Woman Defended: An Anthology of Medieval Texts*, ed. Alcuin Blamires (Oxford: Clarendon Press, 1992), 250–60. For Fiona Somerset's reassessment of the transcripts of Brut's trial and her important conclusions about the limited role of women in Lollardy, see her essay in this volume *"Eciam Mulier:* Women in Lollardy and the Problem of Sources."

15. Vilikovský, *Staročeská lyrika*, 144. My translation.

16. Antonín Škárka, ed., *Nejstarší česká duchovní lyrika* (Prague: Matice Česká, 1949), 76. The translation is mine.

17. For the Latin text of the so-called *Younger Wycliffite Mass*, see František Palacký, *Urkundliche Beiträge zur Geschichte des Hussitenkrieges von Jahr 1419* (Prague, 1873), 2:521–22. For secondary literature, see Zdeněk Nejedlý, *Dějiny husitského zpěvu*, 2nd ed. (Prague, 1955), 3:369–74.

18. "Novissimus autem temporibus non tantum literati phantasticis heu Wiklef insistebant erroribus, verum et laici universaliter singuli sequaces Hussonis, obtusos habentes oculos, quos deus ob individuam suam trinitatem et ob ferventem nostram deprecationem illuminet luce claritis, et ut ecclipsis fidei ipsorum radicitus exstirpetur" (Palacký, *Urkundliche Beiträge*, 522).

19. *Biblia Sacra Vulgata*, ed. Robert Weber (Stuttgart, 1969), 825. *The New English Bible* (Oxford: Oxford University Press, 1972), 422. For the Czech text of *The Daughter*, see Jan Hus, *Sebrané spisy české*, ed. Karel Jaromír Erben (Prague, 1868), 3:104–30. For a brief discussion of its composition at Kozí Hrádek, see Matthew Spinka, *John Hus: A Biography* (Princeton, N.J.: Princeton University Press, 1968), 194.

20. See Jeffrey F. Hamburger, *The Visual and the Visionary: Art and Female Spirituality in Late Medieval Germany* (New York: Zone Books, 1998), 19–21.

21. Šmahel, "Doctor Evangelicus," 19.

22. The standard study of this event is Ferdinand Seibt, "Johannes Hus und der Abzug der deutschen Studenten aus Prag 1409," in *Hussitenstudien: Personen, Ereignisse, Ideen einer frühen Revolution*, Veröffentlichungen des Collegium Carolinum, vol. 60 (Munich: Oldenbourg, 1987), 1–15.

23. Anne Hudson, "Wyclif and the English Language," in Kenny, *Wyclif in His Times*, 85–103 at 87.

24. For relevant bibliographical data on Wyclif's claim, see Anne Hudson, *The Premature Reformation: Wycliffite Texts and Lollard History* (Oxford: Oxford University Press, 1988), 30 and note 127. For its exploitation by Lollard propagandists, see ibid., 248–49.

25. See Andrew Taylor, "Anne of Bohemia and the Making of Chaucer," *Studies in the Age of Chaucer* 19 (1997): 95–119.

26. For more on the Rožmberk sisters see Klassen, *Warring Maidens*, chap. 4 (79–109).

27. For Bohemia, see Thomas, *Anne's Bohemia*, 147–48; for England, see McSheffrey, *Gender and Heresy*.

28. Jan Hus, *Sebrané spisy české*, 3:281–83. For an English translation of this famous letter, see *The Letters of Jan Hus*, trans. Matthew Spinka (Manchester: Manchester University Press, 1972), 165–66.

29. See Katherine Ludwig Jansen, "Maria Magdalena: Apostolorum Apostola" in *Women Preachers and Prophets*, 57–96.

30. Anne Hudson, "*Laicus litteratus:* The Paradox of Lollardy," in *Heresy and Literacy, 1000–1530*, ed. Peter Biller and Anne Hudson, Cambridge Studies in Medieval Literature, vol. 23 (Cambridge: Cambridge University Press, 1994), 222–36 at 234–35.

31. For a commentary on and English translation of this text, see *Cultures of Piety: Medieval English Devotional Literature in Translation*, ed. Anne Clark Bartlett and Thomas H. Bestul (Ithaca, N.Y.: Cornell University Press, 1999), 41–63.

32. Ibid., 8.

33. *Book to a Mother*, ed. Adrian James McCarthy, Studies in the Middle English Mystics 1 (Salzburg, 1981), 39.

34. See John Klassen, "Women and Religious Reform in Late Medieval Bohemia," *Renaissance and Reformation* 5, no. 4 (1981): 203–21 at 205.

35. Robert E. Lerner, "Writing and Resistance among Beguins of Languedoc and Catalonia" in Biller and Hudson, *Heresy and Literacy*, 186–204.

36. Vilikovský, *Staročeská lyrika*, 118–19 (118).

37. See Karma Lochrie, *Covert Operations: The Medieval Uses of Secrecy* (Philadelphia: University of Pennsylvania Press, 1999), 56.

38. *Biblia Sacra Vulgata*, 1533. *The New English Bible*, 729.

39. Quoted from "The Old Czech Life of St. Catherine of Alexandria," trans. Alfred Thomas, in *Medieval Hagiography: An Anthology*, ed. Thomas Head (New York: Garland, 2000), 763–79 at 773.

40. Ibid., 775.

41. Ibid.

42. See Dyan Elliott, *Fallen Bodies: Pollution, Sexuality, and Demonology in the Middle Ages* (Philadelphia: University of Philadelphia Press, 1999), 80–85.

43. Ibid., 114.

44. For the Prague pogrom of 1389, see Miri Rubin, *Gentile Tales: The Narrative Assault on Late Medieval Jews* (New Haven, Conn.: Yale University Press, 1999), 135–40.

45. The *passio* reflected the anger of the church hierarchy against King Wenceslas, who was embroiled in a bitter feud with his archbishop, John of Jenstein, over the Schism and other ecclesiastical matters. This feud would culminate in the king's political murder of the vicar-general of Prague, John of Nepomuk, in 1393. In his time-honored role as the protector of Bohemian Jews (one successfully fulfilled by his more able father Charles IV), Wenceslas was accused of being a "Jew-lover." The resentment of Jewish influence suggested by this epithet clearly articulates the insecurity felt by the church authorities during the reign of Wenceslas. Although anti-Jewish invective was nothing new in medieval Bohemia—earlier examples can be found in texts as disparate as the Latin *Passional of Kunhuta* and the Latin-Czech liturgical play *Unguentarius*—it seems to have escalated in the years following the death of Emperor Charles in 1378, the fateful year in which the Schism also occurred.

46. See chap. four of Thomas, *Anne's Bohemia*.

47. Elliott, *Fallen Bodies*, 56.

48. Ibid, 59.

49. Rita Copeland, "Why Women Can't Read: Medieval Hermeneutics, Statutory Law, and the Lollard Heresy Trials," in *Representing Women: Law, Literature, and Feminism*, ed. Susan Sage Heinzelman and Zipporah Batshaw Wiseman (Durham, N.C.: Duke University Press, 1994), 253–86 at 278.

50. For details about Sophie's life and support of Hussitism, see Klassen, *Warring Maidens*, 231–36.

51. Thomas, *Anne's Bohemia*, 46.

52. Klassen, *Warring Maidens*, 228–29. Quoting the Czech art historian Josef Krása, Klassen reinforces the former's utopian and religious view of the illuminations.

53. See E. Jane Burns, "Refashioning Courtly Love: Lancelot as Ladies' Man or Lady/Man?" in *Constructing Medieval Sexuality*, ed. Karma Lochrie et al. (Minneapolis: University of Minnesota Press, 1997), 111–34 at 128.

54. See Alfred Thomas, *The Czech Chivalric Romances Vévoda Arnošt and Lavryn in Their Literary Context*, Göppinger Arbeiten zur Germanistik, 504 (Göppingen: Kümmerle, 1989).

■ ■ ■

Response to Alfred Thomas's "*The Wycliffite Woman:* Reading Women in Fifteenth-Century Bohemia"

DYAN ELLIOTT

Alfred Thomas's scintillating exposition of *The Wycliffite Woman* points to the centrality of gender constructions at the hands of anti-heretical polemicists. But it also raises an important question—a question possibly not destined for resolution, but that can be wielded as a heuristic device—about the potential correspondence between representation, in this case satirical anti-feminist orthodox polemic, and reality. According to Thomas, *The Wycliffite Woman* "does not necessarily reflect the experience of real women in a direct fashion . . . but rather mediates between standard clerical anti-feminist rhetoric and the specific social reality of fifteenth-century Bohemian women." Thomas thus deploys the poem as an oblique testimony to the threat of the Hussite woman-teacher/preacher—a threat which, accordingly, merited crystallization into the image of the heretic as seductress. This depiction is not without analogues, as Thomas's reference to Beverly Kienzle's discussion of the Waldensian woman preacher as harlot readily suggests. Yet the portrait of *The Wycliffite Woman* has a unique quality that becomes especially pronounced in comparison with the anti-heretical polemic produced in Lollard England—the country that was the matrix for Czech reform and, hence, the natural correlative to the Bohemian situation.

As far as I can discern, English polemic did not muster anything approaching the Czech *Wycliffite Woman*, with its frank presentation of the female heretic as sexual predator. This is, to a certain extent, in keeping with the general nature of anti-Lollard polemic, which rarely ran to impugning the proto-puritanical Lollard sect of sexual immorality.[1] Only a few exceptions come to mind. An orthodox rejoinder was appended to the *Twelve Conclusions of the Lollards*—heretical contentions that were allegedly nailed to the doors of Westminster Hall in an act of Lollard protest.[2] An anonymous orthodox response to the Lollard critique describes the sect as sodomitical—a charge already leveled against orthodoxy in the third of the *Twelve Conclusions,* as well as in innumerable other sources. Thus the orthodox rejoinder mobilizes the predictable strategy of what Carolyn Dinshaw refers to as "reverse accusation."[3]

There is another instance in which heretical study groups are associated with heterosexual promiscuity, hence providing a closer analogue to *The Wycliffite Woman.* This occurs in Friar Daw's reply to Lollard sympathizer Jack Upland's attack on the mendicant orders. The friar is parrying the classic Lollard contention that the mendicant orders were "marrers of marriage." In response to this "aspersion," Friar Daw responds:

> But this arowe shal turne agen to him that it sent. . . .
> Who marrith more matrimonie, ye or the freris?
> With wrenchis and wiles wynnen mennes wyues
> And maken him scolers of the newe scole,
> And reden hem her forme in the lowe chaier;
> To maken hem perfit thei rede you 'r' rounde rollis,
> And call on men for ther lessouns with 'Sister, me nedith!'[4]

As with the Czech poem, a series of double-entendres suggests how study can become a front for seduction. Arrayed in lower seats, women learn "her forme" (i.e., various exercises leading to a degree), in the course of which they perfect the "rounde rollis" of their pronunciation—a more subtle allusion, perhaps, to female curvature than the Wycliffite woman's "two lovely chapters round and bare," but no less effective. The lecherous Lollard, like the roving friar, would further disrupt the family unit by calling at the home of a married woman and professing urgent need for his "sister."

Friar Daw's suggestive scenario is at one with the general tenor of continental anti-heretical discourse. Dominican author, John Nider, for example, consistently represents women as seduced and debauched by spiritual leaders who exploit female religious fervor. Thus Nider invokes the seemingly devout *fraticellus,* who appears with the most subtle books in the vernacular. He enters the house of devout women, sowing the word of God concerning the steps to contemplation and the highest perfection. Urging a transcendence of the passions, he convinces his female dupe to lie naked with him— ostensibly in ascetic chastity. Eventually, however, when least prepared, she falls prey to the inevitable carnal seduction which ensues. Thus religious depravity (in this instance, the antinomian doctrine of the Free Spirit) precipitates sexual license.[5]

As one might predict, such charges are, in many ways, indistinguishable from similar strains in Lollard polemic. Thus Jack Upland will respond impatiently to Friar Daw's depiction of the heterosexual "study groups," asserting that "Your freres ben taken alle day with wymmen & wifes."[6] Other works, such as the anonymous Lollard sermon "Of the Leaven of Pharisees," details how the friars mobilize their learning in ever more ingenious strategies for seduction: "thei feynen hem sotil of fisik and knowynge of wymmenys complexcion and preuyte, seiynge that siche sicknesse or deth schal com to hem in absence of here housbondis but yif thei haue mannus helpe, and thus defoulen on and other."[7]

Not surprisingly, the polemical culture of reverse accusation seems to be a relatively conservative one—bound by certain conventions. Thus while the accusations invariably get reversed, the terms in which these accusations are couched do not. For our purposes, it is worth observing that the gendered roles of male predator and female prey remain remarkably stable. Thus, in contrast to the Bohemian pseudo-*magistra*, her Lollard counterpart never "gets up to dance." Seated in low chairs practicing their oral curvatures, these women are constrained—even in fantasy—so that they will never attain the superior position of master. In other words, the dominant gendered dynamic that emerges in orthodox and Lollard polemic alike closely hugs the contours of 2 Timothy 3:6–7, which impugns heretics "who creep into houses, and lead captive silly women laden with sins, who are led away with divers desires: Ever learning, and never attaining to the knowledge of the truth." In contrast, *The Wycliffite Woman* is an embodiment of the prohibition on female teaching voiced in 1 Timothy 2:12. Operating in the same way as an exemplum, her didactic function is to teach by negative example—a pedagogic role that is a far cry from what she, presumably, imagines for herself.

What, if any, meaning is to be attached to such regional differences in anti-heretical polemic? It would be highly reductionist to posit that the less conventional Hussite imagery, productive of the more active female protagonist, was consistent with the greater threat women posed to orthodoxy. In fact, as Thomas and others have noted, neither movement aimed at or effected comprehensive changes in gender roles. However, at the fringes of Lollardy we discover certain extremists, such as Walter Brut, who launched far-reaching claims on behalf of a female priesthood in terms that actually bring to mind the satirical representation of *The Wycliffite Woman*.

What if we were to understand *The Wycliffite Woman* as a kind of manifesto of political despair that uses gender to signal its despondency? One implacable difference between Lollardy and Hussitism is the disparate degree of success experienced by each group in challenging the status quo. Lollardy was soon quelled by the effective collaboration of a centralized church and state. The Hussite movement, in contrast, brought both church and state to their knees. Perhaps this difference is obliquely represented in the permissible range of polemical expression available to each. The English orthodox polemicist was writing from a position of political strength: the last thing he would be inclined to do was present a woman as priest and *magistra*, even in satire, at a time when certain heretics were imagining precisely this possibility. But his Bohemian counterpart, writing amid political chaos with the world upside down, had less to lose. He may have chosen to signal his distress through the most compelling, chaotic, and carnivalesque impulses that presented themselves. What vehicle would be more appropriate for the symbolic expression of this distress than a thoroughgoing attack on the gender hierarchy? In other words, the creation of the amorous female scholar may be indicative of the Bohemian author's proclivity to use woman "to think with." If this were the case, the poem could be less about the liberties taken by a handful of female aristocrats with heretical sympathies than about the prolonged sufferings of a church and state emasculated by heresy.

Notes

I would like to thank Fiona Somerset and, particularly, Andrew Cole for their immensely helpful suggestions concerning Lollard polemic.

1. This is in spite of the fact that there were a number of idiosyncratic views that would seemingly invite condemnations of immorality. See, for example, the case of the layman William of Ramsbury, who called himself a Lollard priest and was brought before the bishop of Salisbury in 1389. William maintained that "it is permitted to whatsoever priest and any other individual to know carnally whatsoever women—whether nuns, virgins, or wives—and this is for the sake of the multiplication of the human race" (Anne Hudson, "A Lollard Mass," *Journal of Theological Studies* 23 [1972]: 417).

2. For the *Conclusions* and the different Latin and vernacular versions in which they are transmitted to us, see Anne Hudson, *Premature Reformation: Wycliffite Texts and Lollard History* (Oxford: Clarendon Press, 1988), 49 and nn. 225, 226. Hudson, who argues for the primacy of the English version, has edited the *Conclusions* in *Selections from English Wycliffite Writings* (Cambridge: Cambridge University Press, 1978), 24–29.

3. See Carolyn Dinshaw's detailed analysis of the orthodox countercharges of sodomy in *Getting Medieval: Sexualities and Communities, Pre- and Postmodern* (Durham, N.C.: Duke University Press, 1999), 67 ff.

4. *Friar Daw's Reply* 11.94, 99–104, in *Jack Upland, Friar Daw's Reply, and Upland's Rejoinder*, ed. P. L. Heyworth (Oxford: Oxford University Press, 1968), 76.

5. John Nider, *Formicarium* 3.6 (Douai: B. Belleri, 1602), 221–23. See Robert Lerner's account of this movement in *The Heresy of the Free Spirit in the Later Middle Ages* (Berkeley: University of California Press, 1972).

6. He also adds "But of your priuey sodomye speke I not here" (*Upland's Rejoinder* ll. 58–59, in *Jack Upland, Friar Daw's Reply*, 103). See Dinshaw, *Getting Medieval*, 64.

7. F. D. Matthew, ed., "Of the Leaven of Pharisees," c. 3, *The English Works of Wyclif*, Early English Text Society *o.s.* 74 (London, 1880; rev. 1902; Millwood, N.Y.: Kraus, 1973), p. 10; cf. c. 3, p. 12, and c. 2, pp. 6–7 (in the latter instance, the friars are accused of sodomy in conjunction with fornication and adultery). Also see "Of Prelates," c. 35, in ibid., 100.

Playing *Doctor*

St. Birgitta, Ritual Reading, and Ecclesiastical Authority

K A T H E R I N E Z I E M A N

For many women religious, the imperative to perform the liturgy provided the primary motivation to acquire literacy skills. These motivations could extend beyond the desire for spiritual participation, for liturgical performance also provided their primary access to the discourse of clerical letters. As the only definitively clerical practice in which women were regularly allowed and expected to engage, it could even provide access, however limited, to institutional authority. Liturgy was furthermore a decidedly communal activity. Indeed, for some religious communities, such as the Bridgittines who will be the subject of this essay, the liturgy was central to the formation of communal identity and functioned as one of the texts that constituted them as a textual community. The special relation of women to the liturgy has already received some consideration in studies of women such as Hildegard of Bingen and Mechthild of Hackeborn,[1] yet the interest scholars have had in women's liturgical practices has largely concerned their function as either the source or the product of women's writing. While I, too, will be treating the most distinctive feature of Bridgittine liturgy—the lessons that comprise Birgitta of Sweden's *Sermo angelicus*[2]—as a form of writing that articulates some of Birgitta's concerns as a woman, I do so ultimately to situate these texts as *legenda*, "things to be read."

The practice of ritual reading for which the *Sermo angelicus* was composed has been passed over by historians who have hoped to acknowledge women's intellectual accomplishments. Often considered slavish repetition, liturgical performance in general seems the antithesis of the learned engagement with texts enabled by grammatical study. Further, while liturgical reading concerns the vocalization of texts, the voice sacralized in liturgical performance seems the antithesis of the "voice" historians once sought to recover: that principal metonymy of authentic, individual experience. If the reiterative, pre-scripted nature of ritual speech makes it appear an unlikely source from which to derive women's experience, the fact that the ritual performer recited not merely pre-existing texts but texts affirmed by the institutions of official culture makes it seem an even less promising site for those seeking a revisionary history of women's opposition and empowerment. The voice created by liturgy seems the antithesis of the articulatory agency associated with "having a voice" by which one might represent social or political will.

It was nonetheless in the field of the liturgy that Birgitta of Sweden made some of her more radical gestures toward reenvisioning women's relation to both clerical knowledge and ecclesiastical authority. Foremost of these gestures, of course, was the very creation and institution of a distinctive Bridgittine rite. A unique version of the Office of the Virgin performed by the women of the double monastic community, the Bridgittine Office provided a text of divine origin that validated the women's community in particular.[3] The service itself, and especially the lessons of the *Sermo angelicus* read daily at matins, went further to articulate a powerful Mariology that, as I will show, was meant to structure the Bridgittine community to reflect the exemplary authority it granted to the Virgin Mary in the early Christian community. These Marian themes have decidedly less power when perceived as Birgitta's testimony—as her voice. Crucial to their meaning and effect is their repeated rendering in ritual time and space—their liturgical "voicing" that signals not slavish repetition, but participation in a powerful symbolic system.

The "voice" that represents individual agency or intent—a predominantly modern concept, rooted in post-Enlightenment notions of the individuated self and its representation—has also proven a frustrating and ultimately ineffective conceptual tool for women's visionary literature. Without dismissing the constraints of the patriarchal discourse within which women's experience was articulated, it is clear that the complex mediations of the divine, the clerical, and the visionary make the reduction of such texts to an isolatable voice or intent not only impracticable, but undesirable. Interpretation of women's visionary texts rather requires us to conceptualize visionary narration in terms that might show—as Rosalynn Voaden's study has suggested—women's control of visionary discourse if not of their voice.[4] An examination of liturgical discourse—a discourse of voicing rather than one of speaking/writing—provides some alternative models of articulation. Based in the dynamics of performance, this model attends less to the content of an utterance than to the discursive interventions it stages.

Birgitta of Sweden's *Sermo angelicus* is a particularly good example to consider since it is a visionary text modulated into the realm of the liturgical. A product of divine dictation and clerical translation, it could claim the prophetic authority of an appropriately mediated visionary text.[5] There were clearly affinities between the sacred discourses of the visionary and the liturgical that allowed her visions to become liturgical lessons. This transition, however, situated Birgitta's visions within the ecclesiastical structures—most importantly, within institutions of letters—that defined visionary or prophetic discourse dialectically, as that which emanates from outside its boundaries despite their sacred affinities. As a result, the visions participated in a more complex set of tensions internal to ecclesiastical authority, engaging in the kind of dialogue the dialectical construction of visionary discourse prevented. It is from this vantage point that Bridgittine Mariology engages and recasts the terms of visionary experience, clerical literacy, and ecclesiastical authority. More importantly, this engagement was created as an iterable performance that allowed the sisters of the Bridgittine Order to perform Birgitta's visions with the backing of institutional authority, exemplifying for us the potential liturgical performance held for women religious.

Reading in the Liturgy

Liturgical performance of any kind licensed women to disregard the Pauline interdiction against their speaking in church, allowing their speech to enter a complex field of discourse. The liturgy of the Word functioned as an enactment of textual community that ritualized relations between the members of the community in their various hierarchies and groupings as well as relations between the community as a whole and its constitutive texts. Differences in relations could be expressed through differences in gestures, melodic inflection, the spatial disposition of the participants, and, most importantly, voicing. Thus a psalm verse sung antiphonally on a psalm tone by one side of the choir and the same verse sung with a more florid melody by a soloist in the midst of a responsory might celebrate the same text, but the relations performed through its singing in each case would differ. So while the Bridgittine liturgy as a whole allowed the sisters of the Order of St. Savior to speak in church, the meaning of any particular part of the rite depended on its discoursal strategies: who says what to whom on whose behalf.

The *Sermo angelicus* was meant to be read over the course of the week as the lessons of matins.[6] Lessons, or *lectiones,* figured in both the Mass and Office as distinct liturgical speech acts. Unlike psalmody, which was performed in unison by the choir while standing, and ideally from memory, *lectiones* were intoned by a single *lector,* who read from the lectern while the rest of the choir remained seated and silent. While the former practice celebrates the choral community's unified internalization of the text, the latter celebrates their unified subordination to it. *Doctrina* is the term most commentators of the liturgy use to describe this subordination. William Durandus, in his widely read *Rationale divinorum officiorum*, uses the term to refer to the lessons of matins in particular: "the lessons of the night office are our doctrine because through them we are taught to turn our works toward God."[7] Like the modern term "lessons," *doctrina* emphasizes the text's educative function, its embodiment of knowledge.

It is, of course, God's doctrine that is disseminated. Rupert of Deutz, in his *Liber de divinis officiis*, states that after the lesson thanks are given to God "that he deigned to break the bread of his doctrine for us, lest we starve from not hearing the Word of God."[8] Yet even as Rupert equates *lectiones* with the Word of God, his eucharistic language calls attention to the role of the Church and its ministers. Just as the priest is needed for the Host's transubstantiation and fraction, so too is the clergy needed for the mediation and dissemination of doctrine. Commentators consistently emphasize the need for the *lector* to petition a blessing from the officiant (sometimes referred to as the *vicar Christi* or *principatus Ecclesie*)[9] before reading because, as John Beleth says in his *Summa de ecclesiasticis officiis*, "no one ought to read in church unless it has been commanded of or granted to him [to do so]."[10] Durandus goes on to point out that the priest himself does not have the power to bless, but functions as a necessary intermediary in petitioning the blessing from Christ,[11] yet this qualification leaves him in fundamental agreement with the others in the acknowledgment that the practice of ventriloquizing the Word of God must take place only under ecclesiastical auspices.

This assertion, however, is not merely one of clerical power over the laity. Even at the secular institutions that Durandus had in mind, the laity would only be present at matins on feast days, if at all, and yet it is to the lessons of matins that he attributes the greatest edifying function: "just as there are two orders within the Church—the wise and the foolish—so there are two kinds of lessons. The wise are instructed by those lessons read at Mass, whereas the foolish are edified by those read in the night office."[12] Describing the lessons of the night Office as directed toward those in greatest need of instruction suggests that the clergy must submit to doctrine to an even greater degree than the laity. This assertion of humility before the text serves an ideological function: by submitting themselves to doctrine, they sustain it as an objectified power—one that in turn helps objectify the discourse of letters as a primary component of the Church's institutional structure.[13]

Durandus provides an allegorical gloss on the reader's approach to the lectern that makes its symbolic value clear: "So he who is to read the lesson ascends the step as he approaches the book, for a *doctor* ought to transcend the crowd [*uulgos*] by virtue of his perfect life."[14] In actual practice the task of reading was generally deputed to clerks in minor orders, who would have no pretense to doctoral status except that conveyed to them by the doctrinal status of the text. The generalized crowd, by contrast, might include bishops, scholars, or other *viri litterati,* whose accomplishments or accreditation would nonetheless fail to distinguish them in relation to doctrine. Durandus manages to represent the relations of power implicit in this deployment of space as a source of symbolic wish fulfillment in which those of inner perfection are elevated to power. Such transcendence is paradoxically enabled by the self-degradation of those whose ascendancy is ultimately conveyed by the institutions of learning that produce and maintain doctrine in the first place. It is, however, by means of this paradoxical submission that the relations of domination that clerical literacy maintains are rendered opaque even to those who profit by them.

It might then seem odd, if ritual reading serves such an important role, that the task was delegated to lesser members of the clergy: deacons, subdeacons, and clerks in minor orders. Beleth, in fact, objects to priests' serving as readers and states that "reading the lesson is not the priest's duty," a precept that Durandus reiterates, though he makes more elaborate provisions should the priest volunteer to read the lesson.[15] This hierarchy of status and duty is in keeping with both traditional practice (early Christian readers did not even require ordination)[16] and attitudes outside of ritual time and space (where mere reading aloud was considered a relatively menial task). In the late medieval period, however, these practices and attitudes were put to different ideological uses as the relations of the divine, the Word, and the clerisy were resituated and reconfigured in response to shifts in the broader social practices of literacy. As lay participation in spiritual matters became more active and increasingly text based (a trend of which Birgitta was a consummate example), texts that had formerly been the exclusive preserve of the clergy—above all, the Office of the Virgin—came to be used as texts for lay devotion. In reasserting the distinctiveness of their own literacy, the clergy came to distinguish modes of performance and their status more than repertoire. "Devotion" became more frequently articulated as a domestic practice associated with the laity, a practice that, while profitable, did not bear the institutional authority that liturgical performance accrued dialectically. Liturgical reading, by contrast, became the realization of the mystery and power of the Word—a mystery and power that could be revealed only in clerical performance.[17]

This relocation of power was in fact only a modulation of emphasis and was most important for non-biblical texts. The Bible, of course, had long been sacralized through cantillation and liturgy's performative modes had always allowed non-biblical texts to partake of the sanctity of scripture. The assertions and anxieties of liturgical commentators, however, evince a desire to affirm ecclesiastical authority over and through these texts—an authority that, while it is a vicarious form of divine authority, is distinct from it, and one that, while it is wielded by humans, does not emanate from particular bodies. To reassign the power that might otherwise be vested in particular persons—the human author or speaker of the text—commentators often created depersonalizing etiologies of non-biblical texts especially. When Durandus discusses the origin of the liturgy in general, and of common liturgical texts like the *Gloria patri* in particular, the origins he conveys are decidedly corporate: Pope Damasus may have decided to compile and organize the liturgy (to combat the widespread heresy that threatened when early believers were left to their own devices, we are told), but he did so only in concert with "prudent and catholic men," like Jerome, whose work of compilation was later supplemented by such *doctores ecclesie* as Ambrose and Gregory.[18] Association with the *doctores* was a primary mechanism by which earthly texts or textual practices might be invested with authority, but the individual *doctores* were not themselves said to authorize the texts they produced or compiled. Authorship, in these cases, is not simply subordinated, but rather dispersed in order to distinguish it from authority, to ensure that the voice of the liturgy is not that of the text's human author.[19]

If the liturgical text had to be divorced from the voice of its author, it also had to be divorced from the performer who gives it voice. This imperative arises especially around *lectiones*, and around the lessons of matins in particular, since the reading of these frequently non-biblical texts was staged such that it most resembled a singular authoritative voice—the voice, as Durandus figured it, of a *doctor* more than the voice of God. This distance was achieved in part by framing the moment of reading as the performance of a role. The blessing requested of the priest before the reading not only marks the reader's lower station, but also permits his momentary elevation to a higher one. The formulaic ending of the lesson, "Tu autem, Domine, miserere nostri" (But Thou, Lord, have mercy on us), was consistently, if implicitly, glossed as the reader's transition back to his own voice, the first person plural form representing the singular reader and the group of hearers who share his human frailties but perform a different role: "The meaning [of the words]," states Beleth, "is this: 'Lord, while declaiming [the lesson] I have perhaps sinned in reading properly out of desire for human praise, and similarly the hearers, who were distracted by various thoughts and did not grant their attention to the lesson, have also sinned, but ... O Lord, have mercy on us.'"[20] The choir, for their part, is told that even though this supplication concerns them, their communal response—"Deo gratias"—sustains the dialogue, not with the reader, but with the voice of doctrine: according to Rupert of Deutz, "the chorus responds *Deo gratias*, which does not refer to the reader's final prayer, but to the entire lesson."[21] Thus dispersed and deflected, the authority of lessons ultimately resided in the text as the verbal object itself, or, more precisely, in the *performance* of that object as ritual language.

The efficacy of ritual reading, in fact, relied on the fundamental misrecognition that the text conveys authority to its performer, that it allowed the reader to play *doctor*.[22] It was therefore important that the reader not already possess such authority, that he merely play *doctor* under the auspices of ecclesiastical authority. It was equally important that he relinquish the role when the performance of the text ended, such that the text conveyed authority not to particular persons, but to the institutional office: *doctor* is a role—a reproducible relation of power enabled by clerical literacy and instituted in the office of *lector*. Such complex allocations and transactions of power, however, are inherently unstable. The commentators' need to direct speech and persona explicitly attests to the anxieties of attribution that the process invited. These are the instabilities that Birgitta's *Sermo angelicus* was to exploit. The acceptability of reading long, non-biblical texts as lessons during matins allowed Birgitta's visionary experience to be textualized as doctrine. While the emphasis on non-priestly performers may have displayed modes of clerical authority that lay outside the sacramental powers of the priesthood in public performance, it allowed women in the cloister to perform the task of reading the lessons of the Office themselves. The sisters of the Order of St. Savior were thus allowed not simply to speak in church, but to play *doctor*.

Birgitta's Visionary Liturgy

During the protracted struggle over her canonization,[23] several of Birgitta's more radical gestures—particularly gestures that made claims to institutional power—were debated in precisely these terms of speech and authority. The anonymous Perugian "Adversary," whose attacks upon Birgitta are preserved only in Adam Easton's defense against them,[24] denies the authenticity (and therefore the authority) of the Rule of the Order, said to have been dictated to Birgitta by Christ himself,[25] because of the impossibility that such a binding document could be uttered by a woman:

> it is not probable that Christ, by his own mouth, dictated the rule, and that he should have wished to promulgate it through a woman, whom the apostle does not permit to speak in church; and so the men, rather than the women, of that church or monastery are obligated to utter the rule for perpetual observances.[26]

By invoking the Pauline prohibition, the Adversary equates the institution of a rule with its public performance within ritual space. In doing so, he contends not merely that a woman may not impose communal structures, but that she may not even voice such a gesture on Christ's behalf.

Easton attempted to defend Birgitta by introducing nuanced distinctions using terms that approach the conceptual vocabulary of the liturgical commentators. Conveniently confusing the biblical passage the Adversary had adduced, he points out that the Apostle did not say that women could not speak in church, but that they could not teach.[27] He then points to 1 Corinthians 11:5 ("every woman praying or prophesying with her head not covered disgraceth her head") to show that since praying and prophesying cannot be carried out without speaking, some kinds of speech must be permissible. Borrowing an argument from Aquinas,[28] Easton distinguishes the illicit speech act of teaching from praying and prophesying in terms of audience and authority: "a woman is able to speak in church in order to pray and prophesy, according to the agreement given to her, but not to speak in the person of the entire church [*in persona tocius ecclesie*] without a special privilege."[29] Teaching is thus defined as a particular kind of speech act: speaking "in the person of the entire church," a phrase often used by liturgical commentators to describe the public authority of liturgical utterances.[30] In restricting the definition of the interdicted speech act, Easton purposed to make other kinds of speech available to women. Yet in the process he ultimately elaborates the Adversary's stance by supplying the traditional descriptions of women's essential nature that make them unfit to impersonate ecclesiastical authority. "To teach . . . publicly in Church," states Aquinas, "is not the task of subjects, but of prelates." Women, essentially subject "from nature and sex," are therefore ineligible.[31] Easton concedes such claims and generally agrees, along with the *doctores* he cites, that women are incapable of the wisdom that is not merely a prerequisite to, but the very substance of, doctrine. Quoting Nicholas of Lyra, he explains that "to teach is the work of wisdom; but wisdom does not flourish in woman because of the curse."[32] This lack of wisdom, Easton concludes, contributes to a range of deficiencies that disqualify women from wielding the authority to speak in the person of the Church: "woman is fleeting, imprudent, subject, and, by general law, unable to teach publicly as a *doctor* in church."[33]

Easton's well-intentioned but unsuccessful defense of the Rule thus exemplifies the terms and strategies one might use to isolate distinct modes of authority. Although the apology for the *Regula salvatoris* does not itself deal with the liturgy, it does indirectly suggest its potential appeal as a medium of opposition in Easton's final claims. Determined to locate a licit site of articulation for the Rule, Easton finds his answer in Aquinas's distinction between "public" (*publice*) and "domestic" (*domestice*) teaching.[34] While it is true that a woman is not permitted to speak "as a *doctor* in church," she is permitted to teach to small groups in what is understood to be everyday or non-ritual time and space, Easton claims. Defining the promulgation of a rule for a religious community as a domestic, rather than public, speech act thus makes it possible for a woman to voice it. Liturgy, however, could not be as easily categorized as a "domestic" speech act, even when performed within the cloister. Although it might be required by the rule of a particular community, it was meant to benefit all Christians and was performed before God on behalf of the entire Church by definition.

Birgitta gained access to the modes of public authority available in the liturgy from the only mode of public authority available to women: the prophetic authority of visionary discourse. The Bridgittine liturgy was, like the Rule, ascribed to a divine presence experienced in visions. But unlike the Rule, which was simply dictated to Birgitta by Christ himself, the genesis of the liturgy was more complex. Divided into the traditional categories of reading and singing, the sung portions of the liturgy were written by Birgitta's divinely inspired confessor and tutor, Master Peter, while the lessons to be read at matins were dictated to Birgitta by an angel. In a vision recorded in the *Revelaciones extravagantes* (and translated in the Middle English *Myroure of Oure Ladye*, from which I quote), the Virgin Mary shows that the two parts of the Bridgittine rite stemmed from fundamentally different kinds of inspiration:

> First yt semyth to the as a persone shewid the tho thinges that thou hast to say. . . . The seconde wyse yt semyth to thy master as though hys eres & mouthe were fylled with wynde, & as though hys harte were stretched out with brenyng charite to god, as a blather full of wynde. And in that swete harte brenyng he gat knowlege of some wordes & saynges which he coulde not before, & how he shulde make responses, & antemps, & hympnes, & ordeyne the songe in notes. And ether of these twayne is of the holy gost, after the departyng of his verteu, that is to say, to the angell to the shewyng of the lessons, & to the other, that is to master Peter in ordenyng of the songe.[35]

By distinguishing between receiving words and obtaining knowledge, Mary aligns the two liturgical modes of reading and song with two kinds of visionary experience— "spiritual" and "intellectual" visions as defined by Augustine and other church authorities.[36] "Spiritual" visions are those perceived with the spiritual senses in the form of visual or aural images, such as the angel who appeared to Birgitta to dictate the lessons. "Intellectual" visions, by contrast, are those that appeal directly to the intellect, bypassing sensible representation altogether. In Master Peter's case it takes the form of knowledge (*scientia*) with which he is literally inspired. As Voaden's study shows, women, associated as they were with the senses rather than with the intellect, were not thought capable of the superior and more trustworthy intellectual vision.[37] Thus while Mary is chiefly interested in validating Master Peter's experience and involvement in the production of the liturgy in this particular instance, it was Birgitta's experience that was generally in greater need of validation.

Prophetic authority has its source outside of institutions, and for this reason all visionary experience needed to be assimilated into and mediated by ecclesiastical authority under the principles of *discretio spirituum*, the rules by which spiritual and corporeal visions were authenticated.[38] Because spiritual visions appealed to the senses— even the spiritual senses—they were considered more likely to be misconstrued, either because of the fallibility of the senses or because of the potential for demonic intervention to which the senses were more susceptible. Since only male clerics had the knowledge required for such discernment, they were the ones to authenticate, explicate, and disseminate visions. Birgitta's spiritual advisors, including Peter and ultimately Alphonse of Jaén, served this authorizing role for her, first by translating her revelations into authoritative Latin, then by compiling and editing them. This authorizing role had the capacity to subsume that of the visionary, yet a female visionary, such as Birgitta, who was also aware of these conventions, would understand that self-abnegation generally formed a part of self-validation. As Voaden has put it, "a woman visionary who conforms so completely to the principles of *discretio spirituum* as to render herself invisible makes it more likely that the ecclesiastical authorities will hear and accept God's message, and in this way she is empowered."[39] It would therefore have been in the interest of Birgitta and her clerical champions to encourage and make known representations of her visionary experiences that diminished her role.

Such is the case in a depiction of visionary experience recorded in the *Revelaciones extravagantes*. In this vision, Christ provides an exemplum to describe Alphonse's role in editing Birgitta's visions:

> I am like a carpenter, who cuts down some trees, brings them out of the woods into a house, and there makes a beautiful image, decorating it with colors and designs. When his friends, upon seeing the image, note that it might be decorated with even prettier colors, they paint it and apply their own colors.[40]

Although the primary rhetorical gesture in this revelation seems to be to give divine approval to Alphonse, this approval is given in terms that align him with Christ as co-creator of the image that resides within Birgitta, whereas Birgitta's role is subsequently reduced to that of a passive container for the vision-image. This reduction is precisely the kind of staged self-abnegation of which Voaden speaks. Though it would appear merely to transfer articulatory agency to the male cleric, it does so only partially and in the service of an even greater claim to authority. As Christ explicates his exemplum, he likens the inspiration he gives to Alphonse to that given to the evangelists and doctors, and even goes so far as to say that Alphonse himself is fulfilling the role of evangelist (*faciat et impleat officium euangeliste*).[41] This identification validates not only Alphonse, but also the text, which is implicitly lent quasi-scriptural status. While the claim reduces Alphonse's role to that of transmitter, the very extravagance of the visions' scriptural pretensions requires that they be contained.[42] Representing Birgitta as a house serves not only to limit her agency, but also to limit the authoritative claims of the text that resulted from her visions by locating it—in a gesture not unlike Easton's situating of the Rule—within the domestic space of a house. The process by which claims to authority are simultaneously made and contained within visionary discourse does show how self-abnegation can be empowering, yet it also shows the difficulty of negotiating the complex economy of authority that makes up this discourse, and the tenuous nature of prophetic authority in general.

The economy of liturgical authority was no less complex, of course, and it was not an economy to which women had easy access. That Birgitta gained access, however, is less interesting than the difference in the representation of agency—and the status of that agency in relation to her clerical editors—that marks the shift from vision to lesson. The passage from the *Revelaciones extravagantes* describes Alphonse's evangelical function in editing all of Birgitta's revelations, but the anonymous author of *The Myroure of Oure Ladye,* the Middle English translation and explication of Bridgittine liturgy intended for the nuns of Syon Abbey, adapted it to explain and validate Alphonse's contribution to the *Sermo angelicus* in particular. In the process of adaptation, however, the roles shift: editorial changes to the *Sermo* are justified, Christ explains to Birgitta, since "though the Euangelystes wrote the gospelles by the holy goste, yet other doctoures cam after, that by the same spyryte dyscussed and expounded theyr wrytynge moche more playnely and openly, And so yt neded to be."[43] In this case, the unavoidable instrumentality of Birgitta's scribal activity allows her to be an actor rather than the stage. Indeed, she both usurps Alphonse's role as evangelist and obscures Christ's role as the first artist. Alphonse, by contrast, is now grouped with the "other doctoures," who partake of the same inspiration but play a temporally distanced, secondary role.

Birgitta's promotion from house to evangelist is in part explained by the *Myroure*'s later date and provenance, written as it was in England after Birgitta had gained the status and popularity that led to the founding of Syon Abbey. Yet it is also related to the different nature and function of the *Revelaciones* and the *Sermo* as texts. Although the bulk of Birgitta's revelations are recorded as divine speech, this speech is directed toward Birgitta personally—its recording in writing is essentially a form of reportage. The *Sermo,* by contrast, was given to Birgitta as a verbal object—as divine speech not addressed to her directly. It is meant not merely to be heard, but to be used within ritual time and space. As a ritual text, its meaning is neither restricted to nor predicated upon the particularizing context of her presence. The expectation of its perpetual repetition, in fact, lends to it a self-conscious iterability that resists hermeneutic closure. Thus the disappearing act so crucial to successful negotiation of *discretio spirituum* is built into a discourse that, as we have seen, disperses authorial identity. Because the claim of articulatory agency is less, there is less of a need to control her role metaphorically. Birgitta no longer contains the text, but becomes the first in a succession of amanuenses to render sacred language in writing.

It is in its status as sacred language that the *Sermo* effects a reversal of the hierarchy of values encoded in *discretio spirituum.* When considered as revelations, the words Birgitta reports are—as they were depicted in Christ's exemplum—*imagines,* or signifiers, that require interpretation. The visionary's inability to interpret her visions by herself is a sign of their authenticity. In order to explicate the meaning of such visions, the *imagines* must be reduced to their divine signifieds, a task that can be accomplished either by divine interlocutors or knowledgeable and discerning clerics.[44] Even though Christ's exemplum depicts clerical activity as additions to the original image, it is clear that even additions function in the process of substitutions necessary to "clarify obscure things and maintain the catholic sense" of the divine message.[45] In other words, clerical knowledge is employed to constrain the meaning of Birgitta's words that might otherwise produce an excess of interpretations not conforming to institutionally affirmed doctrine. This is simply to say that visions are important for what they mean. While lessons too are important for what they mean, they are also *legenda*—things to be read as ritual language—which equally celebrates the verbal object and its iterability. Although these verbal objects are perhaps not irreducible, they are perpetually reconstituted by repeated performances meant to enact submission to the Word rather than mastery over it. Thus whereas the discourse of *discretio spirituum* would figure Birgitta's inability to interpret her visions—of her rendering of words as unreduced *imagines*—as a virtuous lack that usually needed to be supplied by learned clerics, the discourse of ritual reading celebrates the verbal surface of the text as a sanctified medium through which divine presence and divine truths might be conveyed.

The celebration of the verbal surface of these *legenda* did not, of course, obviate the need for clerical intervention. It was, after all, Master Peter and Alphonse who translated and edited the texts, giving them the form, not to mention the language, in which they would be performed. But whereas within the discourse of *discretio spirituum*, Peter's and Alphonse's tasks would have consisted almost entirely of validation, within liturgical discourse their intervention participates in the dispersal of authorship that texts so often undergo if they are to be included in a ritual repertoire. The editorial history recounted in the *Myroure*, beginning with an angelic but otherwise unidentifiable speaker and proceeding through a succession of amanuenses, mimics the stories of corporate authorship recounted by liturgical commentators and goes further by giving explicitly divine sanction to the editorial enterprise.[46] Although Master Peter's original translation of the *Sermo* was "good and trew, and don by the helpe of the holy goste," we are told that God "wolde that moo men of dyuerse contryes and language shulde labour therin, to theyr more meryte, & to more open shewynge and wytnesse of his maruaylous workeynge."[47] The dispersal of authorship in this account is thus also figured geographically in God's desire to involve clerics beyond the remote locale of Sweden. Even as it elevates Birgitta to an evangelical status, placing her above rather than below her clerical editors, clerical intervention also allows the text out of the house and into public space.

More specifically, it enters the space of public doctrine. Most of the claims I have made so far have focused on the distinction between visionary and liturgical discourse. That Birgitta entered liturgical discourse by writing the *legenda*, however, is itself meaningful. Reading in the liturgy, and especially the reading of lessons at matins, as we have seen, ritualizes the act of teaching. Whereas this teaching represented ecclesiastical authority more than clerical power to those within the clerical realm, to those outside of the clergy the two were inseparable. The staged presence of the book for the reading of lessons further linked these two modes of power with clerical literacy as their primary vehicle. Song also represents a form of lettered knowledge, one that, as we saw with Master Peter, requires *scientia*, yet Peter's *Cantus sororum* never lays claim to the quasi-scriptural status of the *Sermo angelicus*. Its status as a verbal object is generally downplayed, and when it is discussed, it is described in terms that distance it from high literate practice. When the Virgin Mary, for example, reveals her approval of the *Cantus* to Birgitta, she states, "In my songe there be no masterly makynge ne no Rethoryke Latynne, yet thoo wordes endytyd by the mouthe of this my loued frende, plese me more, then sotel wordes of eny worldely maysters."[48]

Mary's words attest to the simplicity that characterizes Bridgittine liturgy as a whole,[49] yet no such statement is made about the *Sermo*. And while associating formal learnedness with worldly pursuits is a common anti-clerical convention, the association of Birgitta's visions with ritual reading seems to place her in the midst of lettered culture, where modes of power depend most upon forms of lettered knowledge. By making her presence in the liturgy most prevalent in the act of playing *doctor*, Birgitta provided commentary on the relation of exclusive forms of knowledge to doctrinal power in a way that neither rejected nor completely embraced clerical literacy. As we shall see in the content of the lessons themselves, Birgitta uses the role of *doctor* to intervene in, and in some measure transform, the clerical discourse of letters.

Maria Doctrix: The Lessons of the *Sermo*

Several of Birgitta's revelations show a disparagement of worldly learning and literacy. Although some other emerging vernacular devotional traditions opposed formal learning (*scientia*) to experiential wisdom (*sapientia*),[50] her visions tend to distinguish between spiritual and temporal wisdom, thereby diminishing the opposition between the two. In one such vision, Mary presents an exemplum that describes a man "desiringe to lere wisedome, seand two maistirs standand bifore him" from which he must choose. The second master, representing temporal wisdom, promises that his followers "sall se outeward shininge clerenes," through his easy teaching, though this wisdom will disappear when one tries to put it to use. Spiritual wisdom, by contrast, is difficult to attain and requires that one give one's will over to God;[51] not only can it be put to use, but it must be, for "it mai noght trewli be called wisedome bot wordes and werkes acorde."[52] Spiritual wisdom thus involves action as well as thought. While the exemplum does associate worldly learning with literacy, defining it as "wisdome with litterature þat sone sall haue ende,"[53] it should not be confused with a celebration of unlearnedness. Mary does not urge Birgitta to consider the example of "Lewed lele laboreres" who "Persen with a paternoster [þe palys of] heuene,"[54] but encourages an arduous intellectual pursuit of an alternative wisdom that maintains its relation—even if a metaphorical one—to institutions of learning. Nor does it necessarily discredit all reading, but rather discourages the reading of unprofitable literature.

It is the case, however, that "wisdom" takes the place of knowledge or letteredness as the goal of learning. And while Birgitta's version of *sapientia* does not necessarily require *scientia*, it does seem to require teaching. In yet another revelation, Christ likens his friends to "scholars"—not those clerks, of course, who acquire learning to use in exchange for earthly wealth and prestige, but those who seek it directly from Christ himself with purity of heart. Such true scholars, Christ states, receive three supernatural forms of knowledge: "first, a perceptive conscience that is beyond the brain's nature; second, a wisdom [achieved] without man['s aid], for I personally teach them inwardly; third, they are filled by a sweetness and a divine love through which they might conquer the devil."[55] These revelations thus promote an ideal spiritual scholarship, the rewards of which go beyond the mystical experience of divine love to include practical forms of knowledge. The first and the last—a supernatural ability to discern right from wrong and the affective tools with which to combat the devil—are the kinds of knowledge required by *discretio spirituum*. But perhaps more interesting is the second reward of wisdom, or rather, of a divine tutorial in wisdom, which rests on the presumption that all of Christ's friends—men and women—might be taught. By associating the quest for wisdom with formal schooling, the vision implies that a woman's search for wisdom might be frustrated not by her organic incapacity, but through her exclusion from the institutions that impart wisdom through learning. It further suggests that by embracing a form of spiritual scholarship, women, too, can acquire it.

Both visions point to Christ as the ultimate source of such wisdom, yet for the Bridgittine Order, the emulatable model of the human pursuit of wisdom was the Virgin Mary.[56] The institutional structure set out in the Rule models the Bridgittine monastery on the post-Ascension community, declaring that each community number eighty-five members to represent the sum of the thirteen apostles (including Paul) and seventy-two disciples.[57] Because it was the Virgin, according to the Rule, who became "the head and the queen of the apostles and disciples of Christ after he had ascended into the heavens," the female abbess, Mary's vicar on earth, was similarly to be head of the monastic community.[58] As Ann Hutchinson has pointed out, the Bridgittine Order was firmly committed to the pursuit of wisdom.[59] Certainly among the men wisdom was pursued by the traditional means of latinate book learning, a practice the Rule encouraged by excepting books from the Order's commitment to poverty.[60] The women, too, engaged in literary activities.[61] The Rule clearly aligns sapiential pursuits with institutionally affirmed modes of learning by providing for four deacons to represent the four *doctores ecclesie*—Jerome, Augustine, Ambrose, and Gregory.[62] These deacons were, nonetheless, numbered within the eighty-five representatives of the post-Ascension

community. The *doctores ecclesie* and their learning are thus situated, by allegorical extension, under Mary's leadership.

It might be more accurate to say that the deacons are placed under Mary's tutelage,
since Mary is upheld—most particularly in the *Sermo angelicus*—as one both skilled in
acquiring wisdom and authorized to disseminate it.[63] The second lesson read at matins
on Thursday, for example, celebrates Mary's powers of understanding and discernment: "No tongue can tell how wisely the sense and intellect of the glorious Virgin fully
comprehended God when first she gained understanding. Especially, the human mind
is too weak to understand the many ways the Virgin subjected her blessed will to the
service of God."[64] This praise of Mary's superior and precocious faculties of recognition
begins a spiritual narrative of discretion and action that continues to the end of the lesson. While Mary begins her life knowing God with *sensus et intellectus* (sense and understanding), it is her *intellectus* that prompts her to give her will over to God and enables
her to strengthen herself against sin such that *intellectus* triumphs over the *sensus*. This
triumph allows her to turn the immediacy of perception with which she began her life
into highly cultivated powers of discernment. As the narrative culminates in the Annunciation, her instantaneous recognition of the angel's divine nature and her submission to God's command is described with climactic *exclamatio*:

> O, quantum appropinquauit hec nauis, scilicet corpus virginis, desiderantissimo
> portui, idest Dei Patris mansioni, quando Gabriel adueniens ait: "Aue gracia plena!"
> O, quam honeste sine viri cooperacione suum Filium Pater Virgini commendauit,
> quando angelo ipsa respondit: "Fiat michi secundum uerbum tuum."[65]

> O how this ship, that is, the Virgin's body, neared that most desirable port, that is,
> the mansions of God the Father, when Gabriel came to her and said, "Hail, full of
> grace!" O how honorably, without the cooperation of man, the Father commended
> his Son to the Virgin when she responded to the angel, "Be it done unto me ac-
> cording to your word."[66]

The parallel syntax of the Latin enhances the sense of immediacy, as does the pairing of
biblical phrases which—like the captioning scrolls of most visual portrayals—edits out
the conversation between Gabriel and a fearful and questioning Mary (Luke 1:28–38).
The Virgin's part in the scene even goes beyond her recognition to suggest the possibility of Marian agency in the Incarnation. Her "drawing nigh" (*appropinquauit*) rhetorically anticipates Gabriel's greeting, and the parallel construction matches the Incarnation itself with her verbal fiat in the second period.[67] Here both word and deed stem from
Mary's discerning knowledge, as she sails her ship into God's harbor. The potential of
causal agency that might well follow from the intensive focus on her will elsewhere in the

lesson is, however, rhetorically contained: word and deed are separated by pairing her action with Gabriel's words and her words with God's action. Any sense of causality is diluted by conjoining each phrase in reverse chronological order by the neutrally temporal "when" (*quando*). Nevertheless Mary's gestures show her to be capable of discerning spirits herself, and able to respond to God's will by exercising her own.

Mary's capacity for the wisdom that might inform such actions becomes the focus of the first lesson at matins on Saturday—the end of the liturgical week and the day on which the Ladymass would normally be celebrated. The text compares her to the Queen of Sheba, who, having tested Solomon, recognized his wisdom. Mary, we are told, similarly exercises her powers of discernment in her pursuit of wisdom: "She sought it with all eagerness . . . until she found the wisdom that is Christ, the Son of God, who is incomparably wiser than Solomon."[68] Mary's skill ultimately allowed her to do more than recognize and acquire wisdom; she also found the capacity to disseminate wisdom in the form of doctrine; indeed, her doctrine is even granted a privileged status due to its efficacy: Mary, we are told, "presented more souls to God with her salutary teaching than anyone else did with all his works."[69] The superlative intercessory effects of her doctrine, according to the lesson, stem from her especially close relation to Christ, which included her knowledge of his divine essence and purpose on earth. So close was this relation, the lesson claims, Mary would have ascended to the heavens with him, were she not needed to lead the community of believers in a number of capacities:

> When her blessed son rose to his glorious kingdom, the Virgin Mary was permitted to remain in this world to comfort sinners and to correct the erring. She was the teacher [*magistra*] of apostles, the comforter of martyrs, the teacher [*doctrix*] of confessors, the most clear mirror for virgins, the consoler of widows, for spouses the most salubrious admonisher, and the most perfect strengthener for everyone in the Catholic faith.[70]

Her qualifications for this series of roles are to some degree related to her maternal bond with Christ, but motherhood could scarcely have given her the accreditation or authority to warrant the titles *magistra* and *doctrix*. The lesson, rather, locates the source of Mary's authority in her wisdom—and in her sagacious recognition of Christ as wisdom itself.

Further still, Mary's superlative wisdom enabled her to be the first of Christ's followers to make this recognition in her perception of his true nature. The first believer and first preacher, Mary alone maintained her faith in the eternal Christ after the death of his humanity and bore witness to his divine nature with her words. If Eve was the first to eat from the tree of the knowledge of good and evil, Mary was the first to use that knowledge to comprehend humanity's redemption. This claim might seem ex-

treme, but it is probably less extreme than the manner in which this position is sub-
stantiated. To support Mary's claim to have the earliest knowledge of the redemption,
the lesson supplies parts of the resurrection narrative that were not commemorated in
scripture: on the day of the resurrection, while the doubtful apostles grieved and the
women searched for Christ's body,

> Although Scripture does not tell anything about her at that time, without doubt
> it is to be believed that she testified that the Son of God was raised in the flesh to
> eternal glory and that death no longer had dominion over him. Scripture says that
> the Magdalene and the apostles saw him first, yet undoubtedly it is to be believed
> that his most worthy Mother truly knew this before them and saw him first, risen
> from the dead, after which she joyfully and humbly praised him, full of jubilation
> in her heart.[71]

The gesture of elaborating the scriptural narrative is itself neither original nor problematic, since it had been preceded by apocryphal stories of Jesus' childhood and the con-
fabulated narratives encouraged in the devotional practice of the Franciscan *Meditations*-
tradition.[72] The Bridgittine lesson, however, differs in that it uses such an elaboration in
the service of a competitive claim about Mary's authority in the context of a liturgical
reading—a text that emphasizes its status as a verbal object of quasi-scriptural standing.
But while this reading does suggest that scripture is incomplete, it does not do so to
challenge scriptural authority. It does so to situate Marian wisdom as anterior to that
of the apostles and evangelists. This privileged position of anteriority, combined with
the emphasis on Mary's power within the post-Ascension community, ultimately allows
Marian doctrine to become a *source* of scripture, a gospel that informed the canonical
gospels found in sacred scriptures. Birgitta's intervention in the clerical discourse of letters thus takes the form of a paradox: as a performance of depersonalized institutional
authority, the lesson celebrates Mary as the founder of the Church; and articulated as it is
from the site of ritualized written authority, the *lectio* is used to situate Mary's doctrinal
authority in the narrative of Christ's resurrection—and in Mary's body—rather than in
the words of the sacralized text.

The lesson's claim, in other words, enacts the obverse of the process by which institutional authority is enacted by ritual reading: rather than relocating power from
the body of the reader to the text, it inserts a very particular body prior to the text—a
body invested with power on account of her corporeal presence among the believers—
in a manner that implies that scripture is lacking. This reversal would not in itself be
oppositional, for its claim is historical. To suggest that the apostles bore authority in
their bodies does not negate the authority of the scriptures that recorded their acts.
Nor does calling attention to scripture's function as historical record necessarily deny

its status as sacred language—Birgitta did, after all, have her own spiritual and institutional investments in the sacralization of verbal objects as a source of authority. But what might otherwise constitute a mere shift in emphasis becomes a radical assertion when a woman's body becomes a locus of authority, doctrinal or otherwise. The discourse of *discretio spirituum*, as Voaden claims, could grant prophetic authority to a woman's words, but only by separating text from body.[73] The Bridgittine *legenda* redeems the body that was often cast as women's impediment to wisdom and intellectual vision, and does so in a medium that links it with the power of clerical literacy and the institutional authority of doctrine.

Such a redemption would, of course, be easier to effect with the body of the Virgin, whose singular virginity might prevent any virtues associated with her body from being emulated, least of all by a woman who had been married and born eight children. Yet just as Birgitta found ways of reconciling her widowhood with her emulation of the Virgin elsewhere,[74] so, too, in the *Sermo* is Mary figured in terms that separate her capacity to teach from the intactness of her virgin body. In the second lesson of the Sunday service, Mary is likened to Noah's ark. The intactness of her body is indeed stressed by describing the holy vessel as "covered with pitch" to the degree "that no bilge-water was able to seep into it."[75] But while the pitch prevents sin from entering the vessel, it does not prevent Christ from leaving it. While Noah simply left the empty ark—or rather "widowed" it (*relicturum*)—when he no longer needed it,[76] Christ remains with Mary: "Although his body would be separated from [Mary's] body at the nativity, he foreknew that he would remain with [her] without end and inseparably."[77] Thus the implicit opposition of virgin and wife gives way to one that contrasts the absence of widowhood with the Virgin's presence, as she continues to bear the Word.

Insofar as Mary is represented as a vessel of God's will, it is as a vessel of transport. The responsory that follows this lesson describes her as a *vehiculum* capable of carrying sinners to grace. Such a depiction diminishes her singular relation to the Word and thus allows for the transferability of her vehicular skills. It is in this aspect—as vessels of God's Word—that Bridgittine liturgy empowered the sisters of the Order to emulate both the Virgin and Birgitta herself. By creating the space for a specifically female voicing in the liturgy, Birgitta altered the terms in which women religious might understand their role in liturgical performance. Performance of the Bridgittine liturgy accentuated women's capacity to participate in the relations of power that outside of the cloister would be open only to male clerics. Although Birgitta herself made no pretensions to the title *doctrix*, the title is conveyed upon her by a memorial antiphon added to the liturgy after her death: "Sponsa regis, doctrix legis / Exempla sequens forcium" (O Byrgytte, kinges spouse, techer of lawe, / folowyng the ensamples of strengthe).[78] While Mary is not explicitly named as the *exempla forcium*, there is an irresistible implication that Birgitta merited the title by following the example of that other *doctrix*, Mary, and, further, that such an honor might await those who follow her example.[79]

It is not surprising that the *Sermo*'s depiction of *Maria doctrix* caught the attention of Birgitta's Adversary, nor that his objections emphatically reassert the distinctions the *Sermo* calls into question. Yet the manner in which both he and Easton attempt to contain the *Sermo*'s disruptive gestures, as well as their ultimate failure to do so, help to sum up the potential liturgy held for women religious. The Adversary, for his part, does allow that Mary had "the gift of wisdom and prophecy," but he clearly distinguishes the two categories from one another: only prophecy can issue in public speech, as it does in Mary's case, he claims, with her canticle (i.e., the *Magnificat*). Prophetic authority is thus reasserted as the only public discourse available to women. What wisdom Mary did possess, he continues, was not to be used in the same manner as Peter, who "in his first teaching and preaching received from the Holy Spirit, converted three thousand souls," but rather to be used, as befits a woman, in contemplation, which is exemplified by Mary's response to Elizabeth's greeting when the two pregnant women met: "But Mary kept all these words, pondering them in her heart" (Luke 2:19).[80] By using Peter's Pentecostal sermon as his example of wisdom used in public teaching, the Adversary not only reestablishes doctrine as an exclusively male prerogative, but also reestablishes Peter as the founder of the Church. The appropriate use of wisdom for women is no longer exemplified by the post-Ascension *Maria doctrix*, but by the pre-natal Mary the contemplative, whose wisdom is manifested not in speaking words, but in withholding them.

To figure Mary as one whose task it is to withhold words is at some level to silence her in response to the threat Birgitta's *Maria doctrix* posed to the Church's institutional structure. This silencing, however, does not have the same meaning in a culture that does not perceive language as self-originating. The Adversary does not deny her self-expression so much as he denies her the use of language as a medium of relation. And while the relation established by doctrine is a relation of power, it conveys only instrumental agency, such that its power is measured not in terms of its content (we are not told precisely *what* Mary teaches), but in terms of the number of souls converted by means of it. Its power is, in other words, based in performance as such. Easton understood this, yet his inability to imagine a woman performing in such a manner causes him—as before—merely to elaborate the ideology of his Adversary even as he tries to defend Birgitta. Invoking once again Aquinas's distinctions, he attempts to replace the Adversary's opposition between doctrine and contemplation with one between public and private teaching. For Easton, Mary did teach, but her teaching was strictly domestic; it was the task of the apostles and disciples to promulgate her doctrine publicly. Thus, according to Easton, Mary could fittingly appropriate the words of Christ: "He that heareth you heareth me" (Luke 10:16), for she is responsible for all souls converted by the apostles. Easton's invocation of the gospel passage does identify Mary with Christ as origin of the doctrine that the apostles ventriloquize, and yet it is clear—especially in light of scripture's failure to commemorate her teaching—that Mary's doctrine would not be known had the apostles not promulgated it publicly: one can no longer be in the presence of her speech. Indeed, to an even greater degree than the Adversary's claims required Mary's silence, Easton's apostolic doctrine is predicated on her absence.

Both of these arguments, however, adduce Mary's canticle—the *Magnificat,* sung daily at vespers—to substantiate their claims, and therefore invoke the liturgical context that the words of the lesson do not by themselves suggest. In both cases, the *Magnificat,* when considered a liturgical text (as it inevitably was), undermines the very distinctions it was meant to exemplify in a manner similar to the *Sermo*'s intervention in the Office as a whole. The Adversary's claim that the *Magnificat* represents prophecy was surely a pre-emptive explanation of a glaring exception to Mary's pondering of words in her heart, but even if considered as prophecy, its status changes when—like the prophetic *Sermo*—it is regularly performed in a ritual context. As Easton was quick to point out, "many have been converted to the Lord" through the canticle, and such perceptible effects are precisely what defines doctrine for the Adversary.[81] Easton himself actually does refer to it as "public doctrine," though he is not able to generalize from what appears to him to be an exceptional case, and one that clashes with his claims for Mary's domestic teaching elsewhere.[82] If the apostles' public doctrine required Mary's absence, the performance of the canticle invokes her presence. This presence might not negate apostolic doctrine, but it does generate conflict for a cleric who wishes both to celebrate the Virgin's deeds and, at some level, to uphold the power that accrues to liturgical texts though decontextualization and depersonalization. The convoluted syntax of Easton's fullest formulation encapsulates this conflict, as he refers to the "*Magnificat . . .* through the public doctrine of which canticle, the entire church of God is instructed in faith and morals through the Virgin."[83] Whereas liturgical commentators tried to attribute agency to the lesson instead of the reader, Easton's argument requires him to attribute it simultaneously to the doctrine itself and to Mary, such that in his reading the canticle paradoxically appears to celebrate not simply the Virgin, but the Virgin's continuing instruction.

The *Sermo,* I have claimed, similarly invokes Mary's presence within a community far less invested in disembodiment. The *Sermo*'s preoccupation with bodily presence, in fact, lent special meaning to the experience of playing *doctrix.* Yet the *Magnificat* differs significantly from the *Sermo,* for it is not a *lectio,* but a canticle—a song that would have been sung antiphonally by the entire choir, most likely from memory. Its performance enacted the community's internalization and appropriation of the text—a speech dynamic that differs from that of doctrine, though one that was equally powerful as a performance of community. Although the reading of *lectiones* and doctrine play a distinctive role in Bridgittine liturgy, it is important to remember that liturgy gave access to more than "public discourse," or to institutionally authorized language that would bear its fullest authority only within the confines of the monastery. Liturgical performance, as I have said, articulates not subjectivity, but subject position; not self, but relation, and it does so less by means of the voice than through the readerly practice of voicing. As such, it enabled women to inhabit an entire range of subject positions, none of which were generally available to them otherwise. It further allowed, or rather required, women to navigate among these sites and to master the fluidity of the various relations that they articulated. Such mastery could surely be cultivated at any religious community of women where the liturgy was celebrated, and perhaps beyond those enclosed communities.[84] It is, in this sense, possible to overemphasize the particularity of the Bridgittine community or the practical power of its liturgy. Yet it is also possible—and has been the general tendency of scholarship—to underestimate the complexity of the field in which Birgitta intervened and the imaginative possibilities it could offer.

Notes

1. Treatments of Hildegard's music and its place in the liturgy are too numerous to mention, though a useful introduction can be found in materials by Barbara Newman and Marianne Richert Pfau in their preface to Newman's edition and translation of Hildegard's *Symphonia*, 2nd ed. (Ithaca and London: Cornell University Press, 1990), 12–32, 74–94. More recently, Bruce W. Holsinger has provided an innovative analysis of the place of the liturgy's music in Hildegard's community in *Music, Body, and Desire in the Medieval Culture: Hildegard of Bingen to Chaucer* (Stanford, Calif.: Stanford University Press, 2001), 87–136. Mechthild's position as *Domna cantrix* is discussed by Theresa A. Halligan in her edition of *The Booke of Gostlye Grace of Mechthild of Hackeborn* (Toronto: Pontifical Institute of Mediaeval Studies, 1979), 36–37. See also Anna C. Sander, "Music and Liturgy in the Visions of Mechthild von Hackeborn" (MPhil diss., University of York, 2003).

2. The full Latin text of the *Sermo*, along with Alphonse of Jaén's introduction, can be found in *Den Heliga Birgitta Opera Minora II: Sermo Angelicus*, ed. Sten Eklund, Svenska Fornskriftsällskapet Samlingar, ser. 2, Latinska Skrifter 8:2 (Uppsala: Almquist and Wiksell, 1972). This text is also available on-line at Julia Bolton Holloway, *Birgitta of Sweden Website* (6 January 2003, accessed 19 February 2003, http://www.umilta.net/bk11.html). The Latin text also appears in its liturgical context in A. Jefferies Collins, ed., *The Bridgettine Breviary of Syon Abbey*, Publications of the Henry Bradshaw Society 96 (Worcester: Henry Bradshaw Society, 1969). Here I provide the text in English translation from John E. Halborg, trans., *The Word of the Angel* (Toronto: Peregrina, 1996) with the Latin from the SFSS edition in the notes, along with page references from the *Breviary*.

3. For a description of the unique features of the Bridgittine rite, see Collins, *Breviary*, ix–xv, xx–xxii, and Anne Bagnall Yardley, "Bridgettine Spirituality and Musical Practices at Syon Abbey," in *Studies in St. Birgitta and the Brigittine Order*, ed. James Hogg, 2 vols., Analecta Cartusiana 35:19 (Salzburg: Institut für Anglistik und Amerikanistik, 1993), 2:199–214. For a more general overview of the various textual and musical forms of the liturgy, see Andrew Hughes, *Medieval Manuscripts for Mass and Office: A Guide to Their Organization and Terminology* (Toronto: University of Toronto Press, 1982), 21–40.

4. Rosalynn Voaden, *God's Words, Women's Voices: The Discernment of Spirits in the Writing of Late-Medieval Women Visionaries* (Woodbridge, Suffolk: York Medieval Press, 1999).

5. The story of the *Sermo*'s origin is related in Alphonse of Jaén's introduction to the *Sermo* (75–76 in the SFSS edition) and analyzed in Collins, *Breviary,* xvi–xx, xxiv–xxx.

6. For the structure of matins and its lessons, see Hughes, *Medieval Manuscripts for Mass and Office,* 53–66.

7. William Durandus, *Rationale Divinorum Officiorum,* ed. A. Davril and T. M. Thibodeau, 3 vols., Corpus Christianorum Continuatio Mediaevalis 140–140B (Turnholt: Brepols, 1995–2000), 2:35 (5.2.604–6): "lectiones nocturnales sunt doctrina nostra quia per eas docemur opera nostra retorquere ad Deum."

8. Rupert of Deutz, *Liber de Divinis Officiis,* ed. H. Haacke, Corpus Christianorum Continuatio Mediaevalis 7 (Turnholt: Brepols, 1967), 12 (1.14.221–23): "Gratias namque agimus Deo, quod doctrinae suae panem nobis frangere dignatur, ne fame audiendi uerbum Dei pereamus."

9. *Vicar Christi* occurs in the *Speculum de Mysteriis Ecclesie,* wrongly attributed to Hugh of St. Victor, *PL* 177, col. 342A; *principatus Ecclesie* occurs in Durandus, *Rationale Divinorum Officiorum,* 2:35 (5.2.615).

10. John Beleth, *Summa de Ecclesiasticis Officiis,* ed. H. Douteil, Corpus Christianorum Continuatio Mediaevalis 41–41A (Turnholt: Brepols, 1976), 1:52 (25.36–37): "nullus in ecclesia nisi iussus debeat legere uel concessus."

11. Durandus, *Rationale Divinorum Officiorum,* 2:35 (5.2.616–19).

12. Ibid., 2:37 (5.2.682–85): "sicut in Ecclesia duo sunt ordines: sapientes et insipientes, sic due sunt lectionum manieres. In illis enim lectionibus que ad missam leguntur sapientes instruuntur; in hiis uero que in nocte recitantur, insipientes erudiuntur."

13. My discussion here and in the following few paragraphs concerning the objectification of relations of power enacted in ritual reading is generally indebted to Pierre Bourdieu, *Language and Symbolic Power,* ed. John B. Thompson, trans. Gino Raymond and Matthew Adamson (Cambridge, Mass.: Harvard University Press, 1991), 107–16; and to his *Outline of a Theory of Practice,* trans. Richard Nice, Cambridge Studies in Social and Cultural Anthropology 16 (Cambridge: Cambridge University Press, 1977), 184–87. In the latter, Bourdieu describes "social formations in which, mediated by objective, institutionalized mechanisms, such as those producing and guaranteeing the distribution of 'titles,' . . . relations of domination have the opacity and permanence of things and escape the grasp of individual consciousness and power. Objectification guarantees the permanence and cumulativity of material and symbolic acquisitions which can then subsist without the agents having to recreate them continuously." For more on the speech dynamics of liturgical performance, see K. Zieman, *Reading and Singing: Liturgy, Literacy, and Literature* (University of Pennsylvania Press, forthcoming).

14. Durandus, *Rationale Divinorum Officiorum,* 2:35 (5.2.44): "Lecturus ergo lectionem, ad librum accedens, super gradum ascendit, quia doctor perfectiori uita uulgos transcendere debet."

15. Beleth, *Summa de Ecclesiasticis Officiis,* 1:59 (30.32–33): "legere lectionem non est officium sacerdotis, sed lectoris." Durandus repeats this passage more or less verbatim within his discussion (*Rationale Divinorum Officiorum,* 2:36 [5.2.638–54]). The remark is prompted in both cases by the disruption to ecclesiastical hierarchy that occurs if a priest or bishop should choose to read. For Beleth, a priest should not need to ask a blessing, since as a priest he is always licensed to read and therefore should be giving rather than receiving the blessing (*Summa de Ecclesiasticis Officiis,* 1:59 [30.27–28]). The structure of blessing is more important to Durandus, however, such that he lists numerous performative options that would allow the blessing to be given without unsettling the

decorum of hierarchy (e.g., a cleric in lower orders can bless a petitioning bishop by speaking "in persona ecclesie"). This fluidity of *persone* is less likely to occur in the Mass since the reading of epistle and gospel lessons is more clearly delegated to subdeacons and deacons, respectively.

16. The practice has its roots in the Jewish *Keriat Hatorah*. Getting *aliyah*, which included pronouncing a blessing over the reading, required membership in the adult male community, but was nonetheless a "lay" practice. Information about early Judeo-Christian practice here is based on Cyrille Vogel, *Medieval Liturgy: An Introduction to the Sources*, trans. William Storey and Niels Rasmussen (Washington, D.C.: Pastoral Press, 1986), 301–302 and nn. 378–79.

17. The development of a dialectical relationship between liturgy and devotion and its consequences for women religious is treated more fully in K. Zieman, "Reading, Singing, and Understanding: Constructions of the Literacy of Women Religious in Late Medieval England," in *Learning and Literacy in Medieval England and Abroad*, ed. Sarah Rees Jones (Turnhout: Brepols, 2003), 97–120.

18. Durandus, *Rationale Divinorum Officiorum*, 2:14–15 (5.2.2–4); Beleth, *Summa de Ecclesiasticis Officiis*, 1:41 (19.10–33).

19. This is not to say that they did not acknowledge human agency in the production of liturgy, or that they did not acknowledge that new rituals (such as the feasts of newly canonized saints) were still being produced. But because the gestures are meant to vest authority in the texts' *institution* rather than its author, liturgical texts are in some sense treated as if always already written. Devotional texts, by contrast, such as those that appear in devotional miscellanies and books of hours, are often prefaced by particularlizing descriptions that mention the writer, the time at which the prayer was conceived or authorized, the particular results of the prayer (especially those with indulgences attached). Particularizing of this sort is ultimately what marks the difference between devotion and liturgy: devotion is the gesture of the individual soul, located in secular history, towards the divine; liturgy is the commemoration and reenactment of salvation history in which all souls have always and will always play a part.

20. Beleth, *Summa de Ecclesiasticis Officiis*, 1:52 (25.55–59): "Et est sensus: Domine, ego forsitan peccaui in legendo modulate pronuntians humane cupidine laudis, et auditores similiter peccauerunt variis cogitationibus intendentes et lectioni non tribuentes auditum. *Autem* pro sed: sed, o tu Domine, miserere nostri." Cf. Durandus, *Rationale Divinorum Officiorum*, 2:36 (5.2.655–61).

21. Rupert of Deutz, *Liber de Divinis Officiis*, 12 (1.14.220–21): "*Deo gratias* succinit chorus, non ad ultimam precem lectoris, sed ad totam lectionem respicit"; cf. *Speculum de Mysteriis Ecclesie*, col. 875B; Beleth, *Summa de Ecclesiasticis Officiis*, 1:52 (25.60–62); Durandus, *Rationale Divinorum Officiorum*, 2:36–37 (5.2.660–66).

22. This misrecognition is similar to that articulated by Bourdieu, *Language and Symbolic Power*, 116.

23. For more on these debates, see Bridget Morris, *St. Birgitta of Sweden* (Woodbridge, Suffolk: Boydell Press, 1999), 152–59; Claire L. Sahlin, *Birgitta of Sweden and the Voice of Prophecy* (Woodbridge, Suffolk, and Rochester, N.Y.: Boydell Press, 2001); and in England in particular, F. R. Johnston, "English Defenders of St. Bridget," in *Studies in St. Birgitta and the Brigittine Order*, ed. James Hogg, 2 vols., Analecta Cartusiana 35:19 (Salzburg: Institut für Anglistik und Amerikanistik, 1993), 1:263–75.

24. The *Defensorium Sancte Birgitte* has been edited and translated by J. A. Schmidtke in "Adam Easton's Defense of St. Birgitta from Bodleian MS Hamilton 7, Oxford University" (PhD diss., Duke University, 1972). Translations of the text quoted here are Schmidtke's unless noted otherwise.

25. The story of the Rule's origin is related in the *Revelaciones Extrauagantes*, ed. Lennart Hollman, Svenska Fornskrifsällskapet Samlingar, ser. 2, Latinska Skrifter 5 (Uppsala: Almquist and Wiksell, 1967), 161–62. See also the opening chapters of the Rule itself in *Den Heliga Birgitta Opera Minora I: Regula Saluatoris*, ed. Sten Eklund, Svenska Fornskriftsällskapet Samlingar, ser. 2, 8:1 (Lund: Berlingska, 1975), 99–101.

26. Schmidtke, "Adam Easton's Defense," 60; "Non est veresimile quod Christus ore proprio dictaverit regulam et eam voluerit publicari per mulierem quam apostolus in ecclesia loqui non permittit et tam viros quam mulieres illius ecclesie sive monasterii ad dictam regulam servandam perpetuo obligari" (ibid., 185).

27. Here he confuses 1 Cor. 14:34 and Tim. 2:12.

28. Thomas Aquinas, *Summa Theologiae*, ed. and trans. Thomas Gilby, 61 vols. (Cambridge: Blackfriars; New York: McGraw-Hill, 1964–1976), 45:132–33 (2a2æ.177.2). The question concerns the nature of speech: "whether the charism of wisdom, speech, and knowledge pertains to women also" (translation slightly modified from Gilby's; "utrum gratia sermonis, sapientiae et scientiae pertineat etiam ad mulieres"), where "speech" (*sermo*) is equated with teaching. It therefore does not distinguish teaching from praying and prophesying, but rather distinguishes public from private teaching, as Easton eventually does as well.

29. Schmidtke, "Adam Easton's Defense," 61; "mulier potest loqui in ecclesia orando et eciam prophetando, iuxta convenienciam sibi datam, non tamen forsan in persona tocius ecclesie sine privilegio speciali" (ibid., 186). The phrase "in persona tocius ecclesie" appears to be Easton's, although the argument is based on Aquinas, *Summa Theologiae*, 45:132–33 (2a2æ.177.2): "Dicendum quod sermone potest aliquis uti dupliciter. Uno modo privatim ad unum vel paucos, familariter colloquendo, et quantum ad hoc gratia sermonis potest competere mulieribus. Alio modo publice alloquendo totam Ecclesiam, et hoc mulieri non conceditur." (Speech can be used in two ways. In one way privately, to one or a few, in familiar conversation. In this way the grace of speech becomes a woman. The other way publicly, addressing oneself to the whole Church. This is not conceded to women.)

30. The phrase is used by Durandus, for example, to explain how a clerk in minor orders may be authorized to give the blessing petitioned by the bishop if he is thought to be speaking "in persona ecclesie" (*Rationale Divinorum Officiorum*, 2:36; 5.2.649). Beleth uses it several times (e.g., *Summa de Ecclesiasticis Officiis*, 1:265; 136.86–87), along with the phrase "uox ecclesie" to denote utterances in the name of or on behalf of the Church (e.g., *Summa de Ecclesiasticis Officiis*, 1:52; 25.61). Although these phrases are not used to discuss the reading of lessons, they emphasize impersonation and voicing as facets of liturgical discourse.

31. Aquinas, *Summa Theologiae*, 45:132–33 (2a2æ.177.2): "Docere . . . publice in Ecclesia non pertinet ad subditos, sed ad praelatos; magis tamen viri subditi ex commissione possunt exequie, quia non habent hujusmodi subjectionem ex naturali sexu, sicut mulieres, sed ex aliquo accidentaliter superveniente."

32. Schmidtke, "Adam Easton's Defense," 61; "docere est opus sapientis; sapientia vero non viget in mulieribus de consequenti cursu" (ibid., 186).

33. Ibid., 61; "mulier est fragilis, inprudens, subiecta, et de iure communi inabilis ad docendum publice tamquam doctor in ecclesia" (ibid., 186).

34. Aquinas, however, uses the term *privatum* rather than *domestice.*

35. Hollman, *Revelaciones Extrauagantes*, 230–31: "Primo videtur tibi, quod quasi aliqua persona demonstrat tibi ea, que dictura es. Secundo modo magistro tuo videbatur, quod quasi

aures eius et os cum vento replerentur et cor eius sicut vesica, repleta ex ardenti caritate ad Deum, extendebatur, et in illa cordi dulci fragracione optinuit ipse scienciam aliquorum verborum et diccionum, que prius nesciuit, et quomodo ipse responsoria, antiphonas et ympnos deberet componere ac cantum in notis ordinare. Ideo vtraque ista duo sunt ex sancti spiritus induccione secundum virtutis sue distribucionem, illi, scilicet angelo, ad leccionum promulgacionem, et alteri ad cantus ordinacionem." The Middle English translation has been quoted from *The Myroure of Oure Ladye*, ed. John Henry Blunt, Early English Text Society *e.s.* 19 (London, 1873), 17–18.

36. On the distinction between types of visions, see Voaden, *God's Words*, 9–12.

37. Ibid., 12–19, passim.

38. Ibid., 46–72. For a history of the development of the doctrine of *discretio spirituum*, see Nancy Caciola, *Discerning Spirits: Divine and Demonic Possession in the Middle Ages* (Ithaca, N.Y.: Cornell University Press, 2003).

39. Ibid., 74.

40. Hollman, *Revelaciones Extrauagantes*, 165: "Ego sum similis carpentario, qui prescindens ligna de silua deportat in domum et inde fabricat ymaginem pulchram et ornat eam coloribus et liniamentis. Cuius amici videntes ymaginem, quod adhuc pulchrioribus coloribus ornari posset, apposuerunt et ipsi colores suos depingendo super eam."

41. Ibid., 166.

42. Apparently this containment was not entirely successful, since Birgitta's writings were sometimes granted the authority of scripture; critics at the Council of Basle (1431–49) objected to claims such as this that likened the *Revelaciones* to the gospels. See Morris, *St. Birgitta*, 158.

43. Blunt, *Myroure*, 20.

44. Voaden's account of Birgitta emphasizes the fact that her visions are interpreted by divine interlocutors rather than by herself (*God's Words*, 99–104). While divine interlocutors are a far cry from male clerics, my chief point here is that visions must be interpreted by another. Without dismissing the divine explicators of Birgitta's visions, however, it is worth pointing out that even divine explications would still be subject to the validation of learned clerics, who are presumed to have the knowledge required for discernment.

45. Hollman, *Revelaciones Extrauagantes*, 165–66: "obscura elucidet et catholicum sensum spiritus mei teneat."

46. Alphonse's preface to the *Sermo* (translated in the *Myroure*) also has the angel himself give approval, describing the ritual text as "a cote to the quiene of heven, the mother of god" and enjoining her to revise it: "Therefore sowe ye yt togyther as ye may" (Blunt, *Myroure*, 19); "Ecce, iam ego sarsi tunicam regine celi, matri Dei; vos ergo eam, sicut poteritis, consuatis" (*Sermo*, 76).

47. Blunt, *Myroure*, 20.

48. This version is found in Blunt, *Myroure*, 17, and translates the speech as it is found in one redaction of the *Revelaciones Extrauagantes* (Hollman, 230n): "In cantu meo non est compositum magistrale et rethoricum Latinum, tamen magis placent michi verba illa de istius amici mei dilecti ore dictata quam subtilia aliquorum magistrorum mundialum." A different redaction, however, prefaces the claim of simplicity with a stronger claim for doctrinal authority, and thus treats doctrine and learning separately. After instructing that the *Cantus* should be given to Bishop Hemming to inspect, Mary states that he may change it, with one exception: "totum autem, quod ibi de infancia mea scriptum est, verum est. Et huic ecclesie contradicere non potest. Et quamuis ibi non sit

magistrale Latinum, pocius tamen mihi verba placent ex ore istius dilecti amici mei quam ex ore alicuius magistri mundani" (230).

49. Yardley, "Bridgettine Spirituality," 199–201, passim, calls attention to the ideal of simplicity in the Bridgittine liturgy.

50. Nicholas Watson, "The Middle English Mystics," in *The Cambridge History of Medieval Literature*, ed. David Wallace (Cambridge: Cambridge University Press, 1999), 551.

51. *The Liber Celestis of St. Bridget of Sweden: The Middle English Version in British Library MS Claudius B.i.*, ed. Roger Ellis, Early English Text Society *o.s.* 291 (Oxford: EETS, 1987), 174–75. The revelation comes from Book 2, ch. 22 of the *Reuelaciones*, of which there is no modern edition. The text of the editio princeps (1494), however, can be found at the *Birgitta of Sweden Website*, http://www.umilta.net/bk2.html: "Unde per exemplum dico tibi, quasi esset unus, qui volens addiscere sapienciam vidit duos magistros ante se stare. . . . Respondit alter magistrorum: 'Si meam sapienciam sequi volueris, ducet te in altissimum montem, sed in via duricia lapidum est sub pedibus, difficultas et preruptum est in ascensu'. . . . Secundus magister ait: 'Si sapienciam meam secutus fueris, ducet te in vallem floridam et ex omni terre fructu amenam. Mollicia est in via sub pedibus et in descensu modicus labor. Si perstiteris in ista sapiencia, habebis, quod extra est fulgidum, sed cum frui eo volueris, fugiet a te. Habebis eciam, quod non durat sed statim finitur.'"

52. "Non enim veraciter sapiencia dici potest, nisi cum verbis concordat opus."

53. "sapienciam cum lectura finituram."

54. William Langland, *Piers Plowman: The C Version*, ed. George Kane and George Russell (Berkeley: University of California Press; London: Athlone, 1997), C.11.293–94.

55. *Revelaciones: Book I*, ed. Carl-Gustav Undhagen, Svenska Fornskriftsällskapet Samlingar, ser. 2, Latinska Skrifter 7:1 (Uppsala: Almquist and Wiksell, 1978), 336 (1.33): "primo conscienciam intelligentem supra naturam cerebri, secundo sapienciam sine homine, quia personaliter doceo eos intus; tercio pleni sunt dulcedine et diuina dileccione, qua vincent diabolum." Cf. *Liber Celestis*, 59: "first, a conninge consciens abouen þe kinde of brayne, þe seconde, a wisdome withoute man, for I in persone teches þaime inward in saule, þe þirde, þai are full of swetenes and of Godes lufe, for þai sall ouircome þe deuell."

56. Ann M. Hutchinson, "*The Myroure of Oure Ladye:* A Medieval Guide for Contemplatives," in *Studies in St. Birgitta and the Brigittine Order*, ed. James Hogg, 2 vols., Analecta Cartusiana 35:19 (Salzburg: Institut für Anglistik und Amerikanistik, 1993), 2:218–19.

57. *Regula Salvatoris*, 118, 159.

58. *Regula Salvatoris*, 161: "ipsa Virgo, cuius abbatissa gerit vicem in terris, ascendente Christo in celos caput et regina extitit apostolorum et discipulorum Christi." Cf. ibid., 120.

59. Hutchinson, "*Myroure of Oure Ladye*," 217.

60. Noted by Hutchinson, "*Myroure of Oure Ladye*," 219.

61. For a partial catalogue of books in the Vadstena library, see Margarete Andersson-Schmitt, Monica Hedlund, et al., eds. *Mittelalterliche Handschriften der Universitätsbibliothek Uppsala: Katalog über die C-Sammlung*, Acta Bibliothecae R. Universitatis Upsaliensis 26, 8 vols. (Stockholm: Almqvist, 1988–95). See also D. N. Bell, *What Nuns Read: Books and Libraries in Medieval English Nunneries*, Cistercian Studies 158 (Kalamazoo, Mich.: Cistercian Publications, 1995), 74–74; 171–210, who provides a catalogue of the extensive library of Syon Abbey.

62. *Regula Salvatoris*, 118, 159.

63. The association of Mary with wisdom already had a long tradition. Hildegard of Bingen perhaps provides the most compelling example, particularly in light of its connections with her understanding of music. See Barbara Newman, *Sister of Wisdom: St. Hildegard's Theology of the Feminine* (Berkeley and Los Angeles: University of California Press), 160–80 and throughout. For an example that concerns the reading of liturgical lessons, see 179–81.

64. Halborg, *Word of the Angel*, 48; "Nulla lingua narrare sufficit quam prudenter sensus et intellectus gloriose virginis ipsum deum in eodem puncto comprehendit, quo primo eius cognicionem habuit, presertim, cum omnis humana mens ad excogitandum debilis sit, quam multiformiter eiusdem virginis benedicta uoluntas dei seruicio se subiecit" (*Sermo*, 113; cf. Collins, *Breviary*, 73).

65. *Sermo*, 115; cf. Collins, *Breviary*, 74.

66. Halborg, *Word of the Angel*, 49–50.

67. Newman, *Sister of Wisdom*, 194–95, shows Hildegard of Bingen suggesting the same creative power for Mary's fiat.

68. Halborg, *Word of the Angel*, 61; "omni auiditate quesiuit . . . solicite inuestigauit, donec ipsam sapienciam, scilicet Christum, Dei Filium, qui incomparabiliter Salamone sapiencior est, sapienter inuenit" (*Sermo*, 128; cf. Collins, *Breviary*, 99).

69. Halborg, *Word of the Angel*, 62; "plures animas suas salutari doctrina ipsi Deo presentabat quam aliqua persona post christi mortem vniuersis suis operibus" (*Sermo*, 129; cf. Collins, *Breviary*, 99).

70. Halborg, *Word of the Angel*, 62; "Ascendente vero suo benedicto Filio ad suum regnum gloriosum, Virgo Maria in hoc mundo ad bonorum confortacionem et errancium correccionem remanere permissa est. Erat enim magistra apostolorum, confortatrix martirum, doctrix confessorum, clarissimum speculum virginum, consolatrix viduarum, in coniugio viuencium saluberima monitrix, atque omnium in fide catholicum perfectissima roboratrix" (*Sermo*, 129–30; cf. Collins, *Breviary*, 99–100).

71. Halborg, *Word of the Angel*, 62; "tunc virgo mater, quamuis Scriptura eo tempore ipsam aliquid locutam non commemorat, sine dubio tamen credendum est, quod ipsa Dei Filium in carne ad eternam gloriam resurrexisse testificata est et quod mors de cetero illi nunquam posset amplius dominari. Item quamuis eciam Scriptura dicat, quod christi resurreccionem magdelena et apostoli prius viderunt, sine dubio tamen credendum est, quod sua mater dignissima antequam illi veraciter hoc sciebat et priusquam illi eum viuum resurrexisse a mortuis vidit, propter quod iubilo cordis plenissima, ipsum humiliter collaudauit" (*Sermo*, 129; cf. Collins, *Breviary*, 99).

72. For more on these traditions, see Elizabeth K. Schirmer, "Orthodoxy, Textuality, and the 'Tretys' of Margery Kempe," *Journal X* 1 (1996): 31–55.

73. Voaden, *God's Words*, 74.

74. For a fuller treatment of Birgitta's relationship with the Virgin as expressed in the *Revelaciones*, see Claire Sahlin, "The Virgin Mary and Bridget of Sweden's Prophetic Vocation," in *Maria i Sverge under tusen år. Föredrag vid symposiet i Vadstena 6–10 oktober 1994*, ed. Sven-Erik Brodd and Alf Härdelin, 2 vols. (Skellefteå: Artos, 1996), 1:232–40, to which my reading is partly indebted.

75. Halborg, *Word of the Angel*, 18; "Letabatur Noe eo, quod archa sua interius et exterius ita bituminanda erat, quod sentina aliqua in eam nequiret instillare" (*Sermo*, 82; cf. Collins, *Breviary*, 18).

76. Halborg, *Word of the Angel*, 18: "Nouit se Noe relicturum archam suam vacuam, quando ab ipsa discederet, et ad eam deinceps minime reuersurum" (*Sermo*, 83; cf. Collins, *Breviary*, 18).

77. Halborg, *Word of the Angel,* 18; "Et quamuis corpus suum a tuo corpore in sua natiuitate separaretur, nichilominus tamen te presciuit secum sine fine inseparabiliter permansuram" (*Sermo,* 83; cf. Collins, *Breviary,* 18).

78. Collins, *Breviary,* 23; Blunt, *Myroure,* 136.

79. This Bridgittine tradition might in part help explain the "misplaced" chapter in the *Book of Margery Kempe:* after Christ has compared her favorably to Birgitta ("'My dowtyr, Bride, say me neuyr in þis wyse'") and has personally authenticated Birgitta's *Reuelaciones* in the previous chapter, chapter 21 goes on to exonerate Kempe for her lack of virginity (what made Birgitta such a powerful model for her) which is immediately followed by the Virgin Mary's claim to be her teacher: "'Dowtyr, I am thy modyr, þi lady, and thy *maystres* for to teche þe in al wyse how þu schalt plese God best'" (*The Book of Margery Kempe,* ed. Sanford B. Meech and Hope E. Allen, Early English Text Society *o.s.* 212 [London: Oxford University Press, 1940], 38, 47, 50, my emphasis).

80. Schmidtke, "Adam Easton's Defense," 139; "Maria absque aliquo dubio accepit excellenter donum sapientie et prophecie . . . non tamen sic accepit ut haberet omnes usus harum et consilium graciarum sicud habuit Christus et eius apostoli, quorum princeps scilicet Petrus in sua doctrina prima et predicacione recepto Spiritu Sancto convertit tria milia animarum . . . sed huiusmodi gracias et usum accepit Virgo Maria excellenter secundum quod conveniebat condicioni ipsius sapiencie enim usus habuit in contemplando secundum Lucam ii: 'Maria autem conservabat verba hec conferens in corde suo'. . . . usum autem prophecie habuit ut patet in cantico illo quod fecit: 'Magnificat anima mea Dominum'" (ibid., 251).

81. Schmidtke, "Adam Easton's Defense," 140; "Ipsa enim publice docebat in cantico suo unde plures ad Dominum sunt conversi" (ibid., 251).

82. Easton's summation of the argument shows his inability to integrate the "public" quality of Mary's *Magnificat:* "potest dici . . . quod Virgo Maria 'plures animas salutari doctrina ipsi Deo presentabat quam aliqua alia persona post Christi mortem universis suis operibus,' quia quod fecit Petrus ipsa eciam faciebat, quia doctrina Petrus publica, a doctrina Virginis domestice orta fuit ut superius dictum fuit. Ipsa enim publice docebat in cantico suo unde plures ad Dominum sunt conversi ut patet Lucis ii [*sic*] capitulo. Et non dicit articulus de publica doctrina Marie sed de salutari doctrina ipsius, qua propter obieccio adversarii nichil facit" (Schmidtke, "Adam Easton's Defense," 251–52).

83. Schmidtke, "Adam Easton's Defense," 138; "Magnificat . . . Per cuius cantici doctrinam publicam tota Dei ecclesia in fide et moribus per quam Virginem erudiri" (ibid., 250).

84. For evidence of the spread of the Syon community and its practice beyond the monastery, see Catherine A. Grisé, "Syon Abbey in Late-Medieval England: Gender and Reading, Bodies and Communities, Piety and Politics" (PhD diss., University of Western Ontario, 1998).

■ ■ ■

"Voices Magnified"

Response to Katherine Zieman

MARGOT E. FASSLER

There has been much written in recent years about the ways in which the inability to participate in the Eucharist as clergy—or sometimes even as communicants—affected medieval Catholic women.[1] Women from across a spectrum of lifestyles, from impoverished hermits to wealthy laity, experimented with ways of redefining human relationships to sacramental action and to the elements of bread and wine, elements they could not draw near to, let alone bless, distribute, or, even, in many circumstances, receive as often as they desired.[2] In some cases, the reshaping of eucharistic understanding stimulated a gendered concentration upon eucharistic elements in particular, and more generally upon food and nurture. A variety of women learned to compensate for their powerlessness and lack of presence around the communion table through various modes either of deprivation or of excess, and sometimes of both; some women addressed the imbalance of power within the Church through renewed understandings of the divine encounter, both within the cloister or sanctuary and without it. Ideas of what the Host was and its centrality in defining not only religious practices but social ordering as well put yet further emphasis upon the reception of the blessed meal.[3] The modes of redress adopted by those who felt powerless in the wake of late medieval clericalism and sacramental straight-jacketing demonstrate that many women in the later Middle Ages wished to find ways of entering into the heart of religious mysteries, those of Eucharist and those of divine encounter more generally.

The Divine Office seems to have offered more opportunities for female participation than did the Mass, at least in the central Middle Ages when most female religious followed the Benedictine Rule, and before the time of the friars and the communities of women directly affiliated with them or supervised by them in some variety of ways. The communal prayer of the Office did not require ordained clergy for its celebration. The Benedictine Office offered nuns direct access to texts and chants and provided opportunities for them to play major roles in direction and execution. Whereas nuns had to import male clergy for the celebration of Mass, they needed no men to celebrate the Office. The extreme importance praying the Office had for one particular female community is demonstrated in a famous letter by Hildegard of Bingen. When her community was placed under indiction and lost its right to sing the Divine Office, Hildegard wrote a scathing critique of those who robbed the nuns of the heart of their purpose. Without communal prayer, sung communal prayer, they ceased to function: full liturgical participation was required to fulfill vows in accordance with the Benedictine Rule. Indeed Hildegard the composer had written the great majority of her musical works for the Office, and for herself and other women to sing.[4]

When it came to the hours of daily prayer throughout the central Middle Ages, religious men and religious women with appropriate linguistic and musical training approached God as liturgical equals. The Benedictine Rule and early interpretations of it gave monks and nuns positions that were not inferior to those of the priestly cast. The burst of interest in the education of nuns in the Rhineland in the twelfth century rested in part upon expectations of full participation in the *opus Dei* with its psalmody and a full cycle of eight monastic hours per day, composed of various combinations of chants, prayers, and intoned readings.[5] Surely one of the reasons Hildegard wished to establish her own community apart from the monks of the Disibodenberg was this need for an Office she could shape along particular lines and in accordance with the tenets of her theology. Singing the Office, however, required the training built into monastic education and witnessed to by the customaries.[6] The immense learning provided to those who sang the Office was fully open only to those who could read Latin and who could sing.

In her essay "Playing *Doctor*" Katherine Zieman posits the reader within liturgical circumstances far removed from those of Hildegard's twelfth-century Benedictine community in the Rhineland. For the specialist accustomed to the rigors of earlier monastic rules and customaries it is not particularly striking to learn that the Bridgittine Order in England at Syon Abbey had a separate Office for men and for women. Comparatively little work has been done on the liturgical practices of double monasteries in any age, but the Bridgittine Order offers some of the best evidence available for a late strain of double monastic life, existing long after many earlier forms of the life had fallen into disuse. What is initially striking, troubling even, about the Bridgittine double Office is the fact that the men sang the full secular Office of Sarum, the ornate and complex set of cathedral hours that was a close kin to the Benedictine Office, whereas the women rendered a version of the Little Office of the Blessed Virgin.[7] In fact, the women followed each hour sung by the men with the appropriate section of this Little Office.[8] It seems at first examination that the exclusion of women from ecclesial power, familiar when regarding the Mass liturgy, has extended to the Office as well in this practice.

Before one studies—or even defends—the powerful female "voice" emitting from the Bridgittine choir loft, we need to take stock of what was lost in the movement from the singing of the Benedictine monastic cursus or the secular Office, such as that of Sarum, to the recitation of the Little Office of the Blessed Virgin Mary, even as recast by St. Birgitta and her associates.[9] The Little Office of the Blessed Virgin developed in the course of the Carolingian period as a set of special devotions to be prayed by monks and nuns at the close of regularly appointed Office hours. Among religious it was designed to enhance the standard *opus Dei,* in which all 150 psalms were sung each week, and which offered a rich array of patristic texts and saints' lives for the readings of the night Office, matins. For Benedictines, then, the Little Office merely supplemented a larger and more complex organization of chanted psalms, readings, and prayers. It was lacking in the variety of the Benedictine Office: in many later recastings—as psalters with little hours became replaced by hours alone in the course of the thirteenth and early fourteenth centuries—the psalmody was set for three-day cycles or even for daily cycles that varied but little throughout the week; the lessons were consistently the same. The sameness of the texts, which were cycled through week after week, made this an appealing vehicle of prayer for the laity. The truncated form and the simplicity of the Little Office made good sense for a man or woman who lived in the secular world and who did not have the time, energy, or musical and linguistic skills necessary for the *opus Dei.* As is well known, the Little Office of the Blessed Virgin became the standard text for medieval books of hours and for a variety of later prayer books as well. As such, it is the most richly illumined of any Christian prayer text.[10] In most of its guises, it evolved as a spoken or silently read *text.* The musical and communal dimensions of the Benedictine Office were not present for most people who prayed it in the later Middle Ages. Even though the texts for chants, antiphons, responsories, and even hymns, are found in the Little Office, they are usually present to be read by an individual rather than sung in community, at least by mid-fourteenth century when the Bridgittine liturgy was first revealed to its holy founder, and then further developed and standardized by her teacher Master Peter.[11]

As we continue to reflect upon the manner in which the Bridgittines found their liturgical voice through their customized mode of prayer, I would suggest that this voice was heard through a practice that was repetitive and lacking in many of the elements that made the Benedictine Office a vehicle not only for prayer but also for learning. The Middle Ages has been seen as a time in which there was a steady march of regress for woman, in power, in learning, and in tolerance. It has been opined that Hildegard's learnedness was what made her less popular as an author in later centuries than her less intellectual sisters. Surely Zieman's work points us toward a major reason than women writers in the later Middle Ages often appear as contemplatives who concentrate almost exclusively on the inner life of the soul; the soul, often their own souls in particular, became the primary material available for their study. Women who lost connections to and participation in the Benedictine Office or other more complex practices of prayer, lost the chance to be schooled in language, music, scripture, and patristic writers. The Divine Office was the great textbook of the Middle Ages, the major compendium of learning for most people until the schools developed other regimes of learning from the mid-twelfth century forward that either supplemented or rivaled it.

The Bridgittine community accepted the Little Office of the Blessed Virgin, but transformed it into something that was their own. But the complexities of learning available through it were not great if one compares it with the full monastic or cathedral hours of prayer. Before we see how the women and the male scholars who aided them redeemed this Office for daily use, it should be said at the start that the Little Office was in need of redemption as a full set of sung monastic hours, a purpose for which it was never originally intended.

The disconnect not only in content, but also in practice, between the Benedictine Office and the Little Office as prayed by laity, alone in their homes or on the road, was deliberately exploited in the Bridgittine Office, which placed the two side by side, day in and day out. It is easy to suppose only that the yin and yang approach was an imaginative exercise, but one which offered the women but the short end of a once-blooming liturgical rod. Yet because it was the stub that lay women knew and cherished, to turn it into a monastic rule was a way to make a profound liturgical statement as well, and in the hands of their founders, one worthy of respect. It offered powerful solidarity with the laity, and underscored the nature of the founder, once a lay woman, and the mother of eight children. The Little Office of the Blessed Virgin was not only the framework but also the guiding inspiration for a new program of readings and chants, chief among them the readings for matins received from an angel by St. Birgitta, and the chants and hymns written by Master Peter, St. Birgitta's teacher.[12]

Zieman demonstrates the ways the readings adapted for the Little Office of the Blessed Virgin by the Bridgittines saved the service of prayer for the women who prayed and sang what might have become a female liturgical afterthought without attention and expansion. In the realm of Bridgittine liturgical practice, Zieman asks the reader to consider the cycle of liturgical readings attributed to Birgitta herself, the *Sermo angelicus*, "a visionary text modulated into the liturgical." It is a cardinal principle in the study of the liturgy to distinguish between what is the inherited practice of a particular community, and what texts and music were created by members of the community itself.[13] These latter are sure places for locating whatever special sense of communal identity was imparted by the liturgy. The creation of a daily set of readings for matins of the Little Office of the Blessed Virgin Mary from the writings of the founder, readings that unfolded throughout the week and were repeated week by week throughout the year, is an extraordinary development in and of itself. Such an unusual practice is surely evidence of the highest order for coming to understand how this community defined itself. It also means that the festive cycle of the church year, one that brought an Office liturgy that was calendrical and shaped by the feasts of the temporale and the sanctorale, was truncated, offering a different and more static sense of history and the unfolding of time.

Zieman points to the ways in which the introduction of St. Birgitta's readings into matins of the Little Office of the Virgin offered her voice authority and power. Zieman is right that this is the place in the liturgy where the fathers were intoned and studied in liturgical context in the Benedictine and secular Office. To replace them with St. Birgitta's does give her the role of a doctor of the church and pride of place. However, because it is an "all-girl show," the force of her accomplishments are not the same as they would be if the materials had been adapted for the Benedictine or secular Office. It is clear that Birgitta's *Sermo angelicus* also offers an interpretation of Mary's position regarding the Trinity and Creation, her experience of Christ's birth, passion, and resurrection, and then depicts the Virgin as leader of the Apostles in the post-Pentecost community. Bridgittine communities were set up so that the abbess was the highest authority, the leader of both the men and women in the monastery. The *Sermo* becomes the key text in the establishment of this custom, and not only magnifies a particular view of the Virgin, but also provides a kind of liturgical customary, explaining her historical powers and defining the kinds of people who followed her. The text in turn defines the power of the abbess, and the nature of the women who are mirrors of the Virgin in community.

It is an important aspect of the way the liturgical voice operates to notice the ways in which the themes established by the *Sermo* are magnified by other prayers and chants, the most important among them, the hymns.[14] Master Peter's twenty-seven originally composed hymns tie the liturgy together, offering places in every hour of the Office for the entire community to proclaim the central theme of the day, themes operating in the readings as well.[15] Thus through the hymn texts, the message of St. Birgitta's matins readings were spread throughout the Office, and they would have been the loudest and most clearly proclaimed of all parts of the liturgy. The hymns are shaped to form a communal megaphone for the *Sermo angelicus,* making the voice established by St. Birgitta much louder. In the Office for Monday, for example, Birgitta's readings are about the angels and their relationship to the Virgin, as the opening of the story demonstrates:

> It was love that led God to create. There could be nothing lacking in God, nothing wanting to his goodness or his joy. It was out of love alone that he willed creation, that there might be beings, apart from himself, who would partake of his infinite

goodness and joy. So the Angels came to be, created by God in countless numbers. To them he gave free will. . . . In their contemplation of God, the Angels saw with wonder a throne placed next to that of God himself. . . . Mary, you were the chosen one, destined for that throne near to the throne of God. It was you the Angels loved, after God, from the first moment of their creation, seeing in the contemplation of God, how beautiful he had made themselves, but how much more beautiful he would make you. . . .[16]

In his hymns for this day, Peter restates and expands upon Birgitta's ideas, weaving them into sung, poetic statements about the angelic hosts and their reverence for God and the mother of God. Yet other references to the angelic tribes operate in the prayers and the chants as well, but the hymns were sung by all in community, and were written especially for the purpose of allowing all the women to voice the strain.

The sonic reverberation of Birgitta's themes were especially favored in this practice, and there were profound reasons for this which go beyond the identity-building exercises provided by well-constructed liturgical practices. Through the *Sermo*, the chants, and the hymns, and the prayers, the cult of the Virgin and the cult of St. Birgitta were entwined, forming the undergirdings of liturgical and devotional life, both for the women who were most intimately involved by singing these texts, for the men who sustained them and prayed alongside them, but also for the laity as well. The women's liturgy became, I would argue, primarily a sonic and secondarily a visual testimony to cult, and a tool for teaching what the Office texts the laity said were really about. Their sung prayer was designed to embody beliefs about cult not only through the Office, but in other unique aspects of their liturgical practices as well, practices that relied upon church architecture and which allowed for the reception of laity to *hear* but not to *see* the nuns as they sang.

A description of the architecture necessary to make this sonic icon present to the laity and brethren as well is found in Collins's speculative reconstruction of the inner structure of Syon Abbey:

The church, in which both communities worshipped, stood between and separated the two sets of conventual buildings. . . . The choir of the sisters, mainly a wooden structure, was raised high above the centre of the nave (by 7 ells); it apparently occupied the second and third (of the five) bays and was supported by their six pillars which pierced its floor. The sisters would seem to have entered the church from their convent through a door in the upper part of the north wall, whence they reached the choir by crossing a bridge over the north aisle. There was other access. Eastwards from the choir they looked upon the Lady-altar, at which a priest-brother celebrated for them the daily Mary-Mass. . . . We are concerned only with the upper choir. In it, invisible to the seculars, perhaps also to the brethern, the sisters sang the Hours of this Breviary and their part of the Mary-Mass; they also saw the ceremonies performed at the High-altar and could hear the brothers as they chanted in their stalls.[17]

The entire liturgical package surrounding St. Birgitta's *Sermo angelicus* made the community a kind of living reliquary from which the spirits of the saints, especially of the Virgin Mary and Birgitta, but of also St. Anne and Birgitta's daughter St. Catherine, could shine forth on the breath of those who drew near to God through their presences. This was a "relic" that could be heard by the laity and appreciated by them because they themselves prayed the Little Office of the Virgin and knew it by heart in many cases. Thus there would have been deep sensitivity to changes and expansions within it. The more focused of those who came to sit below the nuns' gallery and hear the chanted form of a prayer they knew very well could have appreciated every nuance. The importance placed on the Ladymass at the high altar, a service at which they sang the chants, underscores the women's liturgical potency.[18] Later in the day, processions to High Mass would have formed an announcement, not only for the nuns themselves, but also for their varied audiences, the brethren, and the laity.[19] The sisters could see the action of this High Mass, and achieve closeness to the ritual usually denied to women of this period. Through their unusual liturgical actions, the transformed Little Office of the Virgin, their chanting at the Ladymass and their witness to it and to the High Mass, the Bridgittines offered interpretations of women's importance in the Church and its liturgy, and explored the meanings of both Office and Mass from a fresh perspective. Laity who heard them sing were provided yet another way of understanding the purpose and meaning of liturgical action, and surely could join in their prayers and devotional actions with fuller fervor. They could hear the voices of women who saw God, and who partook fully in a liturgical Office of prayer they themselves could recite at home. The Bridgittines offered yet another way of linking laity to clergy, a linking much to be desired in the fourteenth and fifteenth centuries. The "voice" so well described by Zieman was not only a learned one that wrote lessons for the Office. Through its carefully coordinated liturgical settings it rang in the gallery. Its sounds could be carried home and, through the exercise of memory, provide a new context for the much prayed text of the Little Office of the Blessed Virgin Mary.

Notes

1. When the notes for this response refer to bibliography already cited by Zieman, the citations are not given in full. For an introduction to the Eucharist in the Middle Ages, see Gary Macy, *Treasures from the Storeroom: Medieval Religion and the Eucharist* (Collegeville, Minn.: Liturgical Press, 1999).

2. See Caroline Walker Bynum, *Holy Feast and Holy Fast: The Religious Significance of Food to Medieval Women* (Berkeley: University of California Press, 1987), a work which inspired many other studies.

3. See Miri Rubin, *Corpus Christi: The Eucharist in Late Medieval Culture* (Cambridge: Cambridge University Press, 1991).

4. For discussion of this passage and of Hildegard's music in the context of the Office, see Margot Fassler, "Composer and Dramatist, 'Melodious singing and the freshness of remorse,'" in *Voice of the Living Light: Hildegard of Bingen and Her World*, ed. Barbara Newman (Berkeley: University of California Press, 2000), chap. 8.

5. For a window into this life, see the *Speculum Virginum*, now available in a scholarly edition prepared by Jutta Seyfarth (Turnholt: Brepols, 1990).

6. See Margot Fassler, "The Office of the Cantor in Monastic Rules and Customaries: A Preliminary Investigation," *Early Music History* 5 (1985) and Susan Boynton, "Training for the Liturgy as a Form of Monastic Education," in *Medieval Monastic Education*, ed. Carolyn Muessig and George Ferzoco (Leicester, London, and New York: Leicester University Press, 2000), 7–20.

7. The Sarum rite has been much studied and its major texts edited. It is commonly thought to have emanated from Salisbury Cathedral and was the liturgy that dominated in English cathedrals throughout the later Middle Ages. For a brief introduction, see Philip Baxter, *Sarum Use: The Development of a Medieval Code of Liturgy and Customs* (Salisbury, 1994).

8. For discussion of the liturgy of the Little Office, especially in one of its most important centers of development, see Rebecca A. Baltzer, "The Little Office of the Virgin and Mary's Role at Paris," in *The Divine Office in the Latin Middle Ages: Methodology and Source Studies, Regional Developments, Hagiography*, ed. Margot Fassler and Rebecca Baltzer (New York: Oxford University Press, 2000), 463–84.

9. For a brief summary of the salient features of the hours of the Divine Office, including comparison between the monastic and secular orderings, see Lila Collamore, "Prelude: Charting the Divine Office," in *The Divine Office in the Latin Middle Ages: Methodology and Source Studies, Regional Developments, Hagiography*, ed. Margot Fassler and Rebecca Baltzer (New York: Oxford University Press, 2000), 3–11.

10. For an introduction to medieval books of hours, see two studies by Roger Wieck: *Time Sanctified: The Book of Hours in Medieval Art and Life* (New York G. Braziller, 1988) and *Painted Prayers: The Book of Hours in Medieval and Renaissance Art* (New York: G. Braziller, 1997). Several sources available on the web for the study of medieval books of hours are supplied in my "Psalms and Prayers in Daily Devotion: A Fifteenth-Century Devotional Anthology from the Diocese of Rheims, Beinecke 757," in *Worship in Medieval and Early Modern Europe: Change and Continuity in Religious Practice*, ed. Karin Maag and John D. Witvliet (Notre Dame, Ind.: University of Notre Dame Press, 2004), 15–40.

11. See Collins, *Breviary*, xvi–xxxi. St. Birgitta appears to have received the divine command to found an order and the revelation of the rule to govern it in 1346. Two men were involved with the process of transcribing and translating this and other of her works and aiding her with the process of making a liturgy for the Order. Both of them were named Peter Olafsson. Prior Petrus Olavi of the Cistercian Abbey of Alvastra made the first translation of the Rule from Swedish to Latin, and later worked with the other Peter on the breviary edited by Collins. Magister Petrus Olavi (who had been a secular priest at Skänninge, near to Linköping) began to serve as the saint's teacher,

the transcriber and translator of her works, and her partner in liturgical creation after Birgitta left Sweden for Rome to visit the pope in 1349. She was never to return to her native land and died in the Eternal City in 1373. Master Peter died not long after, serving the nuns of the Order and the head of the monks at Vadstena in 1378, a close collaborator with Prior Peter.

12. As pointed out by Helen Redpath in her study of St. Birgitta (Helen M. D. Redpath [Sister M. Dominic, O. Ss. S.], *God's Ambassadress, St. Bridget of Sweden* [Milwaukee: Bruce, 1947]), "the psalms at Compline in the Bridgettine breviary are those also found in the Little Office of Our Lady in the Dominican rite and nowhere else." A. Jefferies Collins, citing this passage, points out that Master Peter had ministered in a Dominican House of Studies at Skänninge. It was Dominicans who often watched over communities of beguines, and Peter may have been inspired by them in his careful attention to St. Birgitta and her fledgling experiment in devising a new form of monastic life based on the Little Office of the Virgin.

13. An analysis of the ways of studying liturgical change is laid out in Margot Fassler, *Gothic Song: Victorine Sequences and Augustinian Reform in Twelfth-Century Paris* (Cambridge: Cambridge University Press, 1993; 2nd ed. Notre Dame, Ind.: University of Notre Dame Press, forthcoming).

14. For discussion of Master Peter's *Cantus sororum*, see Anne Bagnell Yardley, "Bridgettine Spirituality and Musical Practices at Syon Abbey," in *Studies in St. Birgitta and the Brigittine Order*, 2, ed. James Hogg, Analectia Cartusiana 35:19 (Salzburg: Institut fur Anglistik und Amerikanistic, 1993), 199–214.

15. For the importance of the hymn repertories and their interpretations for the formation of Benedictine monasticism, see Susan Boynton, "Glossed Hymns in Eleventh-Century Continental Hymnaries" (PhD diss., Brandeis University, 1997).

16. Various scholarly editions of the *Sermo angelicus* are referenced by Zieman. There is also a modern English translation by John Halborg (Toronto: Peregrina, 1996), and this is available on the *Birgitta of Sweden Website* (http://www.umilta.net/bk11.html). I have quoted from it here.

17. Collins, *Breviary*, xii, xiii, and xiv.

18. This Mass was sung after their prime, which was itself sung after the brethern's terce. Thus the Ladymass in the brothers' liturgy had the place normally given to the High Mass in monasteries and cathedrals. The High Mass was sung after the women's terce. This kind of reversal would have been interesting, if not ironic, to those participating in or observing the liturgy who had knowledge of other practices.

19. Several Bridgittine Processionals survive. Their repertories, unlike the chants Master Peter composed for the Mass and Office, are primarily borrowed from the standard medieval repertories.

Reading Lessons at Syon Abbey

The Myroure of Oure Ladye *and the Mandates of Vernacular Theology*

ELIZABETH SCHIRMER

Just over seventy years ago, R. W. Chambers set out to write an introduction to Nicholas Harpsfield's life of Thomas More and produced, instead, a history of medieval English prose styles. As he found himself drawn inexorably back across the disciplinary boundary-line that divides medieval from Renaissance, Chambers came to stress the importance of women readers in assuring the "Continuity of English Prose from Alfred to More and His School."[1] English historical writing, he concluded, effectively disappeared after the Norman Conquest, not to revive in any significant form until the sixteenth century. The rise of "official" English in the late fourteenth century, in turn, gave birth to an aureate prose style (mirrored in the verse of Lydgate) whose magniloquence sought to compensate for the perceived inferiority of English. But all the while, an unbroken tradition of Middle English devotional writing reached back through the English works of Richard Rolle, the *Ancrene Wisse*, the Blickling Homilies, and the sermons of Aelfric, to its roots in the works of Alfred the Great in the ninth century. These religious texts (argues Chambers) preserved a balanced, mature native prose style, grounded in preaching and indebted to alliterative verse. The majority were written specifically for women: initially for nuns or anchoresses, who lived contemplative lives but had little or no Latin, and ultimately for a much broader audience including significant numbers of secular women interested in the possibility of a "mixed life." Chambers sees in these women readers the conduit, or impetus, for an unbroken native prose tradition linking

345

the two great periods of medieval English literary production, Anglo-Saxon and late fourteenth century.

Most literary historians today are (justifiably) skeptical of broad historical narratives such as this one.[2] But Chambers's claim about the importance of women audiences has come to seem, if anything, more current in recent years as we have sought to understand the significant roles played by women—as patrons, book-owners, and members of key interpretive communities—in the development of vernacular textual culture in late medieval England.[3] Chambers's approach leads us into slightly murkier evidentiary territory, inviting us to consider the agency exercised by women *as readers* in the period.[4] To what extent did the literary tastes and spiritual needs expressed by women shape Middle English religious writing, and through it vernacular reading and writing generally? Is readerly agency legible in the devotional texts that have come down to us, and does it matter that so many of the people who read these texts were women? How can examining these texts in light of their female audiences help us rethink the nature of literacy and literate practices in the period? While definitive answers are, of course, beyond the scope of this essay, these are the kinds of questions I hope to illuminate here.

Nowhere was the agency of late medieval women readers more apparent than at the Bridgittine double monastery of Syon Abbey, founded in 1415 by Henry V as part of his far-reaching plan to reform and revitalize English spiritual life (while at the same time consolidating Lancastrian power).[5] Reading, both liturgical and devotional, was central to the lives of the nuns of Syon, who lived in a world dominated to an unusual extent by female textual authorities (such as Birgitta herself, whose Rule and Office they used) and female authority-figures (the abbess was the head of the entire monastery). While their Bridgittine Office (as Katherine Zieman argues elsewhere in this volume) gave the sisters access to cleric-like liturgical roles, "enabl[ing them] to inhabit an entire range of subject positions" not generally available to women,[6] their Rule placed a strong value on non-liturgical reading: strict injunctions to poverty limit the number of liturgical books the abbey may possess to those absolutely necessary to its functioning, but no limits are imposed on other books for devotional reading and instruction.[7] Thus encouraged, the Syon nuns were soon among the most avid readers and book-collectors of the early fifteenth century, in possession of a remarkable library of religious texts in English, acquired, copied, translated, and composed for the spiritual benefit of the sisters.[8] In fact, David Bell notes that of all the English-language volumes traceable to, or known to have been owned by, medieval nunneries, roughly a third hail from Syon;[9] while seventeen of the library's twenty-three (known) "theological" volumes are in English. Figures like these amply support Bell's assertion that the nuns of Syon "stood at the forefront of English spirituality."[10]

Not surprisingly, Syon looms large in recent studies of late medieval women as patrons and audiences of vernacular texts.[11] The abbey has also been central to emerging debates about the nature and extent of women's readerly agency in the period. Felicity Riddy, for example, offers an image of late medieval women readers as effective co-producers of the texts written for them: "In relation to the male clerks and their female readers," she writes, "it must often have been difficult to determine who followed and who led."[12] In sharp contrast, Denise Despres emphasizes the *limitations* of Syon reading models when compared with their continental counterparts.[13] Focusing on the *Orcherd of Syon,* a translation of Catherine of Siena's *Dialogues,* she finds that the Syon text replaces Catherine's invitation to evangelical charity, dramatic penitential suffering, and imitative mystical and paramystical experiences with an essentially conservative model of monastic *lectio divina.* For Despres, it is precisely the *Orcherd*'s Carthusian emphasis on contemplative reading, at the expense of mendicant-inspired acts of "radical charity," that defines the English text's "devotional paternalism."[14] I want to suggest that it is precisely this tension—between empowering the women of Syon as readers and containing and controlling their readerly agency—that characterizes the textual culture of Syon Abbey. This characteristic tension, I contend, reflects a moment of crisis in Middle English textual culture, sparked by the controversy over the Lollard heresy.

The emphasis placed on reading as the central spiritual practice of the sisters of Syon Abbey has roots, not just in monastic *lectio divina,* nor even solely in the Bridgittine Rule, but in the loose tradition of insular vernacular theology as it developed over the course of the fourteenth century. Long before Syon, indeed long before Lollardy, Middle English religious writing was engaged in distinctive ways with questions of readerly agency. From early compendia that work to convert their "lewed" readers' taste for romances by casting biblical stories and saints' lives in octosyllabic verse;[15] to allegories of Christ as book, or of his crucified body as legal document;[16] to penitential manuals and treatises on the discerning of spirits that offer guidance in the reading of the self;[17] to Franciscan-inspired devotional works that teach reading as imaginative, affective engagement with the events of Christ's life, passion, and death, Middle English religious texts persistently invoke and, more importantly, seek to educate the reading habits of the vernacular audiences they helped to create. Spiritual instruction blends with lessons in reading in these texts until salvation itself comes to seem a hermeneutic problem, spiritual rectitude a matter of right reading. Characterized by a tendency to see reading itself as the vernacular subject's primary means of achieving spiritual progress, Middle English religious writing might best be described, not as a textual culture, but as a culture of reading.[18]

At the time when the *Orcherd of Syon* and other early Syon texts were produced, this vernacular culture of reading was facing a serious challenge in the form of an increasingly aggressive royal and ecclesiastical campaign against Lollardy. The Lollards themselves were, notoriously, a people of the English book, developing schools and scriptoria to propagate their distinctive brand of biblical literalism; and to a devastating extent they succeeded in making the English book their own. Their emphasis on biblical reading, driven by their particular brand of literalist exegesis, came packaged with a virulent anti-clericalism and skepticism about the efficacy of church sacraments and church structures. Early Syon texts, written in the first half of the fifteenth century, were produced in the face of a heightened campaign against Lollardy that rendered vernacular textuality itself officially suspect. Most famously, Archbishop Arundel's anti-Lollard *Constitutions* of 1409 forbid unauthorized access to "any book or tract" containing Englished biblical material made in the time of Wyclif or since (one would have been hard pressed to find an English text that did not contain such material).[19] The campaign against Lollardy, like the founding of Syon itself, was central to Lancastrian efforts to consolidate power. While apparently only sporadically enforced, Arundel's legislation, especially when seen as part of that larger royal agenda, makes the library developed by the sisters of Syon and the English texts produced for them all the more remarkable.[20] This essay seeks, in part, to understand the phenomenon of textual production and consumption at Syon Abbey in the early fifteenth century, given the general atmosphere of censorship and persecution attending its foundation.

The explanation I propose is twofold. It concerns, first, the status of the sisters themselves. As aristocratic women patronized by royalty, and as women religious occupying a kind of liminal space between the increasingly contested categories of cleric and lay—not to mention their association with the celebrated visionary Birgitta of Sweden—the nuns of Syon were shielded on several fronts from suspicion of heresy. Their prestigious abbey was thus uniquely situated to provide a safe haven for the culture of reading at the heart of insular vernacular theology. The second explanation concerns the specific models of reading developed for the sisters in the abbey's early years. I argue that early Syon texts, by striking a delicate balance between granting the sisters readerly agency and controlling the ways in which they exercise that agency, work to preserve the distinctive insular culture of reading they inherit, *without* raising the specter of heresy. In the process they transform, not only the continental texts and traditions they appropriate (as Despres and others have noted),[21] but also the insular tradition they seek to preserve. Nicholas Watson, in a seminal article on the effects of the anti-Lollard campaign on vernacular theology, has argued that Arundel's *Constitutions* functioned effectively as censorship, stifling production of original religious writing and "sealing off the canon" of Middle English vernacular theology.[22] Texts written at Syon under the shadow of Arundel's legislation both refute and support Watson's claim. I hope finally to demonstrate that the sisters of Syon Abbey were instrumental *as readers* in shaping the canon he describes, as well as in determining the direction devotional writing in English would take when it emerged again into more general view—largely through Syon efforts and via Syon texts—toward the end of the fifteenth century.

I take as my central object of study the *Myroure of Oure Ladye*, a translation and explanation of their Bridgittine Office made for the first or second generation of Syon nuns following the abbey's enclosure in 1420.[23] I choose this text, both because it is one of the earliest produced at Syon (written by one of the brethren and possibly even by the Confessor General) and because of the thorough and pervasive interest it takes in the sisters' readerly practices. The *Myroure of Oure Ladye,* in its entirety, is constituted by lessons in reading.[24] Its anonymous author does not simply provide the sisters with an Englished version of their service; nor is he content to explain its literal and expound its various spiritual senses—though he does both at length. Rather, he offers detailed instructions on *how* the Office should be read. By informing their understanding, training their will, and relentlessly orchestrating their response to each element of their service, the *Myroure* works to bring its readers' minds into accord with their tongues in the daily reading of the Office, and thereby to bring all their inner, spiritual faculties into accord with the true meaning or referent of the service itself. In other words, it conducts the spiritual education of the sisters of Syon precisely by educating them as readers. Reading, devotional as well as liturgical, is how God speaks to us, the thing that makes of prayer a two-way conversation; for "Lyke as in prayer man spekyth to God, so in redynge God spekyth to man" (66).[25]

In offering his audience lessons in reading as a means of spiritual progress, the author of the *Myroure of Oure Ladye* announces his investment in the mandates of Middle English vernacular theology, as I began to describe them above. Before looking in detail at the *Myroure* itself, then, it will be helpful to articulate those mandates more fully. What follows is a brief and, perforce, rather schematic account of the culture of religious reading that flourished in late medieval England,[26] a loose but distinctive tradition that, I contend, the *Myroure* both transforms and works to preserve.

I suggested above that the writers and readers of Middle English religious texts created a culture in which readerly agency becomes the vernacular subject's primary means of achieving salvation, of moving closer to the divine. This emphasis on reading as a means of spiritual and theological growth owes much, of course, to the bibliocentric culture of the Latin Middle Ages. But Latin textual culture, unlike (the bulk of) its vernacular analogue, centered on the reading of the Bible: whether through exegesis, to discover the literal and spiritual meanings that grounded theology and doctrine; or through *lectio divina,* a meditative practice setting the reader on the contemplative path to union with the divine.[27] This direct engagement with the biblical text is replaced, in most Middle English texts, with a strong sense of pastoral vocation. No longer addressed to scholars, monks, and priests struggling to engage with the Bible in the most productive way, these texts practice the cure of souls. Their authors, generally male clerics, think of themselves as translators, explicators, commentators, even preachers. While they often express a pastoral (and frequently purely conventional) anxiety about their performance of these writerly functions, they stay focused for the most part on the readers whose spiritual progress they have taken into their care.[28] As such, the texts they produce threaten always to supplant author and pastor alike, becoming themselves the primary conduit between reader and God.

Indeed texts in this culture of reading frequently aspire to render even *themselves* superfluous. Unlike exegesis, the reading practices taught by these pastorally minded, reader-focused texts are almost purely formative. Their readers are asked to imitate, to practice, to be moved, to take a moral to heart or convert to a better way of life. In this these vernacular reading models are akin to *lectio divina.* But with the Bible removed as its central object, vernacular reading tends to come unmoored from texts altogether. Textual reading becomes a means of educating wider-ranging hermeneutic competencies, helping its practitioners move towards God by teaching them to narrow, through parallel readerly activities, the (ultimately unbridgeable) gap between the human and the divine. Members of this newly expanded vernacular audience, increasingly comprised of laypeople, learn to be active readers not just of texts, but of themselves as penitent sinners and potential mystics, of a world that reflects the image of its creator but only darkly, of the multiple ways in which God communicates with fallen human beings. Whether the immediate object of an individual act of reading is one's sins or the Passion, the ten commandments or the joys of heaven or the life of a saint, this kind of reading seeks always to form the reader's own "outward works" and "inner life"— and, especially, to create the crucial accord between the two that renders the reader herself virtuously legible.[29] Ideally, texts that teach reading on this model come to function as pastoral agents in their own right—agents whose success, moreover, is often measured by their readers' ability to do without them.[30]

This way of thinking about reading invites us, in turn, to think of the spread of literacy in late medieval England less in terms of lay access to textuality and more as an expansion and diversification of the readerly strategies available to vernacular audiences.[31] As those audiences, originally confined primarily to parish priests and women religious, expanded to include a more diverse lay readership—as English as a textual language began (in Nicholas Watson's phrase) to "connote universality"[32]—writers of religious texts increasingly seem to have found existing texts and genres inadequate to their readers' needs. As the works of Richard Rolle, for example, became popular outside the cloister and the anchorhold, fueling interest in the possibility of a "mixed life," and as pastorally minded writers like Robert Mannyng of Brunne began to address both meditations on the life of Christ and penitential manuals directly to "lewed" readers rather than to their parish priests,[33] lay readers would have encountered an increasing variety of textual modes and models of reading, not all of them mutually compatible, and many of them developed originally with a much narrower audience in mind. In an effort to meet the evolving needs of their ever-expanding audiences, late fourteenth-century religious writers mine a wide variety of texts and traditions, creating texts that are diverse, multi-generic, and theologically distinctive.[34] These include the relatively well-known works of such "Middle English mystics" as Walter Hilton, the author of the *Cloud of Unknowing,* and Julian of Norwich, as well as many early Lollard sermons and tracts, along with a variety of less-studied texts that do not fit neatly into either category, such as the *Pore Caitif* and the *Prickynge of Love*.[35]

To render more concrete this culture of reading, I want now to turn briefly to one of these less easily categorizable texts, written (its editor argues) on the eve of the Lollard controversy. The *Book to a Mother* was written by an anonymous priest in the West Midlands, probably in the 1370s or early 1380s.[36] It is an insistently biblical discourse on the nature of true religion addressed primarily to the author's widowed mother, apparently to dissuade her from entering a monastery (a popular choice for widows in these increasingly pious times). Multi-generic, and built around a multivalent metaphor of Christ as book, the *Book to a Mother* pushes to its logical extreme the tendency of Middle English religious writing generally to divorce reading as practice from text as object. Anticipating the Lollards (or complementing them—the dating is uncertain), the author of the *Book to a Mother* restores the Bible as the primary object of textual reading. He insists, moreover, as the Lollards were perhaps just beginning to insist, that his secular lay audience is capable of reading the Bible as well as—indeed better than—any clerk. But the Bible he offers them is not the clergy's Bible: he teaches neither exegesis nor *lectio divina*. Instead, drawing on the resources of the vernacular tradition, he develops a formative model of biblical reading, grounded in a dazzling multilayered allegorizing of textuality itself, that seeks finally to render even the biblical text itself redundant, replaced with the Word of God written in the reader's own heart.[37]

The author of the *Book to a Mother* begins by insisting, Lollard-like, that the true Bible is not the words on the page but the life and teaching of Christ.[38] As he explains this central tenet, moreover, it becomes clear that by "þis bok" he means at once the Bible, Christ, and the *Book* itself. For "þis bok," and the central object of all true reading, is "Christ, Godis sone of heuene, wiþ his conuersacioun þre and þrytti wyntur, i-write wiþinne and wiþoute with humilite to hele Adames pride and oures, wiþ wilful pouerte to hele þe synne of proprete, wiþ chastite to hele fleschliche lustis" (31). Here (as in much Lollard thinking) one kind of (mere) text collapses into another, such that the Bible itself comes unmoored from its own textuality. Reading, in turn, becomes a metaphor and a means for imitating and loving Christ—imaged, in a final twist, as *writing* the self.[39] Taken to its logical extreme (as Watson points out), this model of reading replaces the material text of the Bible with the "true" Bible that is Christ himself, written through imitation and love in the soul of the reader, ultimately striving to render text— of the Bible, of the *Book*—obsolete.[40] Textuality thus becomes in the *Book to a Mother* at once an instrument for encountering Christ and a pure metaphor for how he chooses to reveal himself in his incarnation—just as reading and writing image how one chooses to respond to him so revealed.

The *Book to a Mother*, in the model of reading it constructs, walks a fine line between asserting the spiritual value of texts and of textual reading, and representing the best texts as curiously transparent: requiring of the reader imitation and love rather than interpretation, and working best when they efface themselves. A similar tension is reflected in the *Book*'s treatment of genre. Like the *Pore Caitif*, a roughly contemporary collection of treatises (and one that inspired Lollard interpolation),[41] the *Book to a Mother* moves through a range of textual modes, arranged, ladder-like, to lead the reader to an ever higher and more sophisticated spiritual awareness. But where the *Pore Caitif* presents itself clearly as a collection of distinct treatises, the *Book to a Mother* in no way marks the boundaries of the genres it appropriates, never highlights or glosses its own structure. Nicholas Watson has argued that the *Book* is not just multi-generic (like so many late Middle English texts, religious and literary) but *anti*-generic, mixing the genres and scrambling the matter of the genres it evokes until it becomes almost completely astructural. Christ-as-book supplants all genres: he is "þe beste remedie and þe beste rule and þe beste mirour þat mai be to ouercome synne" (31). Watson traces the *Book*'s appropriation of each of these three central genres of Middle English religious writing—remedy, rule, and mirror—and concludes that its author rejects all three, offering the-Bible-as-Christ as the true alternative to all conventional genres as well as all religious orders.[42]

I think the *Book to a Mother* draws on an even wider array of discrete vernacular textual modes than Watson's analysis suggests. The text opens with a section on the elements of the faith (roughly parallel to the opening two treatises of the *Pore Caitif*, on the Creed and the Ten Commandments, respectively). It then enacts a shift from instruction to imitation, introducing the narrative of Christ's life and enjoining its readers to imitate Christ's key virtues of humility, poverty, and chastity. We are reminded here of the immensely popular Franciscan model of devotional meditation on the life and passion of Christ. After presenting a series of analogies explaining the "religion" of Christ (including a version of the well-known conceit of the four principle virtues as the walls of a cloister), he then builds a kind of penitential manual out of allegorical readings of selected gospel elements: the four people Christ raised from the dead represent four "manners" of sins, the three ointments of Mary contrition, devotion, and pity, and so on. This condensed and often disjointed tour through the major textual modes and reading models of vernacular theology culminates, finally, in a collection of minimally commented New Testament translations, described as the "sentence" and "doom" of the "sixe hiȝe iustices of the heiest king" (Christ, John, Jude, James, Peter, and Paul; 191). It is as if all the lessons in reading gestured towards so far were meant to converge upon this experience of reading the text of the Bible itself. Just as the reader is ultimately meant to replace the text of the Bible with the internally written Word, so that text itself must first subsume *and* supplant all other modes of religious writing and reading. In the model of reading constructed here, *all* genres are equally necessary, and equally insufficient.

In fact I want to suggest that it is precisely through the deployment of genre itself—not just the conventions of specific textual modes, but the notion of generic meaning-making—that the author of the *Book to a Mother* enacts the subtle tension between the need for textuality and the need to move beyond reading. For example: much of the *Book* is structured loosely around the narrative of Christ's life, but there is little here beyond that narrative framework to remind us of the affective meditation popularized by the *Meditationes Vitae Christi* and inspiring so much Middle English lyric. Indeed the gospel material emphasized in the *Book,* combined with its injunctions to imitate Christ's virtues, align it more closely with Lollard models of reading the life of Christ that emphasize his ministry and his teaching rather than his passion.[43] Structurally, however, the *Book* presents us with a loose amalgamation of the two, each constantly interrupting the other, as if to suggest that it is precisely the ability to negotiate both models and the disjunctions between them that enables true biblical *imitatio.*

Just as he adopts all genres only to discourage reliance on any single model of reading, so the author of the *Book to a Mother* addresses both one and everyone. Throughout most of the text, the author addresses "my leue dere moder." At the beginning of Chapter III, in a passage that reads very much like a typical vernacular prologue,[44] he explains that his purpose in writing the *Book* is to fulfill the biblical commandment to honor our parents.[45] But in the opening lines of Chapter I, where we should expect such a prologue, he makes a different and much more expansive statement of purpose: "To knowe þe bettere my purpos in þis boke, wite ȝe wel þat I desire *euerych man and womman and child* to be my moder, for Christ seyþ: he þat doþ his Fader wille is his broþer, suster, and moder" (1; my emphasis). The *Book* is for the author's mother; but in accordance with the very principles of biblical reading he advocates throughout, *every* Christian should be his mother, and so co-addressees with her. Now it is reasonable to assume that the author addressed his mother most specifically but hoped, indeed expected, that his work would reach a larger audience.[46] But this curiously doubled prologue, with its echoing biblical resonances,[47] provides a striking parallel to the *Book*'s complex treatment of genre. The author gestures towards the definition of audience and purpose proper to prologues only to refuse to define them at all: his audience is both an individual and every individual, his purpose absorbed into Christ's.

The *Book to a Mother* thus capitalizes on the "universal[ity]" of audience created by the explosion in Middle English religious writing, relying on a widespread facility with different genres and models of reading in order to reject the delimiting and mediating functions of genre altogether, replacing them with a universalized model of biblical reading as imitation, love, and self-formation. This complex project epitomizes in many ways the potentials of vernacular theology before the crisis over Lollardy (so much so, in fact, that its modern editor takes 1382, the date of the condemnation of Wyclif's key ideas at the Blackfriars Council, as its *terminus ad quem*).[48] As such it makes an excellent foil for the *Myroure of Oure Ladye,* showing up two of the key ways in which the later text transforms the tradition it inherits.

First, and most striking, the *Myroure* is addressed exclusively to the sisters of Syon, never explicitly invoking an audience outside the monastery walls.[49] By limiting its audience in this way the *Myroure* reverses (at least in its rhetoric) the "universalizing" trend of so much fourteenth-century religious writing, re-enclosing vernacular theology within the walls of religious institutions, where it had its origins over a century before, and restricting it to the women religious who had been its earliest and most influential audience. Second, in a parallel move, the reading practices taught by the *Myroure* are almost entirely restricted to textual objects. Where the *Book to a Mother* works to render even biblical texts superfluous by teaching the reader to re-write herself, the *Myroure* sees the constant, attentive reading and re-reading of liturgical and (to a lesser extent) devotional texts as precisely the site of spiritual progress.

This distinction is clearest in the *Myroure*'s model of liturgical reading, on which its author expends the bulk of his considerable instructional energy. Part I of the *Myroure,* entitled "Of Diuine Seruice," teaches the sisters to use the information the rest of the texts provides in an effective act of liturgical performance. The first element of such an act, as the *Myroure* presents it, is understanding. The sisters must understand the words of their Divine Office, its various literal and spiritual senses, its divine origins, and the "causes and meanings" of each of its individual elements. Knowledge alone, however, is not enough: the sisters must learn how to mean what they say, a much trickier business and a problem that exercised many vernacular theologians in the period. The readers of the *Myroure* are trained to discipline their inner faculties so as to bring them into line with the true meaning or referent of the text they read and sing. The *Myroure*-author terms this orchestrating of faculties "entendaunce." An active, participial form of "entente" or intent—encompassing both intending (willing) and attending (listening attentively, paying attention)—"entendaunce" refers to an effort of the will with regards to the meaning of the text one is most immediately reading, an effort that both grows from, and seeks to form, an inner, spiritual life. Enabled by understanding, "entendaunce" is the means by which the reading sisters achieve the crucial "accord" between mind and tongue, heart and mind, reader and text, which is the ultimate goal of the *Myroure*'s lessons in reading.

There is something circular about this solution to the problem of "accord" (as we might call it), and about the model of liturgical reading it animates. In order to derive spiritual benefit from a given act of reading, the sister must work to conform her inner faculties to the meaning of the service, for "thentente gyueth euery good dede hys ryght name" (60). But in order for those efforts to succeed, she needs to form her inner faculties—and she does *that* precisely by reading the Office correctly: with a clean conscience, precisely and attentively, with a stable heart and mind, and with the proper pronunciation. Inner and outer, performance and spirit continually inform and enable each other, chicken-and-egg-like, as the sisters labor to say the Office with "inwarde besynes to haue deuocyon in harte" and "*also* in syngynge and redyng with tongue, and in other outwarde obeseruance" (22; my emphasis). While this model derives from *lectio divina* it is far more self-contained than its Latin antecedent: where traditional contemplative models see reading as the first step on a ladder to higher spiritual activities—in the classic Benedictine formulation the reader moves from *lectio* to *oratio* to *contemplatio*—the *Myroure* makes of reading the sole contemplative exercise of the sisters of Syon Abbey. It is through proper reading that each sister achieves the gifts of "sprytuall loue, & inwarde delyte and deuocyon" (3), and through reading that the sisters as a community achieve their primary purpose of praising Mary, benefiting not only themselves and their own community but their nation and the Christian community at large. Like so many other Middle English religious texts, the *Myroure of Oure Ladye* locates the sisters' spiritual progress precisely in the act of reading itself, and educates their reading practices accordingly. But where most fourteenth-century reading lessons expand beyond the boundaries of texts, focusing readerly activity on the self, on the passion of Christ, on the world, the *Myroure* instructs the readers exclusively in the reading of texts. The reading lessons offered by the *Myroure* are contained within textual boundaries as surely as their invoked audience is bounded by the walls of Syon Abbey itself.

In these two parallel moves—drawing vernacular theology back inside the monastery, and containing its reading lessons within the boundaries of texts—we can, I believe, begin to see the *Myroure* responding to the campaign against Lollardy as it impacted English reading and writing in the years following Arundel's *Constitutions*. I want now to consider the strategies of that campaign briefly, so as to illuminate more clearly the ways in which the *Myroure* worked to evade them.

Archbishop Arundel's anti-Lollard *Constitutions* of 1409 are most famous for restricting lay access to vernacular texts, rendering official an existing, pervasive association between English textuality and heresy. Much recent discussion of Arundel's legislation reads it as an act of censorship. The *Constitutions* can, I think, help make sense of the relative paucity of new religious texts produced in the early fifteenth century, as Nicholas Watson argues in his seminal piece on "Censorship and Cultural Change" in the period.[50] But, as Steven Justice points out in his response to this article, it is hard to track the effects of this legislation as censorship with any evidentiary certainty. Justice finds only two texts that refer specifically to the *Constitutions*—Nicholas Love's *Mirror of the Blessed Life of Jesus Christ* (to which we will return in a moment), and the *Myroure of Oure Ladye* itself, both texts that "ostentatiously conformed to [Arundel's] demands."[51] The *Myroure*'s "conformity" is hardly surprising, given how central the institution of Syon Abbey was to the same royal program of reform that included the campaign against Lollardy. What interests me here is the pressures placed on a specific textual community that felt both bound by the spirit of Arundel's project, and invested in a culture of reading whose orthodoxy his legislation brought into question.

Arundel's anti-heretical project itself reflects an awareness of its target as, precisely, a culture of reading—rather than, say, a series of heretical tenets to be stamped out (the *Constitutions* mention none), or even a specific group of texts to censor (here again the legislation is deliberately broad). As I have argued in greater detail elsewhere,[52] the *Constitutions* participated in an official attempt to control not just *what*, but *how* lay-people read. Arundel worked to shore up crumbling literacy barriers, which had tradi-tionally separated cleric and lay, by legislating the modes of textual engagement prac-ticed by laypeople, redrawing the line between laypeople and clerics as a boundary between two distinct interpretive communities. This strategy is most evident in the first English text (as far as we can tell) that Arundel authorized under the new legisla-tion, Nicholas Love's *Mirror of the Blessed Life of Jesus Christ.* Love's text is an overtly anti-Lollard translation of the pseudo-Bonaventuran *Meditationes Vitae Christi.* Seventeen of its manuscripts record Arundel's explicit authorization and his direction that the text be published widely "for the edification of the faithful and the confutation of all false heretics and Lollards" (puplice communicandum fore decreuit & mandauit, ad fidelium edificacionem, & hereticorum siue lollardorum confutacionem).[53] Love and Arundel here pick one genre of Middle English religious writing (Franciscan-style de-votional meditation on the life and passion of Christ), render its model of reading ex-plicitly orthodox, and canonize it for secular laypeople.

Michael Sargent describes the *Mirror* as an anti-Lollard laicization of contemplative models. Indeed the text, dotted throughout with marginal notes drawing attention to this or that passage *contra lollardos*,[54] reads as a kind of layperson's liturgy for private reading, dividing its narrative of Christ's life into devotional readings for each day of the week and encouraging the re-reading and meditation associated with *lectio divina.* But Love is very clear that his secular audience differs in crucial ways from both clerical and monastic readers. He characterizes his readers as "symple creatures the whiche as childryn hauen nede to be fedde with mylke of lyȝte doctryne & not with sadde mete of grete clargye & of [hye contemplacion]" (10). Lay readers are fundamentally unequipped to grapple with the "great learning" reserved for clerics; nor should they aim for the "high contemplation" sought by religious. Instead they should restrict themselves to "light doc-trine" appropriate to their inherently "fleshly" state. In that spirit, Love offers his lay read-ers what he terms "diuerse ymaginacions of cristes life" (11). This key phrase encapsulates Love's model of lay reading. By engaging imaginatively with the events he narrates, his lay readers will be stirred to the love of God and the desire of heavenly things (10) through a program of meditative reading appropriate to their status.

Moreover these imaginations are "diuerse": Love regularly takes liberties not only with the *Meditationes* but with the details of Christ's life as narrated in the gospels. He invites his readers to take the same kinds of liberties, re-imagining the events he narrates in any way that makes them more vivid and inspires more devotion—just as long as they are "not aȝeyns the byleue or gude maneres" (11). Partly, Love tells us, this imaginative model of reading reflects the nature of Christ's life itself, which "may not be fully discriueded as þe lifes of oþer seyntes, bot in a maner of liknes as þe ymage of mans face is shewed in þe mirroure" (11). We hear echoes here of contemplative models that value affective engagement with the biblical text over its exegetical counterpart, love over knowledge. At the same time, we are not so far from the controlling metaphor of the *Book to a Mother*, with its emphasis on readerly engagement with the material of the Bible rather than on the text itself. But there remains a tantalizing irony in the fact that a church hierarch willing to burn heretics over fine semantic distinctions regarding the nature of consecrated bread would authorize a gospel harmony presenting two competing versions of the crucifixion and inviting the reader to choose between them[55]—that he would champion such a text, moreover, as an orthodox alternative to biblical translation.

What we are seeing here, I think, is the construction of a dichotomy between two distinct models of biblical reading, one designed to be appropriate for laypeople, the other reserved to the clergy. The laity are to engage the Bible imaginatively, affectively, as a structure of narratives that inspires devotion. The clergy read it intellectively, as a structure of words that provides the basis for theology and doctrine. In short, laypeople can have the narratives of the Bible—and within reasonable doctrinal limits they can do with them what they will—but they cannot have the words. This implicit dichotomy between intellective and affective reading, words and narrative, interpretation and devotion, works to create a boundary between lay and clerical interpretive communities, each defined by its own texts and readerly strategies.

In canonizing Love's version of devotional meditation for lay readers, Arundel reveals an uneasiness, born of the Lollard controversy, with the relatively unchaperoned proliferation of texts and readerly strategies among an expanding and diversifying lay audience. Many fifteenth-century religious texts written in English seek to quiet those fears, in part by practicing their own version of generic containment: explaining their purpose carefully in formal prologues, and targeting specific, narrowly defined audiences for the reading lessons they develop. The *Myroure of Oure Ladye* is an exemplary instance of the ways in which texts written in the shadow of the *Constitutions*—even, as in this case, invested in some aspects of their anti-Lollard project—manipulated the generic resources at their disposal in the creation of ingenious models of reading, designed to quell any suspicion of heresy while at the same time preserving the mandate of Middle English vernacular theology to teach reading as a basic means of spiritual progress.[56]

For example: in place of the odd and ambiguous double opening of the *Book to a Mother*, the *Myroure of Oure Ladye* bristles with explanatory front matter, its extensive explanations working to minimize any threat of heresy that might be felt to inhere in the vernacular reading lessons it offers. After the life of St. Birgitta that opens the manuscript, the text of the *Myroure* proper begins with not one but two prologues, the first on the importance of understanding liturgical texts, and the second on the difficulties of translation. Part I, "Of Diuine Seruice," itself introduces the translation and commentary that follow, explaining both why and how the service should be read. Part II then opens with a brief treatise (given the editorial title "Of Redynge") on how to read non-liturgical texts—including this one. The degree to which the *Myroure*-author justifies and analyzes his project makes even Love's prologue seem minimal and unself-conscious by comparison. Where the *Book to a Mother* deliberately muddied its genre and confused its statements of purpose and audience address, incorporating the new "universality" of English into a universal, secular vision of the religious life and a parallel model of lay biblical reading, the *Myroure of Oure Ladye* works within a well-established textual tradition (the *expositio missae* or liturgical treatise),[57] restricts its audience to a single community of women religious, and devotes fully a fifth of its length to an in-depth discussion of its own purposes and methods. The *Myroure*'s version of "universal" reading, in stark contrast to the *Book to a Mother*'s, is liturgical and monastic, grounded in the traditional notion of liturgical performance as speaking for the Church, the *opus Dei* as prayer for the world.

The specific audience the *Myroure* invokes, moreover, evades the terms of Arundel's and Love's regulatory dichotomies. The political status of the sisters of Syon—patronized by royalty and many of them related to the royal family—along with their spiritual status as members of the rigorous Order of St. Birgitta, went a long way toward protecting them from the harshest effects of Arundel's legislation, just as their collective wealth contributed to the size of their library. Moreover simply *as* women religious, the sisters of Syon occupy a liminal space between cleric and lay, fitting neatly into neither of the two mutually exclusive interpretive communities Arundel and Love seek to establish. Denied the priesthood, they nevertheless exercised certain key clerical functions, notably the *opus Dei* itself (which they perform moreover, cleric-like, "in the person of Holy Church").[58] By restricting his audience to the nuns of Syon and focusing his reading lessons on the Office, the *Myroure*-author invokes the protection of this liminal, quasi-clerical status, keeping the models of spiritual reading he crafts out of the direct line of Arundel's polarizing efforts.[59]

It is, moreover, precisely the careful distinguishing of audience and genre (arguably itself a "narrowing" impulse) that enables the author of this early Syon text to offer his readers unprecedented agency as readers. To begin with, he provides the sisters of Syon with a greater understanding of their Divine Office than had ever been made available to women religious in England, placing the nuns in a much more cleric-like relation to their liturgical texts. The opening assertion of the *Myroure* is that understanding is key to transforming liturgical reading into the efficacious praise of Mary, grounded in accord between word and meaning, that is the main purpose of the nuns of Syon Abbey.[60] For "[h]ow shall ye then condewly shewe by outwarde praysyng the excellent hyghnes and worthynes of the moste blyssed heuenly quene, oure reuerente lady, as yt is full fayre expressed in al youre holy seruyce: but yf ye haue fyrste syghte therof by inwarde vnderstandinge." (2). Understanding provides the reader with a "sight" of the praise already contained in the service itself, so that they can then express that praise in their own readerly performance. However intuitive this conflation of reading and understanding may seem to a modern literate subject, it was a novel one—even, potentially, a subversive one—to propose to ground the liturgical reading of women religious in late medieval England. Here the value of the sisters' liturgical reading is defined precisely in terms of a level of understanding that had previously been reserved for male clerics.

If vernacular textuality was one prominent site of contest over the boundaries between cleric and lay in late medieval England, liturgy (as Katherine Zieman demonstrates) was another. In this arena, according to Zieman, the grammatical understanding of liturgical texts was increasingly constructed as authoritative clerical literacy, to be carefully distinguished from the purely "liturgical literacy" of women religious.[61] The nature of women religious' understanding of the liturgical texts they read remained an area of redefinition and contest throughout the period. We can see this contest develop in vernacular writings addressed to women religious which take a specific interest in their liturgical practices. Very early in the Middle English period, for example, before literacy was at all widespread amongst secular laypeople (and long before the Lollards came on the scene), English texts for women religious evince little interest in the question of liturgical understanding. The first book of the *Ancrene Wisse*, for example, is quite similar generically to the *Myroure of Oure Ladye*, providing a detailed choreography of prayer liturgical and devotional as well as a rationale for some its elements. But while the author assumes his anchoress addressee is literate, telling her to say her hours as she has them written down,[62] he is far more concerned with accuracy than with comprehension. He advises his reader to substitute Paters and Aves for any prayer she does not know;[63] and he never suggests that she should remedy her ignorance. The concept of accord between reader and text, grounded in understanding, so crucial to the *Myroure*'s model of liturgical reading, is entirely absent here.

The Chastising of God's Children, written much earlier in the period for the nuns of Barking Abbey, does raise the question of liturgical understanding affirmatively— though it comes to very different conclusions than does the *Myroure*. Barking was a more venerable and in many ways more traditional women's institution than Syon, and almost as wealthy and prestigious; it also possessed an impressive library of English books.[64] The *Chastising* is, in essence, a treatise on the causes, benefits, and remedies of temptation, developed largely out of the work of Ruysbroec and other continental writers, including Alphonse of Jaén, one of Birgitta's male clerical supporters. Like the *Book to a Mother,* the *Chastising* evokes Lollardy only in the most limited and perfunctory way, if at all; this has led its editors to date it relatively early, to the 1380s or 1390s,[65] while suggesting to Steven Justice, in his response to this article, a (probably later) audience of "goostli liuers" only minimally engaged with Lollardy and its effects. The *Chastising* and its model of liturgical reading serves me here as a point of comparison for the *Myroure*, whose author(s) and readers alike seem to have felt the Lollard controversy to be an unavoidable circumstance of English reading and writing.

The author/translator of *The Chastising of God's Children* is content to have the sisters of Barking Abbey read translations of their Office on their own time, as devotional reading. But he insists that liturgical reading must take place "in þe maner as it was ordeyned," that is, in Latin (221). He does imagine the sisters may wonder (as doubtless we wonder, and as the *Myroure*-author begins his treatise by wondering) how it is possible to read a text devoutly and "ententifly" without understanding it. His reply reflects a position diametrically opposed to the *Myroure of Oure Ladye*'s:

> I answere ȝou þerto and seie þat for þe uertue of þe wordis and ȝoure lownesse and obeisaunce to holi chirche, wiþ a feruent desire upward to god aftir ȝoure entent, þouȝ ȝe vndirstonde no word þat ȝe seie, it may be to ȝou more medeful, and more acceptable to god þanne grete deuociouns þat ȝe wene ȝe haue in oþer preuy deuocions. (222)

Liturgical reading in this model requires no interaction between the sisters' (inner) understanding and the words they (outwardly) read and sing. Its value relies instead upon the quasi-sacramental virtue inherent in the Latin words themselves, and in the parallel but distinct virtue of the sisters' obedience and desire. In fact, the lack of any connection between the virtue of the singer and the virtue of the words can even *magnify* the spiritual benefits of liturgical reading. (It does, after all, render attentive devotion that much more of a challenge—though its value is never explained in these or any other psychological terms.) For the *Myroure*-author understanding enables the reading sister to create the crucial accord between inner and outer, heart and tongue required to render the service spiritually efficacious. For the author of the *Chastising* it is precisely the gap between outward praise and inward comprehension that can render the Office more "medeful" to the reader and more "acceptable" to God than private devotions.

This difference of opinion about the role of understanding in liturgical reading reflects a larger difference in what we might think of as these two texts' theologies of reading. In the course of teaching the sisters of Barking to read temptation fruitfully, *The Chastising of God's Children* raises a question that haunts Middle English vernacular theology generally: given that reading is our primary means of making spiritual progress and moving toward the divine, how can we be sure that we are reading productively? This question becomes more urgent given the diversity of readerly strategies available to lay readers by the end of the fourteenth century, raising widespread anxieties about the correspondence between signifier and signified, inner truth and outward appearances; heart and tongue, "entente" and deed. The *Chastising* in particular returns again and again to the potential for misreading the self. At his most pessimistic the author even speaks of self-deceived religious, whom he calls "spiritual lecher[s]" (135); these live in great penance and believe they have achieved the true rest of God when in reality they are wallowing in sin-inducing "natural" rest.[66] Yet despite all this epistemological uncertainty, the *Chastising*-author exhorts us to keep reading. Regardless of our "werkis outward" (despite, for example, any mystical gifts we might receive), we must continue to "sliȝli serche oursilf þat we see and knowe what we be wiþinne" (184). The text moves continually back and forth between these injunctions to read, supplemented by long lists of tokens and symptoms to help us, and warnings that we can never rely entirely on the legibility of outward behavior, outward signs—or even our own conscience.[67]

The *Chastising*-author resolves this paradox by developing a practical hermeneutic of humility. This model of reading transforms the ultimate illegibility of the world, even potentially of the reader's own inner state, into a spiritual advantage:

> First I counceile euery man to rette it to his owne defaute þat grace is wiþdrawe, bi sum maner necligence, or for a special defaute, bi dissolute berynge, or for wiþdrawynge the hert fro god bi diuerse veyne þouȝtis, and þouȝ his conscience deme nat this alweis in special, ȝit goode it is to drede, and as openli as he can ofte declare his conscience to his goostli fadir, in special if he kan, or ellis in general wordis; and þis is a souereyn remedie to al temptacions. (111)

Here the self-knowledge that the reader is enjoined throughout the text to seek diligently, and yet warned that she can never fully possess, is subordinated to a healthy "dread" that leads her to the Church—and to clerics—as mediators of divine grace. Confession is not only an antidote to individual sins but a "sovereign remedy" to any temptation. In this passage the theology behind the *Chastising*'s paradoxical reading lessons leaps into focus. There is a moral obligation to read diligently as a means of self-improvement (or self-formation), and an equal obligation to respect the mystery of God's judgment. Into the gap between these two contradictory obligations step the Church and its sacraments, making salvation possible for fallen readers. In the roles assigned by the *Chastising* to lay reading and clerical mediation, respectively, I think we can catch a glimpse of why the proliferation of models of spiritual reading in English did not strike the ecclesiastical establishment as dangerous before Lollardy. Ironically (once again), what redeemed spiritual reading in the vernacular was its very diversity and uncertainty. If reading is always difficult, and always imperfect—always fallen—then there will always be a need for the Church's professional readers, and of the sacraments only they can administer. One relies upon the virtue of the sacraments much as upon the virtue of the Latin words of the Office; both depend in turn upon the reader's good faith efforts to perform them properly, but the virtue of neither derives ultimately from those efforts, which are by the nature of fallen readers and fallen language doomed to fail.

The *Myroure of Oure Ladye,* reflecting a much greater consciousness of the anti-Lollard campaign, takes a very different route to orthodoxy. It does away with the *Chastising*'s pure reliance on the inherent virtue of the Latin words of the service (though it does insist liturgical performance be in Latin) and narrows the gap between the sisters' liturgical knowledge and that of the brethren. Zieman argues that the *Myroure* treats the sisters of Syon more like clerics than like women religious,[68] and to a larger extent than any earlier text I know it certainly does. But if the *Myroure*-author enables the nuns to *understand* their liturgical texts to an unprecedented extent, he does not ever encourage them, nor indeed does he leave them any room, to *interpret* what they read. The understanding he provides them is so exhaustive that their sole intellectual responsibility becomes the absorption of the (transparent) meaning laid out in the English text.

This paradox emerges in the opening pages of the first prologue, in the author's enumeration of the various kinds of understanding his text provides. The levels of meaning delineated here derive ultimately from biblical exegesis and more immediately from Latin liturgical treatises (such as Durandus's widely circulated *Rationale divinorum officiorum*)—both solidly clerical traditions. First (the *Myroure*-author tells us) *translation* ensures literal understanding of the text, endowing the words the sisters sing and read with their most basic level of meaning: for "many of you, though ye can synge and rede, yet ye can not se what the meanynge therof ys" (2). *Exposition* supplements this basic understanding "where the naked letter ys thoughe yt be set in englyshe, ys nat easy for some symple soulles to vnderstonde" (3). Finally, a *rationale* or explanation of the various elements of the liturgy (the "causes and the meanynges of eche parte therof"), such as psalms and hymns, or the traditional times for each hour, enables the sisters to have "the more sprytuall loue, & inwarde delyte and deuocyon, in thys holy seruyce" (ibid.). To acquire the spiritual gifts associated with liturgical prayer, the sisters must understand it thoroughly, not just its text but its structure and elements. But while the "symple soulle" who learns to read from this text is invited to a higher level of understanding than her predecessors (or colleagues?) at Barking Abbey, she is never left to discover, say, a layer of spiritual meaning on her own. All the dark passages in the text of the Office have already been made open in the *Myroure* itself. Nor are common exegetical terms like "spiritual sense" or "mystical sense" employed in this discussion. Nothing challenges the transparency or the finality of the *Myroure*-author's exposition. The sisters of Syon are offered clerical information, even arranged in clerical ways, but they are quietly steered away from the exercise of clerical skills.

In place of those clerical skills, instead of learning to interpret the text, the sisters are taught to *create* accord between themselves as readers and the liturgical meanings provided them. This kind of reading is formative, locating the *Myroure* and its readers within the culture of vernacular reading fostered by Middle English religious writing. If it does not teach clerical skills, it does require not only knowledge but skills and discipline. While understanding enables the unity of mind and tongue that makes devotion possible, God regards not only the mind but the heart and the will as well. The good reader therefore "dressyth hys harte to god at the begynnyng of hys seruyce, with wyll and purpose to keep hys mynde stable thervpon" (41). It is this "dressing" and "stabling" of the inner faculties that constitute "entendaunce," the central concept in the *Myroure*'s model of liturgical reading. Like the understanding that enables it, "entendaunce" is multi-layered, tracking the various levels of meaning in the text as well as the reader's skill levels and her various outer and inner faculties. Some "simple souls" can derive "sauour and deuocion" from their reading if they simply "kepe the mynde vpon the selfe wordes wythout eny vnderstandynge" (49). This, essentially, is the model offered by the *Chastising;* it is strongly implied that the sisters of Syon can and should aspire to more. Second, it is possible to "take hede to the letter only, after the lytterall vnderstondynge" (ibid.). This kind of "entendaunce," enabled by translation and some simple exposition when the letter is "dark," is preferable to the first but "barren" where the letter is. The third and by far the best level of "entendaunce" is to stay focused on "the inwarde gostly vnderstondynge of the wordes that ar sayd or songe" (ibid.). Here the spiritual understandynge provided in the author's commentary enables the reader to bring her inner faculties into accord with the most "inward" meaning of the service she reads.

We are far here from Love's model of imaginative reading, involving a purely devotional movement of the affect. The sisters are taught a sophisticated and multi-layered model of reading, grounded in a distinctive, quasi-clerical solution to the perennial problem of "accord," and demanding a range of readerly skills. But just as there is no liberty here to reinvent the liturgy (as Love's readers can, within the parameters of "the belief and good manners," reinvent pieces of the narrative of Christ's life), so there is no room for any *interpretive* agency on the part of the sisters. As if these general instructions were not detailed enough, they are supplemented in the translation and commentary that follows with explicit directions as to what to think, feel, and intend at each point in the service. Legibility is never an issue in this text: accord is something created by the act of reading, not something discovered through it. Misreading is of course possible (indeed it requires a great deal of effort and skill to avoid it) but consists in a failure on the part of the reading sisters to learn the meanings provided her and discipline her inner faculties appropriately—rather than, as in the *Chastising,* the inevitable hermeneutic failure of fallen humans seeking to discover spiritual truths in a fallen world.

On the one hand, then, the sisters of Syon are offered a depth of knowledge and a range of readerly skills that far exceed not only those designated by Love and Arundel for "symple soulles," but even those offered to women religious in the relatively carefree years of the late fourteenth century. But the knowledge and skills these reading lessons provide are balanced by their restriction to Syon Abbey, by containment within the discernable boundaries of texts, and (above all) by a level of detailed instruction that not only discourages, but obviates the need for interpretive agency. It is, then, precisely when it is most empowering, offering the sisters the most information about the Office and the widest array of readerly strategies, that the *Myroure of Oure Ladye* is most controlling of their actual engagement with the liturgical text.

This balance is more difficult to achieve with non-liturgical texts. Non-liturgical reading is far less (re-)iterative than its liturgical counterpart; where the latter multiplies instances of reading a single (collective) text, the former can multiply its (individual) texts. Given the sisters' propensity for book-collecting, the *Myroure*-author could hardly hope to comment exhaustively on every text they might encounter. But his goal remains the same. The model of reading presented in the brief treatise "Of Redynge," which is sandwiched between Parts I and II of the *Myroure* (65–71) and proposes to teach the sisters "how ye shall be gouerned in redynge of this Boke and of all other bokes" (65), is strikingly similar to the liturgical model described in such detail in the previous section: formative rather than interpretive, asking the reader to bring her inner faculties into accord with the meaning of the text she reads. The same double impulse to educate and to control can be felt, both in the author's need to teach the sisters how to read the *Myroure* itself—reading lessons on reading lessons—and in his parallel claim to universality, to teach them how to read *all* books not covered by the *Myroure*'s liturgical instruction. These devotional reading lessons are even full of key phrases and ideas familiar from the discussion of liturgical reading, such as the injunction to "dyspose you thereto with meke reuerence and deuocyon" and the emphasis on self-governance and self-formation rather than the discovery of meaning.

But there is one key difference: in addition to understanding and "entendaunce," non-liturgical reading requires the exercise of "dyscression," the ability to determine precisely what kind of text one is reading, and to govern one's reading accordingly. In place of choreographing the sisters' interaction with each elements of a given *text,* the *Myroure*-author here teaches them how to read specific *genres.* He groups non-liturgical texts into three basic categories, distinguishes their methods and goals, and enumerates a controlled array of readerly strategies appropriate to each, educating the sisters' "dyscression" to choose between them. This is canonization of a different sort from that practiced by Arundel and Love. Where the anti-Lollard campaign designated one strand of vernacular religious writing as orthodox and appropriate for lay readers, allowing Lollardy to taint the rest of the tradition, the *Myroure of Oure Ladye* preserves the tradition's diversity of reading strategies by gathering them together into carefully unimpeachable genres.

Each of these non-liturgical genres incorporates both some key strand of Middle English vernacular theology and some key element of the *Myroure*'s model of liturgical reading. The first consists of those texts that seek to "enfourme" the reader's "vnderstondynge" (68)—which was, we recall, the first, crucial element of liturgical reading. These books explain what to believe and teach holy doctrine; the reader is instructed to examine herself to see if she lives as they counsel. What is formed here is not spiritual delight but moral behavior. In this category we can recognize the range of texts, including penitential manuals and treatises on the elements of the faith, that grew out of post-Lateran programs of pastoral instruction and reform.

Texts in the second group, by contrast, serve to "quyken & to sturre vp the affeccyons of the soule" (68–69). These texts are designed to form an inner, spiritual state and require an answering motion of the affect and the will not unlike "entendaunce." Here the reader is enjoined to "laboure in your selfe inwardly, to sturre vp youre affeccyons accordingly to the matter that ye rede" (69). She must also use discretion to choose among these texts carefully by subject matter, according to her immediate mood or spiritual state. If she is feeling "drawen downe in bytternes of temptacyon or of trybulacyon," for example, it is hardly "spedefull" to "study in bokes of hueynes & drede" which will only invite despair (ibid.). This second group of texts reflects the vernacularization of contemplative matter, originally for women religious, and increasingly for secular lay readers. Into it, one might imagine, would fall devotional texts ranging from Franciscan-style devotional meditations like Love's to the more complex texts we label "mystical." The latter were especially popular at Syon.[69]

These two categories of texts, then, distinguish two basic modes or impulses in Middle English religious writing: one moral, engaging basic intellective faculties; the other contemplative, engaging the affect. If we listen closely enough, we can hear in them echoes of Love's and Arundel's dichotomy between intellective reading (reserved for the clergy) and affective reading (appropriate for laypeople). But here the terms of that implied dichotomy are stripped of their regulatory energy and transformed into a series of readerly options, in a passage reminiscent of sixteenth-century discussions of poetic decorum. Nor is there any hint that either of the genres discussed demand rigorous intellectual engagement in traditionally clerical modes—moral and doctrinal understanding is not, after all, the same thing as exegetical practice or speculative theology. There is no mention of biblical reading here at all; nor is there any indication that the sisters will take on the specific hermeneutic role quietly reserved throughout the *Myroure* for the clergy. The threat of heresy has been efficiently, but silently, erased.

The *Myroure* does, however, acknowledge that generic boundaries of the kind it traces here were fluid in Middle English textual culture, that the two categories outlined so far (like Arundel's dichotomy) constitute an oversimplification. The third group of texts distinguished in this remarkable passage is made up precisely of those that do not fit neatly into either of the previous two categories. They are hybrids, sometimes addressing themselves to the understanding and sometimes to the affect. In this case the reader must exercise her "dyscression" from one part of the text to the next: "ye oughte to dyspose you to bothe as the matter asketh" (70). Into this third, hybrid category might fall some penitential manuals (I am thinking here especially of *Handlyng Synne,* whose rhetorical complexities Mark Miller has explored so compellingly)[70] and works on the last things, such as the immensely popular *Pricke of Conscience,* texts that both appeal to the understanding to impart doctrine and play on the emotions to induce the reader to amend her life. But in this last category we can also see the effects of the proliferation and intermingling of a variety of genres of religious texts within a single, rapidly expanding literary marketplace. It would incorporate the multi-generic, often theologically ambitious texts of the last quarter of the fourteenth century, such as the *Book to a Mother* and, to an only slightly lesser degree, *The Chastising of God's Children.*

To summarize: the sisters of Syon Abbey in its early years were in a unique position as readers to create a safe haven for vernacular theology. Birgitta's advocating of non-liturgical reading and learning, combined with the sisters' own avid interest in Middle English religious writing, motivated the sisters and those who wrote for them to preserve their embattled textual culture. The author of the *Myroure of Oure Ladye* evades Arundel's efforts to winnow and curb that tradition in three ways. First, he restricts his audience to the sisters of Syon: protected by class, patronage, and Order from persecution under the *Constitutions,* and evading by virtue of their profession the strict dichotomy between lay and clerical readers which Arundel sought to enforce. Second, while adopting the basic principle of spiritual reading central to Middle English vernacular theology, making reading itself the sisters' primary means of spiritual progress, he tweaks that principle to render it less threatening to clerical authority: containing the sisters' reading practices within textual boundaries and focusing their efforts on the creation of accord between reader and text rather than the discovery of meaning.[71] In doing so he strikes a delicate balance between granting the sisters unprecedented readerly agency, providing them with access to "clerical" information and developing for them a challenging and complex model of reading, and controlling their actual engagement with texts, precisely through the level of detailed information and instruction he offers them. Finally, the *Myroure* preserves the diversity and complexity of Middle English religious writing by canonizing it: systematizing its genres and readerly strategies, grouping them into three non-threatening categories, and preserving certain hermeneutic skills to the clergy. I want to conclude by suggesting briefly that, having thus succeeded in preserving this rich textual culture, Syon Abbey played a central role in the reemergence of vernacular theology into more general view at the end of the fifteenth century, as the Lollard threat waned.

The production of vernacular texts at Syon and the development of the sisters' library seem to fall into two periods: one in the early to mid-fifteenth century, and the second in the decades around the turn of the sixteenth century. In the first period, as far as we can tell from fairly scant evidence, the abbey was primarily involved in collecting and producing vernacular theology for the use of the sisters themselves,[72] and in teaching them how to read it.[73] The producers of these texts do not, however, seem interested in circulating texts to a wider lay readership.[74] Most of the books David Bell has traced to the sisters' library date from the second period, as do most of the texts produced by the Syon brothers.[75] Many of these later texts *were* intended explicitly for lay audiences beyond the walls of Syon itself. Whytford's works, for example, were bestsellers in the late fifteenth and early sixteenth centuries;[76] John Fewterer's encyclopedic harmony of devotional materials on the passion dates from this period;[77] and even the *Myroure of Oure Ladye,* keyed so specifically to the sisters' Office and circumstances that it is hard to imagine how a secular layperson would use it, was printed at the instigation of Syon's abbess and confessor general, Agnes Jordan and Fewterer, in 1430, possibly with a larger audience in mind.[78] These two groupings of texts strongly suggest that the abbey began, in the fraught years of the early fifteenth century, to collect vernacular theological works and to produce English texts at least partly concerned with how such works should be read. When English reading and writing had outlived its association with heresy, and the printing press had made wider dissemination relatively easy and appealing, the monastery took the lead in providing English religious texts to a lay readership, actively shaping lay devotional practices and vernacular textual culture.

Notes

An earlier version of this essay was presented at the MLA in San Francisco in 1998, as part of a panel on Syon Abbey as a women's interpretive community. I am grateful to Katherine Zieman for organizing the panel and to her and the other panelists (Laura King and Catherine Grisé) and attendants for their comments. Thanks are also due to Anne Middleton and Alistair Minnis for their attentive readings of an earlier draft and help in revision; and to Steven Justice for a thought-provoking response that returns me to the material with new eyes.

1. R. W. Chambers, *On the Continuity of English Prose from Alfred to More and His School,* Early English Text Society *o.s.* 119A (1932; reprint, London: Early English Text Society, Oxford University Press, 1957), xc and passim; see especially xc–cxxxiv.

2. One is reminded of theory positing an unbroken oral poetic tradition linking *Beowulf* to the fluorescence of alliterative long-line verse in the fourteenth century.

3. Much of this interest was generated by a volume of essays, edited by Carol Meale, on *Women and Literature in Britain, 1150–1500* (Cambridge: Cambridge University Press, 1993); see especially Felicity Riddy's seminal article in that volume, "Women Talking of the Things of God," 104–27. See also Susan Groag Bell, "Medieval Women Book Owners: Arbiters of Lay Piety and Ambassadors of Culture," *Signs* 7, no. 4 (1982): 742–68; Josephine Koster Tarvers, "'Thys ys my mystrys boke': English Women as Readers and Writers in Late Medieval England," in *The Uses of Manuscripts in Literary Studies: Essays in Memory of Judson Boyce Allen*, ed. Charlotte Morse et al. (Kalamazoo, Mich.: Board of the Medieval Institute, 1992). For a full-length study pursuing many of the implications of Chambers's claim, see Elizabeth Robertson, *Early English Devotional Prose and the Female Audience* (Knoxville: University of Tennessee Press, 1990). Recent work in this vein is well represented by the essays in Rosalynn Voaden's collection, *Medieval Women: Texts and Contexts in Late Medieval Britain: Essays for Felicity Riddy* (Turnhout: Brepols, 2000), and those in Denis Renevey, ed., *Writing Women Religious* (Toronto: University of Toronto Press, 2000).

4. This question evokes a larger critical effort to recover agency of any kind for women in a culture whose means of textual production were controlled largely by men. This strand of feminist inquiry frequently falls back upon an impulse to assess texts, institutions, reading models, and so on as either positive, offering women greater opportunity to exercise agency, or negative, tending to restrict women's agency and self-expression. I do not claim fully to escape these tendencies here, but I want to be attentive to the value structures this kind of intuitive categorizing (even when not fully articulated as such) imposes upon its objects of study, and its potential to obscure distinctive late medieval constructions of agency, gender, and textuality.

5. For the classic account of the abbey's foundation, see Margaret Deanesley, "The Foundation of Sion Abbey," in *The Incendium Amoris of Richard Rolle of Hampole* (Manchester: Manchester University Press, 1915), 91–144. For an analysis of Henry's mixed political and religious motives in the foundation of the abbey, see Catherine Annette Grisé, "Syon Abbey in Late-Medieval England: Gender and Reading, Bodies and Communities, Piety and Politics" (PhD diss., University of Western Ontario, 1998). See also Jeremy Catto, "Religious Change under Henry V," in *Henry V: The Practice of Kingship* (Oxford: Oxford University Press, 1985), 97–115.

6. Zieman, 327.

7. See Ann Hutchison, "What the Nuns Read: Literary Evidence from the English Bridgettine House, Syon Abbey," *Medieval Studies* 57 (1995): 205–22.

8. The brothers and sisters of Syon seem each to have had a library, though only the brothers' formal inventory remains. For a list of the books known to have been in the *sisters'* library, see David Bell, *What Nuns Read: Books and Libraries in Medieval Nunneries* (Kalamazoo, Mich.: Cistercian Publications, 1995), 171–210.

9. Ibid., 38.

10. Ibid., 74. Overall, according to Bell, the sisters possessed forty-eight volumes, twenty-five of them liturgical and twenty-three theological (a generic distinction clearly recognized at the abbey itself—see below); of the latter, seventeen were in English, five in Latin, and one in French.

11. See, e.g., E. Catherine Dunn, "*The Myroure of Oure Ladye:* Syon Abbey's Role in the Continuity of English Prose," in *Diakonia: Studies in Honor of Robert T. Meyer*, ed. Thomas Halton and Joseph P. Williman (Washington, D.C.: Catholic University Press, 1986), 111–26; Hutchison "What Nuns Read"; George Keiser, "Patronage and Piety in Fifteenth-Century England: Margaret, Duchess

of Clarence, Symon Wynter, and Beinecke MS 317," *Yale University Library Gazette* 70 (October 1995): 32–46; J. T. Rhodes, "Syon Abbey and Its Religious Publications in the Sixteenth Century," *Journal of Ecclesiastical History* 44, no. 1 (1993): 11–25.

12. Riddy "Women Talking of the Things of God," 107. Riddy takes Rolle as an example of a male clerical writer who was "socialized" into writing his English epistles (very popular at Syon) by his women readers. See also Dunn (*"The Myroure of Oure Ladye"*), who places Syon at the center of an important school or coterie of writers, probably under royal patronage, and comparable to (but distinct from) Lydgate's coterie. The strong sense of rhetorical decorum that characterizes texts of this Syon school, along with a complex interaction of cognitive and affective address, locate it for Dunn firmly in the broader historical tradition traced by Chambers (*On the Continuity of English Prose*).

13. Denise Despres, "Ecstatic Reading and Missionary Mysticism: The *Orcherd of Syon*," in *Prophets Abroad: The Reception of Continental Holy Women in Late-Medieval England,* ed. Rosalynn Voaden (Cambridge: D. S. Brewer, 1996), 141–60.

14. Despres, "Ecstatic Reading," 25. Despres notes further that none of the nuns of Syon, at least to our knowledge, themselves produced visionary, speculative, or even written devotional responses to Catherine's text so transformed, nor is there any record of mystical or paramystical activity at Syon (ibid., 147).

15. See, for example, the *Cursor Mundi*, ed. Richard Morris, Early English Text Society *o.s.* 57, 69, 62, 66, 68, 99, 100 (London, 1874–93); or the more recent edition of the Southern version by Sarah M. Horrall (Ottawa: University of Ottawa Press, 1978); and *The South English Legendary,* ed. Charlotte d'Evelyn and Anna J. Mill, Early English Text Society *o.s.* 235, 236, and 244 (London: Early English Text Society, Oxford University Press, 1956–59).

16. See especially the group of texts edited by Mary Spalding as the "Middle English Charters of Christ" (PhD diss., Bryn Mawr, 1914); also the *Book to a Mother,* ed. Adrian James McCarthy (Salzburg, 1981), discussed in greater detail below.

17. For the most celebrated Middle English penitential manual, see Idelle Sullens, ed., *Handlyng Synne, by Robert Mannyng of Brunne* (Binghamton, N.Y.: MRTS, 1983). *The Chastising of God's Children,* ed. Joyce Bazier and Eric Colledge (Oxford: Blackwell, 1957) offers the nuns of Barking Abbey, among other things, lessons in reading mystical and paramystical experiences, one's own and others'; parts of this text, too, are discussed in greater detail below, while a more thorough reading is offered by Steven Justice in his response to this essay.

18. Nicholas Watson makes the parallel claim that insular mystical texts, while not constituting a formal tradition, are generally interested less in complex theology around the question of union with the divine, and more in the rhetoric of ecstasy, the ability of words to convey feelings, and the "subjective component of all religious feeling in an affective context." See his article on the Middle English version of Marguerite Porete's *Mirror of Simple Souls,* in *Prophets Abroad: The Reception of Continental Holy Women in Late-Medieval England,* ed. Rosalynn Voaden (Cambridge: D. S. Brewer, 1996), 141–60.

19. For the Latin text of Arundel's *Constitutions,* see David Wilkins, ed., *Consiliae Magnae Britanniae et Hiberniae* (London: Sumptibus R. Gosling, 1737), 3:314–19. The sixth and seventh address English reading and writing specifically. Anne Hudson paraphrases the *Constitutions* and discusses their significance, particularly for textual culture, in her *Lollards and Their Books* (London

and Ronceverte: Hambledon, 1985), 146–49. For instances of English books destroyed or confiscated on suspicion of heresy, see 7, 125, and 242–43; for instances of the possession of English books taken as evidence of heresy, see 149 and 182. Hudson even cites one occasion on which possession of the *Canterbury Tales* was cited as evidence of heresy (142).

20. It is worth noting in this regard that Despres attributes the "devotional paternalism" of the *Orchard* in part to the dampening effects of that campaign, arguing that Carthusian translators transformed and diffused continental mysticism for "a spiritual elite beyond suspicion of heresy" (145).

21. In addition to Despres's article cited above, several of the other essays in Voaden's *Prophets Abroad* address this transformation. Kathryn Kerby-Fulton places English religious writing in this vein in its larger continental context elsewhere in this current volume, emphasizing transformation less than participation. Without denying the embeddedness of Syon Abbey and its texts in the nexus of "rival enthusiasms and concerns" that Kerby-Fulton articulates, many of them broadly European rather than narrowly insular, I want to stress that the emphasis placed on reading as a spiritual practice at Syon, while influenced by monastic *lectio divina,* has its roots in the rich and distinctive tradition of English vernacular theology (Kerby-Fulton, "When Women Preached," 37).

22. Nicholas Watson, "Censorship and Cultural Change in Late-Medieval England: Vernacular Theology, the Oxford Translation Debate and Arundel's *Constitutions* of 1409," *Speculum* 70 (1995): 822–64.

23. For theories of authorship and date see Ann Hutchison, "Devotional Reading in the Monastery and the Late Medieval Household," in *De Cella in Seculum: Religious and Secular Life and Devotion in Late Medieval England,* ed. Michael Sargent (Cambridge: D. S. Brewer, 1989), 215–27, along with Blunt's introduction.

24. In this it is both like other early Syon texts and surpasses them. Early Syon texts are rife with reading lessons similar to the *Myroure*'s, though none are devoted so exclusively to readerly instruction. The *Orchard of Syon,* for example, as we have seen, allegorizes Catherine of Siena's *Dialogues* as an orchard and devotes its prologue to teaching the sisters how best to browse in it and eat its fruit. More explicitly still, a rubric in one Syon manuscript of vernacular religious texts, containing excerpts from writers like Suso, Rolle, Hilton, and Birgitta herself, instructs: "We shulde rede and vse bokes to þis ende and entente: for formys of preysynge and preyynge to god, to oure layde, seynte marye, and to alle þe seyntes; þat we myȝte haue by þe forsyd vse of redyge vnderstondyge of god, of hys benefetys, of hys lawe, of hys seruyce, or sume oþer goodly and gosteley trowþþis; or ellys þat we myȝte haue good affeccyon to ward god and hys seyntes, and hys seruice to be gendryd and geten" (MS Harley 1706, f.212 v., quoted in Hutchison, "Devotional Reading in the Monastery," 215–27).

25. This and all quotations from the *Myroure of Oure Ladye* are taken from the edition of John Henry Blunt, Early English Text Society *e.s.* 19 (London, 1873; reprint 1998).

26. For a more detailed discussion of this tradition, see my "Genre Trouble: Spiritual Reading in the Vernacular and the Literary Project of the Pearl-Poet" (PhD diss., University of California at Berkeley, 2001), esp. chap. 1, "Genre and Trouble in Middle English Religious Writing," 22–86.

27. The classic account of these two Latin models of reading is Beryl Smalley's, in her *Study of the Bible in the Middle Ages* (Oxford: Oxford University Press, 1941). See especially chap. 1, on "The Fathers" (though the distinction between these exegesis and *lectio divina* structures much of the

book). Notably absent from Smalley's study is a detailed study of *liturgical* reading; Katherine Zieman's article in this current volume provides a good introduction to the topic, which is essential to a reading of the *Myroure of Oure Ladye.*

28. For an invaluable collection of excerpts from a wide array of vernacular religious texts, focusing on those moments when English writers reflect on their own methods and goals, see Jocelyn Wogan-Browne, Nicholas Watson, et al., eds., *The Idea of the Vernacular: An Anthology of Middle English Literary Theory, 1280–1520* (University Park: Pennsylvania State University Press, 1999).

29. I adopt these terms from *The Chastising of God's Children,* to which we shall return in a moment.

30. It is worth noting in this regard that a second strand of vernacular theology, developing in tandem with writings for women religious, was designed to help minimally literate parish priests perform their pastoral obligations as outlined in the Fourth Lateran Council. The seminal text here is Thoresby's Middle English translation of Pecham's "Syllabus" laying out the articles of the faith; see Thomas Frederick Simmons Nolloth and Henry Edward, eds., *The Lay Folks' Catechism* (Millwood, N.Y.: Kraus Reprints, 1972).

31. Two studies of lay reading in late medieval England bear mention in relation to my project here. The first is Joyce Coleman, *Public Reading and the Reading Public in Late Medieval England and France* (Cambridge: Cambridge University Press, 1996). Coleman's study is grounded in the distinction between silent, "dividual" reading and the reading aloud of texts, which she labels "prelection"; she argues that the latter dominated literary reception well into the fifteenth century (though she focuses more on secular reading of literary, than on cloistered reading of religious, texts). My interest, by contrast, is in readerly skills more broadly conceived, and in what we might call the theologies of reading that proliferate in Middle English religious writing. In this my approach is closer to that of Steven Justice in his *Writing and Rebellion: England in 1381* (Berkeley: University of California Press, 1994). Justice is interested not so much in textual access or literacy rates narrowly defined as in textual competencies. In this study of the rebels' "insurgent" use of writing in the 1381 Rising, Justice traces what he terms the "documentary literacy" of the lay rebels, demonstrating that the rebels knew what kinds of documents to target to achieve their ends, and knew their way around the bureaucracies that produced and held those documents—even if they couldn't write them, or even necessarily read them, themselves. Justice's work is useful in pointing us towards the *kinds* of literacy possessed by various social groups, and, above all, the uses to which particular literacies are put.

32. Nicholas Watson, "The Middle English Mystics," in *The Cambridge History of Middle English Literature,* ed. David Wallace (Cambridge: Cambridge University Press, 1999), 539–65.

33. I refer here to two texts attributed to Mannyng; one of those attributions is sure while the other is not, but the point about their address to laypeople holds in any case. The sure attribution is of *Handlyng Synne,* in whose prologue Mannyng identifies himself by name (see note 17 above). Less certainly Mannyng's, but dating from the same period, is the *Meditations on the Supper of Our Lord and the Hours of the Passion,* ed. J. Meadows Cowper, Early English Text Society *o.s.* 60 (London, 1875), perhaps the earliest Middle English translation of (part of) the pseudo-Bonaventuran *Meditationes Vitae Christi* (more on this below).

34. Nicholas Watson has worked productively to articulate what is theologically distinctive about Middle English religious writing. See, for example, his "Visions of Inclusion: Universal

Salvation and Vernacular Theology in Pre-Reformation England," *Journal of Medieval and Early Modern Studies* 27, no. 2 (1997): 145–87; and his "Conceptions of the Word: The Mother Tongue and the Incarnation of God," in *New Medieval Literatures I*, ed. Wendy Scase et al. (Oxford: Clarendon, 1997).

35. For the former see Mary Theresa Brady, ed., "*The Pore Caitif*" (PhD diss., Fordham University, 1954); for the latter, Harold Kane, ed., *The Prickynge of Loue* (Salzburg: Institut für Anglistik und Amerikanistik, 1983).

36. I cite throughout from McCarthy's edition of the *Book to a Mother*. Nicholas Watson is less certain about the dating of the *Book*; see his "Fashioning the Puritan Gentry-Woman: Devotion and Dissent in the *Book to a Mother*," in *Medieval Women: Texts and Contexts in Medieval Britain: Essays for Felicity Riddy*, ed. Jocelyn Wogan-Browne et al. (Turnhout: 2000), 169–84.

37. For an account of this multiple allegorizing of the text that influences my reading here, see Watson ("Fashioning the Puritan Gentry-Woman").

38. The *Book*'s articulation of this tenet, as a reversal of the traditional Gregorian maxim that images are the books of the laity, brings him strikingly in line with the Lollards' particular brand of biblical literalism: "bokis þat men wryten ben no Holi Writ," he says, "but as images ben holi, for þei bitokeneþ holi seintes; but Crist Godis Sone, he is uereiliche Holi Writ" (30).

39. The author enjoins his mother to "be write wiþinne and wiþoute wiþ pulke þre [i.e., poverty, humility, chastity] as Crist was" (ibid.); her goal should be to "lerne aftir þi samplerie to write a feir trewe bok and better konne Holi Writ þan ony maister of diuinite þat loueþ not God so wel as þou" (39).

40. For "the author's book" (says Watson), "like the Bible, can only serve a mediating function. . . . It follows that while the *Book to a Mother* needs to include a good deal of the Bible within it, it can substitute for the Bible as an exposition of 'God's law,' since both texts are only pointers to Christ. It also follows that to serve as an effective pointer the book must, as a structure always in danger of substituting for the reality it represents, seek to disappear" (Watson, "Fashioning the Puritan Gentry-Woman," 178).

41. See Teresa M. Brady, "Lollard Interpolations and Omissions in Manuscripts of the *Pore Caitif*," in *De Cella in Seculum: Religious and Secular Life and Devotion in Late Medieval England*, ed. Michael Sargent (Cambridge: D. S. Brewer, 1989), 183–203.

42. See Watson, "Fashioning the Puritan Gentry-Woman," 175–78 and passim.

43. For a useful account of different late medieval English representations of the humanity of Christ, Lollard and orthodox, see David Aers and Lynn Staley, *The Powers of the Holy: Religion, Politics, and Gender in Late Medieval English Culture* (University Park: Pennsylvania State University Press, 1996), part 1.

44. Jocelyn Wogan-Browne et al., *Idea of the Vernacular*, provides a useful introduction to this tradition in the form of a plethora of relevant excerpts drawn largely from Middle English religious texts.

45. The relevant passage is as follows: "My leue dere moder, hauyng reward to þe grete godeness þat I haue recyued þorow þe of oure Lord Ihesus Crist, þenkynge and desiryng how I myȝte most sikerly, vereily and best worschipe þe as it were most to Gods worschipe—fulfillynge þe ferþe heste of God þat comaundeþ to worschipe fader and moder—not folewynge foles þat so myche setten her likynge in fals worschipe of þis world þat þei sechen not þe worschipe of God, for alle suche

Crist reproueþ in þe gospel . . . þerfore to be syker at the Day of Dome fro þe scornynge wretthe and wodenes of God and fro alle oþere parels, before alle oþer bokes oon I chese þat techeþ euery man and womman þat wol do after him to be Cristes broþer, sister and moder, and eir with him of al heuene and erþe. And what more worschipe myght a child desire to his moder?" (16–17).

46. By the time he was writing there would have been ample precedent for books written for one audience, often women religious, or even a single nun or anchoress, to enter the wider literary marketplace; the *Ancrene Wisse* (which was not only transmitted widely but translated in Anglo-Norman and Latin) and the English works of Richard Rolle are the most notable examples.

47. In the passage in question from chapter 3 the author asserts that he has chosen to present to his mother that book "þat techeþ euery man and womman þat wol do after him to be Cristes broþer, sister and moder" (17).

48. McCarthy, *Book to a Mother*, xxx–xxxiv.

49. My point here is about the rhetoric of the *Myroure* more than about its actual audience, though there seems little reason to doubt the author's own statements in this regard. It is, however, interesting to note that the *Myroure of Oure Ladye* was one of the first Syon texts to be printed, perhaps supporting Margot Fassler's argument elsewhere in this volume that the Syon Office (as a version of the Marian Little Hours upon which books of hours were based) was particularly appealing to, and educative for, laypeople. For a discussion of later dissemination of early Syon texts, see below. I am grateful to Kathryn Vulic for sharing with me her (as yet unpublished) theories about the address to women religious as a trope, rather than a literal element, in Middle English religious writing.

50. See Watson, "Censorship and Cultural Change."

51. Justice, 387.

52. See my "Orthodoxy, Textuality, and the 'Tretys' of Margery Kempe," *Journal X* 1, no. 1 (autumn 1996): 31–56.

53. Michael G. Sargent, ed., *Nicholas Love's Mirror of the Blessed Life of Jesus Christ* (New York: Garland, 1992), 7. I cite throughout from Sargent's edition of Love's text.

54. Sargent gives a substantial list of places where Love has altered or augmented his source text with explicitly anti-Lollard material, particularly on the topics of obedience to ecclesiastical hierarchy (including corrupt priests), alms, confession, and, especially, the Eucharist—to which he devotes an entire treatise appended to the end of the *Mirror*. Some of these passages contain language echoing Arundel's authorization, suggesting that perhaps the two men worked together; all of them are marked with marginal notes.

55. See Sargent, *Nicholas Love's Mirror*, 176–77.

56. This tendency was not restricted to Syon texts, nor even to monastic ones. For a fifteenth-century text addressed to secular laypeople which makes similar gestures of containment, see *Dives and Pauper*, as discussed in my "Genre Trouble," 126–31.

57. For an overview of this genre see Timothy Thibodeau, "*Enigmata Figurarum:* Biblical Exegesis and Liturgical Exposition in Durand's *Rationale*," *Harvard Theological Review* 86, no. 1 (1993): 65–79.

58. See, e.g., Sargent, *Nicholas Love's Mirror*, 81 and 93. For a more detailed discussion of this aspect of the sisters' liturgical performance see Katherine Zieman's article in this volume.

59. It is interesting to note in this regard that in Love's source, the pseudo-Bonaventuran *Meditationes*, the "simple souls" in question are not laypeople but women religious (as Love himself notes; see Sargent, *Nicholas Love's Mirror*, 10). Love's text thus enacts the move of contemplative/meditative

texts from a narrow audience of women religious to a much broader lay readership; while ironi-cally, in the same gesture, Love transforms his source into a narrowly orthodox model of reading for secular laypeople. This irony is further compounded when we consider that it is precisely *as* women religious (the pseudo-Bonaventure's original, narrow audience) that the sisters of Syon evade the very dichotomizing project that Love's translation works to enact. The paradoxical transformations here are dizzying; to trace them is to trace in miniature one history of Middle English religious writing.

60. See Sargent, *Nicholas Love's Mirror*, 1–2.

61. See Katherine Zieman, "Reading, Singing, and Understanding: Constructions of the Lit-eracy of Women Religious in Late Medieval England," in *Learning and Literacy in Medieval England and Abroad*, ed. Sarah Rees Jones (Turnhout: Brepols, 2003), 97–120.

62. "Euchan segge hire ures as he haued iwriten ham" (15). I cite, here and throughout, from J. R. R. Tolkien's edition of the *Ancrene Wisse*, Early English Text Society *o.s.* 249 (London: Oxford University Press, 1962).

63. E.g., "þe ne con oþer uhtsong oþer ne bute slepen mei hit seggen segge for ughsong þritti pater nostres. & Aue Maria efter euch pater noster. & gloria patri efter euch aue. Aleast oremus hwa se con. Deus cui proprium est. Benedicamus deo. Anime fidelium. for euensong twenit. for euch oþer tide segge fiftene o þis ilke wise" (28).

64. For a list of Barking-related manuscripts, see David Bell, *What Nuns Read*. We might note here that at Barking, unlike Syon, we can identify at least one or two women *writers*, though those we can identify wrote early on, and in Anglo-Norman rather than English. See, for example, "Writ-ing in the Textual Community: Clemence of Barking's Life of St. Catherine," *French Forum* 21, no. 1 (1996): 5–28.

65. See the introductory discussion of dating in Joyce Bazire and Eric Colledge, eds., *The Chastising of God's Children* (Oxford: Blackwell, 1957). Justice challenges their dating in his response to this article. I cite throughout from Bazire and Colledge's edition of the *Chastising*.

66. This kind of self-deception makes it difficult for the author even to narrate the potential for self-deception. At one point he refuses to tell an exemplary tale specifically addressing "hou ful hooli men han be bigiled," (197) precisely because such tales are so often misread by those who cannot even see their own sinfulness: "for sum whanne þei rede suche ensamplis þat bien writen for goode entent, þei turne it aftir þeir nyce conceytis, and make þerof boordes and scornes; and þe cause is for þei bien so blynded þat þei mowen nat (ne can not se) her owne infirmyte" (198).

67. The best example of this is the lengthy section on the discerning of spirits, which trans-forms Alphonse of Pecha's defense of St. Birgitta's revelations into a hortatory discourse on the dan-gers of false mysticism. We are warned sternly and repeatedly to subject any mystical experiences to rigorous examination, and we are provided with seven "tokens" by which to judge them (see 177–82; in general, the authenticity of a vision is legible in the visionary's virtuous life and obedience to her confessor, as well as in the conformity of the visions themselves to the teaching of the Church). But in the next chapter we are warned, just as sternly, never to assume that our own genuine mystical ex-periences are signs of virtue. For "alle þese and suche oþer preuen nat a man ne womman hooli ne parfite, for a repreuable man may haue al þese uertues and manye oþer" (183). We should never pre-sume to have access to the "preuey doom of god" (185). We must always read, but we can never as-sume we are reading correctly—even (indeed especially) when we are reading ourselves.

68. Where *The Chastising of God's Children* (Zieman argues) constructs its version of liturgical literacy in response to affective and devotional excesses—as an alternative to a frightening mystical literacy—thinking of its audience more as lay than as cleric, the *Myroure* views its audience as clerical performers whose prayers have formal intercessory powers. However their understanding is supplied by translation, not grammar, contributing to a "split consciousness," on the sisters' part, "the maintenance of both a liturgical latinity and a vernacular interiority" ("Reading, Singing, and Understanding, 115 and 119).

69. For a list of English mystical texts owned by the sisters or associated closely with the abbey, see Phyllis Hodgson, "The *Orcherd of Syon* and the English Mystical Tradition," *Proceedings of the British Academy* 50 (1964): 229–39. For a full list of texts, including those of continental mystics, see David Bell, *What Nuns Read.*

70. See Mark Miller, "Displaced Souls, Idle Talk, Spectacular Scenes: *Handlyng Synne* and the Perspective of Agency," *Speculum* 71, no. 3 (1996): 606–32. Miller argues that the quasi-literary use of narrative in *Handlyng Synne* offers the reader, not rules and regulations, but a practical (readerly, I would say) skill that engages the territory of agency. In this text (Miller claims) reading exemplary narratives becomes both a model for, and a means of, the ever-shifting acts of self-reading required for true penitence.

71. Cf. Lee Patterson on the "disambiguating" of the *Troilus* in the *Disce Mori* (another Syon text): "Ambiguity and Interpretation: A Fifteenth-Century Reading of *Troilus and Criseyde*," in *Negotiating the Past: The Historical Understanding of Medieval Literature* (Madison: University of Wisconsin Press, 1987), 115–56.

72. In addition to the *Myroure*, texts from this period include the *Orcherd of Syon* (see above); the Life of Saint Jerome written by the Syon brother Simon Wynter for Margaret Holland (on which see Keiser, "Patronage and Piety"); the controversial *Additions to the Rule of St. Savior* (on which see Hans Cnattingius, *Studies in the Order of St. Bridget of Sweden: The Crisis in the 1420's* [Stockholm: Almqvist and Wiksell, 1963]); a copy of Walter Hilton's *Ladder of Perfection,* British Library MS Arundel 146 (see David Bell, *What Nuns Read,* 188); and Rolle's psalter (referred to famously in the *Myroure* itself). Some of the liturgical texts in David Bell's reconstruction of the sisters' library—processionals, psalters and breviaries, hours of the Holy Spirit, and so on—certainly date from this period. We know, for example, that Henry V gave several books to the abbey, including a *magne biblia,* and that his son the duke of Bedford who, like his father, evinced a continuing involvement in Syon and its affairs, donated two service books (Hutchison "What Nuns Read," 206).

73. See note 24 above.

74. Wynter's life of St. Jerome is the exception that proves the rule. Margaret (whose formal association with Syon began in 1428) is asked by its author "first to rede it and to do copye hit for yourself, and syth to lete oþer rede hit and copye hit, who so wyll" (cited in Keiser, "Patronage and Piety," 41). The text survives in four fifteenth-century manuscripts, at least three of them definitely or probably associated with Syon, and one of them (also containing Lydgate's *Life of Our Lady* and various saints' lives) possibly written for Henry V (confirming yet again the monastery's close ties to the Lancastrian king). Despite the injunction to publish, then, we have no evidence that the text traveled far beyond the monastery's walls—or at least no farther than to its king and patron. It was, however, printed in 1499 by de Worde (four years, Keiser tells us, after Margaret's granddaughter Lady Margaret Beaufort ordered the publication of Hilton's *Scale*), supporting my theory that the

turn of the sixteenth century witnessed a new trend in textual dissemination from the abbey. Hutchison ("Devotional Reading") mentions this text as well.

75. Notable are the works of Richard Whytford, John Fewterer, and the compiler of the *Disce Mori*. For further information on the dissemination of vernacular texts from Syon in the sixteenth century see J. T. Rhodes, "Syon Abbey and Its Religious Publications."

76. See Martha W. Driver, "Pictures in Print: Late Fifteenth- and Early Sixteenth-Century English Religious Books for Lay Readers," in *De Cella in Seculum: Religious and Secular Life and Devotion in Late Medieval England*, ed. Michael Sargent (Cambridge: D. S. Brewer, 1989), 229–44, at 233.

77. Fewterer's text has yet to be edited; for a description see J. T. Rhodes, "Prayers of the Passion from Jordanus of Quedlinburg to John Fewterer of Syon," *Durham University Journal* 54, no. 1 (1993): 27–38.

78. Hutchison ("Devotional Reading") points out that the *Myroure* was printed in 1530 at the request of Agnes Jordan, abbess of Syon, and John Fewterer, its confessor general, and may have been prepared for a more general audience.

"General Words"

Response to Elizabeth Schirmer

STEVEN JUSTICE

Schirmer elicits hard paradoxes from the *Mirror of Our Lady*. Its englishing and exegesis of the Latin hours, while apparently signaling some newly generous vernacular access to Latin thought and worship, show to her closer regard how the ambitions of some "vernacular theology" contracted after Arundel's *Constitutions*. The very comprehensiveness of the book's proffer, she argues, constrains the interpretation it enables, indeed dominates and absorbs the reading self, as if without remainder. Although she notes also the rearguard resourcefulness of the *Mirror* and the nuns for whom it was written, it is the final retrenchment that is most striking. Odd and provocative inferences suggest themselves: that the *Constitutions* had created a situation in which the more of systematic and practical use vernacular writing might be, the more it would conform to their repressive force; even that the Syon nuns' "safe haven" stymied one of vernacular theology's chief energies, a provocation of readers to use and then abandon its written discourse. The monastery wall gives the essay its embracing paradox: enclosure both preserves vernacular theology and peremptorily aborts its promise of access; it protects the nuns' reading, and also contains it.

This seems to me a brilliant and, once encountered, nearly inevitable reading. What is it evidence for? I want to approach that question at a slant, treating another work Schirmer discusses: *The Chastising of God's Children*, a treatise written for a "religious sister,"[1] patched together from translations of Ruysbroec, Alphonse of Jaén, Suso, and others, though patched to strikingly original effect. Schirmer's account of the work differs in tone from a more enthusiastic one briefly adumbrated by Nicholas Watson, in his brilliant revisionist essay on the *Constitutions*, who finds it "remarkable" for its picture of men and women prompted by visionary experience to write: it vividly evokes the "relatively unregulated preaching and writing by women and *rustici*" that provoked clerical opposition to vernacular franchise.[2] Schirmer's *Chastising* is darker. Though the perspectives feel different, they are not incompatible. I quibble with both, but my modest purpose for most of this essay is to bring them into productive relation to each other and argue that the book's stringencies are built upon a deeper assumption of its readers' freedoms, and that it presupposes the existence of a network of such readers, whose shared texts and practices bespeak a form of theological and spiritual experimentation that was (so to speak) discursively nearly invisible to official orthodoxy and official Lollardy in their fierce mutual fascination.[3]

Liturgy brings the *Chastising* into Schirmer's account: while the *Mirror* offers to educate its Syon readers that they may understand their liturgical hours, the *Chastising* seems shockingly unconcerned that its readers may not. Schirmer observes that this author binds his reader to recite her hours in Latin, assuring the unlatinate that "the uertu of the wordes" and "ȝoure lownesse and obeisaunce to holi chirche" may render uncomprehended prayers more profitable "þanne grete deuocioun þat ȝe wene ȝe haue in oþer preuy deuocions" (222), an assurance insinuating that the reader cannot even assess her own experience: she maybe only *thinks* that "preuy devocions" profit more than liturgical ones. And while reassuring her that distractions suffered in such prayer are the guiltless upshot of circumstance and human finitude, he "napeles" enjoins her to mention "alle such negligence" in each confession. Schirmer finds here the goal of the interminable self-analysis which the *Chastising* would enforce, and whose very freedom and directionlessness seem designed to baffle its reader back to the reassuring surveillance of confession. She quotes the author's earlier counsel: the reader should blame himself for any feelings of spiritual desolation, and "as openli as he can, ofte declare his conscience to his goostli fadir, *in special, if he kan,* or ellis in general wordis" (111). Self-exploration is finally "subordinated to a healthy 'dread' that leads her to the Church—and to clerics—as mediators of divine grace."[4] So far so good, but what does "in special, if he kan" mean? "Special" is paired antonymically with "general," and so means "specific";[5] the syntax distributes the substantive to both adjectives, so distinguishing *special words* from *general words*. But why "if he kan"?

A later passage tacitly answers the question. Although temptation is not sinful when unwilled and unwelcome, we should still assume blame for it—and go to confession:

it is nedeful to showe it to oure confessours—*or in general wordis or in special,* for suche a confessour it myȝt be þat it were nat spedeful to shewe hym al such goostli temptacions in special þat falle or mow falle to a goostli lyuer. Þerfor to suche a confessour it sufficieþ to speke of temptacions generalli, into tyme þat a man mow comune and aske counseil of anoþer man more discreet and more expert in suche matiers. (202)

Both passages speak of confession; both counsel one to assume a formal and hypo-thetical responsibility for one's temptations and to confess them; both say that this will sometimes be in "general" words, sometimes in "special." It is clear that this latter pas-sage can be taken as a gloss of the first: one should confess in "special" words, in detail, if the priest is up to it. That, then, must be what the earlier passage means by "if he kan": the penitent should be candid if he judges candor expedient ("spedeful") with this priest; if not, he should adopt a bowdlerizing generality.

So the penitent silently judges the priest, and may dissemble the very matter of the confession. Imagine such a case. Approaching him with "goostli temptations" on the mind, the penitent finds words roundabout enough to serve the turn, confesses, and is absolved. The priest does not know what has transpired: does not know that he has been weighed and found wanting, or indeed that he has been weighed; does not know that absolution has been pried from him in what he would have to think bad faith. (His ignorance may be a persistent state: the terms "confessour" and "goostli fadir" can suppose a continuing relationship.) This is what the *Chastising* directs; yet it also directs the reader to confession as to a positive good. The practice counseled is not that of Mar-gery Baxter, for example, who, disdaining the sacrament, confessed falsely to the Dean of St. Mary in the Fields, "so that he would think her of good life."[6] Those suspect of heresy, as she was, sometimes made fictive confession because confession was unavoidable, but, thinking it valueless, could use it instrumentally and (on an orthodox view) cynically to escape detection. One receptive to the *Chastising*'s injunctions will not contemn the absolution of unapt priests, or attack or seek to reform them, or reject or minimize their sacramental power, but will use such power for the good of the inner life one veils from them until one may "comune and aske counseil of anoþer man more discreet" (202). This inner life, which one saves for sharing with the like-minded, does not even reveal its existence to such a confessor.

The passage on liturgical prayer with which we began explains both the importance of confession and this pragmatically flexible approach to it. We confess distractions at prayer "to stonde þe more clier and ful clier in conscience, for oure owne demyng in open confession putteþ awei drede of conscience" (223). The passage has already explained "drede of conscience": there are religious who, when their attention falters, start their prayers again, straining to concentrate; they may spend day and night in this painful exercise "þat her conscience myȝt be discharged," but remain plagued by "grete *drede in conscience*, and . . . a tedious trauaile bi temptacions in þouȝtis" (222). We should confess to find remedy, not for some guilt of imperfect attention, but for the *sense* of guilt and the imprisonment in compulsive fear it brings in tow; and it is our "owne demyng," not the priest's (who may not know what he is "demyng"), that clears the conscience and frees from compulsion. Heretics seek freedom from prosecution in fictive confession; the reader here is to seek in authentic but prudently formulated confession a freedom from stultifying self-surveillance.[7]

It is this logic that requires the reader to say the hours in Latin and not in English. The author uses an analogy from confession:

> if a mannes confessour ʒiuieþ him in penaunce to seie his sautir wiþoute ony oþer wordis, and he gooþ forþ and seiþ it in englisshe and nat in latyn as it was ordeynd, þis man, I wene, dooþ nat his penaunce.

A confessor who enjoins recitation of the psalter, without qualification ("wiþoute any oþer wordis"), plainly means the Latin psalter; to substitute an English psalter would leave the penance unperformed, the sacrament unaccomplished, and the conscience therefore unrelieved. Just so, the routine obligation to recite certain hours plainly means the Latin hours. The analogy with confession thus understood suggests why the author insists on this obligation, and why it is those specifically ("namly") whose regular status binds them to recite their hours that he insists must so recite them: she should not substitute English for Latin prayers, because prescribing for oneself an exception one knows to be illegitimate binds one to that compulsive self-monitoring and self-justification that the *Chastising* invokes confession to remedy. The vernacular is not the issue at all.[8] The author does not impose the requirement of Latin, but enjoins recognition of a requirement already imposed. Evading obligations, he suggests, traps the mind in compulsive repetition, while pragmatically fulfilling them leaves one free.

Free for what? So far I have simply ignored the very different understanding of this work advanced in Colledge's learned, indispensable, and very influential introduction. As Colledge reads it, the *Chastising* wants mainly to stop things, to preserve its readers from the threat of unregulated experience. Its author, he says, omits Ruysbroec's treatment of unitive prayer because he thinks it "quite unsuitable for simple-minded nuns, already too prone to 'enthusiasm'" (47), and omits from Alphonse of Jaén's *Epistola solitarii* the defense of Birgitta of Sweden's visions, lest it encourage visionary activity they are only too likely to seek anyway. Freedom would not be the aim of such a work; but such is not the work its author wrote. This author expects his reader to counsel others on the same difficult matters on which he counsels her (110); he worries, not that his theology will be too stark for "simple-minded nuns," but that it might seem insultingly elementary;[9] the severe criteria he prescribes for testing the authenticity of private revelations not only (as Watson implies) presuppose that revelations will be had, but places the conventionally clerical activity of discernment in the hands of the nuns and other readers.[10] And caution hardly governs his doctrine of the spiritual life. Praying not to be led into temptation, he says at the start, means praying to resist, not to avoid it (97); it is profitable "moche to be tempted and to be troubled," which we see in the Virgin Mary, "which passid al other in hoolynesse, and most was troubled" (97).[11] He shows what "troubling" means when he introduces his main subject, which is, in its broader outlines, conventional enough: God first gives "gostli swetnesse" to those "which bien goostli lyuers"—what exactly this last phrase means will emerge—but eventually withdraws himself, sending first "outward" trials (gossip, scorn, and so on), and then "goostli roddis" with which he "bringeþ hem in grete drede," and sometimes "in dredeful doutis" (114).

This life is nothing so tame as Colledge suggests. "Drede" and "doutis," apparently, are what "troubled" the Virgin, and what the reader must expect will trouble herself. This is why the book so insistently urges one to shed "drede of conscience" in confession: that moral timorousness narrows experience and counterfeits the more spacious dangers met in true prayer, dangers like visions ("orribil stis"), auditions ("wondirful heerynge"), sensations ("dredeful bodili felynge"), and coercive chains of association ("imagynacions of dredeful þinges whiche þei mow nat put awei" [117–18]). These become matter for the reader's own theologizing: they bring more than terror, amazement, or any other sensation: they bring conceptual content, "þouȝtes" (119). The author grows reticent at their mention, unwilling to "specifie" that content lest they infect a reader who has not experienced them.[12] But he specifies enough to show that dread and doubt are bedfellows. Some, for example, will "imagyne of predestinaciouns, and of the prescience or of þe foreknowynge of god" (119). But worry over one's own predestination is not the only trial that thoughts of predestination might evoke: "suche men sum tyme bien dredeful for synnes don bifore, and sum tyme to dredeful" (119–20). *Sometimes* it is consciousness or overconsciousness of sin that predestination evokes; sometimes, therefore, it is not, and he makes clear what else it can be as he moves from species to genus: "Summe also bien traueiled wiþ poyntes of þe feiþ" (120). As dread touches doctrine it becomes doubt; here predestination seems to evoke questions about free will, perhaps, or the doctrine of final judgment.[13] The *Chastising* author assumes that imaginative and intellectual risk come with the territory of prayer: contending with sights and hearings and trains of thought that push at the darkest and hardest elements of doctrine, even finding oneself to doubt them, seems to this author normal. And good: the "temptacioun" (118), the "synne" (119), on such occasions is not doubting, but wishing the doubts away, except as it might please the God who sends them. Troublings "of feiþ or of any drede," or despair or blasphemy, serve to exercise "þe wil of reason" which "fiȝtiþ þerwiþ," he insists later (201). Those given to prayer will be exposed to doubts and trials as a mountain is to wind (97), and the Virgin Mary, "most . . . troubled," models and authorizes exposure to emotional and intellectual struggle with points of the faith.

So far I have offered a reading of the *Chastising* in a familiar thematic mode, tracing out its ideas about the practice of confession and prayer; from it, the decline to the hand-holding of the *Mirror of Our Lady* seems the steeper. But this, like any reading, can detect only the author's prescriptive fantasies. Is it possible to see anything more? Return for a moment to where the author says that the reader should confess to his spiritual father "in special [wordis] if he kan." I adduced a passage much later in the work to discover what "if he kan" means. But that is a scholar's way of answering a scholar's question; it is not what the work asks of the reader. The "religious sister" is not expected to scan the book for some gloss by which she can understand the phrase; she is expected already to understand it. Nor is our initial incomprehension a merely modern bafflement before medieval convention: medieval pastoralia do not conventionally suggest hiding from one's confessor what he might misunderstand or mistrust.[14] The author can use the shorthand "if he kan" because he can expect that she will be familiar with such a practice. But this cannot be the whole explanation for this shorthand, because she is not his only reader. It is a commonplace that medieval works expect audiences beyond their explicit addressees,[15] but this author takes an especially systematic care to cover the varying circumstances of a wider readership. He speaks throughout of "men or women" in his audience (101–21), and varies formulae to include priests as well as nuns ("þe tyme þat we *seien* masse *or hier*" [221; see also 127]). Intriguingly, he works also to address states of life not comprised by male and female monastics. The first chapter lays out temptations that befall "men or wymmen of religion *or of any parfeccion*" (97)—in religious orders or any other course of perfection. His very attentiveness to audience suggests that what he does not say can stand as evidence for what he does not think he needs to say. Whoever these other readers are (and one *is* curious about those "of any parfeccion")[16] he expects them *also* to understand "if he kan" unglossed, which no reader, however informed and sophisticated, would likely do without already sharing such a practice and its guiding maxims. But if he believes that he can predict who his audience will be, then he knows (or thinks he knows) how the book will be circulated, expects that it will be transmitted along a network of readers who share interests and vocabularies and practices, and therefore knows (or thinks he knows) that such lines of contact and knots of community exist.

Such contact with a network of fellow contemplative practitioners is written into the work's vocabulary and assumptions. When wrestling with temptations to despair, he says (chapter 14), "it is goode to shewe it to a mannes confessor, or ellis to oon or tweyne oþer goostli lyuers" (135); as before, talking to one's confessor is optional. But talking is not. While garrulous religious (especially women religious) chatting their way into waste and sin is a stock image,[17] sociability ("commoning") in the *Chastising* is more than permitted, and is more than incident to the life it describes. When tempted to despair (chapter 13), or when experiencing visions (chapter 19), the contemplative who talks to others is safe: "þer falliþ no man ne womman in myschief but suche þat goon forþ and will not shewe her harte to no man" (135).[18] Later, the author revises Alphonse of Jaén's insistence that a visionary must live under the obedience and teaching of his spiritual father, adding "*or* under the counceil and techyng of sum sad preuen man, discreet and uertuous and of gostli lyueng" (177).[19] He cares less whether the visionary is under formal obedience than simply whether she is talking regularly to somebody, not necessarily a priest. Schirmer brilliantly describes how labyrinthine the individual human mind is for the *Chastising*, how dense its complexities are and how large a laboratory of self-deception it proves: but the corollary is that the individual scarcely seems a complete unit of existence: the "goostli" life is one with habitual recourse to others.

And, as the author's expectation of a network of readers suggests, he thinks of books and commoning in the same breath and as the same sort of thing. One can "dryue awei heuynesse" of an overburdened spirit by "preier or meditacioun, redyng or writynge, or ellis goode comuning" (111) and some grow proud over special grace "þat þei haue to conforte oþer bi writynge or commonynge, or for reuelacions or visions" (121). Reading, copying, and talking cluster together, and this is not just an idealizing quirk of the author's imagination; it is also a pragmatic assumption he makes about his book's circulation; and it makes sense of some circumstances that can be known or inferred. Colledge guesses that the *Chastising* achieved its popularity because it offered the most advanced continental thinking on prayer and discernment in its use of Ruysbroec and of Alphonse. It is a plausible suggestion. But the *Chastising* nowhere mentions Ruysbroec or Alphonse, or almost any other modern authority (it does cite Aelred and Aquinas by name, and mentions Hildegard and Birgitta). If market demand for currency drove up its stock, readers who welcomed the book were informed enough to recognize its currency without being given explicit notice of its sources. Indeed, the author seems confident about what his readers have read: despite what Colledge says, he omits to describe Birgitta of Sweden's visions not because he would suppress them but because his readers know of them already: "Of þis *ʒe han* ensample of þat hooli ladi, seint and princesse seint bride" (178). Another author assumes the same of the *Chastising*: the author of *The Cleansing of Man's Soul*, owned at and likely written for nuns of Barking Abbey, who mentions a "bok of englisch" that "ʒe haue . . . , *I trowe*, which is cleped amonges ʒow þe chastising of goddes children."[20] And Barking nuns did circulate or exchange books, at least with Dartford Priory.[21] The sort of network mentioned above is a part of the apparently informal contact that comprises the life imagined in the *Chastising*.

But for all the informality he approves, and his uninterest in clerical supervision, the *Chastising*'s author still expects procedural clarity on important issues. Visionaries must follow the guidance of spiritual fathers "or of oþer discreet and sad goostli lyuers" (174), while their visions should stand to examination by "wise men and lettered and discreete and goostli lyueng men" (175). Clearly these are two different functions:

spiritual guidance by directors, and probation of visions by others. Procedures like this suppose a known community, for which the book has a name: these people are always *goostli lyueres*. In this section of the book, the phrase translates Alphonse of Jaén's *spiri-tuales* and *personae spirituales*,[22] but the author uses it throughout as a term of precise application, which he expects his readers precisely to understand. It is a title conferred by community: "suche folke þat *bien holden* goostly lyuers" (112) are "goode . . . to aske . . . of her counseil" (112). The author consults their experience as a collective authority: he cites Cassian and Birgitta on submission to others' discernment, but adds, "And þis is a general techinge among goostli lyuers" (178). But the procedures cited above suggest that degrees of accomplishment and authority obtain, signaled by additional adjecti-val phrases: "oþer *discreet and sad* goostli lyuers" (171); "a man *more discreet and expert* in suche matiers" (202; see also 177). "Goostli lyueres" are not themselves precisely the sources of wisdom and discernment, but the population within which the wise and discerning are to be found.

Cumulatively these passages suggest that "goostli lyueres" constitute not only a popu-lation of contemplative practitioners (nuns, priests, and those "of any parfeccion")—people tested by visions and other spiritual visitations and by "dredful doutis" (114), those who "don her besynesse to come to parfite loue" (117)[23]—but also a population which is known to itself, and recognized by itself as practicing a distinct form of life.[24] Odd evidence for this emerges in chapters 9–12, which discuss (following Ruysbroec) delusive and heretical forms of spirituality. In chapter 9, those who practice a certain discipline of clearing the mind "seemen ful goode and parfite of lyueng," but "lyuen contrariousli to al manner of uertues" (130), and this, he concludes (in an addition to Ruysbroec), is "o grete errour þat sum tyme falliþ *among goostli lyuers*" (134). The follow-ing chapters treat others, some of whom he fears are "messagiers of antecrist" (144); but he closes this, and the whole discussion of errant contemplatives, saying that he has now showed "hou manye perels and disceites fallen and haue falle *to goostli lyuers*" (145). Its neutral and descriptive sense here is the best evidence that he uses this title as virtually a technical term: it describes heretics as well as readers of the *Chastising*, be-cause it denotes those practicing a distinct and voluntary form of life,[25] who have dis-tinctive and explicit models, practices, doctrines, and vocabularies that distinguish them from other contemplatives and from each other. Clearly none of these groups is for-mally incorporated as an institution; but each clearly has real existence, distinct from others, enacted in the sharing of texts, terms, and techniques of the spiritual life, and in established modes of authority that, without erecting formal institutions, function institutionally.

There are two obvious objections to the picture emerging. First, this passage is taken almost whole from Ruysbroec; we cannot assume automatically that it describes English conditions. Second, one wonders why such groups, if they existed, left so little trace.

To the first: the *Chastising* adapts Ruysbroec's descriptions in ways that are hard to explain except as adjustments to local conditions. Two large instances will show what I mean.[26] The passage in Ruysbroec from which the *Chastising* draws its criticism of the first misguided group (those who seek natural rest) in fact does not describe a group, or even a deliberate practice, but merely a tendency of the soul: a gravity that draws the indolent mind into a natural rest, a pleasing exhaustion of thoughts and images which has nothing to do with the love of God.[27] The *Chastising* author, by contrast, is quite clear that he means a population holding a distinct theory of, or at least a distinct ambition to, contemplative union: "I speke of hem at þis tyme whiche in himself *seeken* þe reste of kynde" (130). Most dramatically, near the end of chapter 11, which describes those who claim freedom of spirit and unmediated union with God, he adds to Ruysbroec the comment that "þer han bien suche but late in our daies, and aftir haue bien turned and com aȝen into þe riȝt wei" (141–42). His telegraphic reference expects readers to know whom he means, and therefore expects them to have had access to the channels of interested discussion on matters connected with their distinctive form of life, to news of an event that seems otherwise to have left no trace in records.

There has been one guess about the identity of these people: Colledge believes that that last passage refers to "the sensational Lollard recantations" of William Swinderby and of John Aston and Philip Repingdon in 1382, shortly after which (he therefore argues) the work must have been written (35). Recent observations about the work's date make this unlikely,[28] but it is improbable on its face: Colledge must assert that the author sloppily hangs Ruysbroec's discussion of the "free spirit" on English Wycliffites, who would be surprised to hear that they claimed superiority to God's commandments, or that they refused on principle to practice virtues (139–40). The suggestion might be less surprising to the recipient of Hilton's *Epistola de leccione*, a priest, now "enclosed," who has turned from the "coverts of error" (*latebras erronee persuasionis*) but who distresses Hilton by meddling still with speculations and speaking in a way "scarcely intelligible to anyone." Hilton's description makes the error sound more like what the *Chastising* attributes to those claiming "fredom of spirit" (138); and urging his correspondent to pray his hours as he is bound to, Hilton adverts to "the heretic" who would dismiss the duty: "That contemplative is deceived who thinks that he has acquired the spirit of freedom [*spiritum libertatis*], and as if with zeal for greater perfection, overskips the canonical hours."[29] That the *Chastising* author could be thinking about Lollards and Lollard recantations is more than improbable, in fact, because he says he is not. He concludes chapter 12 with this passage (which has no source in Ruysbroec):

> *Many mo I miȝt shewe* to make ȝou be war of hem, *as of sum* that now holden
> plainly . . . aȝens confessions and fastynges, aȝens worshippyng of ymages, and
> shortli, as men seien, aȝens al states and degrees and lawe and þe ordynaunce of

hooli chirche. But al þese I leeue, bicause it nediþ nat greteli, for I trowe here bien rehersid þo þat bien most in our knowyng to be dred. (145)

Now *here* we have Lollards, offered as an instance of the "many mo" whose description the author omits, as being "nat greteli" needful. (It is not Lollards, but the heretical groups he *has* described, who have what his readers might be misled into thinking they want.) If he gives reasons in chapter 12 why he has left them undescribed, then he has not described them in chapter 11; and if it is not them he has described, it is someone else, someone unknown to us but not to his readers, and not perhaps to Hilton.[30]

Which brings us to the second objection. It is helpful to discover clerics and laity who, though aware of Lollardy, found it neither alluring nor threatening but merely impertinent. It reminds us how Lollards and inquisitors shared a fierce concentration on each other, not necessarily shared by everyone else, which determined what would be remembered in official record. Look for heretics in episcopal registers, and you find Lollards, because it is Lollards that bishops were looking for. We should wonder at least whether the mechanisms of English inquisition, devised and refined to detect and persecute Lollardy, were simply less well tuned to detect anything else (one listening for the fatal words "accident" and "subject" was not listening for "union" or "freedom of spirit").[31] Lollardy, as I have argued, attracted the allegiance of some freelance anti-clerical dissenters as it gained prominence;[32] we must also assume that it cast other kinds of doctrinal freedom into a shade. Two particular episcopal habits of thought about Lollardy made it improbable that the sort of groups the *Chastising* discusses would be noticed by them. First, the episcopacy liked to think of heresy as a problem of public disorder and sedition.[33] The groups described in the *Chastising*, by contrast, threaten not public disorder but secret infidelity: they obey no one, prelate or priest, "natwiþstondyng þat sum of hem *shewen otherwise outward*"; it is "inward" that they "wolen be suget to no man" (140–41). This is not rebellion waiting to happen, but out-ward conformity maintained for the sake of private freedom.

Second, in response to the Lollard program of textual access and propagation, the episcopacy learned to focus attention on the written word,[34] especially as a medium of biblical translation and a vehicle of certain heterodox teachings. Arundel's strictures on biblical translation are the logical upshot of such episcopal suspicion, and not only because they sought to institutionalize book surveillance. Arundel formed his idea of what orthodox books should be in response to the books he wanted to suppress, and thereby mirrored their ideas of vernacular textuality and its uses. This is a complex matter, which I can barely outline. Wycliffite vernacular writing does not submit texts for the empirical processing Schirmer finds in the *Chastising* and the *Book to a Mother;* the centrality they give not merely to quotation but to precise citation in a scholastic manner shows that they treat texts as units of public discourse, valued not as they present themselves to personal absorption, but as they act as points of mutual understanding, or of demonstration on publicly accepted grounds.[35] Lollard writing keys itself to biblical and patristic texts, and texts of theology and canon law, teaching discursive and argumentative skills and supplying a repertory of authoritative passages and clerical gestures to be made with them. This seems to be what the *Constitutions* have in mind when forbidding translation of "any text [*aliquem textum*] of holy scripture . . . by way of book, booklet, or treatise":[36] the concern is with a kind, not simply with the fact, of quotation, and in its turn a style of writing, characteristic of Lollard texts. If they were looking for such a style of writing, then texts like the *Chastising,* and whatever else might be read by the contemplatives who seem so concretely to populate its pages, would not seem to offer themselves for detection by suspicious bishops.

These are concrete reasons why networks and communities and circulating texts of the sort the *Chastising* describes might not be documented where we seek documentation. The reasons may look sophistical, taking as I do a minimizing approach to the effect the *Constitutions* had outside the group they were designed to persecute. But I do so because, outside that group, there is evidence of only minimal effect. No evidence has been adduced to show that violation of Arundel's provisions was brought against any work not either itself a biblical translation or of Lollard origin, except in the cases of those suspected of Lollardy on other grounds.[37] It is also not clear that, apart from the obviously exceptional case of Bishop Pecock, any author, even any Lollard author, was ever prosecuted for authorship.[38] Of course, as Coetzee observes, censorship's greatest success is its own obsolescence,[39] and the *Constitutions* may indeed have chilled the enthusiasm of vernacular authors, but it is hard to sort the premises from the conclusions of that argument.[40] Nothing suggests that the *Constitutions* inhibited the circulation of vernacular theological texts; the circulation of texts both bespoken and instanced by the *Chastising,* as far as we can tell, went untouched and uncircumscribed.[41] In fact, the only clear evidence of authors who thought about the *Constitutions'* restrictions are the statements of the two who ostentatiously conformed to their demands: Nicholas Love, author of the *Mirror of the Blessed Life of Jesus Christ,* and the author of the *Mirror of Our Lady.* To orthodox authors, the *Constitutions* were perhaps less a threat than an occasional opportunity. (And conversely, the best evidence of the influence for the *Constitutions'* motivation of censorship has to do precisely with Love's *Mirror,* the safest of orthodox vernacular books: the unauthorized contamination by the *Meditationes de passione Christi* was physically excised from one manuscript.)[42] The authors of these two *Mirrors* could invoke the *Constitutions* to undergird and exemplify the reading process Schirmer describes, using or supposing surveillance as a balk, not against episcopal persecution, but against resistance to their own authority.

In either case, Love's *Mirror* and the *Mirror of Our Lady* partake of the character of "Lollard biblical scholarship" (as Hudson calls it) in a way that most Middle English religious prose does not. The former, from one point of view, is to the Gospel *narrative* what the Wycliffite Bible is to the *text* of the Latin Bible, a point-to-point parallel. And what the latter offers is almost indistinguishable in one way from what Lollard texts offered: a translation, keyed to the original in a way that emphasizes the integrity and indeed the textuality of the text. Both reproduce the textual habits of Lollard writing in a way that evades, or claims to evade, what makes those habits dangerous. The shift in the object of reading that Schirmer's essay describes in the *Mirror*—no longer a reading of the self, meditation is now a loss of the self in a text—may be plausibly claimed, as she does, to be a reaction to and fulfillment of the *Constitutions'* strictures. But precisely for that reason these works obey a logic far closer to what they were trying to suppress than do texts like the *Book to a Mother* and *Chastising,* books that remained available to fifteenth-century readers. And that they did marks one limit to the ability of the *Mirror of Our Lady* to mold its readers' minds after an Arundelian logic. There are other limits: one could notice that the logic of the *Mirror*'s ambition to fill its readers' minds with sanctioned exegesis, leaving the nuns no room for thoughts of their own, defeats itself: the more alternative exegeses are disclosed, the more visible will exegetical principles become to anyone who cares to observe them. One could guess further that the author knows this and hopes for it, wearing a poker face for the benefit of any ecclesiastical overseers. But neither resisting readers nor subversive authors are my concern here; them we know. I am more interested in urging the unsubtle observation that any act of reading happens among other acts of reading, and thoughts and actions, and within a culture of reading that gives them meaning. Readings like Schirmer's of the *Mirror* and mine of the *Chastising, as* readings, alike assume what their forms demand they heuristically assume, that the relation of reader to text is absorbing and exclusive: and readings that discover the reader being interpellated and those that discover the text being appropriated differ from each other only in who is given the edge. But through its reading, Schirmer's essay also makes the challenging point that this is not a neutral assumption; in the early fifteenth century, at least, it seems just the sort of reading Arundel wants.

But while Arundel may have wanted it, he did not necessarily get it, even from the Syon readers of the *Mirror*. After all, like them, the reader to whom the *Chastising* addresses itself—who has access to a quasi-institutional community of "goostly lyueres" not officially appointed to her but who can participate in the sharing of books and counsel, and is in receipt of the gossip that obtains in networks of shared interest—is a nun, and the picture elicitable from the *Chastising* describes their experience more plausibly than the more hermetic fantasies of the *Mirror.* The author of the *Mirror* may have wished to think of the monastery walls as an impregnable barrier that could contain and protect the nuns' vernacular reading, but such walls impressed other contemporaries chiefly by their permeability. The busy traffic through convent gates could be regretted as an irregularity,[43] but it was an unavoidable fact of life;[44] more, it could be religiously motivated,[45] and can figure in hagiography as a natural if ad hoc path by which counsel and sanctity might be transmitted.[46] If we attend to the possibilities the *Chastising* can assume are open to nuns, we can conclude not only that the Syon nuns, like other women, kept, not merely talking, but reading and thinking about the things of God,[47] but that it was less their walls that allowed them to do so than the very inquisitorial conventions that could not see the dense culture of theological reading, writing, commoning, counseling, and books.[48] At least the *Chastising*, which requires the assumption of this culture even to be understood, was meaningful enough to them that two copies of the de Worde print were in the sisters' library at Syon a century later.[49]

Schirmer's essay pointedly returns us to local histories of writing, translation, reading, and circulation—to which it makes an important contribution—by making us ask how far our procedures of reading, through which we would discover the constraints on thought, conform themselves to those constraints. Her essay also reminds us that the vernacular has in itself no fixed ideological function; it means and accomplishes what it does as local contexts and particular choices determine. So therefore—something it seems harder to remember—does Latin. A longer response might notice that, just as the *Mirror of Our Lady* on this view shows how a broad-minded clerical generosity can (or can try to) foster dependence and discourage speculation, the *Chastising* suggests how a high-minded clerical stringency can provoke, can even deliberately provoke, resistance; it might wonder how far the formal rather than the social properties of the vernacular— what can be said by its means, rather than to whom it can be said—draws clerical writers to it; and wonder, too, therefore, not only how clerical writers try to teach a laity by its means (or how the laity resists its teaching), but also how using the vernacular lets them take instruction from common usage. But these are questions for another time.

Notes

My thanks to Adrienne Williams for her learned help on this essay.

1. Joyce Bazire and Edmund Colledge, eds., *The Chastising of God's Children* (Oxford: Blackwell, 1957), 95. Remaining citations are given parenthetically. All emphases are of course mine, and I have sometimes silently adjusted punctuation to clarify sense. When referring to readers of the *Chastising,* I am following the work itself in its varying use of pronoun gender and number.

2. Nicholas Watson, "Censorship and Cultural Change in Late-Medieval England: Vernacular Theology, the Oxford Translation Debate, and Arundel's Constitutions of 1409," *Speculum* 70 (1995): 848. Another appreciative notice of the *Chastising* appears in Anne Clark Bartlett, "'A reasonable affection': Gender and Spiritual Friendship in Middle English Devotional Literature," in *Vox mystica: Essays on Medieval Mysticism in Honor of Professor Valerie M. Lagorio,* ed. Anne Clark Bartlett et al. (Cambridge: Cambridge University Press, 1995), 131–45.

3. Walter Brut, whom Kathryn Kerby-Fulton's essay in this volume shows to have been touched by some of the continental movements with which the *Chastising* is partly concerned, is an exception whose near inexplicability to scholarship does prove the rule. I am encouraged to find that my conclusions are generally congruent with hers, and that we have independently come to the same understanding of a passage from chap. 12, discussed below.

4. Schirmer, 361.

5. *MED s.v.* "special(e," n., 3.a., b., a sense the author uses elsewhere; see 119, quoted note 12 below.

6. "Dixit eciam dicta Margeria isti iurate quod ipsa fuit sepius ficte confessa decano de Campis ad finem quod ipse decanus reputaret eam esse bone vite" (Norman Tanner, ed., *Norwich Heresy Trials, 1428–31* [London: Office of the Royal Historical Society, 1977], 48–49).

7. Compare Julian's "doughtfulle drede," "þat lettyth vs, *by þe beholldyng of oure selfe and of oure synne afore done*," to which (in the long version, which I here quote) she adds, as something distinct, the "every day synnes," in which "we holde nott oure promise nor kepe oure clennes" (Edmund Colledge and James Walsh, eds., *A Book of Showings to the Anchoress Julian of Norwich* [Toronto: Pontifical Institute of Mediaeval Studies, 1978], 2:668).

8. In fact, the author in this passage both links this issue with that of biblical translation and dissociates himself from the latter's opponents, while emphasizing, as its proponents did, that the Vulgate was itself a translation. His discussion of whether to recite in English or Latin has specifically to do with *private* recitation (this has not been hitherto remarked); although even the Little Office (which he lists here, along with psalter, penitential psalms, and litany) was recited in some communities (John Harper, *The Forms and Orders of Western Liturgy from the Tenth to the Eighteenth Century* [Oxford: Clarendon Press, 1991], 133–34), all these prayers also featured in private devotions; and aspects of this passage (including the picture of the religious stopping and reciting the prayers again and the advice that one try reciting with a companion) can only refer to individual recitation. This whole passage, and the author's attitude to the place of vernacular translation generally, is far too complicated to go into here.

9. There are passages in which he must excuse covering basic material by asserting its usefulness, not for the reader, but for those she might counsel; see 206, 255–56; the most dramatic is in chapter 23, where a discussion of the affections, drawn from Aelred, leads him into a discussion of love for God and neighbor, which he concludes with an apology, in case it seems too tame or elementary: he has spoken of the latter topic "moore . . . þan I was in purpos at þe bigynnyng of þis chapitle: neuerþeles it may profite oþer symple folke, whanne ȝe commune wiþ hem" (196).

10. I do not understand why Watson describes the book's directions on discernment as criteria "by which clerics can assess the validity of visions" (Watson, "Censorship," 848); Alphonse does seem to treat them as clerical tools (Alfonso of Jaén, *Epistola solitarii ad reges*, ed. Arne Jönsson, in *Alfonso of Jaén: His Life and Works with Critical Editions of the* Epistola solitarii, *the* Informaciones, *and the* Epistola serui Christi [Lund, 1989]), but no clerics crowd the passage in the *Chastising*. For helpful discussions of *discretio* and its place as a clerical specialty, see François Vandenbroucke, "Discernement des esprits. III. Au moyen âge," in *Dictionnaire de la spiritualité* 3.1254–66; Rosalynn Voaden, *God's Words, Women's Voices: The Discernment of Spirits in the Writing of Late-Medieval Women Visionaries* (Woodbridge, Suffolk: York Medieval Press, 1999); Deborah A. Fraioli, *Joan of Arc: The Early Debate* (Woodbridge, Suffolk: Boydell Press, 2000).

11. Colledge's note to this passage says, rightly as far as I can tell, that the insistence on the troubling of the Virgin's soul is unprecedented; he does not note that it derives from her response ("turbata est") to the Annunciation (Luke 1:29).

12. 119; "Also, it is perilouse to specifie such þouȝtes, for sum bien traueiled wiþ oo þouȝt þat anoþer man or womman wold neuer, ne parauenture shul neuer imagyne suche a þouȝt, but bi oþer mennys tellynge. Þerfor I wil nat shewe such þouȝtis in special."

13. This latter is an attractive possibility, as relating to the interesting argument of Nicholas Watson, "Visions of Inclusion: Universal Salvation and Vernacular Theology in Pre-Reformation England," *Journal of Medieval and Early Modern Studies* 27 (1997): 145–87.

14. The *impulse* is of course not unknown; see Julian, *Showings,* 1:266: "I wex ryght gretly aschamed, and walde haffe bene schryfenn. Bot I couth tell it na preste, for I thoght, howe schulde a preste leue me?" But this is not offered as advice. For a late instance of a layman encouraged to evaluate the fitness of parochial confessors, see Vincent Gillespie, "Dial M for Mystic: Mystical Texts in the Library of Syon Abbey and the Spirituality of the Syon Brethren," in *The Medieval Mystical Tradition: England, Ireland and Wales: Exeter Symposium VI,* ed. Marion Glasscoe (Cambridge: Cambridge University Press, 1999), 247; but this seems to involve choosing confessors, not choosing what to tell them.

15. On works like the *Chastising,* see, e.g., S. S. Hussey, "The Audience for the Middle English Mystics," in *De cella in seculum: Religious and Secular Life and Devotion in Late Medieval England,* ed. Michael G. Sargent (Cambridge: Cambridge University Press, 1989), 109–22.

16. Obvious possibilities include anchorites/anchoresses and vowed widows, on which latter, see especially Mary C. Erler, "English Vowed Women at the End of the Middle Ages," *Mediaeval Studies* 57 (1995): 155–203.

17. Instances pertinent to the *Chastising* include Aelred, *De institutione inclusarum, PL* 32.1451–52; E. J. Dobson, ed., *The English Text of the* Ancrene Riwle *Edited from BM Cotton MS Cleopatra C.vi* (Oxford: Oxford University Press, 1972), 53 ff.; Boniface VIII's bull *Periculoso, CIC* 2.1053.

18. The importance accorded to consultation addresses a problem that had been, or would shortly be, recognized by the now unknown Carthusian against whom Thomas Bassett defended Rolle. One of the Carthusian's complaints was that Rolle "fecit homines iudices sui" (Michael G. Sargent, "A Diplomatic Transcript of Thomas Basset's *Defense* of Richard Rolle," *Analecta cartusiana* 55 [1981]: 200).

19. The author introduces this distinction; Alphonse's passage asks whether the visionary "viuit sub obediencia et disciplina continua alicuius patris spiritualis discreti, senioris, et virtuosi et expertis in vita spirituali," *Epistola solitarii,* 154; see also an earlier passage in Alphonse (123), which the *Chastising* author also revises to this effect (173–74).

20. Quoted in Colledge's instruction, *Chastising,* 36.

21. A. I. Doyle, "Books Connected with the Vere Family and Barking Abbey," *Transactions of the Essex Archaeological Society* ns 25 (1958): 222–43.

22. Alfonso, *Epistola,* 123–27.

23. The author names "parfite loue" as the goal of contemplation, for which it here stands metonymically: ". . . þer may noþing suffice to a *parfite loue,* ne noþing may hym please, saue oonli o goodenesse þat may nat be comprehendid, which goodenesse is god hymsilf" (136).

*24. That the phrase is "goostli lyueres" suggests that the author may indeed intend just such an assertion by its form; see the reflections on the idea of "life" in Anne Middleton, "Langland's Lives: Reflections on Late-Medieval Religious and Literary Vocabulary," in *The Idea of Medieval Literature:*

New Essays on Chaucer and Medieval Culture in Honor of Donald R. Howard, ed. James M. Dean and Christian K. Zacher (Newark: University of Delaware Press, 1992), 227–42.

25. The book can speak of an experience that may befall "suche men of goostli lyueng, *or* men of goode wil, *or* men þat han assaied of goostli sweetnesse" (124); the presence of these latter two phrases is hard to explain, unless they describe people who pray as "goostli lyueres" do, but who nevertheless do not share their mode of life.

26. Without access to Groote's translation of Ruysbroec, which the *Chastising* used, close comparison cannot be trusted: G. B. De Soer, "The Relationship of the Latin Versions of Ruysbroek's 'Die Geestelike Brulocht' to 'The Chastising of God's Children'," *Mediaeval Studies* 21 (1959): 129–46.

27. See the original passage in Jan van Ruusbroec, *Die geestelike brulocht*, ed. J. Alaerts (Turnhout: Brepols, 1987), 538–39.

28. Roger Ellis argues that the *Chastising* must have been written after 1391, *The Liber Celestis of St. Bridget of Sweden* (Oxford: Oxford University Press, 1987), xii n., endorsed by Nicholas Watson, "The Composition of Julian of Norwich's *Revelation of Love*," *Speculum* 68 (1993): 637–83, 655n.

29. "Fallitur eciam contemplatiuus qui spiritum libertatis adeptum se putat, et tanquam zelo maioris perfeccionis pretermittit horas canonicas," *Walter Hilton's Latin Writings*, ed. John P. H. Clark and Cheryl Taylor (Salzburg: Institut für Anglistik und Amerikanistik, Universität Salzburg,1987), 237. (Other passages quoted from 221, 225.) The similarities between this *Epistola* and the *Chastising* deserve further attention.

30. On the other hand, Hilton's *Eight Chapters* show a less accurate, more stereotyped idea of the free spirit heretics as those who believe "þat þei han so myche grace of loue, þat þei may lyue as hem lust" (Walter Hilton, *Eight Chapters on Perfection*, ed. Fumio Kuriyagawa [Tokyo: Keio Institute of Cultural and Linguistic Studies, Keio University, 1967], 13); but he may here be reproducing the source he is translating.

31. See the lists of questions in Anne Hudson, "The Examination of Lollards," *Bulletin of the Institute for Historical Research* 46 (1973): 145–59.

32. Steven Justice, "Lollardy," in *The Cambridge History of Medieval English Literature*, ed. David Wallace (Cambridge: Cambridge University Press, 1999), 668–69.

33. Margaret Aston, "Lollardy and Sedition," *Past and Present* 17 (1960): 1–44; Paul Strohm, *England's Empty Throne: Usurpation and the Language of Legitimation, 1399–1422* (New Haven, Conn.: Yale University Press, 1998), chaps. 2–3.

34. H. G. Richardson, "Heresy and the Lay Power under Richard II," *English Historical Review* 51 (1936): 1–28; Anne Hudson, "A Lollard Sermon-Cycle and Its Implications," *Medium ævum* 40 (1972): 142–56; and Anne Hudson, "Lollard Book Production," in *Book Production and Publishing in Britain 1375–1475*, ed. Jeremy Griffiths and Derek Pearsall (Cambridge: Cambridge University Press, 1989), 125–52.

35. This seems to me the corollary, in discursive politics beyond the confines of the Lollard community, of the initiation into textual practice brilliantly outlined in Rita Copeland, *Pedagogy, Intellectuals, and Dissent in the Later Middle Ages: Lollardy and Ideas of Learning* (Cambridge: Cambridge University Press, 2002), 122–40.

36. William Lyndwood, *Provinciale, seu constitutiones Angliae* (Oxford, 1679), 3.66.

37. By far the most promising case in the two generations following the promulgation of the *Constitutions* is that of Robert Bert, chaplain, tried at Norwich in 1430 in Alnwick's trials; ownership of *Dives and Pauper* was urged against him. But it was urged, not as violating the ban on scriptural

translation, but as containing "plures errores et hereses quamplures." Bert was released after oath and compurgation; an examination of his vernacular books—which, if *Dives and Pauper* is indicative, presumably contained violations of the prohibition on englishing biblical passages—apparently yielded nothing of significance (Tanner, *Heresy Trials*, 100–102).

38. Although we easily talk about the danger to which authors exposed themselves, it rather looks as though owning a book was more dangerous than writing one: it was the London citizen John Claydon who was killed for the exuberantly heretical *Lantern of Light*, not the cleric who wrote it (E. F. Jacob, ed., *The Register of Henry Chichele, Archbishop of Canterbury, 1414–1433* [Oxford: Clarendon Press, 1938], 4.132–38).

39. "Censorship looks forward to the day when writers will censor themselves and the censor himself can retire" (J. M. Coetzee, *Giving Offense: Essays on Censorship* [Chicago: University of Chicago Press, 1996], 10).

40. For instance, Watson dates the *Chastising* before 1409 ("Censorship," 847)—the date of the *Constitutions'* promulgation—though there is nothing to enforce a date before 1419. (For this *terminus ad quem*, see Colledge's introduction, *Chastising*, 37).

41. This is a difficulty in the argument of Watson, "Censorship." The relevant portion of the *Constitutions* forbade not only the translation of any portion of scripture in any work but also the *reading* of any such work written "jam noviter tempore dicti Johannis Wickliff, sive citra compositus" (Lyndwood, *Provinciale*, 3.66). Therefore manuscripts of vernacular religious writings of the last quarter of the fourteenth century—both those manuscripts produced after the *Constitutions* and those earlier manuscripts that we know survived the period because they are still extant—are evidence of a freedom that the *Constitutions* did not stifle. Obviously caution is required here. For one thing, there is nothing to which the number of such manuscripts could be compared. For another, Hudson has demonstrated how spottily even episcopal registers record Lollard heresy trials known from other sources, so that we cannot assume that even the registers that survive give a reliable indication of surveillance and prosecution of dissent, perceived or real (Anne Hudson, *The Premature Reformation: Wycliffite Texts and Lollard History* [Oxford: Oxford University Press, 1988], 32–42). At the same time, the disappearance of trial records must be weighed against the disappearance of manuscripts that must axiomatically be assumed, which would of course include manuscripts of those works that violated the letter of the *Constitutions*.

42. M. B. Parkes, "Punctuation in Copies of Nicholas Love's Mirror of the Blessed Life of Jesus Christ," in *Nicholas Love at Waseda: Proceedings of the International Conference 20–22 July 1995*, ed. Shoichi Oguro, Richard Beadle, and Michael G. Sargent (Cambridge: D. S. Brewer, 1997), 57–58. That this was the effect of Chichele's anti-Lollard initiatives in the 1420s is Parkes's guess, though the recognition of an interpolation in an authorized text might, without any particular worries, motivate its removal.

43. On this see Eileen Power, *Medieval English Nunneries c. 1275 to 1535* (Cambridge: Cambridge University Press, 1922), esp. chap. 9, and Elizabeth Makowski, *Canon Law and Cloistered Woman: Periculoso and Its Commentators, 1298–1545* (Washington D.C.: Catholic University of America Press, 1997).

44. See, recently, Marilyn Oliva, *The Convent and the Community in Late Medieval England: Female Monasteries in the Diocese of Norwich, 1350–1540* (Woodbridge, Suffolk: Boydell Press, 1998), 111–83, and Paul Lee, *Nunneries, Learning and Spirituality in Late Medieval English Society: The Dominican Priory of Dartford* (Suffolk: York Medieval Press, 2001), 46–55, 67–106.

45. Syon had a better reputation than many for the integrity of its enclosure; but its very prominence, and its proximity to Sheen, made it a center of attraction for dévots who would live in its vicinity or visit it for its indulgences (VCH Middlesex 1.185–88); widows vowing chastity but not assuming monastic vows lived among them (Erler, "English Vowed Women").

46. Any number of texts could be cited; for two clear examples, immediately pertinent to our inquiry, see the network unselfconsciously outlined in the *legenda* of Richard Rolle—for which see the summary in Hope Emily Allen, *Writings Ascribed to Richard Rolle Hermit of Hampole and Materials for His Biography* (New York: Oxford University Press, 1927), 55–61—and the convent audience to which Hilton addressed his "lost letter" (Hilton, *Latin Writings*, 329–33).

47. My allusion is of course to Felicity Riddy, "'Women Talking about the Things of God': A Late Medieval Sub-Culture," in *Women and Literature in Britain, 1150–1500*, ed. Carol M. Meale (Cambridge: Cambridge University Press, 1993), 104–27, whose influence on this essay should be evident.

48. For late medieval instances of such relations of exchange, see Doyle, "Books Connected"; Mary C. Erler, "Exchange of Books between Nuns and Laywomen: Three Surviving Examples," in *New Science Out of Old Books: Studies in Manuscripts and Early Printed Books in Honour of A. I. Doyle*, ed. Richard Beadle and A. J. Piper (Aldershot: Ashgate, 1995), 360–73; Oliva, *Convent and the Community*, 69–70.

49. David N. Bell, *What Nuns Read: Books and Libraries in Medieval English Nunneries* (Kalamazoo, Mich: Cictercian Publications, 1995), 182, 87.

The Making of *The Book of Margery Kempe*

NICHOLAS WATSON

"I xal spekyn of God"

In the summer of the year 1417, the bourgeois Englishwoman Margery Kempe—wife of John Kempe and daughter of John Brunham, former mayor of Bishop's Lynn, but according to her and her supporters also a chosen spouse and prophet of Christ—was arrested by the mayor of Leicester, John Arnesby, as she was beating an indirect path home from a pilgrimage to the shrine of St. James, Compostella in Spain, with a chaperon called Thomas Marchale. During the next months she was repeatedly detained against her will, not only by the mayor (who called her "a fals strumpet, a fals loller, and a fals deceyver of the pepyl") but at the orders of no less than John, duke of Bedford, a brother of King Henry V (112).[1] She was also questioned, abused, once threatened with rape, repeatedly threatened with burning, denounced from pulpits, and publicly examined on four separate occasions on suspicion of heresy, insurrection, unlawful preaching, and leading women astray: once by the Augustinian abbot, Richard Rothley, before a large crowd in the Church of All Hallow's, Leicester; once, again before a large crowd, by a group of secular canons in the chapterhouse at York Cathedral; and twice at the hands of an increasingly irritated archbishop of York, Henry Bowet. Each of these encounters ended in her release. Even so, it was at least six months before she was able to return home, armed with testimonials not only from her old acquaintance Philip Repingdon, bishop of Lincoln, and from Bowet, but from no less than the archbishop of Canterbury, Henry Chicheley. After she at last found her way back to Lynn, it was years before she apparently left it again.[2]

To some extent, this series of setbacks may have been a mere by-blow of the flurry of official activity following the rebellion of the Lollard knight, Sir John Oldcastle. (This event, perhaps the creation of government propagandists, ended in Oldcastle's execution in London in December 1417, when Kempe was also in London, awaiting the arrival of her husband and Chicheley's letter of safe conduct.)[3] It is true that the recurring accusation that Kempe was a Lollard, though almost plausible, never stood up to theological examination, while the slander that she was one of Oldcastle's letter-bearers who had tried to persuade John of Gaunt's granddaughter to leave her husband was ludicrous. At the same time, however, nobody was under the illusion that Kempe was a cipher, a convenient scapegoat at a time of crisis. Five years of penitential and proselytizing tours around England and as far afield as Jerusalem and Rome had made her many friends; she names as her closest allies in the north the York canon John Aclom, the vicar-choral Sir John Kendale, and her confessor in Bridlington, William Sleightholme, but there were others, both there and in Bristol, far off in the West Midlands.[4] These tours were undertaken with the approval of at least some of her circle of well-educated supporters in Lynn and Norwich, who included: the Carmelites Alan of Lynn and William Southfield; her Lynn confessors Robert Springfield and the Dominican anchorite, "M of P," her special friend; the ageing anchoress Julian of Norwich; and the saintly Norwich priest, Richard Caister, who once stood by her when she was called to "answer to certeyn artyculys" by officers of the bishop of Norwich (40).[5] Moreover, the very fact of her arrest in Leicester—once her white clothing and passionate crying before a crucifix had identified her to the authorities in a town she may never had visited before—suggests that this middle-aged mother of fourteen was considered a force to be reckoned with by some of the most powerful people of her day. All through England she met people of every class who already held strident views about her, either as saint or as seducer of men's wives, darkly suspected of counselling women to give up sex with their husbands to follow Christ. In these closing months of 1417, and in a society increasingly nervous about dissent, whose commonest attitude to women's roles is summed up in the advice, "damsel, forsake this lyfe that thu hast, and go spynne and carde as other women don," Margery Kempe was everywhere treated as a miracle, a scandal, a *cause celèbre* (129).

Margery Kempe has also been controversial in modern times. But the discussion she has inspired since the rediscovery of the *Book* in 1934 has not always found ways of including this vital aspect of her career: the consciousness she shared with her supporters of having a ministry to teach others and the publicity this attracted. All her readers are preoccupied (as she was) with her intensely physical devotion to Christ, her weeping, and the outrage she caused among many people who encountered her. But the persecuted, maladroit, self-justifying figure conjured up by focussing on these themes has never been easy to reconcile with the self-assured and coherent teacher the *Book* also reveals to us: with the woman who insists to the archbishop of York himself that "I xal spekyn of God," who is summoned by the abbess of Denny to talk with her and her nuns, and whom an English priest travels all the way to Rome to meet (126, 202, 96). In this essay I thus want to approach the problems involved in linking Kempe's tears with her ideas—her elevation of the physical and the visual with her *Book*'s use of the intellectual and the verbal—by asking two questions: by what processes was *The Book of Margery Kempe* written? And to what end was it written: to what doctrinal or spiritual insights does it direct readers?

The first question has pressed upon scholars ever since John Hirsh suggested in 1975 that the second of her two scribes was a co-author of the *Book*, in an argument that (as we shall see) draws much of its power from the sense of difficulty many people have felt in trying to imagine Margery Kempe as an author at all.[6] Yet there have been few attempts to address Hirsh's argument on its own terms. Lynn Staley Johnson and Diana Uhlman have characterized the second scribe's voice not as a historical problem but a *trope*, while elsewhere Staley has developed an influential reading of the *Book* that circumvents the issue by making an absolute distinction between Kempe the author and Margery the protagonist.[7] Since there has been no direct response to Hirsh's argument, there has also been no sustained attempt to take stock of the evidence the *Book* furnishes for the circumstances under which it was written and rewritten.[8] By appraising this evidence, I hope to establish that Kempe herself, not her scribe, was primarily responsible for the *Book*'s structure, arguments, and most of its language, and to suggest why it might have been important to her self-understanding that this be so.

Answers to the larger question about the *Book*'s theology are equally sparse. There is good writing on Kempe's spirituality—its themes, models, and tensions—but much of this writing treats the *Book* as a window on her life rather than an exploration of the theological issues that life raises.[9] As the opening of this essay implies, my discussion accepts that the *Book*'s narrative bears a real relation to history, so that the context in which it was written can be deduced from the mass of circumstantial, often inconsequential detail provided by the text itself. However fictionalized (or hagiographized) it may be, the *Book* does often describe what happened; my discussion thus deliberately blurs the roles of author, narrator, and protagonist literary criticism often separates.[10] This positivistic attitude to some of the text's historical claims puts me at odds with the model Staley proposes in *Margery Kempe's Dissenting Fictions*, in which the *Book* has no relation to actual events, and is indebted to the scholars who argue that Kempe's learning, literacy, and linguistic skills were more sophisticated than often thought.[11] At the same time, my reading of the *Book* takes it seriously as argument as well as narration: an argument that uses Kempe's life to explore ideas about the inscrutability of the divine will, about the relation between embodiment, worldly living, and holiness, and about suffering prayer as a path to divine mercy, while also using those ideas to reflect on the puzzling *miraculum* that was her life. Invaded by visions, voices, and fits of prophetic knowing, flooded by bouts of weeping that were hard to read as lucid signs of God's presence, a conundrum to herself and her community, Kempe refused any of the easy resolutions offered her: to be silent; to treat her tears as illness; to regularize her life as anchoress or nun; to reject, or even (after a period) doubt, her revelations. Just so her *Book*, written and rewritten in old age when many of her allies were dead, explores but never resolves the view of the world it thinks through. What is it to be holy in a world that is unholy? If the holy do not separate themselves from the world, can they use it to burnish, rather than tarnish, their perfection? And if the holy cannot let the world go its own way, can they redeem it? Like Langland's *Piers Plowman* in the tenacity of its searching and in its willingness to make demands on readers, *The Book of Margery Kempe* faces us with more questions than answers: its theology less a set of claims than an expression of the hopes built on Kempe's relation to her celestial spouse; less a system of ideas than a hauntingly earthbound verbal icon.

"Hir writer cowde not sumtyme kepyn hymself fro wepyng"

According to the second scribe's long prologue, Kempe originally dictated the *Book* to an Englishman returned from East Prussia "wyth hys wyfe and hys goodys," who "dwellyd wyth the forseyd creatur tyl he had wretyn as mech as sche wold tellyn hym for the tyme that thei wer togydder; and sythen he deyd" (4). Circumstantial evidence establishes that this man was her son, a merchant whose return to England with his wife and death a month later is described in Part II (chapter 2): both son and scribe come from Germany with a wife, leaving a child behind, to lodge with Kempe, and both die in approximately the same year.[12] The prologue also claims that long before (as early as 1413, four years after her conversion) Bishop Repingdon and Alan of Lynn independently suggested that Kempe have a book written of her experiences, but "sche was warnyd in hyr spyrit that sche xuld not wryte so sone" (3, 34, 6).[13] If this is true, then, Margery Kempe knew for two decades before she wrote that she had a mission not only to the present but to the future, as one of the "approvyd wymmen" visionaries (like her model, Birgitta of Sweden) whose accounts of their experiences enriched the Church's understanding of Christ's life and works.[14] Once it was time to write, however, she either had difficulty in finding a cleric to act as a scribe or decided she did not want one.[15] The result was that the first draft of her book was written using an unfamiliar spelling system, in a merchant's script that to the priest who became her second scribe looked half way between English and German, its letters "not schapyn ne formyd as other letters ben" (4).[16] Faced with the task of copying this unorthodox production, whose existence was another of Kempe's bracing challenges to Lynn's establishment, the priest delayed more than four years (some of it taken up by Kempe's impromptu pilgrimage to Prussia and desperate journey home), before setting to work in 1436 (6). After finishing his task, he added a second part, "aftyr hyr owyn tunge," bringing the narrative up to date with an account of the death of her son and last pilgrimage, and rounding the book off with a long prayer (which may have started life as an independent composition) (221).[17] All this was finished before her death, not recorded in the *Book*, but known from guild records to have taken place after 1438–39.

So what happened as this priest scribe worked his way through the first draft of Kempe's book, with the aid of a shoddy pair of spectacles and the prayers and clarifications of the author? Hirsh argues that, as the scribe wrote "aftyr the informacyon" provided by the draft, he also rewrote it, structuring a brief, inchoate narrative as a systematic account of a mystic's progress: an account that, for all its imagining of Kempe's life, owes its authority and most of its language to the priest's knowledge of convention (6). In effect, the priest turned a messy scribble, all too evocative of Kempe's messy religiosity (which Hirsh, quoting Edmund Colledge, characterizes as foolish, wearisome, distracting, obsessive, and sincere) into a real didactic book. Thus "the second scribe, no less than Margery, should be regarded as the author of *The Book of Margery Kempe*," and a Gordian knot of interpretive and historical problems that the *Book* ties is cut.[18]

There is a sense in which this argument might be thought not to need refutation. There is only one piece of evidence for the brevity of the first draft of the *Book*, and that is much less convincing than it looks. This is the fact that the *Book*'s prologue describes this draft as having been written after the first scribe came home from Germany with his wife, where Part II records the same homecoming, which took place soon after a longer earlier visit made on his own, as leading directly to his illness and death, long before he could have had time to take down many thousand words of complex prose (4, 223–25). Hirsh attempts to reconcile these stories by belittling Kempe's first draft, scratched out, as he assumes, during the agony of the last month of the first scribe's life. Yet not only could Kempe's son never have copied any version of the eighty-nine chapters of Part I as he lay dying in bed, he could hardly have written a word, unless it was a will dictated to someone else.[19] This suggests that the second scribe has made a mistake, and the easy mistake for him to have made is that of eliding the son's second, fatal visit with the longer one he survived in the previous year. During this visit, according to Part II of the *Book*, the son so impressed his mother that after watching him carefully, "sche openyd hir hert to hym, schewyng hym and enformyng how owr Lord had drawyn hir thorw hys mercy and be what menys, the whech he seyd he was unworthy to heryn" (224). Indeed, this passage reads like a veiled allusion to the composition of the first draft, one that movingly represents the *Book* as a mother's confession to her son. *Pace* both Hirsh and the prologue to the *Book*, it is only on this visit that the complicated process of writing the *Book* described in Part I, chapters 88–89 can have taken place, involving Kempe in such absorbing work that it interrupted her devotions and spoiled her concentration in church, making her ill until she could get back to the job, and bursting out in "a flawme of fyer abowte hir brest" so powerfully that "he that was hir writer cowde not sumtyme kepyn hymself fro wepyng" (216, 219). Ignoring the evidence these chapters provide about the lengthy period "whan this booke was first in wrytyng," Hirsh also ignores the evidence I describe below for the sophistication of this draft (216).[20]

Yet the power of Hirsh's argument may reside less in its reasoning than in its deployment of assumptions about the intellectual capacities of illiterate medieval women that are easier to recognize than to undo, deeply embedded as they are in our models for thinking about the past. We know that many medieval women visionaries had their books written down for them;[21] we think we know that Kempe was not one of the more learned of these visionaries and got much of her religious information from sermons, consultations with clerics, and having books read her; we know a priest was involved in the final version of the *Book,* and made a number of additions. Could not her priest scribe, then, have been more fully involved than the *Book* admits: silently rewriting, adding most of the *Book*'s references to learned ideas, honing the accounts of Kempe's disputes with her interrogators to an edge of theological precision? Might a "soft" version of Hirsh's thesis not be preferable, for example, to Staley's efforts to make the second scribe disappear? Since there are no simple answers to these questions, no easy means either of depriving Hirsh's argument of authority or of deciding how far to credit it, the only way forward is by detailed analysis. As it turns out, such an analysis finds grounds for supposing that, however much she involved her community in thinking out what she meant to them, Kempe retained a closer control over the interpretation of her calling as a *miraculum* (as God's sign to her community) than her modern readers might suspect.

"Aftyr hys sympyl cunnyng"

Kempe's second scribe seems to have proceeded page by page or chapter by chapter, perhaps copying directly from his exemplar onto the paper or parchment she provided him, perhaps working through the intermediary stage of a draft copy on wax tablets. He tells us that, once he realized the task before him had God's blessing—"when he had wretyn a qwayr," likely consisting of about the first sixteen chapters—he added the long prologue on a loose leaf he then attached to the front of the book, in front of his earlier prologue.[22] In the long prologue he also records reading the *Book* through with her, "sche sumtym helpyng where ony difficulte was," before or as he wrote (5). (This system need not have been followed consistently during the twenty months Part I perhaps took to copy,[23] since he must have become accustomed to the orthography of his exemplar, but the passage does suggest that some of the changes he made could have been initiated by Kempe.) Again, eighty-nine chapters in, he notes the point near which the first scribe died, using this moment to punctuate the *Book* by calling what follows *Secundus liber*, restarting the chapter numbers, and closing Part I and opening Part II with an explicit and incipit:

> Her endith this tretys. For God toke hym to his mercy that wrot the copy of this boke. And, thow that he wrot not clerly ne opynly to owr maner of spekyng, he in hys maner of wrytyng and spellyng mad trewe sentens. The whech, thorw the help of God and of hirselfe that had al this tretys in felyng and werkyng, is trewly drawyn owt of the copy into this lityl boke.

The public respect for the first scribe shown here is supplemented by a private tribute, for the one long episode recorded in Part II grows out of the account of the conversion of Kempe's son and of how his death left her the task of chaperoning his widow back to her distant home. Apart from the final prayer, this episode takes up the whole of Part II (although Part II never identifies the son with the *Book*'s first scribe). While there is room for maneuver in the priest's claim that Part I has been "trewly drawyn owt of the copy into this lityl boke," the obvious inference here is that all of Part I is indeed a transcription, however modified, of the first scribe's draft.

The more delicate question, of course, which will take much more space to address, is how extensively *was* this first draft modified? Copying from beginning to end as he must have done, the priest scribe was in a good position to make silent changes and add his own material, but poorly placed to intervene much in the overall structure of the draft. Indeed, at times this fact evidently irked him, for he complains about the *Book*'s lack of chronological exactitude, explaining as early as the prologue that "thys boke is not wretyn in ordyr, every thyng aftyr other as it wer don, but lych as the mater cam to the creatur in mend whan it schuld be wretyn. For it was so long er it was wretyn that sche had forgetyn the tyme and the ordyr whan thyngys befellyn" (5). Versions of this complaint recur in Part I, notably in the direction "Rede fyrst the 21st chapetre and than this chapetre [chapter 17] aftyr that," crammed in at the end of chapter 16 after someone noticed chapter 21's reference to Kempe's last pregnancy, late enough in the book to compromise readers' belief in her vow of chastity (38). Like the hint in the prologue and in the explicit of Part I that the original draft ended when it did because the first scribe died, not because it was done, the complaint is part of the priest's occasional presentation of the *Book* as lacking a formality that he has been helpless, given his position as copyist, to bestow on it.

Yet even if the priest could hardly rethink Kempe's entire presentation of her life, he could still in principle have been responsible for several more local structuring devices, whose cumulative effect is considerable: (1) the *Book*'s division into numbered chapters; (2) its recourse to phrases like "as is wrete beforn" to provide cross-references;

(3) its use of the third person to describe Kempe, particularly in the phrase "this creatur," which does so much to conventionalize the narrative into something approxi-
mating a saint's life; (4) its rare use of first-person pronouns to characterize the narratorial voice; (5) its habit of suspending the moment-by-moment narration of events to
reflect on their significance in Kempe's life as a whole: a device that elevates certain
scenes to the status of hermeneutic keys to the rest of the *Book*. These devices might be
taken as signs of the priest's desire to give a fluid oral report a formal tone, as Felicity
Riddy argues Julian of Norwich and her putative amanuenses textualized successive
versions of *A Revelation of Love*.[24] But the prologue is unjust in presenting the original
draft as structured around the vagaries of Kempe's memory, which is notably precise
even about chronology.[25] Moreover, all these local structuring devices could derive
from the original draft, not from the revision.

(1) The chapter numbers as we now have them belong to the second version, since
the priest scribe is explicit about having added more than one chapter. But the chapter divisions shadow the *Book*'s episodes so closely that most must be original. Moreover, these divisions suggest the care with which Kempe constructed her text out of
units of nearly equal length.[26]

(2) Some of the references to writing in the *Book* do betray links between first draft
and added materials (as will become clear), but there is reason to think that others
were in the earlier version. For example, when chapter 3 describes John Kempe's reluctance to live chastely, glancing forward to chapter 15 with the words "and 3 or 4 yer
aftyr, whan it plesyd ower Lord, he made a vow of chastyte, as schal be wretyn aftyr
be the leve of Ihesu," the last phrases make much more sense as part of the original
draft—as an expression of Kempe's desire that the pages beginning to accumulate on
her son's desk grow into a book—than as an addition by the second scribe (12). Again,
in chapter 18, when we are told that the fulfilment of the anchorite's prophecy about
the broken-backed man, "as I trust, xal be wretyn more pleynly aftyrward," the passage
is incomprehensible without the forward reference, while the phrase "as I trust" suggests that the later chapter referred to (chapter 30) had not yet been written (44).

(3) As to the *Book*'s use of the third person to describe Kempe, there is one certain shift from third-person to first-person narration, when the Kempes take their vow
of chastity before Repingdon, after which the *Book* reports that "the bysshop dede
no more to us at that day, save he mad us rygth good cher and seyd we wer rygth wol-
come" (34). But while this might be thought evidence that Kempe dictated her account
in the first person (so that here alone the priest scribe failed to translate her voice into
the third person), the consistency of the narrative makes it more likely she described
herself as "she" from the start, slipping into the first person only at this dramatic moment when she and her husband declare a new kind of union in their decision to give
up sex. Just before this, when Kempe finds herself "mech mad of " and worries over
"veynglory," Jesus responds with ringing words: "I xal take veynglory fro the; for thei

that worshep the, thei worshep me . . . and thei that heryn the, thei heryn the voys of God" (22–23). There is great pressure on an account that would refuse vanity at the same time as raising its protagonist to such a height, and it seems likely that third-person narration provided Kempe with a means of easing that pressure.[27]

(4) However, if Kempe did refer to herself as "this creatur" in the draft, there is no reason to think she could not have deployed the narratorial "I"-voice as it is used to introduce chapter 4:

> Ower mercyful lord Crist Ihesu . . . sent hir, as is wrete before, 3 yer of greet temp-tacyon, of the whech on of the hardest I purpose to wrytyn, for exampyl of hem that com aftyr that thei schuld not trostyn on her owyn self . . . And so he leyd be-forn this creatur the snar of letchery. (14)

In the form we have it, the voice in this passage seems to be the priest's, and it is possible that this whole chapter was added in the revised version; the end of chapter 3 and opening of chapter 5 fit together well enough. Yet not only does this seem early in the narrative for the priest to be speaking out; the voice of the chapter as a whole is clearly Kempe's, for the chapter's dominant note is its brilliant evocation of her despairing lust. Moreover, this narratorial "I"-voice never establishes itself as a separate entity, recurring only twice in the entire *Book* (44, 214).

(5) Finally, one of the narrative climaxes in Part I does indeed precipitate a passage of general reflection that must be the priest's, yet close reading of the passage suggests that it is no more than an extension of a set of reflections already present in the original draft. The passage, in chapter 28, is a defence of Kempe's gift of tears as she first experiences it at Calvary, which chastises readers for being more willing to weep for worldly griefs than for the death of God:

> It is nowt to be merveyled yyf this creatur cryed and made wondirful cher and cun-tenawns whan we may se eche day at eye bothe men and women . . . for inordinat lofe and fleschly affeccyon, yyf her frendys er partyn fro hem, thei wyl cryen and roryn and wryngyn her handys. . . . Alas, alas for sorwe! That the deth of a creatur, whech hat oftyn synned and trespasyd ageyn her maker, xal be so unmesurably mornyd and sorwyd—and it is offens to God and hyndryng to the sowlys on eche syde—and the compassyfe deth of owyr Savyowr, be the whech we arn alle restoryd to lyfe, is not had in mende of us unworthy and unkende wretchys, ne not we wylle supportyn owyr Lordys owyn secretariis, whech he hath indued wyth lofe, but rathar detractyn hem and hyndryn hem in as mech as we may. (70–71)

The priest's voice is evident in the Latinate vocabulary ("inordinat," "compassyfe," "sec-retariis," "indued"), in the union of narrator and reader in a preacher's exhortative "we," and in the attack on secular mourning. Yet his defence is not precipitated by the moment of weeping the chapter describes (weeping at the scene of Christ's suffering requires no defence) but by the account of Kempe's afflicting gift of tears that grows out of this description. This account gives a preview of the history of this gift and people's reactions to it as these will be analysed in a later section of Part I (chapters 56–71; the passage runs from 68.23–70.5). With its distance from the moment, its precision about places and times, and the control over the narrative of Kempe's life it exhibits, this is the kind of passage that fits easily into our picture of a cleric transforming narration into written text. But the priest's intervention soon after this passage in her defence shows that the passage was already there in the text he was given to copy.

In short, although the priest played some part in creating the interplay between oral and textual voices Uhlman traces through *The Book of Margery Kempe*, he did not invent this effect. Kempe was fully capable of dictating text, not simply narrating story. Not only could she howl at the memory of the beatings given Christ, every time she saw "a man bett a childe befor hir er smet an hors er another best wyth a whippe," she could analyse the causes, effects, history, and significance of her response; indeed, the *Book* must have been written at least as much to explain as describe (69). This conclusion is reinforced by reading the other long passage of general reflection in the pilgrimage section of the *Book*, following her mystical marriage to God the Father at the Church of the Holy Apostles in Rome (chapters 35–37), in which the narrator's account of the "comforts" and "tokens" Kempe experienced "every day the terme of 25 yere whan this boke was wretyn" are interwoven with speeches by Christ about the meaning of the event (88). The reference to a period of "25 yere" (presumably, from Kempe's conversion around 1409) belongs to the revision. One passage at the beginning of this sequence—which describes how "sche was so meche affectyd to the manhode of Crist" that she cried every time she walked the streets of Rome gazing at the beautiful Italian men and pretty children—has the structure of an explanatory gloss and may also have been added (86.24–87.3).[28] Despite its allusions to Rolle's *Incendium amoris*, however, the rest of this reflection is of a piece with Kempe's literalizing of even the most elevated spiritual experience, and could have been transcribed more or less as is from the original draft. Her versions of Rolle's *fervor, dulcor,* and *canor* involve "hete brennyng in hir brest" as real fire burns a finger or hand, "thow the wedyr wer nevyr so colde"; "swet smellys wyth hir nose"; and "sowndys and melodiis" heard "wyth hir bodily erys" and so loud "that sche myth not wel heryn what a man seyd to hir" (88, 87).[29] She sees little white angels "flying al abowte hir on every syde as thykke in a maner as motys in the sunne"; she hears the Holy Spirit in her ear like bellows, or the voice of a dove, or of "a lityl bryd whech is callyd a reedbrest"; she is invited by Christ to take him into her bed and kiss his whole body as though it was really there (88, 91, 90). This sequence, which may have embarrassed the priest, has many resonances with later moments in the *Book* (especially the final section of Part I), and seems from the start to have been an integral part of Kempe's project.

"To prevyn this creaturys felyngys"

Two preliminary findings present themselves, then: first, that the original draft of the *Book* may indeed have looked very similar to Part I of the revised version; second, that when the revised version did make changes or additions, as perhaps with chapter 4 or the interpolation at the beginning of chapter 35, the priest was not necessarily in full charge of the process. Like most of Part II, which also begins with a gesture of priestly control, both these passages read like a close transcription of an oral narration. When we turn to the passages that are explicit about having been added by the priest, and to a few other passages that seem also to have been added silently, we find that, except in the last few chapters of Part I, the priest rarely tries to dominate the *Book* and its meanings, contenting himself with his role as a witness to or defender of the holiness of Kempe's experiences and practices. Although such passages can certainly be used to suggest that there are other changes to the original draft that cannot now be traced, an analysis of their place in the *Book* also gives information about how the priest and Kempe understood the structure and meaning of the original draft, as well as about the processes involved in revising it.

The first explicit scribal interpolation in the *Book*, chapters 24–25, is a case in point, for it helps us to understand a structural division between the first and second long sections of the original draft.[30] Chronologically, the *Book*'s opening section deals with the period before Kempe's pilgrimage to Jerusalem (from 1413 on): comprising her breakdown, conversion, early revelations, vow of chastity, and travels around England with her husband to discuss her experiences with various people and engage in acts of evangelism and other moral interventions. Thematically, this section deals in particular with the verification of her "felyngys," from her declaration of her revelations to the anchorite of Lynn— who sets in motion her long search to find out "whethyr thei ben of the Holy Gost or ellys of yowr enemy the devyl"—to her conversation with the anchoress, Julian of Norwich, the *Book*'s strongest proponent of Kempe's conviction that this attitude of doubt is the same as a lack of trust and must be done away with (18, chapter 18). Chapter 23 is the last of several chapters containing anecdotes confirming her prophetic abilities once she had accepted this truth and become "mor bold than sche was beforn" (45). Its own collection of anecdotes are followed by a passage that begins:

> Many mo swech revelacyons this creatur had in felyng; hem alle for to wryten it xuld be lettyng peraventur of mor profyte. Thes be wretyn for to schewyn the homlynes

and the goodlynes of owr mercyful lord Crist Ihesu, and for no commendacyon of the creatur. (54)

The chapter ends by noting that "sche had sumtyme so gret trubbyl wyth swech felyngs . . . that hir confessowr feryd that sche xuld a fallyn in dyspeyr therwyth," but that she always understood them in the end (54–55). Chapter 26 then opens, "Whan tyme cam that this creatur xuld vysiten tho holy placys wher owyr Lord was whyk and ded, as sche had be revelacyon yerys aforn," a formal opening that declares the beginning of a long new section that takes the narrative all the way to Kempe's trials for Lollardy and eventual return to Lynn (in chapter 55) (60).

The interpolated chapters deal with the priest's own testing of Kempe and, for all his worries about chronology, they both describe episodes that took place much later, perhaps in the early 1430s. One concerns the priest's attempts to "prevyn this creaturys felyngys" while he was making up his mind to copy the *Book*, how he lent money against her advice to a cleric supposedly on the run for accidental murder and then almost fell victim to a humiliating book-selling scam (55). The other offers an example of Kempe's prophetic intervention in a parish squabble, which the priest says "is wretyn her for convenyens, inasmech as it is in felyng leche to the materys that ben wretyn beforn, notwythstondyng it befel long aftyr the materys whech folwyn" (58).[31] The nature and placing of this interpolation suggests two things. First, the careful transition between sections marked by the ending of chapter 23 and opening of chapter 26 belongs to the original draft: although chapter 23 states that it would be pointless to add more revelations, the interpolated chapters proceed to add several. Second, the priest recognized that, despite its anecdotal qualities, this draft did have a thematic structure, one that required keeping "materys" that were "in felyng leche" to each other together, even at the cost of chronology. In the light of this evidence for the formal structure of the original draft, we can better evaluate Kempe's own departures from chronological order in the first section, as when she claims to the Norwich priest Richard Caister that her experiences can be equalled by those described neither in "Hyltons boke, ne Bridis boke, ne *Stimulus amoris*, ne *Incendium amoris*," even though she was not to encounter any of these books for perhaps a decade after this conversation took place (see chapter 58) (39). Kempe is not muddled or forgetful here, but is showing her awareness of different traditions of devotional writing at a moment in her narrative when she is testing her own "felyngys." It seems evident that she, too, had a formal and thematic sense of her *Book*'s structure and would have understood the rationale for the priest's disruptive interpolation.

Chapters 24–25 could nonetheless have been written without Kempe's help and suggest she did not dominate the rewriting process. Other passages in which the priest's voice seems to be heard produce a more mixed impression. Like the interpolations in chapters 28 and 35 described above, two passages have the priest speaking up for Kempe at times of crisis or stepping in to explain her actions. One of these is the interpolation in chapter 62 that describes his abandonment of her cause under the influence of William Melton's attacks on her weeping, and his reconversion to belief in the truth of her after he discovered precedents for her gift in the *Vita* of Mary of Oignies and several other texts (the interpolation probably runs from 152.32–154.17). As with chapters 24–25, this passage tells us little about Kempe's self-understanding; as a whole, the *Book* shows small interest in finding *precedents* for her tears. But it tells us a good deal about how the clerics of Lynn sought to account for this, her most oppressive spiritual gift, just as it does about the priest's awareness that here (as with the scenes on Calvary and in Rome) he was transcribing one of the *Book*'s central episodes.

The other passage is a description of Margery and John Kempe's living arrangements in chapter 76, written to account for her absence from John's home when he fell on the stairs (179.29–180.16). Like the interpolation about Kempe's devotion to Christ's humanity in chapter 35, this passage is structured as a gloss, this time on the threatening sentence, "And than the pepil seyd, yyf he deyd, hys wyfe was worthy to ben hangyn for hys deth, forasmeche as sche myth a kept hym and dede not."[32] Once again, this interpolation reflects the priest's anxieties about her propensity to cause scandal. Like two shorter passages, one offering the priest's testimony to a miracle in chapter 75, the other bringing the story of John's last illness up to date, the interpolation may also show how, as his copying of the *Book* continued, he grew less self-conscious about adding material (178.36–179.5, 180.36–181.15).[33] Nonetheless, none of them do more than to point up a structure that is already firmly in place.

"Grawntyng hym a grett symme of good for hys labowr"

For the most part, the priest's recopying of *The Book of Margery Kempe* thus seems to have worked as a successful collaboration between an author and a scribe who shared a common sense of the text's structure and meaning. Indeed, his fidelity to this audacious account of a bourgeois saint's progress is so strange as to demand explanation. Not only does the narrative the priest copied see Kempe through early trials, troubled pilgrimages, arrests at the hands of his own episcopal superiors, and the crisis of her crying seizures; almost his only intrusions are for the sake of chronicling his lapses from true belief in her, and how these led to the strengthening of his faith in her holiness and the power of God's purpose. Nothing further from Hirsh's vision of the priest as ghostwriter can be imagined. Why was the priest scribe so compliant?

I suggest that a possible answer to this question is simply this: that the priest was not mainly writing in his capacity as a priest but in that of a scribe, and that he thought of himself in that way because he was being paid for the job Kempe had persuaded him to perform. These are not claims that can be made dogmatically, since the priest constructs his relation to Kempe in more than one way, nor ones that can be proved. But they can be backed up, and make sense of the data we have. The priest was a skilled and self-conscious copyist who imposed a high degree of conformity on the text, despite his difficulties with eye-strain (perhaps a professional deformity), and who used a highly regular spelling system: one consistent with those found in linguistically self-conscious texts produced in Lynn around the same time (5).[34] As Sandford Meech points out, the passages added by the priest are linguistically identical with those he copied from the original draft: a fact for which Meech gives credit to the priest himself, rather than the copyist of the surviving manuscript, Salthows, another Lynn scribe who had a training similar to the priest's (viii–ix, 254). The priest was given to professional grumblings about other copyists, especially Kempe's son, whose uncouth script had caused him so much trouble, and he ends the part of his task involving transcription not only by acknowledging the "trewe sentens" the son had achieved after his amateurish lights but by laying proud claim to have "trewly drawyn" the son's written account "owt of the copy into this lityl boke" (220). Despite her increasing age, Kempe was willing to lay siege to him for several years in order to secure his services in producing what she saw as the definitive copy of her *Book,* a copy from which others, like the one that survives to us, could readily be made. There is no reason to think she had no choice of other copyists (indeed, she had at least one alternative), and she probably wanted him because he was the best-qualified scribe available for her long prose text.

Money may not have been involved in their relationship, which the long prologue claims was based on friendship ("Than was ther a prest whech this creatur had gret affeccyon to" [4]). But the evidence of the *Book* suggests they were not in fact close friends. The priest cannot be identified with any of the named clergy in the *Book,* although we know he was in Lynn by the early 1420s, when Melton was preaching against Kempe, and that at different times he took both sides in the controversy over her weeping (chapter 62). He seems not to have completely understood the circumstances under which the original draft was produced; and according to chapters 24–25, he was sufficiently unconvinced of her authenticity as a prophet when she was asking him to copy the book that he imposed tests on her "to prevyn this creaturys felyngys" (55). Moreover, for all his use of the language of spiritual friendship to describe their relationship, the priest is vividly aware that other scribes are paid for what they do. When Kempe despairs of him and briefly takes her project elsewhere, to a scribe who used to know her son, the priest notes that she offers this other man "a grett summe of good for hys labowr" (after which the priest quickly agrees to look at the project again), while the short prologue's recollection of Alan of Lynn's much earlier offer to write down her revelations is that he "proferyd hir to wryten *frely* if she wold," as though it would have been more natural even for the saintly Carmelite to charge for his services (4, 6).[35] Reading between the lines of chapter 58's account of how Kempe finds an unbeneficed priest (living in lodgings in Lynn with his widowed mother) to read and translate to her from books she provided for him, the *Book* offers evidence of a parallel instance in which a priest is paid to work for her, although the financial details are shrouded in the language of courtesy and spiritual profit (142–44). Might not the priest scribe have been reconciled to his status as copyist through much of the *Book* because that was the most important aspect of the role he had made a financial contract with Kempe to adopt?

If the answer to this question is "yes," the priest may have taken as much professional pride in replicating Kempe's words through most of the *Book* as he took in rectifying the first scribe's howlers, and it might seem that our model of the officious clerical amanuensis to a woman visionary is irrelevant in assessing an arrangement that worked along different lines. Yet we have already seen that the priest did sometimes add his own material, throwing a specifically clerical kind of support behind Kempe's project, and it seems prima facie unlikely that this support was part of what she wanted from him. Her earliest recorded literary accomplishment in the *Book* is a letter of repudiation sent to a certain widow ("On clause was that the wedow xuld nevyr han the grace that this creatur had"), to write which she uses the services of "a maystyr of dyvynite": hardly a neutral choice (45). In her negotiations with the priest scribe, she willingly submits to the tests he set her prophetic powers, courting him for all her worth. For his part, the priest is concerned to stress the clerical rectitude of his decision to work for her and identifies with her project wholeheartedly by the act of adding the long prologue, with its official-sounding opening: "Here begynnyth a schort tretys and a comfortabyl for synful wrecchys, wherin thei may have gret solas and comfort to hem and undyrstondyn the hy and unspecabyl mercy of ower sovereyn savyowr Cryst Ihesu, whos name be worschepd and magnyfyed wythowten ende, that now in ower days to us unworthy deyneth to exercysen hys nobeley and hys goodnesse" (1). His opening flourish in Part II is more domineering, describing how "he held it expedient to honowr of the blisful Trinite" to continue the original draft, a clause in which the topos of the clerical amanuensis is briefly fully articulated (221). At the same time, however, the priest's initial hesitations and the fluid relationship between him and Kempe in the process of copying the *Book* suggest that he continued to find the situation in which she had placed him difficult. He confesses to social embarrassment at having to meet her all the time when there was "so evel spekyng of this creatur and of hir wepyng" in the early 1430s, and the voice he occasionally claims in the *Book* itself quickly wavers; in Part II, Kempe's "owyn tunge" is the one we hear in action, not his (2, 220). I suspect that his humility in the face of his task has to do with his acceptance of his scribal role, with its ethical obligations to copy texts accurately, as secretary of one of "owyr Lordys owyn secretariis," and that he was confirmed in his decision to copy correctly by his discovery of the sheer quality of Kempe's text: a text she wanted to keep a closely guarded secret "as long as sche leved" (71, 4).[36] But his role was nonetheless too ambiguous for him to submit to it entirely or to play it up within limits she assigned to him.

"That sche undirstod bodily it was to ben undirstondyn gostly"

For Kempe and the priest did not see eye to eye all the time. The final section of Part I, which, above all, generalizes the theological significance of her life, makes explicit a disparity between their views which has major implications for the *Book*'s intellectual stance as a whole. The opening of the section (chapter 72) announces that the theme of these last chapters is the holiness she attained after assimilating her gift of tears (which has been the focus from chapter 56 on):

> So, be processe of tyme, hir mende and hir thowt was so joynyd to God that sche nevyr forgate hym, but contynualy had mende of hym and behelde hym in alle creaturys; and evyr the mor that sche encresyd in lofe and in devocyon the mor sche encresyd in sorwe and in contrycyon, in lownes, in mekenes, and in the holy dreed of owr Lord, and in knowlach of hir owyn frelte. (172)

Some of the following chapters, which pull incidents out of her life in careful collage, then offer meditations on portions of Christ's life, especially the Passion (chapters 78–81). These seem designed as perorating counterparts to the Nativity meditations that take up chapters 6–7, and suggest that, in these chapters, Kempe's *imitatio Christi* is to be seen as coming to a culmination. Other chapters tease out the implications both of this *imitatio* and of the form this opening says it took, in her continual "mende" of Christ and ability to see him "in alle creaturys": she beholds Christ in lepers, in a woman suffering from insanity, in her incontinent husband, in small children, when dining (chapters 74, 75, 76, 82). Others still systematize the meaning of her tears, prayers, and charity (chapters 77, 86, 84). Here, God accounts for Kempe to Kempe at length, subdividing the significance of her tears into five "tokens," describing her devotion to Christ, the saints, and the Trinity as a model to others, and explaining how the world benefits from charitable wishes as much as deeds: so that her desire to endow monasteries and redeem those who have fallen into lechery, to be "slayn an hundryd sithys on a day" for God's love, or to welcome the Trinity and the whole court of heaven into the chamber of her soul, is equivalent to doing these things (183, 203–204, 184, 210–11). The spiritual elevation of this phase of her life is conveyed not only by all this praise and the language of continual "mende" (perhaps derived from Rolle),[37] but by recourse to the ineffability topos. Here, as nowhere else, she twice has "many mo holy thowtys

than sche evyr cowde rehersyn," which are "so holy and so hy that sche was abaschyd
to tellyn hem to any creatur"—even if she understands Christ's "swet dalyawnce in hir
sowle as clerly as on frende xulde spekyn to another" (199, 201, 214).

The section (and the original draft of the *Book*) ends with Christ's great speech of
explanation and commendation in chapter 86, followed by a three-chapter coda (chapters 87–89) which describes Kempe's state "whan this booke was first in wrytyng" and
reprises her relationship with Alan of Lynn and Robert Springfield (much of which
could have been added in revision) (216). Near the end of this draft, then, Kempe
placed in Christ's mouth the peroration:

> Also, dowtyr, I thanke the for as many tymys as thu hast bathyd me in thi sowle, at
> hom in thi chambre, as thow I had be ther present in my Manhod. . . . And also,
> dowtyr, I thank the for alle the tymys that thu hast herberwyd me and my blissyd
> modyr in thi bed. For thes and for alle other good thowtys and good dedys that
> thu hast thowt in my name and wrowt for my lofe, thu xalt have—wyth me and
> wyth my modyr, wyth myn holy awngelys, wyth myn apostelys, wyth myn mar-
> tirys, confessowris and virginys, and wyth alle myn holy seyntys—al maner joye
> and blysse lestyng wythowtyn ende. (214)

Here, with Christ's gratitude for her devotion to his human nature, her ability to people
her soul and bed with Christ and his mother, and with the promise of her surpassing reward, Margery Kempe's original draft summed up her life.

Yet in its drawing out of one of these motifs, devotion to Christ's human nature,
this final section seems to have irked the priest, and his revolt against Kempe's understanding of this motif not only causes confusion but raises questions about the section's handling of one other theological theme. The revolt comes at the end of a late
chapter of five miscellaneous visions about the humanity of Christ (chapter 85), each
introduced by the phrase "On a tyme" or "Another tyme," which tells of a vision she experienced "in a maner of slep" (208). In this vision, "sche sey owr Lord standyng ryght
up ovyr hir, so ner that hir thowt sche toke hys toos in hir hand and felt hem, and to hir
felyng it weryn as it had ben very flesch and bon" (208). The text generalizes the significance of this experience, then suddenly veers off on an embarrassed tangent in a
passage that has all the hallmarks of a scribal interpolation:

> And than sche thankyd God of al. For thorw thes gostly sytys, hir affeccyon was al
> drawyn into the Manhod of Crist and into the mynde of hys Passyon—unto that
> tyme that it plesyd owr Lord to yevyn hir undirstondyng of hys inundirstondabyl
> Godhed. As is wretyn beforn, thes maner of visyons and felyngys sche had sone
> aftyr hir conversyon, whan sche was fully set and purposyd to servyn God wyth al

hir hert into hir power . . . and most specialy in Lent tyme, whan sche wyth gret in-
stawns and mech preyer had leve of hir husbond to levyn chast and clene, and
dede gret bodily penawns, er sche went to Jerusalem. But aftyrwardys, whan hir
husbond and sche wyth on assent had mad avow of chastite, as is beforn wretyn,
and sche had ben at Rome and Jerusalem . . . owr Lord of hys hy mercy drow hir affeccyon into hys Godhed. And that was mor fervent in lofe and desyr, and mor
sotyl in undirstondyng, than was the Manhod. And nevyrthelesse the fyr of love
encresyd in hir, and hir undirstandyng was mor illumynyd and hir devocyon mor
fervent than it was befor, whyl sche had hir meditacyon and hir contemplacyon
only in hys Manhod. Yet had sche not that maner of werkyng in crying as sche had
before, but it was mor sotyl and mor softe and mor esy to hir spiryt to beryn, and
plentyuows in teerys as evyr it was beforn. (208–209)

Even if we accept its claim that this late chapter is out of chronological order, this passage plays havoc with the *Book*'s thematization of Kempe's spiritual history. Implying
that her interest in Christ's toes had something to do with the difficulty of shifting to
a life of chastity, the passage refers back to her mystical marriage to the Godhead (described in chapter 35) to suggest that this incident fundamentally changed the tone of
her spirituality, increasing its fervor by making it "mor sotyl in undirstondyng," and
softening the violence (although not lessening the quantity) of her tears. But this is
nothing like what the *Book* says happened. While the mystical marriage is one of the
Book's climaxes, we saw that this event is immediately followed by a speech in which
Christ invites her to "take me" (not the Father) "to thi weddyd husbond, as thy derworthy derlyng, and as for thy swete sone," and "boldly take me in the armys of thi
sowle and kyssen my mowth, myn hed, and my fete" (90). This is one of the devotional
exercises for which Christ thanks her in the peroration of chapter 86 (quoted above),
and the exercise traces its *beginning*, not its shift into something more "sotyl," from the
episode of the mystical marriage. Her relation to the Godhead, throughout the *Book*,
remains a matter of God's exercise of power over her, in giving her the spiritual experiences of song, sweet smells, and fire (also described in chapter 35), and in the majes-
tic interventions whereby he illuminates her with the unwelcome gift of prophecy and
forces her to weep. It is these interventions Christ in his Godhead later compares to
thunder, storms, and earthquakes, and that draw her back to the world, her physical
senses, and the ways her life turns the "erthe" of her heart "upsodown," not away from
these things (181–82).[38] Moreover, far from coinciding with the end of Kempe's most
intense periods of crying, the mystical marriage occurs soon after the first time "sche
myt not kepe hirself fro krying and roryng thow sche xuld a be ded therfor" (68), and
at least a decade before the ferocity of this gift or curse was diminished; that is, indeed,
what the entire previous section of the *Book* has been about (chapters 56–71). The

phrase "mor sotyl and mor softe and mor esy" bears no relation to the terror, the violent physicality, and the sheer volume of the bawling and thrashing the *Book* has described, and whose meaning had long preoccupied the clerisy of Lynn.[39]

In this passage, then, we seem to have a direct testimony to the priest scribe's difficulties in accepting a central aspect of the *Book's* presentation of Kempe's spiritual progress. Eighty-five chapters into his task, the priest still read the career of its protagonist through a model of spiritual living characterized by a stage-by-stage ascent away from the carnal towards the spiritual, away from the "milk" of Christ's humanity towards the "meat" of his divinity. This is the model sustained by two of the texts Kempe lists as parts of her spiritual reading in chapter 58, Walter Hilton's *Scale of Perfection* and Richard Rolle's *Incendium amoris,* which promote the death of fleshly desire as a precondition for holy living or union with the divine;[40] this is also the model I believe Kempe's *Book* was written partly to combat. The absurdity of the priest's attempt to apply the model here, so late in the *Book,* is a testimony to the forcefulness of his objections to some of its meanings. For him the mystical marriage *had* finally to involve a progressive movement away from the world and her tears to be part of that movement. All along, apparently, he had been assuming that this was how the *Book* would turn out. Instead, however, the text comes to a close with scene after scene of unblushingly carnal religious devotion, whose effect is to bring the text in a great circle back to, not away from, scenes like that of Christ's first appearance to Kempe right at the beginning of the *Book,* "in lykenesse of a man, most semly, most bewtyuows, and most amyable . . . clad in a mantyl of purpyl sylke, syttyng upon hir beddys syde" (8). The very chapter after the episode of the toes obliged him to copy a scene in which the holy Trinity is seen sitting in her soul—after the whole court of heaven has helped her adorn it "wyth many fayr flowerys and wyth many swete spicys"—on "a cuschyn of gold, another of red velvet, the thryd of white sylke" (210).[41] Unable to identify the language of the *Book's* final section with any model of holy living he recognized, the priest tried briefly to force Kempe's account of herself, to stand in front of her and to speak for her.

In a sense, this passage is a mere ripple on the surface of *The Book of Margery Kempe,* which obscures the theological logic but might otherwise be thought an isolated outburst. As we shall see, the great prayer that concludes Part II of the revised version reiterates many of the themes of the final section of Part I, while Part II's failure to move beyond the models offered in Part I has often been remarked. In most respects, in other words, the priest fell back into line.

Yet there is one other passage in the coda of Part I (chapters 87–89) which exhibits a similar inconsistency with the *Book's* theology. The coda partly sums up twenty-five years of Kempe's religious experiences (chapter 87), partly describes the period when the original draft was being written and her relationship with her confessors: a conjunction that is perhaps meant to reassure us that her confessors approved of her literary project (chapters 88–89). While it is hard to be sure, much of it may have been added in the revision. (Chapter 87 itself shows some signs of revision and ends with the words, "Therfor, Lord, as thu wilt so mote it be" [216], a sentence found elsewhere in Middle English as part of a perorating couplet that concludes "Amen, Amen, par charite"; perhaps these were the final words of the original draft.) Some passages in these chapters pick up themes that have been introduced earlier, such as Kempe's anxiety about giving too much emphasis to meditation, despite Christ and her confessor's insistence that she pray less (216–17, see 89–90). Others read like intrusions from the priest, such as the claim that "visitacyons and holy contemplacyonis" like Kempe's "wil be had but in gret qwyet of sowle thorw long excersyse," a statement that describes conventional accounts of spiritual exercise but is hard to align with the eruptive force of Christ's invasions of the soul described in the *Book* (214).[42] And one passage seems clearly marked by the priest's anxieties. This passage is part of the inconsequential anecdote that closes Part I concerning Kempe's desire that "Maistyr Aleyn" preach a fine sermon, her statement to three priestly friends that God had told her he would do so, and how she was seized by anxiety until the sermon was preached:

> And, whan sche had telde hem hir felyng, sche was ful sory for dreed whethyr he schulde sey so wel as sche had felt er not, for revelacyons be hard sumtyme to undirstondyn. And sumtyme tho that men wenyn wer revelacyonis it arn deceytys and illusyons. And therfor it is not expedient to yevyn redily credens to every steryng but sadly abydyn and prevyn yf thei be sent of God. Nevyrthelesse as to this felyng of this creatur, it was very trewth schewyd in experiens, and hir dred and hir hevynes turnyd into gret gostly comforte and gladnes. Sumtyme sche was in gret hevynes for hir felyngys, whan sche knew not how thei schulde ben undirstondyn many days togedyr, for drede that sche had of deceytys and illusyons, that hir thowt sche wolde that hir hed had be smet fro the body tyl God of hys goodnesse declaryd hem to hir mende. For sumtyme that sche undirstod bodily it was to ben undirstondyn gostly. And the drede that sche had of hir felyngys was the grettest scorge that sche had in erde, and specialy whan sche had hir fyrst felyngys, and that drede made hir ful meke, for sche had no joye in the felyng tyl sche knew be experiens whethyr it was trewe er not. But evyr blissyd mote God ben! For he mad hir alwey mor myty and mor strong in hys love and in hys drede and yaf hir encres of vertu with perseverawns. Here endith this tretys. . . . (219–20)

This sombre discussion conflates two interpretive difficulties Kempe had with her visions and prophetic insights, one hermeneutic, the other to do with doubts about diabolic interference. As the passage admits, these difficulties are mainly associated in the *Book* only with her "fyrst felyngys"; this is especially true of the second, diabolic difficulty, which most of the *Book* keeps separate from the first: even if, as the story about "Maistyr Aleyn" suggests, she continues to have trouble interpreting her intuitions correctly. So why are the two brought up again here as though they were the same? The rest of the section goes out of its way to stress the lucidity of God's communications with Kempe, while an important passage in chapter 83 claims that the one hindrance to her constant reception of divine grace was "whan sche dowtyd er mistrostyd the goodnes of God, supposyng er dredyng that it was the wyle of hir gostly enmy to enformyn hir er techyn hir otherwyse than wer to hir gostly hele": that is, when she confused her difficulty in understanding the divine with what this passage presents as the diabolic temptation to believe that she was being subjected to demonic influence (201). Against a lively conservative tradition of *discretio spirituum* (exemplified in Alphonse of Pecha's *Epistola solitarii*) that would render all visionary experiences suspect until rigorously tested, the final section of Part I of the *Book* repeats the lesson Kempe presents herself being taught earlier by Julian of Norwich, quoting the Epistle of James: that "he that is evyrmor dowtyng is lyke to the flood of the see . . . and that man is not lyche to receyven the yyftys of God" (42).[43] Only here (pages after the coda itself has reiterated that "sche stabely and stedfastly belevyd that it was God that spak in hir sowle and non evyl spiryt") are the warnings about diabolical deception and the dangers of misconstruing visions reinstated, in language so shifting as to betray a rare sense of awkwardness (215).

It seems that either the last section's deliberate elisions of "bodily" and "ghostly" modes or, perhaps, Kempe's presentation of herself as a mirror to others, revived in the priest a professional caution about the spiritual realm that was no part of her own thinking. This passage again suggests a willingness on the priest's part to defy Kempe's theological logic when it unnerved him. No doubt he intended to protect her from scandal and justify her ways to women and men, even to burnish the mirror she presented to their lives. Nonetheless, as elsewhere, his intervention here is damaging to our sense that the *Book* has anything consistent to say.

"Thu art to me a synguler lofe, dowtyr"

But in what sense *does* the *Book* have anything consistent to say? After all, it conveys plenty of puzzlement about what Kempe's life is about, even on her own part: "Lord, why wilt thu yyf me swech crying that the pepil wondryth on me therfor?" she has herself ask in chapter 77 (181). When the *Book* is not puzzled, it sometimes seems defensive, fending off from a pressure of opposition and confusion many readers feel is understandable and to which even the second scribe succumbed. Nor is it easy to come at the logic that binds Kempe's ideas and experiences together; especially if, like the second scribe, we try to align her with the theological systems of her contemporaries. Like one of the "symple creatures" for whom Nicholas Love's *Mirror of the Blessed Life of Christ* was written, she adores Christ's body and meditates constantly on Christ's life, seeing this acted out by everyone she meets as though Lynn was the permanent scene of a cycle of mystery plays.[44] Yet she identifies these exercises not with spiritual simplicity but with the life of perfection, ignoring all the calls to ascend to contemplation of the heavenly city or God in his essence enunciated by texts like *The Scale of Perfection*. As we saw, even her versions of Rolle's spiritual experiences are brought down, literally, to earth; and these experiences are hard to integrate with her devotion to Christ's humanity.[45] Her prophetic gift, which involves encounters with God's "privities" very different from those of her contemporary, Julian, belongs in a Bridgittine spiritual tradition.[46] Her intense dislike of swearing, her concern with the morality of others, and her desire to evangelize aligns her with the Lollards; her universalism with Langland, Julian, and Sir John Mandeville.[47] Despite all medieval and modern efforts to find parallels, her crying aligns her with nobody.[48] Passionate pilgrim, part-time pauper, proponent of purgatory, self-proclaimed martyr, honorary virgin, spouse of two persons of the Trinity and vehicle for the third, she could easily be seen as a chameleon saint: a little bit of this and a little bit of that. Perhaps her *Book* also has to be seen as a medley, its arguments motivated more by what Karma Lochrie calls "the marginal woman's quest for literary authority" than by an urgent need to enunciate any particular religious teaching.[49]

Although the *Book* is much more theologically coherent than this, it does have a magpie quality, partly because Kempe wanted to say and be something "synguler" (50)—someone defined much of the time by what she was *not*—partly because inclusiveness was close to the heart of her religious praxis and she could not bear to throw anything away. Above all else, she would not throw away the world, or the self that had grown to middle age in the world. The body that had borne more than a dozen children in as many years and enjoyed "many delectabyl thowtys, fleschly lustys, and inordinat lovys" towards her husband's "persone"; the body that briefly yearned, during a time of marital tension, to be taken by another man, and that soon after broke away from human lovers, as the love of Jesus turned her heart and her life upside down: this body and its history remained the locus for all her feeling and thinking, the bridge of sighs between an impure world and a pure, but still perpetually longing, God (181, 15, 182). Weeping ever for her own sins as well as others', to the very end of the *Book* she identifies with sinner saints—"I blisse the, Lord, for Mary Mawdelyn, for Mary Egipcyan, for Seynt Powle, and for Seynt Awstyn"—and asks God to "qwenche in me al fleschly lust, and in alle tho that I have beholdyn thi blisful body in" (253, 249).[50] The gaze that turned all men into the image of Jesus was never quite clean in motive or effect, and even the bitter tears that came after the gaze gave her bodily release, leaving her "bareyn" when they were taken away (199). Yet it is within the soul's chamber in this impure body that the whole court of heaven comes and the Holy Trinity deigns to sit on its colored cushions (210–11). It is through this body's liquefaction into tears, through Kempe's wish to have herself "leyd nakyd on a hyrdil" to be ridiculed by men, through her desire to put her mouth on the sores of lepers and be "hewyn as smal as flesch to the potte" for God's love, that her labor for the salvation of all gains souls for the kingdom of God—"etyn and knawyn of the pepul of the world" though she is "as any raton knawyth the stokfysch" (184, 176–77, 142, 17). Finally it is into the soul in this body, swollen by love, that the *Book*'s final prayer imaginatively summons all creation to the worship of an unimaginable God:

> Here my preyeris. For thow I had as many hertys and sowlys closyd in my sowle as God knew wythowtyn begynnyng how many xulde dwellyn in hevyn wythowtyn ende; and as ther arn dropys of watyr, fres and salt; cheselys of gravel, stonys smale and grete; gresys growyng in al erthe; kyrnellys of corn; fischys, fowelys, bestys, and leevys upon treys whan most plente ben; fedir of fowle er her of best; seed that growith in erbe er in wede in flowyr, in lond er in watyr whan most growyn; and as many creaturys as in erth han ben and arn er xal ben and myth ben be thi myth; and as ther arn sterrys and awngelys in thi syght; er other kynnes good that growyth upon erthe; and eche wer a sowle as holy as every was our lady seynt Mary . . . I may rith wel thynkyn in myn hert and spekyn it wyth my mowth as this tyme in worschip of the Trinite and of al the cowrt of hevyn . . . that alle thes hertys ne sowlys cowde nevyr thankyn God ne ful preysyn hym . . . for the gret mercy that he hath schewyd to me in erth that I can not don ne may don. (252)

Here, in her fantasy union with all God's creation (including the beings he might have made and did not) and in this creation's everlastingly inadequate praise of God for his mercy to her, is the apotheosis of the "creatur": reaching up to God with all the power she can command; still falling short; still reaching up. Here are the questions at the heart of the *Book:* how can finitude aspire to infinity? How can holiness inhabit a sinful body? How can this body redeem the world?[51]

Most mystical texts ask one of these questions, and some ask all three: like the *Revelation of Love,* whose theology is organized around the ways in which perfection and imperfection include and enclose each other, so that God already lies nestled at the centre of creation and the human soul. Julian's solution to the anxiety of contingency is that imperfection is not in the end real. There is a changeable sensuality to human behavior, but at the root of sin and pain is the unwavering substance of the soul, ever united with God, incapable of incurring final blame.[52] What makes *The Book of Margery Kempe* distinctive is the form of its refusal of this harmonizing vision, its identification both of itself and of the "creatur" who "had al this tretys in felyng and werkyng" with the limitations of fleshliness and the impurity it is heir to (220). Kempe presents her life as following two, apparently contradictory, trajectories: towards ever greater perfection on the one hand, and towards ever closer identification with the sinful world around her on the other. As we have seen, she also manages to present these opposing movements very much like standing still, more a matter of an intensification of her being than a progression from one state of soul to another. The incongruities that arise from this way of being and writing put huge pressures on the *Book:* pressures of inadequacy or absurdity, only partly explained by the way they mirror the earthly life of her divine lover, Christ. Speaking herself relatively unmediated by her priestly scribe or the mediation provided by the Church and its sacraments—for all the intensity of her formal observance, she remains a secular figure, a municipal saint—Kempe offers the reader the same puzzle she offered herself and her community. She is, indeed, a "synguler lofe," a startling fusion of opposites that ought to repel, not attract. If she is impure—unlike the virgins who "dawnsyn now meryly in hevyn," their innocent joy a manifestation of the purity Julian would attribute to the substance of every saved soul—she is also, *for that reason,* uniquely desirable to God. "I have ronnyn awey fro the," she says, "and thow hast ronnyn aftyr me," as though God responds to her flight from him as titillation: for all that she must remain to the end anxiously ashamed of her continuing sinfulness, fearful of the purity of God's perfection, shudderingly aware of his willingness to punish as well as pleasure (50).[53] What creates her singularity is not only her status as God's chosen vessel but also her role as a sinning Everywoman, her capacity to be bound more closely to the world than others, at the same time *and in the same way* as she is bound more closely to God.

"For I am an hyd God in the"

Much of *The Book of Margery Kempe*'s own singularity lies in the ways it heightens our sense of the incongruities that cluster around its protagonist, rather than trying to resolve them. Even its most persistent theological themes are shot through with paradox. For example, one of the main ways Kempe as author and protagonist aspires to understand, explain, and influence the divine is by quantitative reckoning. Like many other participants in a mercantile late medieval religious culture imbued with the financial imagery of recompense and satisfaction—numbering masses for the dead and years in purgatory and reciting Aves and Pater Nosters by the hundreds in expiation of sin—she finds aesthetic and spiritual comfort in the process of enumeration.[54] The *Book* is full of assertions such as that particular spiritual experiences have recurred "more than xxv yer whan this tretys was wretyn, weke be weke, and day be day" (214), as though each repetition, and by a set amount, increases the experience's legitimacy. Although the rhetoric of excess is a constant presence, the experiences themselves can likewise be preoccupied with numbers. At the scourging of Christ, Kempe sees "sextene men wyth sextene scorgys, and eche scorge had 8 babelys of leed on the ende, and every babyl was ful of scharp prekelys as it had been the rowelys of a spor, and tho men wyth the scorgys madyn comenawnt that ich of hem xulde yevyn owr Lord 40 strokys": more than five thousand spiked "babelys" descend on Christ's skin, leaving ten times that number of wounds (191). When Kempe weeps every Good Friday for ten years for "5 er 6 owrys togedyr," she does so not just for her own sins but "an owr for the synne of the pepil, . . . another owr for the sowlys in Purgatory, another owr for hem that weryn in myschefe, . . . another owr for Jewys, Sarazinys, and alle fals heretikys," carefully distributing the abundance from her "welle of teerys" to gain the maximum benefit from God (140–41). When she signs half the credit balance in her personal treasury of merits over to her confessor, Master Robert, or imagines expensive deeds of charity she cannot afford to perform, she shows the same mix of prudence and extravagance, the same investment in a spiritual economy of exchange, she attributes to God (20–21, 216, 203–204). Even the lyrical summoning of the creation into herself quoted above evokes a huge, but still finite number as the measure of divine plenitude. Read one way, much of the *Book* seems trustingly confident in the adequacy of number as a way of calculating the relation between earth and heaven.

Read another way, however, all the language of enumeration in the *Book* is there precisely in order to expose its own inadequacy and reveal the absurdity of trying to count to infinity. Even distended by as many souls as there are objects in creation, Kempe can still not praise God enough for his mercy to her alone; limited as she is, she cannot encompass eternity or yet creation. As the rhetoric of excess in the *Book* signs for us, and as the bodily contortions that are so important to her spiritual experiences show, she can never love enough, pray enough, cry enough; on earth there are always more sinners than her tears can redeem, in heaven there is always more holiness than she can match. However she amasses spiritual wealth, spends it on others, or enumerates the sufferings of her divine lover, her desire is set on the infinite reaches of understanding which lie beyond number, and one of whose outlets in the *Book* is her frustrated desire for death: told that she has to live fifteen more years, she replies "A, Lord, I schal thynkyn many thowsend yerys" (176). For all she owes to the world of chantry chapels and indulgences, or finds comfort in the pardon or "plenowr remissyon" she is granted one "Seynt Nicholas Day" and hands on to readers, her use of quantitative measurements in thinking through the complexities of human sin, retributive justice, mercy, and even heavenly reward is rhetorical (175). The numbers are there because they point with manifest inadequacy at something else.

This failure of number, combined with Kempe's personal awareness of limitedness, is why the *Book* must set such store on simile, on the tags "as" and "as if," as the closest it can come to imagining adequacy. "As" and "as if" have multivalent signifi-cance in the *Book*'s usage. First, according to "as if," desire itself—which for Kempe, as for Rolle, can be, or at least symbolize, the infinite, if only because it always yearns for its own increase—becomes the bridge between earth and heaven mere enumeration fails to be, by a divine dispensation which reckons the will to do something as though it were the deed: as God promises Kempe at a crucial moment late in the text, "Dow-tyr, thow xalt han as gret mede and as gret reward wyth me in hevyn for thi good servyse and the good dedys that thu hast don in thi mynde and meditacyon *as yyf* thu haddyst don tho same dedys wyth thy bodily wittys wythowtyn-forth" (203). One of the exemplary lessons Kempe hopes to teach readers is that their actual state of living is of small importance compared to how they desire to live. A married woman of lim-ited means but with a fulsome desire to love God, she can will as highly and be rewarded as richly as any: "*Forasmech as* thu art a mayden in thi sowle," Christ promises Kempe, "so xalt thy dawnsyn in hevyn wyth other holy maydens"; and he will hear anyone who, after her death, "aske the any bone and belevyth that God lovyth the," as he hears those who pray to "Seynt Kateryne, Seynt Margarete, Seynt Barbara, and Seynt Powle" (52). Backed by such a guarantee, this "as if" annihilates spiritual and earthly rank, render-ing inner aspiration more real, more *effective,* than outer reality.

A different manifestation of "as if" annihilates time, leaping the gap between the past of Christ's life and death and the present of its re-enactment by Kempe: "Hys deth is *as* fresch to me *as* he had deyd this same day, and so me thynkyth it awt to be to yow and to alle Cristen pepil," she retorts to a priest who finds her weeping in the church-yard of St. Stephen's, Norwich; and in Rome she famously begins to respond to boy babes in arms by crying "*as thei* sche had seyn Crist in hys childhode," a practice she keeps up for the rest of her life (148, 86). Her contemplative recreations of the Passion bridge past and present in a related way, as she travels back in time in her body as well as soul, playing the part of a mourner when Christ is taken from the cross, and dis-playing her intense emotions to the church congregation among whom she is seated as they simultaneously enact the same events in a liturgical mode (191–94). The emo-tional and structural centre of the first half of Part I is the conflation of past and pres-ent and inner and outer space that takes places for Kempe at Golgotha, where for the first time "sche myt not kepe hirself fro krying and roryng *thow* sche xuld a be ded ther-for" (68). For those around her, as for the reader, Kempe here and elsewhere lives, suf-fers, and responds with an intense empathy that is a third, implied kind of "as if," al-beit one on which the *Book* puts great pressure. Her tears are a form of *imitatio Christi,* and by reading about them and her we can learn to experience the meaning of Christ's life translated into the world of fifteenth-century England: "Sadly he trad it and dewly he went beforn" as the second scribe puts it in his long prologue, as he explains how slander and suffering could be for her "*in a maner of* solas and comfort" (2). By presenting herself journeying to Jerusalem and being persecuted at the hands of others, and by structuring the *Book* as a *vita Christi,* Kempe indeed goes to great lengths to stress the correspondences between herself and Christ. As her insistence that her tears can intercede with God to save sinner shows, she believes with Julian that by participating in the Passion she helps complete it.[55]

The topos of "as if" has far more power in the *Book* than quantitative language, both because it often functions as the form in which Christ makes promises to Kempe and because of its intrinsic confidence that earth and heaven can be bridged by desire or divine fiat: that finite humans can aspire to infinitude. "As if" allows her to persist in her spirituality of embodiment and resist the pressure towards upward spiritual ascent her priest scribe wants her to map out for her readers. Just as, in the logic of simile, a concrete object is a more comprehensible point of comparison for an abstraction than is another abstraction, so in the *Book* the physical is in many ways actually closer to the infinite than the spiritual. "As if" equally legitimates the play of fantasy in which Kempe can enact the roles of saints, virgins, martyrs, and other exemplary characters, be chopped up like a stew for the salvation of souls, and become a figure for the whole of creation, as she unsuccessfully yearns to praise God aright (in the closing prayer) or as she is tossed this way and that by the earthquakes and thunderstorms of divine omnipotence (chapter 77). Kempe is vividly alive to the dangers that inhere in the proximity of her "as if" to that other "as if" enacted by the hypocrite she is accused of being; indeed, a whole episode of Part II is devoted to her defence of her reputation against a trivial charge of double-think (Part II, chapter 9). But as Rolle claims in *Incendium amoris* that even venial sin cannot last long in the contemplative consumed by burning love, so she has Christ assure her that any recipient of his unpredictable gift of tears is by definition authentic (205). Holy tears cannot be faked. Secure in this guarantee, after all the storm-tossed travels of her years of evangelism, pilgrimage, and trial, in which she physically enacts different religious roles (preacher, pilgrim, pauper, prophet) in the face of constant accusations of falsity, the "as if" of devout fantasy becomes Kempe's means of being many people in many places, and so lays the foundation of her claim to intercede for all.[56]

But even when God himself uses the phrase, "as if" is always as much about difference as it is about equivalence in *The Book of Margery Kempe.* Indeed, the uncertainty engendered by the "as if" of fantasy and role-play is pivotal to the *Book*'s teaching. This uncertainty is at least twofold, affecting Kempe's relationship both with God and with her community and readers. In her relationship with God, as we have seen, fantasy and desire are ascribed great performative power: enough to begin to remake the soul, the creation, and heaven itself. But even this power is limited by God's predestining will. When God says to her "Dowtyr, aske what thu wylt, and thu schalt have it," she begs him to have mercy on all, extrapolating with as much boldness as Julian from his love for her as a sinner to the demand that he forgive even Jews, Saracens, and heretics (141). But she can never wrest from God the "all shall be well" that allows Julian to proclaim an end to the anxiety that besets her. However often Kempe raises the issue, God insists on the reality of damnation—as in the sharp lesson he teaches her in chapter 59, with its grotesque diabolic visions of prick-wagging monks, priests, and Saracens—or evades her: "Dowtyr, thu xal wel seen whan thu art in hevyn wyth me that ther is no man dampnyd but he that is wel worthy to be dampnyd" (159). Nor can she wrest from him control of her tears: "Thu xalt not han thy desyr in this, thow my modyr and alle the seyntys in hevyn preye for the, for I xal make the buxom to my wil" replies the Godhead grimly to her plea to be left alone, and she must continue to walk the streets of Lynn in a body that may at any moment manifest to all that see the irresistible arbitrariness of his might (182). Uniquely privileged in her intimacy with Christ's Manhood (God's own "as if"), she is uniquely burdened in her relation to his Godhead. If Kempe is "a merowr" for others "that thei myth therthorw be savyd" (186), the divine image she refracts is multiple, showing fear as well as love. For all God promises her, he pledges nothing to humankind as a whole, and the pattern for holy living the *Book* draws offers hope of salvation only to those who, like her, submit themselves to the uncertainty of God.

For Kempe's community, and in very much the same way for her readers, to submit to the uncertainty of God was, and in part still is, to submit to the uncertainty of Kempe, whose life and claims for its meaning are the most flagrant examples of the "as if" topos in the *Book*. To live with her as husband or son, travel with her to Jerusalem, hear her confession in Bridlington, put her on trial in York, or submit to her sermon-busting crying in Lynn was to make and remake decisions about a person who imposed demands on those around her "as if" she were indeed a "synguler lofe." Even the characters in her visions sometimes have to puzzle her out, as when, at the Ascension, she sharply reproves the apostles who order her "to cesyn and be stille," or when St. Paul apologizes for the damage his injunction against women preaching has done her career (275, 160). Kempe is nothing if not self-conscious about her effect on those around her. As the history of modern reactions to it attests, reading the *Book* still involves making decisions about her today.[57] To refuse "as if"—for example, by refusing to work through the *Book* "as if" we were members of Kempe's community of supporters—is to refuse who she is. Yet much in the *Book* encourages us to make that refusal with a version of the accusations hurled at her by her mighty enemy, the preacher-friar William Melton: that she suffers "a cardiakyl er sum other sekenesse," or "hath a devyl wythinne hir" (151, 165).

There are, of course, signposts that point the discerning towards acceptance of Kempe's special status. God sends tokens to the people of Lynn to help them read her "as if" aright. The Carmelite Alan treasures one of these, the stone that knocked her down when it fell from the vault of the church of St. Margaret, understanding it as a "token of mercy," where the people obstinately take it as "a tokyn of wreth"; and after a period of being forbidden to speak with her he gives her "a peyr of knyvys, in tokyn that he wolde standyn wyth hir in Goddys cawse as he had don beforntyme" (22, 170).[58] Kempe's petitions to God on behalf of her community also serve to validate her; her prayers and advice help extinguish the fire that burned Lynn's guildhall to the ground, and she is the one to calm a woman driven mad, as she was herself, after the birth of her first child (162–64, 177–78). Her prophecies occasionally have social usefulness, but seem intended for the most part to draw community attention: to be tokens pointing to Kempe as God's token to Lynn, the city where she insists she will continue to live "as long as God wolde," however "meche pepyl was ageyn hir" (46–47, 154). On a structural level, the first section of the *Book* provides a different kind of token for readers, by convincing them of the intensity of Kempe's own enquiry into her visionary validity and the authority of her decision to push away doubt. Kempe is herself the *Book*'s bridge between earth and heaven, and to believe in her, as God promises, is to have available a secure means of crossing that bridge: "Thei that belevyn that God lovyth the thei xal ben blyssed wythowtyn ende" (52). For readers to repudiate her, on the other hand, is to risk having applied to them God's terrifying words about Melton: "Dowtyr, thu xalt be in cherch whan he xal be wythowtyn. . . . Ther is no clerk can spekyn agens the lyfe whech I teche the; and yyf he do he is not Goddys clerk, he is the develys clerk" (156, 158).[59] The hermeneutic instructions provided readers by the *Book* are thus no different from those that God offers Kempe. Just as she only receives God's grace when "thorw the mercy of owr Lord Ihesu Crist" she is "compellyd to belevyn stedfastly wythowtyn any dowtyng that it was God spak in hir," so it is for readers, who benefit from the *Book* only if they imitate those people in Lynn who realize that it is better not to "dowtyn not ne mystrostyn" in her, for "to hem that litil trostyd and lityl belevyd, peraventur was litil encres of vertu and of merite" (201).

Yet none of this means that accepting Kempe at God's estimation of her was ever easy. The *Book* depicts her and her closest allies themselves struggling from time to time with doubt or puzzlement. For all her determination to trust in God, sometimes Kempe's belief in her revelations must be "compellyd" by Christ. She experiences the knowledge that particular individuals are damned as "gret ponyschyng and a scharp chastisyng," bitterly resisting the pressure of divine certainty; and she never accepts the turmoil caused by her weeping or her prophetic gift (144, 219). Everywhere in the *Book* we see Kempe's ambitious self-understanding maintained through struggles kept visible in the long periods of anxiety, fear, and sickness that she suffers. On her return from her examinations from heresy in 1418, "God ponyschyd hir [for what?] wyth many gret and diver siknes" for eight years, and she is suffering from sporadic ailments as she dictates Part I to her first scribe five years after that (137, 219). Even before old age adds its burden, being Margery Kempe is a costly experience for the Godhead turns her life upside down with the storms of his omnipotence not once but over and over. If Julian's injunction that she must learn to trust her divine calling goes on being hard to put into practice, it is not surprising that Kempe's sense of difficulty is shared by her friends and by readers of the *Book*. Despite the ubiquity of revelation, in her life and *Book* God remains to a startling extent "an hyd God" whose reality must be found again and again (30). The *Book* demands readers believe in Kempe, but it also gives them every opportunity to number themselves among her doubters or opponents: "Margery, what xal ye now do?" says her confessor, at a point when even her priest scribe has turned against her; "Ther is no mor agen yow but the mone and vii sterrys" (155). For the whole sublunary order, believing in Margery Kempe, like holding onto any other manifestation of the "as if" that allows created beings to trust in the divine, can be tough work.

"Qwyke and gredy to hy contemplacyon in God"

Here, then, is the thinking that grounds the didacticism of *The Book of Margery Kempe* and gives the work its engagement with the complexities of its protagonist's life: Kempe's perception that the very difficulties she has had need to be shared with her readers in the same way they have been with her community, since such experiences are at the centre of Christian living. Kempe's life is a sign of the divine character, and the *Book* is meant to be such a sign as well. But even lucid signs are often rendered illegible by a sinful creation's distance from God. Thus Christian living consists of a process of decipherment, in which the light shone on the world by God's special friends, the saints, is an ever-present aid. The *Book* shines with this light, as Kempe shines for the people of Lynn. But unlike most saints, such as the virgin martyrs (who live a continual and so inimitable display of purity), Kempe's clarity of understanding must be fought for over and over again, like that of any ordinary Christian. Despite her singularity she remains just that: a type of devout lay living, a worldly sinner in need of God's pardon.

Unlike a saint's *vita, The Book of Margery Kempe* similarly invites readers to struggle with it in order to be edified by it. Not only does Kempe show herself, God's friend, fighting this struggle; she shows her supporters and the whole of Lynn doing the same. In this way, the *Book* continually tempts readers into refusing her, should their faith and trust not be supple enough to withstand, inviting them to play the part of her (and Christ's) persecutors. But it rewards readers' fidelity with an understanding of Christ as she and her *Book* reveal him, and with the promise of salvation, if they can become, like her, "qwyk and gredy to hy contemplacyon in God" (253). At least in this respect, the *Book* is more like *Piers Plowman*, in its attempt to absorb the reader into its inner processes by breaking down the distinction between reading and living, than any other Middle English religious work I know.[60]

Margery Kempe's paradoxical self-understanding and magpie-like approach to spiritual experiences do make singular sense and her *Book* makes sense too as a coherent literary project. Given the way it fashions meanings, it is also possible to guess part of the reason why the *Book* primarily presents itself as it does. Despite distancing devices (third person singular, passages of general exhortation), the *Book*'s overwhelming effect is one of immediacy, "as if" a voice is talking, rather than a pen writing. Uhlman is far from being the only scholar to comment on this effect.[61] The *Book* makes us feel we were there. Because this sense of "thereness" was vital to the *Book*'s purpose—because in it Kempe wanted to engage the reader in the texture of experience—it needed not to be written in a clerical voice whose note must be one of authority: of truth pre-known and pre-approved, not subject to testing. This may have been why she dictated her account to her son in the first instance, why the *Book* suppresses all mention of her discussions with the likes of Alan as she worked, and why her second scribe was so compliant even in Part II. For her readers' sakes as well as her own, Kempe needed to speak for herself, her God, and her community; the voice in her *Book* needed to proceed not only from sanctity and knowledge of God's privities but from her sense of herself as Everywoman.

Beyond these concerns, we can see in Kempe's project, in her way of getting it written down, and in its density of detail, the lineaments of a firmly local way of thinking. Despite its concern for humanity and creation, and despite its depiction of her travels, Kempe's *Book* is very much a book about Lynn and her place there. Even though the surviving manuscript was owned by the Carthusians of Mount Grace, in Yorkshire, it would have been for the people of Lynn that the *Book* was initially written, with the help of a priestly scribe qualified to produce an exemplar for future copyists in the town's dialect: the dialect that identifies "Mar. Kempe of Lynn" to the "dissolute personys" she encounters in London after her last pilgrimage (243). Presupposing a reader's knowledge of local geography, history, and politics, the *Book* might be seen as a Pentecostal gift by its author to the townsfolk who had reviled, gossiped over, used, and venerated her. Once she was gone, the *Book* would represent her like a relic or saint's *vita* with its promises to those who invoke the holy dead. And since Kempe's saintliness was the thing of paradox we have seen it to be, her textual relic would be the same: more a bone of contention than a thing of any inherent power to those unable to read aright, more a sign of the difficulties of earthly living than a promise of resolution. Alan of Lynn was precise in his choice of token to represent alliance with this two-edged sword of a woman: "a peyr of knyvys" (170).

Some of the knife-work the *Book* invites readers from Lynn to perform might seem at first to be for the sake of mere community pride. Kempe could have had confidence that most such readers would be her partisans during the first third of the *Book*, as they follow her career across England and Europe as their representative (and mayor's daughter), thrilling with xenophobic glee as she stands unabashed by bishops and archbishops, or insults the mayors of rival towns. But after the scene moves to her retirement in Lynn in 1418, which she refuses to leave even when Melton (a community outsider) threatens to displace her, the local reader's faith is tested. Not only is the community of

426 ■ VOICES IN DIALOGUE

Lynn represented as divided by the *Book,* it comes to represent in itself the division between false and true Christians: between the scribes and pharisees, with their horde of
followers and the faithful group of Christ's persecuted disciples. As we have seen, however clearly we are given to understand who is on God's side, who against him, such a
representation does not make faithfulness to Christ any easy task for the reader.

In the end it is the mystery plays that provide the closest analogy to *The Book of
Margery Kempe*'s theologizing of community and the "as if" that holds Kempe's career
together. Here, as in the plays, Jerusalem comes to England in all its doubleness (city of
sin and of redemption) and is reenacted by a local cast who confirm their solidarity with
themselves and Christian history and ritualize their conflicts and lapses from community. Kempe offers to sacralize Lynn for her readers as she did for her contemporaries by
treading in Christ's footsteps there. She perceives its people, its liturgical celebrations,
its streets irradiated by the haunting near-presence of the lamb of God. As any towns-
person might, she thinks of God partly through numbers, investing in the "as if" of devout fantasy for unimagined profit, working her spiritual business of intercession for
others more successfully than she ever worked her milling and brewing operations, but
according to an analogous logic, as the guilds in York performed plays appropriate to
their craft. She offers herself up for the reverence or scorn of readers like the figure of
Christ or Mary Magdalene, inviting the whole of her community, present and future, to
join with her in the "as if" of participation in holy living that is its redemption.

■ ■ ■

Defending herself that summer of 1417 against the charge of being a wolf in sheep's
clothing ("Thu wolf, what is this cloth that thu hast on?"), in brittle conversation with
a priest in York Minster, Kempe is at first silent (it is passing children who give the
answer, "Ser, it is wulle"), then reproves him for the "many gret othis" with which he
has berated her for not answering, exhorting him to "kepe the comawndmentys of
God and not sweryn so necgligently as ye do." In reply to his officious question—"the
preste askyd hir hoo kept the comandmentys?"—she states with sardonic simplicity,
"thei that kepyn hem." When the priest asks, "kepyst thu hem?" her final remark draws
all humankind, with fierce charity, into a single community of obligation: "Syr, it is my
wille to kepyn hem, for I am bownde therto, and so are ye and every man that wil be
savyd at the last." The priest "jangles" with her some more and then, like a demonic
temptation once it has failed, disappears suddenly, "that sche wist not wher he becam"
(120). Whether by men or by demons disguised as men, questioning Margery Kempe
in this tone never pays off, for she always wins a war of words. Yet as the anecdote
makes clear, *The Book of Margery Kempe* is not finally about words or the propositions

they make, for on their own these always turn into the sheepskin that hypocritically covers the wolf the "jangling" priest shows himself to be. The *Book* is about the demands made on Christians, alone and in community, and the powerful obligations that bind them to the difficult work of obedience to God.

Notes

Thanks to Amy Appleford, Ruth Evans, Claire Fanger, Richard Green, Fiona Somerset, and Jocelyn Wogan-Browne for their help with this essay, and Heather Hill for providing me with a sanctuary in which to write it. I dedicate it to Richard and Fiona, my wonderful former Middle English colleagues at the University of Western Ontario, who read it with their usual care when it was first finished in 1999, shortly before we began to scatter to the winds. *In memoriam.*

1. Quotations are from *The Book of Margery Kempe,* ed. Sanford Brown Meech and Hope Emily Allen, Early English Text Society *o.s.* 212 (Oxford: Oxford University Press, 1940); thorn, yogh, and u-v i-j variations have been modernized, the ampersand has been expanded to "and"; punctuation is my own. Chapter references are to chapters in Part I unless otherwise stated. For convenience, I prefer "Part" to "Book" in referring to the *Book*'s main subdivision.

2. For the events in this paragraph, see chapters 46–55. A good analysis is Ruth Shklar, "Cobham's Daughter: *The Book of Margery Kempe* and the Power of Heterodox Thinking," *Modern Language Quarterly* 56 (1995): 277–304. Kempe says she did leave Lynn to visit the tomb of Richard Caister in Norwich, shortly after his death in 1420 (147), and sometime in the 1420s ventured as far as Denny Abbey, near Cambridge (202–203), but these are local excursions.

3. See Paul Strohm, *Sir John Oldcastle: Another Ill-Framed Knight,* William Matthews Lectures 1997 (London: Birkbeck College, 1997).

4. In Bristol she meets Thomas Marchale (from Newcastle, chapter 44) and her former companion, Richard, the broken-backed man (first encountered in Rome and originally from Ireland) and dines with the bishop of Worcester (76, 109–10).

5. For Kempe's supporters, see D. S. Ellis, "Margery Kempe and King's Lynn," in *Margery Kempe: A Book of Essays,* ed. Sandra McEntire, Garland Medieval Casebooks 4 (New York: Garland, 1992), 139–59; Janet Wilson, "Communities of Dissent: The Secular and Ecclesiastical Communities of Margery Kempe's *Book,*" in *Medieval Women in Their Communities,* ed. Diane Watt (Toronto: University of Toronto Press, 1997), 155–85. There are hints in chapters 10–11 that, around 1412–13, Lynn clerics were actively promoting Kempe's trips to Norwich, York, and Bridlington. Not only does Christ tell Kempe that "My servawntys desyryn gretly to se the," after which "was sche wolcomyd and mech mad of in dyvers placys," as though "my servawntys" designates a network of devout people who are warned in advance of her coming, or who pass her from person to person (as happens in Norwich in chapters 17–18) (22). Chapter 11 describes this group as "Goddys servawntys, bothen ankrys and reclusys and many other of owyr Lordys loverys, wyth many worthy clerkys, doctorys of dyvynyte, and bachelers also in many dyvers placys," offering another term ("owyr Lordys loverys," also used by Julian of Norwich and Richard Rolle) for this same network (25). Caister's intervention on Kempe's behalf before the bishop of Norwich's officials apparently took place in 1413 (since after it

she prophesies his death seven years later), the year he met her, well before her other examinations (40). If there were "envoys pepyl" willing to have her summoned by "certeyn offycerys of the bysshop" this early, this strengthens the supposition that Kempe's career was a part of a larger devotional movement in Lynn and Norwich, and that her examinations had wider political implications.

6. On "author" applied to early women writers, see Jennifer Summit, *Lost Property: The Woman Writer and English Literary History, 1380–1589* (Chicago: University of Chicago Press, 2000). On the issue of authority in the text, see Sarah Beckwith, "Problems of Authority in Late Medieval English Mysticism: Agency and Authority in *The Book of Margery Kempe*," *Exemplaria* 4 (1992): 171–200.

7. John C. Hirsh, "Author and Scribe in *The Book of Margery Kempe*," *Medium Aevum* 44 (1975): 145–50; Lynn Staley Johnson, "The Trope of the Scribe and the Question of Literary Authority in the Works of Julian of Norwich and Margery Kempe," *Speculum* 66 (1991): 820–38; Diana R. Uhlman, "The Comfort of Voice, the Solace of Script: Orality and Literacy in *The Book of Margery Kempe*," *Studies in Philology* 91 (1994): 50–69; Lynn Staley, *Margery Kempe's Dissenting Fictions* (University Park: Pennsylvania State University Press, 1994).

8. Studies which touch on this matter include Clarissa Atkinson, *Mystic and Pilgrim: The Book and the World of Margery Kempe* (Ithaca, N.Y.: Cornell University Press, 1983); John Erskine, "Margery Kempe and Her Models: The Role of the Authorial Voice," *Mystics Quarterly* 15 (1989): 75–85; Wendy Harding, "Body into Text: *The Book of Margery Kempe*," in *Feminist Approaches to the Body in Medieval Literature,* ed. Linda Lomperis and Sarah Stanbury (Philadelphia: University of Pennsylvania Press, 1993), 168–87.

9. Much of the best work on Margery Kempe operates along these lines. See, e.g., Sarah Beckwith, "A Very Material Mysticism: The Medieval Mysticism of Margery Kempe," in *Medieval Literature: Criticism, Ideology, and History,* ed. David Aers (New York: St. Martin's, 1986), 34–57; Susan Dickman, "Margery Kempe and the English Devotional Tradition," in *The Medieval Mystical Tradition in England,* ed. Marion Glasscoe (Exeter: Exeter University Press, 1980), 156–72; Anthony Goodman, "The Piety of John Brunham's Daughter of Lynn," in *Medieval Women: Essays Dedicated and Presented to Professor Rosalind M. T. Hill,* ed. Derek Baker (Oxford: Basil Blackwell, 1978), 347–58.

10. See the helpful discussion of this issue by Sarah Salih, in her *Versions of Virginity in Late Medieval England* (Cambridge: D. S. Brewer, 2001), 170–72, who performs a version of the same conflation. For a critique, see Felicity Riddy's response to the present essay.

11. See David Lawton, "Voice, Authority, and Blasphemy in *The Book of Margery Kempe*," in *Margery Kempe: A Book of Essays,* ed. Sandra McEntire, Garland Medieval Casebooks 4 (New York: Garland, 1992), 93–115; Melissa Furrow, "Unscholarly Latin and Margery Kempe," in *"Doubt Wisely": Papers in Honour of E. G. Stanley,* ed. M. J. Toswell (London: Routledge, 1996), 240–51; Josephine K. Tarvers, "The Alleged Illiteracy of Margery Kempe: A Reconsideration of the Evidence," *Medieval Perspectives* 11 (1996): 113–24.

12. In Part II, written after the death of the first scribe, Kempe's son returns home with his wife but without their child, who has been left "in Pruce wyth her frendys" (also "Duchelond"); in the prologue, the English merchant has "a wyf and a chyld" in "Dewchlond," but comes to England with wife but without child (225, 4). The date of the scribe's death in 1431–32 can be estimated from evidence provided by the prologue: it happened more than four years before the revision of the *Book* was begun in the summer of 1436 (4, 6). The son likewise died in the summer or fall of 1431 (see note 19 below), shortly before his father John, who died after the draft was done (see 225, 30). Further, the prologue suggests a date around 1429–31 for the composition of the draft, "xx yer and

more" after Kempe's first visions, which coincided with her conversion, "3 or 4 yer" before her vow of chastity was taken in the summer of 1413 (3, 12, note to 33.24–25). The only consistent scenario is that the first scribe and Kempe's son are one and the same.

13. Bishop Repingdon and Alan of Lynn could have been responding to the surge of popularity of the writings of Birgitta of Sweden in the early fifteenth century, and the official approval her writings garnered, especially in relation to the foundation of the Bridgittine Syon Abbey in 1413, the year Kempe may have spoken with Repingdon. For the importance of Birgitta's writings, see Roger Ellis, "'Flores ad Fabricandum . . . Coronam': An Investigation into the Uses of the Revelations of St. Bridget of Sweden in Fifteenth-Century England," *Medium Aevum* 51 (1982): 163–86. Elizabeth of Hungary had also been quasi-officially recognized before 1413 by the inclusion of a passage of her *Revelations* in Nicholas Love's *Mirror of the Blessed Life of Jesus Christ,* ed. Michael G. Sargent, Garland Medieval Texts (New York: Garland, 1992), 18–20, another sign that women visionaries were at that moment held in high esteem by the orthodox (see further, next note). See also Rosalynn Voaden, ed., *Prophets Abroad: The Reception of Continental Holy Women in Late Medieval England* (Cambridge: D. S. Brewer, 1996).

14. The term "approvyd wymmen" is taken from an early fifteenth-century Life of Christ, the *Speculum devotorum* (1413–25), probably written for one of the first nuns of Syon Abbey, which uses the revelations of Birgitta of Sweden and Elizabeth of Hungary as a biographical source for Christ's life; see Jocelyn Wogan-Browne, Nicholas Watson, Andrew Taylor, and Ruth Evans, eds., *The Idea of the Vernacular: An Anthology of Middle English Literary Theory, 1280–1520* (University Park: Pennsylvania State University Press, 1999), Part I, excerpt 12:74. For Kempe's admiration for Birgitta, see, e.g., Gunnel Cleve, "Margery Kempe: A Scandinavian Influence in Medieval England?" in *The Medieval Mystical Tradition in England, V,* ed. Marion Glasscoe (Cambridge: D. S. Brewer, 1992), 163–78.

15. Despite the prologue's assertion that Kempe "had no wryter that wold fulfyllyn hyr desyr ne yeve credens to hir felyngs" (4), the first scribe was not chosen *faux de mieux;* the prologue is offering a thematically appropriate explanation for her choice as part of its presentation of her as a persecuted holy woman.

16. The second scribe's problems with his exemplar involved spelling and orthography, not morphology and vocabulary, despite his exasperated statement "it was neithyr good Englysch ne Dewch"—obviously this cannot mean that the original draft was written in a mixture of English and German (4): see the explicit to Part I, where the first scribe is said not to have written "clerly ne opynly to owr maner of spekyng" but to have made "trewe sentens" in his "maner of wrytyng and spellyng" (220). Kempe's son presumably used a script with German orthographic conventions and had trouble spelling words he did not use in his professional life (compare the second scribe's difficulty with German placenames in Part II) (233).

17. The closing prayer is not numbered as one of the chapters in Part II, and the chapter before it concludes with "Amen" (247). The prayer may have been part of the original draft, concluding what is now Part I of the *Book,* or be a product of the period between the two drafts.

18. Hirsh, "Author and Scribe," 150; Edmund Colledge, who actually intends a compliment to Kempe (and does not use all these epithets quite at once), is quoted from "Margery Kempe" in *Pre-Reformation English Spirituality,* ed. James Walsh (New York: Scribner, 1961), 222–23.

19. The *Book* states that the son and his wife "com hom on Satyrday," and that he fell sick at Sunday lunch "and leyd hym on a bed," after which he languished a month and died (225). It is hard to see how he could have written anything. (Despite this, Hope Emily Allen's note to *Book,* 225.11

also assumes the original draft was dictated during this brief period.) In the prologue, the second scribe's concern is not with how the original draft was composed but with explaining his delay in copying the *Book*. Kempe probably asked him to do this shortly after her son's death (before her departure for Prussia with her daughter-in-law eighteen months later), knowing the *Book* needed recopying and perhaps revision: since she did not initiate recopying *before* the son's death, she may already have wanted to supplement her draft. At all events, the draft and the circumstances of the son's death might remain associated in the second scribe's mind.

20. Even the dates do not fit. The son's death can be reliably dated to summer or fall of 1431, since it was around Easter 1433, eighteen months or more after his death, that his widow and Kempe embarked from Ipswich on their way to Danzig (notes to 225.13–14, 229.11–12). Yet Part I has Kempe working on the draft "the tyme of Advent befor Cristmes" (219).

21. Recent studies of the visionary-scribe relationship are in Catherine M. Mooney, ed., *Gendered Voices: Medieval Saints and Their Interpreters* (Philadelphia: University of Pennsylvania Press, 1999). Most of the essays in this volume construct a far more male-dominated picture of the writing relationship than I argue is visible in the *Book*.

22. See Wogan-Browne et al., *Idea of the Vernacular*, Part I, excerpt 1.15, note to 125.

23. Part I was begun in 1436, on 24 July (the day after the feast of Mary Magdalene), Part II on 23 April (St. Vital's Day) (6, 221). There may, of course, have been a gap between the copying of Part I and the composition of Part II.

24. Felicity Riddy, "Julian of Norwich and Self-Textualization," in *Editing Women: Papers Given at the Thirty-First Annual Conference on Editing Problems, University of Toronto, 3–4 November 1995*, ed. Ann M. Hutchison (Toronto: University of Toronto Press, 1998), 101–24.

25. *The Book of Margery Kempe* is full of indications of time, from the general "Another tyme" to the less general "Sone aftyr" to the specific "It befel upon a Fryday on Mydsomyr Evyn" (20, 21, 23). Indeed, the priest's only way of knowing that chronology was not being observed may have been the care the draft takes to point this out. A few chapters are much out of temporal sequence, like chapter 77, set "Whan the seyd creatur had first hyr wondirful cryis" but placed in a part of the book associated with a period more than a decade later (181). Others, especially the accounts of her travels and trials, follow chronological order over a long stretch. In either case, however, Kempe has thematic reasons for her placing of episodes, and the priest's suspicions about her memory bespeak his early difficulties in understanding the nature of her project.

26. Chapters often begin "On a tyme," "On a day," or with other markers that a new episode is beginning; their length varies, but sixty lines is typical. A few chapters seem arbitrarily divided or require subdivision. The long chapter 18 contains a passage beginning "On a tyme" that could have started life as an independent chapter. However, there seems to be wider confusion here (compare the anecdote at 45 with the incident raised at 38); perhaps a leaf containing a chapter division was lost in the exemplar. Divisions between chapters 35, 36, and 37 also seem forced.

27. The tonal importance of third-person narration in the *Book* is made startlingly clear by John Skinner's translation, *The Book of Margery Kempe*, Book-of-the-Month Club Spiritual Classics (New York: Book of the Month Club, 1999), which *silently* renders the text into the first person.

28. The passage is a defence of Kempe's fear of marriage to the Godhead that is easy to separate from its context, ending with a sentence that seems designed as a transition back to this context: "And therfor it was no wondyr yyf sche were stille and answeryd not the Fadyr of heveyn whan

he teld hir that sche xuld be weddyd to hys Godhed" (87). "It was no wondyr" parallels the phrase that opens the interpolation in chapter 28, "It is nowt to be merveyled" (70).

29. For Rolle's accounts of these experiences, see Nicholas Watson, *Richard Rolle and the Invention of Authority*, Cambridge Studies in Medieval Literature 13 (Cambridge: Cambridge University Press, 1991), chap. 2. Kempe's allusion to *fervor* quotes directly from *Incendium amoris* in its "as verily as a man schuld felyn the material fyer yyf he put hys hand or hys fynger therin"; compare "sicut si digitus in igne poneretur fervorem indueret sensibilem, sic animus . . . ardorem sentit veracissimum" (quoted in Watson, *Richard Rolle*, 113) (88). However, where Rolle is using a metaphor, Kempe literalises the image with her addition of "thow the wedyr wer nevyr so colde," just as she literalises references to *dulcor* and *canor*.

30. For another attempt to describe the structure of the *Book*, see Sue Ellen Holbrook, "Order and Coherence in *The Book of Margery Kempe*," in *The Worlds of Medieval Women: Creativity, Influence, and Imagination*, ed. Constance Berman et al. (Morgantown: West Virginia University Press, 1985), 97–110.

31. The events described in chapter 25 took place in 1431–32; see Meech and Allen, *Book of Margery Kempe*, Appendix 7, 373–74.

32. The gloss reveals its status as interpolation when its shifts back to the original narrative by repeating the sentence on which it comments: "And therfor, whan he had fallyn and grevowsly was hurt, as is seyd beforn, the pepil seyd, yyf he deyid, it was worthy that sche xulde answeryn for hys deth" (180).

33. John is alive in chapter 86 ("also thu askyst mercy for thyn husbonde") but dies at the end of chapter 76: the latter is thus obviously a silent addition to the original draft (212, 181).

34. As Meech notes, the works of John Capgrave are also products of Lynn, as is the English-Latin dictionary *Promptorium parvulorum*, compiled by the Dominican anchorite Galfridus Grammaticus, and are generally similar linguistically to one another and to both the *Book* and the *Gild Records* (x–xxxii). These documents attest to a standardization of written Lynn English at a time when the majority of Middle English texts were being copied in one or another version of Central Midlands Standard. For an analysis of Capgrave's language, see the introduction to his *Abbreuiacion of Cronicles*, ed. Peter J. Lucas, Early English Text Society *o.s.* 289 (1983).

35. For this sense of *frely*, see the *Middle English Dictionary* (*MED*), Frely 2. b.(c): "Without price or recompense, gratis," citing, e.g., *The Wycliffite Bible* (LV), Exodus 21:11.

36. Kempe's demand that her text be kept secret is not made to the priest but to his temporary replacement, but it still seems likely that the priest's role was meant to include those of literary executor and publicist.

37. The theme of the continual memory of Christ is found in a number of Anglo-Latin religious texts from the hymn *Dulcis Ihesu memoria* on, but was especially associated with Rolle, in part through the compendium of passages from two of his works called *Oleum effusum* (see Watson, *Richard Rolle*, 150–54, 301 n. 2). The *Book* does not name this work, but it is a common manuscript companion of *Incendium amoris*, described as read to Kempe in chapter 58.

38. Kempe interprets her mystical marriage to the Godhead partly within a mystical and erotic framework—Katherine of Alexandria, the original recipient of this spiritual grace, is present at the ceremony—but mostly in terms of a traditional association between God the Father and power (87). As a result, her marriage to the Godhead has the compulsory submissiveness of Griselda's

marriage to Walter in Chaucer's *Clerk's Tale,* with the compensation that she retains an erotic relationship with Jesus. For the theology of weather here, see *The Vision of Piers Plowman,* ed. A. V. C. Schmidt, Everyman Books (London: Dent, 1995), V.13–20.

39. The priest's desire to make Kempe's tears "mor sotyl" as her devotion becomes "mor fervent than it was befor" has some relation to discussions of the varieties of tears in texts such as Henry Suso's *Horologium sapientiae* (drawing on Cassian's *Collationes*). See, e.g., the distinction between fleshly and spiritual tears drawn from Suso in *The Chastising of God's Children,* ed. Joyce Bazire and Eric Colledge (Oxford: Blackwell, 1957), 186: "It is harde to knowe of suche maner teeris whiche bien of kynde and whiche bien aboue kynde." For the priest's use of "sotyl" here, see *MED* sotil 3. c.(b), citing Rolle's *English Psalter* (497): "My thoght and myn entent ere purgid of vile lustis . . . and made sutil and semely in the luf of ihu crist."

40. The death of fleshly desire is an important theme in *Incendium amoris* (see, e.g., chapter 11, in Watson, *Richard Rolle,* 128–29), while Rolle and Hilton agree that devotion to Christ's human nature belongs to a low level of the spiritual life. See, e.g., *Scale of Perfection,* Book I, chapter 35, which offers the famous formulation: "For a man schal noght comunly come to gostly delite in contemplacion of the godhed bot if he come first in ymaginacion by bitternes and compassion of his manhed"; and chapter 36, which explains that, in order to appear to the apostles in spiritual form, "it was spedefull to hem that [Christ] schuld withdrawye the bodily fourme fro here sight" and adds that the same is true for the devout (quoted from the forthcoming critical edition by S. S. Hussey and Michael G. Sargent; see also the single-manuscript edition by Thomas Bestul, TEAMS Middle English Texts [Kalamazoo, Mich.: Medieval Institute Publications, 2000]).

41. Contrast Julian's insistence that her assertion that the Son now sits on the Father's right hand, instead of standing at his left, is metaphorical: "But it is nott ment that the Sonne syttyth on the ryght hand besyde, as one man syttyth by an other in this lyfe. For ther is no such syttyng, as to my syght, in the Trynyte. But he syttyth on his Faders ryght honde, that is to sey, ryght in the hyest nobylyte of the Faders joy" (Edmund Colledge and James Walsh, eds., *A Book of Showings to the Anchoress Julian of Norwich,* 2 vols., Studies and Texts 35 [Toronto: Pontifical Institute of Mediaeval Studies, 1978], 2.544–45 [Long Text, chapter 51]).

42. Compare many passages of *Scale of Perfection,* Book II, although Kempe's and Hilton's versions of "visitacyons and holy contemplacyonis" of course differ markedly.

43. For *discretio spirituum* in late medieval England, see Rosalynn Voaden, *God's Words, Women's Voices: The Discernment of Spirits in the Writings of Late-Medieval Woman Visionaries* (Cambridge: D. S. Brewer, 1999). The discourse may have been more varied than this useful book suggests; Voaden focuses on the consciously conservative material stemming from the campaign to canonize Birgitta of Sweden, but both Julian and Kempe were evidently working in a less restrictive tradition, perhaps exemplified by two minor treatises of the *Cloud*-author, *Discretion of Spirits* and *Discretion of Stirrings.* Julian is quoting James 1:6.

44. Kempe's possible indebtedness to (and intertextual relationship with) Love's *Mirror* is discussed by Lawton, "Voice, Authority, and Blasphemy." For the discussion of the *Mirror's* intended readers as "symple creatures," see *Mirror of the Blessed Life,* 10. For Love's relation to the miracle plays, see Richard Beadle, "'Devoute ymaginacioun' and the Dramatic Sense in Love's *Mirror* and the N-Town Plays," in *Nicholas Love at Waseda: Proceedings of the International Conference, 20–22 July 1995,* ed. Shoichi Oguro, Richard Beadle, and Michael G. Sargent (Cambridge: D. S. Brewer, 1997), 1–17.

45. In Rolle's most systematic theological work, the twelve-stage account of spiritual ascent entitled *Emendatio vitae,* devotion to Christ's humanity is discussed as a branch of *meditatio* in chapter 8, while *fervor, dulcor,* and *canor* are given pride of place in chapters 11–12, after the earlier devotions have been left behind. See Watson, *Richard Rolle,* 207–21.

46. On Kempe as a prophet, see the excellent study by Diane Watt, *Secretaries of God: Women Prophets in Late Medieval and Early Modern England* (Cambridge: D. S. Brewer, 1997).

47. See Nicholas Watson, "Visions of Inclusion: Universal Salvation and Vernacular Theology in Pre-Reformation England," *Journal of Medieval and Early Modern Studies* 27 (1997): 145–87.

48. The most sustained attempt to explicate Kempe's tears theologically is Sandra J. McEntire, *The Doctrine of Compunction in Medieval England: Holy Tears* (Lewiston, N.Y.: Edwin Mellen Press, 1990), which cites a body of earlier studies. Parallels are sometimes drawn with women visionaries from continental Europe, especially Marie of Oignies, mentioned in the *Book* itself, but the fact that the priest scribe cites the *Stimulus amoris* and Rolle's terminology of *clamor* from *Incendium amoris* (where it has no reference to tears) besides his references to Marie of Oignies and Elizabeth of Hungary (153–54) suggests he is not aware of any single tradition that explains her behavior. For further discussion, see Roger Ellis, "Margery Kempe's Scribes and the Miraculous Books," in *Langland, the Mystics, and the Medieval English Religious Tradition: Essays in Honour of S. S. Hussey,* ed. Helen Phillips (Cambridge: D. S. Brewer, 1990), 161–76.

49. See Karma Lochrie, "*The Book of Margery Kempe:* The Marginal Woman's Quest for Literary Authority," *Journal of Medieval and Renaissance Studies* 16 (1986): 33–55.

50. I thank Andy Cockbain for pointing out to me how this passage presents Kempe's gaze at her fellow humans as sexualizing as well as sexualized.

51. On several of the issues raised in this and the next sections, see, Salih, *Versions of Virginity;* Janet Dillon, "The Making of Desire in *The Book of Margery Kempe,*" *Leeds Studies in English, n.s.* 26 (1995): 114–44.

52. See Julian, *A Book of Showings,* 2.486–89 (Long Text, chapter 45).

53. Kempe apparently assumes that her sinfully active sexual past makes her more alluring to God as well as to her fellow-humans; indeed, she seems to imagine that this past gives her a sexual advantage over the virgin martyrs that partly compensates for her lack of purity.

54. See Nona Fienberg, "The Thematics of Value in *The Book of Margery Kempe,*" *Modern Philology* 87 (1989): 132–41. For the specifically late medieval spiritual logic outlined in this section, see the important essay by Thomas Lentes, "Counting Piety in the Late Middle Ages," in *Ordering Medieval Society,* ed. Bernhard Jussen (Philadelphia: University of Pennsylvania Press, 2001), 55–91; also Eamon Duffy, *The Stripping of the Altars: Traditional Religion in England, c. 1400–c. 1580* (New Haven, Conn.: Yale University Press, 1992).

55. There are differences, however, between Julian's and Kempe's response to the Passion. Julian builds on her notion of the Passion as a manifestation of divine love which can become the basis, through empathetic participation, for human union with the divine. Kempe presents the event as so overwhelming that the only possible response is tears, not theology, and her picture of Christ as lover and judge owes little to meditation on his suffering.

56. "As if" also legitimates the recreation of Kempe's life in the *Book* as a work whose dialogues and presentation of events are primarily for edification. Vividly recreating reality in the manner of a *vita Christi,* Kempe presents her life "as if" it were more patterned than it was. A possible parallel

might be *The Testimony of William Thorpe*, whose protagonist is given just the sharp rejoinders and ability to take charge of events Kempe attributes to herself in all her trial scenes; see Anne Hudson, ed., *Two Wycliffite Texts*, Early English Text Society *o.s.* 301 (New York: Oxford University Press, 1993).

57. For a survey of modern reactions to Kempe, see McEntire, *Margery Kempe*, introduction.

58. For the use of tokens in late medieval England, see Richard Firth Green, *A Crisis of Truth: Literature and Law in Ricardian England* (Philadelphia: University of Pennsylvania Press, 1999), 264–82.

59. However, the *Book* never threatens recalcitrant readers with damnation. While Christ's speeches sometimes come close to this, the text always pleads for mercy. Hearing Christ's "And therfor I xal chastisyn hem [for refusing to acknowledge Kempe] as it wer for myself," she says, "Nay, derworthy Lord Ihesu, chastise no creatur for me. Thu wost wel, Lord, that I desyr no veniawns but I aske mercy and grace for alle men yyf it be thy wille to grawnte it" (159).

60. For analysis of *Piers Plowman* along these lines, see Nicholas Watson, "Conceptions of the Word: The Mother Tongue and the Incarnation of God," *New Medieval Literatures* 1 (1997): 85–124.

61. See Uhlman, "Comfort of Voice, Solace of Script."

Text and Self in *The Book of Margery Kempe*

FELICITY RIDDY

I have only once made a statement to a policeman, in which I described a road accident I had seen and he took it down in longhand. I was a practised talker, he a practised recorder, and the language that emerged was a peculiar mixture of idioms that wholly belonged to neither of us. The constraints must have included, now that I look back on it, his awareness of the audience we were writing for, which I only partly understood; my distress at what I had seen; his concern to establish whether I was credible or not; mine to underestimate my driving speed; his official authority; our different levels of education; our genders; the time available between the other pressures on our lives; the not wholly private place we met in. Between us and all this we brought into being the story of a death.

I think of this when trying to imagine the genesis of the text we call *The Book of Margery Kempe*, which is the title Wynkyn de Worde gave to the first printed version, not so much shortened as gutted. My statement, like the *Book*, was the product of the occasion of its creation, with all the constraints I have listed and probably more, and it was relational, in the sense that it arose out of and was embedded in social interaction: people meeting and talking at a particular time in a particular place. The story of the death was truthful, as I remembered seeing it out of the corner of my eye, which anyway is a slantwise position, but I have no way of knowing if it was true, and the language of the statement was not "mine"—it was the statement's. All this makes me think that Meech's question about Margery Kempe's book, which is also Watson's—"Whose language is it?"—is unanswerable, or can only be answered by "no-one's" and so is probably the wrong one to ask.[1]

Nicholas Watson, like Lynn Staley in her important book, *Margery Kempe's Dissenting Fictions*,[2] seems to need an author for *The Book of Margery Kempe*. This title is, of course, ambiguous: is it by her or about her? Is it like "the book of Troilus" or "the plays of Shakespeare"? This indeterminacy seems to dog much of our thinking. For Staley, the author is apparently a real woman called Margery Kempe who has written a work of biographical fiction in a realistic mode whose central character is also called Margery Kempe. The author's purpose in creating this character is to address contemporary social and religious issues. For clarity, Staley calls the author "Kempe" and the protagonist "Margery," and makes no claims for the veracity of Margery's story. The scribe, she suggests, is probably no more than a rhetorical trope; certainly his visibility in the prologue is intended as an authorizing device. It is not always clear whether Kempe is understood to be fictionalizing her own life (as many first-time authors do), or whether she has made up everything except the name of the central character and the historical personages whom the character encounters. Nor is it clear, once we have gone down this route, why we should not follow Sarah Rees Jones in arguing that the author is not a woman at all, but a cleric who has made up the story of a woman's life for his own purposes: "a book written by clergy, for clergy, and about clergy."[3] Ironically, perhaps, Staley's "Kempe" is a construct, if anyone is: we have a "Mar. Kempe of Lynne" in the text, but no evidence at all for an author of this name outside it.[4]

Nicholas Watson takes quite a different, more straightforward, and in some ways more old-fashioned view: instead of separating author and protagonist, he conflates them. Where Staley's interest in the *Book* is politico-religious, Watson's is theological. He needs an author, like Staley's, of the old humanist kind that knew what it wanted to say and said it; there is no room in either of their readings for a textual unconscious. Watson thinks the author is a real person called Margery Kempe who has composed an autobiographical narrative about herself in the third person; that it is a more or less accurate record of actual events; and that the text was transcribed, first by one scribe and then by a second, verbatim from Margery's dictation. Occasionally the second scribe has intervened in the organization of the original text he received, and has inserted some passages he has composed himself, as well as others composed by Margery Kempe (including the whole of book 2), but most of the text is hers. Although Watson imagines a scene of composition, it seems much less complicated than the one I have described above: she utters an unstinting flow of reminiscence and he writes it down in silence.

Can it possibly have been like this? The first version of the *Book* claims to have been written while the "creatur" was also looking after her infirm and incontinent husband: this means her ear must have been cocked while she talked, to listen for sounds of his distress; she must have broken off to feed him, or to catch him before he relieved himself in his chair, or to make sure his fire didn't die down; she must have had charge of the running of the house. Caring for him "lettyd hir ful meche fro hir contemplacyon" (181), we are told; it must also have interfered with the writing of the book itself. The present in which the *Book* was first written in the early 1430s was one in which its elderly protagonist fulfilled the role of Martha—of active domestic service—while the life that the text creates and yearns for is that of Mary—of contemplative interiority.[5] Moreover, this version was, as Watson argues persuasively, most probably dictated to the son, who must have triangulated the process in unspoken ways.[6] We are told something of his difficult relationship with his mother,[7] but nothing of his relationship with his father, although according to the *Book* they were all together in the house: the born-again son who had caused his parents such distress, the mother with her compulsion to get her life written, and the senile father in need of constant care. Producing a book in these circumstances must have been a physically and emotionally fraught business. It is the domestic product of the nuclear family that is brought into being with such economy at the beginning of chapter 1: "Whan this creatur was twenty yer of age or sumdele mor, sche was maryed to a worschepful burgeys and was wyth chylde wythin schort tyme, as kynde wolde" (6). The *Book* is a record of the mother's memories of trying all her adult life to escape the inevitabilities this sentence sets up—of marriage (note the passivity of "was married") and of motherhood, of the nuclear family itself. And of course the fact that the text does not explicitly identify the first scribe as the son, but leaves only a trail of suggestion, effaces its own origins in the inescapable nuclear family and implies instead that it has come into being through the kindness of strangers, to which the "creatur" habitually commits herself. By the time the second version came to be written, the situation had changed: son and husband were dead and the widowed "creatur" had her freedom at last, which she used to undertake the final reckless journey to Danzig. This version is represented as the product of the relationship with a priest that had its own fraught history, and they presumably worked on it, again, in the "creatur's" chamber in a house in Lynn during the spare time she had set aside for prayer. For both versions, the dictation model suggested in the first proem seems too simple: the prose has none of the repetitions and hesitations, the confusions of syntax, the "oh, sorry, I forgots" that we would expect if it were a verbatim record.[8]

That different kinds of language are used in the *Book* seems undeniable; it is nothing if not polyvocal, criss-crossed by all that direct speech with its conflicting subjectivities. I would prefer not to explore this in terms of authorship, though, but in terms of discourse.[9] The passage that Watson singles out at the end of chapter 28—the defence of Margery's roaring—is a case in point: not direct speech but a place where the narrative mode is temporarily suspended and moves into a different, preacherly voice. For Watson, this is not only preacherly discourse (which is how I would talk about it) but is literally an interpolation by the priest. He cites Latinate items of vocabulary— "inordinate," "compassyfe," "secretariis," "indued"—as evidence of this, without commenting on the fact that three of these four words occur elsewhere in the *Book*.[10] This approach, whereby pieces of text are allocated to different people, is necessary for Watson because he wants an author to whom he can attribute intentions and to whom he can ascribe a theology. Identifying an *auctor* to whom *intentio* can be attributed is, of course, a thoroughly medieval way of proceeding, and the strict separation of Margery Kempe from the scribe is endemic in discussions of the *Book*'s origins. I, on the other hand, want a text, produced I do not know how; I do not care if it is the combined work of a woman remembering and breaking off to do other things, a man asking questions, both of them searching for and arguing over the words to say it with: indued, inordinate, compassive, secretaries.[11]

In trying to explain why I prefer this kind of approach, it is worth rehearsing some of the peculiarities of the narrative, familiar though they are. The text names itself in the opening sentence of the first proem as a "tretys" (1), a term used of both writing and speech, which takes us straight to the heart of its ambiguities.[12] The proem goes on to emphasize its origins in different kinds of talk: "slawnder and repref," "wonderful spechys and dalyawns" (2), speaking and saying and counseling and communing (3–4). At the same time, it foregrounds its writtenness: it is a "boke" (5) whose production has entailed deciphering difficult handwriting in another "boke" (4), as so many medieval books must have done. The proem, most unusually, also describes the processes of re-composition that bring together oral and written modes: "And so he red it ouyr be-forn þis creatur euery word, sche som-tyme helping where ony difficulte was" (5). There is a temptation to bifurcate orality and writtenness, and then to align them with gender and estate—the laywoman talks, the priest writes.[13] This bifurcation has become very familiar in discussions of the relation between visionaries and their confessors/scribes.[14] Perhaps, though, we should pay heed to the doubleness of "tretys" and try to keep them together. The proem to the *Book* records what some sociolinguists now call "literacy events," embedded in sociability.[15] Instead of distinguishing oral and literate, this approach invites us to see reading and the production of texts as arising out of social relationships and situations that are established and maintained through talk, like my interview with the policeman. Literacy is not separate from orality, and "literacy practices" are shared by those who can and cannot read and write. In this case, the complex "literacy event"—a reading back to her, and rewriting of, the book of a woman's life, prompted by her recall both of the book and the life—is represented as the product of an equally complex set of personal relationships characterized by affection, obligation, timorousness, reproachfulness, guilt, and gratitude. The *Book*, that is, understands that texts are embedded in the processes of getting on with other people, getting them to do what we want, and doing things together with them; indeed, texts are themselves a mode of social interchange.

This model enables us to understand what looks like an odd blurring: writing seems to be represented as something that both the literate and the non-literate can do, which makes a nonsense of our categories: "Sum proferyd hir to *wrytyn* hyr felyngys wyth her owen handys, and sche wold not consentyn in no wey, for sche was comawndyd in hir sowle that sche schuld not *wrytyn* so soone" (3; my italics). The first "wrytyn" seems to mean "write down," and the second "compose." The latter sense recurs a little later, when we are told: "And sche was warnyd in hyr spyryt that sche schuld not *wryte* so sone. And many yerys aftyr sche was bodyn in hyr spyryt for to *wrytyn*" (5; my italics). But "wrytyn" cannot simply mean compose, of course; it must mean compose in written form, and thus conflates the processes of composition with those of copying, or simply does not want to distinguish between them. It is not only the "authorial" activity that conflates these two, however; the "scribal" activity is understood in this way as well. This is how the first proem ends: "And for this cause, whan he [the priest, that is] had *wretyn* a qwayr, he addyd a leef therto, and than *wrot* he this proym to expressyn mor openly than doth the next folwyng, whech was *wretyn* er than this" (5). The first "wretyn" seems to mean "written out," while "wrot" means "composed in written form." And what of the second "wretyn," which could mean either or both? The text that "was wretyn er than this" is the earlier version of the proem. If we interpret "wrot" as meaning that the scribe composed the first proem, then why not interpret "wretyn er this" in the same way? My point is that the text itself seems to be the product of a less clear sense of the distinction between composing and copying, between author and scribe, than Watson brings to it. All this confirms what I have already said: that trying to answer the question: "Whose language is it?" by separating the archaeological layers of its composition may be doomed to failure.

Better questions to ask—because they are answerable—might be narratological ones: "who speaks?" and "who perceives?" When we open the *Book* and begin reading the first proem, what voice do we encounter? Through whom are events focalized?[16] The first question is not a difficulty for Watson, who is clear that the voice at this point is the scribe's, while Staley thinks it is Kempe's pretending to be the scribe's. I am not sure that it is either. We might expect the pronouns in the opening sentence to be some help, bearing in mind Emile Benveniste's definitions, borrowed from Arabic grammarians: the first person is "the one who speaks"; the second is "the one who is addressed," and the third is "the one who is absent."[17] Here we have first and third, but not second:

> Here begynnyth a schort tretys and a comfortabyl for synful wrecchys, wherin *thei* may have gret solas and comfort to *hem* and undyrstondyn the hy and unspecabyl mercy of *ower* sovereyn Savyowr Cryst Jhesu, whos name be worschepd and magnyfyed wythowten ende, that now in *ower* days to *us* unworthy deyneth to exercysen hys nobeley and hys goodnesse. (1; my italics)

This sentence apparently begins from some position in which the "synful wrecchys," who are the implied readers, are "thei" or "hem" as distinct from the narratorial "us." Where the actual reader is positioned is not clear. Since there is no "yow" on offer, does the reader belong with "hem," the sinful wretches, or with the inclusive-sounding "ower" of the narrator? As the sentence proceeds, "we" and "they" seem to collapse into one another anyway: "to us unworthy" does not seem much different from "synful wrecchys," and if "thei" need Christ's "unspecabyl mercy," his "nobeley" is conferred on "us" without our meriting it either. So there isn't after all a real choice: this is not a text in which "we" are going to give advice to "them." The speaking position does not seem to be privileged, and as it goes on the voice continues to blur the boundaries between narrator and reader:

> Alle the werkys of *ower* Saviowr ben for *ower* exampyl and instruccyon, and what grace that he werkyth in any creatur is *ower* profyth, yf lak of charyté be not *ower* hynderawnce. (1)

The story that is going to be told, of the specific case of the "grace that he werkyth in any creatur," is for "ower exampyl and instruccyon" and "ower profyth": teller and reader are both included in those "owers." The narrating voice then goes on to say that the narrative will show "how mercyfully, how benyngly, and how charytefully he meved and stered a synful caytyf unto hys love." The "synful caytyf" harks back to the "synful wrecchys" of the opening sentence: now the readers and the read are barely distinguishable either. All this is very different from, say, *The Cloud of Unknowing*, which also starts with "Here beginneth":

> Here biginneth the prolog. In the name of the Fader and of the Sone and of the Holy Goost. I charge thee and beseche thee, with as moche power and vertewe as the bonde of charite is sufficient to suffer, what-so-euer thou be that this book schalt have in possession . . . .[18]

Here we have an utterance confidently positioned between "I" and "thee": an authoritative-sounding first-person narrator or speaker and a second-person narratee, bound by the reciprocal relations of first- and second-person pronouns, as well as by the "bonde of charite." The "I" in *The Cloud of Unknowing* appears frequently and invites identification with the author:

> Some might think that I do litil worship to Martha, that specyal seinte, for I lickyn hir wordes in pleining of hir sister unto these worldly mens wordes, or theirs unto hirs. And trewly I mene none unworschip to hir ne to theim.[19]

All of this is unlike the proem of *The Book of Margery Kempe*, which goes on to describe how it came to be written, and the priest who writes it becomes part of the story it tells. He, too, is presented in the third person as "the preste," not as "I," and he is not named. Who, then, is the "I" who makes a fleeting intervention in the text at the point at which it is describing the arrival of the first scribe?

> a man dwellyng in Dewchlond whech was an Englyschman in hys byrth . . . havyng good knowlach of this creatur and of hir desyr, *meved I trost* thorw the Holy Gost . . . . (4, my italics)

This "I" (though it may of course not be the same "I," since there are no guarantors of identity here), recurs at three other points in the text, as Watson points out (14, 44, 214).[20] He wants to allocate these "I"s to real people outside the text, to know where he stands and who is talking to him. I differ: they seem to me the product of the blurred boundaries between writing, narrating and reading, of a text for which authorship is not claimed.

This is, then, a curious textual world of first and third persons that merge into one another and in which "yow" is absent. The first person "who speaks" is barely a *person* at all: it cannot be identified with either Margery Kempe or the scribe, and does not engage in a relation with a second-person narratee. "I" is emptied of personal reference, and the assurance in the first-person pronoun that, to quote Benveniste again, "in saying 'I,' 'I' cannot *not* be speaking of myself" does not seem to hold, because there is no self for the "I" to speak of.[21] No-one occupies the narratorial subject position; that "I" is only a hallucinatory trick of syntax.

The third person is, says Benveniste, "not a 'person'; it is really the verbal form whose function is to express the *non-person*"; it is "one who is absent."[22] The treatise tells an anonymous life-story in which the narrator never refers to the protagonist, through whom the action is largely focalized, by her name. She is addressed as "Margery" by other characters within the text, but not until chapter 17 do we learn, almost by chance, it seems, that the "worschepful burgeys" to whom she is married is called "John" (34); not until chapter 45 do we learn from a remark attributed to the bishop of Worcester that she is "John of Burnamys dowtyr of Lynne" (109); and not till very near the end of the second book do we discover that her married name is "Kempe" (243). The current critical visibility of the person "Margery Kempe" is quite at odds with the indirect narrative strategies of the *Book*. (This is, incidentally, a difficulty with Watson's argument that the text is intended as a local saint's life, because saints, as we know from the litany, are nothing without their names.) The protagonist is always referred to by the narrator as "the creatur," "this creatur," or "the seyd" or "forseyd creatur." "Creatur" was used in religious contexts to mean "something created" (as distinct from the Creator), but it also simply meant "person." It seems to have been a slightly formal or distancing word, without indications of gender and not even used exclusively of human beings.[23] "Forseyd" gives the voice an official textual timbre, and "this" reinforces it: it is the "this" of legal depositions—"this deponent said"—which seems to indicate presence or at least adjacency.[24] The story is that of someone else nearby: readers are not invited to identify the protagonist with a narrating "I" who can in turn be identified with the author.

All this is related to the question of genre. Watson calls the *Book* an autobiography, and he also argues that it is a saint's life. Staley describes it as "sacred biography," though this seems to me to ignore the question of "who perceives?"[25] The *Book* is focalized almost entirely through the "creatur," who is presented from the inside as well as externally. Other characters are represented from the outside only, and from the "creatur's" perspective: their inner lives are not revealed, except insofar as they articulate these in direct speech.[26] The only exceptions are parts of the proem and some passages, such as those in chapters 24 and 25 discussed by Watson, that are focalized through the priest.[27] That is, the perspective is autobiographical, except there is the formal oddity that the narration is in the third person and not the first, keeping "who speaks?" and "who perceives?" distinct. In autobiography we are accustomed to first-person narration: the "autobiographical pact," in which author, narrator, and protagonist are identical, has been proposed as a hallmark of the genre.[28] More recently, the opening up of autobiography to include different kinds of life-writing, including diaries, memoirs, and letters, has eschewed these prescriptive approaches. Caesar refers to himself in the third person in *De bello Gallico;* Gertrude Stein is a character in her own life. Feminist criticism, moreover, has drawn our attention to the problems women have traditionally had in claiming the autobiographical "I."[29] Watson, who thinks that Margery Kempe dictated the story of her life in the third person, claims that "There is great pressure on an account that would refuse vanity at the same time as raising its protagonist to such a height." He does not ask, though, whether this pressure might be gendered. It is not, after all, a pressure felt in the most influential spiritual autobiography of all, Augustine's *Confessiones*, where the autobiographical pact is never in question; nor is "I" a problem in the memoirs of Guibert de Nogent or Peter Abelard. All of these describe their own remembered powerlessness, sinfulness, and humiliation, certainly, but from a present of writing in which their identities are shored up by their institutional roles as bishop and abbots. We might recall what Virginia Woolf says as she reads the new novel by the distinguished Mr A:

> Back one was always haled to the letter 'I'. One began to be tired of 'I'. Not but what this 'I' is a most respectable 'I'; honest and logical; hard as a nut, and polished for centuries by good teaching and good feeding. I respect and admire the 'I' from the bottom of my heart. But . . . the worst of it is that in the shadow of the 'I' all is shapeless as mist. Is that a tree? No, it is a woman.[30]

Making one's intimate life public in order to exemplify holy living; teaching; drawing moral distinctions about human conduct; criticizing those in authority: the things the *Book* seems to want to do were allowed to women much less readily than to men. The issue of the "I" seems to be not so much one of ungendered vanity as one of gendered access.

Treating the text as autobiographical does not mean treating it as historically true, however, as Watson seems to do. He says early on that he accepts that "the *Book* does often describe what happened" (397), and he opens with an account of "what happened" that ignores autobiography's slantwise view. Autobiography, or "periautography," which is James Olney's new-old word for it, is about the self rather than the world;[31] it is not about events but about the memory of events.[32] The *Book*'s main subject is the protagonist's "mende," a word which recurs and which means "mind," "contemplation," and "memory."[33] The lived life is a continuous and inchoate process, not meaningful or coherent in itself; the remembered life is made up of bits and pieces of the past that remain accessible to consciousness, some of them recuperative in a Wordsworthian way, while others, in Paul Valéry's words, "mordent nos coeurs dans l'ombre."[34] Autobiography—the textualization of memory—gives those bits and pieces a shape, but it is the shape that texts have, not that lives or memories have. Moreover, its emotions are the present emotions of recall, not those of experience. Over the last forty years or so there have been many challenges to the old humanist model of the coherent, pre-textual self that was apparently waiting to be written and could be read as unproblematically true, which is, I think, the model Watson uses. Against this, "The autobiographical subject," says Leigh Gilmore, "is produced not by experience but by autobiography."[35] It is in writing that the self is made, and postmodern accounts of the subject make it look much less stable than it used to be. Nevertheless, the autobiographical self that is brought into being by writing does not come from nowhere, either at the verbal level or at the level of narrative structure: it is fashioned out of whatever cultural bric-à-brac is to hand.[36] Watson suggests that at one point the priest tries to impose on the "creatur's" narrative a pattern of "a stage-by-stage ascent away from carnal towards the spiritual" (413) that contradicts the events, but of course this imposition need not be solely the priest's. We might think of it as part of the cultural bric-à-brac available to an elderly woman recalling her life, especially her inner life, and trying to explain it; one of the possible shapes to try on or discard.[37] Its source is clerical, of course, but since I think of selfhood in this text not as integrated and consistent but as in process—experimental, tentative, and contradictory—I do not need to account for the fact that a pattern is simultaneously asserted and belied by attributing this to the woman and that to the priest.

The fact that this model does not fit is related to the problem of the shadowiness of female selfhood. What other sources of the self were there? Women's lives clearly could not be shaped in terms of the ages of man—three, four, six or whatever—which were widely used throughout the Middle Ages.[38] The "ages of man" model provided the male poets of the previous generation—Chaucer, Gower, Langland, the *Gawain*-poet—with ways of thinking about the relation between the male body and its experience of time.[39] In some manuscript illuminations of the wheel-of-life motif, in which the ages of man are depicted in little roundels on a wheel, the nursing mother appears with her child in her arms, but as an illustration of infancy, not of motherhood.[40] That is, motherhood is represented as part of the male life-course (as it is in the autobiographies of Augustine and Guibert de Nogent), not the female one. No allowance is made in the standard depictions of Youth—Juventus, the phase when one is in one's twenties and early thirties—for fourteen pregnancies.

There were other templates that men used for women's retrospection, of course: the poets loved old women recalling their pasts. We might think here of the "Wife of Bath's Prologue" (or a nastier variant of it in Dunbar's "Tretis of the Twa Mariit Wemen and the Wedo"), which use what can be called the sexual reminiscence format.[41] This has a long history starting with Ovid and passing through the *Roman de la Rose*. In this tradition the elderly woman, like the Wife of Bath, recalls her sexual experiences in explicit terms, and the pleasures it offers are those of listening to a woman talking dirty. In *The Book of Margery Kempe* there is a fragmented history of this kind—the story of the "creatur's" sexual relations with her husband, an account of an affair that came to nothing, and of her sexual fantasies. It is not a dirty story, though, but a sad and comic one, in which the identities of wife and mother cannot be kept apart as they are with the Wife of Bath, but are inseparable. One problem for the "creatur" about her sexuality is not that it is pleasurable, as it is represented as being for the Wife of Bath, but that the outcome of that pleasure is fourteen children and going "owt of hir mende."[42]

Another problem, as many commentators have pointed out, is that sexuality produces the text's unappeasable sense of its protagonist's defectiveness. By the second chapter of book 2, the "creatur" is represented as a widow living on her own in Lynn; since the beginning of book 1 she has been a wife. Understood as a life-cycle phase—as in the triad, maid-wife-widow—wifehood in late medieval England usually seems to have meant social adulthood and the status that derived from a legal and spiritual relationship with a man. The *Book*'s opening sentence, which I have already quoted, resonates with this optimistic secular status: "sche was maryed to a worschepful burgeys." Conflicting with the social esteem in which bourgeois wifehood was held, though, was the disparagement produced by another medieval triad, the spiritual hierarchy, virgin-widow-wife, that circulated in clerical discourses. As a way of categorizing female sexuality, this triad had been a commonplace of Christian thought since the fourth century; according to this valuation, virginity earned the hundredfold reward of the parable of the sower, continent widowhood the sixtyfold, and chaste marriage only the thirtyfold. In terms of this triad, being a wife—or rather not being a virgin—is a failure; it is the lowest rung of the hierarchy, producing an insatiable guilt that ravages the heart. Yet, of course, these two accounts of wifehood are in constant tension within the text: the spiritual may be the one that is explicitly endorsed, but the claims of secular wifehood are also constantly and ac-cusingly voiced—through John Kempe, through the people who are baffled by the white clothes, through the husbands who fear she is leading their wives away, through the men who tell her to go and card and spin like other women do.[43]

The piece of cultural bric-à-brac through which remembered guilt can be spoken is, of course, confession. Within the *Book*, right from the start the "creatur's" practice of confession is represented as a mode of self-narration: the opening crisis is precipi-tated when "sche . . . sent for hir gostly fadyr . . . in ful wyl to be schrevyn of *alle hyr lyfe-tym* as ner as sche cowed" (7; my italics). Later the "creatur" is given permission to go to confession several times a day, and she seems to be driven by a desire to tell and retell her own life. She pins down the vicar of St. Stephens, Norwich, for example, and "schewyd hym al hyr maner of levyng *fro hyr chyldhod*" (38; my italics). She does the same thing with an English friar in Constance: "Than sche went to that worshepful man and schewyd hym hire lyfe *fro the begynnyng unto that owyr* as ny as sche mygth in confession" (63; my italics). Subsequently, the reader is told of a priest attached to a chapel in St. Mar-garet's, Lynn, to whom

> sche schewyd *al hir lyfe as ner as sche cowde fro hir yong age*, bothe hir synnes, hyr labowrys, hir vexacyons, hir contemplacyons, and also hir revelacyons and swech grace as God wrowt in hir thorw hys mercy, and so that preyste trustyd ryth wel that God wrowt ryth gret grace in hir. (169; my italics)

The telling of her life-story is part of the "creatur's" life: she is represented as a com-pulsive autobiographer.

The "creatur's" written confessional narrative of selfhood begins, not with her "chyldhod" but with the terrible first experience of childbirth.[44] This can be linked with Watson's emphasis on the embodiedness of the *Book*'s protagonist, which he does not present as gendered either. It is, of course, a specifically female crisis, in a way that the initiating illness in Julian of Norwich's *A Revelation of Love* is not. Afraid that she is going to die, the "creatur" is tormented by the need to make her confession to a priest, in particular to confess "a thyng in conscyens whech sche had nevyr schewyd beforn that tyme in alle hyr lyfe" (6–7). She is unable, though, to express the unconfessed sin; she wants to speak her whole life—"alle hyr lyfe-tym"—but is unable to do so. She is pre-vented, the reader is told, by her confessor's disapproval, which carries with it a whole history of male silencing of women's lives: he "gan scharply to undyrnemyn hir er than sche had fully seyd hir entent, and so sche wold no mor seyn for nowt he mygth do" (7). It is at this moment of speechlessness that selfhood dissolves into breakdown. The "crea-tur" is released from dissolution by her first vision, and here the text uses another source of selfhood: that offered by holy women's visionary writing. Like confession, this writing interiorizes, but it provides a very different subject position, releasing the "creatur" from guilty and submissive creatureliness. The first vision is of Jesus, who sits on her bed in a purple robe and says to her: "Dowtyr, why hast thou forsakyn me, and I forsoke nevyr the?" (8) This is the first "I" in the narrative, apart from that non-personal narratorial "I" that flickered on to the page once in the proem. Jesus's voice is part of an internal dialogue that runs through the *Book;* his utterances and the discussions the "creatur" has with him are a means whereby the protagonist speaks to, for, and about herself.[45] A very striking feature of the *Book*'s visions, as compared with those of other holy women that were in circulation at the time—the revelations of Birgitta of Sweden and Julian of Norwich, for example—is that in this text they are so exclusively focused on the personal. Speaking as Christ, the protagonist—because Christ is always represented as part of her inner experience—claims the first person. And his words, "Dowtyr, why hast thow forsakyn me, and I forsoke nevyr the?" explain why the first person has hitherto been personless and the second person absent: "thou" and "I," and "thee" and "me" are needed to bring the protagonist's riven selfhood into communion with itself. To quote Benveniste again: "neither of the terms ["I" and "you"] can be conceived of without the other; they are complementary, . . . opposite, and at the same time, they are reversible."[46] They are not used to establish a relationship between narrator and narratee or reader, with which, as I have already intimated, the text is remarkably unconcerned. Rather they are a means of simultaneously figuring selfhood as internally fragmented and of holding out the possibility of connectedness.

Perhaps we can see this as a form of late medieval lay selfhood produced by changes in the theory and practice of confession. Linda Georgianna has elegantly charted the development of a subjective and internalized "contritionist" theory of confession in the twelfth century, to which the necessity for absolution from a priest was added at the Fourth Lateran Council in 1215.[47] By the fourteenth century, it seems, vernacular manuals for laypeople had produced an interiorized selfhood that was characterized by the tender conscience, watchfully in judgement on remembered actions, and the contrite heart, confident of release from the burden of that judgement. Georgianna writes of confession as producing "an internal voice, operating constantly, that urges repentance and simultaneously assures forgiveness through God's mercy."[48] This seems to apply directly to the "creatur," except that for her there is not one voice but two, and except that Georgianna's analysis does not take account of how far apart repentance and forgiveness may be. Repentance is the powerless position in the internal dialogue—it is the position of the "creatur"—while forgiveness is the Creator's unreachable position of power. The odd episode in which the "creatur" saw Jesus standing above her "so ner that hir thowt sche toke hys toos in hir hand and felt hem, and to hir felyng it weryn as it had ben very flesch and bon" (208), about which Watson is faintly ironic, may draw on standard depictions of the Ascension in which he is already disappearing out of sight and only his feet are still within the pictorial frame.[49] "Homly" and intimate though he may be, his forgiveness seems always just about to go out of reach. Watson seems to be responding to the text's riven selfhood when he says that "Kempe presents her life as following two, apparently contradictory, trajectories: towards ever greater perfection on the one hand, and towards ever closer identification with the sinful world around her on the other" (418). When he says that "she can never love enough, pray enough, cry enough," he catches very well the unappeasableness that Jesus never fully assuages.

"For despite her singularity," Watson writes, "she remains [an ordinary Christian]: a type of devout lay living, a worldly sinner in need of God's pardon." I wonder whether the type of devout lay living that the text adumbrates is as ordinary as it seems. A feature which is reported but never explained is the bellowing that develops in the Holy Land and which lasts for years. The bellowing is different from the weeping, which has an established pedigree as a sign of holiness and contrition: the bellowing is reported as terrifying even to the "creatur" herself. She turns the colour of lead with the effort to keep the noise in check, but it bursts out of her. It signals the limits, in so loquacious a text, of what can be articulated, but is quite unlike the "unspeakability" trope that is used on occasion to suggest the point at which the human cannot utter the divine. Pascal has suggested that "In all autobiographies there is a cone of darkness at the centre, even in those so outstanding as psychological documents . . . . It seems to be required of the autobiographer that he [*sic*] should recognize that there is something unknowable in him."[50] The holy woman as bellower seems to suggest such a cone of darkness. An English mid-fourteenth-century confessors' manual, advising priests on what sins to expect from different estates, has a section "Concerning married women and also widows and other sexually-experienced women."[51] The confessor is to ask, among other things, "if they have worn extravagant, vainglorious, outlandish and inordinate apparel on their heads"; "if they have not obeyed their husbands . . . because many women despise their husbands and withdraw from them, dwelling apart"; if they have committed adultery; if they are hypocritical, "because many women pretend they are holy, simple and devoted to God and his saints, greatly frequenting churches and praying and fasting, and yet inwardly they are full of the demon."[52] The limited self-understanding of the "creatur" in the *Book of Margery Kempe* can be read as the product of assumptions about married women of this kind, no doubt shared by clerics and laypeople alike. The sins that she accuses herself of seem remarkably like those on this list: the "creatur" assents to the ways in which her culture defines her. The bellowing, though, suggests that there is something else to which she does not assent, which she tries to repress and which is too unspeakable to be put into words. Are these roars of rage at the good husband who was never quite good enough, and lived too long? At year in, year out of childbearing? At being Martha and wanting to be Mary?

There is a famous passage to which I have already referred in passing, when, making for Beverley after being cleared of heresy at York, the local men whom the "creatur" meets say to her: "Damsel, forsake this lyfe that thu hast, and go spynne and carde as other women don, and suffyr not so meche schame and so meche wo" (129). This life that she has, which is so unlike that of other townswomen, is the mixture of "synnes, . . . labowrys, . . . vexacyons, . . . contemplacyons, and . . . revelacyons" which she had confessed to the priest of St Margaret's, Lynn. The conversations with Jesus elicit his approval for the singular form of contemplative lay piety that this life represents. At one point he distinguishes between the external life of fasting, penance, prayer, and almsgiving[53] and the internal life of "thynkyng in thy mende" (90):

> For I telle the, dowtyr, thei that arn gret fastarys and gret doers of penawnce thei wold that it schuld ben holdyn the best lyfe; also thei that gevyn hem to sey many devocyons thei wold han that the best lyfe, and thei that gevyn mech almes thei wold that that wer holdyn the best lyfe. And I have oftyntymes, dowtyr, told the that thynkyng, wepyng, and hy contemplacyon is the best lyfe in erthe. (89)

It is not surprising that Jesus, the product of the text's focus on the "mende," should be made the advocate of a contemplative way of life. *The Book of Margery Kempe* does not revalue the active life, as some other late medieval writers were doing, nor does it exemplify the mixed life that Walter Hilton had defined in a text written only a generation earlier. Instead it argues, conventionally, for the primacy of the contemplative life but, wholly unconventionally, locates that life in the born-again mother of fourteen bellowing her way round Europe. As if.

Notes

1. "One cannot present facts of the language in the extant manuscript of *The Book of Margery Kempe* until one has given the best answer one can to the question, 'Whose language is it?'" See *The Book of Margery Kempe*, ed. Sanford Brown Meech and Hope Emily Allen, Early English Text Society *o.s.* 212 (Oxford: Oxford University Press, 1940), vii.

2. Lynn Staley, *Margery Kempe's Dissenting Fictions* (University Park: Pennsylvania State University Press, 1994).

3. Sarah Rees Jones, "Margery Kempe and the Bishops," in *Medieval Women: Texts and Contexts in Late Medieval Britain*, ed. Jocelyn Wogan-Browne et al. (Turnhout: Brepols, 2000), 377–91.

4. There is documentary evidence that a woman named Margery Kempe was living in Lynn in the spring of 1438 when she joined the Trinity Guild. (See Meech and Allen, *Book of Margery Kempe*, 358–59.) There is no evidence that this woman was the author of the *Book* or that it is about her life. Even if we assume (as I do) that the *Book* is autobiographical and the name of the protago-

nist a way of letting us know the name of the author, then there is still no reason why Margery Kempe, author, should be the person who joined the Trinity Guild. Why not a daughter-in-law? Sister-in-law? Cousin? Niece?

5. For a historical overview of the idea of the two lives of action and contemplation, see Giles Constable, "The Interpretation of Mary and Martha," in *Three Studies in Medieval Religious and Social Thought* (Cambridge: Cambridge University Press, 1995), 1–141.

6. Watson's argument that the first scribe was the reprobate son, and that the writing was done while he was on his first visit to England rather than his second, is, I think, persuasive. The proem says he "dwellyd wyth the forseyd creatur tyl he had wretyn as mech as sche wold tellyn hym for the tym that thei wer togydder. And *sythen* he deyd" (4; my italics). The common assumption that the son wrote it during his second visit, while on his deathbed, seems to rest on interpreting "sythen" as implying that the death was sequential upon the writing. Elsewhere in the text, "sythen" can mean "later" and is used for events that are far apart in time. See a few lines previously: "a man dwellyng in Dewchlond whech was an Englyschman in hys byrth and *sythen* weddyd in Dewchland" (4).

7. At the time of writing mother and son were reconciled, but relationships carry their pasts with them.

8. The proem says that the first scribe was a layman from Lynn working in Germany and ignorant of local orthographic conventions who wrote "as mech as sche wold tellyn hym" (4). Watson's argument that this first version "may have looked a lot like Part I of the revised version" is a difficulty. Could an amateur scribe have written from dictation, not an easy thing to do? And who eliminated the verbal and syntactical hallmarks of the verbatim utterance? These questions are more easily answered in respect of the second scribe, who may (as Watson suggests) have been a professional. He could have had experience of preparing documents for an ecclesiastical court. Witnesses' depositions were told in the first person and translated into the third person by the scribe, as part of the process of rendering them into legible and succinct prose. (See *Love and Marriage in Late Medieval London*, ed. and trans. Shannon McSheffrey [Kalamazoo, Mich.: Medieval Institute Publications, 1995], for a convenient assemblage of such texts.)

9. I am obviously influenced here by the last paragraph in Michel Foucault, "What Is an Author," trans. J. Harari, in *The Foucault Reader*, ed. Paul Rabinow (Harmondsworth: Penguin Books, 1991), 101–20, at 119–20.

10. See the following passages: "delectabyl thowtys, fleschly lustys, and inordinat lovys" (181); "thei toke her leve eythyr of other wyth compassyf treys" (19); "to prechyn mech of hys Passyon so compassyfly and so devowtly that sche myth not beryn it" (167); "for grace and vertu wyth whech sche was indued thorw the strength of the Holy Gost" (2); "sche was wel lernyd in the lawe of God and indued with grace of the Holy Gost" (40). "Compassyfe," according to *Middle English Dictionary*, occurs only in *The Book of Margery Kempe* and once in Guy de Chauliac, while this example of "compassyfly" is unique. (Harder to account for than these examples, I think, is the little English phrase "at eye," which seems to occur only here. The text's usual preposition is "with".) All my quotations are from Lynn Staley, *The Book of Margery Kempe* (Kalamazoo, Mich.: Western Michigan University for TEAMS, 1996), though page references are to the EETS edition (see note 1) in conformity with Watson's practice. I should like to record my gratitude to Professor Staley and TEAMS for publishing this edition in electronic form at http://www.lib.rochester.edu/camelot/teams/tmsmenu.htm, thereby making a searchable text available to the scholarly community.

11. Robert C. Ross, "Oral Life, Written Text: The Genesis of the Book of Margery Kempe," *Yearbook of English Studies* 22 (1992): 226–37, is one of the few critics to suggest that the text is the product of collaboration between a questioning priest and a remembering woman.

12. "Tretys" in Middle English is used both of written documents and conversation: Chaucer uses it in both senses. See *Middle English Dictionary*, tretis(e n. 1. (a) and 2. (a), and quotations.

13. Diana R. Uhlman, "The Comfort of Voice, the Solace of Script: Orality and Literacy in *The Book of Margery Kempe*," *Studies in Philology* 91 (1994): 50–69, addresses the "Great Dichotomy" between oral and literate which until recently has dogged literacy studies.

14. See the nuanced discussions in Catherine M. Mooney, ed., *Gendered Voices: Medieval Saints and Their Interpreters* (Philadelphia: University of Pennsylvania Press, 1999).

15. See, for example, David Barton and Mary Hamilton, "Literacy Practices," in *Situated Literacies: Reading and Writing in Context*, ed. David Barton, Mary Hamilton and Roz Ivanič (London and New York: Routledge, 2000), 7–15.

16. "Point of view," the tool put to such effective use by Wayne Booth in *The Rhetoric of Fiction* (Chicago: University of Chicago Press, 1961), has now been divided between narration and focalization, between "who speaks?" and "who perceives?" See Gérard Genette, *Figures III* (Paris: Editions de Seuil, 1972), trans. Jane E. Lewin as *Narrative Discourse* (Ithaca, N.Y.: Cornell University Press, 1980); see also Mieke Bal, *Narratology: Introduction to the Theory of Narrative*, trans. C. van Bohemmen (Toronto: University of Toronto Press, 1985). Focalization is the angle from which the story is told, the prism on events.

17. My starting-point here is James Olney's discussion of Benveniste in *Memory and Narrative: The Weave of Life-Writing* (Chicago: University of Chicago Press, 1998), 245–46. See Emile Benveniste, *Problems in General Linguistics* (Coral Gables, Fla: University of Miami Press, 1971), 197. This work has been drawn on regularly in autobiography studies, from Lejeune to Gilmore.

18. Phyllis Hodgson, ed., *The Cloud of Unknowing and The Book of Privy Counselling*, Early English Text Society *o.s.* 218 (London: EETS, Oxford University Press, 1943), 1.

19. Ibid., 49–50.

20. Ross adds 59.23, "my Lord of Norwych Alnewyk"; at 34.25–26 "us" and "we" are also used.

21. Benveniste, *Problems in General Linguistics*, 197.

22. Ibid., 198.

23. See *Middle English Dictionary*, creature n. 1. (a) and 2. (b).

24. See the useful discussion of anaphoric "this" in David Burnley, *The Language of Chaucer* (London, 1983), 23–25. I am grateful to my colleague Matthew Townend for this reference.

25. Staley's claim that "Margery's experience is described by an omniscient, third-person narrator" (*Margery Kempe's Dissenting Fictions*, 35) ignores the issue of focalization, which is a limit on omniscience.

26. Those great fourteenth-century narratives of the inner life—Langland's *Piers Plowman* and Chaucer's *Troilus and Criseyde*—are both quite different in this respect. *Piers Plowman* uses a narrating "I" who is also the protagonist through whom the inner and outer action is focalized. The "I" of *Troilus and Criseyde* is not the protagonist but an omniscient narrative position, with access to the unspoken thoughts of Troilus, Criseyde, and Pandarus alike, so the focalization constantly shifts. (There are, of course, moments in the poem when this "omniscient narrative position" imposes limits on itself and claims not to know the characters' motives.) The poem's mode of narra-

tion allows for irony, in the sense that it presents other views of the characters than their own. In *The Book of Margery Kempe*, focalization through the protagonist produces a character who is created without irony (which is often read as lack of self-awareness), although not without dissension: other views of her than her own are presented frequently in the direct speech addressed to her.

27. It would be easier to think of the text as biographical, rather than autobiographical, if access were granted to the thoughts of other characters and if we were told what they were doing when the protagonist is not there. It is often commented on that John Kempe, for example, makes only sporadic entry into the text and only in relation to the protagonist. He has no independent existence as father, merchant, parishioner, or citizen. It is striking that the only actions that take place outside the purview of the protagonist are those of the priest, her collaborator. His account of his experiences is of course part of her experience, so not independent either.

28. "Pour qu'il y ait autobiographie (et plus generalement littérature intime) il faut qu'il y ait identité de *l'auteur*, du *narrateur* et du *personage*" (In order for there to be autobiography [and intimate literature more generally], *author, narrator* and *protagonist* must be identical) (Philippe Lejeune, *Le Pacte autobiographique* [Paris: Editions de Seuil, 1975], 15). Lejeune has since modified this position.

29. See the works cited below in note 31.

30. Virginia Woolf, *A Room of One's Own* (London: Grafton Books, 1977), 95.

31. Roy Pascal, *Design and Truth in Autobiography* (London: Routledge and Kegan Paul, 1960). The "centre of interest [of autobiography] is the self, not the outside world, though necessarily the outside world must appear so that, in give and take with it, the personality finds its peculiar shape" (9). Despite the fact that Pascal's humanist approach is at times oppressively masculinist and judgmental, nevertheless his book foreshadows the redirection of autobiography studies that took place from around 1970 under the influence of structuralism, post-structuralism, and feminism. Some of the seminal work (apart from works cited in other notes) is: James Olney, *Metaphors of Self: The Meaning of Autobiography* (Princeton, N.J.: Princeton University Press, 1972); Philippe Lejeune, *Le Pacte autobiographique* (Paris: Editions de Seuil, 1975); and Philippe Lejeune, "Le pacte autobiographique (bis)," in *Moi aussi* (Paris: Editions de Seuil, 1986); James Olney, ed., *Autobiography: Essays Theoretical and Critical* (Princeton, N.J.: Princeton University Press, 1980), which includes Georges Gusdorf's article "Conditions and Limits of Autobiography," trans. James Olney, first published in French in 1956; Domna Stanton, ed., *The Female Autograph* (Chicago: University of Chicago Press, 1984); Sidonie Smith, *A Poetics of Women's Autobiography: Marginality and the Fictions of Self-Representation* (Bloomington and Indianapolis: Indiana University Press, 1987); Shari Benstock, ed., *The Private Self: Theory and Practice of Women's Autobiographical Writings* (London: Routledge, 1988); Bella Brodzki and Celeste Schenck, eds., *Life/Lines: Theorizing Women's Autobiography* (Ithaca, N.Y. and London: Cornell University Press, 1988); M. Freeman, *Rewriting the Self: History, Memory, Narrative* (New York: Routledge, 1993); Leigh Gilmore, *Autobiographics: A Feminist Theory of Women's Self-Representation* (Ithaca, N.Y., and London: Cornell University Press, 1994); Kathleen Ashley, Leigh Gilmore, and Gerald Peters, ed., *Autobiography and Postmodernism* (Amherst: University of Massachusetts Press, 1994); P. J. Eakin, *How Our Lives Become Stories: Making Selves* (Ithaca, N.Y.: Cornell University Press, 1999). There is a valuable narratological discussion of "Récit fictionnel, récit factual" in Gérard Genette, *Fiction et diction* (Paris: Editions de Seuil, 1991), 65–96.

32. James Olney, *Memory and Narrative*, xv.

33. See *Middle English Dictionary*, mind(e n. 1. (a); 2; and 3. (a, b, c).

34. I owe my knowledge of Valéry's line "Nos plus chers souvenirs mordent nos coeurs dans l'ombre" to its quotation by Olney in *Memory and Narrative*, 374. Olney translates it brilliantly as "Our dearest memories ravage our hearts in the darkness." It is from Paul Valéry, *Moi*, trans. M. and J. Mathews, *Collected Works of Paul Valéry*, 15 vols. (Princeton, N.J.: Princeton University Press, 1975), 15:288.

35. Gilmore, *Autobiographics*, 25.

36. This is now a commonplace of life-writing studies. See, for example, the introduction to *Getting a Life: Everyday Uses of Autobiography*, ed. Sidonie Smith and Julia Watson (Minneapolis: University of Minnesota Press, 1996), 1–24.

37. Another possible shape is that offered by Passion narratives: see Gail McMurray Gibson, "St Margery: *The Book of Margery Kempe*," in *The Theatre of Devotion: East Anglian Drama and Society in the Late Middle Ages* (Chicago and London: University of Chicago Press, 1989).

38. See John Burrow, *The Ages of Man: A Study in Medieval Writing and Thought* (Oxford: Clarendon Press, 1985); Mary Dove, *The Perfect Age of a Man's Life* (Cambridge: Cambridge University Press, 1986); Elizabeth Sears, *The Ages of Man: Medieval Interpretations of the Life Cycle* (Princeton, N.J.: Princeton University Press, 1986).

39. See Burrow, *Ages of Man*, and Dove, *Perfect Age*.

40. See, for example, a single leaf by William de Brailes depicting the "Wheel of the Ages of Man and of Fortune" (Cambridge, Fitzwilliam Museum, MS 330) and the "Wheel of the Ten Ages of Man" in the De Lisle Psalter (London, British Library, MS Arundel 83, fol. 126v); for illustrations see Lucy Freeman Sandler, *The Psalter of Robert de Lisle in the British Library* (London and Oxford: Harvey Miller and Oxford University Press, 1983), plate 4.

41. A very different (humanist-Marxian) comparison between the Wife of Bath and Margery Kempe is Sheila Delany, "Sexual Economics, Chaucer's Wife of Bath and *The Book of Margery Kempe*," in *Writing Woman* (New York: Schoeken, 1983), 76–92.

42. For a different emphasis, see Rosalynn Voaden, "Beholding Men's Members: The Sexualising of Transgression in *The Book of Margery Kempe*," in *Medieval Theology and the Natural Body*, ed. Peter Biller and Alastair Minnis (Woodbridge: York Medieval Press, 1997), 175–90.

43. Clarissa W. Atkinson has stressed the extent to which virginity was being revalued in the later Middle Ages; nevertheless, she shows that Birgitta of Sweden and Margery Kempe illustrate "the persistence of conflict over the condition of married women." See her "'Precious Balsam in a Fragile Glass': The Ideology of Virginity in the Later Middle Ages," *Journal of Family History* 8 (1983): 131–43.

44. This significance of this episode is stressed in Smith, *Poetics of Women's Autobiography*, 64–83.

45. See Sarah Beckwith, "Problems of Authority in Late Medieval English Mysticism: Language, Agency, and Authority in the Book of Margery Kempe," *Exemplaria* 4 (1992): 171–99. Beckwith uses Bakhtin and de Certeau to address "the riven subject matter of [Kempe's] book—its subject as both God and herself" (180). I have borrowed her word "riven."

46. Benveniste, *Problems in General Linguistics*, 225.

47. Linda Georgianna, *The Solitary Self: Individuality in the* Ancrene Wisse (Cambridge, Mass. and London: Harvard University Press, 1981); Peter Biller, "Confession in the Middle Ages: Introduction," in *Handling Sin: Confession in the Middle Ages*, ed. Peter Biller and A.J. Minnis (Woodbridge: York Medieval Press, 1998), 1–33, and references.

48. Georgianna, *Solitary Self*, 101.

49. For the Anglo-Saxon tradition, see M. Schapiro, "The Image of the Disappearing Christ: The Ascension in English Art around the Year 1000," *Gazette des beaux arts* 23 (1943): 135–52. For later English examples, see Lucy Freeman Sandler, *The Peterborough Psalter in Brussels and Other Fenland Manuscripts* (London: Harvey Miller, 1974), 41, 55, 57.

50. Pascal, *Design and Truth*, 184–85.

51. Michael Haren, "The Interrogatories for Officials, Lawyers and Secular Estates of the *Memoriale presbitorum*," in *Handling Sin: Confession in the Middle Ages*, ed. Peter Biller and A. J. Minnis (Woodbridge: York Medieval Press, 1998), 123–63.

52. See Haren, "Interrogatories," a. xli, pp. 157–61.

53. These forms of piety, appropriate to the active life, were commonly practised by male and female townspeople: for evidence of almsgiving from York, see P. H. Cullum and P. J. P. Goldberg, "Charitable Provision in Late Medieval York: To the Praise of God and the Use of the Poor," *Northern History* 9 (1993): 24–39.

■ ■ ■

Afterwords

FELICITY RIDDY AND NICHOLAS WATSON

Our contributions to this volume see us far apart, not only on how the *Book of Margery Kempe* was produced, but also on the question of what can be known, even what it is desirable to know, about the text's composition. Rather than seeking to reconcile these views, we decided to end with a joint statement that points up our differences without giving either a last word. It is worth pointing out that we have had a version of this argument before, over Julian of Norwich, whose *Revelation of Love* is also treated as a single-author work by Watson, a social and collaborative composition by Riddy (see note 24 in Watson's essay). Watson's subsequent response to Riddy's critique in this case has been to pay more attention to the voices audible in Julian's text, granting that the process of the *Revelation*'s composition must have been social, but representing these voices less as coauthors than as "research assistants." Since the main object of his work on the *Revelation* and the *Book* is the exploration of their respective theologies, an investigation that begins from what Riddy here frames as the "medieval" premise that these may be coherent, this approach seems to him self-consistent and necessary, at least at this stage of his research on the two texts. Riddy's work, on the other hand, focuses on the social spaces in which vernacular texts circulated and her account of the production of the *Book*, like that of the production of the *Revelation*, is consistent with that interest. Part of the difference in our methodologies, though by no means all, comes down to a difference of approach.

Watson: Closely reading parts of the *Book* through its accounts of how it was written, in an attempt to reconstruct its compositional history and especially its original form, I treat the text as, for the most part, the composition of an elderly Margery Kempe. In my view, Kempe dictated a text she may have long had largely written in her head (and in prose, not speech) to her son over a period of some months. While we cannot know whom she consulted as she worked—it seems unlikely that close friends and mentors like Robert Springfield and Alan of Lynn were not involved at some level—she never publicly ceded responsibility for it to anyone, and specifically did not involve the second scribe as a significant coauthor. This is a difficult scenario to believe because an established community view of Kempe assumes that she did not have the level of literacy to carry such a project through, but the text offers evidence for it and I stand by its plausibility. In elucidating that evidence, I understand the text as an account based on actual historical events, although I do not regard this claim as inconsistent with Riddy's observation that retelling shapes history; for the most part, my argument relies on the near-accuracy only of incidental details about the text's genesis. Indeed, since I read the text in part as theological reflection or performance, my essay ultimately invites a reading of much of the *Book* within the framework of the theology of "as if." (It is worth noting that Riddy's response also treats much of the text as factual, or, as she would prefer it, "factual.")

Riddy considers this approach improperly humanistic, uninformed as it is by narratological theory or by critical work on modern autobiography, a mode of self-telling shaped by the post-medieval genre of the novel. I have outlined my critical approach in an article entitled "Desire for the Past" (*Studies in the Age of Chaucer* 21 [1999]: 59–98), where I indeed argue for a scholarship that uses the past's own tools, particularly the mode of thinking and knowing we now term "empathy," to study the past. The first part of Riddy's counterproposal, which uses the language of postmodern theory to describe the text as indeterminately "polyvocal" and its "autobiographical self" as "fashioned out of whatever cultural bric-à-brac is to hand," seems to me to bear my argument out, for the view of the *Book* it offers is oddly similar to the view of the protagonist as a religious "magpie" that my essay suggests is typical of scholarly attitudes to the *Book*'s thought. By inviting interpretations of the text that take it for granted that neither it nor its protagonist—whether textual "creatur" or the woman named Margery Kempe—has anything intellectually coherent to say, these attitudes seem to me to obscure our understanding of the *Book*'s intervention in fifteenth-century religious culture. In places my essay no doubt misrepresents that intervention too, especially when my arguments depend on a speculative reconstruction of the *Book*'s original draft, but that is the risk of historical scholarship, a risk well worth taking if the prize is a better knowledge of one of the first women writing in English to whom the word *author* might apply.

In the second half of her response, however, Riddy takes a surprising turn, evolving a reading of the *Book*'s composition and thematics about which I have more mixed feelings. Once one has substituted unconscious for conscious intentions, this reading seems every bit as biographical and intentionalist as my own. Riddy's "Margery Kempe" is a gloomier figure than mine, a figure who expresses a pent-up rage at her repeated subjection to maternity and the cultural incoherence forced on her by her gender that I find it hard not to interpret, in places, as anger at my own more optimistic reading of the text. If my reading runs the risk of being "medieval," hers runs the risk of presentism. I read the text "backward" from its concluding paeon to the Creator's goodness, where Kempe sees her life and body as containing metonymically the whole history of the cosmos. Riddy reads the text "forwards" from "Kempe's" first childbirth and later experience of "roaring," which becomes Riddy's metonymy for the repressed "cone of darkness" that it is the text's unconscious agenda to express. Our approaches are so different as to be methodologically incommensurable. Thus I suggest that Riddy's deconstruction of my reading is premature, if it has the effect of short-circuiting the hermeneutic project of my essay, which would be more productive to read in its own terms. At the same time, however, I find aspects of Riddy's counterproposal so impressive in their dark poetry and novelistic evocations of a social model of textual composition that I hope she or others will want to pursue them further. Synthesis, at this stage, seems as undesirable as it is unlikely.

Riddy: I start from a similar premise to Watson's: I too regard the text as autobiography, though of a curious kind. We have no way of telling, of course, whether or not an autobiography is fictional; what we can say, however, is that it is a mode that presents itself as fact. When we read the opening of *The History of Mary Prince, a West Indian Slave, Related by Herself* ("I was born at Brackish-Pond, in Bermuda, on a farm belonging to Mr Charles Myners. My mother was a household slave . . ."), we assume that the "Mary Prince" of the title page, the "I" who narrates the story, and the protagonist of the narrative are all the same person. The text refers to real geography; it mentions living people; it deploys factual details: these are all authenticating features that seem to be characteristic of the mode. The text sets up an implicit pact with the reader that it is a true story, told by Mary Prince herself. This "autobiographical pact" does not in fact verify anything, of course; it offers a semblance, rather than a guarantee, of veracity. *The Book of Margery Kempe* is like and unlike this. It reads "as if" it were told from a first-person perspective (because it knows all about what is going on in the protagonist's "mende" and, mostly, nobody else's), though the narratorial "I" hardly occurs and the protagonist is presented as if from the outside, in the third person. Furthermore, the ambiguities of the Middle English verb "wrytyn" were such that the text itself does not distinguish between composing and copying, and so we cannot extrapolate from it a modern idea of authorship. This autobiographical text does not conflate author, narrator, and protagonist, as Watson assumes, moving as he does from one to the other without distinction and reading the narrative as unproblematically true.

Watson is right to say that my approach short-circuits his hermeneutic project, and if he sounds aggrieved, it is not without justification. He has, after all, devoted many years now to developing influential ideas about vernacular theology in late medieval England, and this essay on *The Book of Margery Kempe* is part of that wider endeavour. It goes without saying that he knows far more than I do about the religious writings of this period. I am not sure, though, that we are agreed about the nature of our disagreement. My argument with him is only partly about gender; more fundamentally, it is about the nature of the autobiographical text. I believe that literary critics and literary historians working on medieval texts should pay attention to what our colleagues in adjacent fields are up to. There is now an immensely impressive body of work on life-writing of all kinds, including women's autobiography, that has problematized this whole field; as professionals, we should be aware of it. If my willingness to use contemporary tools of analysis is presentism, I can only reply, first, that the present is where we are, and second, that the coherent liberal humanist self is not medieval either. I do not call my protagonist "Margery Kempe" but the "creatur," the product of retrospection and writing: not a person, but a piece of text. Nevertheless, because I think the *Book* is autobiographical, it follows that I think a woman was crucially involved in its composition— it is an account of her life—and I am willing to speculate on how it might have come into being. I cannot accept the simple dictation model—she speaks, he writes—because the syntax is obviously not that of speech, and so it must have gone through a process of modification. We cannot know what role the priest played in composition or whose language we are reading: with Foucault, I believe that "Who is the author?" is not the important question.

Moreover, I think we should respect the text's unwillingness to conflate author, narrator, and protagonist. Such an approach is, in the end, more accommodating to Watson's aims than he sees: unlike him, I think synthesis may be possible, with the second part of his essay, at least. I do not see why it is necessary to attribute the optimistic theology to Margery Kempe, particularly since this entails unproblematically identifying the author with the protagonist and the text with the life. The story of the "creatur" is not the story of Margery Kempe: the latter's life began when she was born, while the former comes into being in the account of giving birth for the first time. I read the narrative forwards, stressing this point of origin, but Watson is right to emphasize the prayer with which it ends. There, in the present of old age, is the true starting point of autobiography, the already known outcome towards which the "creatur's" story unfolds. As I see it, the optimistic theology that Watson discovers in it is the text's, produced by this extravagantly peopled narrative of inner and outer events, conjured out of those fraught and obsessive meetings between an old woman and a priest.

Stepping into the Pulpit? Women's Preaching in *The Book of Margery Kempe* and *The Examinations of Anne Askew*

GENELLE GERTZ-ROBINSON

Poised on either side of an event as cataclysmic as the Reformation, Margery Kempe's autobiographical *Book* (c. 1438) and Anne Askew's *Examinations* (1546, 1547) introduce the subject of women's preaching in remarkably similar ways. In each text heresy investigators accuse the woman protagonist of preaching, and while she necessarily denies the act, she also asserts her right to preach by defining it as something else. In *The Book of Margery Kempe*, when a priest at Archbishop Henry Bowet's court lifts up a book and "ley(s) Seynt Powwyl for hys party a-geyns hir that no woman schulde prechyn," Kempe responds with an equivocal answer. She insists "I preche not ser, I come in no pulpytt. I vse but comownycacyon & good wordys, & þat wil I do whil I leue" (126).[1] By defining preaching as the occupation of a pulpit and all other speech "comownycacyon & good wordys," Kempe reserves for herself the possibility of preaching in other public settings.[2]

Likewise, in her first recorded trial before Bishop Edmund Bonner's chancellor, Anne Askew receives a reprimand for disobeying St. Paul.[3] Askew, a reformer and possible associate of reform-minded women in Katherine Parr's circle, stands trial for sacramentarianism, or the belief that the host is a sign of Christ's body.[4] After the chancellor informs her that "S. Paule . . . forbode women to speake or to talke of the worde of God," Askew responds with a technical interpretation of Paul's epistle to the Corinthians:

I answered hym, that I knewe Paules meanynge so well as he, whych is, i. Corinthi-
orum xiiii. that a woman ought not to speake in the congregacyon by the way of
teachynge. And then I asked hym, how manye women he had seane, go into the
pulpett and preache. He sayde, he never sawe non. Then I sayd, he ought to fynde
no faute in poore women, except they had offended the lawe. (30)[5]

Without any apparent knowledge of Kempe's *Book,* Askew adopts Kempe's strategy, assuming that preaching must be defined by location—by the actual habitation of a pulpit. Her interpretation of 1 Corinthians 14 (itself an exegetical gesture) continues the
strategy of narrow definition so as to free up other areas for women's teaching. Counter
to the chancellor's assertion that Paul did not permit women "to speake or to talke of the
worde of God," Askew adds a qualification: "a woman ought not to speak *in the congregacyon* by the way of teachynge" (my emphasis).[6] Under Askew's distinction, any place
but the congregation, and perhaps all congregational space outside the pulpit, would
be permissible for women's speech.

When read together, the *Book of Margery Kempe* and the *Examinations of Anne Askew*
supply evidence for identifying important continuities between the Lancastrian and
Tudor periods, especially within women's literary history. I will suggest throughout
this essay that Kempe's and Askew's texts carve out a space for women's preaching by
employing a similar rhetoric of evasion that nonetheless signals homiletic intentions.
At the very points when they deny preaching, both protagonists draw on recognized
rhetorical forms unique to the disciplines of preaching and public instruction.

Similar historical conditions, moreover, contribute to the parallel rhetorical choices
of both texts. Though *The Book of Margery Kempe* affirms orthodox tenets such as the
efficacy of purgatory, affective meditation, and eucharistic devotion, and though Askew's
Examinations deny these principles and expound reformed doctrine, both texts rely on
similar strategies of evasion in order to negotiate the demands of religious censorship.
In both the Lancastrian and Tudor periods, the vernacular Bible came under varying
degrees of censorship. Kempe writes in the wake of Archbishop Arundel's 1409 ruling
that the possession of vernacular Bibles was grounds for heresy, itself an offense newly
punishable by execution.[7] Askew's heresy trials occur after the 1543 Act for the Advancement of True Religion, which decreed that no women, dependents, or servants, and no
one below the status of yeoman, could read the English Bible in public or private. An
added clause made an exception for women of the gentry by allowing them to read the
Bible in private.[8]

Underlying motivations for censorship, as Elizabeth Schirmer and others have indicated in this volume, derived from clerical fear over Lollardy's (and later, the reformers') denial of differences between laity and the priesthood on the matter of preaching.
As discerned in the chancellor's response to Askew, knowledge of scripture proved sus-

picious in the minds of authorities precisely because it enabled lay preaching.[9] Especially in conventicles, or non-church gatherings where first Lollards and then Henrician reformers engaged in scriptural interpretation and discussion, lay preaching was thought to take place.[10] What Kempe's and Askew's texts suggest about this phenomenon is that lay preaching could be differently interpreted when applied to women. When accusing women of preaching, examiners could use the Pauline text exclusively against them and never assume that clerical office would be an option. For lay men, the priesthood and eventual procurement of a preaching license were technically open to all, though social and financial constraints did limit access, especially to peasants. Yet, for as many institutional doors that stood closed to them, Kempe's and Askew's insistence that they never enter the masculine space of the pulpit shows that women could use Paul's proscription for their own purposes. They might claim that whatever they did was obviously not preaching because they were women.[11]

The need to rely on such inventive measures, of course, arose from the high degree of religious surveillance in both periods. Kempe's and Askew's texts reflect this circumstance in their frequent recourse to the experience of heresy trial. As Nicholas Watson comments in his essay in the present volume, no fewer than four separate trials punctuate the events of Kempe's life. Askew's *Examinations* display even greater interest in the scene of trial by excluding every element about her life except her heresy investigations and imprisonment.[12] In this essay, as I discuss homiletic rhetoric in Kempe's and Askew's texts, I consider how the account of the trial, even as it assumes to record accurately the exchanges of the courtroom, relies on literary constructions. Characterization, setting, and dialogue reshape the content and space of the trial, transforming the courtroom audience into a congregation responsive to the defendant-preacher's clerical skills.

What this suggests, I think, is a tradition within early women's writing that draws upon an emerging genre that we might call the "trial narrative."[13] Rita Copeland has discussed a Lollard version of this genre, adopted by Richard Wyche and William Thorpe, in which both authors portray their trials as disputational exchanges.[14] These autobiographical trial accounts, Copeland suggests, draw upon stories of trial and imprisonment in Acts, but also they consciously incorporate disputational rhetoric from the universities, establishing their protagonists as teachers and dissenting intellectuals in spaces outside the academy. What, then, does it mean for lay women to adopt the trial narrative? Contrary to male counterparts like Wyche and Thorpe, Kempe and Askew lacked university or clerical training. In their hands (as well as the hands of their possible collaborators),[15] the portrayal of the heresy trial is crucial not just because it transforms interrogation into an academic or ecclesiastical setting (as for Wyche and Thorpe), but also because it relies on dialogic form to produce female speech. Without the academic qualifications enjoyed by dissidents like Wyche and Thorpe, Kempe and Askew depend especially on the double possibilities of trial to establish their authority. They need an inquisitor to pronounce the official word that women cannot preach because this very proscription, bound within the dialogic exchange of the trial narrative, ironically generates their speech. In the ensuing discussion, I show how *The Book of Margery Kempe* and the *Examinations of Anne Askew* convey women's homiletic rhetoric through the conveniently ambiguous form of the trial narrative.

I

Doubtless in response to groups such as the Waldensians, the Humiliati, and the Lollards, all of whom encouraged lay preaching, a steady output of treatises and quodlibetical discussions of preaching appeared throughout the thirteenth and fourteenth centuries. In an influential treatise on preaching written around 1200, the Cistercian Alan of Lille defined preaching as "an open and public instruction in faith and behavior, whose purpose is the forming of men."[16] Alan separated preaching from other activities such as teaching, prophesying, and speech making, not distinguishing these by office, but by the context of audience and topic. Only the act of preaching required a public audience to be addressed in matters of belief and behavior. In another section of his treatise, however, Alan specified qualifications for preaching, limiting them to office: "Preaching ought to be the work of prelates, and sermons should be delivered by prelates."[17]

Later in the same century Gauthier of Chateau-Thierry, a secular master who became chancellor of the University of Paris, returned to the question of who was authorized to preach. In the formulation of his answer Gauthier decided that preaching could be distinguished from recitation (of prayers, the creed, etc.) as well as exhortation to good behavior because it alone concerned the expounding of scripture. For Gauthier the expounding of scripture could only be performed by clerics and specifically involved the reading of the Bible publicly in a loud voice, followed by interpretation in the allegorical, anagogical, and moral senses.[18] He reserved for women and laymen the related instructional practices of recitation of the creed and exhortation to moral conduct.

The Franciscan Eustache of Arras, in the period between 1263 and 1266, also addressed the question of women's instructional domain. More progressive than Gauthier, Eustache invoked the examples of preaching women saints, such as Mary Magdalene and Katherine of Alexandria, arguing that they derived authority for public instruction directly from the Holy Spirit. Accounting for the examples of Katherine and the Magdalene, he maintained that Paul's admonition to women to be silent in the churches applied to married women only. By implication unmarried women were allowed to speak in public when divinely inspired.[19]

As Kerby-Fulton discusses in the introduction to the present volume, Thomas Aquinas, in *Summa theologiae* (1266–1272), also recognized the biblical precedent of women teachers. He identified them as prophets, noting that divine illumination transcended gender, but at the same time held that these prophets did not constitute precedents for women's preaching.[20] Additionally, Aquinas made reference to the lay gift of "grace" (1 Peter 4:10) as an authorization of women's teaching, but he determined that women's subjection to men as accounted in Genesis, their sexually arousing speech, and their "generally" insufficient wisdom required that, if given the gift of teaching, they should only use it within the household.[21]

In the 1320s Robert of Basevorn flatly disagreed with Eustache's exception concerning women's public instruction and even dismissed the Thomistic possibility of women's divine illumination. He wrote in his preaching manual, "No lay person or Religious, unless permitted by a Bishop or the Pope, and no woman, no matter how learned or saintly, ought to preach. Nor is it enough for one to say that he was commissioned by God, unless he clearly proves this, for the heretics are wont to make this claim."[22]

The *Speculum Christiani,* an English pastoral manual compiled some time between the 1360s and 1370s, also stated that preaching required the authority of ordination, but, in distinction with earlier manuals on which it was based, it allowed the laity an instructional privilege similar to that of the ordained.[23] Preaching, the *Speculum* asserts, "es in a place where es clepynge to-gedyr or foluynge of pepyl in holy dayes in chyrches or othe[r] certeyn places. . . . And it longeth to hem that been ordeynede therto, the whych haue iurediccion and auctoriete, and to noon othyr." Teaching, on the other hand, may be practiced by the laity. A teacher "may enforme *and* teche hys brothyr in eu*ery* place *and* in conable tyme, os he seeth *that* it be spedful. For this is a gostly almesdede, to whych eu*ery* man es bounde that hath cunnynge."[24] The practices of "informing" and "teaching" are provocatively vague here, not nearly as specific as Gauthier's definition of lay instruction as creedal recitation and moral exhortation. Nor is the definition of preaching concerned with any form of instructional practice; it only specifies qualification (authority through ordination) and locale.[25] As Vincent Gillespie has shown, the content of the *Speculum* itself was adapted from preaching manuals so as to suggest the extra-ecclesial didactic purposes of the material.[26]

A later treatise composed in the late fourteenth or early fifteenth century limited the work of "ghostly almsdeeds," or lay religious instruction, to private circumstances.[27] The treatise, British Library MS Harley 31 (discussed in the present volume by Somerset and Kerby-Fulton), may have been written in refutation of the Lollard Walter Brut's argument (during his heresy trials in 1391–93) that women had the power to preach.[28] The Harley author maintained that women's teaching, though allowed as one of the seven works of Spiritual Mercy, should be restricted to private occasions. That Brut, like Eustache of Arras and Aquinas, referred to the precedent of earlier women preachers (whom the Harley author assumed to be Mary Magdalene and Martha) was also not convincing.[29] As Henry of Ghent had argued in a compilation of his Paris lectures dating from 1276–1292,[30] the Harley author affirmed that women's position in the apostolic church was exceptional rather than exemplary, due to the newness of the church and its shortage of able preachers.[31] The Harley author also maintained, as Henry had before him, that women were not qualified to preach because Genesis and Paul denied them authority over men, and because they lacked the vigor necessary to defend virtues and expose vices, instead possessing voices that naturally incited male audiences to sexual desire. Unlike Henry, and in reaction to the Lollard reverence for vernacular scriptures, the Harley treatise claimed that women should not have access to the Bible in the vernacular because they were unable to understand higher things.[32]

Taken together, these arguments and definitions of preaching are remarkable for their relative cohesion.[33] Several of the treatises maintain the laity's right to some form of instruction. The *Speculum* seems to give the most leeway on what lay teaching might include, but Aquinas, Gauthier of Chateau-Thierry, and the Harley author acknowledge the laity's right to instruction as either a work of mercy or a parental duty.[34] Many also assume that public audiences distinguish the activity of preaching from other modes of instruction (which explains why women, in their definitions, are relegated to teaching in private domains). Thus Alan of Lille, Gauthier, and the *Speculum* emphasize the public context of preaching, while Gauthier specifies the reading of scripture aloud in public, followed by interpretation, as the particular task of preachers. Finally, among those who acknowledge the example of saintly women (Aquinas, Robert of Basevorn, Eustache of Arras, Henry of Ghent, and the Harley author), Eustache alone assumes that this authorizes contemporary women (albeit virgins) to speak in public.

All of this illuminates Kempe's and Askew's decisions to deny that they preach by specifying public speaking as habitation of a pulpit (the tactic of the *Speculum*), and, for Kempe, to claim the lay privilege of "communication and good words" (something akin to a work of mercy or gift of grace).[35] As we shall see, this history of definitions at the same time qualifies several of their speech acts as *de facto* preaching. Speaking within the public domain, reading or reciting the Bible aloud, expounding the scriptures, and reproving the moral errors of an audience are all activities selected as unique to the preaching role. I will now turn to a discussion of how the *Book of Margery Kempe* and *The Examinations of Anne Askew* deconstruct their protagonists' claims to a minor teaching role by depicting their fulfillment of several preaching forms.

II

Two central scenes encapsulate the range of Kempe's preaching forms, and in each one, accusations that she preaches or should not be allowed to speak of religious matters in public invite homiletic presentations.[36] We can return to the trial before Henry Bowet to analyze the variety of preaching forms Kempe uses during her trial, and then after this (but chronologically before the trial in the *Book*) an encounter between Kempe and monastics at Canterbury, which exemplifies similar features.

Establishing the public context of the trial space, Kempe's interrogation by Bowet begins with descriptions of the courtroom cast. Men in service to Bowet are the first to address her, taunting her with the prospects of condemnation as a "lollar" and "here-tyke," and swearing "many an horrybyl othe þat sche xulde be brent" (124). Undaunted by such hostility, Kempe warns her accusers that they are sinning by making false oaths, and in this rebuke (discussed later) she exercises homiletic privilege. After Bowet conducts a brief interview and apparently orders that Kempe be put in fetters, he makes a grand re-entrance into the courtroom, trailed by "many worthy clerkys." Bowet dramatically takes his seat, and his assistants find their places as well, "iche of hem in hys degre." Meanwhile, unnumbered "pepil" gathered in the audience air their opinions about Kempe's character ("sum sayd sche was a good woman, & sum seyd nay"). Introducing the court scene in this way, the *Book* presses the importance of Kempe's speech for public audiences in general: not only does she have to persuade her interrogators, but also, and perhaps more importantly, she must win the favor of "meche pepil beyng present" (124).

As the interrogation develops, it is this very audience, and Kempe's implied influence over audiences within the diocese of York, that directs the line of questioning. For, as Bowet himself comments after quizzing Kempe on the articles of faith, she "knowith hir Feyth wel a-now." But other "clerkys" respond that it is her influence which is objectionable: "þe pepil hath gret feyth in hir dalyawnce, and perauentur sche myth peruertyn summe of hem." Enacting a formula that appears frequently in the *Book,* the question of Kempe's public authority here comes under scrutiny as a way of introducing her homiletic language. Bowet commands Kempe, "Þow schalt sweryn þat þu [ne] xalt techyn ne chalengyn þe pepil in my diocyse" and after submitting that she cannot so swear, and claiming that God forbids no one to speak of him, Kempe supports her position with scriptural quotation and exegesis. "[Þ]e Gospel makyth mencyon," she begins,

> þat, whan þe woman had herd owr Lord prechyd, sche cam be-forn hym wyth a lowde voys & seyd, "Blyssed be þe wombe þat the bar & þe tetys þat gaf þe sowkyn." Þan owr Lord seyd a-ȝen to hir, "Forsoþe so ar þei blissed þat heryn þe word of God and kepyn it." And þerfor, sir, me thynkyth þat þe Gospel ȝeuyth me leue to spekyn of God. (126; Luke 11:27–28)

Karma Lochrie has pointed out that one of the arguments used by the Lollard Walter Brut during his heresy trial cites this same passage in defense of women's right to preach.[37] Brut uses the passage in a different way than Kempe, however. He takes Christ's response to the woman as preliminary evidence for the following conditional argument:

"If they are blessed who hear and keep the word of God, they are even more blessed who preach and keep it, because it is more blessed to give than to receive."[38] Lochrie has further noted that Kempe, on the other hand, seems to assume that Christ's response to the woman authorizes her to speak about him, which in itself blatantly ignores his instruction that people should only *hear* and *keep* the word of God (my emphasis).[39] Beyond this subversion, we should realize that Kempe's quotation is significant because of its methodology. Her answer relies on the homiletic privilege of exegesis, which, we have just seen, was conceived as central to the preaching role by theologians such as Gauthier of Chateau-Thierry.[40] Kempe quotes scripture, immediately affixes its meaning—"And þerfor, sir, me thynkyth þat þe Gospel ʒeuyth me leue to spekyn of God"—and confirms her intentions a moment later in the trial by using another preaching tool, the exemplum.

This later moment follows the pivotal scene, discussed in the opening of this essay, when a book-wielding clerk charges by the authority of St. Paul "þat no woma*n* xulde pre*char* chyn." Here again, a proscription against preaching authorizes sermon rhetoric. After arguing that she does not preach because she cannot enter the pulpit, Kempe is conveniently accused of telling anticlerical stories by a priest who had formerly interrogated her. Obliged by Bowet, who "comawnd(s) hir to tellyn þat tale," Kempe expands her homiletic repertoire by telling and interpreting an exemplum.[41] Her story,[42] in which a priest happens upon a bear who turns "hys tayl-ende in þe prestys presens, voydy[ng] . . . owt" his meal from "þe hyndyr party," surprisingly wins court approval. Though her interpretation confirms the former interrogator's accusation by revealing the bear's desecration as symbolic of the priest's sin, Bowet does not take offense. He "likyd wel þe tale & comendyd it, seying it was a good tale," while his chastened colleague, already established as a kind of professional rival to Kempe by virtue of his accusation against her, is forced to admit "Ser, þis tale smytyth me to þe hert" (127).

By the end of her trial at York, Kempe has won over the audience described so carefully at the beginning as either ambivalent or extremely hostile. The clerk who accuses her of slandering the priesthood not only comes to appreciate the power of her stories, but also acknowledges her spiritual authority. Kempe goes on to test his appreciation of her exemplum by quoting what "a good pre*char*" says "many tymes in þe pulpit" at Lynn, namely, that whoever dislikes his preaching no doubt suffers from guilt over committed sins. As if the connection were not explicit enough—that Kempe has just said something reserved for the place of the pulpit—she tells the clerk that he has behaved towards her in the same manner as the guilty members of her parish. She declares, "And ryth so, ser . . . far ʒe be me [so you treat me], God forʒeue it ʒou" (128). Making herself a proxy for her parish preacher, Kempe essentially ascends the stairs of the pulpit while her interrogator observes the rites of this poetic justice by dutifully pleading for her forgiveness and prayers. Drawing the whole scene to a perfect close, the ambivalent audience referred to at the beginning is replaced by a supportive crowd outside the cathedral which waits to greet Kempe: "Than sche . . . was receyued of mech pepil & of ful worthy clerk*ys*."

Like her trial at York, Kempe's confrontation at Canterbury establishes a rivalry between Kempe, the lay woman preacher, and learned men who hold ecclesiastical office. Abandoned by a husband who cannot endure censure of her loud crying, Kempe stands on her own in a chapel at Canterbury Cathedral. This trial-like scene opens with a hostile question that nevertheless invites her speech:

> an eld monk, whech had ben tresowrer w*yth* þe Qwen whyl he was in seculer clothyng, a riche man, & gretly dred of mech pepyl, toke hir be þe hand, seying vn-to hir, "What kanst þow seyn of God?" "Ser" sche seyth, "I wyl boþe speke of hy*m* & heryn of hy*m*," rehersyng þe monk a story of Sc*ri*ptur. (27)

As at York, Kempe here stresses speaking of God, this time also asserting her right to "hear" the word of God (perhaps referring to the eleventh chapter of Luke, which she quotes for Bowet). She supports this claim by reciting scripture, and the term for her quotation of scripture—"rehearsing"—was used specifically to describe preaching rhetoric. The *Middle English Dictionary* lists as its second meaning for "rehearse" (after that of narration) the act of imparting information or explaining a point within the contexts of disputation, proclamation, the statement of a decision, or the declaration of a sermon text.[43] Attendant to all these meanings of the word is a setting of public address, whether governmental, scholastic, or ecclesiastical. But more pertinent to this study is the last meaning, which confirms that Kempe's speech should be understood within the narrative as preaching.

Again mirroring her experience at York, Kempe's audience at Canterbury confirms the instructional effect of her words. Just after citing scripture to the old monk, and in response to a younger monk's declaration that she must be either spiritually inspired or demonically possessed to hold such scriptural knowledge,[44] Kempe launches into another exemplum, proving her pedagogical intentions. She tells the gathered group of monastics a story about a man who served penance for one year in which he paid other men to slander and criticize him. After the completion of his penance, when he encountered a company of people who used sharp words against him (Kempe makes an aside at this point that she stands before a similar company), he began to laugh. When the people demanded to know why he laughed, he told them that for a whole year he had paid men to chide him for his sins, but now he remembers that he can keep his money in his purse.

After repeating the story, Kempe expounds it by making direct application to members in her audience. She remarks that whereas before she had despaired that she suffered no "schame, skorne, & despyte as [she] was worthy" now she can thank them for enabling what she had desired (28). Her listeners in turn demonstrate their understanding of her point, proving the effectiveness of her words by reacting negatively. They follow her out of the monastery, yelling after her, "Þow xalt be brent, fals lollare" (28). By the violent nature of their response, the monks and the laity exhibit their feelings of conviction; most notably, a group of men who should be cool-headed contemplatives rage with anger because someone of mean authority—a woman no less—has challenged them.

But still other preaching forms appear in Kempe's speech before the monks at Canterbury. At the time in which she seeks to convict her audience—that is, during the interpretation that applies the story to the immediate context—she addresses her listeners with a sermon vocative. She pronounces, "I sey to ȝow, *worshepful serys*, whyl I was at hom in myn owyn contre day be day w*yth* gret wepyng & morny*ng*, I sorwyd for I had no schame, skorne, & despyte as I was worthy. I thank ȝow all, *serys*, heyly what fore-noon & aft*yr*-noon I haue had resonably þis day, blyssed be God þ*er*of" (28, my emphasis). By calling members of her audience "sirs" Kempe uses one of the most common forms of address in late medieval English sermons.[45]

Though Kempe practices the rhetoric of preaching in many other contexts,[46] I have limited my discussion to the episodes at York and Canterbury in order to demonstrate the overall coherence of Kempe's performances. In each place the sum effect of Kempe's preaching skills proves greater than the parts because it demonstrates a pattern of rhetorical calculation, and an awareness of the variety of ways a preacher attempts to command the attention of an audience. At York and Canterbury Kempe moves from quoting and interpreting scripture to telling exempla, applying them to her audience, and, in the process of application, formally invoking her audience in the manner of a preacher. The rhetoric of reproof, discussed in Edwin Craun's work as part of the practice of fraternal correction, also appears in both passages, as when Kempe first sees Henry Bowet's men and upbraids them for swearing, and when she denounces the older monk at Canterbury who, after hearing her story of scripture, wishes that "'no ma*n* speke w*yth* [her]'" (27).[47] In return, Kempe admonishes him: "'A, ser . . . ȝe schuld meynteyn Godd*ys* s*er*vawnt*ys*, & ȝe arn þe fyrst þ*at* heldyn a-ȝens hem. Owyr Lord amend yow'" (27). Undoubtedly, the very locations in which Kempe speaks confirm her preaching powers. Standing in ecclesiastical strongholds like the cathedral at York or monastic house in Canterbury (both cities, incidentally, that housed the seats of archbishops), the contiguity of her own position with that of clerics draws attention to her priestly skills. Nothing but office, or indeed, the pulpit, distinguishes her from her male counterparts.

III

Though always contentious, and teetering on the brink of catastrophic outcomes, Kempe's trials lead to her release and return to supportive communities. Eventually, she wins ecclesiastical sanction for her lay ministry in the form of letters granted by Henry Bowet and Archbishop Chichele.[48] In contrast, Anne Askew enjoys no such clerical support. Her text records only two of her trials before Henry VIII's bishops and councilors, narrating her imprisonment, illegal racking in the Tower, and final sentence of heresy. Foxe describes her last moments at the stake, where, supported by a chair because she had been racked, she called out objections to Nicholas Shaxton's sermon: "There, said she, he misseth, and speaketh without the booke."[49] Ironically, Shaxton had recanted in the same round of investigations that led to Askew's final trial and condemnation.[50]

Contributing to a foreboding sense of Askew's eventual death are frequent allusions throughout the *Examinations* to a biblical story of trial and martyrdom. As narrated in Acts 7, Stephen's interrogation and condemnation by a rabbinical council suggest the ending of Askew's own trial, but more remarkably, they inform her interpretation of the Eucharist and provide an example of someone who transformed the occasion of trial into a platform for delivering a sermon.[51]

The first words Askew utters in her trial connect her story with the story of Stephen. Responding to his solicitation of her views concerning the real presence, Askew serves her interrogator, Christopher Dare, a question rather than an answer: "Then I demaunded thys questyon of hym, wherfore S. Steven was stoned to deathe?" (20).[52] This response appears unrelated to Dare's question, but later passages in the *Examinations* reveal that Stephen's argument concerning the Temple—"he that is hyest of all, dwelleth not in temple made with hondes"—supports Askew's sacramentarian view of the Eucharist.[53] In the *lattre* examination, Askew applies this passage to the Eucharist, assuming Christ cannot dwell in bread because it, like the Temple, is a created substance. She writes, "it is playnelye expressed . . . in the Bible, that God dwelleth in nothynge materyall," and her proof is Stephen's argument that "God wyll be in nothynge that is made with handes of men. Acto. 7" (106).

If we return to the opening moments of the trial—before Askew has fully connected Stephen with her view of the Eucharist—we find that she also uses his case as an opportunity to display her exegetical powers. When Christopher Dare follows up Askew's question about Stephen with a report "that there was a woman, whych ded testyfye, that [Askew had] reade, how God was not in temples made with handes," Askew responds by identifying two scriptural passages in which this statement appears. She says that she "shewed [Dare] the vii and the xvii. Chaptre of the Apostles actes, what Steven and Paule had sayd therin" (20 f.). Here Askew not only represents herself quoting scripture to her interrogator and thus adopting one role of the preacher, but also, her choice of vocabulary for describing the manner in which she provides these quotations (her "showing" of them), emphasizes her instructive role.

The theme of public instruction appears in still another aspect of Askew's opening response to Dare. The very texts she quotes for him are themselves sermons given before audiences, either in court (Stephen) or the streets of Athens (Paul). Tyndale glosses Acts 7 with the marginal heading, "The sermon of Stephin," while Acts 17 contains Paul's sermon on "the unknown god."[54] Like Kempe, who repeats words her hometown preacher dispenses from the pulpit, Askew's quotation of biblical sermons before her court audience essentially re-performs them. In order to demonstrate the detailed manner in which Askew draws upon the sermons of Stephen and Paul elsewhere in her text, I will now discuss the biblical accounts of Stephen's and Paul's sermons.

Brought to trial to answer the question of whether he has committed blasphemy against Moses and God, Stephen, in Acts 7, delivers a history of Judaism ranging from the Abrahamic covenant to the Exodus, to the building of the Temple. He asserts as the culmination of this history the crucifixion and resurrection of Christ. What Stephen emphasizes throughout his sermon is the rejection of God's revelation by Israel, especially the revelation given to them through Moses. The Israelites demonstrate this rejection in their worship of the golden calf, and in a current application of the story, Stephen names as contemporary idolators those who would locate God's presence in the Temple rather than in the person of Christ. In demonstration of this, he interprets a text of Isaiah for the council, charging "he that is hyest of all, dwelleth not in temple made with hondes, as saith the Prophete: Heven is my seate, and erth is my fote stole, what housse will ye bylde for me sayth the Lorde? Or what place is it that I shuld rest in? hath not my honde made all these thinges?"[55] He ends his sermon by employing prophetic rebuke, applying the lesson of biblical history directly to the members of his examining council. "Ye stiffenecked and of vncircumcised hertes and eares," he charges, "ye have all wayes resisted the holy goost: as youre fathers dyd, so do ye. Which of the prophetes have not youre fathers persecuted?"[56]

Demonstrating a thorough awareness of Stephen's story, Askew includes many of Stephen's exact words in portions of her *Examinations*. Twice in a confession of faith written in Newgate prison and included in the *lattre* examination, she quotes Stephen's proclamation that "God wyll be in nothynge that is made with handes of men. Acto. 7" (106, 109). Against her examiners, she invokes the same words of reproof that Stephen pronounces at the end of his sermon, exclaiming, "Oh what styffnecked people are these, that wyll alwayes resyst the holye Ghost. But as their fathers have done, so do they, by-cause they have stonye hartes" (106). In the same confession she again takes up Stephen's words, quoting the passage in which he interprets Isaiah, and thereby repeating his strategy of quotation and explication. She notes, "Salomon (*sayth S. Steven*) buylded an howse for the God of Jacob. Howbeyt the heyest of all dwelleth not in templẽs made with handes. As *sayth the prophete*, Esa. 66. Heaven is my seate and the earth is my fotẽ stole. What howse wyll ye buylde for me? Sayth the lorde, or what place is it that I shall rest in? hath not my hande made all these things? Acto. 7" (109, my emphasis). Askew's identification of Stephen's use of Isaiah 66 demonstrates her awareness of his method of scriptural quotation. By including his quotational strategies, she authorizes her own use of scriptural passages in other parts of the *Examinations.*

Stephen's sermons also inform Askew's quotation of other biblical texts. In a sly diagnosis of Lord Chancellor Wriothesley's spiritual state, for instance, Askew alludes to the story of Elijah and the prophets of Baal. In the *lattre* examination, after Wriothesley has begun another round of interrogation concerning the sacrament of the altar, Askew replies: "Then I axed hym, how longe he wolde halte on both sydes?" Perplexed at her meaning, he desires to know "where [Askew had] founde that?" and she replies "in the scripture 3 Reg. 18" (97).[57] In 1 Kings 18 the prophet Elijah challenges the people of Israel to a test of their spiritual allegiance, addressing them in the presence of four hundred and fifty prophets of Baal and four hundred prophets of Asherah. Elijah asks: "howe longe halte ye betwene two opinions? If the Lorde be God, followe hym: but if Baal be he, then go aftyr him."[58] When no one answers, he invites his coreligionists to a competition. Each side is to prepare a sacrifice for his god but withhold the fire, and the god who answers by sending fire will be proven the true god. While Baal fails to assist his priests, the God of Israel answers and sends a fire that consumes all the contents of the sacrifice, including the stones on which it was built. Especially because Askew alludes to this story after Wriothesely has returned to more questions on the sacrament, she implies through her quotation that his views amount to idolatrous veneration of the host. (Her last confession of faith reveals the "Masse . . . to be the most abhomynable ydoll that is in the worlde" [144].) In repeating Elijah's challenge to Wriothesley, Askew invokes the power of prophetic rebuke, once again implying her own position as a preacher within the courtroom.[59]

The subject of idolatry also appears in Paul's sermon to the Athenians, recorded in Acts 17. In Athens Paul finds an altar to an "unknown god," and delivers a spontaneous sermon that, in its condemnation of idolatry, repeats Stephen's argument. Paul exclaims, "God that made the worlde and all that are in it, seynge that he is Lorde of heven and erth, . . . dwelleth not in temples made with hondes, nether is worshipped with mennes hondes."[60] Besides repeating this text before Christopher Dare, as we have already seen, Askew pairs this passage with Acts 7 at other points during her trial. One example occurs in the *lattre* examination just before Askew is condemned by the Privy Council for denying Christ's presence in the host. When asked "Wyll you planelye denye Christ to be in the sacrament?" Askew tells the council "I bel[ieve] faythfullye the eternall sonne of God not to dwell there." She supports this statement by aligning Paul's and Stephen's sermons next to one another along with other texts concerning the destruction of the Temple. Adopting the same description for her discourse as Kempe, she "re[cites]" for the council "the hystorye of Bel, and the xi. Chaptre of Daniel, the vii and the xvii. of the Actes, and the xxiiii. of Matthew" (114). Quoted rapidly in succession, these passages illustrate again Askew's command of scripture, and connect her exegetical method with apostles such as Paul.

In missionary activity preceding his visit to Athens, Paul attracts audiences by entering synagogues and disputing the interpretation of scriptural passages. For three days in a Thessolanica synagogue Paul "declared oute of the scripture vnto them . . . that this Iesus was Christ, whom (sayd he) I preache to you" and again in Beroea, Paul and Silas "entred into the sinagoge off the Iewes" and with them "searched the scriptures dayly whether those thinges [i.e., that Jesus was the Christ] were even so."[61]

Similarly, Askew recounts in the *first* examination that she has traveled to Lincoln Cathedral and "read . . . upon the Byble" (56).[62] Contemporary accounts of reformers in London and Calais reveal that lay persons were entering churches where the English Bible had been set up and attracted crowds of listeners by their loud reading and exposition of the text.[63] Cranmer's preface to the Great Bible, first included in the 1540 printing, complains that such Bible-readers "abuse the king's grace's intent . . . in his grace's injunctions . . . which permit the bible to be read, not to allure great multitudes of people together." He further dismisses the possibility "that any such reading should be used in the church, as in a common school, expounding and interpreting scriptures, unless it be by such as shall have authority to preach and read."[64] While Askew neither explains whether she read aloud from the cathedral Bible nor identifies when she visited, accounts of other reformers who did so, as well as her own frequent quotation and expounding of the Bible during trial, lend considerable suggestiveness to her Lincoln visit.[65]

Whether or not she read aloud at Lincoln, Askew's report of her confrontation with several priests there further indicates the symbolic power she invests in the act of Bible reading. Before traveling to Lincoln, Askew reports that she had received warning from friends that "if I did come . . . the prestes wolde assault me," but she makes the journey anyway, "rema[ining] there vi. dayes, to se what wolde be sayd unto me" (56). As she was reading the Bible in the minster, Askew recalls, priests "resorted unto me by ii. and by ii. by v. and by vi. myndynge to have spoken to me, yet went . . . theyr wayes agayne with out wordes speakynge" (56). Crucial to this account is the sequence Askew provides of the events. Already knowing that cathedral priests "were bent agaynst" her, Askew travels to the cathedral and makes an appearance before the Bible.[66] In effect, she stages her meeting with the priests around the Bible, suggesting that she has drawn them to herself, rather than the possibility that they summoned her. In this scene, moreover, the authority of Askew's faith as represented in her individual reading of the Bible stands in dramatic contrast with the authority of the silent priests. Perfectly allegorizing the slogan of the Reformation (*sola scriptura*), Askew peers into the text without priestly assistance. As if in recognition of their redundancy, the nearby priests decide not to address Askew and part quietly, "going theyr wayes agayne with out wordes speakynge."

The *Examinations* thus present Askew as a preacher by establishing a public audience for her speech in both trial and cathedral scenes. Before the trial audience, Askew uses the process of interrogation to preach, including in her responses frequent quotation and interpretation of scripture. Before the priests at Lincoln, Askew reads from the Bible, suggesting her likeness to other reformers who were reading aloud and explicating Bible passages for gathered crowds. In addition to providing explication, Askew also invokes the language of prophetic rebuke. She re-enacts the sermons of Stephen, Paul, and Elijah, appropriating their prophetic authority against that of her interrogators.

IV

It is now clear that knowledge of scripture plays a crucial role in both Kempe's and Askew's narratives, providing an authority based upon textual rather than exclusively visionary knowledge. As we have seen, quotation of scriptural passages itself enables further speech and writing by requiring interpretation and application. These scriptural uses acquire even more significance because both authors wrote during periods of ecclesiastical censorship of the vernacular Bible.

While both Kempe and Askew bravely employ biblical knowledge in the face of censorship, their texts convey different points about women's acquisition and exercise of biblical literacy in the Lancastrian and Tudor periods. The *Book of Margery Kempe* highlights the possibilities open to industrious laity who might take advantage of conferences with priests, in addition to constant attendance of sermons, to acquire biblical and other forms of religious education.[67] But at the same time it demonstrates the severe limits of this educative path, recording Kempe's difficulty in finding and retaining sympathetic ecclesiastics like Alan of Lynn who take time to instruct her. This friar, in fact, falls under punishment for his generosity, receiving instructions from Thomas Netter, provincial prior of the English Carmelites and polemicist against Lollard women's preaching, to withhold from "enformyn [Kempe] in . . . text*y*s of Sc*r*iptur" (168).[68] Kempe expresses her devastation at the loss of Alan's instruction, complaining to God, "Now haue I . . . no co*m*fort neiþyr of man ne of childe" (168).

By featuring the practical and political obstacles threatening Kempe's instruction, the *Book* foregrounds the fact that attainment of biblical literacy often involves difficulty. Kempe wins biblical knowledge through hardship, and continues to endure that hardship through her engagement with publics who disapprove of her possession and use of such knowledge. One might ultimately say that the *Book* makes heroic both the pursuit of education and the practice of such skills once they have been acquired.

In Askew's *Examinations*, however, biblical access is never in jeopardy. Because vernacular Bibles were available even though limitations had been placed upon reading and annotating them, Askew uses scripture much more frequently than Kempe. She in fact theorizes her relation to the Bible as one allowing direct communication between herself and God. She proclaims, "loke what God hath charged me with hys mouthe, that have I shutte up in my harte" (118) and again, "loke what he hath layed unto me with hys owne mouth, in his holye Gospell, that have I with Gods grace, closed up in my harte" (143). Here the implication of "shutting" God's words within does not suggest silence, but rather internalization to the point of frequent and easy recall.

Thus, even as Askew's text informs the study of how early modern people read their Bibles, what both *The Book of Margery Kempe* and the *Examinations of Anne Askew* demonstrate about textual access is its social applicability. Essentially, to argue that Kempe and Askew preach is to show that they read or listen to biblical texts in order to use these texts in public settings. The strictures against conventicles in the Lancastrian and Tudor periods, and the 1543 Act for the Advancement of Religion, we have seen, assumed the greater efficacy of biblical interpretation within a community rather than individually. Henry Bowet confronts Kempe not on her knowledge of scripture, but upon her teaching of the people "in [his] diocyse" (126). Similarly, Askew's inquisitors worry not only about what she thinks, but also about what she tells other people. The second question she receives in examination follows from a report that she had been reading the Bible to another woman: Christopher Dare "sayd, that there was a woman, whych ded testyfye, *that I shuld reade,* how God was not in temples made with handes" (20, my emphasis).

Through their demonstration of familiarity with texts, on the one hand, and their emphasis upon the oral dissemination of texts within communities on the other, Kempe's *Book* and Askew's *Examinations* exemplify the cultural effects of the rise of literacy as theorized by Richard Firth Green. In *A Crisis of Truth: Literature and Law in Ricardian England,* Green proposes that in the late fourteenth century a shift of cultures began between one that assumed truth was constituted in the community, registered in the spoken and public trothplight, to one that assumed it originated in "the judicially enforced written contract."[69] Both Kempe and Askew seem to be straddling this divide, aware that truth rests in texts of scripture as much as personal revelation, yet eager to represent the efficacy of textual authority within oral, and thus communal, contexts. Their narratives entrust the written word within the service of the spoken, casting their teaching not in the formally arranged manner of a treatise, but as a speech made before a public audience.

In assuming that the scriptures could be as powerful as lives, and indeed, carry authority over lives, Kempe and Askew portrayed the dissemination of scripture as autobiography. Both engaged scriptural texts through the medium of personal stories—Kempe standing before Bowet's court repeating the words of the woman who cried out to Christ in Luke 11, or Askew recalling the challenge of Elijah when she demanded of Wriothesley "how long he [would] halt on both sides?" Under the heady immediacy wrought by the newly translated Bible and other devotional texts, Kempe and Askew literally made God's words their own, incarnating them twice in female form: in the mother tongue, and in the voice of the woman preacher.

Notes

For their comments on earlier drafts of this essay I would like to thank Reid Barbour and Lynn Robinson. Additionally, I owe thanks to Wendy Scase and Emily Steiner, both of whom responded to my argument about Kempe at the 2000 International Medieval Congress. This essay has further benefited from the criticism of Elaine Beilin, Clare Costley, Kathryn Kerby-Fulton, John Fleming, Linda Olson, Nigel Smith, Vance Smith, and members of the Princeton Medieval and Early Modern Studies reading group. I also wish to thank David Wallace for his care in reading and responding to my work.

1. This and all subsequent quotations are taken from *The Book of Margery Kempe*, ed. Sanford Brown Meech and Hope Emily Allen, Early English Text Society *o.s.* 212 (London: Oxford University Press, 1940).

2. The phrase "comownycacyon & good wordys" may reference a traditional lay right of instruction. See Helen Spencer, *English Preaching in the Late Middle Ages* (Oxford: Clarendon Press, 1993), 51–54, for a discussion of how Margery Kempe's practice follows and sometimes exceeds this traditional lay role. See also Alcuin Blamires, "Women and Preaching in Medieval Orthodoxy, Heresy, and Saints' Lives," *Viator* 26 (1995): 135–52, esp. 140 and 150, for a tradition of preaching as a work of mercy, and thus, a social obligation required of all Christians. See also Alcuin Blamires and C. W. Marx "Woman Not to Preach: A Disputation in British Library Harley 31," *Journal of Medieval Latin* 3 (1993): 34–63. Discussion of varying definitions of preaching in the Middle Ages appears below in section I.

3. Askew mentions only her first (March 1545) and third (June 1546) trial hearings in *The Examinations*. She omits her second hearing in June 1545 in which she was acquitted for sacramentarian beliefs. See *The Examinations of Anne Askew*, ed. Elaine Beilin (Oxford: Oxford University Press, 1996), xx–xxii.

4. It is hard to determine the exact influences upon sacramentarian thought in the 1520s, 30s, and 40s. It could have Lollard, Lutheran, or Zwinglian roots. See *Oxford English Dictionary*, "sacramentarian," 1.a and Susan Brigden, *London and the Reformation* (Oxford: Clarendon Press, 1988), 124.

5. This and all subsequent quotations are taken from Beilin, *Examinations of Anne Askew*.

6. Askew's qualification correctly follows the fourteenth chapter of Corinthians in Tyndale's 1534 translation of the New Testament. Tyndale uses the phrase "in the congregation" twice: "Let youre wyves kepe silence in the congregacions. For it is not permitted vnto them to speake: but let them be vnder obedience, as sayth the lawe. If they will learne eny thinge, let them axe their husbandes at home. For it is a shame for wemen to speake in the congregacion" (*The newe Testament*, 2nd ed. [Antwerp, 1534] fol. cclv v. STC 2826). All subsequent quotations of Tyndale's New Testament are from this text. The word "congregation" as a translation of "ecclesia" was a point of controversy between evangelicals and traditionalists in the early 1540s. In the Bishop's Convocation of 1542 Stephen Gardiner included "congregation" in a list of several key words that should be changed in a revised translation of the 1541 English Bible (not drastically altered since Tyndale) to better reflect the Vulgate. As a translation for "ecclesia," the word "congregation" seems suggestive of evangelical gathered communities while the alternative, "church," connotes a larger institution with its leadership hierarchy and system of governance. For an account of Gardiner's list, which has now been lost, see James Arthur Miller, *Stephen Gardiner and the Tudor Reaction* (London: Society for the Promotion of Christian Knowledge, 1926), 104–105. For a different assessment of Askew's

interpretation of 1 Cor. 14:34–35, see Susan Wabuda, "The Woman with the Rock: The Controversy on Women and Bible Reading," in *Belief and Practice in Reformation England: A Tribute to Patrick Collinson from His Students* (Aldershot: Ashgate Press, 1998), 55.

7. Arundel legislated against the possession of vernacular Bibles in the *Constitutions* (drafted in 1407 and formally issued in 1409) and declared heresy punishable by burning in *De Heretico Comburendo*, 1401.

8. 34 and 35 Henry VIII c. 1 in *The Statutes of the Realm*, vol. 3 (London, 1810–1822), 896: "everye noble wooman and gentlewooman maie reade [the Bible] to them seules and not to others." For discussion of this act see Brian Cummings, "Reformed Literature and Literature Reformed," in *The Cambridge History of Medieval English Literature*, ed. David Wallace (Cambridge: Cambridge University Press, 1999), 843. See also Diarmaid MacCulloch, *Thomas Cranmer: A Life* (New Haven, Conn.: Yale University Press, 1996), 311, and Wabuda, "The Controversy on Women and Bible Reading," 54–55.

9. On the similarities between scriptural citation and the act of preaching, see Anne Hudson, *The Premature Reformation* (Oxford: Clarendon Press, 1988), 190: "memorization was a skill deliberately chosen for its evangelizing potential." In the *Repressor of Overmuch Blaming of the Clergy*, Reginald Pecock complained of persons who "neuere leerned ferther in scolis than her grammer" but through memorization of scripture "bi herte and bi mouth" understood how to "preche full gloriosely into plesaunce of the people." Pecock describes how this occurred at public venues such as the ale house: "thei kunned bi herte the textis of holi scripture, and dunned lussche [pour] hem out thikke at feest, and at ale drinking, and vpon her highe benchis sitting" (quoted in Hudson, *Premature Reformation*, 190–91). See also Claire Cross, "'Great Reasoners in Scripture:' The Activities of Women Lollards, 1380–1530," in *Medieval Women: Essays Dedicated and Presented to Professor Rosalind M. T. Hill*, ed. Derek Baker (Oxford: Basil Blackwell, 1978), 359–80, and Shannon McSheffrey, *Gender and Heresy: Women and Men in Lollard Communities, 1420–1530* (Philadelphia: University of Pennsylvania Press, 1995), for a revision of Cross's thesis. I discuss reading aloud of the Bible in Henrician London at greater length in chapter three of my dissertation, "Trying Testimony: Heresy, Interrogation, and the English Woman Writer," Princeton University, 2003.

10. According to Hudson, in "the section of the Decretals *De Hereticis*," within the twelfth chapter, "the term *conventicula* covers the heretical activities of translation into the vernacular, the discussion of questions concerning scripture amongst lay people, and preaching by the laity." After 1401 "conventicles and schools" became the standard description of Lollard meetings, and in these meetings group instruction took place in which men and women were sometimes learners, sometimes teachers. By the early sixteenth century, conventicles or schools were also referred to as "lectures" and "readings" at which local people, including women, recited and interpreted scripture. See Hudson, *Premature Reformation*, 176–83. Also, David Wallace has shown that the word "conventicle" applied to trade associations as well as religious groups in fourteenth-century London. See Wallace, *Chaucerian Polity* (Stanford, Calif.: Stanford University Press, 1997), 171–72. The word "conventicle" in the fifteenth and sixteenth centuries referred generally to an "assembly," but by Henry VIII's reign it had acquired a specific religious sense. In religious contexts it meant "a religious meeting or assembly of a private, clandestine, or illegal kind; a meeting for the exercise of religion otherwise than as sanctioned by the law." See *Oxford English Dictionary*, "conventicle," 4.a. Susan Brigden describes the "Protestant underground" conventicles gathering in London in the early 1540s in *London and the Reformation*, 328–29.

11. This claim resembles the early modern phenomenon Natalie Zemon Davis discusses as the usefulness of the "female persona" in authorizing acts of resistance. When rioting men dressed up as women, or women themselves participated in riots, they could hide behind the supposed weakness of the female gender, assuming that whatever they did was of little consequence because it was initiated by "mere women." See "Women on Top" in *Feminism and Renaissance Studies*, ed. Lorna Hutson (Oxford: Oxford University Press, 1999), 176 (reprinted from *Society and Culture in Early Modern France* [Polity Press, 1965], 124–51).

12. See Theresa D. Kemp, "Translating (Anne) Askew: The Textual Remains of a Sixteenth Century Heretic and Saint," *Renaissance Quarterly* 52 (1999): 1021–43, for the argument that Askew documents her trial as a way of addressing conflicting reports produced about her by evangelicals and traditionalists.

13. For discussion of trial accounts as literature, see Beilin, "Anne Askew's Dialogue with Authority," in *Contending Kingdoms: Historical, Psychological, and Feminist Approaches to Literature of Sixteenth-Century England and France* (Detroit: Wayne State University Press, 1991), a reading of Askew's *Examinations* within the tradition of Renaissance dialogues; John Knott, *Discourses of Martyrdom in English Literature, 1563–1694* (Cambridge: Cambridge University Press, 1993), 8, an identification of trial accounts as "a distinct genre"; and Ritchie D. Kendall, *The Drama of Dissent: The Radical Poetics of Nonconformity, 1380–1590* (Chapel Hill: University of North Carolina Press, 1986), a discussion of trial narratives as forms of drama from Lollardy to Puritanism.

14. Rita Copeland, *Pedagogy, Intellectuals, and Dissent in the Later Middle Ages: Lollardy and Ideas of Learning* (Cambridge: Cambridge University Press, 2001), 141–219.

15. I assume the relative autonomy of Kempe and Askew as authors of their texts, but see David Wallace's response to my essay as well as the articles in the present volume by Nicholas Watson and Felicity Riddy. As with most medieval and Renaissance texts, we have no autograph manuscripts for either Kempe or Askew. The manuscript on which all editions of Kempe's *Book* are based, British Library Additional 61823, is a copy. As both Watson and Riddy note, the *Book* itself claims Kempe's illiteracy and describes a collaborative relationship between Kempe and her scribes wherein she dictates her experiences, hears the text read back, and offers suggestions. In Askew's case, there is no manuscript of her text. All editions of her *Examinations* are based on John Bale's *first* and *lattre examinacyon of Anne Askew* (Wesel, 1546 and 1547 respectively). It is therefore possible that Kempe's scribes emended her dictation and that Askew's editor, John Bale, made changes to her manuscript. I do, however, want to claim that both Kempe and Askew exercised some degree of agency in the writing of their texts—Kempe in dictating narratives to her scribes and Askew in writing and sending out manuscripts that were edited by Bale. For arguments concerning the likelihood of Askew's authorship, see Leslie Fairfield, *John Bale: Mythmaker for the English Reformation* (West Lafayette, Ind.: Purdue University Press, 1976), 133–35; Diane Watt, *Secretaries of God: Women Prophets in Late Medieval and Early Modern England* (Cambridge: D. S. Brewer, 1997), 94–95; and Thomas Freeman and Sarah Elizabeth Wall, "Racking the Body, Shaping the Text: The Account of Anne Askew in Foxe's 'Book of Martyrs,'" *Renaissance Quarterly* 54 (2001): 1165–96. (Though Freeman and Wall caution that Foxe, especially, took minor liberties with Askew's text, such liberties by no means discount the existence of Askew's original manuscript. This original text is simply filtered through the interests of her editors.)

16. Alan of Lille, *The Art of Preaching*, trans. Gillian R. Evans (Kalamazoo, Mich.: Cistercian Publications, 1981), 16–17. "Praedicatio est, manifesta et publica instructio morum et fidei, informationi hominum deserviens" (*Summa de arte praedicatoria, Patrologia Latina*, 210, col. 111).

17. Lille, *Art of Preaching*, 142. "Praelatorum debet esse praedicatio, et ab eis est proponenda" (*Summa de arte praedicatoria, Patrologia Latina*, 210, col. 182d).

18. From Nicole Bériou, "The Right of Women to Give Religious Instruction in the Thirteenth Century," in *Women Preachers and Prophets through Two Millennia of Christianity* (Berkeley: University of California Press, 1998), 138. Bériou refers to the transcription by M. Peuchmaurd, *Sacerdoce et prédication* (unpublished thesis for the degree of Reader, Paris, 1961), t. 2, annexe 2.

19. Bériou, "The Right of Women to Give Religious Instruction," 138. "dicendum quod auctoritatem habuerunt a Spiritu Sancto ipsis instigante et specialiter mittente, sicut apparuit per officium: ubi enim fides periclitabatur, igitur a Spiritu Sancto sunt missae; et quod dicit Apostolus, dicendum quod loquitur de mulieribus nuptis, quia sunt in statu communi mulierum, non autem de illis quae omnino specialiter electae fuerunt et privilegiatae, et sic etiam intelligitur" (Jean Leclercq, "Le magistère du prédicateur au xiiie siècle," *Archives d'Histoire doctrinale et littéraire du Moyen Age* 15 [1946]: 105–47, at 120).

20. Blamires, "Women and Preaching," 146. "Gratia prophetiae attenditur secundum mentem illuminatam a Deo; ex qua parte non est in hominibus sexuum differentia.... Sed gratia sermonis pertinet ad instructionem hominum, inter quos differentia sexuum invenitur" (quoted by Blamires from the *Summa theologiae* 2a2ae.177.2, gen. ed. Thomas Gilby, O.P., 60 vols. [London, 1963–], 45:134).

21. Blamires, "Women and Preaching," 145. Insufficient wisdom: "Communiter mulieres non sunt in sapientia perfectae, ut eis possit convenienter publica doctrina committi"; subjection to men: "Principaliter proptet conditionem foeminei sexus, qui debet esse subditos viro, ut patet *Gen*. Docere autem et persuadere publice in Ecclesia non pertinet ad subditos, sed ad praelatos" (quoted by Blamires from Gilby, *Summa theologiae*, 45:132). See also Blamires and Marx, "Woman Not to Preach," 41–42.

22. Basevorn, *The Form of Preaching*, trans. Leopold Krul in *Three Medieval Rhetorical Arts*, ed. James A. Murphy (Berkeley: University of California Press, 1971), 124. "Nullus laicus vel religiosus, nisi per Episcopum vel Papam licentiatus, nec mulier quantumcumque docta et sancta, praedicare debet. Nec sufficit alicui dicere quod sit a Deo missus, nisi hoc manifeste ostendat quia hoc solent haeretici dicere" (*Artes praedicandi: Contribution à l'histoire de la rhétorique au moyen age*, ed. Th.-M. Charland [Paris, 1936], 241–42).

23. *Speculum Christiani: A Middle English Religious Treatise of the 14th Century*, ed. Gustaf Holmstedt, Early English Text Society *o.s.* 182, reprint 1988 (London: Oxford University Press, 1933), clxxvi.

24. *Speculum Christiani*, 2.

25. Karma Lochrie posits a similarity between the *Speculum Christiani*'s definition of preaching and Margery Kempe's answer about whether or not she preaches. See *Margery Kempe and Translations of the Flesh* (Philadelphia: University of Pennsylvania Press, 1991), 111.

26. Gillespie, "*Doctrina* and *Predicacio:* The Design and Function of Some Pastoral Manuals," *Leeds Studies in English* 11 (1980): 36–50. See p. 42.

27. On the manuscript's composition date see Blamires and Marx, "Woman Not to Preach," 38–39.

28. Brut's testimony as recorded in the trial proceedings of the bishop of Hereford's register is printed in *Registrum Johannis Trefnant*, ed. W. W. Capes, Canterbury and York Society 20 (1916): 285–358. See also Blamires, "Women and Preaching," 136 n. 5, and Blamires and Marx, "Woman Not to Preach," 39.

29. Also in "Women and Preaching," Blamires argues that the Harley author's identification of the cases of Mary and Martha was itself a demonstration of the widespread credibility of de Voragine's *Life* of the Magdalene, which depicts Mary preaching to the king of France. See Jacobi a Voragine, *Legenda aurea vulgo historia lombardica dicta*, ed. T. Graesse, 3rd ed. (1890; reprint, Osnabruck, 1965), 409: "Post hoc autem advenit princeps provinciae illius cum uxore sua, ut pro habenda prole ydolis immolaret. Cui Magdalena Christum praedicans sacrificia dissuasit."

30. *Summa quaestionum* 1.11.2, *Utrum mulier possit esse doctor seu doxtrix huius scientiae*, cited by Blamires in "Women and Preaching," 139, from *Magistri Henrici Goethals a Gandavo . . . Summa in tres partes*, 3 vols. (Ferrara: F. Succius, 1642–1646).

31. Blamires, "Women and Preaching," 147.

32. Blamires and Marx, "Woman Not to Preach," 45–46.

33. They are also notable for the fact that some of them were formed in response to heretical claims for women and laymen's right to preach, which suggests that women's preaching, or at least the advocacy of it, was itself responsible for calling the definition of preaching into question.

34. Gauthier cited Titus 2:3–4, where Paul advises older women to educate young girls, as an example of an acceptable teaching role for women. See Bèriou, "The Right of Women to Give Religious Instruction," 138.

35. Blamires, "Women and Preaching," 150 n. 77, applies the history of preaching definitions to Kempe's answer.

36. Anthony Goodman, Karma Lochrie, and Lynn Staley have all briefly suggested that Margery Kempe preaches. They assume a loose definition of preaching, however, specifying it only as speaking about religious matters in public. My argument expands their inquiry, proposing that a greater understanding of the rhetorical figures of preaching will allow us a fuller picture of how the *Book* intends its audiences to recognize Kempe as a preacher. What Kempe's preaching capacities reveal is a dependence upon textual and rhetorical learning, which ultimately suggests her desire to participate in clerical culture rather than bypass its authority by recourse to visionary knowledge alone. See Goodman, "The Piety of John Brunham's Daughter of Lynn," in *Medieval Women: Essays Dedicated and Presented to Professor Rosalind M. T. Hill*, ed. Derek Baker (Oxford: Basil Blackwell, 1978), 354; Lochrie, "*The Book of Margery Kempe:* The Marginal Woman's Quest for Literary Authority," *Journal of Medieval and Renaissance Studies* 1 (1986): 33–55, esp. 42–47; and Staley, *Margery Kempe's Dissenting Fictions* (University Park: Pennsylvania State University Press, 1994), 55.

37. Lochrie, "Marginal Woman's Quest," 44–45, and *Translations of the Flesh*, 109–11.

38. Quoted and translated in Lochrie, *Translations of the Flesh*, 110. "si beati qui audiunt et custodiunt, magis beati qui predicant et custodiunt verbum Dei, quoniam beacius est magis dare quam accipere" (Capes, *Registrum Johannis Trefnant*, 345).

39. Lochrie, *Translations of the Flesh*, 110.

40. The classic text on medieval preaching, G. R. Owst's *Preaching in Medieval England*, identifies three basic sermon forms: the text- or scripture-based form, the sophisticated university-style sermon consisting of divisions and themes, and the more popular sermon style based on fable or story. The text-based sermon form obviously makes scriptural interpretation its main objective. Under discussion of this style, Owst quotes Dominican Thomas Wallys as well as Oxford Chancellor Thomas Gascoigne, both of whom emphasize the importance of textual explication included in

the sermons of the church fathers. See Owst, *Preaching in Medieval England* (Cambridge: Cambridge University Press, 1926), 310–13.

41. The exemplum was a stock component of popular-style sermons. John Mirk's *Festial*, a widely copied sermon collection, includes an exemplum, or "narracio," in every sermon. A famous Chaucerian "ensample" is the Pardoner's tale, which seeks to persuade listeners against avarice even as the Pardoner himself pursues it.

42. Lynn Staley discusses this story as evidence of Kempe's apparent orthodoxy in comparison with Lollards. "Mendicants and other popular preachers," she notes, "were more likely to weave stories into their sermons." Staley does not discuss, however, how Kempe's use of the exemplum establishes her homiletic authority. See *Margery Kempe's Dissenting Fictions*, 120.

43. "rehersen," 2.b.

44. The young monk tells Kempe, "'Eyþyr þow hast þe Holy Gost or ellys þow hast a devyl wyth-in þe, for þat þu spekyst her to vs it is Holy Wrytte, and þat hast þu not of þiself'" (28). And as she defends her right to speak of God in Bowet's court by quoting Luke 11, other clerks argue "'sche hath a deuyl wyth-inne hir, for sche spekyth of þe gospel'" (126). Anne Hudson notes that as early as Bishop Alnwick's investigations "the ability to recite from memory passages from the bible was regarded as evidence of heresy" and that in the later hearings under Bishop Longland "recitation and readings are constantly mentioned." See Hudson, *Premature Reformation*, 166.

45. Spencer, *English Preaching*, 112 and 406 n. 138. "Sirs" was not exclusively used in sermons; it also applied generally to other public occasions of address.

46. See, for example, Kempe's castigation of swearing (101, 124, 127), which many critics have taken as evidence for Lollard sympathies. Swearing was, however, censured in many preaching manuals. Owst (*Preaching*, 182) notes the prominence of swearing among lists of vices in several preaching manuals. John Mirk catalogues swearing as breaking the second commandment in his *Instructions for Parish Priests*, ed. Gillis Kristensson (Lund Studies in English, 1974), 119.

47. See Edwin D. Craun, "*Fama* and Pastoral Constraints on Rebuking Sinners: *The Book of Margery Kempe*," in *Fama: The Politics of Talk and Reputation in Medieval Europe*, ed. Thelma Fenster and Daniel Lord Small (Ithaca, N.Y., and London: Cornell University Press, 2003), 187–209.

48. She obtains a written license to move freely about England without being taken in for heresy investigation. She asks Henry Bowet for a "lettyr & . . . seyl in-to recorde þat I haue excusyd me a-geyn myn enmys & no-thyng is attyd ageyns me, neiþyr herrowr ne heresy þat may ben preuyd vp-on me" and Bowet "ful goodly grawntyd hir al hir desyr" (134). Henry Chichele, the successor to Arundel as archbishop of Canterbury (1414–1443), also grants Kempe a letter, apparently upon Henry Bowet's request (135–36).

49. John Foxe, *The seconde volume of the Ecclesiasticall historie conteyningthe acts and monuments of martyrs* (London, 1597), 1130.

50. Brigden, *London and the Reformation*, 374.

51. Elaine Beilin first argued for the importance of Stephen as a model for Askew in "'Readynge upon the Bible': Anne Askew's Journey to Lincoln" (paper presented at the Sixteenth Century Studies Conference, Toronto, October 1998). Beilin's work on Stephen forms part of a larger project that examines representations of Askew from the sixteenth century to the present. I have benefited from discussions with Beilin about Stephen and the role of biblical typologies in Askew's *Examinations*. For discussion of Stephen as an apostolic model for Askew's writing and

self-representation see Gwynne Kennedy, *Just Anger: Representing Women's Anger in Early Modern England* (Carbondale and Edwardsville: Southern Illinois University Press, 2000), 145–48. My analysis of Stephen's role in the *Examinations* differs with Beilin's and Kennedy's in its focus upon Stephen's words as sermon rhetoric, and consequently, upon Askew's quotation of his words as preaching.

52. Beilin and Megan Matchinske have both noted the "wiliness" of Askew's character, chiefly evidenced in her refusal to play by the rules of interrogation. They emphasize that Askew asks (instead of answers) questions of her interrogators, makes deliberately ambiguous responses, and frequently employs irony. See Beilin, *Redeeming Eve: Women Writers of the English Renaissance* (Princeton, N.J.: Princeton University Press, 1987), 35, 37, 40; and Matchinske, *Writing, Gender and State in Early Modern England: Identity Formation and the Female Subject* (Cambridge: Cambridge University Press, 1998), 45–47.

53. Tyndale, *newe Testament*, 1534, fol. Clxvii r. I quote from Tyndale's 1534 translation of the New Testament because it alone, of the Coverdale Bible of 1535, as well as the Matthew Bible of 1537 and the Great Bible of 1539, 1540, nd 1541, contains marginal commentary (besides scripture references) on Stephen's sermon in Acts 7. In addition to identifying Stephen's speech as a sermon, Tyndale's 1534 translation includes a star after the word "temple" in Acts 7. The margin reads, "God dwelleth not in temples or churches made with ha(n)des" (fol. Clxvii r). Tyndale does not, however, directly reference the source text for Paul and Stephen (Isa. 66) in the margin.

54. Tyndale, *newe Testament*, 1534, fol. Clxxxiiii r.

55. Tyndale, *newe Testament*, fol. Clxvii r and v.

56. Tyndale, *newe Testament*, fol. Clxvii v.

57. Here, as in her earlier exchange with Christopher Dare, Askew's quotation of scripture is solicited by her examiner's inability to identify a biblical text.

58. *The Byble in Englysh* (London, 1541), fol. lviii r and v.

59. Of Askew's quotation of 1 Kings 18, Kennedy also observes that "Askew aligns herself with Elijah as God's spokesperson and defender" (*Just Anger*, 149).

60. Tyndale, *newe Testament*, fol. Clxxxiiii r and v.

61. Tyndale, *newe Testament*, fol. Clxxxiii r.

62. Margaret Bowker records that Bishop Longland placed a vernacular Bible (the Great Bible) in Lincoln Cathedral in 1541. See Bowker, *The Henrician Reformation: The Diocese of Lincoln under John Langland, 1521–1547* (Cambridge: Cambridge University Press, 1981), 170.

63. For London: John Foxe, *seconde volume of the Ecclesiasicall historie*, 1097, 1101, the account of Mrs. Castle and John Porter. For Calais: *Letters and Papers, Foreign and Domestic of the Reign of Henry VIII*, vol. 14, pt. 1 (London, 1894), no. 1351.

64. *Miscellaneous Writings and Letters of Thomas Cranmer*, ed. John Cox (Cambridge: Parker Society, Cambridge University Press, 1846), 122.

65. As explained in section I, under the 1543 Act for the Advancement of Religion, gentlewomen were barred from reading the Bible in public settings. Beilin notes, "If [Askew's] trip to Lincoln occurred after the passage of this Act . . . [she] was deliberately defying the law when she read the Bible so publicly in Lincoln minster" (xxvi).

66. Beilin suggests that the Lincoln Bible could have "been placed either in the choir (where indeed a Bible now stands on a late seventeenth-century reading desk) or . . . where a reading desk

was later customarily positioned opposite the pulpit in the nave before the screen." From her un-published paper, "'Readynge upon the Bible,'" 4.

67. One priest reads to Kempe "many a good boke of hy contemplacyon & oþer bokys, as the Bybl wyth doctowrys þer-up-on, Seynt Brydys boke, Hyltons boke, Bone-ventur, Stimulus Amoris, Incendium Amoris, & swech oþer" (143). On the growing number of orthodox vernacular texts in the fifteenth and early sixteenth centuries, see Eamon Duffy, *The Stripping of the Altars: Traditional Religion in England, 1400–1580* (New Haven, Conn., and London: Yale University Press, 1992), 53–87, and Vincent Gillespie, "Vernacular Books of Religion" in *Book Production and Book Publishing in Britain, 1375–1475,* ed. Jeremy Griffiths and Derek Pearsall (Cambridge: Cambridge University Press, 1989), 317–44. On Lollard vernacular writings and Lollard uses of orthodox vernacular texts, see Margaret Aston, *Lollards and Reformers: Images and Literacy in Late Medieval Religion* (London: Hambledon Press, 1984), 101–33, 194–217.

68. Netter's condemnation of Lollard women appears in his *Doctrinale antiquitatum fidei Catholicae Ecclesiae,* 3 vols., ed. F. Bonaventura Blanciotee (Venice: Antonio Bassanesi, 1759; reprint, Farnborough, 1967), 1:636 ff. and passim. Alan of Lynn compiled indices to Birgitta of Sweden's *Revelations* and the *Prophecies.* See *The Book of Margery Kempe,* n. 22/11–12, p. 268.

69. Richard Firth Green, *A Crisis of Truth: Literature and Law in Ricardian England* (Philadelphia: University of Pennsylvania Press, 1999), xiv.

■ ■ ■

Response to Genelle Gertz-Robinson

"Stepping into the Pulpit?"

DAVID WALLACE

Genelle Gertz-Robinson here subtly teases out the maneuverings of a complex feminine *occupatio:* women who preach while denying their discourse the status of preaching. Crucial here is their common insistence "that preaching must be defined by location— by the actual habitation of a pulpit" (p. 460). Both women recognize the pulpit as a highly charged social space that confers authority upon a speaker and what he, norma- tively he, has to say. Chaucer's Pardoner, famously, deploys a whole range of gestural techniques with which to spellbind audiences from a pulpit ("And lo, sires, thus I preche," 3.915). Chaucer himself, represented as author in the famous Corpus Christi frontis- piece, is imagined in a pulpit-like structure that lends authority to his narrating.[1] Preach- ers, especially in Italy, would address large crowds from pulpits built out over public squares, and the rulers of Florence would similarly expose or display themselves from the *ringhiera* or external platform of the Palazzo Publico to the masses below.[2] Both Margery Kempe and Anne Askew, Gertz-Robinson observes, neatly exploit their very absence from such a delimited masculine space as a means of enabling, of allowing continuance to, their religious discourse: "I preche nat ser," says Kempe, "I come in no pulpytt" (126); "and then I asked hym," says Askew (defending herself under interroga- tion), "how manye women he had seane, go into the pulpett and preache" (30).

I have referred here to "Kempe" and "Askew" as we typically do, bracketing out complexities of textual transmission in order to suggest a cleaner or more immediate encounter with historical protagonists. In the case of Kempe and Askew, however, it seems especially important to dwell on such complexities for a moment: for there is often a strong pull to make clean distinctions between the textual operations of male amanuenses and editors and the authentic "voices" of remarkable women such as Askew and Kempe. Margery, as she herself tells us, employed a series of male amanuenses. There was nothing especially glamorous, as Hoccleve reminds us, about scratching a pen across animal skin to record other people's inspirations: such activity was more artisanal than artistic.[3] Margery evidently maintained close control over the production of her text (which could be read back to her as she went along). Kempe's text, as Gertz-Robinson convincingly demonstrates, deploys a wide range of preaching forms, such as exempla, expoundings of Scripture, and sermon vocatives. Such forms had doubtless been impressed upon Margery's consciousness through hundreds of hours of pulpit preachings. At the same time, these same forms might also have comprised part of the scribe's mental furniture; experiences narrated by Kempe might thus have assumed peculiarly literary shape or inflection at the moment of writing. And, on hearing them read back, Kempe might have felt (like any of us, subjected to good copyediting) that gains outweighed losses. Kempe's *Book* is (like almost all medieval texts) constitutively multi-voiced, multi-authored, and (to extend a medieval metaphor) hermaphrodite, middle-chambered, owing something to both male and female.

The same holds for Askew's text, or texts, although it is more difficult to conceive this as a liberating possibility over which, ultimately, Askew retains control: for many parties have designs on Askew and her life's narrative, a story which can only attain full historic charge if Askew dies, and dies young. For the Catholic faction in the latter years of Henry VIII, Askew's torture and execution serve *encourager les autres*.[4] For the Protestants assembling in the wings around teenage Edward, Askew's violent demise holds promise of Protestant martyrological narrative. The fact that it is John Bale who takes control of Askew's afterlife (as he assumes control of John Leland's) should certainly give us pause: Bale's radical self-introjection into Askew's narrating almost certainly extends (so Claire Costley convinces us) to putting words in her mouth.[5] And yet, such suspicions seem not to diminish the allure of Askew's text: indeed, the very fragility of her historical record—threatened by encroachments from "friend" and foe alike—make her appear the more poignant and compelling as historical actor: "Thus fare ye well. Quod Anne Askew."[6]

Texts representing women who preach (while ostensibly confining themselves, as Kempe has it, to "comownycacyon & good wordys") have implications, then, not only for women but for the men who share in their production and dissemination. Chaucer, writing and disseminating at about the time the Lollard Walter Brut is on trial for championing women preachers, has his pilgrim Pardoner recognize his Wife of Bath *as* a preacher ("Ye been a noble prechour in this cas," 3.165). Chaucer does not, of course, have his Wife ascend a pulpit, although her verbal performances in her favored locus do seem (to adapt a term from Judith Bennett) pulpit-like.[7] This locus is, of course, the bed: a site where women (medieval confessors recognized) might effectively sermonize their husbands.[8] Women, we have heard Askew say, do not actually "go into the pulpett and preache"; and yet both Askew and Kempe knew of preaching women from centuries past (particularly those glorious early Christian centuries to which Catholic, Lollard, and Protestant cultures alike perennially itched to return). St. Catherine, dedicatee of so many medieval guilds and educational foundations, preached to and confounded fifty orators. St. Cecelia, freshly brought to Henrician England by William Thynne's editions of 1532 and 1542, climaxes her earthly life by preaching from a place that, again, seems pulpit-like, namely, her bath. This liminal structure, located between life and death (as lifeblood flows from the female saint, along with her language) shares something of the symbolic charge of the anchorhold: a space forming part of the physical fabric of the church from which a woman might address the world (as Julian of Norwich spoke to Margery Kempe, chap. 18). Here again, it is the very thoroughness with which male clerics attempted to regulate this aperture for feminine "comownycacyon & good words" which suggests its social efficacy.

Such struggles to regulate and exploit women's access to, and strategic disavowal of, pulpits and pulpit-like structures are worked out in the visual arts as well as in writing. Here I would like to consider just one example, a painting from the Philadelphia Museum of Art (figure 1) that negotiates many of the issues raised by Gertz-Robinson's account of Kempe's *Book* and Askew's *Examinations*.[9] The date ascribed to this work, c. 1500–1520, splits that of our two literary texts but the painting speaks to them both. From its background scenes it is evident that this depiction, like so many others from this period, follows the *Legenda Aurea* of the Dominican Jacobus de Voragine (or one of its numerous derivatives). Friar Jacobus, originally from the coastal town of Varazze to the west of Genoa, compiled his lives of saints from the lectionary between 1259 and 1266. His work, translated across Europe, became vastly influential: Chaucer borrowed from it for his St. Cecelia story (and perhaps for his Magdalene legend); Caxton drew from versions in Latin, French, and English to produce his own translated edition (subsequently reprinted by Wynkyn de Worde, Pynson, and Notary).[10] According to the *Legenda Aurea*, then, Mary Magdalene and her entourage were bundled onto a pilotless boat by unbelievers fourteen years after the death of Christ and left to drown. Washing up at Marseilles, Mary preaches to and eventually converts the prince of the region. Flushed with convert zeal, the prince and his pregnant wife embark for Rome in order to see the sights and converse with St. Peter. A storm breaks out, the baby is born and the mother dies in labor (thus making the male child "his mother's murderer," 168). Dead mother and suckling child are then abandoned on an island; the father carries on to Rome, where Peter assures him all will be well and shows him the Christian sights. Returning home two years later, the father calls in at the island and finds the baby—a

FIGURE 1. Master of the Magdalene Legend, "Saint Mary Magdalene Preaching," John G. Johnson Collection, Philadelphia Museum of Art. Reproduced by permission.

very tiny baby, in the painting—playing by the seashore and the mother, still wrapped in his cloak, miraculously preserved. She then awakes singing the praises of Mary Magdalene; the happy troika return to Marseilles, find Mary preaching among her disciples, and destroy all temples of idols in the town.

In our painting, however, this complicated narrative functions as little more than an identifying frieze set above the main visual subject (as named by the painting's catalogue): "Saint Mary Magdalene Preaching." Such a baldly descriptive title establishes the phenomenon of a woman preaching as the painting's subject with a directness that the painter himself (or herself: you never know) contrives to avoid; as with our two literary texts, woman here does and does not preach. Mary Magdalene, of course, had exceptional credentials: Christ made her, the *Golden Legend* tells us, "one of his most intimate associates" (166); in appearing first to her after the resurrection, St. Ambrose maintains, Christ made her *apostolorum apostola*, "an apostle to the apostles."[11] It was thus only fitting that, on reaching Marseilles, "the lips which had pressed kisses so loving and so tender on our Lord's feet should breathe the perfume of the word of God more copiously than others" (167). But there is no suggestion, in the *Legend*, of Mary Magdalene preaching in the kind of rural landscape evoked by our painting: she preaches in cities, first Marseille and later Aix. And is she, in the painting, actually engaged in *preaching?* She seems, rather, to be breathing forth "the perfume of the word of God," as if she has herself become the vessel that is her identifying iconographic sign.[12] She, alone of all the foreground figures, seems withdrawn from the very scene that, visually, she dominates: as if, perhaps, already transported to the next scene of her life, the thirty years' solitariness in a desert landscape where, borne up by angels, she levitates between heaven and earth seven times a day.[13] Women sit at her feet, seeking instruction: one of them supports a baby reaching for an apple (reminding us both of Christ and, perhaps, the male child in the legend); the two others gaze across Mary's body at the two men authoritatively framing the saint, left and right. One of these male figures (possibly a donor portrait?) clasps what might be a pilgrim staff; the other raises his right hand in the classic sermonizing gesture, evidently in response to the questioning implicit in the female figure on his left. Her gesture, it is worth noting, represents a stiff-jointed, left-handed variant of the more supple—but still essentially affective—gesture of the Magdalene herself. The suggestion is, I think, that although the authority of witness emanates from the heavy-lidded female saint, powers of exegesis are to be sought along sight-lines that will lead to masculine figures.[14]

But although the painting busily contrives to augment masculine authority, there is no doubt that this woman, Mary from Magdalum, really is preaching: a fact conceded by her standing in a structure so pulpit-like that it is, indeed, a pulpit. Jean Poyet, painting c. 1500, imagines a similar structure for the rural preachings of his John the Baptist (*Hours of Henry VIII*, fol. 173); the crucial, pulpit-suggesting detail in both works is the wooden crossbar between two tree trunks upon which the preaching saint's left hand lightly rests.[15] Thirteenth-century commentators, especially Dominicans, were willing to concede that Mary Magdalene did, indeed, preach: the verb *nunciare* (to announce) was most often used to characterize her relation to the apostles, but *praedicare* (to preach) was preferred for describing her mission in Marseilles. The phrase "ascending the pulpit" was often used to denote preaching: one notices that, in our painting, the Magdalene is set higher than not only the women at her feet, but also the men at her sides. And there are surviving examples in fresco, carved relief, and embroidery of Mary preaching from more conventional pulpits.[16] Commentators did worry about what precedent such images of a woman preaching might set; their strategy, following that generally applied to the Virgin Mary, was to emphasize the singularity of the woman (the Mary) in question. "One reads that after Pentecost," the Dominican Giovanni di San Gimignano writes, that Mary Magdalene "preached as an apostle to the people. But then it was prohibited to other women by the Apostle saying, 'Let women keep quiet in Church.'"[17] He thus returns us to the Pauline strictures (here 1 Cor. 14) with which, as we have seen, Kempe and Askew are still in delicate negotiation.

Friar Giovanni does, however, open a sight- or time-line to a moment—between the resurrection of Christ and the coming of St. Paul—that might be imagined utopian for preaching women. And perhaps the most appealing and suggestive aspect of the Philadelphia painting, for women of active life, was its opening up of temporal possibilities. Two times are running in the painting: that of the evangelization of Europe, and that of the unfolding historical present. The suggestive simultaneity of heroic past and negotiable present is served by painterly focus upon a precise moment in the Magdalene's life narrative, one that speaks also to the shifting history of her clothes. Illustrations of Mary's early, pre-Christian career favor garish and extravagant outfits; her career to come, in the desert, will see her wearing not much at all, beyond her own luxuriant hair.[18] Here, however, in the phase of public ministry, she wears clothes that are modest but distinctively stylish; the pattern of her dress is shared by no other woman. If the female viewer identifies with the female protagonist's wearing of contemporary dress, she might further imagine the active life to be led within such clothing. Margery Kempe—herself a sometime wearer of garish dress, chap. 2—observed the suggestive lines of such split temporal schemes: while struggling to persist in a difficult historical present, she willingly accepted the invitation (as disseminated by texts such as the *Meditationes vitae Christi*, and its visual and vernacular derivatives) to imagine herself back into the biblical moment, pursuing the *vita activa*. Anne Askew, similarly, could imagine herself reliving moments of biblical drama—most vividly, as Gertz-Robinson observes, as a new Stephen—even by way of enduring the unspeakable harshness of her own historical moment.

It is not clear, finally, whether our painting should be assigned to the canon of medieval or Renaissance art. The illuminations of Jean Poyet, dating from roughly the same period, are ringingly assigned to the Renaissance by the Pierpoint Morgan Library;

justifications for this, beyond matters of marketing, seem slender.[19] "Stepping into the Pulpit?" prompts us to reflect whether equivalent period differentiations prove germane for Askew and Kempe. Distances and differences between the two women have certainly been exaggerated by canonical schemata and by practices of anthologizing. The Longman Annotated Texts series, for example, assigns Kempe to Alexandra Barratt's *Women's Writing in Middle English*, whereas Askew features in Randall Martin's *Women Writers in Renaissance England*. For Martin, the terms "Renaissance" and "Protestant" seem almost interchangeable: his anthology has little to say about those women in sixteenth-century England who persisted in their Catholicism (or who carried it overseas, along with their Englishness). Gertz-Robinson's consideration of Askew and Kempe within a common analytical frame is thus both timely and instructive. I would like to conclude with two short reflections on questions of periodization that arise from her analysis.

The first is to note how this intercalated account of Kempe and Askew prompts us to consider parallels between the political regimes and religious cultures of Lancastrian and Tudor England. Each dynasty is established more by force of arms than by claims of birthright; each is willing to employ religious argument as a means of effecting or obscuring, as instrument or screen, political ends. Margery Kempe has often been written about as if hysterical, but attentive reading of her *Book* reveals that if the term *hysteria* be allowed, it inheres not so much in Kempe as in the greater body of the traumatized kingdom (where Arundel rules the roost; where followers of John, duke of Bedford—he who secures the burning of Jeanne d'Arc—roam the land). Conditions in the very late years of Henry VIII are comparably volatile, although the use of state-sponsored violence to determine matters of religion—as pioneered by the Lancastrians—has become routine.[20] Whereas Kempe, never tortured, survives her interrogations, Askew is tortured so cruelly that she is carried to execution on a chair. There are, nonetheless, continuities in the struggles of Kempe and Askew to survive political coercion that are only obscured by recourse to cultural markers such as "medieval" and "Renaissance."

Last, Gertz-Robinson's reflections upon the kindred ways in which Kempe and Askew defend themselves specifically *as women* prompt us to inquire: when did the need for such techniques arise; when did they become historically redundant? Here again, questions of pulpit privilege prove crucial: for the steady rise of universities, equipping men with technical means and professional opportunities for pulpit and pulpit-like performance, signaled equivalent decline for women. The biological control here, as in so much else, is all that Hildegard and her sisters achieved and enjoyed before the networking of universities routinized masculine domination of learning. The far reaches of this process might be traced forward at least to 1929, as Virginia Woolf—even in preparing to address women's communities within larger university structures—is refused entry to a university library and is yelled at for infringing a lawn.[21] If we wish, then, to name the historiographical frame within which Gertz-Robinson conducts her analysis, we might term it a long (very long) Middle Ages (and since Hildegard is a medieval woman *par excellence,* the denial of pulpit-like performance to women will always appear, under analysis, as a matter of construction rather than ontology). There is, of course, some degree of comfort for us in clustering women together across time: for the most terrible aspect of the brave lives led by Askew and Kempe is their loneliness, a quality that the interrogations described above are designed to produce and intensify. Being completely alone, particularly for a premodern person, was terrifying: a glimpse of how it might feel, perhaps, to be without God. Writing as a respondent within a collective volume such as this provides forms of comfort that these women, we might imagine, would much have appreciated.

Notes

1. Corpus Christi College, Cambridge, MS 61, fol. 1b. See Derek Pearsall, "The *Troilus* Frontispiece and Chaucer's Audience," *The Yearbook of English Studies* 7 (1977): 68–74. "What the painter has represented," Pearsall observes, "understandably enough, since it is the only iconography available for such a picture, is a preacher" (70–71). See further John Burrow, *Gesture and Looks in Medieval Narrative* (Cambridge: Cambridge University Press, 2002).

2. See Stephen Milner, "Citing the *Ringhiera:* The Politics of Place and Public Address in Trecento Florence," *Italian Studies* 55 (2000): 53–82.

3. "We stowpe and stare," Hoccleve says (of himself and his fellow scriveners) "vpon the schepys skyn / And kepe must *our* song and wordys in" (*The Regiment of Princes,* 1014–15, as conveniently available in M. C. Seymour, ed., *Selections from Hoccleve* [Oxford: Clarendon Press, 1981], 35; my emphasis).

4. I employ the terms "Catholic" and "Protestant" here in preference to such terms as "conservative" or "reactionary" (denoting the group ascendant late in Henry VIII's reign) versus "reform"-minded (their antagonists, who will come into political favor with Edward VI), terms employed in Randall Martin, ed., *Women Writers in Renaissance England* (London: Longman, 1997), 58–60.

5. "The Balade whych Anne Askew made and sange when she was in Newgate," as presented by Bale, contains (Costley notes) the kind of apocalyptic imagery to which Bale himself was especially devoted: see *The Examinations of Anne Askew,* ed. Elaine Beilin (Oxford: Oxford University Press, 1996), 149–50, esp. lines 41–48.

6. "Anne Askewes answer unto Jhon Lassels letter," in Beilin, *Examinations,* 188–89 (line 275). Mediation of Askew is in this instance exercised by John Foxe as part of his *Actes and Monuments* (1563).

7. Judith Bennett casually coined the term "lesbian-like" a decade ago, then reclaimed and enlarged upon it at the "Queer Middle Ages" conference, New York, November 1998. "Lesbian-like" carries an epistemological charge quite different from that of "pulpit-like," although both terms simultaneously suggest and deny identifications in ways that prove useful for present purposes. See now Judith Bennett, "'Lesbian-like' and the Social History of Lesbianisms," *Journal of the History of Sexuality* 9 (2000): 1–24.

8. See Sharon Farmer, "Persuasive Voices: Clerical Images of Medieval Wives," *Speculum* 61 (1986): 517–43.

9. John G. Johnson Collection, accession 402, ascribed to the "Master of the Magdalene Legend." Oil on panel, 48 3/8" x 30 3/16".

10. See Jacobus de Voragine, *The Golden Legend: Selections*, selected and translated by Christopher Stace, introduction and notes by Richard Hamer (London: Penguin, 1998), ix–xxiv; Johann Georg Theodor Graesse, ed., *Jacobi a Voragine Legenda Aurea* (Dresden and Leipzig, 1846; 3rd ed. Breslau, 1890). On the defects of Graesse's edition, see Stace, *Golden Legend*, xxxvii; citations in my text follow Stace's volume. Chaucer tells us that he "made" a Magdalene legend (now lost) early in his career: see *The Legend of Good Women*, F 427–28 in *The Riverside Chaucer*, ed. Larry D. Benson (Boston: Houghton Mifflin, 1987); John P. McCall, "Chaucer and the Pseudo Origen *De Maria Magdalena:* A Preliminary Study," *Speculum* 46 (1971): 491–509.

11. She is so cited by the *Golden Legend* (166).

12. For visual representations of the saint with her trademark canister of perfumed ointment, see Johannes H. Emminghaus, *Mary Magdalene* (Recklinghausen: Bongers, 1967); on her wider symbolic associations, see Helen Meredith Garth, *Saint Mary Magdalene in Mediaeval Literature* (Baltimore, Md.: Johns Hopkins Press, 1950).

13. *Golden Legend*, 170–72. This scene is neatly depicted in a miniature from a German devotional manuscript, now British Library MS Add. 15682 (fol. 105r.): see Katherine Ludwig Jansen, *The Making of the Magdalen: Preaching and Popular Devotion in the Later Middle Ages* (Princeton, N.J.: Princeton University Press, 2000), 133 (figure 21).

14. Thus the exegete Rabanus Maurus observes that when Mary and her sister Martha sailed westward, "the Western land was illuminated by their corporeal presence and their holy relics" (rather than by their preaching and exegesis) (*Patrologia Latina* 112, cols 1492–93; Garth, *Magdalene*, 44).

15. See Roger S. Wieck, William M. Voelkle, and K. Michelle Hearne, *The Hours of Henry VIII: A Renaissance Masterpiece by Jean Poyet* (New York: George Braziller, in association with the Pierpoint Morgan Library, 2000). John the Baptist's hand gestures, particularly the downward pointing right hand, compare with those of the bishop of Rouen, preaching a crusade, in British Library MS Royal 20. C.vii, fol. 7b (reproduced in Pearsall, "*Troilus* Frontispiece," plate III).

16. See Jansen, *Making of the Magdalen*, 62–76.

17. Biblioteca Apostolica Vaticana Barb. lat. 513, f. 98v., as cited by Jansen, *Making of the Magdalen*, 66.

18. One fifteenth-century ecclesiastical cope features, among ten scenes from her life, Mary in extravagant headdress beset by animal-headed suitors. See Jansen, *Making of the Magdalen*, 145–96, esp. figures 4, 27. For a later but nonetheless extraordinarily fanciful rendition of the Magdalene's hair and clothes, see the frontispiece to Jacques de Voragine, *La Legend de Sainte Marie-Magdeleine*, trans. Claude Terni, illus. Louis Malteste (Paris: Maurice Glomeau, 1921).

19. The exhibition at the Pierpoint Morgan Library, New York, said much about Poyet's use of color and *contrapposto* and less about his adherence to thoroughly traditional typological and iconographic schemes.

20. See Paul Strohm, *England's Empty Throne: Usurpation and the Language of Legitimation, 1399–1422* (New Haven, Conn.: Yale University Press, 1998).

21. *A Room of One's Own* (London: Hogarth Press, 1959).

❖ CONTRIBUTORS ❖

ALISON I. BEACH is Assistant Professor of Religious Studies at the College of William and Mary in Williamsburg, Virginia. Her research focuses on religious women in twelfth-century Germany, particularly on the uses of literacy in the creation of community. She is the author of *Women as Scribes: Book Production and Monastic Reform in Twelfth-Century Bavaria* (Cambridge, 2004).

DAVID N. BELL is University Research Professor and Professor of Religious Studies at the Memorial University of Newfoundland (Canada). He is the author of some fourteen books and more than seventy substantial articles on Cistercian studies, Coptic studies, and patristic and medieval theology. One of his better-known books is *Many Mansions: An Introduction to the Development and Diversity of Medieval Theology, West and East* (Kalamazoo, 1996). His most recent work, at present in press, is a study of the seventeenth-century Cistercian reformer, Armand-Jean de Rancé, abbot of La Trappe.

ALCUIN BLAMIRES is Reader in English at Goldsmiths' College, University of London. His most recent book is *The Romance of the Rose Illuminated* (MRTS, 2002), but he is particularly known for his writings on debate about women in medieval writings, both as chief editor of *Woman Defamed and Woman Defended: An Anthology of Medieval Texts* (Oxford, 1992) and as author of *The Case for Women in Medieval Culture* (Oxford, 1997). He is currently preparing a book on Chaucer, gender, and ethics.

GILES CONSTABLE is Professor Emeritus at the Institute for Advanced Study in Princeton, N.J. He works on the religious history, especially monastic life and thought, of the eleventh and twelfth centuries, but has also worked on the early and late Middle Ages, the Crusades, and the history of letters. Among his publications are *Monastic Tithes* (1964), *The Letters of Peter the Venerable* (1967), *Letters and Letter-Collections* (1976), *People* *and Power in Byzantium* (with Alexander Kazhdan) (1982), *Three Studies in Medieval Religious and Social Thought* (1995), *The Reformation of the Twelfth Century* (1996), and five volumes of reprinted essays and articles.

CATHERINE CONYBEARE is Assistant Professor of Classics on the Rosalyn R. Schwarz Lectureship at Bryn Mawr College, where she specializes in teaching Late Latin. Her first book, *Paulinus Noster: Self and Symbols in the Letters of Paulinus of Nola*, was published by Oxford University Press in 2000. It examines the nexus of ideas about friendship and selfhood developed in early Christian letter writing, an interest reflected from another angle in her essay for this collection. A book on the early thought of St. Augustine, *The Irrational Augustine*, will appear from the same press in 2005.

DYAN ELLIOTT is Professor and the Ruth N. Halls Chair of History at Indiana University. She is the author of *Spiritual Marriage: Sexual Abstinence in Medieval Wedlock* (1993); *Fallen Bodies: Pollution, Sexuality, and Demonology in the Middle Ages* (1999); and *Proving Woman: Female Spirituality and Inquisitional Culture in the Later Middle Ages* (2004). She is currently working on two projects: one concerning the ramifications of Latin Christendom's encounter with dualism, and a second involving the impact of the matrimonial template on medieval culture.

MARGOT E. FASSLER, Director of the Institute of Sacred Music at Yale University, is the Robert S. Tangeman Professor of Music History. A historian of music and liturgy, her special fields of interest are medieval and American sacred repertories. Her book *Gothic Song* won the Nicholas Brown Prize of the Medieval Academy and the Otto Kindeldey Prize of the American Musicological Society. She has recently finished a book on the Virgin of Chartres (Yale University Press) and is now writing a book on Hildegard of Bingen. *Psalms in Community: Jewish and Christian Textual, Liturgical, and Artistic Traditions*, which she co-edited with Harold W. Attridge, was published in 2004 by the Society of Biblical Literature.

GENELLE GERTZ-ROBINSON is Assistant Professor of English at Washington and Lee University in Virginia where she teaches courses on early modern literature and history. She has published work on theories of martyrdom and interrogation in Milton, and is currently writing a book on women preaching and heresy in England from the late Middle Ages to the seventeenth century.

C. STEPHEN JAEGER is Gutgsell Professor of German and Comparative Literature at University of Illinois. He has published on medieval vernacular and the culture of courts and cathedrals. His publications include *The Envy of Angels: Cathedral Schools and*

Social Ideals in Medieval Europe, 950–1200 (1994) and *Ennobling Love: In Search of A Lost Sensibility* (1999).

STEVEN JUSTICE, Associate Professor of English at the University of California, Berkeley, is author of *Writing and Rebellion: England in 1381* (Berkeley and Los Angeles, 1994) and some essays.

KATHRYN KERBY-FULTON is Professor of English and Medieval Studies at the University of Victoria (Canada). She has written or edited several books and articles on medieval literary writers and their reception, especially the visionaries William Langland and Hildegard of Bingen. She is author of *Reformist Apocalypticism and Piers Plowman* (Cambridge, 1990), and, with Denise Despres, *Iconography and the Professional Reader: The Politics of Book Production in the Douce Piers Plowman* (Minneapolis, 1999).

MARY JANE MORROW is Adjunct Assistant Professor of History at Duke University. Her work includes studies of English women's religious practice, social implications of monastic Latin literacy among female and male communities c. 11th–13th centuries, and the development of monastic devotional prayer.

BARBARA NEWMAN is Professor of English and Religion at Northwestern University, where she holds the John Evans Chair of Latin Language and Literature. Her most recent book, *God and the Goddesses: Vision, Poetry, and Belief in the Middle Ages,* was published by University of Pennsylvania Press in 2002. She is also the author of *Sister of Wisdom: St. Hildegard's Theology of the Feminine* (Berkeley, 1987) and *From Virile Woman to WomanChrist: Studies in Medieval Religion and Literature* (Philadelphia, 1995); editor and translator of *Hildegard of Bingen's Symphonia* (Cornell, 1988); and editor of *Voice of the Living Light: Hildegard of Bingen and Her World* (Berkeley, 1998). Newman has held fellowships from the American Council of Learned Societies, the Guggenheim Foundation, the National Endowment for the Humanities, and the Alice Berline Kaplan Center for the Humanities at Northwestern. She is a Fellow of the Medieval Academy of America.

LINDA OLSON specializes in medieval Latin and English literature and literacy, with a particular focus on spiritual and autobiographical writings. She is the author of "Reading Augustine's *Confessiones* in Fourteenth-Century England: John de Grandisson's Fashioning of Text and Self" (*Traditio* 1997), and other articles on the reception of Augustine among male and female readers in the Middle Ages. She teaches English and Medieval Studies at the University of Victoria (Canada), and is currently writing a historical novel set in twelfth-century Yorkshire.

FELICITY RIDDY is Deputy Vice-Chancellor and Professor of English of the University of York, UK. She has written extensively on medieval English and Scottish literature, including Arthurian literature, romance, gender studies, and manuscript studies. Recently her interest in urban culture (stimulated by the Centre for Medieval Studies interdisciplinary urban household research group) has produced articles on courtesy texts, romances, devotional reading, and domestic authority. She is working on a book on urban domesticity, which links with her publications on women's reading and writing.

ELIZABETH SCHIRMER is Assistant Professor of English and Medieval Literature at New Mexico State University. Her research centers on cultures of lay reading and vernacular writing in late medieval England. Schirmer received her PhD in 2001 from the University of California, Berkeley, where she wrote a dissertation on the literary theology of the Pearl-poet. Her current book project, tentatively entitled "Canonizing Narratives: Inventing English Textuality from Arundel to Pecock," reconsiders the impact of the Lollard controversy on vernacular reading and writing under Lancastrian rule.

FIONA SOMERSET is Associate Professor of English at Duke University. She is author of *Clerical Discourse and Lay Audience in Late Medieval England* (Cambridge, 1998), as well as several articles on late medieval vernacular and Latin writings, and editor (with Nicholas Watson) of *The Vulgar Tongue: Medieval and Postmedieval Vernacularity* (Penn State University Press, 2003), as well as (with Jill C. Havens and Derrick G. Pitard) *Lollards and Their Influence in Late Medieval England* (Boydell and Brewer, 2003). She is also editor (with Andrew Cole and Lawrence Warner) of the *Yearbook of Langland Studies*.

ALFRED THOMAS is Professor and Head of Slavic and Baltic Languages and Literatures at the University of Illinois at Chicago. He is a specialist in medieval and modern Czech literature. His books include *The Czech Chivalric Romances Vévoda Arnošt and Lavryn in Their Literary Context* (Kümmerle, 1989), *The Labyrinth of the Word: Truth and Representation in Czech Literature* (Oldenbourg, 1995), *Anne's Bohemia: Czech Literature and Society, 1310–1420* (Minnesota, 1998), *Cultures of Forgery: Making Nations, Making Selves* (Routledge, 2003) (co-edited with Judith Ryan), and *Embodying Bohemia: Gender, Sexuality and Society in Modern Czech Culture* (Wisconsin, forthcoming 2005). He is presently working on a book provisionally entitled "Bohemia on the Sea: England and East-Central Europe from Chaucer to Shakespeare."

JOHN VAN ENGEN is Professor of Medieval History at the University of Notre Dame, and was director of its Medieval Institute for twelve years. He has published widely on medieval intellectual and religious history, beginning with a study of Rupert of Deutz (California, 1983) and working more recently on the *Devotio Moderna* in the late Middle

Ages. Recently, he has edited a volume of essays (with Michael Signer) *Jews and Christians in Twelfth-Century Europe* (Notre Dame, 2001), and a collection of his essays, *Religion in the History of the Medieval West* (2004).

MARK VESSEY is Associate Professor of English and Canada Research Chair in Literature, Christianity and Culture at the University of British Columbia. His articles on Augustine have appeared in *Revue des Etudes Augustiniennes, Augustinian Studies, Vigiliae Christianae,* and *Journal of Early Christian Studies.* He is co-editor (with J. W. Halporn) of *Cassiodorus: Institutions of Divine and Secular Learning* (Liverpool University Press, Translated Texts for Historians, 2004) and (with Karla Pollmann) of *Augustine and the Disciplines: From Cassiciacum to "Confessions"* (Oxford University Press, forthcoming).

DAVID WALLACE is Judith Rodin Professor of English, University of Pennsylvania and President of the New Chaucer Society (2004–2006). His most recent book is *Premodern Places. Calais to Surinam, Chaucer to Aphra Behn* (2004). Edited volumes include *The Cambridge Companion to Medieval Women's Writing* (with Carolyn Dinshaw, 2003) and *The Cambridge History of Medieval English Literature* (1999, 2002).

NICHOLAS WATSON is Professor in the Department of English and American Literature and Language at Harvard University. He is the author of *Richard Rolle and the Invention of Authority* (Cambridge, 1991); co-author, with Jocelyn Wogan-Browne, Andrew Taylor, and Ruth Evans, of *The Idea of the Vernacular: An Anthology of Middle English Literary Theory, 1280–1520* (Penn State University Press, 1999); and co-editor, with Jacqueline Jenkins, of *The Writings of Julian of Norwich: A Vision to a Devout Woman and A Revelation of Love* (Penn State University Press, forthcoming 2005). He has also written numerous articles on vernacular religious texts.

KATHERINE ZIEMAN specializes in the literature and culture of late medieval England, with particular attention to issues of literacy and the practices of the liturgy. She has published articles on Chaucer as well as on literature written for women religious and is completing her book *Reading and Singing: Literacy, Liturgy, and Literature in Late Medieval England* (forthcoming from University of Pennsylvania Press). She currently teaches English and Medieval Studies at Wesleyan University.

INDEX OF HISTORICAL NAMES, PLACES, AND TITLES